Real Essays
with Readings

Writing Projects for College, Work, and Everyday Life

THIRD EDITION

Real Essays
with Readings

Writing Projects for College, Work, and Everyday Life

Susan Anker

Bedford / St. Martin's
Boston ◆ New York

For Bedford/St. Martin's

Senior Developmental Editor: Alexis P. Walker
Senior Production Editor: Karen S. Baart
Senior Production Supervisor: Dennis Conroy
Marketing Manager: Casey Carroll
Editorial Assistant: Cecilia Seiter
Production Associate: Lindsay DiGianvittorio
Production Intern: Shannon Walsh
Copyeditor: Rosemary Winfield
Text Design: Claire Seng-Niemoeller
Cover Design: Billy Boardman
Cover Photographs: (top row, left to right) Giovanni Bohorquez, Rose Martinez,
   Monique Rizer; (second row) Irma Karpaviciute; (third row, left to right) Shawn
   Brown, Danita Edwards; (bottom row, left to right) Alex Espinoza, Janice Diamond
Composition: TexTech International
Printing and Binding: RR Donnelley and Sons

President: Joan E. Feinberg
Editorial Director: Denise B. Wydra
Editor in Chief: Karen S. Henry
Director of Marketing: Karen R. Soeltz
Director of Editing, Design, and Production: Marcia Cohen
Assistant Director of Editing, Design, and Production: Elise S. Kaiser
Managing Editor: Elizabeth M. Schaaf

Library of Congress Control Number: 2008925869

Copyright © 2009 by Bedford/St. Martin's

3   2   1   0   9   8
f   e   d   c   b   a

For information, write: Bedford/St. Martin's, 75 Arlington Street, Boston, MA 02116
(617-399-4000)

ISBN-10: 0–312–47574–8   ISBN-13: 978–0–312–47574–1   (Student Edition)
ISBN-10: 0–312–48280–9   ISBN-13: 978–0–312–48280–0   (Instructor's Annotated Edition)

Acknowledgments

Dave Barry. "The Ugly Truth about Beauty." Originally titled "Beauty and the Beast." From
   the *Miami Herald*, February 1, 1998. Copyright © 1998 Dave Barry. Reprinted by permission
   of the author.

*Acknowledgments and copyrights are continued at the back of the book on pages A-20–A-22, which
constitute an extension of the copyright page. It is a violation of the law to reproduce these selections by
any means whatsoever without the written permission of the copyright holder.*

Brief Contents

READINGS

Contents

EDITING ESSAYS

Thematic Contents

(Essays listed in order of appearance)

Preface for Instructors

Too often, students perceive their writing course as something they must put up with in order to move on to "content" courses that will help them get a good job. The aim of *Real Essays*, as indicated by its subtitle, *Writing Projects for College, Work, and Everyday Life*, is to show students that the writing course is a crucial gateway to success in every arena of their lives. To achieve this aim, *Real Essays* casts writing and editing skills as practical and valuable. Further, it sends the message that strengthening these skills is worth the effort because all the roles students will play in their lives—college student, employee, parent, consumer, community member—require that they write often and well.

Real Essays shares an overarching purpose with its companions, *Real Writing: Paragraphs and Essays for College, Work, and Everyday Life* and *Real Skills: Sentences and Paragraphs for College, Work, and Everyday Life*—to put writing in a real-world context. All three books link writing skills to students' own goals in and beyond college. What's more, these books motivate students by introducing them to other people who have struggled with writing, have wondered why it is important, and are learning that good writing is not a mysterious, elusive gift but a skill that can be learned by anyone who is willing to pay attention and practice.

Maintaining a strong connection to the real world, the third edition of *Real Essays* does more to build the skills that are essential for success in the writing course and for other college-level work. Expanded coverage of academic reading, writing, and learning skills gives students practical preparation for college success.

Features

Real Essays presents the information that students need and also shows them how and why writing is relevant to them. Many popular features of earlier editions have been carried over to this edition, with revisions based on suggestions from vast numbers of instructors and students.

Motivates Students with a Real-World Emphasis

- **Profiles of Success show that writing is key to success.** Inspiring case studies of former students, with photos, short autobiographies, and workplace writing samples appear in each of the nine Part Two chapters.
- **Real-world models of writing give students practical examples.** Unique to *Real Essays*, all the assignment chapters include three essay-length samples — one each from college, work, and everyday life. One example is by the subject of the chapter's Profile of Success.

Profile of Success

Shawn Brown
Founder, Diamond Educators

BACKGROUND: I had what is, unfortunately, a poor, urban youth who are caught up in gar brother was murdered in a crossfire, and I li no father around. I was an athlete and got a school. I had my first kid at age fifteen and i a rival who had disrespected me. I didn't, ma my coach, who'd warned me not to leave my Ed Powell, had a saying I still repeat often: " to fail." I was lucky to have Powell and a fev me, help me turn around, and get me on the better life.
A few years ago, I got together a group c

Presents Essay Writing in Logical, Manageable Increments

▦ FOUR BASICS OF GOOD CAUSE AND EFFECT

1. The main point reflects the writer's purpose — to explain causes, effects, or both.
2. If the purpose is to explain causes, it presents concrete causes.
3. If the purpose is to explain effects, it presents real effects.
4. It gives readers clear and detailed examples or explanations of the causes and effects.

In the following paragraph, each number corresponds to one of the four basics of good cause and effect.

1 Little doubt remains that global warming is a threat to our world, but not everyone understands why it is happening and what the effects really are. Many experts believe that this warming trend is largely the result of 2 greenhouse gases, including 4 carbon dioxide emissions, mainly from cars, and pollutants from industrial processes. 2 Deforestation is another

- **A focus on the "four basics" of each type of essay makes writing instruction simple.** Each of the assignment chapters opens with a list (indicated by this symbol: ▦) of four basic features of the type of writing followed by annotated model passages that are color-coded to show how the four basics work in writing.
- **Step-by-step Writing Guides offer real help.** The Writing Guide in every assignment chapter breaks down the process of writing each type

of essay into a series of manageable tasks. Each step is accompanied by clear advice for completing the task.

- **Two chapters help students tackle essay exams, timed writings, summaries, and reports.** Chapter 20, on writing summaries and reports, offers helpful writing guides for these tasks and shows one student's process for writing a book report on Toni Morrison's *The Bluest Eye*.

- **An easy-to-follow chapter presents ten steps for writing research essays.** This chapter follows one student through the research process and culminates in her paper about the benefits of mandatory school uniforms.

- **The section on MLA documentation** has a colored border that makes it easy to find without hunting for page numbers.

WRITING GUIDE: CAUSE AND EFFECT	
STEPS IN CAUSE AND EFFECT	**HOW TO DO THE STEPS**
Focus.	☐ Think about an event or situation that and whether you want to describe its both. Review the four basics of good o page 272.
Prewrite to explore your topic. See Chapter 4 for more on prewriting.	☐ State what your purpose for writing is causes, effects, or both. ☐ Use the ring diagram or clustering to g causes or effects of your topic.
Write a thesis statement. The thesis statement in a cause and effect essay often includes the topic and an indicator of whether you will be discussing causes, effects, or both. Topic + indication of cause/effect = Thesis A blog ruined my marriage.	☐ Write a thesis statement that includes indicator of cause, effect, or both.

Presents Editing in Logical, Manageable Increments

- **The editing section helps students overcome the four most serious errors—and more.** *Real Essays* covers all standard grammar, punctuation, and mechanics topics, but it concentrates first, with fuller coverage, on the errors identified by teachers as the most serious: fragments, run-ons, subject-verb agreement problems, and verb tense problems.

- **References to *Exercise Central* provide ample opportunities for skill practice.** Marginal references throughout the editing section direct students to *Exercise Central* for additional exercises. The largest online bank of editing exercises (with almost nine thousand items), *Exercise Central* offers two levels of skill practice, immediate feedback, and instructor monitoring tools.

- **Review charts at the end of each grammar chapter present key information visually.** For students who are visual learners, the editing section presents concepts and strategies in chapter-ending flowcharts for quick comprehension and practical application.

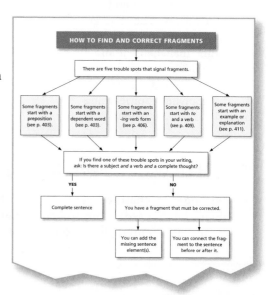

Helps Students with College-Level Reading

- **Chapter 2 gives students strategies for and practice with reading and understanding** a variety of college materials, such as textbook chapters, syllabi, and tests.
- **Reading prompts in the margins of essays help students develop the practice of active reading.** These "Pause" prompts alongside the readings in Part Two and Part Eight ask students to consider key elements of the reading, including their own responses.

New to This Edition

We have included an array of new features to help students become better readers and writers throughout college and beyond.

More Help with College Success

- **A new Chapter 1 on how to succeed in college** offers advice from students who have passed both developmental and college-level writing courses. These students provide concrete, practical advice about the writing and reading they do in composition and other classes. The chapter also includes topics such as time management and note taking, along with a section on understanding and applying your learning style to college work.

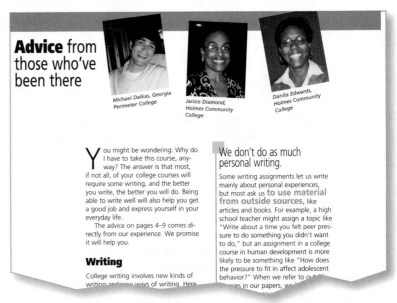

Advice from those who've been there

Michael Dalkas, Georgia Perimeter College

Janice Diamond, Holmes Community College

Danita Edwards, Holmes Community College

You might be wondering: Why do I have to take this course, anyway? The answer is that most, if not all, of your college courses will require some writing, and the better you write, the better you will do. Being able to write well will also help you get a good job and express yourself in your everyday life.

The advice on pages 4–9 comes directly from our experience. We promise it will help you.

Writing

College writing involves new kinds of writing and new ways of writing. Here

We don't do as much personal writing.

Some writing assignments let us write mainly about personal experiences, but most ask us **to use material from outside sources,** like articles and books. For example, a high school teacher might assign a topic like "Write about a time you felt peer pressure to do something you didn't want to do," but an assignment in a college course in human development is more likely to be something like "How does the pressure to fit in affect adolescent behavior?" When we refer to out

More Help with College Writing

- **A stronger emphasis on practicing four key college skills—summary, analysis, synthesis, and evaluation**—develops students' abilities. These skills are introduced in Chapter 2 and reinforced with prompts and questions for writing and discussion in all Part Two chapters.

How to Analyze a Writing Assignment

Getting started can be one of the hardest parts of writing, and one common obstacle to starting is not quite understanding what the assignment is asking you to do. There are ways of translating writing assignments that will help you get started. Let's look at a couple of assignments and the ways you might begin them.

ASSIGNMENT: Discuss the reasons for low employee morale at your workplace.

ANALYZING A WRITING ASSIGNMENT

STEPS	WHAT TO DO FOR THIS ASSIGNMENT
1. Highlight the key words.	Discuss the reasons for low employee morale at your workplace.
2. Get some ideas down on paper or on your computer.	List all reasons you can think of — at your current job, past jobs, or other jobs you know about. (For more on getting ideas, see the next chapter.)
3. Think again. Revise your ideas, and add to them.	Give some details about each reason, and say *how* each contributes to low employee morale. Then reread your list. Do they all contribute to low employee morale? Delete those that now seem irrelevant, and try to say more about the others. Record any other reasons that occur to you in the process.
4. Try out a main point.	Reread your revised list of reasons, and decide on your main point — what you want to say about your reasons. Do they have a common cause? What do they say about the workplace? Can you think of a way to improve morale? To find your main point, think about your audience and purpose. For example, if you are writing a report for your boss, your thesis ~~would not be entirely critical of the co~~

- **Advice on decoding and approaching assignments** helps students understand exactly what they are being asked to do. A new section in Chapter 3, "How to Analyze a Writing Assignment," and "Tips for Tackling [the mode]" boxes in all assignment chapters give students essential strategies.

- **A new sample writing rubric with examples of poor, fair, and good writing** (Chapter 3) helps students gauge the success of their own writing.

- **A new section, "How to Create a Writing Portfolio"** (Chapter 3), helps students evaluate, assemble, and reflect on their own work.

More Help with College Reading

- **New vocabulary prompts for readings** in Part Two writing assignment chapters help students focus on words they need to know.

- **Synthesis prompts** in all Part Two chapters encourage students to link readings from these chapters with those in the "Readings for Writers" section.

- **New "Linked Readings" prompts** at the end of each "Readings for Writers" chapter help students make connections among readings in different chapters, allowing them to explore themes such as "The Pressure to Conform," "Feeling Foreign," and "Stereotypes."

When I got in high school, though I got another hobby which took all my time and money, my car was my new love. It is a Nissan 300 ZX, and it is black with a black interior. It had 16" rims and a sweet body kit. I got it when I was 17 and I put everything I had into it and I loved it almost as much as my girlfriend Kate.

As you can see, by my senior year, my only hobbies were playing baseball for my school team and taking care of the car. I once spent all my time riding my bicycle with my friends but I guess I've outgrown that. The one hobby that has lasted throughout my life is my love for baseball. I will probably play that until I am an old man.

Student essay #2 is better for the following reasons:

- It has a clearly identifiable thesis, introduction, body, and conclusion.
- The body paragraphs are generally cohesive, and the essay shows a chronological (time order) development.
- It has fewer errors in grammar and punctuation than the low-level essay has.

- **A new argument casebook on assisted suicide** offers students perspectives from medical personnel, a patient with terminal cancer, and others.
- **Twelve new readings** in "Readings for Writers" engage students in contemporary concerns.

More Help with Grammar

- **Ten new comprehensive mastery tests at the end of the grammar section** review grammar and other principles of writing.
- **New verb review charts** (Chapter 26) give students a reference tool for correct use of verb tenses and forms along with examples of the most common errors.
- **Expanded ESL coverage** includes new practice sets, more language-specific advice, and simple explanation of difficult concepts.

Note on MLA Documentation

As you may know, the Modern Language Association publishes two versions of its guidelines for documenting sources. The *MLA Style Manual and Guide to Scholarly Publishing* is for scholars and graduate students. The *MLA Handbook for Writers of Research Papers* is for undergraduate and high school students. In May 2008, the guide for scholars was updated with new guidelines for documenting sources. The Modern Language Association strongly discouraged publishers from updating texts intended for undergraduates to reflect the changes in the scholars' guide. Accordingly, the coverage of MLA documentation in *Real Essays with Readings* reflects the guidelines for undergraduates as put forth in the current edition of the *MLA Handbook for Writers of Research Papers*. When the Modern Language Association publishes the new edition of this guide (anticipated in the spring of 2009), student copies of *Real Essays with Readings* will be reprinted to reflect these new guidelines.

Ancillaries

Print Resources

For Students

- *The Bedford/St. Martin's Planner with Grammar Girl's Quick and Dirty Tips* (ISBN 10: 0–312–48023–7 / ISBN 13: 978–0–312–48023–3). This handy resource includes everything that students need to plan and use their time effectively, with advice on preparing schedules and to-do lists and blank schedules and calendars (monthly and weekly) for planning. Integrated into the planner are pointers on fixing common grammar errors, with tips from Mignon Fogarty, host of the popular *Grammar Girl's Quick and Dirty Tips for Better Writing* podcast, and from other podcast hosts. Also included are advice on note taking and succeeding on tests, an address book, and an annotated list of useful Web sites.

- **The Bedford/St. Martin's ESL Workbook, Second Edition** (ISBN 10: 0–312–54034–5 / ISBN 13: 978–0–312–54034–0). This comprehensive collection of exercises covers grammatical issues for multilingual students with varying English-language skills and cultural backgrounds. Instructional introductions precede exercises in a broad range of topic areas.

- **Quick Reference Card on writing, editing, word processing, and research** (ISBN 10: 0–312–40490–5 / ISBN 13: 978–0–312–40490–1). Students can prop this handy three-panel card up next to their computers for easy reference while they're writing and researching.

- **From Practice to Mastery** (for the Florida College Basic Skills Exit Tests; ISBN 10: 0–312–41908–2 / ISBN 13: 978–0–312–41908–0). Full of practical instruction and plenty of examples, this handy book gives students all the resources they need to practice for—and pass—the Florida College Basic Skills Exit Tests on reading and writing.

- **Portfolio Keeping: A Guide for Students, Second Edition** (ISBN 10: 0–312–41909–0 / ISBN 13: 978–0–312–41909–7). Written by Nedra Reynolds and Rich Rice, this guide provides all the information students need to use the portfolio method successfully in a writing course.

For Instructors

- **Instructor's Annotated Edition of *Real Essays*, Third Edition** (ISBN 10: 0–312–48280–9 / ISBN 13: 978–0–312–48280–0). This instructor's edition gives practical page-by-page advice on teaching with *Real Essays*, including discussion prompts, strategies for teaching ESL students, and ideas for additional classroom activities. It also contains answers to all exercises and suggestions for using the other ancillaries.

- **Practical Suggestions for Teaching REAL ESSAYS, Third Edition** (ISBN 10: 0–312–48284–1 / ISBN 13: 978–0–312–48284–8). This guide contains information and advice on working with basic writers, bringing the real world into the classroom, building critical-thinking skills, using computers, teaching non-native speakers and speakers of nonstandard dialects, and assessment. It also includes tips for new instructors and ideas for making the most of *Real Essays*.

- **Additional Resources for Teaching REAL ESSAYS, Third Edition** (ISBN 10: 0–312–48285–X / ISBN 13: 978–0–312–48285–5). This collection of resources supplements the instructional materials in the text with a variety of transparency masters and other reproducibles for classroom use.

- ***Teaching Developmental Writing: Background Readings,* Third Edition** (ISBN 10: 0–312–43283–6 / ISBN 13: 978–0–312–43283–6). This professional resource, edited by Susan Naomi Bernstein, offers professional essays on topics of interest to basic writing instructors, along with editorial apparatus pointing out practical applications for the classroom. The new edition includes revised chapters on technology and the writing process and focuses on topics relevant to non-native speakers of English in the developmental writing course.

- ***The Bedford Bibliography for Teachers of Basic Writing,* Second Edition** (ISBN 10: 0–312–41480–3 / ISBN 13: 978–0–312–41480–1). Compiled by members of the Conference on Basic Writing under the general editorship of Linda Adler-Kassner and Gregory R. Glau, this annotated list of books, articles, and periodicals was selected specifically for its value to teachers of basic writing. (This Bedford Bibliography is also available online at **www.bedfordstmartins.com/basicbib/content.asp**.)

- ***Portfolio Teaching: A Guide for Instructors,* Second Edition** (ISBN 10: 0–312–41911–2 / ISBN 13: 978–0–312–41911–0). Written by Nedra Reynolds and Rich Rice, this guide provides the practical information instructors and writing program administrators need to use the portfolio method successfully in a writing course. Ideal companion to *Portfolio Keeping: A Guide for Students* (see entry under Print Resources / For Students above).

New Media Resources

For Students

- ***WritingClass* with Real Essays with Readings e-Book** (ISBN 10: 0–312–55791–4 / ISBN 13: 978–0–312–55791–1). *WritingClass,* a new online learning space for student writers, comes preloaded with our best media: *Exercise Central,* video tutorials for challenging concepts, writing guides, and more. Best of all, *WritingClass with Real Essays with Readings e-Book* allows you and your students to access a complete, interactive e-book version of *Real Essays:* Students can work through the instruction and exercises online, respond to assignments in writing spaces, take notes, bookmark important sections, and more. Students stay focused because assignments, grades, and writing instruction are all in one place. It's easy for you to monitor student progress and offer feedback when it counts most. What could be better? To learn more, visit our book companion Web site at **www.bedfordstmartins.com/realessays**.

- *Real Essays* **book companion Web site at www.bedfordstmartins.com/ realessays.** This helpful, *free* site provides resources that help students with writing and research. Key features include

  - Annotated model essays
  - Writing for the Workplace advice
  - Graphic organizers for all modes of writing
  - Peer review forms for all modes of writing
  - Exercises with immediate feedback
  - Links to other useful resources from Bedford/St. Martin's

- *Re:Writing Basics* **(www.bedfordstmartins.com/rewritingbasics) for basic writing classrooms, and** *Re:Writing* **(www.bedfordstmartins.com/ rewriting) for composition.** These open-access sites collect the best free resources from our many book companion sites in one convenient location, with assignments, activities, handouts, exercises, and tutorials you can start using right away. You can refer students to the appropriate site or print out what's useful. *Re:Writing Plus,* our premium resource for composition, offers even more: To learn about it, contact your local sales rep or read more online at **www.bedfordstmartins.com**.

- *Make-a-Paragraph Kit* **with** *Exercise Central to Go* **(demo at www .bedfordstmartins.com/paragraphkit;** ISBN 10: 0–312–45332–9 / ISBN 13: 978–0–312–45332–9**).** This fun, animated CD-ROM gives students everything they need to write successful paragraphs. First, students see a paragraph develop and undergo revision as part of an "Extreme Paragraph Makeover" "reality" program. Then, they write their own paragraphs based on a choice of six topics, getting advice and help along the way. Next, animated audiovisual tutorials show them how to find and fix the four most serious grammar errors (fragments, run-ons and comma splices, subject-verb agreement problems, and verb problems). Finally, students can build their own writing and revising checklist and get lots of grammar practice with *Exercise Central to Go,* the entire content of which is on this CD.

For Instructors

- *Real Essays* **book companion Web site at www.bedfordstmartins.com/ realessays.** This companion Web site provides instructors with tools for teaching with *Real Essays,* including downloadable presentation slides for illustrating key grammar concepts, a downloadable version of *Additional Resources for Teaching* REAL ESSAYS, and more.

- **Just-in-Time Teaching: Classroom and Professional Support (www .bedfordstmartins.com/teachingcentral).** Looking for last-minute course materials from a source you can trust? At Just-in-Time Teaching, we've culled the best handouts, teaching tips, assignment ideas, and more from our print and online resources and put them all in one place. Bedford/St. Martin's is committed to supporting the work that teachers do, with something for everyone — from the first-time adjunct to the program director. And, like all of Bedford/St. Martin's professional resources, Just-in-Time Teaching tools are *free* to instructors.

- *Re:Writing Basics / Re:Writing* **instructor resources.** Instructors can access blogs and newsletters for instructors, make use of online bibliographies — *The Bedford Bibliography for Teachers of Writing* and *The Bedford Bibliography for Teachers of Basic Writing* — order free professional resource books for office or home libraries, sign up for exam copies of textbooks, learn about workshops, and more.

- *bits: Ideas for Teaching Composition* **(www.bedfordstmartins.com/ bits).** Need some inspiring ways to get students to use their handbooks? Looking for something to do in class tomorrow? This blog is for you. Every two weeks throughout the school year, our featured author, Barclay Barrios of Florida Atlantic University, posts creative suggestions for teaching a range of composition topics. You can search the collection by category or sign up to have new activities emailed to you as they're posted. After you've tried an activity with your students, come back to the site and let others know how it worked or how you adapted it for your class.

- *Testing Tool Kit: A Writing and Grammar Test Bank* **(demo at www .bedfordstmartins.com/toolkit;** ISBN 10: 0–312–43032–9 / ISBN 13: 978–0–312– 43032–0**).** This CD-ROM allows instructors to build customized tests and quizzes from a choice of nearly two thousand questions on forty-seven writing and grammar topics. The questions are at two levels of difficulty so that instructors can pick just the right level for their classes and goals. Also included are ten ready-to-administer diagnostic tests.

- *Exercise Central to Go: Writing and Grammar Practices for Basic Writers* (ISBN 10: 0–312–44652–7 / ISBN 13: 978–0–312–44652–9). This CD-ROM includes hundreds of practice items to help basic writers build their writing and editing skills and provides audio instructions and instant feedback. Drawn from the popular *Exercise Central* resource, the practices have been extensively class-tested. No Internet connection is necessary.

WebCT and Blackboard content is also available for *Real Essays*.

Ordering Information

To order any of the ancillaries for *Real Essays,* please contact your Bedford/St. Martin's sales representative, e-mail sales support at **sales_support@bfwpub.com**, or visit our Web site at **www.bedfordstmartins.com**.

Use these ISBNs when ordering the following supplements packaged with your students' books:

TITLE	ISBN 10	ISBN 13
WritingClass	0–312–56170–9	978–0–312–56170–3
The Bedford/St. Martin's Planner with Grammar Girl's Quick and Dirty Tips	0–312–56120–2	978–0–312–56120–8
The Bedford/St. Martin's ESL Workbook, Second Edition	0–312–55930–5	978–0–312–55930–4
Quick Reference Card	0–312–55929–1	978–0–312–55929–8
Make-a-Paragraph Kit	0–312–55928–3	978–0–312–55928–1
Exercise Central to Go CD-ROM	0–312–55931–3	978–0–312–55931–1
From Practice to Mastery (for Florida)	0–312–55932–1	978–0–312–55932–8

Acknowledgments

This edition of *Real Essays* is a collaboration among many fine teachers and students across the country as well as the staff at Bedford/St. Martin's. I am grateful to all of these people.

Reviewers

I would like to thank the following people for helping to shape ideas for this edition: Kathryn Barker, Ivy Tech Community College; E. Mairing Barney, Roosevelt University, Truman College; Monica Benton, Georgia Perimeter College–Decatur; Leslie Brown, Georgia Perimeter College; Gloria Burke, Terra State Community College and Lourdes College; James Andrew Clovis, West Virginia University at Parkersburg; Kathleen Collins, SUNY Ulster Community College; Steven Dalager, Lake Superior College; Seth Dugan, Mercy College; Mike Eskew, Chaffey Community College; Roy Freedman, The Citadel and South Wesleyan University; Nicole Grasse, Richard J. Daley College; Kelli Hallsten, Lake Superior College; Kirsi Halonen, Lake Superior College; Rochelle Harden, Parkland College; Judy Harris, Tomball College; Julie Jackson, Gavilan College; Francine Jamin, Montgomery College, Takoma Park/Silver Spring; Billy

P. Jones, Miami Dade College, Kendall; Therese Jones, Lewis University; Mandy Kallus, Kingwood College; J. Damon Kapke, Lake Superior College; Craig Kleinman, City College of San Francisco; Mimi Leonard, Wytheville Community College; Ray Lightburn, Broward Community College; James McKeown, McLennan Community College; Dawn Mizwinski-Wesley, Lackawanna College; Mona Sue Moistner, Ivy Tech Community College; Lisa Oldaker Palmer, Quinsigamond Community College; Barbara Pescar, Cuyamaca College; Dr. Nicolette Rose, Georgia Perimeter College; Jennifer Rossino, Passaic County Community College; Norman Stephens, Cerro Coso Community College; Stephanie Stiles, Dominican College; Ann Stotts, Gateway Tech College; Amy Jo Swing, Lake Superior College; Jennifer Thompson, Richard J. Daley College and Moraine Valley Community College; Carole Thurston, Northern Virginia Community College; Monalinda Verlengia, College of the Desert; and Rhonda Wallace, Cuyahoga Community College.

Students

Many current and former students have helped shape each edition of *Real Essays*. I am very grateful to the following students for helping me write the new first chapter, "How to Succeed in College": Michael Dalkas, Georgia Perimeter College; Janice Diamond and Danita Edwards, Holmes Community College; Irma Karpaviciute, Quinsigamond Community College; Daniel Madrid, East Los Angeles College; Rose Martinez, Passaic County Community College; and Lia Uenohara, Bunker Hill Community College.

The nine former students who are included as "Profiles of Success" are terrific role models for current students, and their examples of workplace writing show students real-world applications of writing principles. The profiles of success are Giovanni Bohorquez, Shawn Brown, Alex Espinoza, Juan Gonzalez, Jolanda Jones, Gary Knoblock, Patty Maloney, Monique Rizer, and Garth Vaz.

Other students and former students generously agreed to share their work: John Around Him, Florence Bagley, Jordan Brown, Roberta Fair, Danny Fitzgerald, Shannon Grady, Messelina Hernandez, Michael Jernigan, Derek Johnson, Dylan Marcos, Luz Medina, Mario Mighlietti, Donnie Ney, Jennifer Orlando, Liliana Ramirez, Tiffany Shale, Silvio Testagrosso, Brenda White, and Carson Williams.

Contributors

I am very lucky to have worked with some of the following contributors over numerous editions and books. Mark Gallaher, an old friend

Advice,
continued

Instructors take off points for grammar errors.

In some of our first writing classes, we had a chance to correct errors before we received a final grade. This isn't the case, though, in other college classes. That means you have to **get it right before you hand in your paper,** so be sure to proofread carefully.

Be careful about using the wrong word.

When your teacher points out a word in your paper that you've used incorrectly, make a note of it, and check for the same error in your next paper. Also, be sure to **reread your paper after using your computer's spell checker.**

Reading and Thinking

You also have to read well to succeed in college. Luckily, most college writing courses offer some help here, too. Here is what you should be prepared for.

We read a lot.

Nearly all of the reading we do is assigned as homework. **A lot of in-class time is spent discussing what we read.** When we haven't done the reading, we can't participate in class—a bad thing, since we are usually graded on our class participation.

We read all kinds of things.

We read a lot—textbook chapters, stories, newspaper and magazine articles, secondary sources about a research topic—**and we have to know how to discuss** and write about all of it. Your writing course will give you some practice doing this, so take advantage of it.

We're expected to remember what we read.

Highlighting as you read will help, and so will taking notes on the following:

- What makes the piece interesting to you?
- What does it teach you, and how does it relate to your experiences?
- What bothers you, confuses you, or excites you?

Proofreading Tips That Work for Us

1. Read your paper line by line, looking carefully at every word.

2. Read your paper out loud, reading every word carefully.

3. Pause at every comma, and come to a full stop at the end of every sentence.

4. Ask someone else to read your paper, looking only for errors, not for overall meaning.

5. If your computer has a speech tool, use it to read your paper back to you.

6. Check for the four most serious errors (Chapters 22–26 in this book).

Irma Karpaviciute, Quinsigamond Community College

Daniel Madrid, East Los Angeles College

Rose Martinez, Passaic County Community College

Lia Uenohara, Bunker Hill Community College

Sometimes, we have to choose our own writing topics.

This can be fun, but it can also be scary. If you draw a blank, here are some ways to get started:

1 First, try thinking about what you, and only you, have to say about a subject. We all have *something* to say that's important.

2 Try some of the prewriting techniques (such as brainstorming and freewriting) that you'll learn in this course. (See Chapter 4 for coverage of prewriting techniques.)

3 Talk over your ideas with a friend. You'll be surprised at what you come up with.

We have less time to write longer pieces and less step-by-step instruction in class.

Your instructors may not spend much in-class time helping you write the papers they assign. **Your chance to learn how to write is now,** in your writing class, so pay close attention to your instructor's comments on your writing. Also, use writing tutors if they are available.

We have to *revise* our work.

All instructors expect us to really "dig into" our ideas. It's almost impossible to do this in a single draft, so learn how to revise. One of the best ways we've found is to read your writing aloud and then ask,

- Can you recognize the main point?
- Do you give good details to back up your point?
- What makes your ideas interesting to you?
- Do you think your reader will be interested, too?

We have to use formal English.

In college, our instructors—all of them—expect us to use formal, academic English—the same kind that's used in newspapers, television newscasts, and radio reporting. **Using formal English in college is not "selling out"** or compromising who you are. It's an opportunity to practice a language that will help you succeed at school, at work, and in all areas of your life.

In our writing courses, we didn't spend much in-class time on grammar.

Our writing teachers would often just point out our errors and refer us to parts of a textbook, to a writing center, to a writing tutor, or to a computer lab for help. This means that **a lot of what you learn about grammar will be up to you.**

Part One

How to Read and Write in College

1

Succeeding in College

What You Need to Know

If you're reading this, you've probably just started a college writing course, and you might not know what to expect. What kind of writing will you have to do? What do you need to know to pass? What will the teacher expect?

In the first section of this chapter, students who have recently completed their first year of college supply answers to these and other common questions. These students were in your exact spot very recently, so they're in a good position to tell you what you need to know.

In the second section of this chapter, you'll learn four strategies that will be critical to your success in all your college courses—how to identify your goals, how to manage your time, how to use the resources available to you, and how to find and use your learning style. Paying attention now to the students' advice and the four success strategies is definitely worth your time.

 PRACTICE YOUR EDUCATIONAL EXPERIENCES . . . .

Write about your educational experiences so far, including things that may help your teacher understand what you've done so far and things that you hope to learn in this course.

■ **IDEA JOURNAL**
Write about some good advice (or some bad advice) you've gotten in the past.

3

Advice from those who've been there

Michael Dalkas, Georgia Perimeter College

Janice Diamond, Holmes Community College

Danita Edwards, Holmes Community College

You might be wondering: Why do I have to take this course, anyway? The answer is that most, if not all, of your college courses will require some writing, and the better you write, the better you will do. Being able to write well will also help you get a good job and express yourself in your everyday life.

The advice on pages 4–9 comes directly from our experience. We promise it will help you.

Writing

College writing involves new kinds of writing and new ways of writing. Here are some of the things we had to get used to.

Essays aren't always just five paragraphs.

Many of us learned to write essays with five paragraphs (introduction, three body paragraphs, and conclusion). That is a great way to learn how to write a basic essay, but in college courses, **you'll hardly ever be assigned a "five-paragraph essay."** Your teachers might give you a target length, but the final length will depend on what you need to develop your ideas.

We don't do as much personal writing.

Some writing assignments let us write mainly about personal experiences, but most ask us **to use material from outside sources,** like articles and books. For example, a high school teacher might assign a topic like "Write about a time you felt peer pressure to do something you didn't want to do," but an assignment in a college course in human development is more likely to be something like "How does the pressure to fit in affect adolescent behavior?" When we refer to outside sources in our papers, we have to *document* our sources. (See Chapter 2.)

We have to know how to narrow broad topics.

We might get a broad assignment like "Write a short essay on religion and culture." We would have to **use some of the techniques we learned in our writing courses** to come up with something manageable—for example, an Eagle Scout's request to restore the previously removed words "to God" to his badge so that it read "For Service to God and Country." (For help on narrowing a topic, see p. 63.)

Every revision of every book is shaped by executives and long-time friends in the Boston office: Joan Feinberg, president; Denise Wydra, editorial director; Karen Henry, editor in chief; and Karen Soeltz, marketing director—this one is no exception. As I've said often, they are a superb team.

I worked for the first time with two other editorial maestre in the New York office: Erica Appel, director of development, and Senior Editor Alexis Walker, both of whom helped immensely with thoughts about this revision. Alexis brought fresh eyes, expert editorial skills, and new ideas to the project, along with a limitless tolerance for a sometimes cranky, Luddite-like author. Thank you, Alexis. I also continue to thank Beth Castrodale, my other editor, for helping supply information that Alexis and I needed and I forgot. I'm a lucky author.

Finally, as always, thanks to my husband, Jim, on whom I depend for the most important things in life.

To all of you, thank you.

—Susan Anker

and talented all-around editor/writer/actor, crafted wonderful questions, prompts, and ideas for the readings. Bruce Thaler contributed exercises, and I marvel at his ability to come up with accurate and interesting practices. Sally Gearhart has become my go-to person for all things ESL, and I continually call on her knowledge and experience. Claire Seng-Niemoeller once again pulled new designs from her magic artist tool kit. Rosemary Winfield eagle-eyed and tamed errors and infelicities in her copyediting of the manuscript.

I thank several other people for their extremely useful and timely contributions for *Practical Suggestions for Teaching REAL ESSAYS.* Craig Kleinman, who has helped me in many ways over the years, wrote a chapter about using writing portfolios, and Linda Nilson allowed me to include her piece "Getting Students to Do the Readings." A person who has not formally contributed to this book but has introduced me to unique students and ideas is Wick Sloane.

Bedford/St. Martin's

As always, I am deeply indebted to the many at Bedford/St. Martin's who collaborate with me. With each successive project, I am more grateful and appreciative, and with each I vow to rein in the kudos. So to all of you, please know that the words don't match the appreciation.

In the editorial department, Cecilia Seiter coordinated many elements of the book and kept things moving along smoothly during the writing. Martha Friedman and Helane Prottas secured art permissions, while Sandy Schechter and Warren Drabek corralled permissions for written material. Billy Boardman patiently and artfully presided over the cover conception and design, and Hope Tompkins produced the illustrative and informative brochure.

The New Media team, all of them, create supersmart and useful tools for teachers and instructors—far beyond what I can even understand. In particular, Dan Cole was instrumental in developing the *Real Essays* e-book and *WritingClass,* and Kamali Thornell oversaw the production of the many Web sites full of terrific information and options.

In the marketing and sales department, too, I owe thanks to whole groups of people; here I'll single out Casey Carroll, marketing manager, who is the perfect connector among salespeople, editorial staff, and me. Along with Casey, Dennis Adams, humanities specialist manager, is a tenacious yet gracious advocate for our books.

I am always greatly delighted to work with Karen Baart in the production department, and working with her on this edition of *Real Essays* more deeply rooted that sentiment. The assistance of Production Associate Lindsay DiGianvittorio was likewise invaluable.

We often talk about how one reading or concept relates to another.

If one reading reminds you of another, make a note, and bring it up in your next class. **Your teacher will be impressed.**

Teacher Expectations

College teachers have definite expectations of us. Basically, being successful is *your* responsibility. That means the following things:

Do Treat your course as seriously as you'd treat a job.

Your boss doesn't *give* you money—you *earn* it, through hard work and professional behavior. Likewise, your teacher doesn't *give* you a grade. You *earn* the grade you get. Think of your course work as a job that can lead to bigger and better things—if you work hard and perform well.

Do Get to class on time, and stay until your teacher dismisses you.

Again, going to class is like going to a job—you have to come and go on the boss's schedule, not yours.

Do Come to class prepared.

You have to do your homework or expect to fail. Even if you've never done homework before and have managed to pass, you won't pass in college. You'll also have points taken off for late homework.

Do Let your teacher know if you have to miss a class, and make sure to contact him or her about work missed.

Some teachers want you to get information about what you missed from a classmate, so ask first.

Do Read the syllabus carefully and hang onto it for the entire semester.

Your teacher will expect you to know what the homework is and when assignments are due: Your syllabus will tell you. Always bring your syllabus to class, in case your teacher announces updates or reminders. (For more on reading a class syllabus, see p. 34.)

Do Pay close attention to the teacher's comments on your work.

Good teachers spend a lot of time commenting on your work. When you get your papers back, don't focus on the grade alone. If you don't carefully read the comments, you'll miss a lot of the value in your courses. Also, each teacher has different priorities, and you can get better grades on your work for the course when you know those priorities.

Advice,
continued

Do Get to know your teacher, and make sure he or she knows you.

Communication is important. If you get a low grade or don't understand something, either ask in class or make an appointment to visit your teacher during office hours. It's up to you to take steps to clear up anything you don't understand.

Do Ask questions if you aren't clear about an assignment.

Your instructor may assume that you know things you don't, so expectations and assignments may not be as clearly spelled out as they were in previous classes. Don't be afraid to ask—if it's not clear to you, chances are it's not clear to at least some of your classmates.

Do Participate in class: Ask questions, answer questions, and make comments.

Don't be afraid of making a stupid comment or giving the wrong answer. That's part of how you learn. Plus, many teachers grade on participation.

Do Listen and take notes.

When the teacher is talking, listen carefully, but don't try to write down every word that he or she says. To figure out what you should make a note of, look at the teacher while she talks. When she says something important, she may make an arm or hand gesture, write something on the board, or change her tone of voice.

Do Sit near the front of the class.

Sitting near the front is important for a number of different reasons:

- The teacher can see you. (When the teacher knows that you're there, he or she will likely get to know you sooner. Sitting in front also signals that you're motivated.)
- You can see the teacher, the board, and any visual aids used in class.
- You're less likely to be distracted by any of your less motivated classmates.

What to Listen for While Taking Notes

1. **What is the teacher talking about?** (Listen for introductions like *today we're going to discuss. . . .*)

2. **What points does she want me to know about that topic?** (Listen for words like *there are five different reasons,* and for transitions between points, like *also, it's important, another thing, remember, then.*)

3. **What's the most important thing about each point?** (Listen for words like *key, critical, this is important because, most important, primary, main.*) If you think one idea relates to another, make a note of it. Making these kinds of connections is what your teacher calls *synthesis.*

4. **What's her wrap-up?** (Listen for words that signal a conclusion like *therefore, so, in essence, in conclusion, finally, as you can see, so that's why, so we need to understand, so the point is. . . .*) Teachers often restate their major points toward the end. If you don't understand or have missed something, this is the time to ask questions.

Don't Sit in the back of the room, text message, or fall asleep.

Doing any of these will create a bad impression, waste your time, and waste your money. If you don't want to be there, stay home.

Don't Make excuses for not having your homework or assignment.

Explain that you don't have it, and tell the teacher when the work will be completed. Then make sure it is done by the date you've promised. (If your teacher does not accept late work, it's not a bad idea to complete the assignment anyway and submit it. It might not count toward your grade, but your teacher will respect your effort—and the writing practice won't hurt.)

A Few Other Things

A few other things that we want you to know don't fit easily into one of the categories above, but they're important.

Your college writing courses are important.

We've said it before, and we really mean it. Don't make the mistake of taking your writing courses lightly. You have to pass them to graduate, and what you learn there will affect how well you do in your other courses. Remember, **you're in charge of your success.** Don't fail yourself.

Keep up with your courses; don't fall behind, because it's really hard to catch up.

When you get home and you're tired, take a short break, but force yourself to do your homework and study. **You have to be mature** about your college responsibilities.

Don't leave big assignments until the last minute.

If you do, either you won't be able to finish, or you'll do a bad job and get a bad grade.

You need to really *think*, not just repeat others' ideas.

Your experience makes you unique, and your ideas will reflect that. Let other people know who you are—in class discussions and in what you write.

Have confidence in yourself.

If you try hard enough, you *will* learn. Even though you'll have to work hard, remember that **what you do will help you in your other courses and in your life.**

Four Strategies for Success

The strategies for success that follow here apply to your college courses, your work, and your everyday life. Before getting into these, though, *remember the number four* as you use this book.

To make remembering some important information easier for you, this book frequently uses the number four, as in these cases:

- Four Basics of Critical Reading (p. 23)
- Four Basics of Good Writing (p. 45)
- Four Basics of [each of the kinds of writing you will do] (Chapters 10–18)
- Four Most Serious Errors (Chapters 22–26)

So *remember the number four,* and when you see one of the charts or lists of Four Basics, make note of the information. It should help you remember it when you need to use it.

Identify Your Goals

You're in college, so we'll assume that one of your goals is to get a college degree. You may even know what kind of degree you want and what type of job you want. It's helpful to have goals for steps along the way to those larger goals, too. For example, you need to pass this course, so start by developing some writing goals. Although this course is new to you, you've written in your previous courses, so you probably have some idea of how you need to improve your writing.

Writing Goals

ACTIVITY: Think about the writing you have done in previous courses. What kinds of writing did you do? What kinds of grades did you get? When you are given an assignment, how do you begin? What problems do you think you have with writing?

Now list at least four writing goals—skills you want to learn, practice, or improve in this course. Be as specific as possible. For example, "Learn to write better" is too general to help you focus on what you need to do. Throughout the course, refer to this list of skills and abilities, and make sure you achieve these writing goals.

1. _____

2. _____

3. _____

4. _____

Degree Goals

If you know what you want to major in, you're already ahead of many other students. However, do you know what courses you need to take to get a degree in that major? They should be listed in the college bulletin, but you should also make an appointment with your academic adviser to plan the sequence of courses that will lead to your degree. Even if you don't yet know your major, the college probably has some core courses that every student has to take to graduate. It would help you to list those courses and the semesters in which you plan to take them.

In the spaces that follow, list your desired major (if you know it) and the courses that you need to take to get a degree in that major. As you reach the end of this term, quarter, or semester, consult this list as you register for more courses. If you're like most students, you're juggling a lot of important things—like a job, perhaps children, and certainly the day-to-day things that keep our lives going. Having a plan to reach your goals will help you achieve them.

I want to major in _____.

Courses I will need for that major (If you don't know your major yet, list the courses that are required for all students.)

_____

_____

_____

_____

_____

_____

_____

Number of courses I can take next term _____

Courses I should take if they fit into my schedule (Remember, certain courses have other courses as a prerequisite.)

_____

_____

Manage Your Time

We all have too much to do to remember everything. Most successful students use a planner of some sort—a calendar or notebook that lists what they need to do and when.

Many Web sites (for example, **calendar.google.com** or **myfreecalendar .com**) offer calendars that are free for you to download, either to use on a computer or to print out. Your e-mail program and cell phone may already have calendars built in. Two examples of calendars follow: a course calendar that lists all the things you need to do for a particular course and a general calendar that integrates school tasks with other tasks.

Make a Course Calendar

A course calendar plots all the work you need to do for a course so that you can see what needs to be done and when you need to do it. Following is an example of a monthly calendar that you might keep for an English course.

College Writing, Tuesday/Thursday, 8:30–10:00 a.m.
Professor Murphy
Office hours: T/Th, 11:00–12:30, and by appointment

		1	**2**	**3**	**4**	**5**
		8:30–10:00: Class. *Draft due, illustration.*	*12:00: Study with Genie.* *Study for test on fragments and run-ons (Chs. 22–24).*	*8:30–10:00: Class. Test, Chs. 22–24.*		*Work on revising illustration essay.*
6	**7**	**8**	**9**	**10**	**11**	**12**
		8:30–10:00: Class.	*11:30: Appt. at writing center.*	*8:30–10:00: Class. Final illustration essay due.*		
13	**14**	**15**	**16**	**17**	**18**	**19**
	Study for test on subject-verb agreement (Chs. 25–26).	*8:30–10:00: Class. Test, Chs. 25–26.*		*8:30–10:00: Class.* *11:00: Appt. with Prof. Murphy.* *Start description essay.*		
20	**21**	**22**	**23**	**24**	**25**	**26**
		8:30–10:00: Class. Draft due, description essay.		*8:30–10:00: Class.*	*Work on revising description essay.*	
27	**28**	**29**	**30**	**31**		
	Study for test on past-tense verbs (Ch. 26).	*8:30–10:00: Class. Test, past-tense verbs.*		*8:30–10:00: Class. Final description essay due.*		

Make a General Calendar

A course calendar helps you manage time for course work, but you should also keep track of every other commitment you have. Be sure to leave some unscheduled time for rest, fun, and unexpected events. If you don't want to make separate calendars, make one master calendar with all of your college, work, and everyday life commitments, and keep it with you wherever you go.

Following is part of the calendar you just saw, with additional appointments and tasks filled in. The student who made this calendar is taking two courses, working, and caring for a two-year-old daughter, Lottie.

		1	**2**	**3**	**4**	**5**
12:00–6:00: Work. 7:00: Mom, dinner. 9:00: Illustration draft.	8:00–4:00: Work. 5:00: Pick up Lottie, day care. 8:00–9:30: Study for math test.	8:30–10:00: English. Draft due, illustration. 12:00–6:00: Work. 7:00–10:00: Math. Test, Chs. 5–6.	8:00–4:00: Work. 12:00: Study with Genie. 4:30: Doctor. 5:30: Pick up Lottie. 8:00: Study for English test. Math homework.	8:30–10:00: English. Test, Chs. 22–24. 11:00: Food shopping. 12:00–6:00: Work. 7:00–10:00: Math.	8:00–4:00: Work. 5:00: Pick up Lottie, get present for birthday party.	Work on revising illustration essay. Clean, do laundry. 6:00: Lottie to party.

Use All Resources

Many students don't know how many campus resources are available to them for free. For example, here is a list of resources most colleges offer:

- Writing Center and writing tutors
- Financial Aid office
- Employment Office
- Office of Student Affairs (with many programs)
- Counseling Office
- Mini-courses or seminars on a wide variety of topics
- Ride-sharing and babysitting exchange boards

Your community also offers many resources. Call your local town or city hall, and ask about the services the town offers. Remember, your tuition and your taxes pay for these services, so take advantage of them.

 ACTIVITY   LOCATING COLLEGE RESOURCES . . . .

Look at your college's catalog or Web site, and list five services that might be useful to you.

. . . .

Find Your Learning Style

People learn in different ways, and knowing how you learn best will help you succeed in college. Take the learning style questionnaire that follows. It will tell you what your learning style is. Then, read about how you can use your learning style in college. Understanding how to use your particular learning style will definitely help you succeed.

Learning Style Questionnaire

For each item on the following questionnaire, circle the answer that is *most* like what you would do. There are no right or wrong answers.

VARK QUESTIONNAIRE ON LEARNING STYLES

1. You are about to give directions to a friend who is staying in a hotel in town and wants to visit you at home later. She has a rental car. Would you
   a. draw a map for her?
   b. tell her the directions?
   c. write down the directions (without a map)?
   d. pick her up at her hotel?

2. You are not sure whether a word is spelled *dependent* or *dependant*. Would you
   c. look it up in a dictionary?
   a. see the word in your mind and choose it by the way it looks?
   b. sound it out in your mind?
   d. write both versions on paper and choose one?

3. You have just planned a great trip, and your friend wants to hear about it. Would you
   b. phone him immediately and tell him about it?
   c. send him a copy of the printed itinerary?
   a. show him on a map of the world?
   d. share what you plan to do at each place you visit?

4. You are going to cook something as a special treat for your family. Do you
   d. cook something familiar without a recipe?
   a. look at the pictures in a cookbook for ideas?
   c. look for a particular recipe in a cookbook?

5. Your job is to help a group of tourists learn about parks in your state. Would you

    d. drive them to a park?

    a. show them slides or go to a Web site that has pictures?

    c. give them some booklets on parks?

    b. give them a talk on parks?

6. You are about to buy a new CD player. Other than price, what would most influence your decision?

    b. the salesperson telling you what you want to know

    c. reading about it in a consumer magazine

    d. trying it out at the store

    a. it looks very cool

7. Recall a time when you learned how to do something, like playing a board game. Try to avoid using a physical skill like riding a bike. How did you learn best? By

    a. looking at pictures, diagrams, or charts.

    c. reading written instructions.

    b. listening to somebody explaining it.

    d. doing it or trying it.

8. You have a knee problem. Would you prefer that the doctor

    b. tell you what is wrong?

    a. show you a diagram of what is wrong?

    d. use a model to show you what is wrong?

9. You are about to learn to use a new computer program. Would you

    d. sit at the keyboard and play with the program's features?

    c. read the manual?

    b. phone a friend and ask questions about it?

10. You are staying in a hotel and have a rental car. You would like to visit friends whose addresses/locations you don't know. Would you like them to

    a. draw you a map?

    b. tell you the directions?

    c. write down the directions (without a map)?

    d. pick you up at the hotel?

11. Aside from price, what would most influence your decision to buy a particular kind of textbook?

    d. the fact that you used a copy before

    b. a friend talking about it

    c. quickly reading parts of it

    a. the way it looks (color, photographs, and so on)

12. What would most influence your decision to go see a new movie?

    b. You heard a review of it on the radio.

    c. You read a review of it.

    a. You saw a preview of it.

13. You prefer a teacher who uses

    c. textbooks, handouts, readings.

    a. diagrams, charts, and slides.

    d. field trips, labs.

    b. discussions, guest speakers.

Now, count how many a's you circled, and write that number in the blank beside the "V" (visual) below. Put the number of b's you circled beside the "A" (auditory), put the number of c's you circled beside the "R" (read/write), and put the number of d's you circled beside the "K" (kinesthetic). Circle the letter next to your highest score. This is your strongest learning style. If you have two scores that are the same, that means that you have two equally strong learning styles, as many people do.

——   **V**   Visual
——   **A**   Auditory
——   **R**   Read/write
——   **K**   Kinesthetic (movement)

Use Your Learning Style in College

To figure out how to apply your learning style in college, look at the following sections, and read the one that matches your style. If you have a preference for more than one learning style, read all the sections that apply.

Visual

Visual learners learn best by drawing, looking at images, or "seeing" things as they read, write, and listen.

USING YOUR LEARNING STYLE	
To read/study →	• Draw pictures or diagrams of concepts. • Use colored highlighters to mark what you want to remember. • Note headings in texts, and look at diagrams, charts, graphs, maps, pictures, and other visuals. • Write symbols that mean something to you in the margins. (For example, write exclamation points by the most important information in a chapter.) • Make your own flowcharts or time lines. • Make outlines in different-colored inks.
To write →	• Use mapping or clustering to get ideas. (See p. 65.) • Use charts or outlines to plan, write, and revise. (See Chapter 7.) • Use correction symbols to edit. (See the symbols at the back of this book.)
To take a test →	• Highlight important information, or put check marks or other symbols by it. • Make a flowchart or outline of your answers.

Auditory

Auditory learners learn best by hearing things.

USING YOUR LEARNING STYLE	
To read/study →	• Read aloud notes, texts, handouts, and so on.
	• Tape lectures and class discussions (but don't forget to take notes, too). Later, you can listen to the recordings.
	• Listen to course-related audio CDs or tapes.
	• Talk to other students about course material.
	• Work with other students to prepare for class, complete activities, and so on.
To write →	• Get ideas by talking to yourself or others.
	• Read your writing aloud as you draft.
	• Read your writing aloud as you revise and edit.
To take a test →	• Read the directions and test items aloud in a quiet whisper.
	• Read your answers aloud in a quiet whisper.

Read/Write

Read/write learners learn best by reading and writing throughout a course.

USING YOUR LEARNING STYLE	
To read/study →	• Read headings, summaries, and questions in books. • Put what you read into your own words. • Take careful notes from books and lectures, and read them later. • Keep and read all handouts. • Highlight when you read. • Describe charts, diagrams, maps, and other visuals in writing.
To write →	• Freewrite or brainstorm to get ideas. (See p. 69.) • Keep a journal. (See p. 72.) • Read and reread what you write, making notes for revision. • Revise your writing several times.
To take a test →	• Read and highlight the directions. • Write an outline for essay questions, or write quickly and revise. • Reread your answers carefully.

Kinesthetic (Movement)

Kinesthetic learners learn by doing and by moving around.

USING YOUR LEARNING STYLE	
To read/study →	• Stand up when you read or study. • Take short breaks, and walk around. • Underline or highlight readings, or make notes. • Make flash cards to study course material. • Make puzzles (like crosswords) to help you remember important concepts. • Make your own study guides. • Relate information to your own experiences. • Mark examples in texts that are relevant to you. • Write out questions that you have, and ask them. • Work with other students to prepare for class, complete activities, and so on.
To write →	• Imagine your topic as a movie to get ideas. • Think of ideas for writing as you walk. • Imagine what pictures could express your ideas. • Write ideas or details for a paper on sticky notes, and move the notes around. • Create a writing notebook with different pockets for different kinds of ideas or writing. • Write and ask questions about your topic.
To take a test →	• Breathe deeply and regularly throughout the test. • Stand up and walk to a different part of the room (after asking your instructor for permission). • Calculate the time you will spend on each part of the test, and time yourself. • Stand and take a deep breath as you review your answers.

2

Reading and Writing in College and Beyond

What You Need to Know

Reading carefully and purposefully can boost your chances of success in college, on the job, and in everyday life. Good readers can find solid, practical information about anything they are interested in — making money, investing, starting a business, finding a job, treating an illness, buying a car at the best price, and so on. Most of us don't need to become lovers of good literature—though some of you may—but we do need to know how to read carefully—in college, at work, and in our everyday lives.

This chapter previews the skills you need to succeed and also shows how they are linked to good writing. So use this chapter's information to help you: Your grades depend on good reading skills.

How to Read in College

In college, you will read a variety of materials — course syllabi, handouts, textbooks, articles, essays, literature, Web sites, and more. While you will read these materials in slightly different ways, they all require you to be able to read closely and critically.

Close reading means paying attention to every word and every point. You should closely read course syllabi, tests, and textbooks, taking in every word and highlighting important points. **Critical reading** requires both close reading and more — asking yourself why the author has made these points in this way, what they mean, and whether you agree. You will apply critical reading to textbooks, articles, essays, and literature.

Critical reading is active. You have to get involved with what you read in order to understand it, and this means being mentally alert. For many people, lying down is not a good way to read because it can cause drowsiness. Instead, read sitting up with a good light source, and have a pencil, pen, or highlighter in your hand. Try reading aloud, too.

The following basics will help you get the most out of the reading you do in this course and others.

■■
■■ **FOUR BASICS OF CRITICAL READING**

1. Preview the essay, article, or chapter.

2. Find the main point and the support for that point.

3. Take notes on paper or in the text.

4. Review and respond to what you have read.

Preview the Reading

Before reading any piece of writing, skim or preview the whole thing, using the following steps.

Read the Title, Headnote, and Introductory Paragraphs Quickly

The title of a chapter, an article, or any other document usually gives you some idea of what the topic is. Some documents are introduced by headnotes, which summarize or provide background about the selection. If there is a headnote, read it. Whether or not there is a headnote, writers often introduce their topic and main point in the first few paragraphs, so read those, and note what you think the main point might be.

Read Headings, Key Words, and Definitions

Textbooks and magazine articles often include headings to help readers follow the author's ideas. These headings (such as "Preview the Reading" above) tell you what the important subjects of the writing are.

Any terms in **boldface** type are especially important. In textbooks, writers often use boldface for key words that are important to the topic. Read the definitions of key words as you preview the writing.

Look for Summaries, Checklists, and Chapter Reviews

Many textbooks (such as this one) include features that summarize or list main points. Review summaries, checklists, or chapter reviews to make sure you have understood the main points.

Read the Conclusion Quickly

Writers usually review their main point in their concluding paragraphs. Read the conclusion, and compare it with the note you made after you read the introduction and thought about what the main idea might be.

Ask a Guiding Question

As the final step in your preview of a reading, ask yourself a **guiding question** — that is, a question you think the reading might answer. Sometimes, you can turn the title into a guiding question. For example, read the title of this chapter, and write a possible guiding question. As you begin your close reading, try to answer your guiding question. Having a guiding question gives you a purpose for reading and helps keep you focused.

Find the Main Point and the Support

After previewing a reading, begin reading carefully for meaning, trying especially to identify a writer's main point and the support for that point.

Main Point

■ For more on main points, see Chapter 5.

The **main point** of a reading is the central idea the author wants to communicate. Writers usually introduce their main point early, so read the first few paragraphs with special care. After reading the first paragraph (or more, depending on the length of the reading selection), stop and write down — in your own words — what you think the main idea is. If the writer has stated the main point in a single sentence, <u>double-underline it.</u>

 PRACTICE 1   FINDING THE MAIN POINT . . . .

Read each of the following paragraphs. Then, write the main point in your own words in the spaces provided.

1. Neighbors who are too friendly can be seen just about anywhere. I mean that both ways. They exist in every neighborhood I have ever lived in and

seem to appear everywhere I go. For some strange reason these people become extremely attached to my family and stop in as many as eight to ten times a day. No matter how tired I appear to be, nothing short of opening the door and suggesting they leave will make them go home at night. (I once told an unusually friendly neighbor that his house was on fire, in an attempt to make him leave, and he still took ten minutes to say goodbye.) What is truly interesting about these people is their strong desire to cook for us even though they have developed no culinary skill whatsoever. (This has always proved particularly disconcerting since they stay to watch us eat every bite as they continually ask if the food "tastes good.")

— From Jonathan R. Gould Jr., "The People Next Door"

■ For online exercises on main points, visit *Exercise Central* at **bedfordstmartins .com/realessays**.

2. Relief from depression may be a mouse click away. Australian researchers have developed Web sites to fight depression. In a study of 525 people, those who visited a site designed to reduce anxiety and develop coping skills (moodgym.anu.edu.au) showed a 25 percent improvement in depression symptoms. Those who visited a site offering information about depression (bluepages.anu.edu.au) improved by 20 percent. A control group who participated in weekly phone discussions improved by only 8 percent. The sites are available online for public use.

— From Kate Dailey, ed., "Health Bulletin," *Men's Health*, June 2004

3. Entrepreneurs have certain traits, such as being creative innovators, moderate risk takers, independent, and determined to achieve success. Also, previous experience in managing a business often helps to make a successful entrepreneur. However, a person who has these characteristics may not be motivated to use them to launch a business until a precipitating event occurs. A **precipitating event** is a change in the environment that spurs an individual to take action. Such events can take various forms. They may be part of an individual's personal life, such as a change in health, family makeup, or financial status. They may be technological innovations that enable a new type of work or work in a new location. Or else they may be job-related events beyond the individual's control — layoffs, mergers, changes in corporate management, market changes, or even a sudden entrepreneurial opportunity.

— From Kenneth H. Blanchard et al., *Exploring the World of Business* (1996)

4. Class attendance and participation are essential since we do many in-class writings and much group work, which are part of a student's grade in the course. If you must miss a class and know this in advance, please contact me so that we can discuss work and assignments that you will miss. For excused absences — student illness, a death in the family, an accident, and religious holidays — you must arrange to make up work missed, and that work must be submitted within a week. Other absences will be considered unexcused absences unless discussed with me. Any student who has more than three unexcused absences will be asked to drop the course.

— From a syllabus for a writing course

Support

■ For more on support, see Chapter 6.

Support for the main point consists of details, explanations, or evidence. The type of support provided depends on the purpose of the piece of writing.

DOCUMENT	SUPPORT
Course syllabus	Details about course objectives, grading policies, classroom rules, and assignment due dates
Textbook	Explanations of topics or concepts in a chapter
Essay	Details, facts, and examples that help explain the author's main point
Short story	Details that reveal characters and situations

■ For online exercises on support, visit *Exercise Central* at **bedfordstmartins .com/realessays**.

PRACTICE 2   FINDING SUPPORT

Go back to Practice 1 (p. 24), where you identified the main point of each passage. Now, underline the support for each main point.

Take Notes

Another way to read critically is to take notes. Taking notes can help you understand a reading and keep you alert. Using check marks and other symbols, underlining, or highlighting can also make important parts stand out. Here are some ideas about how to take notes:

- Note the <u>thesis statement</u> (double-underline it).
- Note the major <u>support points</u> (underline them).
- Note ideas you agree with (put a check mark ✓ in the margin).
- Note ideas you don't agree with or are surprised by (put an **X** or **!** in the margin).
- Note points or words you don't understand (put a **?** in the margin).
- Note information that answers your guiding question (write "guiding question" in the margin).
- Note thoughts or reactions you have while reading.

Review and Respond

Often, your instructor will ask you to answer questions about a reading or to write about it. To do either, you may need to review the reading, looking at your notes and your highlighting before responding. The following Critical Thinking guide will help you.

CRITICAL THINKING: READING CRITICALLY

FOCUS

- Review the reading selection.

ASK

- What is the author's main point?
- What evidence and explanations does the writer use to back the main point?
- Does the support actually help me understand the main point, or am I left with questions and doubts?
- Has the author convinced me of his or her point of view? How has the piece changed my feelings about the topic?
- What do I think about the author's message? Why?
- How does what I've learned connect to other things I know? How does it relate to experiences I have had?

WRITE

- Based on the answers to your questions and your assignment, write a response to the reading selection.

An Active Reader at Work

Before moving to the section on reading college textbooks, read the following piece. The notes in the margins show how one student, Tom, read an essay assigned in a writing course. Many of his comments show how he read critically by thinking about how the writer's points related to his own experiences. Additionally, he noted points that seemed likely to be important for a class discussion or writing assignment. You may want to use this sample as a model for the reading you do in the following chapters.

Deborah Tannen

It Begins at the Beginning

Guiding Question: How do boys and girls differ in their play and the language they use in their play?

Deborah Tannen is a professor of linguistics at Georgetown University in Washington, D.C. Linguistics — the study of human language — reveals much about people and their culture. Part of Tannen's research in linguistics has focused on differences in how women and men use language and how those differences affect communication. The following excerpt, taken from her book *You Just Don't Understand,* describes how girls' and boys' language and communication patterns differ from a very early age.

Thesis

Even if they grow up in the same neighborhood, on the same block, or in the same house, girls and boys grow up in different worlds of words. Others talk to them differently and expect and accept different ways of

✔ Yep—friends are key.

talking from them. Most important, children learn how to talk, how to have conversations, not only from their parents, but from their peers. . . . Although they often play together, boys and girls spend most of their time playing in same-sex groups. And, although some of the activities they play

Still true today?? (computers?)

at are similar, their favorite games are different, and their ways of using language in their games are separated by a world of difference.

Examples (boy's play)—might be part of discussion/quiz.

Boys tend to play outside, in large groups that are hierarchically structured. Their groups have a leader who tells others what to do and how to do it, and resists doing what other boys propose. It is by giving orders and making them stick that high status is negotiated. Another way boys achieve status is to take center stage by telling jokes, and by sidetracking or challenging the stories and jokes of others. Boys' games have winners and losers and elaborate systems of rules, and the players frequently boast their skill and argue about who is best at what.

! But don't boys & girls play together—at least sometimes?

Girls, on the other hand, play in small groups or in pairs; the center of a girl's social life is a best friend. . . . In their most frequent games, such as jump rope and hopscotch, everyone gets a turn. Many of their activities (such as playing house) do not have winners or losers. Though some girls are certainly more skilled than others, girls are expected not to boast about it, or show that they think they are better than the others. Girls don't give orders; they express their preferences as suggestions, and suggestions are likely to be accepted. Anything else is put down as bossy. They don't grab center stage — they don't want it — so they don't challenge each other directly. And much of the time, they simply sit together and talk. Girls are not accustomed to jockeying for status in an obvious way; they are more concerned that they be liked.

More examples (girls' play).

Question: Does Tannen think these differences affect how adult men and women work together?

— Adapted from Deborah Tannen,
You Just Don't Understand (New York:
HarperCollins, 1990)

Reading College Textbooks

Most textbooks have special features to help students find and understand key information. The sections below will give you practice in recognizing these features.

Finding Information

Reading a long, dense textbook can be a challenge, so textbooks use a number of features to help you find your way. The most common of these are described below, with page numbers that direct you to an example of the feature in this textbook.

Table of Contents

If you want to find a particular chapter, use the brief table of contents (pp. v–vi). If you're looking for specific information within a chapter, try the detailed table of contents (beginning on p. vii), which lists chapter titles and major headings.

Index

If you want to find a particular topic, you can also use the index starting on page I-1. Topics are listed alphabetically. To find information on using apostrophes in contractions, look under "apostrophes," and find the subentry "in contractions." The page number will direct you to the right information.

> Anthology, citing, 316
> Apostrophes, 571–579
>   in contractions, 574
>   definition of, 571
>   editing for, 577–579
>   with letters, numbers, time, 576
>   to show ownership, 571–572
> Appositives

Chart of Correction Symbols

Some instructors use symbols to indicate grammar, spelling, or punctuation errors in your writing. You can use the chart at the back of this book to find the meaning of each symbol and a chapter reference for more help.

adj	Use correct adjective form
adv	Use correct adverb form
agr	Correct subject-verb agreement or pronoun agreement
awk	Awkward expression: edit for clarity
cap	Use capital letter correctly

Headings at the Tops of Pages

When you want to know where you are in the book, look at the headings that run along the tops of the pages. The left page gives you the name of the part of the book you're in (for example, Part One • How to Read and Write in College), and the right page tells you which chapter you're in (Chapter 2 • Reading and Writing in College and Beyond).

■ For more practice correcting run-ons, visit *Exercise Central* at **bedfordstmartins .com/realessays**.

___ 9. There are differen
and listening to n
tion from the driv

___ 10. Drivers who love
striction many ot

Marginal Notes

Real Essays includes helpful tips and references printed in the margin. These direct you to additional information or resources in the book or on the book's companion Web site.

■ **PRACTICE 3   FINDING INFORMATION IN TEXTBOOKS** • • • • • • • • • •

Complete the exercises below to practice using the Brief Contents, complete Table of Contents, and Index found in *Real Essays*.

1. **Brief Contents:** In what chapter will you find coverage of *pronouns*?

   _____

2. **Table of Contents (complete):** On what page does coverage of *citing and documenting sources* begin? _____

3. **Index:** On what page will you find out how commas are used in dates?

   _____

• •

Reading Textbook Chapters

In some textbooks, each chapter includes standard features that provide important information. Some of these features are listed below, and you can see examples of each in the excerpt from the textbook *Discovering Psychology*.

At the Beginning of a Chapter

Chapter title: The chapter title announces the major subject of that chapter.

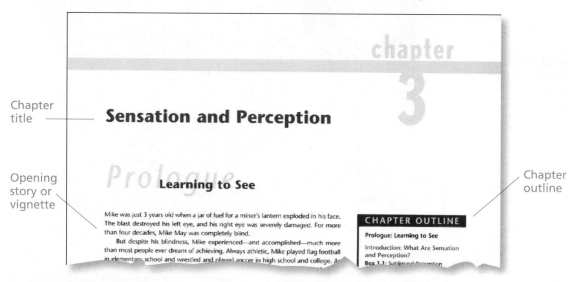

From Don H. Hockenbury and Sandra E. Hockenbury, Discovering Psychology, *4th ed. (New York: Worth, 2007)*

Chapter outline: The outline tells you what major topics will be covered in the chapter and often gives page numbers for those topics.

Opening stories or vignettes: These opening stories sometimes have different titles, but they are often real-world examples that relate to the subject of the chapter.

Throughout the Chapter

Headings: Chapters are divided into sections, and each section has a heading that tells you what's in it and how the topics fit together. Main headings introduce major topics within chapters; subheadings introduce important aspects of each topic.

First main heading sets up first topic: our experience of color.

Subheading raises intriguing question answered in text.

Visual (with explanation) clarifies key concepts.

Boldface emphasizes key words defined in text.

Definitions in the margins explain key terms.

---

94   **CHAPTER 3** *Sensation and Perception*

When Red + Blue + Green = White When light waves of different wavelengths are combined, the wavelengths are added together, producing the perception of a different color. Thus, when green light is combined with red light, yellow light is produced. When the wavelengths of red, green, and blue light are added together, we perceive the blended light as white.

color
The perceptual experience of different wavelengths of light, involving hue, saturation (purity), and brightness (intensity).

The Experience of Color
What Makes an Orange Orange?

To explain the nature of color, we must go back to the visual stimulus—light. Our experience of **color** involves three properties of the light wave. First, what we usually refer to as color is a property more accurately termed **hue.** Hue varies with the wavelength of light. Look again at Figure 3.2 on page 89. *Different wavelengths correspond to our subjective experience of different colors.* Wavelengths of about 400 nanometers are perceived as violet. Wavelengths of about 700 nanometers are perceived as red. In between are orange, yellow, green, blue, and indigo.

Second, the **saturation,** or *purity,* of the color corresponds to the purity of the light wave. Pure red, for example, produced by a single wavelength, is more *saturated* than pink, which is produced by a combination of wavelengths (red plus white light). In everyday language, saturation refers to the richness of a color. A highly saturated color is vivid and rich, whereas a less saturated color is faded and washed out.

The third property of color is **brightness,** or perceived intensity. Brightness corresponds to the amplitude of the light wave: the higher the amplitude, the greater the degree of brightness.

These three properties of color—hue, saturation, and brightness—are responsible for the amazing range of colors we experience. A person with normal color vision can discriminate from 120 to 150 color differences based on differences in hue, or wavelength, alone. When saturation and brightness are also factored in, we can potentially perceive millions of different colors (Bornstein & Marks, 1982).

Many people mistakenly believe that white light contains no color. White light actually contains all wavelengths, and thus all colors, of the visible part of the electromagnetic spectrum. A glass prism placed in sunlight creates a rainbow because it separates sunlight into all the colors of the visible light spectrum.

So we're back to the question: Why is an orange orange? Common sense tells us that the color of any object is an inseparable property of the object (unless we paint it, dye it, or spill spaghetti sauce on it). But, actually, *the color of an object is determined by the wavelength of light that the object reflects.* If your T-shirt is red, it's red because the cloth is *reflecting* only the wavelength of light that corresponds to the red portion of the spectrum. The T-shirt is *absorbing* the wavelengths that correspond to all other colors. An object appears white because it *reflects* all the wavelengths of visible light and absorbs none. An object appears black when it *absorbs* all the wavelengths of visible light and reflects none.

How We See Color

Color vision has interested scientists for hundreds of years. The first scientific

Bold-faced text: Terms in **boldface** emphasize important concepts that are defined in the text, and some books collect these terms in a separate glossary.

Visuals: Visuals (such as photos, illustrations, diagrams, and tables) usually have captions that clarify key concepts. They provide help for all students but especially for those who prefer visual learning.

Information in the margins: Many textbooks use the margins for important information such as **key words, definitions, key concepts, explanatory notes,** and other **study aids** that will help you understand the text material. *Do not skip over the information in the margins:* It may be essential to your understanding of the text material!

End of Chapter

Much of the material at the end of the chapter helps you check your understanding of what is important in the chapter and helps you review for tests or assignments. **Chapter reviews** summarize essential information such as **key points, key terms,** and **key skills. Chapter tests** let you check what information you have mastered and what you need to review.

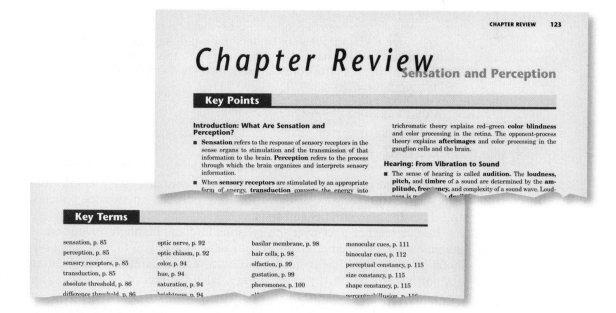

Chapter Review Sensation and Perception

Key Points

Introduction: What Are Sensation and Perception?

■ **Sensation** refers to the response of sensory receptors in the sense organs to stimulation and the transmission of that information to the brain. **Perception** refers to the process through which the brain organizes and interprets sensory information.

■ When **sensory receptors** are stimulated by an appropriate form of energy, **transduction** converts the energy into

trichromatic theory explains red–green **color blindness** and color processing in the retina. The opponent-process theory explains **afterimages** and color processing in the ganglion cells and the brain.

Hearing: From Vibration to Sound

■ The sense of hearing is called **audition.** The **loudness, pitch,** and **timbre** of a sound are determined by the **amplitude, frequency,** and complexity of a sound wave. Loud-

Key Terms

sensation, p. 85	optic nerve, p. 92	basilar membrane, p. 98	monocular cues, p. 111
perception, p. 85	optic chiasm, p. 92	hair cells, p. 98	binocular cues, p. 112
sensory receptors, p. 85	color, p. 94	olfaction, p. 99	perceptual constancy, p. 115
transduction, p. 85	hue, p. 94	gustation, p. 99	size constancy, p. 115
absolute threshold, p. 86	saturation, p. 94	pheromones, p. 100	shape constancy, p. 115
difference threshold, p. 86	brightness, p. 94		perceptual illusion, p. 116

PRACTICE 4 READING TEXTBOOK CHAPTERS . . . .

Using a textbook from another class, review a chapter for its special features. On a separate piece of paper, write the title of the book, the class you are using it in, and a list of its special features.

. . . .

You can use the following Critical Thinking guide when reading textbooks or any other readings assigned in college.

CRITICAL THINKING: READING COLLEGE MATERIAL

FOCUS
- Think carefully about any reading assignment.

ASK
- Why am I being asked to read this? To understand course expectations? To understand certain concepts that I will be tested on? To show what I have learned (on a test or in a writing assignment)? To get background information?
- Given the purpose of this assignment, what parts of the text deserve special attention?
- How can I best use features like headings, boldface type, and summaries to help me understand the selection?

WRITE
- Answer any end-of-chapter or end-of-selection questions to reinforce and improve your understanding of key concepts. If you are asked to do other writing in response to the reading, follow your instructor's directions carefully, and see the Critical Thinking box on page 27.

Reading Course Syllabi

It is important to use your course syllabus. It contains essential information such as the course objectives, grading policies, attendance policies, and dates for assignments and tests.

If your teacher goes over the syllabus in class, highlight or underline the points she or he emphasizes. If your teacher asks you to review the syllabus on your own time instead, read each section carefully, highlighting key policies and dates. If you are using a calendar, record all due dates for assignments, tests, and drafts. (See Chapter 1, p. 13.)

Syllabus
Course name and number
Meeting days and hours

Instructor information
Professor name
Phone number
E-mail address
Office hours

Course description: This course focuses on expository writing. Students will use the writing process and will read, write, and edit effectively as well as use and document library resources.

Course objectives:
- Use a variety of writing strategies.
- Recognize and correct grammar errors.
- Read and think critically and apply information.
- Develop ideas in paragraphs and essays with clear theses.
- *Etc.*

Read carefully. Your grade will depend on how well you achieve these objectives.

Course materials:
Susan Anker, *Real Essays with Readings,* Third Edition

Grading policies (*percentage of grade*):

Papers	60%	Explanation of
Tests	25%	grading policies
Homework	10%	
Class participation	5%	

Grading scale for tests and papers:

A	90–100%	Explanation of
B	80–89%	grading criteria
Etc.		

See handout with grading rubric and examples.

Course policies:
- **Attendance:** Class attendance is required. Students who miss more than one week . . . *etc.*
- **Classroom rules:** Arrive on time, turn off cell phones, . . . *etc.*
- **Late or missed work:** No late work is accepted without my consent . . . *etc.*
- **Academic integrity:** This course adheres to the college handbook, which defines the following criteria: . . . *etc.*   Explanation of course policies

Moving from Reading to Writing

Reading and writing skills are closely related: If you can read critically, you are in a good position to do college writing assignments. (Remember that critical reading means understanding the main point and the support, thinking about how effective the support is, and considering your own response to the reading and how it relates to your own experiences.) In many of your courses, you write about what you read.

Just as you will read many types of documents in college, you will write many types of assignments, such as essays, reports, summaries, reviews, exams, and research papers. Some types of writing will require skills that may be new to you. We introduce those skills here so that you can draw on them when a writing assignment requires them.

Key College Skills: Summary, Analysis, Synthesis, and Evaluation

College writing assignments often require you to demonstrate your deep understanding of subject matter, which you get through critical reading. For example, you may be asked to show some or all of the following about what you have read:

- Your basic understanding of its content (summarizing)
- Your ability to identify its points and parts (analyzing)
- Your ability to relate it to other information and experiences (synthesizing)
- Your ability to judge its effectiveness (evaluating)

The "Writing about Readings" assignments at the end of each chapter in Part Two, Writing Different Kinds of Essays, will call on these key college skills.

Read the passage from *Discovering Psychology* on page 37 and the four sections that follow it. Each section covers one of the skills just described, defines the skill in more detail, and shows how it could be applied in writing about the passage.

Daily Hassles
That's Not What I Ordered!

What made you feel "stressed out" in the last week? Chances are it was not a major life event. Instead, it was probably some unexpected but minor annoyance, such as splotching ketchup on your new white T-shirt, misplacing your keys, or discovering that you've been standing in the wrong line.

Stress researcher **Richard Lazarus** and his colleagues suspected that such ordinary irritations in daily life might be an important source of stress. To explore this idea, they developed a scale measuring **daily hassles**—everyday occurrences that annoy and upset people (DeLongis & others, 1982; Kanner & others, 1981). The *Daily Hassles Scale* measures the occurrence of everyday annoyances, such as losing something, getting stuck in traffic, and even being inconvenienced by lousy weather.

Are there gender differences in the frequency of daily hassles? One study measured the daily hassles experienced by married couples (Almeida & Kessler, 1998). The women experienced both more daily hassles and higher levels of psychological stress than their husbands did. For men, the most common sources of daily stress were financial and job-related problems. For women, family demands and interpersonal conflict were the most frequent causes of stress. However, when women *do* experience a stressful day in the workplace, the stress is more likely to spill over into their interactions with their husbands and other family members (Schulz & others, 2004). Men, on the other hand, are more likely to simply withdraw.

How important are daily hassles in producing stress? The frequency of daily hassles is linked to both psychological distress and physical symptoms, such as headaches and backaches (DeLongis & others, 1988). In fact, the number of daily hassles people experience is a better predictor of physical illness and symptoms than is the number of major life events experienced (Burks & Martin, 1985).

Why do daily hassles take such a toll? One explanation is that such minor stressors are *cumulative* (Repetti, 1993). Each hassle may be relatively unimportant in itself, but after a day filled with minor hassles, the effects add up. People feel drained, grumpy, and stressed out. Daily hassles also contribute to the stress produced by major life events. Any major life change, whether positive or negative, can create a ripple effect, generating a host of new daily hassles (Pillow & others, 1996).

Summary

A **summary** is a condensed version of a piece of writing. It presents the main points and key support in a brief form and in your own words. Think of a summary as making a long story short.

Hockenbury and Hockenbury tell us that daily hassles often cause more stress than major problems do. According to several studies, men and women report different kinds of daily stress and react to stress differently, though both experience psychological and physical symptoms. Some research shows that daily hassles produce stress because their effects are cumulative — that is, they add up over time to create major stress.

[The example identifies the main point and lists the factors that support that main point.]

Analysis

An **analysis** breaks down the points of a piece of writing and considers how they relate to each other. For a writing assignment, you might choose one particular point to analyze.

> We've all read a lot about stress, but Hockenbury and Hockenbury have something new and interesting to say about it: It's not the big life crises but the million petty hassles we face every day that get to us. They mention a number of different studies on hassles and their effects on us. Two of these studies explore gender differences, and they conclude that men and women report different kinds of daily hassles and respond to them differently.
>
> These studies seem to involve only married men and women, however, which raises areas for further exploration. Do *all* men and women really experience and respond to hassles differently? For example, would unmarried male and female students be affected in the same ways that married men and women are? In a future paper, I would like to examine the kinds of daily hassles my college friends — both male and female — react to and what symptoms those hassles produce. The subject of hassles and how we react to them seems particularly relevant to students, whose lives are full of stress.
>
> [The writer discusses one of the major points in the passage and some questions the work raises for her.]

Synthesis

A **synthesis** pulls together information from two or more sources to make a new point that the individual sources have not provided. For example, the student who wrote the above analysis interviewed her male and female student friends and wrote a paper that compared her findings to those of the studies cited in *Discovering Psychology*. Because she wanted to understand the hassles that people experience and the symptoms that they cause, she incorporated additional information from published research.

> In *Discovering Psychology*, Hockenbury and Hockenbury present evidence that males and females react to different sources of stress and respond differently to them. The studies they use as evidence discuss only married couples, however, and they provide few details about the actual kinds and symptoms of stress. Several other studies, as well as original research done among unmarried college students, provide some additional insights into these questions.
>
> In an article on stress published in *Encarta*, Gramling and Auerbach provide many examples of daily hassles that they claim affect adults in

general, including "living in a noisy neighborhood, commuting to work in heavy traffic, disliking one's fellow workers, standing in long lines, and worrying about owing money." The Web site *Diabetes at Work* gives a list of the "Top 10 Daily Hassles," among them illness of a family member, home repairs, too many things to do, and crime. Neither of these sources mentions gender differences in the types of hassles reported.

Gramling and Auerbach list many symptoms of stress. These include nail biting, cold or sweaty hands and feet, dry mouth, and increased heart rate. *Diabetes at Work* adds muscle tension, upset stomach, shortness of breath, and back pain to the list of physical symptoms and forgetfulness, trouble concentrating, trouble making decisions, and short temper to the psychological symptoms. Again, though, neither source mentioned gender differences.

To these sources, I added interviews with eight friends — four men and four women — who all reported these top five daily hassles: worries about money, transportation problems, waiting in lines, unfair bosses, and automated phone systems that take forever and never get you an answer.

The only significant difference in the kind of hassles reported by the men and women I talked to was that several women (but not men) mentioned worries about physical safety (for example, while traveling home from school at night). When I asked my friends to report how they dealt with their stress, they seemed to confirm the Hockenburys' claim that women's stress spills into the family and men tend to withdraw. Two men reported no psychological symptoms of stress, whereas the remaining six people (four women and two men) emphasized both psychological and physical symptoms.

These sources suggest that there might be some gender differences in the hassles that people experience and the symptoms that result from these hassles, but they might not be as major as the Hockenburys' passage led me to expect. Most of the stresses mentioned seem to be caused by having to do too much in too little time. Perhaps this is a comment on the quality of modern life, which affects both men and women equally.

Works Cited

Gramling, Sandra E., and Stephen Auerbach. "Stress (Psychology)." MSN Encarta: Online Encyclopedia. 2007. 4 Sept. 2007 <http://encarta.msn .com>.

Hockenbury, Don H., and Sandra E. Hockenbury. Discovering Psychology. New York: Worth, 2007.

United States. Dept. of Health and Human Services. National Diabetes Education Program. Diabetes at Work. 27 May 2007. 31 Aug. 2007 <http://www.diabetesatwork.org>.

Evaluation

An **evaluation** is your informed judgment about a reading or an issue. It considers the reading or issue independently and also in terms of what else you have learned about it. When you evaluate, you build on what you have discovered through summarizing, analyzing, and synthesizing.

> Hockenbury and Hockenbury present important information and raise some interesting questions about how daily hassles affect our lives. In a few paragraphs, they present a great deal of information on the subject of daily hassles — what they are, who developed the scale of daily hassles, how men and women differ in their reactions to daily hassles, and how the stress of daily hassles negatively affects people. They provide numerous credible references to support their points. Other sources — such as Gramling and Auerbach's entry in *Encarta,* the Web site *Diabetes at Work,* and a gender-based poll I conducted — provide more details about some aspects of daily hassles and raise questions about the extent to which women and men are differently affected by them. However, the Hockenburys present a good overview of the subject in a short piece of writing. I think the authors do a great job of pulling together good information for students.

Critical Reading and Writing: Key College Skills

SKILL	DEFINITION	YOU KNOW THIS
Summarizing	Briefly recapping the main points in your own words	You tell someone what a movie is about.
Analyzing	Closely examining something to understand its parts and the ways they work together	You explain how the music, the look of the film, and the acting worked together to create suspense.
Synthesizing	Bringing together information from several sources to make a new point	You relate the effect the movie had on you to something you read about in a psychology course.
Evaluating	Making an informed and supported judgment	You tell the person why you loved the movie.

■ **PRACTICE 5   SUMMARIZING, ANALYZING, SYNTHESIZING, AND EVALUATING** . . . .

According to your instructor's directions or your own preference, choose one of the following.

1. **Summary:** Summarize the plot of a movie or television program in one paragraph.

2. **Analysis:** Read a letter to the editor in a newspaper or a blog posting on a particular issue. Whether you agree or disagree with the writer, write a paragraph analyzing the points he or she presents.

3. **Synthesis:** Read three letters to the editor or three blog postings on the same subject. In one paragraph, state your position on the subject according to your reading of the letters or blog postings, and explain the range of opinions on the subject.

4. **Evaluation:** Consider your performance in a recent activity, such as a sport, an exam, a party, or a task at work, and write a paragraph evaluating how well you performed in the situation.

. . . .

As you write in response to reading assignments, you may want to refer to the following Critical Thinking guide.

CRITICAL THINKING: WRITING ABOUT READINGS

FOCUS
- Carefully read the writing assignment.

ASK
- Does the assignment include any words that indicate the type of writing required (*summarize, analyze, describe, give examples of, compare,* and so on)?
- Is the writing supposed to be in response to the reading alone, or are you supposed to bring in other sources and points of view?
- Are you supposed to quote from the reading to support your point?
- Does the assignment ask you to evaluate the reading?

WRITE
- Apply your critical reading skills to the reading, and write a response to the reading that fulfills the requirements of the writing assignment.

Documenting Sources

■ For more on
documenting
sources, go to
**bedfordstmartins
.com/rewritingbasics**.

Look back at the example of synthesis on page 38. The writer includes ideas from three sources: a Web site (*Diabetes at Work*), an online encyclopedia entry (Gramling and Auerbach), and a book (Hockenbury and Hockenbury). She introduces her sources in her paper and at the end gives a full citation for each.

College writers have to follow specific rules to document all works they have referred to or quoted from. The writer of the synthesis example uses the documentation system of the Modern Language Association (MLA), which is used in most English courses. Other courses may use other systems, such as that of the American Psychological Association (APA). In this book, assignments that ask you to use an outside source to support your points will require the MLA documentation system, which is detailed in Chapter 21. You can use that chapter to find ways to acknowledge sources within your paper (called *citing sources*) and in a list at the end of your paper (called *Works Cited*).

■   **PRACTICE 6   DOCUMENTING A SOURCE** . . . .

For practice, write an entry for *Real Essays* in a Works Cited list. To do this, look at page iv.

. . . .

Reading and Writing beyond College

Critical reading and writing are not limited to college classes: In many ways, they are even more important outside of college. For example, in 2007, a warning was issued that counterfeit Colgate toothpaste made in China contained a deadly ingredient. The only way that people who used Colgate could tell if their product was genuine was to read the box carefully. Counterfeit tubes had misspellings. Although no one will be grading you when you read real-world documents like these, your ability to understand and act on key information could in this case literally mean the difference between life and death.

Less dramatic examples abound. The following are just some of the documents that you will be expected to read carefully and perhaps write responses to:

• Credit-card applications and statements
• Job applications

AnyBank Card

Statement
Nov. 10–Dec. 13, 2008

SEND PAYMENTS TO:
Box 54321
Anycity

NAME: Josephine Student   **ACCOUNT** #: 54-32-1
CREDIT LIMIT: $2,000   **AVAILABLE CREDIT**: $1,894.00

NEW BALANCE: $105.97   **MINIMUM AMOUNT DUE**: $20.00 —

Wow! This is a lot lower than my balance. But maybe I'll pay more interest this way?

Activity Since Last Statement

Trans	Posted	Description	Amount
11/18		Payment – THANK YOU	−152.43
11/11	11/11	Campus Cafe	12.14
11/20	11/20	Bradley's Hardware	8.00
11/20	11/20	Bradley's Hardware	8.00
11/24	11/24	DiscKing Music	32.59
12/11	12/11	Howard's Books and Stationery	53.24

Two charges for the curtain rod I bought. Must be a mistake!

Total Standard Purchases: $105.97
Cash Advances: $ 0.00

NEXT PAYMENT DUE: January 3, 2009

Account Summary

Previous Balance	152.43	New Balance	105.97
Purchases	105.97	Minimum Payment	20.00
Cash Advances	0.00	Amount Past Due	0.00
Payments	152.43	Amount Over Credit Line	0.00
Late Charges*	0.00	Finance Charges*	0.00

I pay more if I pay late.

Finance Charge Information

	Purchases	Cash Advances
Periodic Rate	.04381%	.05477%
Annual Percentage Rate	15.990%	19.990%

*See the reverse of this statement for an explanation of how finance charges and late charges are calculated.

I read the back and I still don't understand these charges. Better ask customer service.

Questions? Call Customer Service at 800-XXX-XXXX

- Loan or refinance applications
- Forms for setting up a checking account
- Car or apartment leases
- Employment contracts (or other contracts)
- Health insurance forms
- Wills or living wills

Reading such documents carefully is crucial because they are financially or legally binding.

You might want to make notes on important documents, asking questions as they arise. If you need to keep a document free of marks, put your notes on a photocopy or on a separate sheet of paper. The example on page 43 shows some notes that one customer made on one of her first credit-card statements.

PRACTICE 7   READING REAL-WORLD DOCUMENTS . . . .

Bring into class any document such as the ones listed previously. In a small group, highlight the parts of the document that contain important information that could easily be overlooked without critical reading. Then, share what you have found with the rest of the class.

. . . .

3

Writing Basics

Audience, Purpose, and Process

You Know This

You write almost every day, for many reasons.

- You write a note to explain your child's absence from school.
- You e-mail a friend or coworker to ask a favor.
- You text friends to make plans or just to keep in touch.

Most college courses require writing. So do most jobs, which may surprise you. Good communication skills, including good writing, will help you achieve success in life.

Four elements are key to good writing. Keep them in mind throughout the writing process.

■ **IDEA JOURNAL**
Think of something you do well and how you got to be good at it.

■ For more on making a point, see Chapter 5. For more on supporting a point, see Chapter 6.

■■
■■ **FOUR BASICS OF GOOD WRITING**

1. It considers the needs and knowledge of the audience.
2. It fulfills the writer's purpose.
3. It includes a clear, definite point.
4. It provides support that explains or proves the main point.

This chapter discusses audience and purpose first because they are essential to effective writing. Purpose determines what a writer's main point is, and audience determines how the writer makes that point.

The chapter shows you how to structure your writing to meet the four basics of good writing and outlines the steps of the writing process. It also explains the criteria your instructor may use to grade your writing and gives you advice on how to create a writing portfolio.

Understand Audience and Purpose

Audience

Your **audience** is the person or people who will read what you write. Whenever you write, always have at least one real person in mind as a reader. Think about what that person already knows and what he or she will need to know to understand your main idea. In most cases, assume that readers will know only what you write about your topic and main point.

Your writing may be very different for two different audiences. Read the following two examples, which describe the same situation but are written for different audiences. Notice both the tone and the content of each paragraph.

SITUATION: Christiane went to a big party over the weekend. She had a great time and met an interesting guy. She later describes the party in a letter to her grandmother (A) and in a text message to her friend (B):

A.

CHRISTIANE

Dear Avó,

A friend and I went to a great party last weekend. Many of the people there were from my college. I knew them from class and from studying in the library. There was a lot of food, but nothing as good as your empadinhas! I met a really nice boy there. He has a good job and a nice car and really good manners. I know you'd like him! I hope he calls me.

I hope you're doing well! I'll write again soon.

Love,

Christiane

B.

Hey, went to GR8 prty @ Mike's!! Got waaasted, stayed out L8. Met SME1!!! Jon, total QT, drives a BMW! How RU? TTYL

■ PRACTICE 1 **UNDERSTANDING AUDIENCE** . . . .

Reread Christiane's two notes, and answer the following questions.

1. How does the note to Christiane's grandmother differ from the message to her friend?

   _____

2. How do her two audiences affect what Christiane writes (the content) and how she writes (the tone)? _____

   _____

   _____

   _____

3. What words in the note to the friend would have to be changed in a more formal note? _____

. . . .

Purpose

The **purpose** for a piece of writing is your reason for writing it. In college, your purpose for writing often will be either to show something; to explain, analyze, or evaluate something; or to make a convincing argument.

■ PRACTICE 2 **UNDERSTANDING PURPOSE** . . . .

Reread Christiane's notes, and answer the following questions.

1. What is Christiane's purpose in the note to her grandmother? _____

   _____

   _____

2. What is her purpose in the note to her friend? _____

   _____

. . . .

Understand Paragraph and Essay Forms

Throughout college and beyond, you will write paragraphs and essays. Each of these has a basic structure.

Paragraph Structure

A **paragraph** is a group of sentences that work together to make a point. A good paragraph has three necessary parts—the topic sentence, the body, and the concluding sentence. Each part serves a specific purpose.

PARAGRAPH PART	PURPOSE OF THE PARAGRAPH PART
1. The **topic sentence**	states the **main point.** The topic sentence is often either the first or last sentence of a paragraph.
2. The **body**	supports (shows, explains, or proves) the main point. It usually contains three to six **support sentences,** which present facts and details that develop the main point.
3. The **concluding sentence**	reminds readers of the main point and often makes an observation.

Read the paragraph that follows. The parts of the paragraph are labeled.

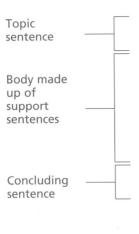

Topic sentence

Body made up of support sentences

Concluding sentence

Asking your boss for a raise doesn't have to be painful if you plan the conversation well, using several simple but effective techniques. First, think about how you will introduce the subject when you talk with your boss. Then, make a list of reasons why you deserve the raise. Be prepared to give specific examples of your achievements. Also, consider the amount you will ask for. Always ask for more than you think you deserve. When your plan is ready, make an appointment to meet with your boss. Your plan will allow you to be confident and will increase your chance of success.

Essay Structure

An **essay** is a piece of writing with more than one paragraph. A short essay may consist of four or five paragraphs, totaling three hundred to six hundred words. A long essay is six paragraphs or more, depending on what the essay needs to accomplish—persuading someone to do something, using research to make a point, or explaining a complex concept.

An essay has three necessary parts—an introduction, a body, and a conclusion.

ESSAY PART	PURPOSE OF THE ESSAY PART
1. The **introduction**	states the **main point,** or **thesis,** generally in a single strong statement. The introduction may be a single paragraph or multiple paragraphs.
2. The **body**	supports (shows, explains, or proves) the main point. The body generally has at least three **support paragraphs.** Each support paragraph begins with a **topic sentence** that supports the thesis statement and continues with facts and details that develop the main point.
3. The **conclusion**	reminds readers of the main point. It may summarize and reinforce the support in the body paragraphs, or it may make an observation based on that support. Whether it is a single paragraph or more, the conclusion should relate back to the main point of the essay.

The parts of an essay correspond to the parts of a paragraph:

- The **thesis** of an essay is like the **topic sentence** of a paragraph.
- The **support paragraphs** in the body of an essay are like the **support sentences** of a paragraph.
- The **conclusion** of an essay is like the **concluding sentence** of a paragraph.

Read the following essay, in which the parts are underlined and labeled. It is about the same topic as the paragraph on page 48, but because it is an essay, it presents more details.

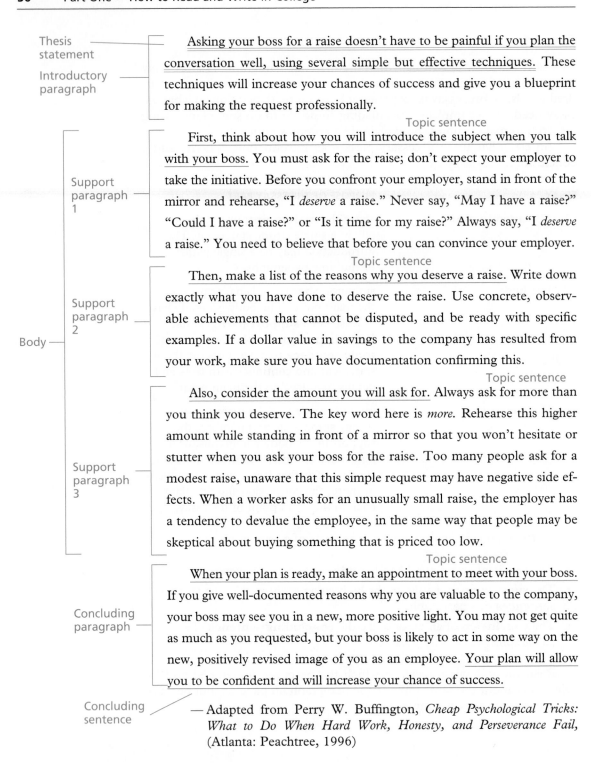

Thesis statement

Introductory paragraph

Asking your boss for a raise doesn't have to be painful if you plan the conversation well, using several simple but effective techniques. These techniques will increase your chances of success and give you a blueprint for making the request professionally.

Topic sentence

Support paragraph 1

First, think about how you will introduce the subject when you talk with your boss. You must ask for the raise; don't expect your employer to take the initiative. Before you confront your employer, stand in front of the mirror and rehearse, "I *deserve* a raise." Never say, "May I have a raise?" "Could I have a raise?" or "Is it time for my raise?" Always say, "I *deserve* a raise." You need to believe that before you can convince your employer.

Topic sentence

Support paragraph 2

Then, make a list of the reasons why you deserve a raise. Write down exactly what you have done to deserve the raise. Use concrete, observable achievements that cannot be disputed, and be ready with specific examples. If a dollar value in savings to the company has resulted from your work, make sure you have documentation confirming this.

Topic sentence

Body

Support paragraph 3

Also, consider the amount you will ask for. Always ask for more than you think you deserve. The key word here is *more*. Rehearse this higher amount while standing in front of a mirror so that you won't hesitate or stutter when you ask your boss for the raise. Too many people ask for a modest raise, unaware that this simple request may have negative side effects. When a worker asks for an unusually small raise, the employer has a tendency to devalue the employee, in the same way that people may be skeptical about buying something that is priced too low.

Topic sentence

Concluding paragraph

When your plan is ready, make an appointment to meet with your boss. If you give well-documented reasons why you are valuable to the company, your boss may see you in a new, more positive light. You may not get quite as much as you requested, but your boss is likely to act in some way on the new, positively revised image of you as an employee. Your plan will allow you to be confident and will increase your chance of success.

Concluding sentence

— Adapted from Perry W. Buffington, *Cheap Psychological Tricks: What to Do When Hard Work, Honesty, and Perseverance Fail,* (Atlanta: Peachtree, 1996)

RELATIONSHIP BETWEEN PARAGRAPHS AND ESSAYS

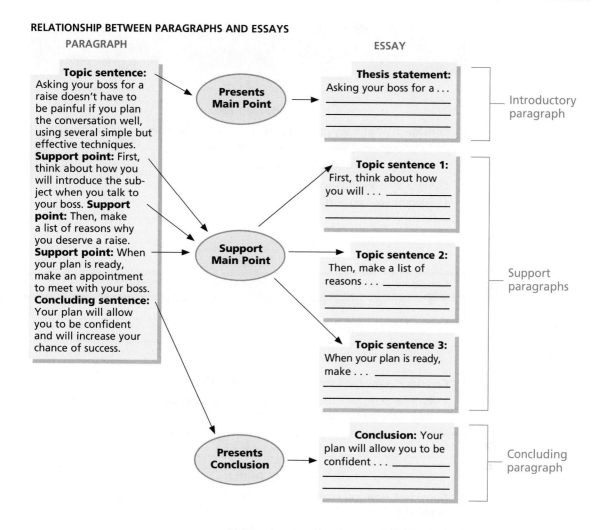

PARAGRAPH

ESSAY

Topic sentence: Asking your boss for a raise doesn't have to be painful if you plan the conversation well, using several simple but effective techniques.

Support point: First, think about how you will introduce the subject when you talk to your boss. **Support point:** Then, make a list of reasons why you deserve a raise. **Support point:** When your plan is ready, make an appointment to meet with your boss. **Concluding sentence:** Your plan will allow you to be confident and will increase your chance of success.

Presents Main Point

Support Main Point

Presents Conclusion

Thesis statement: Asking your boss for a . . .

Introductory paragraph

Topic sentence 1: First, think about how you will . . . _____

Topic sentence 2: Then, make a list of reasons . . . _____

Topic sentence 3: When your plan is ready, make . . . _____

Support paragraphs

Conclusion: Your plan will allow you to be confident . . . _____

Concluding paragraph

Understand the Writing Process

The **writing process** consists of five basic stages—generating ideas, planning, drafting, revising, and editing.

Whenever you are first learning to do something—playing a sport, driving a car, riding a bicycle—the steps seem complicated. However, after you practice them, the individual steps seem to blend together, and you just do them. The same thing will happen as you practice the steps in the writing process.

THE WRITING PROCESS

Generate Ideas

Consider: What is my purpose in writing? Given this purpose, what interests me? Who will read this? What do they need to know?

- Find and explore your topic (Chapter 4).
- Make your point (Chapter 5).
- Support your point (Chapter 6).

Plan

Consider: How can I organize my ideas effectively for my readers?

- Arrange your ideas, and make an outline (Chapter 7).

Draft

Consider: How can I show my readers what I mean?

- Write a draft, including an introduction that will interest your readers, a strong conclusion, and a title (Chapter 8).

Revise

Consider: How can I make my draft clearer or more convincing to my readers?

- Look for ideas that don't fit (Chapter 9).
- Look for ideas that could use more detailed support (Chapter 9).
- Connect ideas with transitional words and sentences (Chapter 9).

Edit

Consider: What errors could confuse my readers and weaken my point?

- Find and correct errors in grammar (Chapters 22–33).
- Look for errors in word use (Chapters 34–35), spelling (Chapter 36), and punctuation and capitalization (Chapters 37–41).

The flowchart on page 52 shows the five basic stages of the writing process and the steps within each of those stages. The remaining chapters in Part One cover every stage except for editing, which is detailed later in the book. You will practice each stage, see how another student completes the stage, and write your own essay using the writing process.

Before moving on to those chapters, read the following advice on analyzing writing assignments, understanding grading criteria, and creating a writing portfolio.

How to Analyze a Writing Assignment

Getting started can be one of the hardest parts of writing, and one common obstacle to starting is not quite understanding what the assignment is asking you to do. There are ways of translating writing assignments that will help you get started. Let's look at a couple of assignments and the ways you might begin them.

ASSIGNMENT: Discuss the **reasons for low employee morale** at your workplace.

ANALYZING A WRITING ASSIGNMENT	
STEPS	**WHAT TO DO FOR THIS ASSIGNMENT**
1. Highlight the key words.	Discuss the reasons for low employee morale at your workplace.
2. Get some ideas down on paper or on your computer.	List all reasons you can think of — at your current job, past jobs, or other jobs you know about. (For more on getting ideas, see the next chapter.)
3. Think again. Revise your ideas, and add to them.	Give some details about each reason, and say *how* each contributes to low employee morale. Then reread your list. Do they all contribute to low employee morale? Delete those that now seem irrelevant, and try to say more about the others. Record any other reasons that occur to you in the process.
4. Try out a main point.	Reread your revised list of reasons, and decide on your main point — what you want to say about your reasons. Do they have a common cause? What do they say about the workplace? Can you think of a way to improve morale? To find your main point, think about your audience and purpose. For example, if you are writing a report for your boss, your thesis should not be entirely critical of the company:

continued

STEPS	WHAT TO DO FOR THIS ASSIGNMENT
4. Try out a main point (cont.).	• Main point (for boss): Super Java has some good employee benefits, but several conditions here negatively affect the working experience. If you are writing for your teacher, you might be more candid: • Main point (for teacher): It's a myth that Super Java is a great employer. Employee morale is low, and for very good reasons. *or* • Company policies at Super Java guarantee low employee morale.
5. Jump in.	You have some ideas to start writing about, so get started.

PRACTICE 3   ANALYZING A WRITING ASSIGNMENT . . . .

Fill in the chart that follows, using this assignment:

ASSIGNMENT: **Discuss the challenges of juggling work and school responsibilities.**

STEPS	WHAT TO DO FOR THIS ASSIGNMENT
1. Highlight the key words.	
2. Get some ideas down on paper or on your computer.	
3. Think again. Revise your ideas, and add to them.	
4. Try out a main point.	
5. Jump in.	

Grading Criteria

Many instructors use a **rubric,** which is a list of the categories on which your writing is graded. If your instructor uses a rubric, it may be included in your course syllabus, and you should refer to it each time you write. A sample rubric follows to show you some of the categories you may be graded on. Rubrics often differ from one instructor to another, so this example will give you an idea of some of the kinds of elements you might be graded on. The importance of each element in determining the final grade will also vary by instructor. The elements listed in the rubric will be covered in Chapters 4 through 9.

Sample Essay Rubric

ELEMENT	GRADING CRITERIA
Relevance or appropriateness	• Did the student follow the directions in writing the essay? • Are the topic, length, and so on appropriate?
Introduction	• Does the introduction give the reader a preview of the subject? • Does it include a clear and definite thesis?
Thesis	Does the thesis clearly state a main point and use a complete sentence?
Support	• Is there enough support for the thesis statement? • Is the support presented in paragraph form with topic sentences that relate to the thesis statement?
Organization	• Is the structure logical? • Are transitions (both transitional words and transitional sentences) used to help move the reader from one idea to the next?
Conclusion	• Does the conclusion remind the reader of the main point? • Does it make an observation based on the information the writer has presented in the essay?
Coherence	Does the essay stay on topic throughout?
Grammar	• Is the essay free of the four most serious errors? • Are all words correctly spelled? • Are all punctuation and mechanics correct?
Timeliness	Was the essay submitted on time?
Other:	

Sample Student Essays

The following examples and analyses of each example will help you understand how rubrics may be used to evaluate student essays. For a key to the correction symbols used, see the chart at the back of this book.

TOPIC: As we mature, our hobbies and interests are likely to change. In an essay of no more than five hundred words, describe how your interests have changed as you have gotten older.

STUDENT ESSAY #1

> <u>I had many hobbies over the years.</u> *(tense)* I use to play T-ball but I moved on to playing real Baseball. *(lc)* I played baseball for more than ten years finaly *(sp)* I became a pitcher for my High School *(lc)* varsity squad. *(fs)*
>
> The one hobby that I can think of that I use to have *(tense)* that I don't do *(awk)* anymore is riding bicycles. My friends and I cruised *(dic)* all over our neighborhood on our bicycles looking for trouble to get into all the time and once even running *(con t)* from the cops, who caught my friend Jimmy, who was the leader of our so called gang. *(-)* When I got in *(dic)* *(u)* high school, though I got another hobby which took all my time and money, *(cs)* my car was my new love. I got it when I was 17 and I put everything *(coord)* I had into it and I loved it almost as much as my girlfriend Kate. As you can see, by my senior year, my only hobbies were playing baseball for my school team and taking care of my sweet car. *(dic)*

Student essay #1 likely will not pass, for the following reasons:

- It's a single paragraph. The assignment called for an essay.
- There is a thesis (double-underlined on p. 56), but it's too general. A more compelling thesis would explain how (and perhaps why) the writer's interests changed.
- There is no real conclusion. The paragraph simply stops.
- The writer gives examples of hobbies but few supporting details.
- It doesn't have a clear pattern of organization, and the writer strays from the point occasionally (see "u" on p. 56).
- The sentence structure is unvaried and contains few transitions. There are a number of grammar and spelling errors (marked on p. 56), and the language is too informal for an essay.

STUDENT ESSAY #2

Everybody has some kind of hobby, whether it is playing piano, or skiing. People's hobbies change sometimes over the years as they change too. This is certainly true for me. I have had many hobbies over the years, and they have certainly changed.

As a child, I played T-ball, and I eventually moved on to playing real baseball. I played baseball for more than ten years; finally, I became a pitcher for my High School varsity squad, and I played during my junior and senior years. I am looking forward to pitching in the college ranks.

The one favorite hobby I used to have that I don't have anymore is riding bicycles. My friends and I cruised all over our neighborhood on our bicycles looking for trouble to get into all the time and once even running from the cops, who caught my friend Jimmy, who was the leader of our so called gang. I eventually outgrew this hobby, as it was replaced by a new more exciting vehicle.

continued

When I got in high school, though I got another hobby which [,] took all my time and money, [cs] my car was my new love. It is a Nissan [tense?] 300 ZX, and it is black with a black interior. It had 16" rims and a [combine] sweet body kit. [dic] I got it when I was 17 and I put everything I had into it and I loved it almost as much as my girlfriend Kate. [coord]

As you can see, by my senior year, my only hobbies were playing baseball for my school team and taking care of the car. I once spent all my time riding my bicycle with my friends [,] but I guess I've outgrown that. The one hobby that has lasted throughout my life is my love for baseball. I will probably play that until I am an old man.

Student essay #2 is better for the following reasons:

- It has a clearly identifiable thesis, introduction, body, and conclusion.
- The body paragraphs are generally cohesive, and the essay shows a chronological (time order) development.
- It has fewer errors in grammar and punctuation than the low-level essay has.

The following areas still need improvement:

- The thesis (double-underlined on p. 57) could be more specific. Again, a more compelling thesis would explain how (and perhaps why) the writer's interests changed.
- The writing strays from the topic in a few areas and could use several more transitions between paragraphs.
- The language is too informal in spots.
- Most of all, the essay needs more supporting details about the writer's hobbies and changes in them over the years.

STUDENT ESSAY #3

Everybody has some kind of hobby, whether it is a craft, a musical instrument, or a sport. While some hobbies last a lifetime, many fade or appear at different times during our lives. Some people play sports as youngsters that they cannot play later in life, and some people adopt new hobbies as adults that they would never have enjoyed as a young person. This is certainly true for me. I have had many hobbies over the years, and as I have gotten older, they have changed. <u>As I have grown, I have lost my interest in riding bicycles, gained a love for cars, and undergone some changes in the way I play baseball, the one hobby I have always enjoyed.</u>

My earliest hobby was one that I outgrew some time during junior high school: riding bicycles with my friends. As a child, my bicycle was my only real means of independence. My friends and I rode all over our neighborhood, looking for trouble to get into and even tangling with the police on one occasion. As I got older and my friends began to get cars, this hobby faded and a new one emerged, featuring a new type of vehicle.

Working on my car is my new interest, and it is a hobby that grew from my love for my bicycle. The car is a Nissan 300 ZX, and it is black with a black interior, sixteen-inch rims, and a beautiful body kit. I got it when I was seventeen, and, for the past two years, I have put all of my time and money into it. My high school friends joked that I loved it almost as much as my girlfriend, Kate. It offers me the same sense of freedom as the bicycle, and I feel the same pride in keeping it in perfect shape.

My one love that has remained throughout my life is baseball, but even that hobby has undergone some changes as I have matured. As a young child, I played T-ball and quickly grew to love it. I eventually moved on to playing real baseball and played second base and shortstop in little league for more than ten years. After ten years of hard work, I became a pitcher for my high school varsity squad, and

continued

I pitched in the starting rotation for both my junior and senior years. I am looking forward to pitching in college and beginning a new stage in my baseball "career."

My hobbies have changed as I've matured, but in many ways, they have stayed the same. My first hobby, riding my bicycle, grew into my love for my car, and in many ways, the change from two wheels to four wheels reflects my growing maturity. My one lifetime hobby, baseball, has evolved as well, as I've lost the "T" and changed positions. One day, I may play another position or even another sport. However, like my love for speed, my love for competition will always define my hobbies.

Student essay #3 is clear, effective, and well supported. All the essential elements are present:

- The thesis is specific and clearly sets up the rest of the essay.
- The writer has described the hobbies in a clear chronological order, and he uses transitions effectively.
- Descriptions of the hobbies are detailed. They use more varied and exciting language and sentence structure than the previous sample essays.
- The writing stays on topic throughout and answers the essay question thoughtfully and thoroughly.

How to Create a Writing Portfolio

Your instructor may want you to create a writing portfolio. This is a collection of the writing you do in the course that shows your writing progress. Usually, a portfolio will include drafts, revisions, and final copies of certain assignments. To create the portfolio, you should print out copies of all the drafts you do of each assignment and keep them in an organized folder. You should also create a Writing Portfolio folder on your computer with subfolders for each assignment. Use a shortened version of the title of the assignment (for example, "Why Trans Fat Should Not Be Banned") to name your computer files, and include both the assignment step and the date they were created:

- Trans Fat prewriting 3/6/09
- Trans Fat draft 1 3/13/09
- Trans Fat draft 2 3/18/09
- Trans Fat revision 1 3/23/09
- Trans Fat revision 2 3/28/09
- Trans Fat final paper submitted 4/1/09

As always, make sure that you back up any work that you do on the computer.

In some cases, your instructor will select the assignments that should be added to your portfolio. If you are responsible for deciding which assignments to add, you should choose pieces that you're proud of but also those that show improvement in your writing. Look not only at the final grade you earned but also at the changes you made from draft to final copy:

- Review your instructor's comments on your draft.
- See the changes you made in your revised paper (those that your instructor suggested and those that you decided on yourself).
- Read your instructor's comments on your final paper.

Most instructors who assign portfolios will also ask you to write statements in which you reflect on your writing process—what you think you did well, what still needs improvement, and what you have learned about writing. Some teachers ask students to write reflective statements or a letter to the teacher for each assignment, along with one end-of-semester reflection statement. Others may ask for just an end-of-semester statement that might include the following:

- A detailed description of your writing process
- An evaluation of your best piece of writing in the course—what is good about it, why it is good, and examples from the actual piece of writing
- A comparison of your worst piece of writing to your best, with specific examples of why one is better than the other
- A letter written to your instructor about what you have learned and how your writing has improved during the semester
- A paper describing how what you have learned about writing will help you in the future
- A discussion of which of your writing goals you have achieved or how you would modify those goals

You Know This

You recognize top-ics when you talk, read, or watch television.

- You read about hot topics such as sex scandals, cults, and execu-tions.
- You talk with a friend about the topic of athletes' salaries.

4

Finding and Exploring Your Topic

Choosing Something to Write About

Understand What a Good Topic Is

A **topic** is what or who you are writing about. A **good topic** for an essay is one that interests you, that you know something about, and that you can get involved in.

Any topic that you choose to write about should pass the following test:

QUESTIONS FOR FINDING A GOOD TOPIC

- Does this topic interest me? If so, why do I care about it?
- Do I know something about it? Do I want to know more?
- Can I get involved with some part of it? Is it relevant to my life in some way?
- Is it specific enough for a short essay?

Choose one of the following topics or one of your own, and focus on one aspect of it that you know about and are interested in. (For example, focus on one specific pet peeve you have, one personal goal, or one aspect of male/female relationships that interests you.)

My goals

Pet peeves

Personal responsibility

Taking risks

Male/female relationships

Something I'm really good at

Something I'm proud of

Something I'm really interested in (what I do in my spare time)

Family roles

Reality TV

Popular music

 PRACTICE 1 FINDING A GOOD TOPIC . . . .

Ask the Questions for Finding a Good Topic (p. 62) about the topic you have chosen. If you answer "no" to any of the questions, look for another topic, or modify the one you chose.

MY TOPIC: _____

Keeping in mind the general topic you have chosen, read the rest of this chapter, and complete all of the practice activities. When you finish, you will have found a good topic to write about and explored ideas related to that topic.

Narrow Your Topic

To **narrow** a topic is to focus on the smaller parts of a general topic until you find a more limited topic or an angle that is interesting, familiar, and specific. In real life, you narrow topics all the time: You talk with friends about a particular song rather than music, about a particular person rather than the human race, or about a class you're taking rather than about every class the college offers.

In college writing, you often need to do the same thing. A professor may give you a broad topic like "religion and culture," "cheating in our society," "TV: good or bad?," or "goals in life." If you tried to write about one of these topics without narrowing it, you couldn't possibly dig deeply into it in a few pages. Fortunately, there are lots of ways to narrow broad topics, some of which are shown in the next few pages.

Ask Yourself Questions

Shannon Grady was assigned the broad topic "religion and culture" for an essay. What follows shows the process she used to narrow the topic to something she could write about. Here Shannon is sharing what's going on in her mind—how she *thought* about the broad topic and the kinds of questions she asked to make it manageable.

> First, I think about the words that are important. Here, that's <u>religion</u> and <u>culture</u>.
>
> Then, I ask questions. For some reason, jotting them down usually helps more than just doing this part in my head. At first, the questions are all over the place, and I want to quit. But I tell myself I can't stop until I have something that might work, or else I know I'll be too frustrated to come back to it later.
>
> • <u>What religion—mine?</u> I don't go to church too often. But my grandmother's very religious. She came to this country from Ireland, and she always talks about her church back there. Plus, she goes to church here every single morning.
>
> • <u>Whose culture—mine? This country's? Another country's? Now or in the past?</u> If I stick with my grandmother, she can tell me stuff about religion back there and why she came to this country and how people treated her (Irish and Catholic) when she got here and settled in Lowell, Massachusetts. She loves to talk about her life in "the old country," and she has great stories.
>
> • <u>What kind of culture—like art? Politics?</u> Well, Gran and all of her friends love storytelling, dancing, singing, and she's always playing Irish music. I never asked why everyone from Ireland seems to know how to sing, dance, play music, and tell great stories. But lots of the stories and songs are really sad—why?
>
> • <u>Serious religion? Or things like Christmas music? Maybe both?</u> Talk with Gran. Ask her about the church in Ireland, and here.
>
> Then, I take stock. <u>What do I have here so far?</u> I've got two big topics to put together somehow:
>
> • The Catholic church in Ireland (Gran's version)
>
> • The Irish tradition of music, dance, storytelling, singing
>
> How long is the paper supposed to be? Five pages.
>
> How about:
>
> • <u>My grandmother's religion?</u> No, this isn't really the topic.
>
> • <u>The role of Catholicism in Ireland?</u> Too big.
>
> • <u>Church and culture in small-town Ireland: One woman's story?</u> OK, try this as a start. I can talk to Gran about her town, her church,

> why the church was important, and how it relates to all the song, dance, music, storytelling. Maybe a separate paragraph for each?
>
> <u>Finally, I ask myself the questions for a good topic:</u>
>
> 1. <u>Does the topic interest me?</u> Yes, I love my grandmother, and I can find out stuff I don't know about her!
> 2. <u>Do I know something about it?</u> Yes. <u>Do I want to know more?</u> Yes.
> 3. <u>Can I get involved in some part of it?</u> Yes. <u>Is it relevant to my life in some way?</u> Yes.
> 4. <u>Is it specific enough for a short essay?</u> (Five pages is short??) I think it's specific enough, and it's a whole lot better than the boring "how religion influences culture"!!
>
> <u>Done for now!!</u>

Map Your Ideas

Use circles and lines to help visually break a general topic into more specific ones. Start in the center of a blank piece of paper, and write your topic. In the example below, the topic is "cheating." Circle your topic, and ask yourself some questions about it, such as "What do I know about it?" or "What's important about it?" Write your ideas around the topic,

■ For online mapping tools, see **www.bubbl.us** and **www.rev2 .org/2007/06/04/9**.

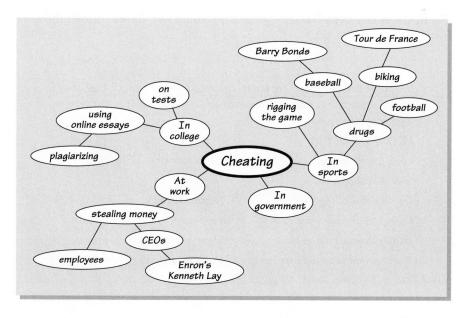

drawing lines from your topic to the ideas and then circling them. Keep adding ideas, connecting them with the lines and circles. This technique of mapping out your ideas is called **mapping** or **clustering**. After mapping, look at each cluster of ideas, and consider using one of the narrower topics. In the example above, the student, Paul Desmots, ended up writing about steroid use in sports and focused on recent examples in baseball.

List Narrower Topics

A student, Roberta Fair, was assigned a short essay on the general topic "personal goals." First, she listed specific personal goals.

> PERSONAL GOALS
>
> Lose some weight   Stop smoking
>
> Get a better job   No beer
>
> Get a college degree   No deadbeat guys
>
> Learn to use my time better   Be nicer
>
> Stay patient with my kids   Clean my house more often
>
> Don't argue with my mother   Don't buy things I don't need

Then, she asked herself some questions to help her choose one of the narrower topics on her list.

> • **Which of the narrowed topics is the most important to me?** They're all important, but some of them aren't as important as others, so I'll cross those out.
>
> PERSONAL GOALS
>
> Lose some weight   Stop smoking
>
> Get a better job   ~~No beer~~
>
> Get a college degree   ~~No deadbeat guys~~
>
> Learn to use my time better   ~~Be nicer~~
>
> Stay patient with my kids   ~~Clean my house more often~~
>
> ~~Don't argue with my mother~~   Don't buy things I don't need

- *Is it the right size for a short essay? Not really sure.*
- *Is it broad enough that I can make at least three or four points about it? I think so.*
- *Is it narrow enough that I can "dig deeply" and give good details in a short essay? I think all of these topics are.*
- *Which one is most important to you? They all are, in different ways.*

  Losing weight would make me look better and maybe feel better.

  A better job would give me more money.

  A college degree would get me a better job, and I'd feel like I'd done something important.

  To get a college degree, I have to learn to use my time better.

  Maybe I'd be more patient with my kids if I had a better job and more money.

  Stop smoking. Right now I'm not ready.

  If I had a degree, a better job, and more money, I could buy things I want and not feel guilty.

Looking them all over again, though, I think the college degree would get me other things that are important — like a better job, more money, maybe more patience with my kids. I'm going to go with that.

Roberta then chose "Getting a college degree" as her narrowed topic.

TOPIC	NARROWED TOPIC
A personal goal	*Getting a college degree*

PRACTICE 2   NARROWING A TOPIC

Use one of the three methods on pages 63–67 to narrow your topic. Then, ask yourself the "Questions for Choosing a Narrowed Topic." Write your narrowed topic below.

NARROWED TOPIC: _____

Explore Your Topic

Explore a topic to get ideas you can use in your writing. **Prewriting techniques** are ways to come up with ideas at any point during the writing process—to find a topic, to get ideas for what you want to say about the topic, and to support your ideas.

QUESTIONS FOR EXPLORING A TOPIC

- What interests me about this topic?
- Why do I care about it?
- What do I know?
- What do I want to say?

Use prewriting techniques to find the answers.

Use Prewriting Techniques

You can explore your narrowed topic using one or more of several prewriting techniques, three of which (questioning, clustering, and listing) you've seen used on pages 63–67. Writers don't necessarily use all of these. Instead, they choose the ones that work best for them after considering their assignment, their purpose for writing, and their audience.

- Freewrite
- List/brainstorm
- Question
- Discuss
- Cluster/map
- Use the Internet

While exploring ideas, just think; don't judge. You can decide later whether your ideas are good or not. At this point, your goal is just to come up with as many ideas as possible. Get your brain working by writing down all the possibilities.

The following sections detail techniques for exploring ideas and show how Roberta Fair used each one of them to get ideas about her topic, "Getting a college degree."

Freewrite

Freewriting is like having a conversation with yourself on paper. To free-write, just start writing everything you can think of about your topic. Write nonstop for at least five minutes. Don't go back and cross anything out, and don't worry about using correct grammar or spelling; just write.

> *I don't know, I don't think about goals more than just handling every day—I don't have time. The kids, my job, laundry, food, school, it's a lot. So I just get by day by day but I know that won't get me or my kids anywhere. I really do wish I could get a better job that was more interesting and I sure wish I could make more money and get my kids better stuff and live in a better place and not be worried all the time about money and our apartment and all that. I really do need to get that degree cause I know we'd have a better chance then. I know I need to finish college.*

List/Brainstorm

List all the ideas about your topic that you can think of. Write as fast as you can for five minutes without stopping.

> *So hard to find time to study*
> *Good in the long run*
> *Lots of advantages*
> *Better job*
> *Better place to live*
> *More money*
> *More opportunities*
> *A big achievement—no one in my family's ever gotten a degree*
> *But they don't give me support either*

Ask a Reporter's Questions

Ask yourself questions to start getting ideas. The following reporter's questions—Who? What? Where? When? and How?—give you different angles on a narrowed topic, but you can also use other kinds of questions that come to you as you explore your narrowed topic.

> *Who? Me, a single mother and student*
>
> *What? Getting a college degree*
>
> *Where? Stetson Community College*
>
> *When? Taking classes off and on now, want a degree in next couple of years*
>
> *Why? Because I want more out of life for my kids and me*
>
> *How? Working like a dog to finish school*

Discuss

When you discuss ideas with someone else, you get more ideas and also feedback on them from the other person.

Team up with another person. If you both have writing assignments, first discuss one person's topic and then the other's. Ask questions about anything that seems unclear, and let the writer know what sounds interesting. Give thoughtful answers, and keep an open mind. It is a good idea to take notes when your partner comments on your ideas.

> *Roberta: I guess my personal goal is getting a college degree.*
>
> *Maria: Why?*
>
> *Roberta: Well, I think it would help me.*
>
> *Maria: How?*
>
> *Roberta: You know, I have a lousy job, no money, the kids, stuff like that.*
>
> *Maria: Yeah, so how will a college degree help?*
>
> *Roberta: I know I could get a better job that paid more, so I wouldn't have to work so much. I could spend more time with the kids, and we could live in a better place, you know.*
>
> *Maria: You sound pretty convinced. So what's the problem?*
>
> *Roberta: Doing it. Time, money. But I know it's worth it for a while, just till I get the degree.*

Cluster/Map

You saw an example of clustering, also called mapping, on page 65. Here is Roberta's cluster.

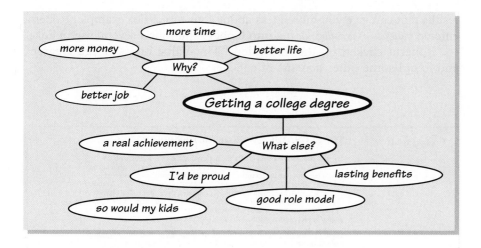

Use the Internet

Go to a search engine such as Google, and type in key words related to your topic, being as specific as possible. The search will probably yield a lot of

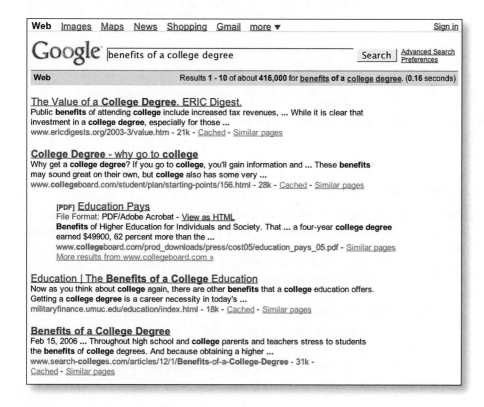

results that can give you more ideas about your topic. For example, Roberta entered *benefits of a college degree* into Google and found several useful links.

Roberta clicked on the link titled "The Value of a College Degree" and found some other benefits of college.

Privacy Policy

Resources for
Library Instruction

Information
Literacy Blog

THE ECONOMIC VALUE OF HIGHER EDUCATION

There is considerable support for the notion that the rate of return on investment in higher education is high enough to warrant the financial burden associated with pursuing a college degree. Though the earnings differential between college and high school graduates varies over time, college graduates, on average, earn more than high school graduates. According to the Census Bureau, over an adult's working life, high school graduates earn an average of $1.2 million; associate's degree holders earn about $1.6 million; and bachelor's degree holders earn about $2.1 million (Day and Newburger, 2002).

These sizeable differences in lifetime earnings put the costs of college study in realistic perspective. Most students today-- about 80 percent of all students--enroll either in public 4-year colleges or in public 2-year colleges. According to the U.S. Department of Education report, Think College Early, a full-time student at a public 4-year college pays an average of $8,655 for in-state tuition, room and board (U.S. Dept. of Education, 2002). A full-time student in a public 2-year college pays an average of $1,359 per year in tuition (U.S. Dept. of Education, 2002).

These statistics support the contention that, though the cost of higher education is significant, given the earnings disparity that exists between those who earn a bachelor's degree and those who do not, the individual rate of return on investment in higher education is sufficiently high to warrant the cost.

OTHER BENEFITS OF HIGHER EDUCATION

College graduates also enjoy benefits beyond increased income. A 1998 report published by the Institute for Higher Education Policy reviews the individual benefits that college graduates enjoy, including higher levels of saving, increased personal/professional mobility, improved quality of life for their offspring, better consumer decision making, and more hobbies and leisure activities (Institute for Higher Education Policy, 1998). According to a report published by the Carnegie Foundation, non-monetary individual benefits of higher education include the tendency for postsecondary students to become more open-minded, more cultured, more rational, more consistent and less authoritarian; these benefits

---

Keep a Journal

Another good way to explore ideas and topics for writing is to keep a journal. Set aside a few minutes a day, or decide on some other regular schedule to write in your journal. Your journal will be a great source of ideas when you need to find something to write about.

You can use a journal in many ways:

- To record and explore your personal thoughts and feelings
- To comment on things that happen either in the neighborhood, at work, at your college, in the news, and so on
- To examine situations you don't understand (as you write, you may figure them out)

By the time Roberta had used all of the prewriting techniques, she had decided that her narrowed topic (getting a college degree) was a good one and had also generated some ideas to discuss in her essay.

ROBERTA'S JOURNAL ENTRY

> I've been taking courses at the college for a couple of years but not really knowing whether I'd ever finish or not. It's so hard, and I'm so tired all the time that I sometimes think it would be easier (and cheaper!) to stop or to go one semester and not another, but then it's so easy to get out of the habit. I need to decide whether getting a degree is worth all of the effort it will take, and I'm starting to think it is. I don't want to live like this forever. I want a better life.

 PRACTICE 3   PREWRITING . . . .

Choose *two* prewriting techniques, and use them to explore your narrowed topic. Keep your readers in mind as you explore your topic. Find ideas that will be effective for both your purpose and your readers' understanding.

You Know This

You have lots of experience understanding and stating main points.

- You explain to a friend why you are a vegetarian (what the point is).
- You understand the point of a movie.

5

Making a Point

Writing Your Thesis Statement

Understand What a Good Thesis Statement Is

The **thesis statement** of an essay states the main point you want to get across about your topic. It is your position on whatever you are writing about.

Narrowed topic + Main point/position = Thesis statement

Eating disorders are caused by both cultural and psychological factors.

A strong thesis statement has several basic features.

BASICS OF A GOOD THESIS STATEMENT

- It focuses on a single main point or position about the topic.
- It is neither too broad nor too narrow.
- It is specific.
- It is something that you can show, explain, or prove.
- It is a forceful statement written in confident, firm language.

IDEA JOURNAL Think about a song you like. Does it make a point of some kind? What is it?

WEAK THESIS STATEMENT   I think college is good, and there are lots of them.

This statement does not follow the basics of a good thesis statement: It focuses on two points, not one; it is very broad; the word *good* is not specific; and the words *I think* are not forceful or confident.

GOOD THESIS STATEMENT   A college degree brings many concrete benefits such as better jobs, more career choices, and higher salaries.

This statement has all the basics of a good thesis statement. Check the list of basics yourself.

Language Note: In some cultures, people avoid making direct points, either in speech or in writing: It is considered impolite. In the United States, however, writers are expected to make clear, direct points. Readers want to know early on what point the writer will make in the essay, the paragraph, or any nonfiction text.

A good thesis statement is essential to most good essays. Early in your writing process, you may develop a *draft thesis* (or *working thesis*), a first-try version of the sentence that will state your main point. You can revise it into a final thesis statement later in the writing process.

Practice Developing a Good Thesis Statement

The explanations and practices in this section, which are organized according to the basics of a good thesis statement (p. 74), will help you write strong thesis statements.

Write a Thesis That Focuses on a Single Main Point

Your thesis should focus on only one main point. If you try to address more than one main point in an essay, you will probably not be able to give adequate support for all the points. Also, you risk splitting your focus.

THESIS STATEMENT WITH TWO MAIN POINTS

In the next decade, <u>many schools will have a drastic shortage of teachers,</u> and <u>teachers should have to take competency tests.</u>

The two points are underlined. The writer would need to explain why there will be a shortage of teachers and also why teachers should take competency tests. These are both meaty points, and any writer would have trouble supporting them equally in a single essay.

REVISED

In the next decade, many schools will have a drastic shortage of teachers.

or

Teachers should have to take competency tests.

THESIS STATEMENTS WITH TWO MAIN POINTS

My sister showed great bravery during the war, but my family was very worried about her.

Internships offer excellent learning opportunities, and the job market is very tight now.

REVISED

My sister showed great bravery during the war.

or

While my sister was serving in the war, my family worried about her every single day.

Internships offer excellent learning opportunities.

or

The job market for students is very tight, but there are things you can do to help get a job.

Although a good thesis statement focuses on a single main point, it may include more than one idea if these ideas directly relate to the main point. For instance, the last thesis statement above includes two ideas—a tight job market and the "several things" (job-finding tactics) that can be done to get a job. The two points are closely related and essential to the thesis statement.

A good thesis may or may not include other information that the essay will include. If you know the points or examples that you will make to support your thesis, you can include them. For example, see how the following revised thesis statements include some points (shown in *italics*) that support the writer's thesis:

> Internships offer excellent learning opportunities—*seeing how people dress and act in offices, finding out the kinds of jobs the business has, and meeting people who are good future connections for you.*
>
> The job market for students is very tight, but there are things you can do to help get a job in your field, such as *asking for an informational interview, networking, or getting an internship.*

Write a Thesis That Is Neither Too Broad Nor Too Narrow

Your thesis should fit the size of the essay assignment. A thesis that is too broad is impossible to support fully in a short essay: There is just too much to cover well. A thesis that is too narrow doesn't give you enough to write a whole essay on.

TOO BROAD   Family is an essential part of life.

[Both *family* and *life* are broad concepts, and the thesis would be impossible to explain in a short essay.]

REVISED   Time spent with my children is a welcome balance to time spent at work.

TOO BROAD   The Industrial Revolution was important in this country.

[The Industrial Revolution is too broad to cover in an essay.]

REVISED   Women played an important role in Lowell, Massachusetts, during the Industrial Revolution.

A thesis that is too narrow leaves the writer with little to show, explain, or prove. It can also make the reader think, "So what?"

TOO NARROW   My family members all have the same middle name.

[Once the writer says what the middle name is, there isn't much more to say, *unless* there's an interesting family story explaining why everyone has it.]

REVISED   An interesting event from long ago explains why my family members all have the same middle name.

TOO NARROW   I made my blog entry this morning.

REVISED   Blogging connects me to other people and their ideas.

Write a Thesis That Is Specific

A strong thesis statement gives readers specific information so that they know exactly what the writer's main point is.

GENERAL   Writing is important for my job.

[Why is writing important for your job, and what kind of job do you have?]

SPECIFIC   Although my primary job, as a nurse, is to care for others, I've found that I also need good writing skills.

[This thesis tells us that the job is nursing and suggests that the essay will discuss the types of writing a nurse does.]

One good way to be specific is to let your readers know what you will be discussing in your essay. This prepares them for what's to come.

MORE SPECIFIC As a nurse, my ability to write clearly is essential in documents such as patient reports, status notes to nurses on other shifts, and e-mails to other hospital staff.

[This thesis tells the reader specific kinds of writing the essay will discuss.]

GENERAL   Next month is a big one for me.

SPECIFIC   Next month will bring several important events.

MORE SPECIFIC Next month will bring several important events: My family is moving, I will be graduating, and I will be having a baby.

Write a Thesis That You Can Show, Explain, or Prove

If a thesis is so obvious that it doesn't need support or if it states a known fact, you won't be able to say much about it.

OBVIOUS   Most teenagers drive.

Many people own pets.

Guns can kill people.

REVISED   The high accident rates among new teen drivers could be reduced with better and more extended driver training.

In many households, pets get all the respect and privileges of a family member.

Accidental handgun deaths could be prevented through three sensible measures.

FACT   A growing number of American children are overweight.

Our city has reported a 10 percent increase in racial-profiling cases since 2001.

Each year, more companies outsource jobs to foreign workers.

REVISED   We must, as a nation, act to reduce obesity in our children.

Although racial profiling remains a serious problem, our city has taken some innovative steps to address it.

As more companies export jobs to foreign countries, we will see numerous negative effects.

■ Note that the revised thesis statements in this chapter take a clear stand on issues and express a particular point of view. Starting with a topic that you care about can help. For more advice on choosing a topic, see Chapter 4.

Write a Thesis That Is Forceful and Confident

A strong thesis statement should be forceful and definite. Avoid writing a thesis statement that begins, "In this essay I will show. . . ." Don't say you will make a point. Just make it.

WEAK   In this essay, I will prove that high school dropouts have a difficult time in life.

FORCEFUL   High school dropouts can expect to face surprising hardships in life.

Also, some words and phrases—such as "maybe" and "I think"—can indicate you lack confidence in your main point. Avoid them.

WEAK   I think you have to be careful when buying a used car.

FORCEFUL   Before buying a used car, get some basic information so that you don't pay more than you need to.

WEAK   Maybe it is time to evaluate our monthly spending.

FORCEFUL   We need to seriously review our monthly spending.

The practices that follow will help you write a good thesis statement. The first practice will help you develop a thesis statement from a narrowed topic. The rest of the practices focus on the basics of a good thesis statement (p. 74).

PRACTICE 1 DEVELOP A THESIS STATEMENT FROM A NARROWED TOPIC . . . .

For each item, write a thesis statement from the narrowed topic.

EXAMPLE

GENERAL TOPIC	NARROWED TOPIC	THESIS
Foreign languages	Learning a foreign language	Learning a foreign language has many benefits.

> **Language Note:** A verb + -ing can be the subject of a sentence, as "learning" is in this sample thesis.

■ For practice identifying thesis statements, visit *Exercise Central* at **bedfordstmartins .com/realessays**.

GENERAL TOPIC	NARROWED TOPIC	THESIS
1. A memory	My first date	_____
2. Music	My favorite kind of music	_____
3. Friendship	My best friend	_____
4. Owning a car	Costs of owning a car	_____
5. Reality TV	(One show that you watch)	_____

 PRACTICE 2 WRITE THESIS STATEMENTS THAT FOCUS ON A SINGLE MAIN POINT . . . .

Rewrite the following thesis statements so that they focus on just one of the points made. You can add information to make the statements more specific.

EXAMPLE: Juggling college and other responsibilities can be challenging, and rising college costs are putting higher education out of reach for many.

_____

1. Planning for college financial aid should begin long before a student's first year of college, and prospective students should also draw up a budget that includes all of their projected expenses.

_____

2. My first job taught me the importance of cooperation, and I also learned how to manage my time effectively.

_____

3. For several reasons, I'll never own my own business, but I do have what it takes to be a top athlete.

_____

4. Organizations can reduce absenteeism by telling workers about several measures to prevent colds and flu, and they can increase morale by offering benefits such as discounts on gym memberships.

_____

5. Given recent violent incidents, Riverside Mall needs to increase security, and the mall should also do a better job of plowing its parking lots in the winter.

_____

PRACTICE 3 WRITE THESIS STATEMENTS THAT ARE NOT TOO BROAD OR TOO NARROW ·

Read the following thesis statements, and decide whether they are too broad, too narrow, or the right size for a short essay. For statements that are too broad, write "B" in the space to the left; for statements that are too narrow, write "N"; and for statements that are the right size, write "OK."

EXAMPLE: ___N___ My dog will be ten years old next month.

_____ 1. Hinduism is a fascinating religion.

_____ 2. I love food.

_____ 3. Being a vegetarian offers a wide range of food choices.

_____ 4. There are many vegetarians in this country.

_____ 5. Another gourmet coffee shop opened last week, the third one on a single block.

PRACTICE 4 WRITE THESIS STATEMENTS THAT ARE SPECIFIC · · · · ·

Rewrite each of the following thesis statements by adding at least two specific details.

EXAMPLE: Electronic devices in high schools can be a huge problem. *Cell phones* that ring during a high school class disrupt *students' concentration and learning.*

1. I have a lot of useful skills.

   _____

2. Studying is hard.

   _____

3. I have always had trouble writing.

   _____

4. Children have more allergies now than in the past.

   _____

5. After I was robbed, I had many feelings.

   _____

PRACTICE 5 WRITE THESIS STATEMENTS THAT YOU CAN SHOW, EXPLAIN, OR PROVE ·

Each of the following items is either obvious or a fact and therefore difficult to write about. Rewrite each sentence so that it would give you something to write in an essay.

EXAMPLE: I have lived in this town for fourteen years. [Fact]
In the fourteen years I have lived in this town, I've learned a lot about small towns.

1. Many teenagers experiment with drugs.

   _____

2. Every year my college tuition goes up.

   _____

3. I make $8.00 an hour.

   _____

4. I have just finished my first college course.

_____

5. Sports stars make huge salaries.

_____

■ **PRACTICE 6   WRITE FORCEFUL THESIS STATEMENTS** . . . .

Rewrite the weak thesis statements that follow to make them more forceful.

EXAMPLE: In my opinion, my dog, Kayla, understands me better than any human being does.

My dog, Kayla, understands me better than any human being does.

1. I will explain some examples of history repeating itself.

_____

2. This college could have better parking facilities.

_____

3. Given that I've improved my job performance and shown a lot of initiative, I'm pretty sure I'll get a raise this year.

_____

4. It would be a good idea to warn young people about the possible dangers of crystal meth.

_____

5. In this paper, I'll describe three reasons why going to college has been a challenge for me.

_____

■ **PRACTICE 7   REVISING THESIS STATEMENTS** . . . .

In the spaces provided below, revise each of the possible thesis statements that you wrote in Practice 1, improving them according to the basics of a good thesis statement (p. 74). Again, think of a statement that you would be interested in writing about. You may want to add more information to your thesis statements to make them more specific and forceful, but short, punchy thesis statements also can be very powerful.

> **POSSIBLE THESIS:** When the sun is shining, people's moods improve.

> **REVISED THESIS:** Bright sunshine dramatically improves people's moods.

1. _____

2. _____

3. _____

4. _____

5. _____

Write Your Own Thesis Statement

A thesis statement doesn't have to come at the beginning of the first paragraph. Experienced writers may not get to the thesis for a few paragraphs, or they may imply their main point rather than state it in a single sentence. In most college writing, however, you'll need to have a clearly identifiable thesis statement, and it should be either the first or last sentence of your first paragraph. Your instructor may have a preference for putting the thesis statement as the first or last sentence in the first paragraph; if not, you can choose. In the following two paragraphs, one has the thesis statement first, and one has it last.

THESIS FIRST

Bright sunshine dramatically improves people's moods because of its effects on our brains. Most people know this from experience because they tend to feel better during the long, sunny days of summer. In the shorter, darker days of winter, people usually feel more tired and less energetic. Until quite recently, people assumed that this was a psychological reaction, often tied, at least in the United States, with childhood memories of the long, happy, carefree days of summer when schools were shut down. But recently we've learned that feeling better in summer isn't just in our heads.

THESIS LAST

Do you feel different during the different seasons? For many of us, the short, dark days of winter are difficult: We feel tired, and we lack energy. Most of us want to sleep more and eat hearty, hot meals. In the bright, sunny days of summer, though, we come alive. Until quite recently, people assumed that this was a psychological reaction, often tied, at least in the United States, with childhood memories of the long, happy, carefree days of summer when schools were shut down. But recently we've learned that feeling better in summer isn't just in our heads. <u>Bright sunshine dramatically improves people's moods because of its effects on our brains.</u>

What will both essays go on to describe? _____

Remember, the thesis statement you write first is a *draft thesis*: You can modify it as often as you like while you write your essay.

Before selecting a writing assignment, read how a student, Derek Johnson, developed a thesis statement from his narrowed topic. Before writing his thesis, Derek did some freewriting about it.

GENERAL TOPIC   *Reality TV shows*

NARROWED TOPIC   <u>*The Apprentice*</u>

FREEWRITING: *Some people think reality TV is stupid, and some of it is, but there are also some good shows where you can learn a lot. Like <u>The Apprentice</u>. This show shows real business situations and you get to watch really smart people try to figure out how to do something in the business world so they will be chosen as Trump's apprentice. Trump is a very rich man and knows the business world, and working for him would be a great experience and probably have a good salary too. You actually learn stuff while watching TV and it's entertaining too. Other shows like <u>Fear Factor</u> are just dumb but some are excellent.*

Next, Derek decided on what point he wanted to make about *The Apprentice:*

POINT   <u>*The Apprentice* is really a good show.</u>

He then wrote a draft thesis statement:

> **DRAFT THESIS STATEMENT**   *The Apprentice, a reality television show, is good because it can teach you a lot.*

Finally, Derek revised his thesis statement to make it more specific and forceful:

> **REVISED THESIS STATEMENT**   *The Apprentice is an example of good reality television, where viewers can learn many useful lessons about the business world.*

As you write your essay, you will probably tinker with your thesis statement along the way, but the process that Derek followed should get you off to a good start.

WRITING ASSIGNMENT

Write a thesis statement using the narrowed topic and ideas you developed in Chapter 4 or one of the following topics (which will need to be narrowed).

Friendship	Fashion/style	A good cause
Drug use	Computer games	A waste of time
Good gifts	Stolen identity	A news item of interest
Exercise	Foreign customs	Lying

Before writing, read the Critical Thinking box on the next page.

CRITICAL THINKING: WRITING A THESIS STATEMENT

FOCUS

- Read your narrowed topic.
- Decide what you think is important about it. You may want to use a prewriting technique.

ASK

- What is my position or my point about my topic?
- Why is it important to me?
- What do I want to show, explain, or prove?
- Can I think of additional ideas to support it?
- Is my position a single point?
- Is it a complete sentence?

WRITE

- Write a draft thesis statement, and make sure that it follows the basics of a good thesis statement (p. 74).
- Revise your draft statement according to the basics of a good thesis statement, and try to make it more specific and confident.

You Know This

You already know how to support a point you want to make.

- You explain to someone why you think a certain rule is unfair.
- You give reasons for an important decision you have made.

■ IDEA JOURNAL
Write about a time you had to give someone reasons for why you wanted to do something.

6

Supporting Your Point

Finding Details, Examples, and Facts

Understand What Support for a Thesis Is

Support consists of the evidence, examples, or facts that show, explain, or prove your main point, or thesis. **Primary support points** are the major support for your thesis. **Supporting details** (or secondary support points) are specifics that explain your primary support points.

Without support, you *state* the main point, but you don't *make* the main point. Consider the following statements:

I didn't break the plates.

I don't deserve an F on this paper.

My telephone bill is wrong.

These statements may be true, but without support they are not convincing. Perhaps you have received the comment "You need to support (or develop) your ideas" on your papers. This chapter will show you how to do so.

Writers sometimes confuse repetition with support. Using the same idea several times in different words is not support; it is just repetition.

REPETITION, NOT SUPPORT	My telephone bill is wrong. The amount is incorrect. It shouldn't be this much. It is an error.
SUPPORT	My telephone bill is wrong. There are four duplicate charges for the same time and the same number. The per minute charge is not the one my plan offers. I did not call Antarctica at all, much less three times.

As you develop support for your thesis, make sure that each point has the following three basic features.

■ See Chapter 5 for advice on developing thesis statements.

BASICS OF GOOD SUPPORT

- **It relates to your main point, or thesis.** The purpose of support is to show, explain, or prove your main point, so the support you use must relate directly to that main point.

- **It considers your readers.** Aim your support at the people who will read your writing. Supply information that will convince or inform them.

- **It is detailed and specific.** Give readers enough detail, particularly through examples, so that they can see what you mean.

Practice Supporting a Thesis Statement

A short essay usually has between three and five primary points that support the thesis statement. Each primary support point becomes the topic sentence of its own paragraph. Each paragraph presents details that support that topic sentence.

The following sections detail the steps in supporting a thesis statement.

Prewrite to Find Support

Reread your thesis and imagine your readers asking, "What do you mean?" To answer this question and generate support for your thesis, try using one or more of the prewriting techniques discussed in Chapter 4.

■ For more practice with support, visit *Exercise Central* at **bedfordstmartins .com/realessays**.

 PRACTICE 1   PREWRITE TO FIND SUPPORT . . . .

Choose one of the following sentences or one of your own, and write for five minutes using one prewriting technique. You will need a good supply of ideas from which to choose support points for your thesis. Try to find at least a dozen different ideas.

SUGGESTED THESIS STATEMENTS

1. Everyone in my family _____.
2. Online dating services are wonderful for busy people.
3. Online dating services can be very disappointing.

4. Discrimination comes in many forms.

5. I have done some stupid things in my life.

NOTE: Imagine your reader asking, "What do you mean?"

Drop Unrelated Ideas

After prewriting, remind yourself of your main point. Then, review your prewriting carefully, and drop any ideas that are not directly related to your main point. If new ideas occur to you, write them down.

 PRACTICE 2   DROP UNRELATED IDEAS

Each thesis statement below is followed by a list of possible support points. Cross out the unrelated ideas in each list. Be ready to explain your choices.

1. **THESIS STATEMENT:** Written communication must be worded precisely and formatted clearly.

   POSSIBLE SUPPORT POINTS

   use bulleted lists for important short points

   once I wrote a ridiculous memo to my boss but never sent it

   try to keep it to no more than a single page

   write the date

   get it done by the end of the day

   read it over before sending

   hate to put things in writing

   takes too much time

   make a copy

   getting forty e-mails in a day is too many

2. **THESIS STATEMENT:** Just this year, I experienced a day that was perfect in every way.

   POSSIBLE SUPPORT POINTS

   weather was beautiful

   on vacation

we'd had a great meal the night before

slept late

cold but inside fire was burning hot

new snow, all white

the year before we lost electricity

sky cloudless and bright blue

snow shimmering in the sunlight

perfect snow for skiing

no one else on the ski trail, very quiet

next Tuesday the ski resort would close for the season

3. **THESIS STATEMENT:** I know from experience that sometimes the customer is wrong.

   POSSIBLE SUPPORT POINTS

   work at supermarket

   customers often misread sale flyer

   they choose something like the item on sale but not it

   get mad and sometimes get nasty

   why do people bring screaming kids to the supermarket?

   they don't have any right to be rude but they are

   want to argue but I can't

   customers steal food like eating grapes that are sold by the pound

   sometimes they eat a whole box of cookies and bring up the
       empty box

   then the kids are always grabbing at the candy and whining, some-
       times they just rip the candy open or put it in their mouths

   customers misread the signs like ones that say "save $1.50" and think
      the item is on sale for $1.50

   should get a different job

Select the Best Support Points

After dropping unrelated ideas, review the ones that remain, and select the ones that will be clearest and most convincing to your readers. As noted earlier, short essays usually have three to five primary support points. They will become the topic sentences for your support paragraphs.

■ **PRACTICE 3**   **SELECT THE BEST SUPPORT POINTS** . . . .

For each item, circle the three points you would use to support the thesis statement. Be ready to explain your answers.

1. **THESIS STATEMENT:** A college degree should not be the only factor in hiring decisions.

   POSSIBLE SUPPORT POINTS

   job experience

   motivation and enthusiasm

   friends who work at the company

   appearance

   age

   reliability and honesty

   good transportation

   artistic talents

2. **THESIS STATEMENT:** People have a variety of learning styles.

   POSSIBLE SUPPORT POINTS

   learn by doing

   not interested in learning anything new

   learn by seeing

   don't bring their books to class

   disrupt the class

   learn by working with others

   get bored

   bad learners

   gifted students

3. **THESIS STATEMENT:** The beauty and grandeur of the cathedral astonished me.

POSSIBLE SUPPORT POINTS

four hundred feet high

hundreds of tourists

white, pink, and green marble gleaming in the sun

junky gift shops in the circle around it

interior very plain

beautiful warm day

built hundreds of years ago

intricate carving on all sides

. . . .

Add Supporting Details

Once you have chosen your primary support points, you will need to add details to explain or demonstrate each of those points. These supporting details can be examples, facts, or evidence. As the following example shows, a supporting detail is always more specific than a primary support point.

THESIS STATEMENT	I try to eat sensibly, but some foods are just too good to pass up.
PRIMARY SUPPORT POINT	Chocolate in any form is a major temptation for me.
SUPPORTING DETAIL	Peanut M&M's are especially tempting; I could eat a whole pound bag in one sitting.
SUPPORTING DETAIL	Canned chocolate frosting is great; I can eat it with a spoon right from the can.
SUPPORTING DETAIL	Big fat truffles with the creamy centers just melt on my tongue.
PRIMARY SUPPORT POINT	Freshly baked bread calls to me from the supermarket shelves.
SUPPORTING DETAIL	I can smell it as soon as I walk into the store.
SUPPORTING DETAIL	Sometimes it's still warm and soft, with steam on the wrapping.
SUPPORTING DETAIL	It reminds me of my grandmother making rolls for Thanksgiving dinners.

PRIMARY SUPPORT
POINT
I tell myself never to buy boxes of cheese crackers, but sometimes my hand doesn't listen to me.

SUPPORTING DETAIL
Cheddar is my favorite, with lots of salt and shaped in little bite-sized squares.

SUPPORTING DETAIL
Once I open the box, they'll be gone within a day, maybe even within a couple of hours, especially if I'm working at home.

SUPPORTING DETAIL
I start by eating one at a time, but I get into handfuls as I go along.

 PRACTICE 4   **ADD SUPPORTING DETAILS** . . . .

For each primary support point, again imagine your readers asking, "What do you mean?" Add specific details to answer that question.

THESIS STATEMENT
My baking skills are absolutely superb.

PRIMARY SUPPORT
POINT
My chocolate chip cookies are irresistibly delicious.

SUPPORTING DETAIL
I use **extra-large double chocolate chips** that are **soft, gooey, darkly sweet,** and **sinfully rich.**

In the space indicated, write the points you chose in Practice 3, item 1 (p. 92), as the best support. In the space to the right, add three details that would show, explain, or prove each primary support point.

THESIS STATEMENT: A college degree should not be the only factor in hiring decisions.

PRIMARY SUPPORT POINT	SUPPORTING DETAILS
_____	_____
	_____
	_____

PRIMARY SUPPORT POINT	SUPPORTING DETAILS
_____	_____
	_____
	_____

PRIMARY SUPPORT POINT	SUPPORTING DETAILS
_____	_____
	_____
	_____

. . . .

Write Topic Sentences for Your Support Points

Your primary support points will form the topic sentences of the paragraphs that support your thesis statement. Each topic sentence should clearly relate to and show, explain, or prove your thesis.

THESIS STATEMENT	Playing a team sport taught me more than how to play the game.
TOPIC SENTENCE (1st paragraph)	I learned the importance of hard practice.
TOPIC SENTENCE (2nd paragraph)	I also realized that, to succeed, I had to work with other people.
TOPIC SENTENCE (3rd paragraph)	Most important, I learned to be responsible to others.

Once you have developed topic sentences to support the thesis, you will need to back up your topic sentences with supporting details.

■ **PRACTICE 5   WRITE TOPIC SENTENCES AND SUPPORTING DETAILS**

Using the support points you generated in Practice 4, write topic sentences that support the thesis statement. In the space under each topic sentence, list the details you selected. When you have completed this practice, you will have developed support for an essay.

THESIS STATEMENT: A college degree should not be the only factor in hiring decisions.

TOPIC SENTENCE (primary support point 1): _____

_____

SUPPORTING DETAILS: _____

_____

_____

TOPIC SENTENCE (primary support point 2): _____

_____

    SUPPORTING DETAILS: _____

    _____

    _____

TOPIC SENTENCE (primary support point 3): _____

_____

    SUPPORTING DETAILS: _____

    _____

    _____

. . . .

Write Your Own Support

Before selecting a writing assignment, read how a student, Carson Williams, developed support for his thesis.

> **THESIS STATEMENT:** *Although my girlfriend and I are in love, we have some very different ideas about what a "good" relationship is.*

1. To generate ideas that might work as support, Carson used a prewriting technique: listing/brainstorming.

LISTING

She always wants to talk

Asks me how I feel, what I think, what I'm thinking about

Gets mad if I don't answer or thinks I'm mad about something

~~Talks during movies and annoys me~~

~~Puts makeup on in the car~~

Always wants to be affectionate, holding hands, kissing

Wants me to tell her I love her all the time

Wants to hear she's pretty

Gets jealous if I'm looking at another girl even though I'm not interested

~~Always asks me if she looks fat and gets mad whatever I say~~

~~Even when we're out she talks on her cell forever~~

Wants to talk about our "relationship" but I don't have anything to say, it's fine

~~Talks about her girlfriends and their relationships~~

Not wild about cars

~~Loves cats and tiny dogs~~

If I just don't feel like talking, she imagines I'm in a bad mood or mad

Hates TV sports

Wants me to go shopping with her

Doesn't like me going out with the guys

2. Next, Carson read his list and crossed out some things that seemed unrelated to his main point. (See the crossed-out items in the preceding list.)

3. He then reviewed the remaining ideas and noticed that they fell into three categories—differences in expectations about communication, differences about showing affection, and differences about how to spend time.

He grouped the ideas under these category labels and saw that the labels could serve as primary support points for his thesis. These support points could be turned into topic sentences of paragraphs backing his thesis, while the ideas under the labels could serve as supporting details for those topic sentences.

PRIMARY SUPPORT: *Differences in expectations about communication*

SUPPORTING DETAILS

She always wants to talk

Asks me how I feel, what I think, what I'm thinking about

Gets mad if I don't answer or thinks I'm mad about something

Wants to talk about our "relationship" but I don't have anything to say, it's fine

If I just don't feel like talking, she imagines I'm in a bad mood or mad

PRIMARY SUPPORT: *Differences about showing affection*

SUPPORTING DETAILS

Always wants to be affectionate, holding hands, kissing

Wants me to tell her I love her all the time

Wants to hear she's pretty

Gets jealous if I'm looking at another girl even though I'm not interested

PRIMARY SUPPORT: *Differences about how a couple in a "good" relationship should spend time*

SUPPORTING DETAILS

Not wild about cars

Hates TV sports

Wants me to go shopping with her

Doesn't like me going out with the guys

4. Finally, Carson wrote topic sentences for his primary support points.

TOPIC SENTENCES FOR PRIMARY SUPPORT

One big difference is in our expectations about communication.

Another difference is in how we show affection.

Another difference is in our views of how we think a couple in a "good" relationship should spend time.

■   **WRITING ASSIGNMENT** . . . .

Develop primary support points and supporting details for the thesis you wrote in Chapter 5 or for one of the following thesis statements.

William Lowe Bryan said, "Education is one of the few things a person is willing to pay for and not get."

Elderly people in this country are not shown any respect.

Very few people know how to really listen.

Some movies have made me cry from happiness.

There is one book that really made me think and learn.

Before writing, read the following Critical Thinking box.

. . . .

CRITICAL THINKING: SUPPORTING YOUR THESIS

FOCUS

- Reread your thesis.
- Think about the people who will read your writing.

ASK

- What support can I include that will show, explain, or prove what I mean?
- What do my readers need to know or understand in order to be convinced?
- What examples come to mind?
- What have I experienced myself?
- What details could I use to strengthen the support?

WRITE

- Use a prewriting technique to find as many support points as you can.
- Drop ideas that aren't directly related to your main thesis.
- Select the best primary support.
- Add supporting details.
- Write topic sentences for your primary support points.
- Make sure that all of your support points have the basics of good support (p. 89).

■ For examples of prewriting techniques, see pages 68–70.

You Know This

You have experience in planning.

- You make a list of things you need to do, with the most important things first.
- You figure out how to do something step by step.

7

Making a Plan

Arranging Your Ideas

Understand Ways of Ordering Ideas

In writing, **order** means the sequence in which you present your ideas—what comes first, second, third, and so on. Three common ways of ordering your ideas are **chronological order** (by the sequence of time in which events happened), **spatial order** (by the physical arrangement of objects or features), and **order of importance** (by the significance of the ideas or reasons).

Chronological Order

Use **chronological order** (time order) to arrange points according to when they happened. Time order works well when you are telling the story of an event or explaining how to do something. Usually, you go from what happens first to what happens last; in some cases, though, you can work back from what happens last to what happens first.

EXAMPLE USING CHRONOLOGICAL (TIME) ORDER

The cause of the fire that destroyed the apartment building was human carelessness. The couple in apartment 2F had planned a romantic dinner to celebrate the woman's raise at work. They lit candles all over the apartment and then shared a bottle of wine and ate a delicious meal. After dinner, they decided to go out to a club to continue the celebration. Unfortunately, they forgot to blow out all of the candles, and one of them was too close to a window curtain, which caught fire. The fire spread quickly throughout the apartment and then spread to others. By the time another resident smelled smoke, the fire was uncontrollable. The building was destroyed. Fortunately, rescuers were able to save everyone who was in the building. But all of the tenants lost their homes and most of their possessions. Human carelessness caused much human misery.

How does the writer use chronological order to arrange information?

_____

Spatial Order

Use **spatial order** to arrange ideas so that your readers see your topic as you do. Space order works well when you are writing about what someone or something looks like. You can move from top to bottom, bottom to top, near to far, far to near, left to right, right to left, back to front, or front to back.

EXAMPLE USING SPATIAL (SPACE) ORDER

I stood watching in horror while all-powerful flames destroyed an entire building, including my apartment and everything I owned. The first few floors looked normal, except that firefighters were racing into the front entry. A couple of floors up, windows were breaking and gray, foul-smelling smoke was billowing out. I could see shadows of the firefighters moving in and out of the apartments. My eyes were drawn to the top two floors, where flames of orange and white leapt from the windows. A lone dog with brown and white spots barked furiously from the rooftop. Until you have actually witnessed a severe fire, you can't imagine how powerful it is and how powerless you feel in its presence.

What type of spatial order does the writer use?

_____

Order of Importance

Use **order of importance** to arrange points according to their significance, interest, or surprise value. Save the most important point for last to end with a strong point.

EXAMPLE USING ORDER OF IMPORTANCE

Fires caused by human carelessness often have disastrous effects on people's lives. In a recent incident, when an apartment building was completely destroyed by a fire, the owner and tenants had no homes to return to. They also lost all of their possessions: furniture, clothing, and treasured personal items that could never be replaced. Worse than that, however, was that the owner and many of the tenants had no insurance to help them find new housing and replace their possessions. Many had to depend completely on relatives, friends, and a fund that was started for them by neighbors. The most disastrous effect of the fire, however, was that a firefighter lost his life. The thirty-year-old man had a wife and three young children who were robbed of their loved one. Carelessness has no place around fire, which has the power to destroy.

What is this writer's most important point about the effects of fires?

_____

As you arrange your ideas, consider what your purpose for writing is and what kind of organization would work best to make your main point. Some examples follow in the chart.

PURPOSE	ORGANIZATION
To describe an experience	Chronological
To explain how something works	
To explain how to do something	
To help your reader visualize whatever you are describing as you see it	Spatial
To create an impression using your senses—taste, touch, sight, smell, sound	
To re-create a scene	
To persuade or convince someone	Importance
To make a case for or against something	

Practice Making a Plan

When you have decided how to order your ideas, make a written plan—an **outline**—starting with your thesis statement. Then state each of your primary support points as a topic sentence for one of the body paragraphs of the essay. Add supporting details to develop or explain the topic sentence.

Your plan should also include a possible main point for the concluding paragraph. Although your outline serves as a good guide or blueprint, it can be modified as you draft your essay.

Many people find it useful to write complete sentences as they plan so that their outline is a more complete blueprint for the essay.

Also, there is no one right order for any essay. Use the order that will help you make your main point most effectively.

OUTLINE FOR A SHORT ESSAY: The example that follows uses "standard" or "formal" outline format, in which numbers and letters distinguish between primary support points and secondary supporting details. Some instructors require this format. If you are making an outline for yourself, you might choose to write a less formal outline, simply indenting secondary supporting details under the primary support rather than using numbers and letters.

■ For a diagram of the relationship between paragraphs and essays, see page 51.

Thesis statement

I. Topic sentence (primary support point 1)

   A. Supporting detail

   B. Supporting detail (and so on)

II. Topic sentence (primary support point 2)

   A. Supporting detail

   B. Supporting detail (and so on)

III. Topic sentence (primary support point 3)

   A. Supporting detail

   B. Supporting detail (and so on)

Concluding paragraph

■ For more advice on primary support and supporting details, see Chapter 6.

PRACTICE 1 OUTLINING PRIMARY SUPPORT POINTS AND SUPPORTING DETAILS . . . .

Arrange the primary support points and supporting details in the spaces provided, as illustrated in the example below.

THESIS STATEMENT: Being a good customer service representative in a retail store requires several important skills.

ORGANIZATION: Order of importance

PURPOSE AND AUDIENCE: To explain part of the job to someone who is interested in a job as a customer service representative

Filling out paperwork

Looking at person

Listening carefully

Making notes

Asking questions

Being pleasant and polite

Smiling, saying hello

Figuring out how to solve the problem

Calling the right people

Primary support point ——— I.   Being pleasant and polite

Supporting details ———   A.   Smiling, saying hello

    B.   Looking at person

Primary support point ——— II. Listening carefully

Supporting details ———   A.   Making notes

    B.   Asking questions

Primary support point ——— III. Figuring out how to solve the problem

Supporting details ———   A.   Calling the right people

    B.   Filling out paperwork

1. **THESIS STATEMENT:** I didn't think I was college material.

ORGANIZATION: Order of importance

PURPOSE AND AUDIENCE: To explain to a college admissions officer why you took time off after high school before applying to college

No one in my family had gone to college.

I'd goofed off in high school.

I didn't know anyone who could tell me what college was like.

I've been out of high school for a while.

My sister said college was a waste of time and money.

I forgot what school was like.

I didn't have good high school grades.

I didn't care about school.

I'm older than other students.

I. _____

    A. _____

    B. _____

II. _____

    A. _____

    B. _____

III. _____

    A. _____

    B. _____

2. **THESIS STATEMENT:** Avoid being taken by telephone con artists.

    ORGANIZATION: Chronological order

    PURPOSE AND AUDIENCE: To advise consumers on how to avoid getting scammed on the phone

Contact authorities after the call, if you're suspicious.

Can I call you back?

Personal information is private.

Your Social Security number can be misused.

Ask questions from the start.

It's good for authorities to track potential scams.

Your actions could protect other consumers.

Don't reveal personal information.

What is your address?

I. _____

    A. _____

    B. _____

II. _____

    A. _____

    B. _____

III. _____

    A. _____

    B. _____

■ PRACTICE 2 OUTLINING AN ESSAY . . . .

Outline the essay that follows. First, double-underline the thesis statement and the main point in the concluding paragraph. Underline each topic sentence, and put a check mark next to each supporting detail.

We all know people who seem to fall in love over and over. They love being in love. But others have different patterns. Some people seem to fall in love once and stay there. Others avoid long-term commitment. Until now, we had no way to figure out why some people were steady lovers and others not. Some researchers now believe that the amount and type of certain hormones in a person's brain may determine a person's patterns of love.

Using mice as subjects, the researchers found that when two particular hormones (oxytocin and vasopressin) exist in the pleasure centers of the brain, they produce individuals with a pattern of long-lasting love. Male mice with these hormones in their pleasure centers were faithful to their partners. They stayed with their female mouse partners through pregnancy and the raising of offspring.

In contrast, when those same hormones existed outside of the pleasure center, the male mice sought constant sources of new love. They did not have steady partners and did not stick around when a female mouse became pregnant. The mice with hormones in this location were the ones who ran from commitment.

Unfortunately, the research did not deal with the most common love pattern: individuals involved in relationships that last for some time but not for life. In this pattern, people have a series of serious relationships that are often broken off when one person wants a formal commitment and the other doesn't. Perhaps this research will come next, as it is in these relationships where much of the pain of love exists.

Though these behaviors may be built into the brain, scientists are working on ways to modify the effects. They hope to find a balance so that love patterns can be modified. One humorous researcher suggested that before we select our mates, we should ask them to have a brain scan to determine whether they're likely to stay or go.

Write Your Own Plan

Before selecting a writing assignment, read how one student, Roberta Fair, generated an outline on the benefits of a college degree. You saw Roberta's prewriting on this subject in Chapter 4.

After reviewing her prewriting, Roberta saw that she could group her ideas about the benefits of college into three major points: She could get a better job, be a better parent to her children, and feel better about herself. She also used many of her prewriting ideas as supporting details for those three main points, and she added other ideas that occurred to her.

Roberta decided to organize her ideas by order of importance, building up to the most important point.

THESIS (part of paragraph 1): Getting a college degree will help me build a better life for me and my children.

I. **Primary support point 1** (paragraph 2): Could get a better job
    Supporting details:
    A. Get a less boring job
    B. Have more options for jobs
    C. Make more money and work one job, not two

II. **Primary support point 2** (paragraph 3): Be a better parent to my children
    Supporting details:
    A. Spend more time with them because I don't have to work two jobs
    B. Get them some things they want
    C. Live in a better place
    D. Be a good role model for them

III. **Primary support point 3** (paragraph 4): Feel better about myself
    Supporting details:
    A. Get respect from others
    B. Respect myself because I achieved an important goal
    C. Go on to achieve other goals

POSSIBLE POINT FOR CONCLUSION (paragraph 5): Won't be easy, but worth the time and effort involved

▇ WRITING ASSIGNMENT . . . .

Develop a plan for your essay using the support you wrote in Chapter 6 or one of the following thesis statements.

Recently, I've been very worried about _____ because _____.

I am looking forward to _____ because _____.

My brother/sister has just joined the army, and I am _____ because _____.

When I have a conflict, I usually _____.

People think I'm a very strong person because _____.

Before writing, read the following Critical Thinking box.

· ·

CRITICAL THINKING: MAKING A PLAN FOR YOUR ESSAY

FOCUS
• Reread your thesis statement and support points.

ASK
• What would be the best way to organize my support points? (Time? Space? Importance?)
• What point should come first? Next? After that? Last?
• What supporting details will show, explain, or prove each of my main points?
• Will this organization help me get my main point (my position) across? Will it help my readers follow my essay?

WRITE
• Write a plan that shows how you want to arrange your points.

You Know This

You often rehearse in advance.

- Your sports team plays preseason games.
- You practice what you're going to say to someone.

8

Writing a Draft

Putting Your Ideas Together

Understand What a Draft Is

A **draft** is the first whole version of your ideas in writing. Do the best job you can in writing a draft, but remember that you will have a chance to make changes later. Think of your draft as a dress rehearsal for your final paper.

BASICS OF A GOOD DRAFT

■ For more on thesis statements, see Chapter 5. For more on support, see Chapter 6.

- It has a thesis statement that presents the main point.
- It has primary support points that are stated in topic sentences that develop or explain the thesis statement.
- It has supporting details that develop or explain each topic sentence.
- It has an introduction that captures the readers' interest and lets them know what the essay is about.
- It has a conclusion that reinforces the main point and makes an observation.
- It follows standard essay form (introduction, body paragraphs, conclusion) and uses complete sentences.

Practice Writing a Draft

The explanations and practices in this section will prepare you to write a good draft essay.

Draft the Body of the Essay

A good first step in drafting is to refer back to the plan for your essay. The plan should include your thesis statement, the primary support points for your thesis, and supporting details for your primary support points.

■ See Chapter 6 for advice on support and Chapter 7 for advice on planning. For a diagram showing the parts of an essay, see page 51, and for a complete draft of an essay, see page 122.

Referring to the plan, draft complete paragraphs that support your thesis. Each should contain a topic sentence that presents a primary support point as well as supporting details. Usually, your topic sentence should be either the first or the last sentence in the paragraph. At this point, you'll be drafting the body of your essay; you'll write the introduction and conclusion later. In general, essays have at least three body paragraphs, and they may have many more, depending on your assignment and purpose.

If you are having trouble with a word or sentence as you draft, make a note to come back to it and then keep going.

 PRACTICE 1   WRITING TOPIC SENTENCES . . . .

Writing topic sentences for primary support points is a good way to start drafting the body of an essay. Below is an outline that appeared in Practice 1 of Chapter 7. Convert each of the primary support points into a topic sentence that supports the thesis. You can make up details if you'd like.

THESIS STATEMENT: Being a good customer service representative in a retail store requires several important skills.

I. Being pleasant and polite [Primary support point 1]
    A. Smiling, saying hello [Supporting detail]
    B. Looking at person [Supporting detail]

TOPIC SENTENCE I: _____

II. Listening carefully [Primary support point 2]
    A. Making notes [Supporting detail]
    B. Asking questions [Supporting detail]

TOPIC SENTENCE II: _____

III. Figuring out how to solve the problem [Primary support point 3]
    A. Calling the right people [Supporting detail]
    B. Filling out paperwork [Supporting detail]

TOPIC SENTENCE III: _____

Write an Introduction

The introduction to your essay should capture your readers' interest and present the main point. Think of your introductory paragraph as a challenge. Ask yourself: How can I get my readers to want to continue reading?

BASICS OF A GOOD INTRODUCTION

- It should catch readers' attention.
- It should present the essay's thesis statement (narrowed topic + main point).
- It should give readers an idea of what the essay will cover.

The thesis statement is often either the first or the last sentence in the introductory paragraph, though you may find essays in which it is elsewhere.

Here are examples of common kinds of introductions that spark readers' interest.

Start with a Surprising Fact or Idea

Surprises capture people's attention. The more unexpected and surprising something is, the more likely people are to take notice of it and read on.

> I was saved from sin when I was going on thirteen. But not really saved. It happened like this. There was a big revival at my Auntie Reed's church. Every night for weeks there had been much preaching, singing, praying, and shouting, and some very hardened sinners had been brought to Christ, and the membership of the church had grown by leaps and bounds. Then just before the revival ended, they held a special meeting for children, "to bring the young lambs into the fold." My aunt spoke of it for days ahead. That night I was escorted to the front row and placed on the mourners' bench with all the other young sinners, who had not yet been brought to Jesus.
>
> —Langston Hughes, "Salvation" (See pp. 745–48 for the full essay.)

Open with a Quotation

A good short quotation can definitely get people interested. It must lead naturally into your main point, however, and not just be stuck there. If you start with a quotation, make sure that you tell the reader who the speaker or writer is (unless it is a general quote, like the proverb in the following excerpt).

"Grow where you are planted" is an old proverb that is a metaphor for living. Although I had heard it before, it took me many years to understand and appreciate its meaning. If I had listened to that proverb earlier, I would have saved myself and others many painful experiences.
                              —Teresa Fiori, "Appreciate What You Have"

Give an Example or Tell a Story

Opening an essay with a brief story or illustration often draws readers in.

Brian Head saw only one way out. On the final day of his life, during economics class, the fifteen-year-old stood up and pointed a semi-automatic handgun at himself. Before he pulled the trigger, he said his last words: "I can't take this anymore."
                              —Kathleen Vail, "Words That Wound"
                        (See pp. 759–63 for the full essay.)

Offer a Strong Opinion

The stronger the opinion, the more likely it is that people will pay attention.

Sex sells. This truth is a boon for marketing gurus and the pornography industry but a rather unfortunate situation for women. Every issue of *Playboy,* every lewd poster, and even the Victoria's Secret catalog transform real women into ornaments, valued exclusively for their outward appearance. These publications are responsible for defining what is sexy and reinforce the belief that aesthetic appeal is a woman's highest virtue.
                              —Amy L. Beck, "Struggling for Perfection"
                        (See pp. 829–32 for the full essay.)

Ask a Question

A question needs an answer. If you start your introduction with a question, you engage your readers by inviting them to answer it.

If you're a man, at some point a woman will ask you how she looks. "How do I look?" she'll ask.
    You must be careful how you answer this question. The best technique is to form an honest yet sensitive opinion, then collapse on the floor with some kind of fatal seizure. Trust me, this is the easiest way out. Because you will never come up with the right answer.
                              —Dave Barry, "The Ugly Truth about Beauty"
                        (See pp. 817–20 for the full essay.)

■   **PRACTICE 2   IDENTIFY TYPES OF INTRODUCTIONS** . . . .

Read the following three paragraphs. Identify the kind of introduction they use, and write the number in the space to the left of each.

1. surprising fact

2. quotation

3. example or story

4. strong opinion

5. question

_____ Several government studies have reported that the number of over-weight children in the United States has doubled since the 1970s and that 13 to 15 percent of U.S. children are now overweight. The studies cite a number of causes for this increase; however, the biggest factor is simply overeating. The average serving at the leading fast-food restaurants has ballooned with the popularity of "supersize" meals. Many busy families now eat at these restaurants several times a week because the service is fast and the meals are a good value. But overindulging consumers—including children—are paying a severe price in terms of their health, for they face a higher risk of diabetes, heart disease, and other conditions.

_____ The U.S. people must stop wasting the world's resources. Although the United States accounts for less than 5 percent of the world's population, it uses 25 percent of the world's natural resources. One of the worst examples of waste is the amount of gas we consume. The popularity of sport utility vehicles (SUVs) has dramatically increased gas consumption. According to Northeast Environmental Watch, SUVs use 25 percent more gas per mile than the average car. We also waste vast supplies of water by using excessive amounts of water while we wash dishes, brush our teeth, take showers, water lawns, and do other chores. We must stop our excessive use of limited resources.

_____ What does the new business environment mean for college students—for your own education and career choices? A fast-changing business environment creates fast-growth careers at the same time that it turns other careers into dead ends. The conventional wisdom holds that the wisest course is to pick a field that is on the upswing. The conventional wisdom is right—to a degree. However, in a turbulent environment you cannot count on stability—especially in growth projections. Today's hot careers may soon be dead ends, replaced by tomorrow's hot careers. This means that success will come from considering first what you want to do and what you are good at, and then developing a set of all-purpose job skills that you can transfer to the next growth area.

—Kenneth H. Blanchard et al., *Exploring the World of Business* (1996)

PRACTICE 3   IDENTIFY STRONG INTRODUCTIONS . . . .

Find a strong introduction in a newspaper, a magazine, a catalog, an advertisement—anything written. Explain, in writing, why you think it is a strong
introduction.

PRACTICE 4   SELL YOUR MAIN POINT . . . .

As you know from watching and reading advertisements, a good writer can
make just about anything sound interesting. For each of the following topics, write an introductory statement using the technique indicated. Make the
statement punchy and intriguing enough to motivate your readers to stay with
you as you explain or defend it.

1. **TOPIC:** Mandatory drug testing in the workplace

   TECHNIQUE: Ask a question.

   _____

2. **TOPIC:** Teenage suicide

   TECHNIQUE: Present a surprising fact or idea (you can make one up for
   this exercise).

   _____

3. **TOPIC:** Free access to music on the Internet

   TECHNIQUE: Give a strong opinion.

   _____

4. **TOPIC:** The quality of television shows

   TECHNIQUE: Use a quotation (you can make up a good one for this
   exercise).

   _____

5. **TOPIC:** Blind dates

   TECHNIQUE: Give an example or tell a brief story (you can just sum it up).

   _____

 PRACTICE 5   ANALYZING WEAK INTRODUCTIONS . . . .

Read the following three introductions. Then, indicate whether the introductions are weak (W) or okay (OK) by writing those letters in the space to the

left of each passage. For any introduction that you mark as weak, use the spaces under it to explain why you think it is weak.

_____ In this essay I am going to write about my car. It is not new, but it is very important to me. It has a good sound system, and I can listen to music while I drive. Sometimes I open all the windows and turn the volume and bass way up so it sounds like the band is right there in my car. Also, it is pretty good on gas, getting 20 mph in city driving. Before I had a car, I had to take public transportation, which wasn't very reliable, so sometimes I was late for class or for work. It took all of the money I had saved, plus a loan, but my car was worth every penny. It has changed my life for the better.

_____

_____

_____ We have two good friends, quite dissimilar in most ways, who share one common characteristic. They have no sense of smell. Paul is an electrical engineer in his early thirties. Warren is a well-known professor of psychology some twenty years older. Although you might expect this condition to be extremely rare, the inability to smell, called "anosmia," is relatively common, occurring in about 1 in 500 people.

—Don H. Hockenbury and Sandra E. Hockenbury,
Discovering Psychology, 2nd ed. (2001)

_____

_____

_____ "If you can't change your fate, change your attitude" is a quote by the writer Amy Tan. Tan is a good writer, and I agree with her. I have a bad attitude about my job. The place is filthy, and we can't talk to each other.

_____

_____

· ·

Write a Conclusion

Your conclusion should have energy and match the force of your thesis statement; it is your last chance to drive your main point home. Fading out with a weak conclusion is like slowing down at the end of a race. In fact, you should give yourself a last push at the end because people usually remember best what they see, hear, or read last. A good conclusion creates a sense of completion: It not only brings readers back to where they started but also shows them how far they have come.

BASICS OF A GOOD CONCLUSION

- It should refer to your main point.
- It should briefly summarize the support you have developed.
- It should make a final observation.

A good way to end an essay is to refer back to something in the introduction.

- If you asked a question, ask it again, and answer it based on what you've said in your essay.
- If you started a story, finish it.
- If you used a quotation, use another one—by the same person or by another person on the same topic. Or refer back to the quotation in the introduction, and make an observation.
- If you stated a surprising fact or idea, go back to it and comment on it, using what you have written in the body of the essay.
- Remind your reader of your original point, perhaps repeating key words that you used in your introduction.

Look again at three of the introductions you read earlier, each shown here with its conclusion.

OPEN WITH A QUOTATION

INTRODUCTION A: "Grow where you are planted" is an old proverb that is a metaphor for living. Although I had heard it before, it took me many years to understand and appreciate its meaning. If I had listened to that proverb earlier, I would have saved myself and others many painful experiences.

CONCLUSION A: Finally, I have learned to grow where I am planted, to appreciate the good things in my life rather than look for the bad and be angry. I have learned to take advantage of the many opportunities I have for personal and professional growth, right here and now. And I have vowed to help others around me grow also. My life is much richer now that I follow that old wisdom, and I will pass its lesson on to my children.

—Teresa Fiori, "Appreciate What You Have"

START WITH A STRONG OPINION OR POSITION

INTRODUCTION B: Sex sells. This truth is a boon for marketing gurus and the pornography industry but a rather unfortunate situation for women. Every issue of *Playboy*, every lewd poster, and even the

Victoria's Secret catalog transform real women into ornaments, valued exclusively for their outward appearance. These publications are responsible for defining what is sexy and reinforce the belief that aesthetic appeal is a woman's highest virtue.

CONCLUSION B: Women are up against a long history of devaluation and oppression, and, unfortunately, the feminist movements have been only partially successful in purging those legacies. Sexually charged images of women in the media are not the only cause of this continuing problem, but they certainly play a central role.

—Amy L. Beck, "Struggling for Perfection"

ASK A QUESTION

INTRODUCTION C: If you're a man, at some point a woman will ask you how she looks. "How do I look?" she'll ask.

You must be careful how you answer this question. The best technique is to form an honest yet sensitive opinion, then collapse on the floor with some kind of fatal seizure. Trust me, this is the easiest way out. You will never come up with the right answer.

CONCLUSION C: To go back to my main point: If you're a man, and a woman asks you how she looks, you're in big trouble. Obviously, you can't say she looks bad. But you also can't say that she looks great, because she'll think you're lying, because she has spent countless hours, with the help of the multibillion-dollar beauty industry, obsessing about the differences between herself and Cindy Crawford. Also, she suspects that you're not qualified to judge anybody's appearance. This is because you have shaving cream in your hair.

—Dave Barry, "The Ugly Truth about Beauty"

PRACTICE 6 ANALYZE CONCLUSIONS . . . .

After reading the paired introductions and conclusions above, indicate the techniques used in each conclusion to refer back to its introduction.

A. Technique used to link introduction and conclusion: _____

_____

B. Technique used to link introduction and conclusion: _____

_____

C. Technique used to link introduction and conclusion: _____

_____

PRACTICE 7   IDENTIFY GOOD INTRODUCTIONS AND CONCLUSIONS

In a newspaper, magazine, or any other written material, find a piece of writing that has both a strong introduction and a strong conclusion. Answer the following questions about the introduction and conclusion.

1. What method of introduction is used? _____

2. What does the conclusion do? Does it restate the main idea? Sum up the points made in the piece? Make an observation? _____

    _____

3. How are the introduction and the conclusion linked? _____

    _____

PRACTICE 8   WRITE A CONCLUSION

Read the following introductory paragraphs, and write a possible conclusion for each one. Your conclusions can be brief, but they should each include the basics of a good conclusion (p. 117) and consist of several sentences.

1. **INTRODUCTION:** When it comes to long-term love relationships, I very much believe Anton Chekhov's statement, "Any idiot can face a crisis; it's the day-to-day living that wears you out." When faced with a crisis, couples often pull together. A crisis is a slap in the face that reminds you of who and what is important in your life. It is the routine necessities of living that can erode a relationship as couples argue over who does the laundry, who does the cleaning, or cooking, or bill paying. The constant skirmishes over day-to-day living can do more serious damage over the long term than a crisis.

    CONCLUSION: _____

    _____

    _____

2. **INTRODUCTION:** Why do so many people feel that they must be available at all times and in all places? Until recently, the only way you could reach someone was by telephone or by mail. Now if you don't have a cell phone, an e-mail account, a beeper, and call waiting, people trying to reach you

get annoyed. To me this is just a loss of privacy. I don't want to be available twenty-four hours a day.

CONCLUSION: _____

_____

_____

Title Your Essay

Even if your title is the *last* part of the essay you write, it is the *first* thing that readers read. Use your title to get your readers' attention and to tell them what your essay is about. Use concrete, specific words to name the topic of your essay.

BASICS OF A GOOD ESSAY TITLE

- It makes readers want to read the essay.
- It does not repeat the wording in your thesis statement.
- It may hint at the main point but does not necessarily state it outright.

One way to find a good title is to consider the type of essay you are writing. If you are writing an argument (as you will in Chapter 18), state your position in your title. If you are telling your readers how to do something (as you will in Chapter 13), try using the term *steps* or *how to* in the title. This way, your readers will know immediately both what you are writing about and how you will present it. For example, "Five Steps to Financial Independence" may be a more inviting and more accurate title for a process analysis essay than "Financial Independence."

> **Language Note:** A title is centered on the line above the first line of a paragraph or essay. The first letter of most words in a title should be capitalized. (See p. 717 for more details.)

 PRACTICE 9 WRITE A TITLE . . . .

Read the following introductory paragraphs, and write a possible title for the essay each one begins. The first one is done as an example. Be prepared to explain why you worded each title as you did.

EXAMPLE: The origin of this species of rant was a toothbrush—a new toothbrush that came with an instructional DVD. The user of this advanced piece of dental equipment had been brushing his teeth lo these many years without any educational aids at all. But now he was the proud owner of an IntelliCleanSystem equipped with packets of paste to be downloaded into the toothbrush's hard drive.

POSSIBLE TITLE: *Making Life Better through Technology*

1. It is easy to take cheap shots at the owners of cellular phones. But before doing so, you should determine to which of the five following categories they belong.

    POSSIBLE TITLE: _____

2. With the same ethological methods they have long used in studies of animals, scientists are turning their attention to the nuances of human courtship rituals—otherwise known as flirting.

    POSSIBLE TITLE: _____

3. Is a girl called Gloria apt to be better-looking than one called Bertha? Are criminals more likely to be dark than blond? Can you tell a good deal about someone's personality from hearing his voice briefly over the phone? Can a person's nationality be pretty accurately guessed from his photograph? Does the fact that someone wears glasses imply that he is intelligent?

    The answer to all these questions is obviously, "No."

    Yet, from all the evidence at hand, most of us believe these things.

    POSSIBLE TITLE: _____

Write Your Own Draft

Before selecting a writing assignment, read a sample draft by one student, Carson Williams. In Chapter 6, you saw how Carson developed support for this paper. Look back at his final list of primary support points and supporting details (pp. 97–98) and notice what he has kept and what he has changed.

Different but in Love

Introduction
with thesis
(double-
underlined)

Although my girlfriend, Carly, and I are in love, we have some very different ideas about what a "good" relationship is. We both have expectations, but hers demand more of me while mine require very little of her or of me. While you might think these levels of expectations would fit together perfectly (one expects a lot, the other very little), they often cause conflict and misunderstanding (mostly on her part).

Body
paragraphs
(with topic
sentences
underlined)

One big difference is in our expectations about communication. Carly always wants to talk. She asks me what I'm thinking about when I'm quiet. If I just don't feel like talking, she imagines I'm in a bad mood or mad about something. Or she gets mad. She wants to talk a lot about our relationship, and I don't have anything to say about it: It's fine. What else would I want to talk about? One question she asks a lot is how I "feel" about something. That question makes me never want to open my mouth again. I don't think much about how I feel, and I really don't want to have to talk about the subject. Carly wants to keep the communication up 24/7, or she thinks something is wrong. I like a little peace and quiet.

Another difference is how and where we show affection. Carly wants to be openly affectionate all the time, like holding hands wherever we are and kissing. While we're holding hands or kissing, she expects me to tell her I love her all the time. I don't understand why that is necessary: If I've already told her I love her, why does she need to hear it again and again? I haven't changed my mind. And sometimes I just want to walk without holding hands; that doesn't mean I don't love her. Carly expects that love should be reinforced every day, while I think once it's said, it's out there until something big changes.

A final difference is our expectations about how a couple in a "good" relationship should spend time. We're both busy people, with jobs and classes. When I have free time, I like to watch sports on television. Carly hates TV sports and wants to go out and do things. Mostly she wants to go shopping and talk about our future, like what she'd like for our house. I hate shopping and get bored. Or I get annoyed when she wants to try clothes on for me. I just have to sit there in the ladies' department doing nothing until she comes out. Then I'm supposed to be enthusiastic about whatever she has on. But she never believes what I say. She'll always ask, "Do you really like it, or are you lying?" "Are you sure?"

At times like these, I often think I'd rather go out with the guys, who just let me be who I am. But I really do love Carly, and I'm beginning to understand that even though she and I have different expectations, we can still be happy together if we learn to accept—and even appreciate—those differences.

— Conclusion

WRITING ASSIGNMENT . . . .

Write a draft essay using the outline you developed in Chapter 7 or one of the following thesis statements.

These days, teenagers do not do much traditional dating.

Although cartoons are typically intended to entertain, they may also have important messages.

The most important skills a college student should have are
_____.

My college professor does not understand that _____.

Living with roommates requires _____.

Before writing, read the Critical Thinking box on page 124.

CRITICAL THINKING: WRITING A DRAFT ESSAY

FOCUS

- Reread your outline for the essay.

ASK

- Is my thesis clear?
- Are there topic sentences for each body paragraph?
- Do I have supporting details for each topic sentence?
- Is my support arranged in a logical order?
- What introductory technique will get my readers' attention and make my point stand out?
- How can I use the conclusion for one last chance to make my point?
- How can I link my conclusion to my introduction? What is the strongest or most interesting part of the introduction that I might refer back to in my conclusion?
- Will my title make readers want to read my essay?

WRITE

- Write a draft essay.

9

Revising Your Draft

Improving Your Essay

Understand What Revision Is

Revising is looking for ways to make your ideas clearer, stronger, and more convincing. When revising, you might add, cut, move, or change whole sentences or paragraphs.

Editing is correcting problems with grammar, style, usage, and punctuation. While editing, you usually add, cut, or change words and phrases instead of whole sentences or paragraphs (as you might while revising).

Revising and editing are two different ways to improve a paper. Most writers find it difficult to do both at once. It is easier to look first at the ideas in your essay (revising) and then to look at the individual words and sentences (editing). Revising is covered in this chapter, and editing is covered in Chapters 22–41.

No one gets everything right in a draft—even professional writers need to revise. The tips below will help you with the revising process.

■ IDEA JOURNAL
Write about a time you wish you'd said or done something differently, what those differences would have been, and why you think they would have served your purpose better.

TIPS FOR REVISING

- Take a break from your draft—set it aside for a few hours or a whole day.
- Read your draft aloud, and listen to what you have written.
- Imagine yourself as one of your readers.
- Get feedback from a friend, a classmate, or a colleague (see the next section of this chapter).
- Get help from a tutor at your college writing center or lab.

■ For more on purpose and audience, see Chapter 3.

You may need to read what you have written several times before deciding what changes would improve it. Remember to consider your audience (the people who will read your essay) and your purpose (your reason for writing it).

Understand What Peer Review Is

Peer review is the exchange of feedback on a piece of writing among fellow students, colleagues, or friends. Getting comments from a peer is a good way to begin revising your essay.

Other people can look at your work and see things that you might not—parts that are good as well as parts that need more explanation or evidence. The best reviewers are honest about parts that could be better but also sensitive to the writer's feelings. In addition, they are specific. Reviewers who say a paper is "great" without offering further comment do not help writers improve their work.

BASICS OF USEFUL FEEDBACK

- It is given in a positive way.
- It is specific.
- It offers suggestions.
- It may be given orally or in writing.

To get useful feedback, find a partner and exchange papers. Each partner should read the other's paper and jot down a few comments. The first time someone comments on what you have written, you may feel a little embarrassed, but you will feel better about the process once you see how your writing benefits from the comments.

The following box shows questions peer reviewers might consider as they read a draft.

> ## *Questions for Peer Reviewers*
>
> 1. What is the main point?
> 2. After reading the introductory paragraph, do you have an idea of what the essay will cover, and why?
> 3. How could the introduction be more interesting?

4. Is there enough support for the main point? Where might the writer add support?

5. Are there confusing places where you have to reread something in order to understand it? How might the writer make the points, the organization, or the flow of ideas clearer or smoother?

6. How could the conclusion be more forceful?

7. What do you most like about the essay? Where could it be better? What would you do if it were your essay?

8. What other comments or suggestions do you have?

Practice Revising for Unity

Unity in writing means that all the points are related to your main point: They *unite* to support your main point.

Sometimes writers drift away from their main point, as the writer of the following paragraph did with the underlined sentences. The diagram after the paragraph shows where readers might get confused.

Just a few years ago, online dating services were viewed with great suspicion, but they now have millions of subscribers. With an online dating service, people set up their own dates and don't have to cruise the bars. Online dating services also give users the opportunity to screen individuals and contact only those who interest them. That screening saves time and also helps people avoid many awkward first dates. Subscribers can exchange e-mails with prospective dates before arranging a meeting. But sometimes people lie. For example, my friend e-mailed with a guy who said he loved her, but she found out he was also e-mailing the same thing to her cousin! She cut it off right away! With people spending so much time working, it's hard to meet anyone outside of work, so online dating services expand the possibilities. The opportunity to "meet" many people without leaving your home and to screen out obvious duds is, for a growing number of people, the only way to play the dating game.

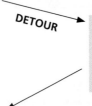

TOPIC SENTENCE: Just a few years ago, online dating services were viewed with great suspicion, but they now have millions of subscribers.

SUPPORT POINT 1: With an online dating service, people set up their own dates and don't have to cruise the bars.

SUPPORT POINT 2: Online dating services also give users the opportunity to screen individuals and contact only those who interest them.

DETOUR

OFF MAIN POINT: But sometimes people lie. For example, my friend e-mailed with a guy who said he loved her, but she found out he was also e-mailing the same thing to her cousin! She cut it off right away!

SUPPORT POINT 3: With people spending so much time working, it's hard to meet anyone outside of work, so online dating services expand the possibilities.

CONCLUDING SENTENCE: The opportunity to "meet" many people without leaving your home and to screen out obvious duds is, for a growing number of people, the only way to play the dating game.

■ **PRACTICE 1 EVALUATE UNITY** . . . .

Read the following two paragraphs, and underline any detours from the main point. In the lines provided at the end of paragraph 2, indicate which paragraph is more unified and explain why.

1. Identity theft is becoming very common in this country, but people can take several precautions to protect themselves. One way is to buy an inexpensive paper shredder and shred documents that contain your Social Security number or personal financial information. Shredded documents don't take up as much room in the trash, either. Another precaution is to

avoid mailing change-of-address postcards. Thieves can intercept these and use them to get mail sent to your old address. Half the time people never keep these cards, so they just waste the postage. It would be better to notify people of your address change by phone or e-mail. When I moved, I sent postcards that had a misprint, so they weren't good anyway. A third way is to avoid ever giving out your Social Security number. Even these precautions don't guarantee that your identity won't be stolen, but they will help prevent what is a time-consuming and expensive problem to set right.

■ For more practice in achieving unity in writing, visit *Exercise Central* at **bedfordstmartins .com/realessays**.

2. Many new markets have appeared to meet the needs of pet owners who treat their pets as if they were precious children. The most thriving market is clothing, especially items that allow owners and their dogs to dress alike. This clothing includes cruisewear, formalwear, and jeweled loungewear. Another big market is made up of hotels all over the world that advertise themselves as pet-friendly. These hotels provide doggie or cat beds, on-site grooming, and pet care professionals. The rooms are uniquely decorated and provide special meals prepared and served to meet the needs of each "guest." Each guest also is treated to an individualized exercise program. These new markets don't cater to the conservative spender: They appeal to those pet owners who seem willing to spend any amount of money on luxuries for their pets. Live and let live, but it all seems mighty crazy to me.

MORE UNIFIED PARAGRAPH: _____

REASONS THAT THIS PARAGRAPH IS MORE UNIFIED THAN THE OTHER: _____

_____

_____

PRACTICE 2   REVISE FOR UNITY . . . .

Each of the following essays includes sentences that are off the main point. Underline those sentences. The main point in each essay is in boldface type.

1. Look for five off-the-point sentences.

Oprah Winfrey is one of the most influential people of our times, but that doesn't mean that life is easy for her. As a child in rural Mississippi, she was dirt-poor and sexually abused. Somehow, she managed to climb out of that existence and become successful. But because she is now a superstar, every aspect of her life is under the media spotlight, and she is frequently criticized for everything from her weight to her attempts to help people spiritually.

Oprah's roller-coaster weight profile is always news. Every supermarket tabloid, every week, seems to have some new information about Oprah and her weight. I can relate to how humiliating that must be. She looked like a balloon in a recent picture I saw, even fatter than my Aunt Greta.

Oprah is also criticized for her wealth, estimated to be at about $800 million. You never hear about the charitable work she does, only about how much money she has. She has a fabulous apartment overlooking Lake Michigan in Chicago. While many businesspeople are as wealthy as Oprah, few are criticized as often—or as publicly—as she is.

Even Oprah's book club and magazine, *O,* bring unwarranted negativity. "Who is she to recommend books?" say some, and "What does she know about publishing?" say others. I especially liked the book *She's Come Undone.* What could possibly be wrong with recommending books and championing literacy? Yet one high-profile author, Jonathan Franzen, said he did not want the Oprah book club logo on his novel *The Corrections* because he thought it would negatively affect his literary reputation. He's a real snob in my mind, and all my friends think so, too.

Oprah Winfrey, despite her wealth and fame, does not have an easy life. Her critics feel free to cut her down at every turn. Instead, why not celebrate her personal and professional achievements? She deserves respect, not ridicule.

2. Look for four off-the-point sentences.

A recent survey of the places students prefer to study revealed some strange results. We would expect the usual answers, such as the library, a bedroom, a desk, the kitchen, and the survey respondents did in fact name such areas. But some people prefer less traditional places.

One unusual place cited was a church. The respondent said it was a great spot to study when services weren't taking place because it was always quiet and not crowded. Some churches are locked during the day because of vandalism. Other churches have had big problems with theft.

Another unusual study area was the locker room during a football game. A problem is that the person would miss the game. Except for half-time, the large area was empty. The person who studied there claimed that there was a high energy level in the locker room that, combined with the quiet, helped him concentrate. I wonder what the smell was like, though.

The most surprising preference for a place to study was the bleachers by the pool of a gym. The light was good, said the student, she loved the smell of chlorine, and the sound of water was soothing.

The results may seem strange—a church, a locker room, and a pool—but they do share some characteristics: quiet, relative solitude, and no interruptions, other than half-time. Perhaps we should all think about new places that might help us study.

Practice Revising for Support and Detail

■ For more on primary support points and supporting details, see Chapter 6.

Support is the evidence, examples, or facts that show, explain, or prove your main point. **Primary support points** are the major ideas developed in the paragraphs that make up the body of your essay. **Supporting details** are the specifics that explain your primary support to your readers.

When you read your draft essay, ask yourself: Do you provide enough information for your reader to understand the main point? Do you present enough evidence to convince your reader of that point? Look for places where you could add more support and detail.

Read the two paragraphs that follow, and note the support the writer added to the second one. Notice that she didn't simply add to the paragraph; she also deleted some words and rearranged others to make the story clearer to readers. The additions are underlined; the deletions are crossed out.

> This morning I learned that my local police respond quickly and thoroughly to 911 calls. I meant to dial 411 for directory assistance, but by mistake I dialed 911. I hung up after only one ring because I realized what I'd done. A few seconds after I hung up, the phone rang, and it was the police dispatcher. She said that she'd received a 911 call from my number and was checking. I explained what happened, and she said she had to send a cruiser over anyway. Within a minute, the cruiser pulled in, and I explained what happened. I apologized and felt very stupid, but I thanked him. I am glad to know that if I ever need to call 911, the police will be there.

REVISED TO ADD SUPPORT AND DETAIL

> This morning I <u>tested the 911 emergency system and found that it worked perfectly. Unfortunately, the test was a mistake.</u> ~~learned that my local police respond quickly and thoroughly to 911 calls.~~ I meant to dial 411 for directory assistance, but <u>without thinking</u> ~~by mistake~~ I dialed 911. I <u>frantically pushed the disconnect button</u> ~~hung up~~ after only one ring because I realized <u>my error.</u> ~~what I'd done.~~ <u>As I reached for the phone to dial 411,</u> ~~A few seconds after I hung up,~~ it <u>rang like an alarm.</u> ~~the phone rang, and it was the police dispatcher.~~ <u>The police dispatcher crisply announced</u> ~~She said~~ that she'd received a 911 call from my number and was checking. I <u>laughed weakly and</u> explained what happened, <u>hoping she would see the humor or at least the innocent human error. Instead,</u>

the crispness of her voice became brittle as ~~and~~ she said she had to send a cruiser over anyway. <u>I went to meet my fate.</u> Within a minute, the cruiser pulled in, and <u>a police officer swaggered toward me.</u> I explained what <u>had</u> happened, apologized, and thanked him very humbly. I felt <u>guilty of stupidity, at the very least.</u> ~~and felt very stupid, but I thanked him.~~ <u>We learn from our mistakes, and in this case</u> I am glad to know that if I ever need to call 911, the police will be there.

PRACTICE 3   EVALUATE SUPPORT ·

In the two paragraphs that follow, the main points are in bold. Underline the primary support points, and put a check mark by each supporting detail. Then, in the lines provided at the end of paragraph 2, indicate which paragraph provides better support and explain why.

1. **Women tend to learn the art of fly fishing more easily than men.** For one thing, they have more patience, which is key to successful fishing. It may take many hours of silent, solitary fishing to catch a single fish. Even long hours may net no fish, and men tend to be more eager for results. This can make them more careless. Women also tend to be more sensitive to subtle movements. This trait helps both in the casting motion and in the reeling in of a fish. Women are more likely to take breaks than men, who continue even when they are frustrated or tired. Women may also spend money on the appropriate attire for fishing, gear that is waterproof and warm. Finally, women are more receptive to fishing advice than are men. These feminine traits make a big difference in fly fishing.

2. **Because they are susceptible to certain safety problems, people over the age of seventy-five should be required by law to take a driving test every year.** Some people believe that such a law would represent age discrimination because many people are great drivers until they are in their nineties. But government statistics indicate that people over seventy-five have more accidents than younger drivers do. One common failing of older drivers is impaired peripheral vision. This makes it

difficult for them to see cars on either side or at an intersection. Another common problem is a longer response time. Although older drivers may know to stop, it takes them much longer to move their foot from the gas pedal to the brake than it does younger drivers. This lengthened response time is the most common cause of accidents among older drivers. The most dangerous failing among older drivers is a loss of memory. Consider this common scenario: The driver starts to back out of a parking space after checking to see that there's nothing behind him. He then notices that his sunglasses have fallen on the floor. He retrieves them and puts his foot back on the gas pedal without remembering that he needs to look again. Because he is still in reverse, the car moves quickly and hits the person or car now behind him. Although it may inconvenience older drivers to take annual driving tests, it will help save injuries and lives.

PARAGRAPH WITH BETTER SUPPORT: _____

REASONS THAT THIS PARAGRAPH'S SUPPORT IS BETTER: _____

■ For more practice in revising for support, visit *Exercise Central* at **bedfordstmartins .com/realessays**.

_____

_____

_____

■ **PRACTICE 4** **REVISE FOR SUPPORT** . . . .

Read the following essay, and write in the space provided at least one additional support point or detail for each body paragraph and for the conclusion. Indicate where the added material should go in the paragraph by writing in a caret (∧).

If it's leather, I love it. Anything made of leather makes me want to spend some time admiring it. This appeal is not just limited to coats and jackets but includes furniture, bags, gloves, boots, and any other leather product I find. To me it's an all-around wonderful experience.

The smell of leather is intoxicating. It seems to hang in the air, inviting me to take a big whiff. I smell the leather, especially soft leather, and it is wonderful. I'd like to bury my nose in a soft leather jacket for hours.

Leather also feels wonderful to the touch. It is smooth and silky. It feels soothing against my cheek and hands. When I'm wearing a leather jacket, I have to stop myself from running my hands up and down the sides and sleeves because it just feels so smooth and soft.

Finally, leather is comfortable, whatever form it comes in. A leather coat or jacket doesn't just look good — it's also very warm. Pull on a pair of leather gloves, and your hands won't be cold. And, best of all, sink into a soft, buttery leather easy chair. I guarantee it will relax you.

Just writing this essay about leather makes me want to put on a leather jacket and some soft leather slippers, and find a great leather chair to curl up in. It's my kind of heaven.

Practice Revising for Coherence

Coherence in writing means that all the support connects to form a whole. In other words, even when the support is arranged in a logical order, it still needs "glue" to connect the various points.

A piece of writing that lacks coherence sounds choppy, and it is hard for the reader to follow. Revising for coherence improves an essay by helping readers see how one point leads to another. The best way to improve coherence is to add transitions.

Transitions are words, phrases, and sentences that connect ideas so that writing moves smoothly from one point to another. Transitions can be used to connect sentences and ideas within a paragraph and also to connect one paragraph to another. The box on page 136 lists some, but not all, of the most common transitions and their purpose.

Common Transitional Words and Phrases

INDICATE SPACE

above	below	near	to the right
across	beside	next to	to the side
at the bottom	beyond	opposite	under
at the top	farther	over	where
behind	inside	to the left	

INDICATE TIME

after	eventually	meanwhile	soon
as	finally	next	then
at last	first	now	when
before	last	second	while
during	later	since	

INDICATE IMPORTANCE

above all	in fact	more important	most
best	in particular	most important	worst
especially			

SIGNAL EXAMPLES

for example	for instance	for one thing	one reason

SIGNAL ADDITIONS

additionally	and	as well as	in addition
also	another	furthermore	moreover

SIGNAL CONTRAST

although	in contrast	nevertheless	still
but	instead	on the other hand	yet
however			

SIGNAL CAUSE OR CONSEQUENCE

as a result	finally	so	therefore
because			

The following essay shows how transitions link ideas within sentences and paragraphs and connect one paragraph to the next. It also shows another technique for achieving coherence: repeating key words and ideas related to the main point. The transitions and key words are underlined.

I thought I would never make it to work today. I had an important meeting, and it seemed as if everything was conspiring against me. <u>The conspiracy started before I even woke up.</u>

<u>I had set my alarm clock, but it didn't go off, and therefore I didn't wake up on time.</u> <u>When</u> I did wake up, I was already late, not just by a few minutes but by an hour and a half. To save time, I brushed my teeth <u>while</u> I showered. <u>Also,</u> I figured out what I was going to wear. <u>Finally,</u> I hopped out of the shower ready to get dressed. <u>But the conspiracy continued.</u>

<u>The next act of the conspiracy</u> concerned my only clean shirt, which was missing two buttons right in front. <u>After finding a sweater that would go over it,</u> I ran to the bus stop.

<u>When I got to the stop,</u> I discovered that the buses were running late. <u>When one finally came,</u> it was one of the old, slow ones, and it made stops about every ten feet. <u>In addition,</u> the heat was blasting, and I was sweating but couldn't take off my sweater because my shirt was gaping open. Now I was sweating, and perspiration was running down my scalp and neck. At least, I thought, I'll dry off by the time the bus gets to my work.

<u>In fact,</u> <u>I did dry off a little, but the conspiracy didn't end there.</u> <u>When</u> I <u>finally</u> got to work, the elevator was out of service, <u>so</u> I had to walk up ten flights of stairs. I was drenched, late, and inappropriately dressed. <u>By the time I got to my desk,</u> I knew that the hardest part of the day was behind me.

▦ PRACTICE 5   ADD TRANSITIONAL WORDS · · · · · · · · · · · · · · ·

Read the following paragraphs. In each blank, add a transition that would smoothly connect the ideas. In each case, there is more than one right answer.

EXAMPLE: Today, many workers are members of labor unions that exist to protect worker rights. _However,_ until the 1930s, unions did not exist. In the 1930s, Congress passed laws that paved the way for unions. *After that,* workers had the right to organize, bargain, and strike. *Today,* unions are a powerful force in American politics.

1. The modern-day vending machine is based on an invention by a Greek scientist named Hero, who lived in the first century C.E. The machine that he invented required that the user insert a coin. _____ the coin fell, it hit a lever. _____ out came the desired product—a cup of holy water.

2. _____ Jackie Robinson joined the Brooklyn Dodgers in 1947, he became the first African American to play major league baseball in the twentieth century. _____ he was the first, he was faced with what was called "breaking the color line" and received many death threats. _____ a few seasons of playing well, he spoke out against discrimination against African Americans. _____ his career, he played in six World Series and won the National League Most Valuable Player award in 1949.

3. Alcohol affects women more quickly than men. This is because women have more fat tissue, ___ men have more muscle tissue, which has more water than fat tissue. _____ men drink alcohol, it is diluted by the water in muscle. _____ when women drink, the alcohol is more concentrated. _____ women get drunk sooner.

■ For more practice in achieving coherence in writing, visit *Exercise Central* at **bedfordstmartins.com/realessays**.

PRACTICE 6   ADD TRANSITIONAL SENTENCES . . . .

Read the following essay. Then, write a transitional sentence that would link each paragraph to the one following it. You may add your transitional sentence at the end of a paragraph, at the beginning of the next paragraph, or in both places.

Many teenagers today do not date in the traditional sense—one boy and one girl going on dates or "going steady." Instead, they go out in groups rather than as couples. This gives many parents a sense that their sons and daughters are safe from premature sex and possible sexually transmitted diseases.

_____

_____

Although teenagers do not pair off romantically, they are getting plenty of sex, just not with people they care about. They care about their friends and don't want to risk ruining friendships, so they "hook up" with strangers they meet while out at night or online. "Hooking up" means having sex with someone, and many teens hook up only with people they have no other contact with, preferably from different schools or towns.

_____

_____

Although teenagers often think that sex without emotional involvement will avoid heartbreak and breakups, many teens, both girls and boys, admit that it is difficult not to develop feelings for someone they are physically intimate with. If one person begins to feel an attachment while the other doesn't, a distancing occurs: That hurts. It's a breakup of a different sort.

_____

_____

Teenagers have always experimented with ways to do things differently than their parents did. Trying new ways to do things is an important stage in teenagers' development. Experimentation is normal and sometimes produces better ways of doing things. According to most teens, however, the "hook-up" isn't the answer to heartbreak: It's just another road to it. Perhaps teenagers are destined to experience some pain as they try out what "love" means.

PRACTICE 7   ADD TRANSITIONS ·

The following essay has no transitions. Read it carefully, and add transitions both within and between the paragraphs. There is no one correct answer.

Skydiving is the most thrilling activity I can ever imagine. I was scared, euphoric, and proud during my one skydive. I would encourage anyone to have the experience of a lifetime.

_____ I was scared as I looked down out of the plane, ready to jump. The ground was barely visible. My instructor gave the ready sign, assuring me that he would be guiding me all the way. I closed my eyes, and we jumped out of the plane together. It felt as if we were dropping very fast. I opened my eyes and saw that, _____ we were. I panicked a little, fearing that the parachute wouldn't open or that my instructor would activate it too late, and we'd be killed.

I was ___ euphoric. My instructor opened the chute, and we just glided silently through the air. It was like flying. It was very peaceful and almost religious. I had never felt this way and knew that this was an important experience.

We landed, and I was proud of myself. It had taken a lot of courage to jump and to trust my life to another individual, my instructor. I had done it and done it well. I had benefited from the experience, mentally and spiritually. It was so thrilling and wonderful I probably won't do it again for fear that the second time would be an anticlimax. Do it!

Revise Your Own Essay

Before selecting a writing assignment, read how Derek Johnson, the student whose writing you saw in Chapter 5 as he developed a thesis, revised his draft essay. Look at the changes that Derek made in his revised essay. They are highlighted in bold.

DRAFT

> *The Apprentice* is an example of good reality television, where viewers can learn many useful lessons about the business world, such as how to dress, what real-world business situations are like, and how to solve problems. Many people criticize reality TV for putting people into unrealistic situations. This criticism is true of programs like *Fear Factor* and *The Swan,* which are for entertainment only. But *The Apprentice* is both entertaining and educational.
>
> Viewers of *The Apprentice* can learn how to dress for the business world. All of the candidates are very well dressed in a formal sense. They all wear suits at the beginning and are very neat.

Also, viewers can learn about real-world business situations. For example, people have to work together in teams. They have to elect a team leader and that person is responsible for the results of the team. And the winning team doesn't win because it is faster but because it uses better strategies. The team is creative. This is true of everything from running a lemonade stand to coming up with a marketing campaign for an airline.

Finally, viewers can learn about problem solving in business. People on the show can't just say they have a problem and expect someone else to fix it. They have to figure out how to deal with the problem as a team. Like in the last episode, Bill was running a golf tournament and the sponsor's sign didn't show up. And Kwame was running a casino event starring Jessica Simpson, who got lost on the way to the event.

Some reality television is really useless, but *The Apprentice* gives viewers an opportunity to learn about business while they are being entertained. In fact, several business school programs have used *The Apprentice* episodes as case studies. I wish there were more of this kind of television.

REVISED (changes in bold)

Many people criticize reality TV for putting people into unrealistic situations. **Although** this criticism may be true of programs like *Fear Factor* and *The Swan,* which are for entertainment only, it does not apply to *The Apprentice,* which is entertaining and educational. *The Apprentice is an example of good reality television, where viewers can learn many useful lessons about the business world, such as how to dress, what real-world business situations are like, and how to solve problems.*

One good lesson viewers of *The Apprentice* can learn is how to dress for the business world. All of the candidates are very well dressed in a formal sense. **For example,** they all wear suits at the beginning, and they are very neat. **The women do not wear big jewelry or have messy hairstyles. Similarly, the men do not have long hair or visible piercings. Seeing how the *Apprentice* contestants dress made me realize that people can't wear**

Thesis (underlined) links to lessons described in later paragraphs; introduction reorganized to build to main point

Links to thesis

continued

everyday clothing at work. Before seeing *The Apprentice,* I didn't know that about business.

Another lesson I learned from *The Apprentice* is that real-world business situations often require people to work together in teams. **First,** the group members have to elect a team leader who is responsible for the results of the team. **Then they have to learn how to work well together. They learn to pool their ideas and listen to each other. Also, they learn to think critically together.** The winning team doesn't win because it is faster but because it uses better strategies. **In addition,** the team is creative. **Good teamwork is important in every situation,** from running a lemonade stand to coming up with a marketing campaign for an airline. **Before seeing *The Apprentice,* I didn't know how important teamwork was.**

The most important lesson I learned was about problem solving in business. People on the show can't just say they have a problem and expect someone else to fix it. They have to figure out how to deal with the problem as a team. **For example,** in the last episode, Bill was running a golf tournament and the sponsor's sign didn't show up. **Instead of panicking and yelling at other people, he organized a search and finally found the sign in a Dumpster.** And Kwame, **the other remaining contestant,** was running a casino event starring Jessica Simpson, who got lost on the way to the event. **Kwame stayed calm as usual and logically made a list of people to contact for information. Even though the problem seemed unsolvable and disaster inevitable, Kwame's strategy worked, and Jessica Simpson was found in time for the show. I know now that getting mad and panicking does not help solve a problem.**

With all that I have learned from watching *The Apprentice,* I truly believe that it is a worthwhile and educational reality TV program. Some reality television is really useless, but

Links to thesis

Links to thesis

The Apprentice gives viewers an opportunity to learn about business while they are being entertained. In fact, several business school programs have used *The Apprentice* episodes as case studies. I wish there were more of this kind of television.

 REVISING ASSIGNMENT . . . .

Revise an essay using the draft you developed in Chapter 8. Before revising, read the following Critical Thinking box.

CRITICAL THINKING: REVISING YOUR ESSAY

FOCUS

- After a break, reread your draft with a fresh perspective.

ASK

- What's my point or position? Does my thesis statement clearly state my main point?
- Does my essay have the following?
  —An introductory paragraph
  —Three or more body paragraphs
  —A topic sentence for each paragraph that supports the main point
  —A forceful concluding paragraph that reminds my readers of my main point and makes an observation
- Does my essay have unity?
  —Do all of the support points relate directly to my main point?
  —Do all the supporting details in each body paragraph relate to the paragraph's topic sentence?
  —Have I avoided drifting away from my main point?
- Do I have enough support?
  —Taken together, do the topic sentences of each paragraph give enough support or evidence for the main point?
  —Do individual paragraphs support their topic sentences?
  —Would more detail strengthen my support?
- Is my essay coherent?
  —Have I used transitional words to link ideas?
  —Have I used transitional sentences to link paragraphs?

REVISE

- Revise your draft, making any improvements you can.

Part Two

Writing Different Kinds of Essays

10

Narration

Writing That Tells Stories

Understand What Narration Is

Narration is writing that tells a story of an event or experience.

▪▪ FOUR BASICS OF GOOD NARRATION

1. It reveals something of importance to you (**main point**).

2. It includes all of the major events of the story (**primary support**).

3. It uses details to bring the story to life for your audience (**secondary support**).

4. It presents the events in a clear order, usually according to when they happened.

In the following passage, each number corresponds to one of the four basics of good narration.

> **1** My guardian angel made sure I got to the interview that changed my life. **2** I went to bed early on the night before the most important job interview I have ever had. I felt that getting this job would be the best thing I would ever do, and I wanted it with all my heart. **3** I had laid my clothes out for the morning, and I had checked my alarm clock twice to

4 Events in chronological order

make sure that I would wake up in plenty of time to get ready and get to the interview on time. Everything was set, and I had no reason to worry.

2 At 2:00 a.m., I sat bolt upright in bed, absolutely certain that I was going to lose my electricity, the alarm wouldn't go off, and I would miss the interview. **3** It was a mild spring night, with no chance of high winds, snow, or lightning—the usual sources of power failure. Nevertheless, I knew I was going to lose power.

2 I was so certain that I called my mother right then and asked her to call me at 6:30 a.m. because I thought I was going to lose my electricity. **3** Groggily, she muttered, "Are you crazy? Why do you think you're going to lose power?" I couldn't really explain, and she thought I was just nervous about the interview. But she agreed to call me. Satisfied, I went back to sleep.

2 I was sound asleep when the phone rang hours later. **3** My mother said, "I am your wake-up call, you worrywart." When I looked at my clock, it was dead: I had indeed lost power. I told her and then asked what time it was. She assured me that it was only 6:35, and I had plenty of time. I had to go to her place to shower and get ready, **2** but I got to the interview on time, got the job, and, as I thought, changed the course of my life. **1** Since then, I've never doubted the existence of my guardian angel.

4 Events in chronological order

Telling stories is one important way in which we communicate with one another. Whether they are serious or humorous, stories provide information and examples that can show, explain, or prove a point.

You can use narration in many practical situations. Consider the following examples:

COLLEGE
: In a U.S. history course, you trace, in your own words, the specific sequence of events that led the United States to enter World War II.

WORK
: A customer becomes angry with you and lodges a complaint with your boss. You recount—in writing—what happened.

EVERYDAY LIFE
: Your wallet is stolen, and you file a written account with the police reporting exactly what happened.

■ For an example of an actual narration written for work, see page 156. The piece was written by the journalist who is profiled in the box on page 155.

Main Point in Narration

Whenever you write a narration, you should have a **purpose** in mind, whether that is to explain what happened, to prove something, or simply to entertain someone. If you don't know the purpose of your narration, your readers won't know it either.

In addition to knowing your purpose, you should also be clear on your **main point**—what is important about the narration. Generally, college instructors will want your main point to indicate what is important to you about a story. Take another look at the passage under the Four Basics of Good Narration (p. 147). What if the main point had been stated as follows?

I lost electricity one night.

You might respond, "So what?" This statement doesn't promise a very interesting story. Now read the actual statement of the main point:

My guardian angel made sure I got to the interview that changed my life.

This statement emphasizes the event's importance to the writer. You need to express your main point clearly in topic sentences (for paragraphs) and in thesis statements (for essays). Topic sentences and thesis statements usually include your topic and your main point.

■ For more on topic sentences and thesis statements, see Chapter 5.

Topic + Main point = | Topic sentence/thesis statement |

| My guardian angel made sure I got to the interview that changed my life. |

Although writers generally reveal the main point either at the beginning or at the end of their narration, we suggest that you state it in the first paragraph and remind readers of it at the end of your writing.

■ For online exercises on main point and support, visit *Exercise Central* at **bedfordstmartins .com/realessays**.

Support in Narration

The **support** for the main point of your narration is the presentation and explanation of the major events in the story, as well as details about those events. Your **point of view** determines how you present these events and details.

Point of View

In a narration, the events you include and the way you describe them create a story that is based on your point of view. For example, two people who witness or participate in the same series of events may give very different accounts, because they perceive what happened differently.

The stories that Gloria and Mason tell in the following two paragraphs reflect their different points of view regarding the same experience.

GLORIA'S STORY

This morning, Mason and I set out for what was supposed to be a great day at the beach, but Mason's stubborn behavior ruined everything. First, he took the longest route, so we hit traffic that we would have avoided by going the short route. Then, we got lost. When I suggested that we stop and ask for directions, Mason refused. After another hour of driving, we passed an intersection that we'd crossed earlier. I again suggested that we stop and ask for directions, but Mason wasn't buying it. So we drove some more. Finally, we were about to run out of gas, so we pulled into a gas station. While Mason was filling the tank, I asked the attendant for directions. I swear, if we hadn't needed gas, we'd still be driving around looking for that beach!

MASON'S STORY

This morning, Gloria and I set out for what was supposed to be a great day at the beach, but Gloria wanted to pick a fight. First, she insisted I was going the wrong way, it was going to take us longer, and we'd hit more traffic. Then, she decided we were lost. I knew where we were going, but Gloria kept on nagging me to stop and ask for directions. When we were almost there, I decided to get gas, and she had to ask the attendant for directions. I don't know what was going on with her, but she was really on my case.

When you write a narration, be careful to describe events in a way that will tell the story you want to tell.

Major Events and Details

The **major events** of a story are your primary support in narration, and they will usually become the topic sentences for the body paragraphs in your essay. Ask yourself what the major events are and what makes them important. To help your readers experience the events as you did, give supporting details that bring the experience to life.

■ For more on supporting a point, see Chapter 6.

For example, one student stated the main point of an event in the following thesis: *The theft of my wallet this morning showed me how easy it is to be deceived.*

The student then did some listing to come up with the major events and details about those events.

■ For more on listing, see page 69.

MAJOR EVENTS (primary support)	SUPPORTING DETAILS (secondary support)
Woman bumped into me	Light bump, but she dropped her folder of papers, and they scattered
I bent down to help her collect the papers.	Wind was blowing, so I had to work fast
A man stopped and asked if he could help.	I didn't get a good look at him because I was trying to get the papers, but he stood close to me and hung around for a minute just watching us. Then, he just left without saying anything.
Woman thanked me, and I said no problem	She had her head down and walked off fast.
When I went to get coffee, I realized the wallet was gone.	I broke into a sweat at the café and had that horrible panicked feeling.
I realized that the man and woman were working together.	Looking back on the details, it was clear how carefully they'd planned the scam.

Organization in Narration

**NARRATION
AT A GLANCE**

**Introduction with
thesis statement**
Says what's
important about
the experience

↓

First major event
Details about the
event

↓

**Second major
event**
Details about the
event

↓

Third major event
Details about the
event

↓

Conclusion
Reminds readers
of the main point
and makes an
observation based
on it

Because narration tells a story, it uses **chronological (time) order**. Start at the beginning of the story, and describe the events in the sequence in which they occurred. See the chart on the left for an overview of the steps in this process.

Time transitions (see the box following this paragraph) are important in narration because they make the order of events clear to readers. Writers of narration use these common transitions not only within a paragraph to move from one detail about the event to the next but also between paragraphs to move from one major event to the next.

Common Time Transitions

after	eventually	meanwhile	soon
as	finally	next	still
at last	first	now	then
before	last	second	when
during	later	since	while

■ For more on
chronological order,
see page 100.

■ For more on
transitions, see
pages 135–37.

Read and Analyze Narration

Before writing a narration essay, read the following three examples of narration—from college, the workplace, and everyday life—and answer the questions that accompany them.

Narration in College

The following essay was written for a college writing course. The assignment was "Write an essay describing an important decision in your life."

A RETURN TO EDUCATION

Jordan Brown

1   For me, college has been an experience marked by anticipation, fear, and pride. I sometimes find myself still surprised that I am really here. The journey to get here has been a long one, but if I can put my fears behind me, I believe I will be able to accomplish something that I can really be proud of.

■ For more examples of narration, see Chapter 43.

2   Finally being able to go to college is something that I have been anticipating for many years. Since I left high school and the California Bay Area behind, I have been on the go in one way or another. After graduation, I felt that I wasn't ready for the commitments or responsibilities of college. Instead, I enlisted in the army. The army provided me with the maturity and self-discipline that I desperately needed in my life; however, being in the army also provided me with very little time or money to go to college, so I put it off until "a later date."

PAUSE: What are the commitments and responsibilities of going to college?

3   After the army, I sought a higher-paying job, first becoming a truck driver. This job provided me with money but no time. Now I work for the railroad, and with my apprenticeship behind me, I have some free time for the first time in my life.

4   What I have been anticipating for years is finally here. I now have the time and money for college, but do I have the ability? It has been eleven years since I last sat in a classroom. This made me question myself: Can I do this? Will I succeed? Will I fail? Am I even capable of learning in a classroom environment? Although I had these questions, I knew that the only way to face my fears was to attack them head-on. I reminded myself that the only thing I could do is try.

PAUSE: As you read the next few paragraphs, think about how your experience compares with Jordan's.

5   When I first walked into Front Range Community College, I was nervous. I couldn't help but notice how young everyone looked. I got to my study skills class, sat down, and looked around. I felt out of place. Most of the people in the class looked as if they had just graduated from high school. When we did our introductions, however, I learned that one of the women sitting across the room had graduated from high school eleven years ago. I started to feel a little younger.

PAUSE: Recall in detail your first college class.

_____

_____

6   When I got to my philosophy class, I watched the other students come in and noticed that not everyone looked like a kid. This class looked very much like an American melting pot, with students of many ages and cultures. As we went around the room introducing ourselves, I felt very much more confident about my decision to try college. Many students were even older than I was. A woman sitting near me, who looked about my mom's age, said she was in college because all of her kids were in college now. She told us that she wanted a college education and a better job. An older gentleman across the room said that he was a business executive from Germany. His job had become boring, and he was looking for something more challenging. By the end of the introductions, I was convinced that this "college thing" might just work.

PAUSE: Are your friends and family supportive of your going to college?

_____

_____

7   Since I have gone back to school, there has been a lot of pride surrounding me. My parents can't stop talking about me and how proud they are. My family and friends are excited for me and congratulate me on my decision. I am also proud of myself for making the tough decision to go back to school. I know that when I get my degree, I will have something to be truly proud of.

8   I still have fears and uncertainties. But I also have positive anticipation and hope. Now, I know that I am on the right course. I know that as long as I have stamina and determination, nothing can stop me from achieving my dream of getting my degree in mechanical engineering.

1. Double-underline the **thesis statement.**
2. Underline each **topic sentence/major event.**
3. Put a check mark (✔) by the **supporting details.**
4. Circle the **time transitions.**

■ For a list of the four basics of good narration, see page 147.

5. Does Jordan's essay have the **four basics of good narration**? Be ready to explain your answer.
6. When you started college, was your experience at all like Jordan's? Why or why not? If you were meeting a new student who felt as Jordan did, what would you say to him or her?

Narration at Work

The following profile shows how a journalist uses narration in her work.

Profile of Success

Monique Rizer
Journalist and
Development
Associate

BACKGROUND: I was the oldest of six children, and before my mother married my stepfather, she was on welfare. She homeschooled me for five years, from grades four through eight, until I begged her to let me go to a public high school. There I made friends with some people who expected to go to college, and I realized I wanted to go, too. I started at Green River Community College, but just then my parents' financial situation got really bad, and the eight of us had to move to a trailer. I stopped going to school and floundered for a while, until I met my future husband, who was going to a community college and encouraged me to go back. I enrolled at Highline Community College, and several months later I became pregnant with my first son. I was determined to stay in college, so I continued and ended up completing one year at Highline. That summer, I had my son, got married, and found loans to transfer to Pacific Lutheran University with my husband. While there, I received one of the first Gates Millennium Scholarships, which made continuing college possible.

Although I moved a few times, I graduated from college and went on to graduate school. After I finished graduate school, I had another son. About two years ago, my husband, children, and I moved to Virginia for my husband's job. A few months after we got there, he was called to active duty and deployed to Iraq, where he spent the next fifteen months. Although he was wounded, he returned home safely.

COLLEGES/DEGREES: B.A., Gonzaga University; M.S., Syracuse University

EMPLOYER: National Military Family Association

WRITING AT WORK: I have done many types of writing for many kinds of audiences. When I worked in marketing at an accounting firm, one of my jobs was to rewrite material the accountants gave me so that it would be appealing, clear, and simple. When my husband was in Iraq, I wrote a newsletter for families of soldiers with advice on finding resources and keeping up morale and with news of what was going on with the soldiers in Iraq.

During that time, I had to find my own resources for military families, and it's not easy. I had to write well, speak well, and be persistent. Even when you don't write for a living, you have to communicate effectively to get what you need in life. Words give you the power to fight for what you want and need. Everything you're learning now, you will need later.

HOW MONIQUE USES NARRATION: Much of the writing I do involves telling people's stories so that readers can understand them and their unique problems.

Monique's Narration

The following is an excerpt from an article, published in *The Chronicle of Higher Education,* that Monique wrote in her profession as a journalist.

VOCABULARY
The following words are *italicized* in the excerpt: *fidgeted, postpartum, intangible.* If you don't know their meanings, look them up in a dictionary.

WHEN STUDENTS ARE PARENTS

1   Crammed behind my desk, I *fidgeted* and shifted my eyes to observe the other students in the room. I tried not to look the way I felt—like I didn't belong there with them. I couldn't help noticing that all the other women were wearing shorts, sandals, flirty summer dresses: appropriate clothes for a warm September day. I tugged at the baggy clothes hiding my *postpartum* weight. I thought of my six-week-old son and hoped I'd make it home to nurse him at the scheduled time.

PAUSE: Have you felt out of place in college or other places?

2   It was the summer of 1998. I was a twenty-year-old new mother and wife, and it was my first day of class, though not my first day of college. I'd begun my long journey through higher education three years before, but my plans to attend full time after high school graduation were put on hold when financial difficulties forced my family of eight to move. I then found a local community college and felt prepared to start again, but instead the registration papers sat abandoned in my car, where I practically lived since home was a 32-foot trailer filled with seven other people. In the summer of 1996, I packed my bags and left to live on my own; I enrolled again the next spring and had my son in July 1998. I knew I had to stay in school and go full time. I wanted more for my son and myself, even though I wasn't sure what exactly "more" was at the time.

PAUSE: How do you think Monique found the strength to go back to school after dropping out?

3   That commitment to finish college has paid off. Now, I have a bachelor's in journalism from Gonzaga University and a master's in information management from Syracuse University. During my years in school, my son kept me focused and ignited my ambition to be a better student. In my experience, there is no better motivation to finish college and to appreciate the full experience than a child whose future depends on

your decisions. I had to continue to use my education to give him a better life and to set an example for him to follow. I also had to finish what my mother didn't: She had me at nineteen and gave in to pressure to quit college and go to work.

4   I feel a tremendous sense of accomplishment: I've learned so many *intangible* lessons about myself; I've decided that I want to help other young parents achieve their educational goals; and I see a better future for my boys (I have two now). And I keep telling my mom that she doesn't have to live vicariously through me: She can return to college any time she wants.

PAUSE: Do you have enough information to understand how Monique got through college?

1. Double-underline the **thesis statement**. Note: It is not in the first paragraph.

2. In which paragraph does Monique give the most **detail** to help us understand her experience? _____

3. What part of Monique's narration could use more detail? _____
_____. Why? _____
_____
_____

4. In Monique's profile, the Background section gives some of the same information that her essay does. How does her essay differ from the background information? _____
_____

5. Does Monique's essay have the **four basics of good narration**? Be ready to explain your answer. _____
_____

6. How does Monique's experience of starting college compare to Jordan's? Which essay gives us more detail? _____

Narration in Everyday Life

The following is a blog written by a young marine who was blinded in 2005 while serving in Iraq. He received a medical retirement from the Marine Corps.

VOCABULARY
The following words are *italicized* in the excerpt: *Braille, battalion, sombrero, adrenaline.* If you don't know their meanings, look them up in a dictionary.

BACK TO SCHOOL

Michael Jernigan

PAUSE: What is the tone of this first paragraph? How does it compare to Monique's first paragraph?

1   Hola, amigos! Greetings from the great state of Virginia. It has been a couple of months since my last post, and during that time I have been on a couple of trips and even attended my ten-year high school reunion in St. Petersburg, FL. It was nice to see some of the people that I have not seen since graduation. I received a very warm welcome from everyone. As it turns out, I am the only one who had a really good reason for having plastic surgery! . . . But in all seriousness, I was very touched to receive a plaque from my class thanking me for my service and sacrifice to our country. They even had it engraved in *Braille* so that I can read it.

2   At the end of June, I went to Jacksonville, NC, for the opening of the new Wounded Warrior Battalion. It was a wonderful ceremony and I was able to meet the *battalion* commander. I ran into some of my friends from National Naval Medical Center in Bethesda, MD and also a young marine, Adam, from my hometown. It was Adam's mom who sent me food from my favorite Cuban restaurant when I was first in the hospital after being wounded.

3   I then went back to Camp Lejeune for the Fourth of July. The unit I had gone to Iraq with had just come back from a deployment to the Mediterranean Sea, and some of the guys and I wanted to welcome them home with a nice party. After that, I was able to come back to Virginia for a few weeks and register for school. I had to take a placement exam and register for all of my classes.

4   In July, my girlfriend Leslie and I . . . took a cruise with my family to Cozumel, Mexico. This was our first family vacation in several years. We had a great time—there was food everywhere and bars on every deck that were all too willing to part me from my money. We enjoyed

spending time with my mom and stepdad and my brother and sisters. I am glad that Leslie enjoyed herself because this was the first time she was around my whole family. You should have seen me on board ship after the day in Cozumel. I went from bar to bar with my *sombrero* speaking my best Spanglish.

5   In August, Leslie and I also went to Albuquerque, NM, where we attended the Blinded Veterans Association's national convention. We were there as part of a program called Operation Peer Support. This program is designed so that newly blinded veterans can meet other veterans who have been at this for a lot longer than we have.

6   During this trip, I went skydiving. It was one of the most fun things I have ever done. I was very calm until they opened the door of the plane. At that moment, I felt something I hadn't felt in a very long time—a strange mixture of *adrenaline*, excitement, and fear. I jumped at 10,500 feet and had a 31-second freefall. On landing, I got my foot caught in the dirt and strained my right knee. As soon as I was off the ground, I was doing a TV interview for a local news channel. It's a good thing they edited it because I had no idea I was being interviewed. Since I could not see the camera and microphone, I just thought a guy was asking me some questions. A family friend called my mom at 12:30 a.m. to see if "Mikey was in Albuquerque" because he had just seen me on the news! It's not the first time that my mom has gotten a call like that.

7   Well, now the school year has started, and I'm currently taking ten credit hours at Northern Virginia Community College and enjoying it. I haven't been in school for ten years, and that would be hard enough, but now I'm doing it blind. Brittani, my guide dog, is my eyes on campus. It is hard teaching her to read the textbooks, but give it awhile and we'll see.

PAUSE: Does Michael give details to help us imagine "doing it blind"?

_____

_____

8   Let me tell you about the frustrations I had at the beginning. In one class, I received textbooks on CDs, only to find that the school had never ordered me the proper reader for the CDs. I am still waiting on three textbooks: I thought six weeks' notice would have been plenty of time for them to get me everything I needed.

PAUSE: What frustrations did you experience at the start of college?

_____

_____

9   I am lucky that all of my classes are in the same building, but it can be stressful going from class to class because the hallways are crowded, and there aren't any landmarks. I have found that my fellow students are very helpful in pointing me in the right direction. And I am extremely lucky that my professors are cooperative and helpful in adapting to my unique conditions.

10   Keep checking and reading my blog, as I will be sharing a lot more with y'all in the near future.

—From "Home Fires: Five Iraq War Veterans on Their Return to American Life," *NYTimes.com*, Sept. 18, 2007

1. Because this is a blog, there is no **thesis statement**. Try writing a thesis statement for the piece. _____

    _____

2. What paragraph has the most vivid details? _____

3. What impression do you have of Michael? Underline some examples that give you that impression.

    _____

    _____

4. Is "Back to School" a good title for this essay? Write another title.

    _____

5. What one word in the essay would be too informal for a formal essay? (Did it stand out as you read it?)

    _____

Critical Reading and Writing: Key College Skills

1. **Summary.** Briefly summarize the three essays in this section, listing major events. At the end, write your impression of each person's experience.

2. **Analysis.** Compare the first paragraphs of each of the three essays. How are they different? The same? All of the authors discuss their return to college. Which gives you the fullest description of their experience? Which essay makes you wish you'd been given more details? Why?

3. **Synthesis.** Using information from all three essays, along with your own experience, write about the different reasons students go to college,

the difficulties of returning to college, or how the first days are always uncomfortable.

4. **Evaluation.** Using the **four basics of good narration** as a measure, decide which of the three essays is the best as a formal narration. Give specific examples to support your choice. Is your choice for best essay different from the one you *liked* most? How?

Write a Narration Essay

■ Use the chart on page 152 to help you organize.

In this section, you will write your own narration essay based on one of the following assignments. Before you begin to write, review the four basics of good narration on page 147. Also, read the Tips for Tackling Narration in the box that follows.

TIPS FOR TACKLING NARRATION

1. Read the assignment carefully, highlighting key words. A narration assignment won't necessarily include the word *narrate*. Instead, it might say *describe* or *recall* or *recount* or *tell about a time.*

2. Then, choose an event or experience. What's important about it? Why? Start out by drafting a thesis statement that states the significance.

3. Work on answering the questions "What happened, and when? Then what?"

4. Ask yourself: So what? Your essay should answer that question.

■ **ASSIGNMENT 1 WRITING ABOUT COLLEGE, WORK, AND EVERYDAY LIFE** . . . .

Write a narration essay on *one* of the following topics or on a topic of your own choice.

COLLEGE

- Write about your first experiences of college, as Jordan, Monique, and Michael did.

- Explain what led you to start college.

- Summarize an interesting story you learned in one of your other classes, such as psychology or history.

WORK

- Tell the story of something positive you did at work (some achievement).
- Explain what you learned from getting or doing your first job.
- Describe an incident that shows your boss as _____ (supportive/unsupportive, fair/unfair, clueless/sharp, realistic/unrealistic, honest/dishonest).

EVERYDAY LIFE

- Recount a time that you took a risk.
- Recount the most embarrassing, rewarding, happy, or otherwise memorable moment in your life.
- Write about a time when you were proud or ashamed of your behavior.

 ASSIGNMENT 2 WRITING ABOUT AN IMAGE . . . .

Write a narration essay about what has happened (or is happening) in the picture on the opposite page. Be as creative as you like, but be sure to follow the four basics of good narration.

ASSIGNMENT 3 WRITING TO SOLVE A PROBLEM . . . .

THE PROBLEM: You order a computer from a mail-order company, but it doesn't work properly. You try every step from the online help guide, but nothing works. Then, after holding for a half hour on the customer-service line, you learn that you "might" get a refund after returning the computer and that the process could take as long as two months. You tell the phone rep that this policy is unacceptable. The rep, who suggests that others have complained about the company's refund practices, urges you to write an e-mail to the company's customer satisfaction service. He adds, "That's definitely gotten results in the past." You decide that's what you'll do.

THE ASSIGNMENT: Working on your own or with a small group, write a courteous but firm e-mail to the company, Computers Inc., describing your problems with the computer and with the company's refund practices. Ask for a replacement, give a desired deadline, and indicate the steps you are prepared to take if you don't get satisfaction.

RESOURCES: Review the chart on pages 868–69 for general advice about problem solving. You might also visit Web sites like *Complaints.com* (**www .complaints.com**) for ideas about how to phrase your complaint and what evidence to include. At *Complaints.com*, see especially the links "Browse Complaints" and the complaint posting guidelines (under "How It Works"). List any Web sites that you use.

■ Be sure to cite and document any sources you use in your papers. For advice, see Chapter 21.

ASSIGNMENT 4 **WRITING ABOUT READINGS** . . . .

The assignments that follow ask you to read at least two different examples of narration and draw from them to write your own essay.

- Read Uzodinma Iweala's essay, "A Close Encounter" (p. 749), and review Jordan Brown's "A Return to Education" (p. 153). What lesson does each learn, and how does each writer's initial assumptions about the situation change? Write an essay about an event or situation where you learned something new, and refer to Iweala's and Brown's essays when possible. Also, consider using dialogue (conversation between characters) as Iweala does. (For information on quoting, see pp. 361–65.)

■ For advice on summarizing, analyzing, synthesizing, and evaluating, see pages 36–40.

- Read the essays in this chapter (Jordan Brown's, Monique Rizer's, and Michael Jernigan's). All are about education, especially the experience of returning to school after an absence. Drawing from each of these pieces, write an essay about situations or circumstances that made you feel odd about being in school or that were difficult for you.

- Read Langston Hughes's essay, "Salvation" (p. 745), and review Jordan Brown's and Monique Rizer's essays in this chapter. These three narratives include the experience of wanting to fit in, but with different outcomes. Write an essay about a time you felt pressured to fit in, the ways you responded, and the outcome. Draw from the readings to relate your experience to that of the other writers.

Follow the steps in the Writing Guide starting below to help you prewrite, draft, revise, and edit your narration. Check off each step as you complete it.

WRITING GUIDE: NARRATION	
STEPS IN NARRATION	**HOW TO DO THE STEPS**
Focus.	☐ Think about who will read your narration and what point you want your readers to understand.
Prewrite to explore your topic. See Chapter 4 for more on prewriting.	☐ Determine your purpose for writing. ☐ Decide what story you want to tell. ☐ Use a prewriting technique to explore your thoughts about what happened; how it affected you or others; and what the story shows, explains, or proves.

STEPS IN NARRATION	HOW TO DO THE STEPS
Write a thesis statement. Topic + <u>main point</u> = Thesis My father <u>has become a stranger.</u> See Chapter 5 for more on writing a thesis.	☐ Decide what is important to you about the story. Imagine a reader saying, "So what?" ☐ Specify the point you want your readers to understand. ☐ Write a thesis statement that will begin or end your first paragraph.
Support your thesis statement. The primary support points in narration are the major events of the story you want to tell. See Chapter 6 for more on supporting a thesis statement.	☐ List all of the major events in the story. ☐ Review your thesis, and drop any events that do not help you explain, show, or prove your main point. Make your thesis more specific. ☐ Choose at least three major events that will help your readers understand your main point. ☐ Add supporting details about each event that will help your readers experience it as you did.
Make a plan. See Chapter 7 for more on planning.	☐ Arrange your major events according to when they occurred (chronological order). ☐ Write a plan or an outline for your narration that includes your main support points (the major events) and supporting details for each event. (See the diagram on p. 152.)
Write a draft. See Chapter 8 for more on drafting.	☐ Write an introduction that gets your readers' interest and presents your thesis statement. See if you can use one of the introductory techniques in Chapter 8. ☐ Using your outline, write a topic sentence for each of the major events. ☐ Write body paragraphs that give specific details that bring the story to life. ☐ Write a concluding paragraph that reminds your readers of your main point and makes a final observation about the importance of the story. ☐ Title your essay.
Revise your draft. See Chapter 9 for more on revising a draft.	☐ Ask another person to read and comment on your draft. ☐ Consider how you can make the point of the story clearer to your readers. ☐ Revise your thesis to make it more forceful. ☐ Make sure all of the events and details support your thesis. Add details that strengthen your support, and cut any details that aren't relevant.

continued

STEPS IN NARRATION	HOW TO DO THE STEPS
Revise your draft (cont.).	☐ Reread your introduction, and make changes if it is dull.
	☐ Reread your conclusion to make sure that it is energetic and convincing and that it reminds your readers of your main point.
	☐ Add transitions (especially time transitions) to connect your ideas.
	☐ Make at least five changes to your draft to improve unity, support, or coherence (see pp. 127–40).
	☐ Check to make sure the draft follows the four basics of good narration.
Edit your draft. See Parts Four through Seven for more on editing.	☐ Use the spell checker and grammar checker on your computer, but also reread your essay carefully to catch any errors.
	☐ Look for errors in grammar, spelling, or punctuation. Focus first on sentence fragments, run-ons, errors in subject-verb agreement, verb errors, and other areas where you know you often make mistakes.
	☐ Ask yourself: Is this the best I can do?

11

Illustration

Writing That Shows Examples

Understand What Illustration Is

Illustration is writing that uses examples to show, explain, or prove a point.

> ■■ **FOUR BASICS OF GOOD ILLUSTRATION**
> ■■
> **1.** It has a point to illustrate.
> **2.** It gives specific examples to show, explain, or prove the point.
> **3.** It gives details to support these examples.
> **4.** It uses enough examples to get the writer's point across.

In the following paragraph, each number corresponds to one of the four basics of good illustration.

What's the strongest predictor of your health? **1** It may not be your income or age but rather your literacy. **2** People with low literacy skills have four times greater annual health costs than those with high skills. Why is literacy so important? **3** Most Americans read at an eighth- or ninth-grade level, and 20% read at just a fifth-grade level or below. However, most health-care materials are written above the tenth-grade

4 Enough examples given to back the writer's main point

167

4 Enough examples given to back the writer's main point

level. **3** As many as half of all patients fail to take medications as directed, often because they don't understand the instructions.

2 Americans can improve their health literacy by asking their doctor or pharmacist **3** three questions: (1) "What is my main problem?" (2) "What do I need to do?" and (3) "Why is it important to do this?" If you're still confused, don't hesitate to ask your doctor, nurse, or pharmacist to go over the information again.

—"Literacy and Health," *Parade* magazine, January 18, 2004

Whenever we explain something, we use examples to show what we mean. Here are some ways you might use illustration:

COLLEGE	In a criminal justice course, you discuss and give examples of the most common criminal violations.
WORK	Your written self-evaluation includes specific and measurable examples of how well (or poorly) you performed.
EVERYDAY LIFE	You take your car to a mechanic and give him or her examples that show how the car is not running properly.

Main Point in Illustration

Look at the opening sentences in the paragraph with the colored shading (p. 167).

What's the strongest predictor of your health? It may not be your income or age but rather your literacy.

In this case, the topic—the strongest predictor of your health—is in the opening sentence, which is followed by a surprising **main point**: that literacy might be a predictor of health. Because the point is surprising, the reader will be interested in reading on to find out how it could be true. The writer demonstrates the main point by giving examples.

Often, a thesis statement in illustration includes the topic and your main point.

Topic + Main point = Thesis statement

■ For more on thesis statements, see Chapter 5.

Learning another language has many benefits, including some you might not expect.

Topic + Main point = | Thesis statement |

| Holistic medicine is gaining support among doctors. |

■ For online exercises on main point and support, visit *Exercise Central* at **bedfordstmartins .com/realessays**.

Support in Illustration

In illustration, the **examples** show or prove your stated main point.

A student who had written the thesis *Homeschooling is beneficial to both the child and the parent* focused her prewriting on finding examples of benefits of homeschooling. Here are some examples from her brainstorming:

individualized to child	*parent and child have control*
parent and child together	*more flexibility*
at child's own pace	*considers child's learning style*
one-on-one	*education is part of regular life*

■ For more on brainstorming, see page 69. For more on supporting a point, see Chapter 6.

An illustration essay usually uses several examples as **support points**. The writer of the prewriting on homeschooling selected "individualized to child" as one support point and asked herself, "What do I mean? How? In what ways?" to find supporting details.

She also chose "parent and child have control" as another major example that would support the thesis. She then asked herself, "How do they have more control?" and listed potential supporting details:

control over materials used (what books, what computer programs, what approach)

control over time of instruction (what hours of the day, based on child's natural rhythms, vacations—not tied to a school's calendar)

Organization in Illustration

**ILLUSTRATION
AT A GLANCE**

Introduction with thesis statement
Says what you want readers to know about the topic

↓

First example
Details about the example

↓

Second example
Details about the example

↓

Third example (often the most powerful)
Details about the example

↓

Conclusion
Reminds readers of the main point and makes an observation based on it

Illustration often uses **order of importance** to organize several examples, often saving the most vivid, convincing example for last. A typical plan for an illustration essay might look like the one on the left.

Transitions are important in illustration because they signal to readers that you are moving from one example to another. Use transitions to move between sentences within a paragraph and also to move from one paragraph to another.

Common Transitions in Illustration

also	finally	for instance	in addition
another	for example	for one thing	one example . . . another example

---

■ For more on order of importance, see page 101.

■ For more examples of illustration, see Chapter 44.

Read and Analyze Illustration

Before writing an illustration essay, read the following three examples of illustration—from college, the workplace, and everyday life—and answer the questions that accompany them.

Illustration in College

The following is part of a report that Luz Medina wrote when she served as a student representative to the division of Student Affairs at her college. Her job was to survey some other students and present a list of suggestions for new services that would help students.

To: Vice President, Student Affairs

Fr: Luz Medina

Re: Suggestions for student services

1   To complete this report, I interviewed twenty-five students, asking them the following questions: (1) Do you know about the student services that are available on this campus? (2) What service or organization would help your college experience and why? (3) Would you be willing to help set up this program? I have attached the complete responses to these questions, but here I will summarize what I found. The responses were both surprising and well worth considering in the future.

2   To my surprise, most of the students I interviewed were not aware of the many programs that are already available to them. For example, several of the students said that they didn't know what to do when they were about ready to drop out. I told them about our Succeeding Together program and gave them the Web site that lists the people and services that are designed just for these situations. I encouraged them to go to these sites for help, telling them that the college works hard to help keep students from dropping out.

PAUSE: Are you aware of services offered on your campus? Name three and their locations.

_____

_____

3   Another area where we have many services that students don't know about is in preparing for a job search. Most students know that there is an office of career planning, but they thought it just posted job announcements. They didn't know about great programs like the Virtual Job Fair or the many mini-seminars on interviewing, making a good first impression, or one-on-one counseling to match students with employers. They also didn't know about the program that gives very specific career counseling that matches student interests with careers and then helps students plan what courses will best help them get started in the career.

4   There were many other services students did not know about. Although they are listed online and we offer an orientation, I think we, as a committee, should figure out how to more successfully let students know what resources they have on this campus.

5   The students offered some good suggestions for new services. One is that we devise an instant-messaging system for communication with advisers. Students said that often they have to wait to see their advisers when they have a question that would take only a minute to ask and answer. One student compared it to standing in a long line to buy a package of gum: It doesn't seem worth the wait.

6   Two other good suggestions regard the problems students often have with transportation and child care. Students suggested that there be a college-sponsored online bulletin board that students can go to to find rides at various times. Students looking for transportation could find other students with cars who would be willing to give students rides for a small fee. The students also suggested a similar child-care bulletin board that might help parents connect to babysit for each other.

PAUSE: Summarize the new ideas the students suggested.

_____

_____

7   A final suggestion that two students made was to have professors record their lectures so that they could be downloaded for students who had to miss a class. Students said that they could already get the homework assignments for a missed class, but they had no way to get the lecture material.

8   Students were surprised that the college already has so many resources, and they gave serious and thoughtful suggestions for new and needed services. I am sorry to report that only five of the twenty-five students said that they would be willing to help set up a new service, but at least those few are willing. Interviewing other students was an interesting project for me, making me think about the importance of student-affairs programs and giving me experience gathering and analyzing information.

1. Double-underline the **thesis statement**.
2. Underline the **topic sentences** in each paragraph.
3. Do you know what student services are available at your college?
4. If you were asked to suggest a student service at your college, what would it be?
5. Does Luz's report have the **four basics of good illustration**? Be ready to explain your answer.

Illustration at Work

The following profile shows how a university vice president uses illustration at work.

Profile of Success

Juan Gonzalez
Vice President of
Student Affairs,
University of
Texas, Austin

BACKGROUND: I grew up in Amarillo, Texas, in a family of ten children. For most of my life, going to college never even occurred to me. I was a marginal student, on the slow track in school. I expected to either join the military or to work with the Rock Island Railroad, as my father did for thirty-seven years.

However, my circumstances changed when I was a sophomore in high school. In that year, my father lost both of his legs in an accident at work. As I sat with him through his long stay in the hospital, I realized that I wanted a different future. I knew then that I had to go to college, but I didn't know how I could accomplish that seemingly impossible goal.

Timing is often miraculous. Soon after making the decision to pursue higher education, I was approached by a TRIO/Upward Bound counselor who asked me to consider participating in their program. I jumped at the opportunity. The TRIO student support services program gave me the support, encouragement, and skills I needed for college work, and I will always be deeply grateful for their help.

COLLEGES/DEGREES: B.A., Texas Tech University; M.Ed., University of Texas, San Antonio; Ph.D., University of Illinois, Urbana-Champaign.

EMPLOYER: University of Texas, Austin.

WRITING AT WORK: Most of the writing I do at work is in creating presentations for a variety of different audiences, reviewing and revising statements of school policy, and writing and updating various reports on student life at the school. I work closely with student leaders, and much of our communication is oral—shared exchanges of ideas during meetings. However, in those meetings I take minutes of what occurs so that I have accurate records. I maintain active correspondence with students, with administrators in other areas of the college, and with faculty. I also spend a good amount of time writing e-mail messages to people at the university, in the community, and to colleagues around the country.

HOW JUAN USES ILLUSTRATION: In reports to administration and in presentations to parents, trustees, and students, I have to give detailed examples of the work that the Student Affairs office does.

Juan's Illustration

The following is from an address Dr. Gonzalez gave to a group of new students.

VOCABULARY
The following words are *italicized* in the excerpt: *embarking, striving, encapsulates, indicators, collaborative, integrated, aspire, complementing, facilitates, foster, engendering, status quo.* If you don't know their meanings, look them up in a dictionary.

1   As new students, you are *embarking* on an incredibly exciting and challenging time, a time of expanding knowledge, relationships, viewpoints, and achievements. In my role as vice president, I am constantly *striving* to match that energy level so that we can offer the highest level of service on this very diverse campus. I frequently marvel at college students who seem to have an unlimited amount of energy that allows them to attend classes, read and study, maintain a social life, run for political office, pursue a hobby, play an intramural sport, volunteer for a worthy cause, hold down a job. We in the Division of Student Affairs strongly encourage activities outside the classroom that enrich the academic experience, as we recognize that a university education is enhanced through involvement in our campus community.

PAUSE: Are you involved in any campus activity? Is there one you might be interested in?

2   Last November, a group of Student Affairs staff, students, and faculty began work on creating a strategic plan for the division. They have been laboring diligently on this document, and I am excited to share with you the fruit of that labor, our newly developed Student Affairs Strategic Plan, which has as its motto "Student Affairs: Where Life and Learning Intersect."

3   This phrase *encapsulates* the driving force behind the Division of Student Affairs. We exist, in essence, to help students succeed and grow, and we believe that growth and success must be measured in many ways. Academic success is one gauge of how well students are performing, but there are a variety of *indicators* other than grades. Those who take the most from their college experience are those who recognize that learning happens both inside and outside the classroom.

4   In fact, I recently had our units count the services they offer that are *collaborative* efforts with the academic side of the family, and a rough survey yielded 140 programs. This idea of *integrated* learning carries through most of what we do, whether it is a program to recruit the best students from around Texas like the Honors Colloquium, the increasingly popular "Academic Community Centers" for studying and advising on site in the residence halls, Summer Orientation, or the professor-led Freshman Reading Round-Up book discussions.

Our Vision Statement

5   Our vision statement lights the path we are following to where we *aspire* to be:

> The Division of Student Affairs at The University of Texas at Austin seeks to become the premier organization of its kind. We envision a network of programs and services that excels in meeting students' out-of-classroom needs, *complementing* their academic experiences, and building community on a diverse campus. In doing so, we will contribute to developing citizens and leaders who will thrive in and enrich an increasingly complex world.

Our Mission

6   Our mission, or the explanation of what we do, is described this way:

> The Division of Student Affairs *facilitates* students' discovery of self and the world in which they live. We enhance students' educational experiences through programs and services that support academic success. We provide for fundamental needs, including shelter, nourishment, and a sense of security. We create environments that *foster* physical, emotional, and psychological wellness, and advance healthy lifestyles. Student Affairs builds communities, both real and virtual, that encourage inclusiveness, invite communication, and add to the cultural richness of the institution. We focus on personal development, including career decision making,

problem solving, and group dynamics, challenging students to work both independently and as part of a team.

7   The work group that wrote the strategic plan also composed a defining phrase to encapsulate Student Affairs: "Our passion is complete learning." These, I hope you will agree, are stirring words. We take our responsibility for providing an environment that is inclusive and promotes a healthy lifestyle very seriously. We are committed to supporting you as you achieve your goals at this university.

Our Core Values

8   Sharing a fundamental belief in the value of Student Affairs and its ability to transform lives, we will pursue our vision by

- Focusing on the lifelong learning and personal growth of all members of the university community;
- *Engendering* a community that is inclusive, accessible, and secure;
- Conducting ourselves and our programs with the highest integrity;
- Enhancing our services by creating opportunities to collaborate and nurture partnerships;
- Challenging ourselves to move beyond the *status quo* and pursue higher levels of excellence with determination and enthusiasm;
- Strengthening a tradition of quality, compassion, and an unwavering belief in students and ourselves;
- Demonstrating the innovation and courage to adapt to changing conditions; and
- Realizing that both action and vision are necessary for a better future.

9   Our society benefits by having everyone educated, and education is a process that requires everyone to be engaged in the advancement of all peoples. The well-being of our state requires the next generation of leaders and scholars to understand our new world. This means looking at the process of education as more than four years in college, the material in textbooks, or the contents of a classroom lecture but as a way to improve the world.

1. What is the motto of the Student Affairs Strategic Plan? _____

_____

2. Underline **four examples** of programs sponsored by the Office of Student Affairs.

3. What are the **three major points** that Dr. Gonzalez writes about?

_____

4. How do you think Dr. Gonzalez's background influenced his career in student affairs?

5. Writing mission and vision statements is a common writing task in the work world. In Dr. Gonzalez's document, are the examples specific or general, for the most part?

_____

Illustration in Everyday Life

The following is an excerpt from Malcolm Gladwell's best-selling book *Blink,* which is about the role of "snap" decisions that we make in life.

VOCABULARY

The following words are *italicized* in the excerpt: *adaptive, unconscious, apparatus, relegating, toggle, spontaneous.* If you don't know their meanings, look them up in a dictionary.

THE INTERNAL COMPUTER

Malcolm Gladwell

1   The part of our brain that leaps to conclusions is called the *adaptive unconscious,* and the study of this kind of decision-making is one of the most important new fields in psychology. The adaptive unconscious is a kind of giant computer that quickly and quietly processes a lot of the data we need in order to keep functioning as human beings. When you walk out into the street and suddenly realize that a truck is bearing down on you, do you have time to think through all your options? Of course not. The only way that human beings could ever have survived as a species for as long as we have is that we've developed another kind of decision-making *apparatus* that's capable of making very quick judgments based on very little

PAUSE: Summarize what the adaptive unconscious is. Give an example from your own experience.

_____

_____

information. As the psychologist Timothy D. Wilson writes in his book, *Strangers to Ourselves,* "The mind operates most efficiently by *relegating* a good deal of high-level, sophisticated thinking to the unconscious, just as a modern jetliner is able to fly on automatic pilot with little or no input from the human, 'conscious' pilot. The adaptive unconscious does an excellent job of sizing up the world, warning people of danger, setting goals, and initiating action in a sophisticated and efficient manner."

2   Wilson says that we *toggle* back and forth between our conscious and unconscious modes of thinking, depending on the situation. A decision to invite a co-worker over for dinner is conscious. You think it over. You decide it will be fun. You ask him or her. The *spontaneous* decision to argue with that same co-worker is made unconsciously—by a different part of the brain and motivated by a different part of your personality.

3   Whenever we meet someone for the first time, whenever we interview someone for a job, whenever we react to a new idea, whenever we're faced with making a decision quickly and under stress, we use that second part of our brain. How long, for example, did it take you to decide how good a teacher one of your professors was? A class? Two classes? A semester? The psychologist Nalini Ambady once gave students three ten-second videotapes of a teacher—with the sound turned off—and found they had no difficulty at all coming up with a rating of the teacher's effectiveness. Then Ambady cut the clips to five seconds, and the ratings were the same. They were remarkably consistent even when she showed the students just *two* seconds of videotape. Then Ambady compared those snap judgments of teacher effectiveness with evaluations of those same professors made by their students after a full semester of classes, and she found that they were also essentially the same. A person watching a silent, two-second video clip of a teacher he or she has never met will reach conclusions about how good that teacher is that are very similar to those of a student who has sat in the teacher's class for an entire semester. That's the power of the adaptive unconscious.

PAUSE: Summarize Nalini Ambady's experiment.

_____

_____

—From Malcolm Gladwell, *Blink: The Power of Thinking without Thinking* (New York: Little, Brown, 2005), pp. 11–12

1. How does the adaptive unconscious help us? _____

   _____

2. What is the **one example** Gladwell gives here of the adaptive uncon-

   scious? _____

3. What is your reaction to that example? Were you surprised?

4. If the teacher was just recovering from the flu when the videotape was made, would the tape still be an effective evaluation of the teacher's ability?

5. Give an example of a time your adaptive unconscious helped you.

6. Why do you think the title of Gladwell's book is *Blink*? What would you expect the book to give examples of?

Critical Reading and Writing: Key College Skills

1. **Summary.** Briefly summarize each of the three essays in this section, including the examples each of them gives to demonstrate the main point.

2. **Analysis.** Does Luz Medina give enough examples to fulfill her purpose (to provide information for the director of Student Affairs)? How does her piece compare to Dr. Gonzalez's?

3. **Synthesis.** Review Luz's and Dr. Gonzalez's writings. Would Luz's findings help achieve Dr. Gonzalez's vision, mission, and core values? How? How could the example that Malcolm Gladwell gives be used to improve the student experience?

4. **Evaluation.** Using the **four basics of good illustration** as a measure, which of the three selections is the best? Why? Give examples to support your opinion.

Write an Illustration Essay

In this section, you will write your own illustration essay based on one of the following assignments. Before you begin to write, review the four basics of good illustration on page 167. Also, read the Tips for Tackling Illustration in the box that follows.

<hr>

TIPS FOR TACKLING ILLUSTRATION

1. Read the assignment carefully, highlighting key words. An illustration assignment won't use the word *illustrate,* but it may say *give examples of* or *use specific examples to, explain,* or *discuss.* All writing assignments, illustration or other types, call for detailed examples.

2. Think of the main point you want to make, and write it down.

3. For each example, think how you can explain it clearly to your readers.

4. Work on answering the questions, "Like what? What do you mean?"

ASSIGNMENT 1   WRITING ABOUT COLLEGE, WORK, AND EVERYDAY LIFE

Write an illustration essay on *one* of the following topics or on a topic of your own choice.

COLLEGE

■ Use the chart on page 170 to help you organize.

- Discuss some of the activities, services, and programs offered on your campus.
- Write about what you expect to get out of college.
- Write about something you learned in another course, and give examples to explain it to a friend who hasn't taken the course.

WORK

- Tell someone applying for a job like yours what his or her typical responsibilities might be.
- Explain to your supervisor your claim that there is too much work to be done in the time allotted.
- Demonstrate to an interviewer the following statement: "I am a very detail-oriented employee."

EVERYDAY LIFE

- Write a letter to your landlord about how your apartment's maintenance needs to be done more regularly.

- Write a letter to a friend in which you explain that your (mother, father, sibling, sweetheart) is the most (selfish, generous, irresponsible, capable) person you know.

- Name the most influential person in your life, and give examples of his or her characteristics.

ASSIGNMENT 2   WRITING ABOUT AN IMAGE . . . .

The public service announcement below uses illustration to express the difference between being "perfect" and being a "perfect parent." Write an illustration essay in which you give examples of the qualities that, in your view, make a "perfect parent."

You don't have to be perfect to be a perfect parent.
There are thousands of teens in foster care who would love to put up with you.

1 888 200 4005 · adoptuskids.org

■ **ASSIGNMENT 3   WRITING TO SOLVE A PROBLEM** . . . .

THE PROBLEM: A good friend of yours is being sexually harassed at work by a supervisor who is not her boss. Although she has tried to let the person know that the advances are not welcome, the offending behaviors haven't stopped. Your friend is afraid that if she complains to her boss, she will be fired. She asks your advice about what to do.

THE ASSIGNMENT: Working on your own or with a small group, give your friend some advice about how she could handle the problem. Try to give her several good resources to think about or use. Don't forget to include resources that her company might offer.

■ Be sure to cite and document any sources you use in your papers. For advice, see Chapter 21.

RESOURCES: Review the chart on pages 868–69 for tips about problem solving. Also, check some Web sites for ideas about dealing with sexual harassment. You can start by typing *advice on sexual harassment* into a search engine. List any Web sites you use.

■ **ASSIGNMENT 4   WRITING ABOUT READINGS** . . . .

Choose one of the following options:

• Read Kathleen Vail's essay, "Words That Wound" (p. 759), and review Juan Gonzalez's piece on page 174. Write a short essay explaining how schools can affect the quality of students' lives. Give examples of both positive and negative effects, drawing from Vail's essay and your own experience. You might want to write a thesis that makes use of Gonzalez's phrase "where life and learning intersect."

• Read Monique Rizer's essay, "When Students Are Parents" (p. 156), and Luz Medina's report (p. 171). Write a letter to Juan Gonzalez that gives examples of programs that the Division of Student Affairs could offer to help students. Include examples from your own experience, too.

Follow the steps in the Writing Guide starting on the next page to help you prewrite, draft, revise, and edit your illustration. Check off each step as you complete it.

WRITING GUIDE: ILLUSTRATION

STEPS IN ILLUSTRATION	HOW TO DO THE STEPS
Focus.	☐ Think about what you want to explain and who will read your illustration essay. Review the four basics of good illustration on page 167.
Prewrite to explore your topic. See Chapter 4 for more on prewriting.	☐ Use a prewriting technique to explore your topic and the things that are important about it to you. ☐ Narrow your ideas to a topic you can write about in a short essay, and generate examples that would demonstrate what you want to say about your topic.
Write a thesis statement. Topic + <u>main point</u> = Thesis Homeschooling is beneficial to both the child and the parent. See Chapter 5 for more on writing a thesis statement.	☐ Decide what is important to you about your topic. ☐ Write a working thesis statement that presents your topic and your point about that topic.
Support your thesis statement. The major support points in illustration are the examples you give to demonstrate or prove your thesis. These examples will become the topic sentences for the body paragraphs. See Chapter 6 for more on supporting a thesis statement.	☐ To come up with examples, assume someone has read your thesis and asked, "What do you mean?" or "Like what?" ☐ Use a prewriting technique to help you get ideas for examples. ☐ Choose at least three examples that will show your readers what you mean. ☐ Reread your prewriting to find supporting details. ☐ Find additional supporting details by asking yourself more questions: What do I mean? How? In what ways? ☐ For each of your examples, add supporting details that will help your readers understand how the example demonstrates your main point.
Make a plan. See Chapter 7 for more on planning.	☐ Arrange your major support examples in order of importance, leading up to the one you think will have most impact on your readers. ☐ Make a plan or outline for your essay that includes your main support points (your examples) and supporting details for each example. (See the diagram on p. 170.)
Write a draft. See Chapter 8 for more on drafting.	☐ Write an introduction that gets your readers' interest and presents your thesis statement. See if you can use one of the introductory techniques in Chapter 8.

continued

STEPS IN ILLUSTRATION	HOW TO DO THE STEPS
Write a draft (cont.).	☐ Using your outline, write a topic sentence for each of the major examples.
	☐ Write body paragraphs that give specific details about each example.
	☐ Write a concluding paragraph that reminds your readers of your main point and makes a final observation.
	☐ Title your essay.
Revise your draft. See Chapter 9 for more on revising.	☐ Imagine that you are a reader, or ask someone else to read and comment on your draft. Look for the following:
	__ Examples and details that don't really demonstrate your thesis
	__ Places where you would stop and think, "I don't get it," because there isn't enough concrete information
	__ Places where the examples need transitions to connect ideas and move a reader smoothly from one idea to the next
	☐ Reread your thesis statement. Revise it so that your point is more concrete and forceful.
	☐ Reread your introduction, and make changes if it is dull or weak.
	☐ Reread your conclusion to make sure it is energetic and drives home your point.
	☐ Make at least five changes to your draft to improve unity, support, or coherence (see pp. 127–40).
	☐ Check to make sure the draft follows the four basics of good illustration.
Edit your draft. See Parts Four through Seven for more on editing.	☐ Use the spell checker and grammar checker on your computer, but also reread your essay carefully to catch any errors.
	☐ Look for errors in grammar, spelling, or punctuation. Punctuation may be a special problem in illustration (see Chapters 37–40).
	☐ Focus also on sentence fragments, run-ons, errors in subject-verb agreement, verb errors, and other areas where you know you often make mistakes.
	☐ Ask yourself: Is this the best I can do?

12

Description

Writing That Creates Pictures in Words

Understand What Description Is

Description is writing that creates a clear and vivid impression of the topic. Description translates your experience of a person, place, or thing into words, often by appealing to the senses—sight, hearing, smell, taste, and touch.

■ **IDEA JOURNAL**
Write about the most beautiful, the most interesting, or the ugliest chair, car, T-shirt, or other object you've ever seen.

▉▉ FOUR BASICS OF GOOD DESCRIPTION

1. It creates a main impression—an overall effect, feeling, or image—about the topic.
2. It uses specific examples to support the main impression.
3. It supports those examples with details that appeal to the senses—sight, hearing, smell, taste, and touch.
4. It brings a person, place, or physical object to life for the reader.

In the following paragraph, each number corresponds to one of the four basics of good description.

1 Nojoqui Falls is a special place to me because it is very beautiful, and I have good memories of visiting the falls with my parents. **2** At the

185

4 All the
details bring
the falls to life.

start of the trail leading to the falls, the smell and sound of oak trees and pine trees make visitors feel they're up for the journey. **3** The sun hitting the trees makes the air fresh with a leafy aroma. Overhead, the wind blows through the leaves, making a soft noise. **2** Closer to the waterfall, the shade from the trees creates a shielding blanket. When the sun comes out, it fills the place with light, showing the vapor coming out of the trees and plants. To the left of the trail are rocks that are positioned perfectly for viewing the waterfall. **3** Water splashes as it hits the rocks. **2** The waterfall itself is beautiful, like a transparent, sparkling window of diamonds. **3** The water is so clear that objects on the other side are visible. It is like a never-ending stream of water that splashes onto the rocks.

— Liliana Ramirez, student

Being able to describe something or someone accurately and in detail is important both in college and in other settings. Describing something well involves using specific, concrete details. Here are some ways that you might use description:

COLLEGE	For a science lab report, you describe the physical and chemical properties of an element.
WORK	You write a letter to your office cleaning contractor describing the unacceptable conditions of the office.
EVERYDAY LIFE	You describe a jacket that you left at the movies to the lost-and-found department.

Main Point in Description

In descriptive writing, your **main point** conveys the way in which you want readers to see your topic. In other words, it conveys the main impression about your topic that you want to get across.

Take another look at the paragraph starting on page 185. What if the topic sentence had been

I love Nojoqui Falls.

You wouldn't know why the writer likes the place. But the actual topic sentence conveys a main impression of the falls and lets you know why this place is important to the writer:

Nojoqui Falls is a special place to me because it is very beautiful, and I have good memories of visiting the falls with my parents.

This statement provides a preview of what is to come, helping the audience read and understand the description.

The thesis statement in description essays typically includes the topic and the main impression about it that the writer wants to convey.

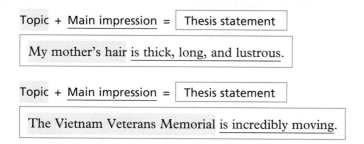

Topic + Main impression = Thesis statement

My mother's hair is thick, long, and lustrous.

Topic + Main impression = Thesis statement

The Vietnam Veterans Memorial is incredibly moving.

■ For online exercises on main point and support, visit *Exercise Central* at **bedfordstmartins .com/realessays**.

Support in Description

Good description uses specific, concrete details to present the sights, sounds, smells, tastes, and textures that contribute to a clear overall impression. These details constitute the **support** for a description. You can use prewriting techniques to recall details that will help readers understand your experience.

SIGHT	SOUND	SMELL
Colors	Loud/soft	Sweet/sour
Shapes	Piercing/soothing	Sharp/mild
Sizes	Continuous/off-and-on	Good (like what?)
Patterns	Pleasant/unpleasant (how?)	Bad (rotten?)
Brightness	High/low	New (like what?)
Does it look like anything else?	Does it sound like anything else?	Does it smell like anything else?

TASTE	TOUCH
Good (What does *good* taste like?)	Hard/soft
Bad (What does *bad* taste like?)	Liquid/solid
Bitter/sugary	Rough/smooth

TASTE	TOUCH
Metallic	Dry/oily
Burning/spicy	Textures
Does it taste like anything else?	Does it feel like anything else?

As you think about the main impression you want to convey, ask yourself: What sensory details might bring this subject to life? Add additional details to convey each sensation more accurately or vividly.

For example, one student wrote this thesis statement:

When I take her coat from the closet, it's as if my grandmother is standing beside me.

To support this main impression, the writer might include sensory details about the smell of the coat (*sweet like Grandma's perfume, with a faint odor of mothballs and home-baked bread*); the feel of the fabric (*nubby and rough, with some smooth spots where the fabric has worn thin*); and the candy in the pocket (*single pieces of butterscotch that rustle in their wrappings and a round cylinder that is a roll of wintergreen Life Savers*).

DESCRIPTION AT A GLANCE

Introduction with thesis statement
Gives a main impression

↓

First major sensory detail
Supporting details

↓

Second major sensory detail
Supporting details

↓

Most important sensory detail
Supporting details

↓

Conclusion
Reminds readers of the main impression
Makes an observation

Organization in Description

Description may use any of the orders of organization, depending on the purpose of the description. If you are describing what someone or something looks like, you might use **spatial order,** the most common way to organize description. If you are describing something you want to sell, you might use **order of importance,** ending with the feature that would be most appealing to potential buyers. At left is a typical plan for a description essay.

Add transitions to be certain that your readers can move smoothly from detail to detail. (See box on the following page.)

> ### Common Transitions in Description
>
> | TRANSITIONS TO SHOW ORDER OF IMPORTANCE | TRANSITIONS TO SHOW SPATIAL ORDER |
> |---|---|
> | more | to the left/right |
> | even more | in front of/behind |
> | the most | beyond |
> | the strongest | above/underneath |
> | the most intense | |

Read and Analyze Description

Before writing a description essay, read the following three examples of description—from college, the workplace, and everyday life—and answer the questions that accompany them.

■ For more examples of description, see Chapter 45.

Description in College

The following description essay was written by a student for a course assignment.

PHOTOGRAPH OF MY FATHER

Florence Bagley

1   This old black-and-white photograph of my father fills me with conflicting emotions. He died very young, and this photo is one of the few that my family has of him. The picture seems to show a strong, happy man, young and smiling, but to me it also reveals his weakness.

2   Looking at this picture of my father, I feel how much I have lost. In it, my father is sitting upright in a worn plaid easy chair. It was "his" chair, and when he was at work, I'd curl up in it and smell his aftershave lotion and cigarette smoke. His pitch-black hair is so dark that it blends into the background of the photo. His eyes, though indistinct in this photo, were a deep, dark brown. Although the photo is faded

PAUSE: What mood has Florence created so far?

_____

_____

around my father's face, I still can make out his strong jaw and the cleft in his chin. In the photo, my father is wearing a clean white T-shirt that reveals his thick, muscular arms. Resting in the crook of his left arm is my younger brother, who was about one year old at the time. Both of them are smiling.

PAUSE: How has the mood changed?

_____

_____

3   However, when I study the photo, my eyes are drawn to the can of beer that sits on the table next to him. Against my will, I begin to feel resentful. I have so many wonderful memories of my father. Whether he was carrying me on his shoulders, picking me up from school, or teaching me to draw, he always made time for me. All of these memories fade when I see that beer. From what I remember, he always made time for that beer as well. The smell of beer was always on him, the cool, sweating can always within reach.

PAUSE: What conflicting feelings does the picture create?

_____

_____

4   In this photo, my father appears to be a strong man; however, looks are deceiving. My father died at the age of thirty-seven because he was an alcoholic. I was eleven when he died, and I really did not understand that his drinking was the reason for his death. I just knew that he left me without a father and the possibility of more memories. He should have been strong enough to stop drinking.

5   In spite of the resentment I may feel about his leaving me, this photo holds many loving memories as well. It is of my father—the strong, wonderful man and the alcoholic—and it is the most precious thing I own. Although I would much rather have him here, I stay connected to him when I look at it.

1. Double-underline the **thesis statement**.
2. Underline each **topic sentence**.
3. Put a check mark (✔) by the **supporting details** that back Florence's topic sentences.
4. Circle the **transitions**.

■ For a list of the four basics of good description, see page 185.

5. Does Florence's essay have the **four basics of good description**? Be ready to explain your answer.
6. What descriptive details does Florence use to show her conflicted feelings about her father?

7. What other kind of sensory details might Florence have used to make her father more alive to you?

8. Among your relatives or friends, whom do you remember vividly? What, if any, photographs do you have of that person?

■ The final question after each reading in this section makes a good essay topic.

Description at Work

The following profile shows how a writer uses description in an excerpt from a novel.

Profile of Success

Alex Espinoza
Writer and Assistant Professor

BACKGROUND: I was born in Mexico, the youngest of eleven children. My father was an alcoholic and was murdered when I was in high school. I didn't do well in school and was placed in the automotive program, where I barely passed my classes. At San Bernardino Community College, I discovered both writing and the Puenté Project. In writing, I found my voice; in Puenté, I found people who encouraged me academically. Although I had a low GPA, I had good recommendations and good grades in writing, so I was accepted at the University of California, Riverside, which has a great writing program. I then went on to get a master's degree in creative writing at the University of California, Irvine, which, although I didn't know it at the time, has one of the most selective creative writing programs in the country. My first novel, *Still Water Saints,* was published in 2007, and I have a contract for a second one.

COLLEGES/DEGREES: A.A., San Bernardino Community College; B.A., University of California, Riverside; M.F.A., University of California, Irvine.

EMPLOYER: California State University, Fresno

WRITING AT WORK: My job is writing and teaching writing, so I'm always writing. Here's some advice I always give my students: When you write, you are putting yourself on the page, and you can control how you are perceived. If you ignore the conventions of writing (like grammar, spelling, and punctuation), you will in turn be ignored by those whose attention you want.

HOW ALEX USES DESCRIPTION: In my own writing, I have to create vivid scenes for my readers. In my teaching, I help students form vivid images in their own writing.

Alex's Description

The following is from Alex's novel *Still Water Saints*. (For another example of Alex's descriptive writing, see pp. 766–69.) Note that there is no thesis statement because this is not an essay but rather part of a novel.

> **VOCABULARY**
> The following words are *italicized* in the excerpt: *bellows, padlock, massacred, lynched, opossum, dingy*. If you don't know their meanings, look them up in a dictionary.

1   The iron security gate unfolded like the *bellows* of an accordion as Perla pulled it along the rail in front of the door. She snapped the *padlock* shut, turned around the corner of the building, and headed home. Her house was close, just across the empty lot next to the shopping center. Wild sage and scrub grew beside the worn path that cut through the field. Boys sometimes rode their bikes there, doing tricks and wheelies as they bumped over mounds and breaks, falling down, laughing and scraping their knees, their faces coated with grime. Their tires left thin tracks that looped around the salt cedar trees, around the soiled mattresses and old washers and sinks that were dumped there.

PAUSE: What impression do you have of the area so far? Why?

_____

_____

2   People told of a curse on these grounds, a group of monks traveling through Agua Mansa in the days when California was still a part of Mexico, back before states were shapes on a map. They said a tribe of Indians *massacred* the monks; they skinned them and scattered their body parts around the lot for the crows. Still others said Mexican settlers had been *lynched* from the branches of the cedars by Anglos who stole their land for the railroads. Seeing a piece of stone, Perla wondered about the monks and those men dangling from branches. *A tooth? Part of a toe?* Empty soda cans and wrappers were caught under boulders and discarded car parts. *What would the monks think about having a tire for a headstone, a couch for a marker?* She thought of her husband, Guillermo, of his tombstone, of the thick, green lawns of the cemetery where he was buried.

3   When she reached her house and stepped inside, the air was warm and silent. Perla put her purse down on the rocking chair near the front door and went around, pushing the lace curtains back and cracking open the windows. She breathed in the scent of wood smoke from someone's fireplace down the street, a smell that reminded her of her father toasting garbanzo beans. She went into the kitchen and looked for something to eat.

PAUSE: How does the impression change here? Why?

_____

_____

4   Dinner was a bowl of oatmeal with two slices of toast, which she took out to the patio. The night was cold, and the steam from the oatmeal rose up and fogged her glasses as she spooned it in her mouth. Police sirens wailed down the street, and dogs answered, their cries lonely and beautiful. She looked up, and in the flashing lights saw a set of glowing red eyes.

PAUSE: How does the last sentence change the mood of the scene?

_____

_____

5   Perla flicked on the porch light. It was an *opossum,* its fur *dingy* and gray, the tips and insides of its ears bright pink. It stood motionless, behind the trunk of the organ pipe cactus, staring at her. It climbed to the top of the fence, making a low, faint jingle as it moved. Perla looked again; a small brass bell was tied to a piece of red yarn knotted around the opossum's tail. She took her spoon and threw it. When it hit the bottom of the fence, the animal darted, the clatter of the bell frantic. The opossum disappeared behind the branches of the avocado tree and down the other side of the fence into the empty lot, the ringing growing fainter and fainter.

6   From under the kitchen sink, behind the pile of cloths and old sponges she could never bring herself to throw away, was a bottle of rum. She poured some into a cup and took a drink. Then she took another. The warmth calmed her nerves.

7   She imagined the ghosts of the dead monks and the lynched men rising up from the ground, awakened by her thoughts. Curls of gray smoke at first, they slowly took human form. They walked in a straight line, one in front of the other. A slow progression followed the opossum's tracks through the lot and back home.

8   She took another drink and closed her eyes. That animal was a messenger. It was letting her know that something was out there. It was coming.

—Alex Espinoza, *Still Water Saints* (New York: Random House, 2007), pp. 11–12

1. In the first paragraph, underline the **details** that create an impression of the area.

2. In paragraphs 3 and 4, underline the **details** that change the impression.

3. What senses does Alex's description use? _____

4. How does Perla's mood change when she sees the opossum?

_____

5. Underline the **details** Alex uses in paragraph 5 to give you a picture of the opossum.

6. Do you think that Perla drinks often? What gives you that impression?

_____

Description in Everyday Life

The following is a letter that Jennifer Orlando wrote to her best friend. Jennifer recently moved to a different state, and she is trying to convince her friend to visit her.

Dear Amy,

PAUSE: What do you expect the rest of the essay will be about?

_____

_____

1   Today I went for an easy hike to Rattlesnake Canyon. I had been a little down this week because I don't really know anyone here and was lonely. I just wanted to get out and forget my troubles. Instead, though, I came back happy and feeling really lucky to be here. The area is incredibly beautiful, and it is completely different from anything I have ever experienced.

2   The path is lined with gorgeous desert plants that go on for acres. There are many varieties of cactus, many with long white spines reaching out of the green "leaves." I never thought of cactus as being colorful, but there can be purple or about five shades of green. Some of them have "flowers" that look like huge, bright red radishes. Others have tiny yellow flowers growing beside the sharp spines, and still others have lavender flowers sprouting. There are all kinds of yellow

flowering plants—some pale, and some darker, like an egg yolk. Swarms of yellow butterflies flutter around them, dancing in and out of the branches. I just started laughing when I saw them; it was so perfect. My favorite plant is sage, again lots of different kinds. Some have billions of little purple flowers, and they're about four feet tall. Others are a silvery green, and when you run your hand over the leaves, they give off this savory scent that is barely sweet and makes me think of my mother's stuffing at Thanksgiving. It's sage, the herb. The air just smells all herby from sage, juniper, and other smells I can't identify. There are some low bushes that have bright red flowers—some scarlet, some rust, and some orangy. I can't believe how beautiful the desert plants are. I'd always thought the desert was just sand.

3   As I went along, I was surrounded by the huge rocks of the canyon; it's like pictures I've seen of the Grand Canyon. At the base, the rocks are a dark, rusty color. As they rise up, they have about ten different layers of color—from a kind of light grey, to darker grey, to pale red, and finally to a brilliant red that shines in the sunlight from flecks of mineral in them. I was literally surrounded by these looming rocks, thousands of feet high.

4   Best of all, though, is the sky. The towering, multicolored cliffs were met by the bluest sky I have ever seen. There were no clouds, and this blue was dark and beautiful against the red of the rock. The sun was bright, as it usually is here, and everything was so big, so colorful, so intense that I felt lucky to be alive. There's something about all this beauty that has been here for millions of years that makes you feel as if your problems just aren't that big.

5   I kept wishing you were here because I know you would feel the same way I do about this area. It is just so beautiful it makes you happy. I took some pictures that I'm sending to you. The pictures aren't nearly as astonishing as the real thing, though. You need to see it for yourself. Please come out soon. I promise you won't be sorry, and maybe you'll decide to move out here. I miss you.

Love,

Jennifer

PAUSE: Why did Jennifer laugh?

PAUSE: Summarize Jennifer's description of the plants in the canyon.

PAUSE: Is there any place that has given you this feeling? Why?

1. Double-underline the **thesis statement**.

2. Which paragraph gives you the strongest impression? Why?

3. What surprises Jennifer about what she sees? _____

    _____

4. What kind of **organization** does Jennifer use? _____

5. What senses does the letter appeal to? _____

6. Does Jennifer's letter have the **four basics of good description**? Be ready to explain your answer.

Critical Reading and Writing: Key College Skills

1. **Summary.** Briefly summarize each of the three examples of description, including the major impression that each creates of its subject.

2. **Analysis.** How is each of the pieces organized? Which piece's organization helps you vividly see the subject? Which is the most complex piece,

    and why? _____

    _____

3. **Synthesis.** Each of the three pieces describes either a place or an object. Think of a place or an object you are familiar with, and look at it as if you've never seen it. How do the techniques that Florence, Alex, and Jennifer use help you take a fresh look at it?

4. **Evaluation.** Using the **four basics of good description** as a measure, which of the three selections is the best? Why? Give examples to support your opinion.

Write a Description Essay

In this section, you will write your own description essay based on one of the following assignments. Before you begin to write, review the four basics of good description on page 185. Also, read the Tips for Tackling Description in the box on page 197.

 ASSIGNMENT 1   WRITING ABOUT COLLEGE, WORK, AND EVERYDAY LIFE . . . .

■ Use the diagram on page 188 to help you organize.

Write a description essay on *one* of the following topics or on a topic of your own choice.

TIPS FOR TACKLING DESCRIPTION

1. Read the assignment carefully, highlighting key words. Often a description assignment includes the word *describe,* but you may need to use description in other kinds of writing, too. As you give examples in your writing, try to imagine them, and use colors, shapes, sizes, smells, textures, tastes to make them clear to readers.

2. Think about your topic and the overall impression that you want to create. For example, if you think the student lounge is a dump, what about it makes it seem so — the condition of the furniture, its arrangement, the color of the walls, the smell? What else?

3. Write down the impression you want to create, and use that sentence as a draft thesis statement.

4. Fill in the details in words, assuming your reader has never seen your subject as you have.

COLLEGE

- Describe your favorite place on campus so that a reader understands why you like to be there.
- Describe what you imagine a character looks like in a novel you have read.
- Describe an event or a setting that you learned about in one of your courses.

WORK

- Describe an area of your workplace that is not worker friendly.
- Describe a product or service that your company produces.
- Describe a specific area at work that you see every day but haven't really noticed. Look at it with new eyes.

EVERYDAY LIFE

- Describe a favorite photograph.
- Describe a favorite food without naming it. Include how it looks, smells, and tastes.
- Describe a local landmark, and have others in the class identify it after reading your description.

ASSIGNMENT 2   **WRITING ABOUT AN IMAGE** . . . .

Write a descriptive essay about the messy space shown below or about a similar space in your own home or workplace. Be sure to use plenty of details.

ASSIGNMENT 3   **WRITING TO SOLVE A PROBLEM** . . . .

THE PROBLEM: A wealthy alumna has given your college money for a new student lounge. The president has selected a group of students (including you) to advise him on the lounge and has asked that the group be as specific as possible in its recommendations.

THE ASSIGNMENT: Working on your own or, preferably, in a small group, write a description of an ideal student lounge to send to the president. Be sure to think about what various purposes the lounge should serve, where it should be located, what it should have in it, and what it should look like.

RESOURCES: Review the chart on pages 868–69 for advice about problem solving. Also, search the Web using the words *student lounges* and *design*. You might also go to the library and look for design or architecture books and magazines. List any Web sites or publications that you consult.

 ASSIGNMENT 4   WRITING ABOUT READINGS . . . .

The assignments that follow ask you to read one or more different descriptions and draw from them to write an essay.

- Read Alex Espinoza's "An American in Mexico" (p. 766), and review his description on page 192. Are there similarities between the two pieces? Drawing from both pieces, write a more detailed description of the neighborhood in which Alex might have grown up. Use your imagination.
- Read Debra Marquart's "Chores" (p. 770). Using her essay as a model, think about an activity that you regularly perform, and describe it in detail. Include what other people are involved, what is most intense about the activity, and how it begins, proceeds, and ends.

Follow the steps in the Writing Guide below to help you prewrite, draft, revise, and edit your description. Check off each step as you complete it.

WRITING GUIDE: DESCRIPTION	
STEPS IN DESCRIPTION	**HOW TO DO THE STEPS**
Focus.	☐ Think about what you want to describe and the overall impression you want to give your readers. Review the four basics of good description on page 185.
Prewrite to explore your topic. See Chapter 4 for more on prewriting.	☐ Write some ideas about impressions you have when you think about your topic. ☐ Use a prewriting technique to explore these impressions, generating details that appeal to the five senses.

continued

STEPS IN DESCRIPTION	HOW TO DO THE STEPS
Write a thesis statement. The thesis statement in description includes the topic and the main impression about it that you want to convey to your reader. Topic + Main impression = [Thesis] My grandmother's coat <u>evokes her image.</u> See Chapter 5 for more on writing a thesis statement.	☐ Review your prewriting, and decide what main impression you want to create. ☐ Write a thesis statement that includes your topic and main impression.
Support your thesis statement. The major support points in description are the sensory details that, together, create the main impression. See Chapter 6 for more on supporting a thesis statement.	☐ Review your thesis statement and prewriting, and make other notes. ☐ Try to find strong sensory details that will support your main impression and make the topic come alive for your readers. ☐ Choose at least three major sensory details that will help to convey your main impression. ☐ Add specific supporting details that bring to life the major sensory details. Try to appeal to the senses—sight, sound, smell, touch, and taste.
Make a plan. See Chapter 7 for more on planning.	☐ Write a plan or an outline for your description that includes your main support points (the major sensory details) and supporting details. ☐ Organize your support using either spatial order or order of importance. (See the diagram on p. 188.)
Write a draft. See Chapter 8 for more on drafting.	☐ Write an introduction that gets your readers' interest and presents your thesis statement. See if you can use one of the introductory techniques in Chapter 8. ☐ Using your outline, write a topic sentence for each of the major supporting details. ☐ Write body paragraphs that give additional details for each of the major support points. ☐ Write a concluding paragraph that reminds readers of your main point and makes a final observation about what you are describing. ☐ Title your essay.

STEPS IN DESCRIPTION	HOW TO DO THE STEPS
Revise your draft. See Chapter 9 for more on revising a draft.	☐ Ask another person to read and comment on your draft. ☐ Consider how you can make your descriptions more vivid for readers. To get ideas, refer back to the categories under Support in Description on page 187 (sight, sound, smell, taste, and touch). ☐ Revise your thesis to make it more forceful and vivid. ☐ Make sure all of the images and details support your thesis. Add details that make your topic more alive for your readers, and cut any details that aren't relevant. ☐ Reread your introduction, and make changes if it is dull. ☐ Reread your conclusion to make sure that it is energetic and convincing and that it reminds your readers of your main impression. ☐ Add transitions (space or importance) to connect your ideas. ☐ Make at least five changes to your draft to improve unity, support, or coherence (see pp. 127–40). ☐ Check to make sure the draft follows the four basics of good description.
Edit your draft. See Parts Four through Seven for more on editing.	☐ Use the spell checker and grammar checker on your computer, but also reread your essay carefully to catch any errors. ☐ Look for errors in grammar, spelling, or punctuation. Run-on sentences and the proper use of adjectives and adverbs can be particular problems in description, so focus first on those. Then, read for fragments, errors in subject-verb agreement, verb errors, and other areas where you know you often make mistakes. ☐ Ask yourself: Is this the best I can do?

You Know This

You use processes all the time.

- You assemble something using the step-by-step directions.
- You follow routine processes, like recycling.

13

Process Analysis

Writing That Explains How Things Happen

Understand What Process Analysis Is

Process analysis explains either how to do something (so your readers can do it) or how something works (so your readers can understand it). Both types of process analysis present the steps involved in the process.

■■ **FOUR BASICS OF GOOD PROCESS ANALYSIS**

1. It helps readers either perform the steps themselves or understand how something works.
2. It presents the essential steps in the process.
3. It explains the steps in detail.
4. It arranges the steps in a logical order (usually in chronological order).

In the following paragraph, each number corresponds to one of the four basics of good process analysis.

4 Steps arranged in a logical order

1 The Web site *MapQuest.com* can get you from where you are to where you want to go in several easy steps. **2** First, type in the Web address (**www.mapquest.com**), and wait for the home page to appear. Then, click on the link titled "Directions." You will be prompted to type your starting address and the address of your destination. **3** It's important to supply complete information, including the street address, city, and state (or zip). **2** Next, click on "Get Directions." This screen will present you with written directions and a map showing the route to take. **3** The written directions guide you step-by-step and include the mileage for each step. The map allows you to zoom in and out to get a better view. Although sometimes I have found errors in them, MapQuest directions are usually correct and take me exactly where I want to go.

4 Steps arranged in a logical order

Whenever you give someone directions about how to do something or explain how something works, you are using process analysis. Here are some ways you might use process analysis:

COLLEGE	In an information technology course, you write an essay explaining the process for implementing a new data management system.
WORK	The office has a new security system, and you are asked to write a memo to employees explaining how to access their work areas during and after normal business hours.
EVERYDAY LIFE	You write directions telling your child how to operate the microwave oven.

Main Point in Process Analysis

Your **purpose** in process analysis is to explain a process so that readers can either do it themselves or understand how it works. Your **main point** lets your readers know what you think about that process—for example, whether it's easy or complicated. The topic sentence of the paragraph on page 202 does just that:

> The Web site *MapQuest.com* can get you from where you are to where you want to go in several easy steps.

A thesis statement for a process analysis usually identifies the process and the point you want to make about it. The thesis should also suggest what you want your readers to know or learn about the process.

Process + Main point = | Thesis statement |

| Wallpapering a room takes careful preparation and application. |

■ For online exercises on main point and support, visit *Exercise Central* at **bedfordstmartins .com/realessays**.

In process analysis, include your thesis statement in your introduction so that readers know from the start what the process and the purpose are.

Support in Process Analysis

A clear process analysis presents all the essential steps in the process; these steps constitute the **major support**. Each step is explained by supporting details. For example, the writer of the thesis *Learning how to use the advanced functions on my computer is frustrating* might identify several essential steps and the details to explain each step.

ESSENTIAL STEPS

- **Step 1:** Using the Help feature

    SUPPORTING DETAILS

    Trying to find the right search terms

    Finding that none work

- **Step 2:** Consulting a reference book such as *Word 2007 for Dummies*

    SUPPORTING DETAILS

    Trying to find the function in the table of contents and index

    First finding advice that isn't really what you need

    Finding the right explanation

    Deciding that you don't want to use the function

- **Step 3:** Trying to undo automatic functions

    SUPPORTING DETAILS

    Reading about the Undo function and trying it with no luck

    Finally calling a friend

    Etc.

Make sure to include all of the essential steps in the process, particularly if you want your readers to be able to do something using only your instructions. Read the following process analysis example. What essential step is missing?

Please do the laundry before I get home. The clothes are in the baskets next to the machine. One of the baskets has all dark clothes. Put these in the washing machine, with the heaviest, biggest items on the bottom. You can fill the machine to the top, but don't mash the clothes down. (If you put in too many clothes, the machine will stall.) After all of the clothes are in, set the level on Extra High. Then, turn the knob on the left to Warm Wash, Cool Rinse. Press the Start button. After about half an hour, the laundry should be done, and you can transfer it to the dryer.

MISSING STEP: _____

_____

_____

Organization in Process Analysis

Because process analysis explains how to do something or how something works, it usually uses **chronological (time) order.** Start with the first step, and then explain each step in the order that it should occur. The plan for a process analysis often looks like the one on the right.

Add transitional words and sentences to your essay to help readers follow each step in the process.

Common Transitions in Process Analysis

after	eventually	meanwhile	soon
as	finally	next	then
at last	first	now	when
before	last	second	while
during	later	since	

PROCESS ANALYSIS AT A GLANCE

> **Introduction with thesis statement**
> Includes the process you are describing

> **First step in process**
> Details about the first step (how to do it or how it works)

> **Second step in process**
> Details about the second step

> **Third step in process**
> Details about the third step

> **Conclusion**
> Reminds readers of the process and makes an observation related to your main point

Read and Analyze Process Analysis

Before writing your own process analysis, read the following three examples of process analysis—from college, the workplace, and everyday life—and answer the questions that accompany them.

Process Analysis in College

■ For other examples of process analysis, see Chapter 46.

The following is an excerpt from a textbook used in the field of interpersonal communication.

VOCABULARY
The following words are *italicized* in the excerpt: *dilemma, accommodate, forsake, ultimate, collaboration, enhance, incompatibility, empathic, stance, maintain, bogged down.* If you don't know their meanings, look them up in a dictionary.

COLLABORATIVELY MANAGING CONFLICT

Steven McCornack

PAUSE: Have you ever had such a conflict? How did you discuss it? What do you expect the rest of this piece will discuss?

1   Imagine that it's a few weeks before Thanksgiving, and you and your new romantic partner are making holiday plans. Each of you has always shared the day with family. But now that you're a couple, you face the obvious *dilemma* of which family to spend the holiday with. You both want to share the day together, but neither of you wants to miss your traditional family gathering. Do you simply ignore the issue, avoiding the conflict until it's too late? Does one of you *accommodate* the other, and agree to *forsake* his or her family's get-together? Do you compete with each other, each person trying to dominate the *ultimate* decision? Or do you search for a solution that will make both of you happy?

2   The most constructive approach for managing conflict is ***collaboration,*** treating conflict as a mutual problem-solving challenge rather than something that must be avoided, accommodated, or competed over. Collaboration tends to increase relationship satisfaction and to *enhance* trust and relational commitment.

3   To use a collaborative approach, openly discuss the *incompatibility* of goals or the competition for resources that has fueled your conflict. Give equal attention to both persons' needs and desires. For example, to collaboratively manage the conflict over Thanksgiving, you would honestly discuss the matter with your partner, expressing *empathic* concern and perspective-taking ("I know this is hard for each of us, and

I completely understand how important our family traditions are"). Also, keep the conversation focused on solutions and take a flexible, respectful *stance* toward your partner ("Let's try to figure out a plan together so we can both end up happy"). Perhaps most valuable, be courteous, respectful, and positive toward your partner, and avoid personal attacks.

PAUSE: Summarize this paragraph in your own words.

4   Communications scholars William Wilmot and Joyce Hocker offer four additional suggestions for collaboratively managing conflict (2001). First, attack problems, not people. When talking about the conflict, separate the problem that's the source of the conflict from the people who are involved. For example, in the Thanksgiving scenario, you would stress that it's the practice of spending the holidays with your families that is the source of the conflict and not the personality, values, or attitudes of your partner. Avoid personalizing the conflict through statements such as "You don't care about my family!" or "You're always out for yourself!" Second, focus on common interests and long-term goals ("I know we both want to *maintain* close ties to our families as well as spend important holidays together"). Arguing over positions ("I want this," "Well, I want that!") endangers relationships because the conflict quickly becomes a destructive contest of wills. Third, create options before arriving at decisions. Identify different possible routes for resolving the conflict, and then combine the best parts of them to come up with a solution. For instance, solutions to the Thanksgiving dilemma might include spending the holiday with one family this year and with the other family next year or eating turkey with one family and having dessert and coffee with the other family. Don't get *bogged down* searching for the one "perfect" solution—it may not exist. Finally, critically evaluate your solution. Ask: Is it equally fair for both of us?

PAUSE: Summarize the four steps in this paragraph.

> —Steven McCornack, *Reflect and Relate: An Introduction to Interpersonal Communication* (Boston: Bedford/ St. Martin's, 2007), pp. 310–13

1. Double-underline the **thesis statement**. Note: It is not in the first paragraph.

2. What important term is defined in this excerpt? _____

3. Underline each of the **steps** of collaboration.

4. Because this excerpt is not a formal essay, it lacks a concluding statement. Write a statement that would effectively conclude the excerpt.

_____

5. Have you ever made a conflict worse by not using collaborative communication to manage it?

Process Analysis at Work

The following profile shows how a nurse uses process analysis at work.

Profile of Success

Patty Maloney
Clinical Nurse
Specialist

BACKGROUND: I was always a terrible student who was shy and lacking in confidence. After high school, I took one course at a community college but quit because I didn't think I could do it.

After working as a typist, I got a job as a nursing assistant at the Shriners Hospital in Boston, a thirty-bed pediatric burn hospital. This motivated me to become a licensed practical nurse (LPN).

As time went on, I wanted more responsibility, so I took courses that led, first, to a registered nurse (RN) degree and, finally, to a master's degree in nursing. In the various nursing degree programs I completed, I had to do lots of writing—long papers, summaries of articles, and analyses of diseases and of case studies.

COLLEGES/DEGREES: Massachusetts Bay Community College, Labouré Junior College, Massachusetts College of Pharmacy (B.S.N.), Northeastern University (M.S.N.)

EMPLOYER: All Children's Hospital, St. Petersburg, Florida

WRITING AT WORK: Observations of patients, notes about patients, memos to colleagues, instructions for junior staff, lots of e-mail

HOW PATTY USES PROCESS ANALYSIS: Notes on treatment are often process analyses. They need to be concise, precise, and clear because both I and others will need to refer to them for patients' further treatment.

Patty's Process Analysis

The following is from a report that Patty prepared for a patient's file to document the steps taken to treat her. The report shows that when a nurse on the team and a resident disagreed as to the treatment called for, the nurse called for another opinion. This type of communication is frequent among medical personnel.

VOCABULARY

The following words are *italicized* in the excerpt: *vital signs, resident, pneumothorax, rupture, attending physician.* If you don't know their meanings, look them up in a dictionary.

1   **Patient:** (name), female, age 8, with tumor and disease progression

2   **Symptoms at arrival:** Child had not eaten much for two days and was withdrawn and uncommunicative.

3   **Treatment process:** First, we needed to determine if the child was in immediate danger or in need of further medications for pain control. We took her *vital signs*, which were within the range of normal for her, with a slightly elevated heart rate. Then we interviewed the child's mother to see if she had administered any breakthrough pain medication during the last 24 hours. We gave the child a short-term pain medication.

4   As a next step, we had a discussion with the doctor in the unit, and we then administered a breakthrough pain medication. We closely monitored the patient's vital signs, particularly noting if the heart rate came down. We were documenting the signs every hour formally but also checked on the child's status in the Intensive Care Unit every 15 minutes.

5   During one check, one of our nurses noted that the child looked pale, and her breathing was somewhat shallow. The nurse knew that the child had fragile lungs and felt that she was at risk of the *pneumothorax* collecting fluid with a possible *rupture* of the lung lining and collapse of the lung. Following procedure, the nurse immediately alerted the *resident*, who felt that the child was fine and suggested that nothing but continued observation was necessary.

PAUSE: What do you think will happen next?

_____

_____

6   The nurse disagreed with the resident's diagnosis and at that point sent another nurse to page the *attending physician* for another opinion. In the meantime, while waiting for the attending, the nurse called for an

x-ray. She then pulled the cart over to the patient in preparation for inserting a tube into the lung cavity to reinflate the lung. When the attending
physician arrived and was briefed, he agreed with the nurse's diagnosis.
The tube was quickly inserted, and the collapse of the lung was avoided.

7   The child continues in observation in the ICU. Her condition is
stable.

1. Underline the **steps** of the treatment process.

2. Though a description of a treatment process, the report does not give
   many details. What is the purpose of the report? _____
   _____
   _____

3. How would the report differ if its purpose was to teach new nurses how
   to do a particular procedure? _____
   _____

4. Write a possible **thesis statement** for the report.

5. Write a possible **concluding statement**.

6. Have you ever witnessed people disagreeing about what to do to help
   you? How would you describe their communication with each other?

Process Analysis in Everyday Life

VOCABULARY
The following words are *italicized* in the excerpt: *options, survey,
glitzy, blog.* If you don't know their meanings, look them up in a
dictionary.

HOW TO CREATE AND USE MYSPACE

Silvio Testagrosso

PAUSE: What do
you think this essay
will be about?

_____

_____

1   A lot of my friends have MySpace pages. I wasn't interested for the
longest time, but lately I started feeling left out. I thought creating my
own page would be a hassle, but it turns out I was wrong. Creating a
MySpace account is simple and fun. You can be creative about how
you want to portray yourself to others, and you can learn about a lot of

new things. Most important, though, MySpace is a great communication tool for keeping up with friends and family and for meeting new people.

2   To start, type "MySpace graphics" into your search engine. From there, you will have thousands of sites that will lead you through creating an account. I used **www.myspacejunks.com**. First, you will have to enter your e-mail address, a password, and a name for your account. Then, if you have entered everything correctly, you can get to the fun part, like choosing a look for your page.

3   Choosing a look is important, and you will have many choices. When you get to the page with *options* for layout, *survey* lots of them before choosing one. As you see images you like, bookmark them so that you can return to them easily when you are ready to make your final choice. Although there are lots of very *glitzy*, animated, and flashing images, don't overuse them, or your page will be irritating to read. Consider the colors you want to use and the overall impression the page will create. What do you want to be—quiet and thoughtful, fun and loud, or something else? Whatever you decide, keep in mind that a prospective employer, a boss, or your mother can access your page as easily as your friends can.

4   Once you have decided on the look, copy and paste the layout code to the "Edit Profile—About Me" section of your MySpace page. Then, consider elements to put into the page, such as information about yourself. Do you want to add your age, schools, interests, or videos of yourself? You have complete choice here: You can tell everything about yourself, including very personal information, or you can keep it to basic facts. Again, though, remember that anyone can read what is there, so don't post anything you wouldn't want everyone to know about you.

PAUSE: Summarize the options for what you can put on a MySpace page.

5   Next, you can start up a *blog* from your page. A blog lets you communicate with everyone about anything. You can talk about what you did last night and include a video or photos, you can ask for other people's opinions or ask for help, or you can just write about what is on your mind on any given day. People who visit your MySpace page can

PAUSE: Have you ever blogged? About what?

comment and respond to your blog, so use it to find out whatever you want to find out about. I've learned a lot by blogging. I've even gotten ideas about assignments for school. Blogging is, for me, the best thing about my MySpace account.

6   Finally, consider meeting new people through MySpace, which is, after all, a social networking site. MySpace has groups for anything you might be interested in—cooking, starting a business, music, and so on. MySpace also has forums that give you a chance to talk with others about issues that are important to you. You can meet and communicate with hundreds of new people and really broaden your horizons.

7   Creating a MySpace account is easy, free, and creative. Using it is informative and fun. Most of all, though, MySpace connects people who might not otherwise meet, and it is one of the best and most enjoyable ways I have found to communicate. I'd recommend creating a page to anyone who doesn't already have one.

1. Double-underline the **thesis statement**.
2. What kind of **organization** does the essay use? _____
3. Circle five **transitions** Silvio uses.
4. Does Silvio's essay have the **four basics of good process analysis**? Be ready to explain your answer.
5. Do you have a MySpace account? How did you set it up, and how do you use it?

Critical Reading and Writing: Key College Skills

1. **Summary.** Briefly summarize each of the three selections, including the major steps of each of the processes described. How is each essay about a communication situation?

2. **Analysis.** Compare the three communications situations the selections describe. Which selection has the most detailed explanation of the communication situation? _____ Which has the least? _____ Why, do you think? _____

3. **Synthesis.** Discuss or write about the following: "Effective communication is a complex skill, and it varies depending on the specific situation and people involved." Draw from each of the selections to give examples.

4. **Evaluation.** Using the **four basics of good process analysis** as a measure, which of the three selections do you think is the best example of a process analysis? Give specific examples to support your choice. Is your choice different from the one you find most useful?

Write a Process Analysis Essay

In this section, you will write your own process analysis essay based on one of the following assignments. Before you begin to write, review the four basics of good process analysis on page 202. Also, read the Tips for Tackling Process Analysis in the box that follows.

TIPS FOR TACKLING PROCESS ANALYSIS

1. Read the assignment carefully, highlighting the key words. A process analysis may ask you to *describe the process of,* but it may also use words such as *describe the stages (or steps) of, how does* _____ *work?,* and *how can one* (for example, use collaboration) *to manage conflict?*

2. Think of the steps involved in the topic.

3. If you are explaining how to do something, pretend your reader doesn't know anything about the process.

4. Give examples of how to do each step or how it works.

ASSIGNMENT 1   WRITING ABOUT COLLEGE, WORK, AND EVERYDAY LIFE ·

Write a process analysis essay on *one* of the following topics or on a topic of your own choice.

COLLEGE

• How to apply for financial aid

• How to study for a test

• How (a process in your major field of study) works

WORK

• How to do one of your major tasks at work

• How to get a job at your place of work

• How to get fired or how to get promoted

■ Use the diagram on page 205 to help you organize.

EVERYDAY LIFE

- How to calm down or how to get to sleep
- How to do (something you do well)
- How to break up with someone

 ASSIGNMENT 2 **WRITING ABOUT AN IMAGE** . . . .

Recipes are common examples of process writing. Take a few minutes to think about the "recipe" presented in the public service ad below. Then, write your own "recipe for disaster"—or, if you prefer, a recipe for happiness. Accompany it with an image if your topic allows it. Then, in an essay, explain what you mean by disaster (or happiness) and why you think following your recipe will lead there.

The "It's Only Another Beer"
Black and Tan

8 oz. pilsner lager
8 oz. stout lager
1 frosty mug
1 icy road
1 pick-up truck
1 10-hour day
1 tired worker
A few rounds with the guys

Mix ingredients.
Add 1 totalled vehicle.

Never underestimate 'just a few.'
Buzzed driving is drunk driving.

Ad Council

U.S. Department of Transportation

ASSIGNMENT 3 **WRITING TO SOLVE A PROBLEM** . . . .

THE PROBLEM: Your friend is in an awful situation. Because of her great grades in high school, she was accepted at an excellent private university and received a lot of money in student aid. Even so, she began falling behind with tuition payments and had to drop out. At this point, her full loan payment came due. She wanted to transfer to a public university where the tuition was much lower; however, when she requested her transcript from the private university, she was told her records would not be sent until she had paid the charges on her loan. She wants to continue her studies but doesn't know how to manage this financially.

THE ASSIGNMENT: Working on your own or in a small group, research the options your friend has, and write some steps she could take to resolve her problem.

RESOURCES: Review the chart on pages 868–69 for advice on problem solving. Additionally, the Internet has many sites that offer advice on repayment of student loans. A good one to start with is at **www.finaid.org.** Or try typing *student loan repayment* into a search engine. List any Web sites that you use.

■ **TIP:** When you refer to an outside source, document it in the text and in a list at the end of your essay.

 ASSIGNMENT 4 **WRITING ABOUT READINGS** . . . .

Communication issues exist in all areas of our lives, as you can begin to see from the selections in this chapter. Choose *one* of the assignments below to explore further communication issues and situations.

• **Nonverbal communication.** Review Silvio Testagrosso's essay on MySpace (p. 210), considering especially how choice of color and image can shape the effect that a page can have. Then, read Daniel Goleman's "For Man and Beast, Language Shares Many Traits" (p. 781) and Amy L. Beck's "Struggling for Perfection" (p. 829). Drawing examples from these selections, discuss how nonverbal communication plays a role in how we perceive ourselves and others.

• **Gender and communication.** Review the textbook excerpt on pages 206–07, considering the different ways that communication affects relationships, especially male/female relationships. Then, read Dave Barry's "The Ugly Truth about Beauty" (p. 817) and Deborah Tannen's "It Begins at the Beginning" (p. 28). Drawing examples from these readings, discuss how men and women communicate differently. You may also want to read Carson Williams's "Different but in Love" (p. 122) and bring in your own experience.

WRITING GUIDE: PROCESS ANALYSIS

STEPS IN PROCESS ANALYSIS	HOW TO DO THE STEPS
Focus.	☐ Think about the process you want to explain to your readers, the steps involved in the process, and the main point you want to make. Review the four basics of good process analysis on page 202.
Prewrite to explore your topic. See Chapter 4 for more on prewriting.	☐ Choose a process you know about and understand. ☐ Use a prewriting technique to jot down some ideas about the steps in the process and ways you can explain the process to readers who aren't familiar with it.
Write a thesis statement. The thesis statement in a process analysis usually identifies the process and the main point you want to make about that process. Process + Main point = ⬚Thesis⬚ ⬚ Communication skills <u>are</u> varied and complex. ⬚ See Chapter 5 for more on writing a thesis statement.	☐ Decide on the main point you want to make about the process. ☐ Decide what you want your readers to know or learn about this process. ☐ Once you know your main point, write a thesis statement that contains both the process (your topic) and your main point about that process.
Support your thesis statement. The major support points in a process analysis are the essential steps involved in explaining how to do the process or showing how the process works. See Chapter 6 for more on supporting a thesis statement.	☐ List all the essential steps in the process. ☐ Review your thesis statement, and drop any steps that are not essential. ☐ Choose the steps that are necessary for readers to perform this activity or to understand how it works. ☐ Add details that describe the steps and that would help your readers do this activity correctly. ☐ Imagine that you are not already familiar with the process, and ask yourself whether you could do it or understand how it works after reading the essay.
Make a plan. See Chapter 7 for more on planning.	☐ Arrange the steps in the process in a logical order (often chronological). ☐ Make a plan for your process analysis that includes your major support points (the steps in the process) and supporting details. (See the diagram on p. 205.)

STEPS IN PROCESS ANALYSIS	HOW TO DO THE STEPS
Write a draft. See Chapter 8 for more on drafting.	☐ Write an introduction that gets your readers' interest and presents your thesis statement. See if you can use one of the introductory techniques in Chapter 8. ☐ Write topic sentences for the essential steps in the process, supported by explanations of those steps. ☐ Add time transitions to move readers smoothly from one step to another. ☐ Write a concluding paragraph that has energy, refers back to your point about the process, and makes a final observation or recommendation. ☐ Title your essay.
Revise your draft. See Chapter 9 for more on revising a draft.	☐ Ask another person to read and comment on your draft. ☐ Revise your thesis to make it more energetic. ☐ Reread the body of your essay to make sure you haven't left out any essential steps. Try to imagine that you have no idea of how to perform the process or how the process works. Add any details that would make the steps clearer, and cut details that aren't relevant. ☐ Reread your introduction, and make changes if it is dull or weak. ☐ Reread your conclusion to make sure that it is energetic and convincing and reminds your readers of your main impression. ☐ Add time transitions to connect your ideas. ☐ Make at least five changes to your draft to improve unity, support, or coherence (see pp. 127–40). ☐ Check to make sure the draft follows the four basics of good process analysis.
Edit your draft. See Parts Four through Seven for more on editing.	☐ Use the spell checker and grammar checker on your computer, but also reread your essay carefully to catch any errors. ☐ Look for errors in grammar, spelling, or punctuation. Fragments and run-on sentences can be a particular problem in process analysis, so focus first on those. Then, read for errors in subject-verb agreement, verb errors, and other areas where you know you often make mistakes. ☐ Ask yourself: Is this the best I can do?

You Know This

You already use classification.

- You use the college bookstore, where books are classified by discipline (English, biology, economics) and by course number.
- You use catalogs that are organized by type of product.

The Gym

athletic footwear for every activity

The Park

the top names in comfort footwear

Image provided courtesy of Zappos .com, Inc. © 2008 Zappos.com, Inc.

■ **IDEA JOURNAL**
Write about the different kinds of friends you have.

14

Classification

Writing That Puts Things into Groups

Understand What Classification Is

Classification is writing that organizes, or sorts, people or items into categories.

The **organizing principle** for a classification is *how* you sort the people or items, not the categories themselves. The organizing principle is directly related to the **purpose** of your classification. For example, you might sort clean laundry (your purpose) using one of the following organizing principles (how you achieve your purpose)—by ownership (yours, your roommate's, and so on) or by where it goes (the bedroom, the bathroom).

> ■■ **FOUR BASICS OF GOOD CLASSIFICATION**
> ■
> 1. It makes sense of a group of people or items by organizing them into useful categories.
> 2. It has a purpose for sorting the people or items.
> 3. It uses a single organizing principle.
> 4. It gives detailed examples or explanations of the things that fit into each category.

In the following paragraph, each number corresponds to one of the four basics of good classification.

All people do not learn in the same way, and **2** it is helpful to know what learning style you prefer. How do you naturally take in and absorb new information? The VARK learning styles inventory is a thirteen-item questionnaire that reveals which **3** learning style a person favors. **1** The first of its four learning styles is visual (V). **4** Visual learners absorb information best by looking at images or by drawing or diagramming a concept. For example, a visual learner may learn more by studying a flowchart of information rather than reading that same information in paragraph form. **1** The second learning style is auditory (A). **4** Auditory learners take in information most efficiently by hearing and listening. They remember information that they hear better than they remember information that they read. Even reading aloud is better than reading silently because hearing is key. Auditory learners benefit from discussion with others rather than working alone silently. **1** The third learning style is read/write (R). **4** Read/write learners learn best by reading written material. They also benefit from writing about what they have read. For example, many read/write learners study by reading and then writing a summary of what they have just read. Many people who are not naturally read/write learners have used that learning style in school because schools are oriented toward reading and writing. For example, a person whose score on the VARK is split evenly between auditory and read/write is probably an auditory learner who has learned to use a read/write learning style for school. **1** The final learning style is kinesthetic (K). **4** Kinesthetic learners learn by doing and by being active. For these learners, experiments in science may be easier to understand than reading a chapter in a book, listening to a lecture, or looking at an image. Kinesthetic learners often need to create activity in order to learn well: They may make flash cards, walk around as they study, or make a static activity interactive in some other way. All learners benefit from learning techniques such as highlighting and making notes, though different kinds of notes work for different learning styles. All learners are active learners: They learn best when they actively involve themselves in a task rather than passively observe it.

2 Taking a learning styles inventory is both fun and useful, particularly for students.

Whenever you organize or sort things to make sense of them, you are classifying them. Here are some ways that you might use classification:

COLLEGE	In a nursing course, you discuss three types of antibiotics used to treat infections.
WORK	For a report on inventory at a software store, you list the types of software carried and report how many of each type you have in stock.
EVERYDAY LIFE	You look at the types of payment plans that are available with your car loan.

■ For an example of an actual classification written for work, see page 226. The piece was written by the consultant who is profiled in the box on page 225.

Main Point in Classification

The **main point** in classification uses a single **organizing principle** to sort items in a way that serves the writer's purpose. The categories must be useful—helping to achieve the **purpose** of the classification. Imagine the following situation, in which a classification system isn't logical or useful.

You go into your video store to find that it has been rearranged. The signs indicating the location of different types of videos—comedy, drama, action—are gone. When you ask the clerk at the desk how to find a video, she says, "The videos over on this side are arranged by length of the film, starting with the shortest. The videos on the other side are arranged alphabetically by the lead actor's last name."

This new arrangement is confusing for three reasons:

- It doesn't sort things into **useful** categories. (Who's likely to select a video based on its length?)
- It doesn't serve the **purpose** of helping customers find videos.

- It doesn't have a **single organizing principle**. (Even if you know the length of the video and the actor's last name, you still don't know on which side of the store to start looking.)

The diagram on the following page shows how videos at most stores are classified.

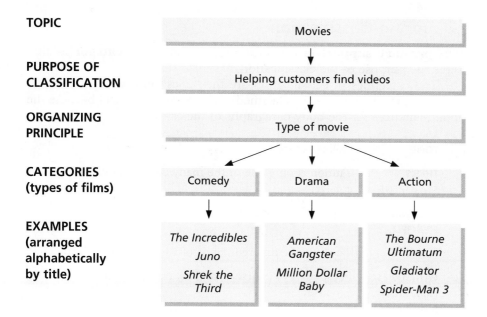

TOPIC	Movies
PURPOSE OF CLASSIFICATION	Helping customers find videos
ORGANIZING PRINCIPLE	Type of movie
CATEGORIES (types of films)	Comedy / Drama / Action
EXAMPLES (arranged alphabetically by title)	*The Incredibles / Juno / Shrek the Third* — *American Gangster / Million Dollar Baby* — *The Bourne Ultimatum / Gladiator / Spider-Man 3*

The following examples show how thesis statements for classification express the organizing principle and purpose.

Organizing principle + Purpose = Thesis statement

> There are several kinds of equipment you will need to enjoy a backpacking trip.

In addition to the purpose and organizing principle, a thesis statement in a classification may also include the categories that will be explained.

Organizing principle + Purpose + Categories = Thesis statement

> There are several kinds of equipment you will need to enjoy a backpacking trip, including proper footwear, versatile outerwear, and decent cooking supplies.

■ For online exercises on main point and support, visit *Exercise Central* at **bedfordstmartins .com/realessays**.

Support in Classification

The **primary support** in classification consists of the **categories** that serve the purpose of the classification.

The categories in classification are the "piles" into which the writer sorts a topic (the items to be classified). These categories will become the topic sentences for the body paragraphs of the essay.

TOPIC	College costs
THESIS STATEMENT	Tuition is only one of the many costs of going to college.
ORGANIZING PRINCIPLE	Types of costs other than tuition
PURPOSE	To show the different kinds of costs and their significance
CATEGORIES/ PRIMARY SUPPORT	Fees, costs of course materials, transportation expenses

The **supporting details** in classification are **examples** or explanations of what is in each category. The examples in classification are the various items that fall within each category. These are important because readers may not be familiar with your categories.

CATEGORY: Fees

    EXAMPLES/SUPPORTING DETAILS: General student fee assessed to each student, lab fees, computer fees

CATEGORY: Costs of course materials

    EXAMPLES/SUPPORTING DETAILS: Costs of books, lab manuals, software

CATEGORY: Transportation expenses

    EXAMPLES/SUPPORTING DETAILS: Costs of gas, parking, bus fare

Organization in Classification

Classification can be organized in different ways depending on its purpose. For example, read the thesis statements and purposes that follow:

THESIS STATEMENT	The high costs of college make higher education impossible for many students.
PURPOSE	To argue that some costs should be reduced

How might this classification be organized? _____

THESIS STATEMENT	My daughter has every kind of mess imaginable in her room, making it clear that she needs a lesson in taking care of her space and her things.
PURPOSE	To prove the need for the lesson by describing the messes

How might this classification be organized? _____

THESIS STATEMENT	During my teenage years, I adopted three distinct clothing styles.
PURPOSE	To show how a person's style changed

How might this classification be organized? _____

The chart on the right shows a general pattern for classification essays.

As you write your essay, you might find the following transitions helpful as you lead from one category to the next or from one example to another.

CLASSIFICATION AT A GLANCE

Introduction with thesis statement:
Organizing principle + purpose OR
Organizing principle + categories + purpose

↓

First category
Examples/explanations

↓

Second category
Examples/explanations

↓

Third category
Examples/explanations

↓

Conclusion
Refers back to the classification's purpose and makes an observation

---

Common Transitions in Classification

another	first, second, third (and so on)
another kind	for example
for instance	

Read and Analyze Classification

Before writing a classification essay, read the following examples—one each from college, the workplace, and everyday life—and answer the questions that accompany them.

Classification in College

The following student essay was written for an English composition class.

VOCABULARY
The following words are *italicized* in the excerpt: *skeptical, validity, strive, trendsetter, ruthless, compassionate, individualists, adaptable, tactful, downside, procrastinate, horoscope.* If you don't know their meanings, look them up in a dictionary.

BLOOD TYPE AND PERSONALITY

Danny Fitzgerald

PAUSE: What do you expect the rest of the essay to be about?

_____

_____

1   In Japan, the question "What's your blood type?" is as common as "What's your sign?" in the United States. Some Japanese researchers claim that people's personalities can be classified by their blood types. You may be *skeptical* about this method of classification, but don't judge its *validity* before you read the descriptions the researchers have put together. Do you see yourself?

2   If you have blood type O, you are a leader. When you see something you want, you *strive* to achieve your goal. You are passionate, loyal, and self-confident, and you are often a *trendsetter*. Your enthusiasm for projects and goals spreads to others, who happily follow your lead. When you want something, you may be *ruthless* about getting it or blind to how your actions affect others.

PAUSE: Do you know people who fall into these categories? Do you think blood type determines what category they fall into?

_____

_____

3   Another blood type, A, is typically associated with a social person. You like people and work well with them. You are sensitive, patient, *compassionate*, and affectionate. You are a good peacekeeper because you want everyone to be happy. In a team situation, you resolve conflicts and keep things on a smooth course. Sometimes type A's are stubborn and find it difficult to relax. They may find it uncomfortable to do things alone.

4   People with type B blood are usually *individualists* who like to do things on their own. You may be creative and *adaptable*, and you usually say exactly what you mean. Although you can adapt to situations, you may choose not to do so because of your strong independent streak. You may prefer working on your own to being part of a team.

5   The final blood type is AB, and if you have this blood type, you are a natural entertainer. You draw people to you because of your charm and easygoing nature. AB's are usually calm and controlled, *tactful*, and fair. On the *downside*, though, they may take too long to make decisions. And they may *procrastinate*, putting off tasks until the last minute.

PAUSE: What is your blood type? Does it match the description given here?

6   Classifying people's personalities by blood type seems very unusual until you examine what researchers have found. Most people find the descriptions fairly accurate. When you think about it, classification by blood type isn't any more far-fetched than classification by *horoscope* sign. What will they think of next? Classification by hair color?

1. Double-underline the **thesis statement**.
2. What is Danny's **single organizing principle**? _____
3. What **introduction techniques** does Danny use to get the reader's attention? _____
4. Underline the **topic sentences** that present the categories.
5. Put a check mark (✔) by the supporting details.
6. Does Danny's essay have the **four basics of good classification**? Be ready to explain your answer.

■ For a list of the four basics of good classification, see page 218.

Classification at Work

The following profile shows how a CEO uses classification at work.

Profile of Success

Giovanni Bohorquez

Chief Executive Officer, Algrita, Inc.

BACKGROUND: At the age of eleven, I left Colombia and came to the United States to live with my father in New Jersey. My family was poor, so I worked at several jobs and was earning significant wages by the age of twelve. After high school, I went to a community college and then transferred to the University of California, Los Angeles (UCLA), where I finished my bachelor's degree. I received a master's degree in business administration (M.B.A.) at UCLA's Anderson School and, after graduation, founded Algrita, Inc.

COLLEGES/DEGREES: El Camino College (A.A.), UCLA (B.S., M.B.A.)

EMPLOYER: Algrita, Inc.

WRITING AT WORK: Proposals, project plan reports, contracts, sales letters, documentation of business processes, e-mail

HOW GIOVANNI USES CLASSIFICATION: My company, Algrita, Inc., is a consulting firm that analyzes other companies and helps them improve their operations. I write reports that suggest the kinds of new technology that a business could adopt, the kinds of changes that could benefit them, and the kinds of services that Algrita offers.

Giovanni's Classification

The following is a description of the types of services that Algrita, Inc., can provide to clients.

VOCABULARY

The following words are *italicized* in the excerpt: *facilitate, synergistic, navigate, resolution, implementation, expertise, penetrate, segmentation, branding, outsourced, breadth, intranet, retain, augmenting, innovative.* If you don't know their meanings, look them up in a dictionary.

PAUSE: What categories of professional services does Algrita specialize in?

1   Algrita Consulting is a professional services firm specializing in strategy, process, and systems consulting. It offers a range of high-quality consulting services that are designed to *facilitate* the exchange of products and services worldwide by providing *synergistic* value in everyone we touch. Our service consultants analyze and learn our clients' businesses and most pressing needs. We help our clients quickly *navigate* the process of targeted solution designs, issue *resolution*, approvals, and *implementation*.

PAUSE: What area of expertise does this paragraph describe?

2   One area of *expertise* we offer is in the area of business services. Algrita offers strategic analysis of the market for your industry. We help our clients identify and *penetrate* new markets, develop new marketing strategies ranging from *segmentation* to *branding*, merge multidivisional companies to allow cross-selling, and effectively tie in leading technologies to stay ahead of the curve. In addition, we have experience leading and transforming businesses in the area of operations management, human resources (employee hiring, training and development), marketing, and financial analysis.

3   Another type of expertise that Algrita offers is in information technology services. Algrita allows you to build solutions in-house with our seasoned professionals, who provide expertise in systems development and integration, while taking advantage of *outsourced* back-end services. Our *breadth* of knowledge is concentrated on the client's best interests, and our methodologies are properly complemented by our systems technology expertise.

PAUSE: What area of expertise does this paragraph describe?

_____

_____

4   By helping you strengthen your technology processes and systems, we make a difference in your interactions with employees, customers, and suppliers. We help you improve *intranet* communications, *retain* intellectual property with knowledge-management tools, streamline processes through centralized systems, and develop Web-enabled solutions to automate or update legacy systems.

5   A third area of expertise is in our outsourcing services. Algrita's international development partners offer world-class infrastructure and technology know-how and can help you deliver results with speed and substantial savings. *Augmenting* your staff for big, short-duration projects allows you to focus your in-house resources on critical areas of the business while enhancing customer service and support.

PAUSE: What area of expertise does this paragraph describe?

_____

_____

6   Algrita services provide practical and *innovative* solutions, allowing you to do more. We look forward to helping you meet new challenges.

1. What is Giovanni classifying? _____

_____

2. What is his **purpose** for writing? _____

3. What are the **categories**? _____

_____

4. What other kinds of **examples** of each category might help? _____

_____

5. Does Giovanni's essay have the **four basics of good classification**? Be ready to explain your answer.

Classification in Everyday Life

In this essay, a student discusses the different types of roommates he has had.

BAD ROOMMATES

Dylan Marcos

PAUSE: What is Dylan's purpose in writing the essay?

_____

_____

1   Over the past few years, I have learned a lot about bad roommates. Although I doubt that I have encountered all types, I certainly know more now than I did before. I'll pass on to you some of what I've experienced, so you can try to avoid the following types of roommates—the romeos, the slugs, and the criminals.

2   The romeos are usually great guys and lots of fun, when they happen to be single—but they're usually not. They always seem to have girlfriends, who basically become nonpaying roommates. The women are mostly nice, but they change the apartment in big ways. First, we have to watch how we act. We can't walk around half-dressed in the morning, for example. Also, we have to get used to sharing: The girlfriends spend hours at a time in the bathroom, doing their hair and putting on make-up. There are always more dishes in the sink when they're around, more food disappears, and even shampoo goes faster than normal. The romeos don't seem to understand that having semipermanent guests in the apartment really changes the way we live.

3   Another type, the slug, is even harder to live with than the romeo because the slugs are slobs. They never wash the dishes or put away food, they leave a trail of dirty clothes behind them, and they completely destroy the bathroom every time they use it. Slugs pretty much live in front of the television, so you'll probably never have a chance to watch what *you* want. The slug is also sloppy about paying rent and bills. Although he usually has the money, he has to be reminded—no, hounded—before he will actually pay what he owes.

4   The worst type of roommate is the criminal, for obvious reasons. I've had only one of these, but one was more than enough. He was a nice guy for about two weeks—clean, not around too much, but good to have a beer with when he was there. One day, though, I came home

after work to find that he was gone, along with everything valuable in the apartment—our laptops, iPods, some cash, a bunch of CDs, and my favorite leather jacket. Although we called the police, I know I'll never get back anything he stole.

5   What I've learned from my experience is that, when I interview potential roommates, I should ask for at least two references, preferably from former roommates, so I can weed out the romeos, slugs, and criminals. That should keep my living situation sane—at least until I meet someone who seems great at first but turns out to fall into another, equally bad category. I'll keep you posted.

PAUSE: What three types of roommate does Dylan identify? Which one does he like least?

1. Double-underline the **thesis statement**.
2. What kind of **organization** does Dylan use? _____

_____

3. Underline the **topic sentences**.
4. Does Dylan's essay have the **four basics of good classification**? Be prepared to explain your answer.
5. What kinds of roommates have you had?

Critical Reading and Writing: Key College Skills

1. **Summary.** Briefly summarize each of the three selections, including the major categories of each classification.

2. **Analysis.** Reread the introductions to each essay. Does each of them set up the classification so that you know what is being classified? What purpose does each of the classifications serve? _____

_____

_____

3. **Synthesis.** Review the paragraph on learning styles (p. 219) and the essay about blood type and personality (p. 224). Drawing from these two pieces and your own experience and knowledge, discuss the variety of methods there are for determining what kind of person you are (hint: horoscopes, colors, and so on).

4. **Evaluation.** Using the **Four Basics of Good Classification** (p. 218) as a measure, decide which of the three essays is the best classification and why. Give specific examples to support your choice. Is your choice for the best classification essay different from the essay you like best?

Write a Classification Essay

In this section, you will write your own classification essay. Before you begin to write, review the four basics of good classification on page 218. Also, read the Tips for Tackling Classification in the box that follows.

TIPS FOR TACKLING CLASSIFICATION

1. Read the assignment carefully, highlighting the key words. They may be *describe* or *discuss the kinds of, what types of, explain the kinds of,* or *identify the kinds of.*

2. List the most important categories and the things that fit into them.

3. Be specific and descriptive.

4. In the end, draw a conclusion about the various types of whatever it is you're describing.

■ **ASSIGNMENT 1   WRITING ABOUT COLLEGE, WORK, AND EVERYDAY LIFE** . . . .

Write a classification essay on *one* of the following topics or on a topic of your own choice.

COLLEGE

- Types of degree programs
- Types of students
- Skim a textbook from another class to find a topic that is broken into categories. Then, summarize the topic.

■ Use the diagram on page 223 to help you organize.

WORK

- Types of work spaces
- Types of customers or clients
- Types of skills needed for a particular job.

EVERYDAY LIFE

- Types of drivers
- Types of restaurants in your town
- Types of cell phones

■ **ASSIGNMENT 2   WRITING ABOUT AN IMAGE** . . . .

This public service ad from the Department of Homeland Security is a reference to the USDA's "food pyramid," which illustrates the different categories of food a person should eat every day. To communicate the idea of being prepared for an emergency, the ad shows us the kind of "food pyramid" most of us could construct from our understocked kitchens. Write an essay in which you

discuss the ingredients necessary for one of the following—being ready for an emergency, being a successful student, running a profitable business, being a good friend, or staying in shape. How many of the necessary ingredients do you have right now? How might you acquire the rest?

 ASSIGNMENT 3   WRITING TO SOLVE A PROBLEM . . . .

THE PROBLEM: When you were a freshman in college, you received a flood of credit-card offers, and you signed up for three. Over time, you have run up a big debt, partly from the charges themselves and partly from the interest. Now you are seriously in debt and don't know how to get out of it.

THE ASSIGNMENT: Working on your own or in a small group, first classify your monthly expenses. Then, divide them into "necessary expenses" and "unnecessary expenses." Once you have done this, write an essay that classifies your expenses. Finally, cite some options you will pursue to pay down your debt.

RESOURCES: Review the chart on pages 868–69 for advice on problem solving. Also, check Web sites for advice about paying down debt without getting into even bigger trouble. You might start by typing in the words *advice on how to pay off credit cards* into a search engine. List any Web sites that you use.

 ASSIGNMENT 4   WRITING ABOUT READINGS . . . .

Read both Scott Russell Sanders's "The Men We Carry in Our Minds" (p. 788) and Amy Tan's "Mother Tongue" (p. 796). Then, write a short paper based on one of the following assignments:

- Both Sanders and Tan describe people who have influenced how they see themselves and the world. Write an essay classifying important people in your life by the ways in which they have influenced you. Begin by summarizing the influences described by Tan and Sanders.

- Tan refers to the "different Englishes" she uses. Analyze Tan's use of this term, and try to come up with your own definition of it. Then, classify the "different Englishes" we use depending on whom we are speaking with (parents, spouses, children, friends, and so on). Be sure to present your definition of "different Englishes" and draw on examples from Tan's essay.

Follow the steps in the Writing Guide below to help you prewrite, draft, revise, and edit your classification essay. Check off each step as you complete it.

WRITING GUIDE: CLASSIFICATION	
STEPS IN CLASSIFICATION	**HOW TO DO THE STEPS**
Focus.	☐ Think about what you want to classify (sort) for your readers and what purpose your classification will serve. Review the four basics of good classification on page 218.
Prewrite to explore your topic. See Chapter 4 for more on prewriting (including clustering).	☐ Select the topic or group that you want to classify. ☐ Decide on the purpose of the classification. ☐ Use a prewriting technique to generate useful categories for sorting your topic. Clustering works well for classification.
Write a thesis statement. Topic + Organizing principle = Thesis Three professions top the list of hot jobs in 2005. Topic + Organizing principle + Categories = Thesis Three professions top the list of hot jobs in 2005: health care, network systems analyst, and home services. See Chapter 5 for more on writing a thesis statement.	☐ Identify the organizing principle you will use to sort your topic into categories. ☐ Write a thesis statement that follows one of the suggested formats in the column to the left.
Support your thesis statement. The primary support in classification consists of the categories into which you sort your topic. See Chapter 6 for more on supporting a thesis statement.	☐ Remind yourself of your purpose and organizing principle. ☐ Choose categories that will serve the purpose of your classification. ☐ Give detailed examples of what fits into each category.

continued

STEPS IN CLASSIFICATION	HOW TO DO THE STEPS
Make a plan. See Chapter 7 for more on planning.	☐ Decide how the categories you have chosen should be arranged. Their arrangement should serve the purpose of your classification (see p. 222). ☐ Make a written plan that includes your primary support points (the categories) and supporting examples for the categories. (See the diagram on p. 223.)
Write a draft. See Chapter 8 for more on drafting.	☐ Write an introduction that includes your thesis statement. See if you can use one of the introductory techniques in Chapter 8. ☐ Write topic sentences for each of the categories. ☐ Write body paragraphs that give detailed examples of what is in each category. ☐ Write a concluding paragraph that makes an observation about the way you have classified the topic and why (your purpose). ☐ Title your essay.
Revise your draft. See Chapter 9 for more on revising a draft.	☐ Ask another person to read and comment on your draft. ☐ Make sure that you have just one organizing principle. ☐ Review the categories you have chosen to make sure they serve the purpose of your classification. ☐ Review the examples you give for each category. Delete any that don't really fit, and add any that you think would give the readers a better idea of what is in the category. ☐ Add transitions to connect your ideas. ☐ Reread your thesis statement. Revise it so that your point is more concrete and forceful. ☐ Reread your introduction, and make changes if it is dull or weak. ☐ Reread your conclusion to make sure it is energetic and drives home your point. ☐ Make at least five changes to your draft to improve unity, support, or coherence (see pp. 127–40). ☐ Check to make sure the draft follows the four basics of good classification.

STEPS IN CLASSIFICATION	HOW TO DO THE STEPS
Edit your draft. See Parts Four through Seven for more on editing.	☐ Use the spell checker and grammar checker on your computer, but also reread your essay carefully to catch any errors. ☐ Look for errors in grammar, spelling, and punctuation. Focus first on sentence fragments, run-ons, errors in subject-verb agreement, verb errors, and other areas where you often make mistakes. ☐ Ask yourself: Is this the best I can do?

You Know This

You already use definition.

- Your child hears the word *hurricane* and asks what it means. You then define it for him.
- A friend new to this country sees a "No Smoking" sign and asks what it means. You define it for him or her.

15

Definition

Writing That Tells What Something Means

Understand What Definition Is

Definition is writing that explains what a term or concept means.

> ■■ **FOUR BASICS OF GOOD DEFINITION**
> 1. It tells readers what term is being defined.
> 2. It presents a clear definition.
> 3. It uses examples to show what the writer means.
> 4. It gives details about the examples that readers will understand.

In the following paragraph, each number corresponds to one of the four basics of good definition.

1 Internet addiction is 2 chronic, compulsive use of the Internet that interferes with the addicts' lives or their relationships with others. 3 For example, addicts may spend so much time online that they are unable to perform as expected at home, work, or school. 4 These addicts may spend hours surfing the Web, playing games, or e-mailing friends and family. 3 In other cases, the Internet addiction can cause financial problems, or worse. 4 For example, online shoppers who go to extremes can find themselves

in debt and, as a result, damage their credit, not to mention personal relationships. 3 Still other Internet addictions involve potentially dangerous or illegal activities. 4 These activities can include meeting people online, gambling, viewing pornography, and engaging in cybersex. However, for Internet addicts, the problem usually isn't *how* they use the Internet; the problem is that they cannot stop using it, even if they want to.

Many situations require you to explain the meaning of a term, particularly how you are using it.

COLLEGE   On a U.S. history exam, you define the term *carpetbagger*.

WORK   You describe a coworker as "dangerous" to a human resources staffer, and the staffer asks what you mean exactly.

EVERYDAY   You explain the term *fair* to your child in the context of
LIFE   games or sports.

Main Point in Definition

In definition essays, your **main point** typically defines your topic. The main point is directly related to your **purpose,** which is to get your readers to understand the way that you are using a term or concept in the context of your essay. Although writers do not always define a term or concept in a thesis statement, it helps readers if they do.

A thesis statement in definition can follow a variety of different patterns, two of which include the term and its basic definition.

1. Term + Means/is + Basic definition = Thesis statement

> Today, marriage means different things to different people.

Term + Means/is + Basic definition = Thesis statement

> My company is customer-oriented: From start to finish to follow-up, the customer comes first.

Term + Means/is + Basic definition = Thesis statement

> I am a neat freak.

2. Term + Class + Basic definition = | Thesis statement |

> Today, marriage is an *institution* that means different things to different people.

Term + Class + Basic definition = | Thesis statement |

> Childhood obesity is a *condition* that threatens the future of our country in many ways.

In essays based on the following thesis statements, readers would expect the italicized terms and concepts to be defined through examples that show the writer's meaning.

What does *marriage* mean today?

I am a *neat freak.*

The concept of *equal pay for equal work* is a joke.

Many people do not understand what *affirmative action* really means.

Support in Definition

If a friend says, "Summer in New York City is awful," you don't know what she means by *awful.* Is it the weather? The people? The transportation? Until your friend explains what she means, you won't know whether you would think New York City in the summer is awful.

Support in definition provides specific examples of terms or concepts to help explain what they mean. Read the two thesis statements that follow and the lists of examples that could be used as support.

THESIS	Today, marriage means different things to different people.
SUPPORT	A union of one man and one woman
	A union of two people of either sex
	A union that is supported by state law
	A union that is supported by both civil and religious laws
THESIS	I am a neat freak.
SUPPORT	I clean compulsively.
	I'm constantly buying new cleaning products.

My cleaning habits have attracted the notice of friends and family.

In both of these examples, the writer would then go on to develop the examples with details.

THESIS	I am a neat freak.
SUPPORT	I clean compulsively.
	DETAILS: I clean in the morning and at night, can't let a spot on the counter go for a second, fret when I can't clean as much as I'd like to.
SUPPORT	I'm constantly buying new cleaning products.
	DETAILS: Every week, I buy new products, have a closet full of them, always think there's something better around the corner.
SUPPORT	My cleaning habits have attracted the notice of friends and family.
	DETAILS: Kids used to appreciate the clean house; now they complain that I'm compulsive; friends tease me, but I wonder if they think I go too far.

Organization in Definition

The examples in a definition essay are often organized by **importance,** or the impact you think the examples will have on your readers. Save the most important example for last.

The plan for a definition essay might look like the diagram to the right.

As you write, add transitions to connect one example to the next. See box on the following page.

**DEFINITION
AT A GLANCE**

Introduction with thesis statement
Defines term or concept

↓

First example explaining the definition
Details about the first example

↓

Second example explaining the definition
Details about the second example

↓

Third example explaining the definition
Details about the third example

↓

Conclusion
Refers back to the defined term/concept and makes an observation about it based on what you have written

---

Common Transitions in Definition

another	for example
another kind	for instance
first, second, third, and so on	

Read and Analyze Definition

■ For other examples of definition, see Chapter 48.

Before writing a definition essay, read the following three examples—from college, the workplace, and everyday life—and answer the questions that accompany them.

Definition in College

The following *Boston Globe* article was assigned to students in a marketing course to demonstrate the concept of product branding.

VOCABULARY
The following words are *italicized* in the excerpt: *familiar, salivating, perception, altered, restrict, marketing, instill, obsessional*. If you don't know their meanings, look them up in a dictionary.

STUDY SAYS ADS TRICK CHILDREN'S TASTE BUDS

Lindsey Tanner

PAUSE: Why would juice and carrots—items that McDonald's doesn't even sell—taste better when packaged in McDonald's wrapping?

1   Anything made by McDonald's tastes better, preschoolers said in a study that powerfully demonstrates how advertising can trick the taste buds of young children. Even carrots, milk, and apple juice tasted better to the children when they were wrapped in the *familiar* packaging of the Golden Arches: such is the power of branding, closely associating a name, logo, slogan, or design with a particular product or line of products or services.

2   The study had youngsters sample identical McDonald's foods in name-brand and unmarked wrappers. The unmarked foods always lost

the taste test. "You see a McDonald's label and kids start *salivating,*" said Diane Levin, a childhood development specialist who campaigns against advertising to children. Levin said it was "the first study I know of that has shown so simply and clearly what's going on with [marketing to] young children."

PAUSE: How does the study show the effect of branding?

3   Study author Dr. Tom Robinson said the children's *perception* of taste was "physically *altered* by the branding." The Stanford University researcher said it was remarkable how children so young were so influenced by advertising. The study involved 63 low-income children ages 3 to 5 from Head Start centers in San Mateo County, Calif. Robinson believes the results would be similar for children from wealthier families.

4   The research, appearing in August's *Archives of Pediatrics and Adolescent Medicine,* was funded by Stanford and the Robert Wood Johnson Foundation. The study will probably stir more debate over the movement to *restrict* ads to children. It comes less than a month after 11 major food and drink companies, including McDonald's, announced new curbs on *marketing* to children under 12. McDonald's says the only Happy Meals it will promote to young children will contain fruit and have fewer calories and less fat.

PAUSE: Why do you think McDonald's made the decision to reduce its marketing to children?

5   "This is an important subject and McDonald's has been actively addressing it for quite some time," said company spokesman Walt Riker. "We've always wanted to be part of the solution and we are providing solutions."

6   But Dr. Victor Strasburger, an author of an American Academy of Pediatrics policy urging limits on marketing to children, said the study shows that too little is being done. "It's an amazing study and it's very sad," Strasburger said. "Advertisers have tried to do exactly what this study is talking about—to brand younger and younger children, to *instill* in them an almost *obsessional* desire for a particular brand-name product," he said. Just two of the 63 children studied said they had never eaten at McDonald's, and about one-third ate there at least weekly.

7   The study included three McDonald's menu items—hamburgers, chicken nuggets, and fries—and store-bought milk or juice and carrots.

Children got two identical samples of each food on a tray, one in McDonald's wrappers or cups and the other in plain, unmarked packaging. The participants were asked if they tasted the same or if one was better. McDonald's-labeled samples were clear favorites. Fries were the biggest winner; almost 77 percent said the labeled fries tasted best while only 13 percent preferred the others. Fifty-four percent preferred McDonald's-wrapped carrots versus 23 percent who liked the plain-wrapped sample. Fewer than one-fourth of the children said both samples of all foods tasted the same.

PAUSE: Summarize the experiment.

_____

_____

8   Pradeep Chintagunta, a University of Chicago marketing professor, said a fairer comparison might have gauged children's preferences for the McDonald's label versus another familiar brand, such as Mickey Mouse. "I don't think you can necessarily hold this against" McDonald's, he said, since the goal of marketing is to build familiarity and sell products.

—From the *Boston Globe*, 7 Aug. 2007, p. A6

1. Underline the **definition** of branding. Now define it in your own words.

2. How does the essay serve as a definition of branding?

3. Does the essay give enough **details** about the experiment? What else would have been helpful? _____

_____

4. Does the essay have the **four basics of good definition**? Be ready to explain your answer.

5. What is another example of branding that you know about? About marketing to children?

Definition at Work

The following profile shows how a business owner uses definition at work.

Profile of Success

Gary Knoblock
Business Owner

BACKGROUND: I grew up in New Orleans, where, after high school, I tried college for a year but was told by a professor that I wasn't college material and should try manual labor. I left college and moved to Fort Worth, Texas, where I became a police officer. During my ten years with the force, I attended a junior college at night, earning an associate's degree. I received numerous promotions at work and eventually became a member of the force's SWAT team. In 1999, I decided to start my own business. I moved to Mississippi and started a sign company, Lightning Quick (LQ) Signs. Since then, the company has grown steadily into a successful business. It was destroyed by Hurricane Katrina in 2005, but I rebuilt and reopened it in 2007.

COLLEGES/DEGREES: Tarrant County Junior College (A.A.)

EMPLOYER: Self

WRITING AT WORK: Proposals to get jobs, advertising copy, follow-up reports and letters, loan applications, correspondence with clients and prospective clients, precise and descriptive specifications for government jobs

HOW GARY USES DEFINITION: I often need to define terms for clients. In addition, the letter about the company that I use in sales situations defines how LQ Signs is customer-oriented.

Gary's Definition

Gary uses this mission statement to get contracts for his sign company.

VOCABULARY

The following words are *italicized* in the excerpt: *fundamental, orientation, prospective, installation.* If you don't know their meanings, look them up in a dictionary.

1   The *fundamental* principle of Lightning Quick (LQ) Signs is customer *orientation*. While most companies claim that they are customer-oriented, most have no idea what that really means. I tell my employees that I would like to have a customer giggle at the completion of the job, delighting in the product and service we have delivered, his every

expectation met and exceeded. For all of us at LQ Signs, *customer-oriented* means that from start to finish to follow-up, the customer comes first.

2   Our customer orientation begins before the job begins. Before doing anything, we interview the customer to learn what his or her needs are and to determine the most cost-effective route to meet those needs. No job for us is "standard." Each is unique.

3   Our customer orientation means that we produce high-quality products quickly. We keep signs simple because our customers want their *prospective* customers to be able to read the sign in a glance. We use the most current digital printing processes to produce sharp, readable signs quickly. Because we have previously determined, with the customer, the most cost-effective method of producing the signs, the high quality and rapid return do not come at extra cost.

4   Our customer orientation means that our products are thoroughly checked for flaws and installed at the customer's convenience. Our signs leave our workshop in perfect condition, as the customer has ordered. Our well-trained team of installers works with the customer to determine the *installation* schedule.

PAUSE: What are three examples of customer-oriented practices?

5   Finally, our customer orientation means that the job is not complete when the sign is in place. We follow up every sale to make sure that the product is in top shape and that the customer is pleased.

6   LQ Signs is truly customer-oriented, from start to finish to follow-up. Our customers are our partners.

1. What is Gary's **purpose**? _____

   _____

2. Double-underline the **thesis statement**.

3. Underline the **topic sentences**.

4. Were you familiar with the term that Gary defined? Restate the meaning of *customer-oriented* in your own words. _____

   _____

   _____

Definition in Everyday Life

VOCABULARY
The following words are *italicized* in the excerpt: *anesthetic, reconstruction, resin, retainer, adhesive, mimic, minimally, invasive, enhanced, persist.* If you don't know their meanings, look them up in a dictionary.

CELEBRITY TEETH
Rebecca Skloot

1   Last year, if you walked into your dentist's office saying, "Hey, Doc, can you make my teeth look like Cameron Diaz's or Brad Pitt's?" the answer would have been, "Yeah, sure—with a lot of *anesthetic,* drilling, and permanent *reconstruction.*" But things have changed.

2   Meet the Snap-On Smile—a thin, flexible, *resin* shell of perfect teeth that snaps over your actual teeth like a *retainer.* No *adhesive,* no drilling. Its inventor, Marc Liechtung, is a dentist at Manhattan Dental Arts, where you can walk in on a Monday, make a painless plaster mold of your teeth, and then pick up your new smile by Friday. All for $1,200 to $1,600. Patients can work with a "smile guide" to choose one of seventeen colors ("yellow-white," "yellow-gray," even "Extreme White Buyer Beware") and eighteen shapes ("squared," "square-round," "pointy"). But many patients just hand Liechtung a celebrity photo and say, "Make my teeth look like this." So he does. But he wants to make one thing clear: "I did not come up with the Snap-On Smile so people could *mimic* celebrities."

3   His goal was an affordable, *minimally invasive* dental tool. "I had patients with almost no teeth who didn't have $20,000 for reconstruction," he says. So this year, after months in the lab, he unveiled Snap-On Smiles. He is licensing them to dentists and has sold more than three hundred to his own patients, many of whom have perfectly healthy (and often straight) teeth.

4   People don't ask Liechtung whether the Snap-On causes permanent damage (it doesn't) or whether you can eat with it (you can—even corn

PAUSE: What do you expect the next paragraph to be about?

———————

———————

PAUSE: Why might he have invented the Snap-On Smile?

———————

———————

PAUSE: Why would someone with healthy teeth buy a Snap-On Smile?

———————

———————

on the cob). "No," Liechtung says, "they just want to know: 'Which is the most popular celebrity?' 'What kind of girls get Halle Berry?' 'Who do guys ask for?'"

5   "In the beginning, it made me sick. I thought I invented some serious medical device, but all people wanted to do was use it to make themselves look like celebrities!" Eventually he thought, Well, why not? "A person comes in, I say I can give them any teeth they want, who are they going to want to look like? Me? No!"

6   Liechtung wears a Snap-On every day. But whose smile is it? "I just made an *enhanced* version of my own," he says. But people rarely believe him. "I hate to admit it," he says, "but when they *persist*, I tell them my teeth are Brad Pitt's, because really, who wouldn't want his teeth?"

—From *The New York Times Magazine,*
11 Dec. 2005, pp. 61–62

1. What is the **term** being defined? _____

2. Double-underline **the sentence where the term is defined**.

3. Underline two **details** about the Snap-On Smile.

4. Does the essay have the **four basics of good definition**? Be ready to explain your answer.

5. If you were choosing a Snap-On Smile, what would it look like? Does the idea appeal to you? Why or why not?

Critical Reading and Writing: Key College Skills

1. **Summary.** Briefly summarize each of the three selections, including the definitions that each essay provides.

2. **Analysis.** Review the introductory paragraphs of each selection. What purpose does each selection have? Do the introductions serve that

   purpose? _____

   _____

   _____

3. **Synthesis.** Review Lindsey Tanner's "Study Says Ads Trick Children's Taste Buds" (p. 240) and Rebecca Skloot's "Celebrity Teeth" (p. 245). Then, drawing from each and your experience, discuss how media affects our choices.

4. **Evaluation.** Using the **four basics of good definition** as a measure, which of the three selections in this chapter is the best example of a definition? Give specific examples to support your choice. Is your choice different from the one you find most informative?

Write a Definition Essay

In this section, you will write your own definition essay based on one of the following assignments. Before you begin to write, review the four basics of good definition on page 236. Also, read the Tips for Tackling Definition in the box that follows.

TIPS FOR TACKLING DEFINITION

1. Read the assignment carefully, highlighting key words. An assignment that uses definition might ask you to *define*, but it might also use words such as *discuss the concept of* _____, *what is* _____ *and how does it work?*, *define and give examples of,* and *what does* _____ *mean in the context of* _____?

2. Figure out what word or concept you need to define.

3. Work out a simple definition, and list examples that demonstrate what the word or concept is in relation to the assignment.

4. Give examples of your understanding of the word or concept.

■ **ASSIGNMENT 1   WRITING ABOUT COLLEGE, WORK, AND EVERYDAY LIFE** . . . .

Write a definition essay on *one* of the following topics or on a topic of your own choice.

COLLEGE

- A term or concept from another course you have taken
- A good/inspiring/motivating teacher
- Cheating

WORK

- Any term you use at work
- McJobs
- A model employee

EVERYDAY LIFE

- An attitude or behavior (such as assertiveness, generosity, negativity, optimism, and so on)
- Morality
- Road rage

 ASSIGNMENT 2   WRITING ABOUT AN IMAGE . . . .

What point is the woman in the following picture trying to make? How might she define *patriotism*? Write a definition essay presenting your definition of *patriotism*.

■ **ASSIGNMENT 3   WRITING TO SOLVE A PROBLEM** . . . .

THE PROBLEM: Your company is putting together a new employee handbook. To make the handbook both realistic and relevant, the company has decided that the contents will come directly from the employees. Your department has been assigned the section on communication.

THE ASSIGNMENT: Working on your own or with a small group, write a short piece defining *good communication skills*, giving detailed examples of how those skills should be applied in your company.

RESOURCES: Review the chart on pages 868–69 for advice on problem solving. You might also

- Set up an informational interview with a human resources worker to find out about your subject.
- Type *definition of good communication skills* into a search engine. Document any Web sites or references you use.

■ **ASSIGNMENT 4   WRITING ABOUT READINGS** . . . .

The assignments that follow ask you to read one or more different definition essays and draw from them to write your own essay.

- Review Lindsey Tanner's "Study Says Ads Trick Children's Taste Buds" (p. 240), and read Juliet B. Schor's "Age Compression" (p. 811). Define the terms *branding* and *age compression*. Then, explain how each essay describes them. Give examples, too, from your own experience or from other things you have read.
- Review Rebecca Skloot's "Celebrity Teeth" (p. 245), and read Dave Barry's "The Ugly Truth about Beauty" (p. 817) and Amy L. Beck's "Struggling for Perfection" (p. 829). Drawing from these three selections to make your point, discuss the pressures that people who live in this society feel to be young and beautiful.

Follow the steps in the Writing Guide on the next page to help you prewrite, draft, revise, and edit your definition essay. Check off each step as you complete it.

WRITING GUIDE: DEFINITION

STEPS IN DEFINITION	HOW TO DO THE STEPS
Focus.	☐ Think about why you are being asked to define a term or concept and what you need to show. Review the four basics of good definition on page 236.
Prewrite to explore your topic. See Chapter 4 for more on prewriting (including clustering).	☐ Make a list of some topics you would be interested in defining—for example, a type of person, a belief that is important to you, or a term that you think is often misused. ☐ Choose one of the topics, and prewrite to come up with ideas about what you are defining. (Clustering works well for definition.) What does it mean to you? Decide on the meaning that you will develop in your essay.
Write a thesis statement. A thesis statement in definition can follow one of these patterns: Term + Means/is + Definition = Thesis Binge drinking is a killer. Term + Class + Definition = Thesis Yoga is an exercise that helps people relax. *Or,* write a thesis statement that names the term and indicates what your essay will say: I am a geek and proud of it. See Chapter 5 for more on the thesis.	☐ Review your prewriting about what your topic means to you. ☐ Write a working thesis statement that includes the term. It also should include either your definition of the term or some idea of what your essay will explain. ☐ Think about your readers, and revise your thesis statement to make it either clearer or more interesting to them.
Support your thesis statement. Support in definition explains what terms or concepts mean by providing specific examples. See Chapter 6 for more on supporting a thesis statement.	☐ Prewrite to find examples that explain how you are defining your topic. ☐ Review the examples, and get rid of any that don't show your meaning of the term. Choose at least three good examples. ☐ With your readers in mind, add details to the examples that show your readers what you mean by your definition. Think about the kinds of examples and details that will make sense to them.

STEPS IN DEFINITION	HOW TO DO THE STEPS
Make a plan. See Chapter 7 for more on planning.	☐ Choose an order for your support points. A definition essay generally uses order of importance and builds up to the example that readers will find most powerful. ☐ Make a written plan that includes the major support points (examples) and supporting details. (See the diagram on p. 239.)
Write a draft. See Chapter 8 for more on drafting.	☐ Write an introduction that includes your thesis statement. See if you can use one of the introductory techniques in Chapter 8. ☐ Write topic sentences for each of the examples. ☐ Write body paragraphs that give detailed explanations of each example. ☐ Write a concluding paragraph that makes an observation about the term based on the examples you have given. ☐ Title your essay.
Revise your draft. See Chapter 9 for more on revising a draft.	☐ Ask another person to read and comment on your draft. ☐ See if your thesis statement and introduction could be clearer or more interesting to your readers. ☐ Reread the body of your essay to make sure that the examples explain your definition and the details explain the examples. Add other examples and details that help explain what you mean by the term. ☐ Reread your conclusion to make sure it reinforces your definition. ☐ Add transitions to connect your ideas. ☐ Make at least five changes to your draft to improve unity, support, or coherence (see pp. 127–40). ☐ Check to make sure the draft follows the four basics of good definition.
Edit your draft. See Parts Four through Seven for more on editing.	☐ Use the spell checker and grammar checker on your computer, but also reread your essay carefully to catch any errors. ☐ Look for errors in grammar, spelling, and punctuation. Run-ons and punctuation errors are common in definition, so check for those first. Then, focus on sentence fragments, errors in subject-verb agreement, verb errors, and other areas where you often make mistakes. ☐ Ask yourself: Is this the best I can do?

You Know This

You already use comparison and contrast to make decisions.

- You compare and contrast features of several cell phones.
- You compare and contrast the prices of various goods.

Annual Cost of Your Caffeine Fix*

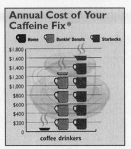

Source: Consumer Reports Money Adviser, October 2004.

16

Comparison and Contrast

Writing That Shows Similarities and Differences

Understand What Comparison and Contrast Are

Comparison is writing that shows the similarities among subjects—people, ideas, situations, or items; **contrast** shows the differences. In conversation, we often use the word *compare* to mean either compare or contrast, but as you work through this chapter, the terms will be separated.

■■ **FOUR BASICS OF GOOD COMPARISON AND CONTRAST**

1. It uses subjects that have enough in common to be usefully compared and contrasted.

2. It serves a purpose—that is, it expresses a main point that helps readers make a decision or understand the subjects.

3. It presents several important, parallel points of comparison and contrast.

4. It is organized either point by point or whole to whole (see pp. 255–56).

In the following paragraph, which contrasts the subjects, each number corresponds to one of the four basics of good comparison and contrast.

1 My current boyfriend **2** is a major improvement over **1** my ex-boyfriend **2** in terms of how he treats me. **3** One difference is that my current boyfriend opens the door when I get in the car as well as when I get out. In contrast, my ex-boyfriend never opened the door of the car or any other door. **3** My current boyfriend likes to tell me that he loves me. For example, we went to the beach, and he screamed that he loved me to the four winds so everyone could hear. My ex, on the other hand, always had a ready excuse for why he couldn't say that he loved me, ever. However, he wanted me to tell him I loved him all the time. **3** Another difference between the two is that my boyfriend spends money on me. When we go out to a restaurant, he pays for the meal. My ex just never seemed to have money to pay for dinner or anything else. He would say he forgot to bring his wallet, and I would have to pay for the food. **3** To me, the most important difference between the two guys is that my current boyfriend is honest. He never lies to me about anything, and he makes me feel confident about our relationship. In contrast, I never could tell if my ex was lying or telling the truth because he often lied about his family and other things, and I never knew what to believe. **2** To sum it all up, my current boyfriend is a gentleman, and my ex was a pig.

4 Uses point-by-point organization (see p. 255).

—Liliana Ramirez, student

Many situations require you to use comparison and contrast.

COLLEGE	In a business course, you compare and contrast practices in e-commerce and traditional commerce.
WORK	You compare and contrast two health insurance options offered by your company in order to select the one that is best for you.
EVERYDAY LIFE	Before choosing a telephone plan, you compare and contrast the rates, services, and options each offers.

Main Point in Comparison and Contrast

A comparison and contrast essay shows readers how two or more subjects are alike or different. The **purpose** of a comparison and contrast essay may be to have readers understand the subjects or to help them make a decision. For example, you might compare and contrast two characters in a book to show that you understand them, or you might compare and contrast breeds of dogs to help a potential owner choose among them.

In comparison and contrast, your **main point** expresses similarities or differences in your subjects. For example, in the paragraph on page 253, Liliana Ramirez contrasts the different ways that her two boyfriends treated her. Her purpose is to help readers understand why one became her "ex."

Typically, thesis statements in comparison and contrast essays present the central subjects and indicate whether the writer will show similarities, differences, or both.

| Subject 1 | + | Subject 2 | + | Indication of similarity or difference | = | Thesis statement |

While on the surface Facebook and MySpace are similar, a recent report indicates that they attract very different kinds of users.

To determine your thesis in a comparison and contrast essay, decide whether you want to show similarities, differences, or both. To make this decision, you need to think about what your purpose is—what you want your readers to understand—and what will be meaningful to those readers.

Support in Comparison and Contrast

The **support** in comparison and contrast demonstrates your main point by showing how your subjects are the same or different. To find support, many people make a list with multiple columns—one for the points that will serve as the basis of the comparison or contrast and one for each of the subjects.

For example, one student, Daniel, wrote the following thesis statement, which indicates that his essay will focus on the differences between the ages of twenty and forty:

The ages of twenty and forty are both enjoyable, but they represent very different stages in life.

To support this thesis, Daniel needs to find several points of contrast between twenty and forty. He generates this list:

> *DIFFERENCES BETWEEN TWENTY AND FORTY*
>
> *appearance*
>
> *place in life*
>
> *perspective*

Then, for each point of comparison, Daniel lists some details that explain the differences:

	AGE TWENTY	*AGE FORTY*
APPEARANCE	*smooth skin*	*some wrinkles*
	trendy haircut	*classic hairstyle*
	rounded features	*well-defined features*
PLACE IN LIFE	*just starting out*	*established*
	single, no children	*married with children*
	living at home	*own home*
PERSPECTIVE	*self-centered*	*more thoughtful*
	choices to make	*many choices made*
	uncertainty	*wisdom*

Organization in Comparison and Contrast

A comparison and contrast essay can be organized in two basic ways: A **point-by-point** organization first compares or contrasts one point between the two subjects and then moves to the next point of comparison or contrast. A **whole-to-whole** organization first presents all the points of comparison or contrast for one subject and then all the points for the second. To decide which organization to use, consider which of the two will best serve your purpose of explaining similarities or differences to your readers. Once you choose an organization, stick with it throughout the essay.

The two organizations look like this:

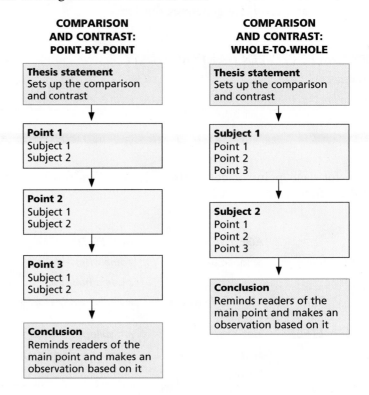

Using **transitions** in comparison and contrast essays is important to move readers from one subject to another and from one point of comparison to another.

Common Transitions in Comparison and Contrast

COMPARISON	CONTRAST
one similarity	one difference
another similarity	another difference
similarly	in contrast
like	now/then
both	unlike
	while

Read and Analyze Comparison and Contrast

Before writing a comparison and contrast essay, read the following three examples—from college, the workplace, and everyday life—and answer the questions that accompany them.

Comparison and Contrast in College

The following is an excerpt from a college textbook.

VOCABULARY

The following words are *italicized* in the excerpt: *disorders, spectrum, distorted, excessive, laxatives, optimal, hallmark, emaciated, purge, enemas, conceal, consumption,* and *genetic.* If you don't know their meanings, look them up in a dictionary.

WHEN THE REGULATION OF EATING BEHAVIOR FAILS: ANOREXIA AND BULIMIA

1   Two life-threatening eating *disorders* are common, especially among females, and while they may have similar psychological causes, the behaviors themselves are quite different. Both of these disorders lie at the opposite end of the *spectrum* from obesity.

2   **Anorexia nervosa** is a potentially life-threatening psychological disorder that involves near self-starvation. This psychological disorder has three key symptoms: The individual refuses to maintain a minimally normal body weight, is extremely afraid of gaining weight or becoming fat, and has a *distorted* perception of the size of his or her body. Approximately 90 percent of cases of anorexia nervosa occur in adolescent or young adult females (American Psychiatric Association, 1994).

3   It is rare for a person with anorexia to lose her appetite completely. Rather, she places herself on a very restricted diet that may be limited to just a few foods. Weight loss is also often accomplished by *excessive* exercise, fasting, self-induced vomiting, or the misuse of *laxatives.* By reducing total food intake, individuals with anorexia drop 15 percent

or more below their *optimal* body weight. Depression, social with-drawal, insomnia, and failure to menstruate frequently accompany the disorder.

4   A *hallmark* of anorexia is distorted self-perception. Despite her *ema-ciated* appearance, the person with anorexia looks in the mirror and sees herself as still overweight. Or she expresses displeasure with certain parts of her body, such as her abdomen or thighs, that are "too fat." Weight loss is viewed with pride and regarded as an act of extraordinary self-discipline. Approximately 10 percent of people with anorexia ner-vosa die from starvation, suicide, or physical complications of extreme weight loss (American Psychiatric Association, 1994).

PAUSE: Summarize the behaviors of anorexia.

5   In contrast, people with **bulimia nervosa** are within their normal weight range and may even be slightly overweight. People with bulimia engage in binge eating and then *purge* themselves of the excessive food consumption by self-induced vomiting. Less often, they may use laxa-tives or *enemas* to purge themselves of the food.

6   People suffering from bulimia usually *conceal* their eating problems from others. Episodes of binge eating typically occur in secrecy. A binge usually includes the *consumption* of high-caloric, sweet foods that can be swallowed quickly, such as ice cream, cake, and candy. Once they begin eating, people with bulimia often feel as though they cannot control their food intake. Sometimes consuming as much as 50,000 calories at one time, they eat until they are uncomfortably, even painfully, full (American Psychiatric Association, 1994; Johnson, Stuckey, Lewis, & Schwartz, 1982).

PAUSE: Summarize the behaviors of bulimia.

7   Diverse cultural, psychological, social, and *genetic* factors seem to be involved in both anorexia nervosa and bulimia nervosa (North, Gowers, & Byram, 1995; Steinhausen, 1994). There is strong cultural pressure, especially for young Western women, to achieve the thinness ideal. The higher incidence of eating disorders among women may be related to their greater dissatisfaction with their appearance. Women are much more likely to have a poor body image than are men of the same age (Feingold & Mazzella, 1998).

References

American Psychiatric Association. (1994). *Diagnostic and statistical manual of mental disorders* (4th ed.). Washington, DC: American Psychiatric Association.

Feingold, A., & Mazzella, R. (1998). Gender differences in body image are increasing. *Psychological Science, 9,* 190–195.

Johnson, C. L., Stuckey, M. K., Lewis, L. D., & Schwartz, D. M. (1982). Bulimia: A descriptive survey of 316 cases. *International Journal of Eating Disorders, 2,* 3–16.

North, C., Gowers, S., & Byram, V. (1995). Family functioning in adolescent anorexia nervosa. *British Journal of Psychiatry, 151,* 82–88.

Steinhausen, H. C. (1994). Anorexia and bulimia nervosa. In M. Rutter, E. Taylor, & L. Hersov (Eds.), *Child and adolescent psychiatry: Modern approaches.* Boston: Blackwell Scientific Publications.

—From Don H. Hockenbury and Sandra Hockenbury, *Discovering Psychology,* 2nd ed. (New York: Worth, 2001)

1. Double-underline the **thesis statement**.

2. Underline each **topic sentence**.

3. Does this piece of writing use point-by-point or whole-to-whole organization? _____

4. Circle the **transition** that the writer uses to move from one subject to the other.

5. What are two main points of contrast in this piece? _____

_____

_____

6. Does this excerpt follow the **four basics of good comparison and contrast**? Be ready to explain your answer.

■ For a list of the four basics of good comparison and contrast, see page 252.

7. In what other ways might you characterize the behavior of someone who is anorexic or bulimic?

Comparison and Contrast at Work

The profile on page 260 shows how a family-practice physician uses comparison and contrast in his work.

Profile of Success

Garth Vaz
Physician

BACKGROUND: I was born in Jamaica, and at school, everyone thought I was lazy because I couldn't read. I knew I worked hard but didn't understand why I had such trouble reading. When it came time to go to high school, I dropped out and moved to Brooklyn, New York. Shortly thereafter, I was drafted and served as a medic in the military, where I got my G.E.D. After completing my service, I went to Central Florida Community College and transferred to the University of Florida. I dropped out eventually and worked for a few years as an orderly.

I was accepted at the University of Florida Medical School but flunked out, at which point I finally discovered that my reading and writing problems were caused not by laziness but by dyslexia. I petitioned the school to return and passed my courses with the help of a note-taking service. But I failed the medical boards twice before I was allowed "accommodation" for dyslexia.

Today I am a doctor working at a community health clinic that, in addition to other medical services, provides care for migrant workers and their families. I also travel and speak extensively on learning behaviors, especially dyslexia and attention-deficit/hyperactivity disorder (ADHD).

COLLEGES/DEGREES: A.A., Central Florida Community College; M.D., University of Florida

EMPLOYER: Community Health Centers of South Central Texas, Inc.

WRITING AT WORK: For work, I write patient reports, speeches, and papers for publication. As a dyslexic, writing is still very difficult for me, though I have learned how to compensate for the difficulty. Because I still make lots of spelling errors, I have to read very carefully and reread anything I write to correct the mistakes.

Garth's Comparison and Contrast

The following is excerpted from an article that Dr. Vaz published on the subject of dyslexia.

VOCABULARY
The following words are *italicized* in the excerpt: *dyslexics, misconception, misdiagnoses, abound, deficient, remediation, diligent, squirm, fidget, excessively, blurts, norms, alienates, shun, ostracism, labored, intervention,* and *contemporary.* If you don't know their meanings, look them up in a dictionary.

1   For decades, *dyslexics* have been one of the most misunderstood groups in our society. *Misconceptions* and *misdiagnoses abound,* as when dyslexics are mislabeled stupid, retarded, or lazy and placed among the mentally *deficient.* Many dyslexics have been placed in special education programs along with the slow learners. Later, after appropriate *remediation,* these same students have gone on to become educators, lawyers, and doctors. It is therefore of great importance that we be aware of the sensitive nature of dealing with these prize products of our society, our dyslexic students. We must be *diligent* in our efforts to help them in their struggle for success.

2   Such misdiagnoses are due to the lack of understanding of dyslexia and conditions such as attention-deficit/hyperactivity disorder (ADHD), childhood depressive disorder (CDD), central auditory processing deficit (CAPD), and many others that share some similarities with common symptoms of dyslexia. I will now list, in brief, some of the differences in behaviors that characterize ADHD and dyslexia in children, particularly children in the elementary school classroom.

3   A young person with ADHD cannot easily sit still, certainly a problem in the classroom. He or she often leaves his assigned seat, running around and attempting to climb on shelves, desks, and the like. When told firmly to remain in his seat, the child will try to obey but will *squirm* and *fidget* almost constantly, clearly in a state of agitation. He acts as if he is driven by a motor.

4   A child with ADHD often talks *excessively* and is unable to wait to be called on: Instead, he *blurts* out answers and responses. He seems to just butt into games and conversations, not observing social *norms* that require a give-and-take among group members. Such behavior often *alienates* other children and frustrates teachers and others who try to maintain control. Other children may *shun* the child with ADHD. This *ostracism,* in turn, results in further negative effects, such as low self-esteem and greater isolation.

PAUSE: Summarize the characteristics of ADHD.

5   In contrast, a young person with dyslexia can sit still but has trouble organizing objects, belongings, and letters. She may mix up sounds,

saying, for example, "plain" for "plan" or "seal" for "soul." She may have a stutter, furthering the frustration and embarrassment she already feels.

6   A dyslexic child typically reads very poorly, confusing the order of letters, for example, in words such as "saw" and "was." Also, she may confuse words that have similar shapes or start and end with the same letters, as in "form" and "from" or the words cited in the last paragraph. While a dyslexic's reading is *labored,* his handwriting and spelling are usually worse. All of these symptoms of dyslexia, while quite different, often result in the same ostracism and loss of self-esteem. These problems then cause other behavior problems that are similar to those shown in children with ADHD and a number of other conditions. This explains why certain conditions are often confused. In addition, many children indeed have more than one condition. For example, over 40 percent of children with dyslexia have ADHD as well.

PAUSE: Summarize the characteristics of dyslexia.

_____

_____

7   Unfortunately, because of budgeting restrictions, dyslexics are sometimes placed among the wrong group for remediation. In order for any *intervention* to succeed, it must be tailored specifically for the dyslexic. There are many improved techniques now being used successfully in reading remediation that are based on the Orton-Gillingham method. Many of these can be obtained on videocassettes and CDs. Arlene Sonday and the Scottish Rite Hospital have such programs on the market, and many other good ones can be located on the Internet (for example, **http://www .interdys.org/**, **http://www.dys.org/**, **http://www.kidshealth.org**/, and **http://www.ninds.hih.gov/disorders/dyslexia**, among many others).

8   There are many successful dyslexics in our society, some *contemporary* and others in the past. Albert Einstein, Benjamin Franklin, and General George Patton are a few who have made history. Athletes Bruce Jenner and Nolan Ryan and entertainers Whoopi Goldberg and Cher are among our contemporaries. Identifying with the successful dyslexic offers some hope to parents and children alike. The book *Succeeding with LD* is a collection of stories of successful dyslexics. The book was authored by Jill Lauren and published by Free Spirit Publishers. Each of these stories could make a book by itself but is short enough for the dyslexic to enjoy reading.

1. What two **subjects** are compared? _____

2. Does this piece of writing use **point-to-point** or **whole-to-whole organization**? _____

3. Circle the **transition** that lets you know that the writer is moving from one subject to the next.

4. Underline two of the ways in which dyslexia and ADHD behaviors differ.

5. Does the essay have the **four basics of good comparison and contrast**? Be ready to explain your answer.

Comparison and Contrast in Everyday Life

VOCABULARY
The following words are *italicized* in the excerpt: *controversial, preferences, dictated,* and *bandwidth.* If you don't know their meanings, look them up in a dictionary.

FACEBOOK OR MYSPACE?

Mario Mighlietti

1   Facebook and MySpace are both popular social networking sites used by millions of people around the world. They both connect people with other people, and they both offer a variety of interest groups and ways to meet others with interests like your own. While on the surface the two sites are similar, a *controversial* recent research report indicates that they attract very different kinds of users.

PAUSE: Do you expect a comparison or a contrast?

_____

2   Danah Boyd, a researcher at Berkeley, analyzed many profiles of both Facebook and MySpace users from all over the United States, and she has interviewed hundreds of users (Boyd 2007). What she has concluded is that, surprisingly, user *preferences* are defined more by social class than by any other factor.

PAUSE: What do you expect the next paragraph to be about?

_____

3   Boyd found that the "good" kids go to Facebook, possibly because it was first started as a college student networking site and is still used by large numbers of college students as a way to meet other college students. Boyd characterizes the typical Facebook user as, "the goodie two shoes, jocks, athletes, . . . the kids who come from families

who emphasize education and going to college. . . . They are in honors classes, looking forward to the prom, and live in a world *dictated* by after-school activities" (Boyd 2007).

4 In contrast, Boyd describes the more typical profile of a MySpace user in the following terms: "MySpace is still home for Latino/Hispanic teens, immigrant teens, 'burnouts,' 'alternative kids,' 'art fags,' punks, Goths, gangstas, queer kids. These are the kids whose parents didn't go to college, who are expected to get a job when they finish high school. These are the teens who plan to go into the military after high school" (Boyd 2007).

PAUSE: Do you agree with Boyd's findings?

_____

_____

PAUSE: Why ban MySpace and not Facebook?

_____

_____

5 Apparently, the military also believes that Facebook and MySpace are very different sites with different purposes and users. In 2007, the military banned soldiers from using MySpace and other networking sites, while saying nothing about Facebook. The reasons given were national security and amount of *bandwidth* available (McMichael 2007).

6 It seems that both Boyd and military commanders consider Facebook and MySpace to be fundamentally different. I disagree. Many people I know belong to both and do the same kinds of things on both. My friends agree that there is very little difference. When I read about what Boyd says and about the military ban, I wonder what information these people have that I don't. More than surprised, I find myself insulted. Their conclusions seem to be just another example of older people making a big thing out of what younger people are doing because they don't really understand.

Works Cited

Boyd, Danah. "Viewing American Class Divisions through Facebook and MySpace." Weblog post. *Apophenia Blog Essay* 24 June 2007. 5 Jan. 2008 <http://www.danah.org/papers/essays/ClassDivisions.html>.

McMichael, William H. "YouTube, MySpace Banned on DoD Computers." *Army Times* 15 May 2007. 6 Jan. 2008 <http://www.armytimes.com/news/2007/05/military_websitesblocked_070514>.

1. Double-underline the **thesis statement**.

2. What two **subjects** are contrasted? _____

3. Circle the **transition** that the writer uses to move from one subject to the next.

4. Does the essay have the **four basics of good comparison and contrast**? Be ready to explain your answer.

5. From what you know of Facebook and MySpace, do you agree with Boyd's findings?

Critical Reading and Writing: Key College Skills

1. **Summary.** Briefly summarize each of the three selections, including the subjects being compared and contrasted in each.

2. **Analysis.** Review the three selections. Do they use point-by-point

   or whole-to-whole organization? _____

   Try changing the organization to the one that was not used in the original. Does it work as well?

3. **Synthesis.** Review "When the Regulation of Eating Behavior Fails: Anorexia and Bulimia" (p. 257) and "Facebook or MySpace?" (p. 263). Both relate to people's images of themselves. Discuss how physical appearance plays a role in social networking, drawing from each of the selections and your own experience.

4. **Evaluation.** Using the **four basics of good comparison and contrast** as a measure, which of the selections in this chapter is the best example of a comparison or contrast? Give specific examples to support your choice. Is your choice different from the one you find most interesting? If so, why?

Write a Comparison and Contrast Essay

In this section, you will write your own comparison and contrast essay based on *one* of the following assignments. Before you begin to write, review the four basics of good comparison and contrast on page 252. Also, read the Tips for Tackling Comparison and Contrast in the box that follows.

■ Use the diagram on page 256 to help you organize.

TIPS FOR TACKLING COMPARISON AND CONTRAST

1. Read the assignment carefully, highlighting key words. An assignment that uses comparison and contrast might actually use the words *compare* or *contrast,* but it might also use words such as *how are _____ and _____ similar (or different)?, discuss the similarities or differences of _____,* or *which _____ is more _____ and why?*

2. Choose the two or more subjects that you need to compare or contrast.

3. List the points of comparison and contrast.

4. Decide whether to use point-by-point or whole-to-whole organization.

  ASSIGNMENT 1   WRITING ABOUT COLLEGE, WORK, AND EVERYDAY LIFE . . . .

Write a comparison and contrast essay on *one* of the following topics or on a topic of your own choice.

COLLEGE

- Two professors
- Two courses you are taking or have taken
- Being an older, returning student versus coming right from high school

WORK

- Two jobs you have had
- Two companies you have worked for
- A job and a career

EVERYDAY LIFE

- Two places you have lived
- Good customer service and bad customer service
- Two of your friends or relatives

ASSIGNMENT 2   WRITING ABOUT AN IMAGE . . . .

The U.S. Army's official recruitment site (**goarmy.com**) offers download-able, interactive games that are based on warfare, including America's Army Game (**goarmy.com/aarmy**). In a short essay, consider the ways that battle is like and unlike a video game. In your conclusion, give your opinion on whether the U.S. Army's comparison between soldiers and gamers makes sense.

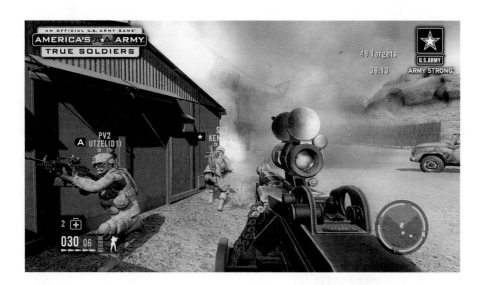

 ASSIGNMENT 3   WRITING TO SOLVE A PROBLEM . . . .

THE PROBLEM: You need a new DVD recorder and decide to look at *Consumer Reports*'s comparison of various models before buying one. You aren't sure if you want a DVD-only model or a combination DVD and VCR model.

THE ASSIGNMENT: Working either on your own or with a small group, write a comparison and contrast essay about three DVD recorders. Use the *Consumer Reports* chart below to write the essay, and, if possible, do some follow-up research online. Keep a list of any Web sites that you use. Try sites that specialize in reviews of technology, like CNET (**http://reviews.cnet.com**), or do a Google search using "ratings DVD players" as key words. Carefully review any site that you use for bias: Beware of advertisements or advertisement-supported sites. In your concluding paragraph, indicate which model you would purchase and why.

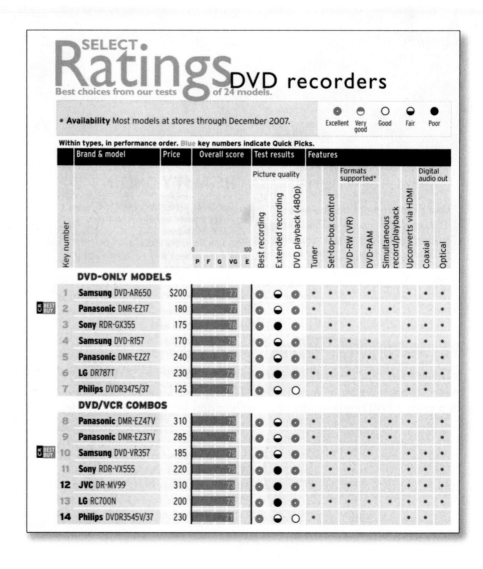

ASSIGNMENT 4   WRITING ABOUT READINGS . . . .

Read "The Ugly Truth about Beauty" by Dave Barry on page 817 and "Struggling for Perfection" by Amy L. Beck on page 829. Next, review the excerpt "When the Regulation of Eating Behavior Fails: Anorexia and Bulimia" by Don H. Hockenbury and Sandra Hockenbury on page 257. Write a brief paper on *one* of the following:

- Although their tones are very different, Barry, Beck, and the Hockenburys make a similar point about women's images of themselves. Explain that point, bringing in references from the three readings. In your concluding paragraph, indicate which of the three makes the point most effectively to you and why.

- Analyze why people are influenced by advertising images and why they hold unrealistic expectations for themselves. To do this, draw on the three sources and on experiences you or people you know have had.

Follow the steps in the Writing Guide below to help you prewrite, draft, revise, and edit your comparison and contrast essay. Check off each step as you complete it.

WRITING GUIDE: COMPARISON AND CONTRAST	
STEPS IN COMPARISON AND CONTRAST	**HOW TO DO THE STEPS**
Focus.	☐ Think about what you want to compare and contrast and the main point you want to make about your subjects. Review the four basics of good comparison and contrast on page 252.
Prewrite to explore your topic. See Chapter 4 for more on prewriting.	☐ Decide on your purpose for the comparison or contrast: to help readers understand the two subjects or to help them make a decision. ☐ Make a side-by-side list of possible parallel points of comparison or contrast between your two subjects.
Write a thesis statement. A thesis statement in comparison and contrast usually presents the central subjects and indicates whether the writer will show similarities, differences, or both. See diagrams on the following page.	☐ Write a thesis statement that includes your subjects and indicates whether you will discuss similarities or differences.

continued

STEPS IN COMPARISON AND CONTRAST	HOW TO DO THE STEPS
Write a thesis statement (cont.). Subject 1/Subject 2 + Indication of similarity/ difference = Thesis Facebook and MySpace appeal to different kinds of people. See Chapter 5 for more on writing a thesis statement.	
Support your thesis statement. The major support for comparison and contrast consists of points of comparison or points of contrast. See Chapter 6 for more on supporting a thesis statement.	☐ Review the list of possible points of comparison and contrast from your prewriting. ☐ Select from your list the points of comparison and contrast that your readers will understand and that will serve your purpose. ☐ Add supporting details and examples to explain the points of comparison.
Make a plan. See Chapter 7 for more on planning.	☐ Decide whether you will use a point-by-point or whole-to-whole organization. ☐ Make a plan or outline that follows the point-by-point or whole-to-whole structure and that organizes support points most effectively (using time order, space order, or order of importance). (See the diagram on page 256.)
Write a draft. See Chapter 8 for more on drafting.	☐ Write an introduction that includes your thesis statement. See if you can use one of the introductory techniques in Chapter 8. ☐ Write topic sentences either for each of the subjects or for each point of comparison and contrast. ☐ Write body paragraphs that give detailed examples to support your topic sentence. ☐ Write a concluding paragraph that makes an observation about the subjects based on the points you have made in your essay. ☐ Title your essay.

STEPS IN COMPARISON AND CONTRAST	HOW TO DO THE STEPS
Revise your draft. See Chapter 9 for more on revising a draft.	☐ Ask another person to read and comment on your draft. ☐ See if your thesis statement could be clearer or more interesting to your readers. ☐ Reread the body of your essay to make sure the points of comparison and contrast are parallel and support your thesis. Add other examples and details that would further show the similarities and differences between your subjects. ☐ Add transitions to connect your ideas. ☐ Reread your introduction, and make changes if it is dull or weak. ☐ Reread your conclusion to make sure it reinforces your main point. ☐ Make at least five changes to your draft to improve unity, support, or coherence (see pp. 127–40). ☐ Check to make sure the draft follows the four basics of good comparison and contrast.
Edit your draft. See Parts Four through Seven for more on editing.	☐ Use the spell checker and grammar checker on your computer, but also reread your essay carefully to catch any errors. ☐ Look for errors in grammar, spelling, and punctuation. In comparison and contrast, some students write fragments and run-ons and make errors in subject-verb agreement. Focus first on these errors, and then edit for verb errors and other areas where you often make mistakes. ☐ Ask yourself: Is this the best I can do?

You Know This

You already use cause and effect to understand things.

- You understand that washing your red shirt in hot water caused white items to turn pink.
- You understand ads that show causes and effects.

Number of ads aired for "junk food" during four hours of Saturday morning cartoons:

202

Percentage of American children ages 6 to 11 who are seriously overweight:

17%

■ **IDEA JOURNAL**
Write about a time when you should have thought before you spoke or acted.

17

Cause and Effect

Writing That Explains Reasons or Results

Understand What Cause and Effect Are

A **cause** is what makes an event happen. An **effect** is what happens as a result of an event.

> ■■ **FOUR BASICS OF GOOD CAUSE AND EFFECT**
> 1. The main point reflects the writer's purpose—to explain causes, effects, or both.
> 2. If the purpose is to explain causes, it presents concrete causes.
> 3. If the purpose is to explain effects, it presents real effects.
> 4. It gives readers clear and detailed examples or explanations of the causes and effects.

In the following paragraph, each number corresponds to one of the four basics of good cause and effect.

1 Little doubt remains that global warming is a threat to our world, but not everyone understands why it is happening and what the effects really are. Many experts believe that this warming trend is largely the result of **2** greenhouse gases, including **4** carbon dioxide emissions, mainly from cars, and pollutants from industrial processes. **2** Deforestation is another

272

significant cause. To date, the United States has refused to ratify the Kyoto Protocol, a worldwide agreement that would limit emissions of the gases that cause global warming. Ironically, if current warming trends continue, the United States is most at risk for **1** negative consequences, although the entire world will be affected. Scientists predict that **3** sea levels will rise dangerously and **4** flood coastal areas. There will also be **3** more droughts and changes in precipitation patterns, **4** such as the rapid sequence of hurricanes in the fall of 2004. In addition and possibly most destructive is the **3** threat to plant and animal life and, consequently, to public health.

Analyzing causes and effects goes beyond asking "What happened?" to also ask "Why?" and "How?"

SITUATION: On a hot summer day, you leave a rented video on the front seat of your car while you are at work. When you come out of work, you find that the video has melted.

The **cause** of the video's melting was **leaving it in a hot car all day**. The **effect** of leaving the video in a hot car all day was that **it melted**.

Jim Rice of Quinsigamond Community College helps his students visualize the cause and effect relationship by suggesting that they think of three linked rings:

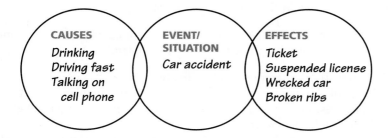

Many situations require you to determine causes or effects.

COLLEGE	In an information technology course, you must discuss the effects of a virus on a local-area computer network.
WORK	You analyze the likely effects of laying off 15 percent of your department's employees.
EVERYDAY LIFE	You try to figure out what is causing your computer to freeze.

Main Point in Cause and Effect

The **main point** in a cause and effect essay should reflect your **purpose**. For example, if you are writing about why a certain event in history happened, your main point would be to explain the causes. If you are writing about what happened as a result of that event, your main point would be to explain the effects. Consider the following thesis from an essay on drunk driving:

Topic + cause + effect = | Thesis |

| Drunk driving destroys thousands of lives every year. |

The main point of the essay is to discuss the effects of drunk driving—thousands of destroyed lives. The body of the essay will give examples.

Sometimes a thesis statement for a cause and effect essay will include both what caused the topic and what resulted from the topic. The topic sentence in the paragraph on page 272 follows this pattern:

Topic + cause + effect = | Thesis |

| Little doubt remains that global warming is a threat to our world, but not everyone understands why it is happening and what the effects are. |

Sometimes the writer does not directly indicate causes or effects in the thesis statement, as in the following example:

> Until local police departments enforce restraining orders, women and children will continue to be the victims of violence.

■ For online exercises on main point and support, visit *Exercise Central* at **bedfordstmartins .com/realessays**. Also visit **bedfordstmartins .com/rewritingbasics**.

Although the writer does not indicate a specific cause or effect, the main point of the essay is clear—to discuss how unenforced restraining orders have resulted in violence. The body of the essay will likely give examples of such situations.

As you begin to write cause and effect essays, you might find it helpful to include both the topic and an indicator of cause or effect in your thesis statement.

Support in Cause and Effect

In a cause and effect essay, **support** consists of explanations of causes and effects, and it demonstrates the main point stated in your thesis. Take, for example, this thesis statement:

> Irresponsible behavior caused my car accident.

The writer supported this thesis by presenting the causes with details that explain them.

CAUSE	Driving too fast	CAUSE	Talking on my cell phone

DETAILS:

Rainy and slippery
Going too fast to control car
Couldn't stop

DETAILS:

Not paying close attention
Hit a curve while laughing
Didn't react fast enough

CAUSE	Drinking

DETAILS:

Not focused
Slowed reaction time

When you are writing about causes, be careful that you don't say something caused an event or situation just because it happened beforehand. For example, many of us have gotten sick after a meal and assumed that the food caused the sickness, only to find out that we'd been coming down with the flu even before the meal.

When you are writing about effects, do not confuse something that happened after something else with the effect. To return to the previous example, just as the meal didn't cause the illness, the illness was not the effect of the meal.

Organization in Cause and Effect

Cause and effect essays are organized in different ways depending on their purpose.

MAIN POINT	PURPOSE	ORGANIZATION
Global warming is a serious threat to life as we know it.	To explain the effects of global warming	Order of importance (saving the most serious effect for last)
Global warming will flood many coastal states.	To describe how the U.S. map eventually might look	Space order
Over the next century, the effects of global warming will be dramatic.	To describe the effects of global warming over the next 100 years	Time order

CAUSE AND EFFECT AT A GLANCE

Thesis statement
Indicates causes, effects, or both

↓

Cause 1 or effect 1
Detailed explanation or example of the first cause or effect

↓

Cause 2 or effect 2
Detailed explanation or example of the second cause or effect

↓

Cause 3 or effect 3
Detailed explanation or example of the third cause or effect

↓

Conclusion
Reminds readers of your main point and makes an observation about it based on what you have written

A typical plan for a cause and effect essay is on the left.

As you write your essay, add transitions to show how each cause or effect relates to your main point. Here are some common transitions that are used in cause and effect writing.

Common Transitions in Cause and Effect

one cause, reason, effect, result	as a result
also	because
another	thus
first, second, third, and so on	

Read and Analyze Cause and Effect

Before writing your own cause and effect essay, read the following three examples—from college, the workplace, and everyday life—and answer the questions that accompany them.

Cause and Effect in College

The following is an excerpt from a college textbook.

VOCABULARY
The following words are *italicized* in the excerpt: *developmental, thrive, generativity, maturity, anthropologists, cohort, contemporary, ambivalence, extent, equity,* and *adept.* If you don't know their meanings, look them up in a dictionary.

WHAT MAKES MARRIAGES WORK?

PAUSE: Do you have thoughts about what makes a successful marriage or partnership?

1   From a *developmental* perspective, marriage is a useful institution: Children generally *thrive* when two parents are directly committed to their well-being, and adults thrive if one other person satisfies their need for intimacy and for *generativity.* Yet, clearly, not all marriages accomplish these goals. Why do some marriages work well, while others do not?

2   One developmental factor that influences the success of a marriage is the *maturity* of the partners. In general, the younger the bride and

groom, the less likely their marriage is to succeed (Amato, Johnson, Booth, & Rogers, 2003). That may be because, as Erikson pointed out, intimacy is hard to establish until identity is secure. Thus, in a series of studies, college students who were less advanced on Erikson's identity and intimacy stages tended to define love in terms of passion, not intimacy or commitment—butterflies and excitement, not openness, trust, and loyalty (Aron & Westbay, 1996).

PAUSE: What does *intimacy* mean here?

3   A second influence on marital success is the degree of similarity between husband and wife. *Anthropologists* distinguish between **homogamy**, or marriage within the same tribe or ethnic group, and **heterogamy**, or marriage outside the group. Traditionally, homogamy meant marriage between people of the same *cohort*, religion, socioeconomic status, ethnicity, and education. For *contemporary* marriages, homogamy and heterogamy refer to similarity [and difference, respectively] in interests, attitudes, and goals (Cramer, 1998).

PAUSE: What are homogamy and heterogamy?

4   One study of 168 young couples found that **social homogamy**, defined as similarity in leisure interests and role preferences, is particularly important to marital success (Houts, Robins, & Huston, 1996). For instance, if both spouses enjoyed (or hated) picnicking, dancing, swimming, going to the movies, listening to music, eating out, or entertaining friends, the partners tended to be more "in love" and more committed to the relationship. Similarly, if the two agreed on who should make meals, pay bills, shop for groceries, and so on, then *ambivalence* and conflict were reduced.

PAUSE: Why is social homogamy important?

LANGUAGE NOTE
Eating out means eating at a restaurant.

5   A third factor affecting the success of a marriage is **marital equity**, the *extent* to which the two partners perceive a rough equality in the partnership. In many modern marriages, the *equity* that is sought is in shared contributions. Both partners expect equality and sensitivity to their needs regarding dependence, sexual desire, shared confidences, and so on, and happier marriages are those in which both partners are *adept* at emotional perception and expression (Fitness, 2001). What matters most is the perception of fairness, not absolute equality.

PAUSE: What is marital (or relationship) equity?

References

Amato, P. R., Johnson, D. R., Booth, A., & Rogers, S. J. (2003). Continuity and change in marital quality between 1980 and 2000. *Journal of Marriage and Family, 65,* 1–22.

Aron, A., & Westbay, L. (1996). Dimensions of the prototype of love. *Journal of Personality and Social Relationships, 70,* 535–51.

Cramer, D. (1998). *Close relationships: The study of love and friendship.* New York: Oxford University Press.

Fitness, J. (2001). Intimate relationships. In J. Ciarrochi, J. R. Forgas, & J. D. Mayer (Eds.), *Emotional intelligence in everyday life: A scientific inquiry* (pp. 98–112). Philadelphia: Psychology Press.

Houts, R. M., Robins, E., & Huston, T. L. (1996). Compatibility and the development of premarital relationships. *Journal of Marriage and the Family, 58,* 7–20.

—From Kathleen Stassen Berger, *The Developing Person through the Life Span,* 6th ed. (New York: Worth, 2005)

■ For a list of the four basics of good cause and effect, see page 272.

1. Double-underline the **thesis statement** (the sentence indicating whether the piece will discuss causes or effects).

2. Put a check mark (✔) by each **cause** or factor affecting marital success.

3. Why do you think certain words are in bold type? _____

_____

_____

■ The final question after each reading in this section makes a good essay topic.

4. Circle the **transitions**.

5. Does the piece have the **four basics of good cause and effect**? Be ready to explain your answer.

6. What do you think are the most important factors for a marriage or other committed relationship?

Cause and Effect at Work

The following profile shows how an attorney, consultant, and city councilor uses cause and effect.

Profile of Success

Jolanda Jones

Attorney, Houston City Councilor, and Consultant

BACKGROUND: I grew up in a housing project in Houston, Texas, where I lost several relatives to street violence. I always did well in school, however, as a student and an athlete. I eventually graduated magna cum laude from the University of Houston, where I was a three-time NCAA heptathlon champion, and afterwards enrolled in law school. In 1996, I qualified for the U.S. Olympic Team trials, and I won the high jump, beating Jackie Joyner-Kersee, who went on to win the gold medal. However, my brother was murdered at about this time, and for a variety of reasons, I did not do well in the rest of the trials. In 2000, I received the NAACP's Award for Legal Excellence for dedication to community service. I started my own consulting business, along with a law practice, and in 2007, I won a highly contested seat on the Houston City Council. Along the way, I was a contestant in season 10 of *Survivor*.

COLLEGES/DEGREES: B.A., University of Houston; J.D.L., University of Houston, Bates School of Law

EMPLOYER: Self

WRITING AT WORK: Legal briefs, proposals, letters, Web site content, speeches, presentations

HOW JOLANDA USES CAUSE AND EFFECT: As part of my community service and consulting, I speak to inner-city youth. When I address students, I emphasize the importance of understanding that for every action they take, there is a consequence they should consider. During my election campaign, I emphasized to voters how a vote for me would result in many changes in the city of Houston.

The following is a talk that Jolanda Jones gives to students.

VOCABULARY
The following words are *italicized* in the essay: *consequences, abusive, coward, aspirations, humiliated,* and *capable.* If you don't know their meanings, look them up in a dictionary.

1   Some of the worst life situations I've seen were caused simply by people failing to consider the effects of their actions. Each of you in this room must learn for yourselves that every single decision you make has *consequences.* It is important that you think about the decisions you make **before** you make them because if you don't, then you will end up somewhere you didn't plan for.

PAUSE: What do you expect the next paragraph to be about?

_____

_____

2   My best decisions are the ones I make when I think my grandmother might find out about them. If I would be proud for her to know the decision I've made, then it's probably a good decision. If I have to sneak or would be ashamed for her to know my decision, then it is probably a bad decision. In any case, here are some examples of the thought process in good decision making. They show what happens when you don't consider consequences.

LANGUAGE NOTE *Break up with* means to end the relationship. *Prude* means too proper.

3   Some of you girls might be getting pressured by your boyfriends to have sex. What should you think about? Well, you're probably wondering what he'll say if you don't sleep with him. Will he break up with you or call you "prude"? Well, don't let him define you. What if you get pregnant? What if you get a sexually transmitted disease? What if you get AIDS? What if you break up after you have sex with him? Will he tell everyone how good you were in bed? Will everyone know your business?

4   Single parenthood is hard. I know from personal experience. I had graduated from college, was working as a minority recruiter and admissions counselor, and was training for the Olympics. I also planned to go to law school at Stanford. Then, I got pregnant without planning for it. Suddenly, I was expecting a child with a man who was both *abusive* and unsupportive. I was not married. I was disappointed in myself. I was ashamed of the shame I brought on my grandmother. I was a *coward*. I fled the United States and hid my pregnancy in Spain. I absolutely love my son, but I gave up my Olympic *aspirations* and Stanford Law School.

LANGUAGE NOTE A *crackhead* is a person who is addicted to crack cocaine. *On welfare* means getting financial assistance from the government.

5   Some of you might be thinking about using drugs. Think long and hard. I have crackheads in my family whose lives have been destroyed. Some are homeless. Some are dying of AIDS. My aunt was murdered in a drug house. My brother was murdered buying marijuana. I have an alcoholic cousin who does not take care of her children, and she is on welfare. People who do drugs come to love drugs more than they love anyone or anything else. Then, the drugs control you. You lose control of your life.

6   What about crime—just little stuff, like shoplifting that little pair of earrings at the neighborhood Target? When I was sixteen, I'd worked to earn money to buy stuff I wanted. I wanted a pair of jeans. Instead, my mother took my check for herself. I still thought I was entitled to the jeans, so I went to Target and took a pair. I got caught. I was arrested, handcuffed, put in the back of a patrol car, and detained. I ducked my head down in the back of the patrol car. I just knew the whole world was looking at me. I was *humiliated.* I should have thought about the consequences. It wasn't right to steal from Target even if my mother took my check. You best believe I've thought about that ever since that date because I've never shoplifted again. I even told my son about it. I don't want him to make the same mistake that I did.

7   You have choices in life, and it's up to you to make the decisions that will most positively benefit your life. We are all *capable* of thinking through stuff and making the right decision. The question is: Are you going to do it, or are you going to just take the easy road through life? My grandmother said, "If you make a bad decision, learn from it and move on; that way it's not your fault. If, however, you make the same mistake twice, you're stupid and it is your fault." I don't know about you, but I'm not stupid.

LANGUAGE NOTE
Take the easy road means not making hard choices.

8   I've made good and bad decisions in my life. Thankfully, I've made more good ones than bad. I hope to continue to make good decisions by considering consequences and learning from my mistakes. I hope that's your philosophy too.

1. What grade level of students do you think Jolanda is addressing? _____

_____

2. What is Jolanda's **purpose**? _____

_____

3. Double-underline the **thesis statement** (the sentence indicating whether the piece will discuss causes or effects).

4. Underline each **topic sentence**.

5. Use ring diagrams to show one of the situations Jolanda presents, along with the causes or effects.

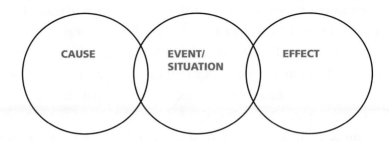

6. Double-underline the sentence in the concluding paragraph that restates Jolanda's <u>**main point**</u>.

7. Write about a time when you didn't consider the negative consequences of an action.

Cause and Effect in Everyday Life

The following example of cause and effect writing appeared in a newspaper article.

VOCABULARY

The following words are *italicized* in the essay: *peer pressure, conserve, consumption, herd, intensifying, activists, oblivion, productive, insights, quirks, psyche, immobilize, irreplaceable, heritage, symbolically, compliance, manipulate, coincidentally,* and *scrupulous.* If you don't know their meanings, look them up in a dictionary.

IN PRAISE OF PEER PRESSURE

Christopher Shea

1   *Peer pressure* gets bad press, but in some cases more of it might make the world a better place. In California, psychologists recently found that they could get people to *conserve* electricity with a simple notice, delivered to their doorstep, telling them how their *consumption* compared with the neighborhood average. In the weeks that followed, homeowners who were consuming more electricity than their neighbors cut back—presumably because they were embarrassed to be out of step with the *herd*.

2   The research, reported in *Psychological Science,* reflects growing interest in what's known as "social-norms marketing"—attempting to change behavior by telling people what their peers do. The basic concept is about two decades old, but psychologists have been *intensifying* efforts to find more effective ways of using it. And now, with a growing recognition of the limits of browbeating, a wide range of groups—from climate-change *activists* to college deans trying to keep students from drinking themselves to *oblivion*—have been making peer pressure their ally.

PAUSE: What is social-norms marketing?

3   "The norm is like a magnet," says Robert Cialdini, a professor at Arizona State University who is an author of the new study. "What's appropriate to do, in most people's minds, is what other people like them do."

4   The social-norms approach is part of a general movement to make *productive* use of *insights* into the *quirks* of the human *psyche.* For example, psychologists have found that presenting people with a wide range of choices (about almost anything) can frustrate and *immobilize* them, so that they end up making no choice at all or a bad choice. Supermarket managers and policy experts designing health plans have taken note.

PAUSE: Why would supermarket managers want to think about this?

5   Cialdini's work tends to focus on the environment. In a paper from 2003, he identified a problem with signs in the Petrified Forest National Park, in Arizona, intended to discourage the theft of ancient, *irreplaceable* wood. The signs sternly warned that America's "*heritage*" was being "vandalized" by "theft losses of petrified wood of 14 tons a year."

6   That sent the message that pocketing souvenirs was the norm for tourists, Cialdini argues. In an on-site experiment, he and his coauthors demonstrated that by making use of new signs that stressed how few people removed items from the park and that by *symbolically* isolating those who do (on the sign, thieving stick figures had red slashes through them), the park could cut vandalism substantially.

7   In another experiment, Cialdini has shown that hotels will have more success encouraging their clients to reuse towels if they alter the wording of their appeals. "Join your fellow guests in helping to save the

environment: A majority of our guests use their towels more than once" works better than any other approach.

PAUSE: Can you think of an example of a positive effect of peer pressure?

8   In Minnesota, a study by the Department of Revenue found that informing taxpayers that most people don't cheat on their taxes improved tax *compliance* more than stressing the link between taxes and popular public programs.

9   The field is still in flux: The effects of peer pressure remain hard to measure and hard to *manipulate*—yet the tug of the herd mindset is everywhere. *Coincidentally,* I recently came across a survey that found that 80 percent of adult males in the United States have six or fewer drinks in a week. I was taken aback, assuming the average was higher. I skipped wine with dinner a few times that week.

PAUSE: What is he going to think about?

10   Later that same week, I read in an economics journal that freelance businessmen—I'm a freelancer—report only about 60 percent of their income, according to IRS estimates. Yet I'm *scrupulous* to the penny. Do I want to remain abnormal? Does anyone? I filed for an extension, so I've got some time to think about it.

—From the *Boston Globe*, 29 April 2007: E4–5

1. Double-underline the **thesis statement**.

2. Underline two examples of the positive **effect** of peer pressure.

3. In paragraphs 5–7, what positive effects of peer pressure are desired?

_____

4. Does the essay have the **four basics of good cause and effect**? Be ready to explain your answer.

5. Give some other examples of the effects of peer pressure, either negative or positive.

Critical Reading and Writing: Key College Skills

1. **Summary.** Briefly summarize each of the three selections, including the subject of each and examples of causes and effects.

2. **Analysis.** Review the three selections, focusing on the thesis statements and topic sentences in each. Which of the three has the clearest structure in the body paragraphs? Why?

3. **Synthesis.** Discuss or write about the following: Each essay mentions the importance or influence of a group and being similar or different than the group. What does each essay say about how a group can influence or affect an individual? How does that fit in with your own experiences?

4. **Evaluation.** Using the **four basics of good cause and effect** as a measure, which of the three selections do you think is the best example of a cause and effect essay? Give specific examples to support your choice. Is your choice different from the one you like the best? If so, why?

Write a Cause and Effect Essay

In this section, you will write your own cause and effect essay based on *one* of the following assignments. Before you begin to write, review the four basics of good cause and effect on page 272 and the diagram on page 276. Also, read the Tips for Tackling Cause and Effect in the box that follows.

TIPS FOR TACKLING CAUSE AND EFFECT

1. Read the assignment carefully, highlighting the key words. The assignment calling for cause and effect may use words such as *identify and discuss the cause (or effects) of X, what led to or were the effects of X?*, or *what resulted from or were the effects of X?*

2. Think of what actually caused the event to occur or what happened as a direct result of it.

3. List specific examples of causes, effects, or both. Use the ring diagram to help you.

4. Think about *how* something caused or resulted from something else, and explain it to your reader.

ASSIGNMENT 1 WRITING ABOUT COLLEGE, WORK, AND EVERYDAY LIFE . . . .

Write a cause and effect essay on *one* of the following topics or on a topic of your own choice.

■ Use the diagram on page 276 to help you organize.

COLLEGE

- The immediate effects of being in college or the desired long-term effects of going to college
- Causes of a legitimate absence that resulted in your missing a test (directed to your professor)
- From another course you are taking, the causes or effects of something that was discussed in the course or the textbook

WORK

- Causes of low employee morale
- Causes, effects, or both of a situation at work
- Effects of juggling work, school, and family

EVERYDAY LIFE

- Causes of an argument with a friend or a member of your family
- A good decision or a bad one
- Effects of sleep deprivation (look for articles or Web sites)

■ **ASSIGNMENT 2**   **WRITING ABOUT AN IMAGE** . . . .

This photograph was taken at a summer camp for overweight youth. Write a cause and effect essay about either the causes or effects of childhood obesity.

ASSIGNMENT 3   WRITING TO SOLVE A PROBLEM . . . .

THE PROBLEM: Your child has been diagnosed with attention-deficit/hyperactivity disorder (ADHD), and the doctor has recommended that he take the drug Ritalin. The doctor assures you that Ritalin is very commonly prescribed for children with ADHD, but you are uncomfortable giving your child a drug that you know little about.

THE ASSIGNMENT: Working on your own or with a small group, write a paper that discusses the effects of Ritalin on children with ADHD. In your conclusion, indicate whether you will put your child on Ritalin or not, based on what you now know.

RESOURCES: Review the chart on pages 868–69 for general advice on problem solving. Also, type *effects of Ritalin on children with ADHD* into a search engine and view some of the Web sites on the subject. Make sure that the Web sites you consult are sponsored by medical organizations rather than drug companies. List any Web sites you use.

 ASSIGNMENT 4   WRITING ABOUT READINGS . . . .

Society's (or a group's) standards of who and what are good or bad are reflected in television, magazines, music, and virtually every other type of media. Media images affect us all, whether or not we are aware of it, and several of the readings in this book deal with how people can be harmed by them. Choose one of the reading pairs below, and write an essay on the topic that follows it.

1. Amy L. Beck's "Struggling for Perfection" on page 829 and Don H. Hockenbury and Sandra Hockenbury's "When the Regulation of Eating Behavior Fails: Anorexia and Bulimia" on page 257

   • Discuss the issue that Beck raises and how the Hockenburys' piece on anorexia and bulimia supports her point. Refer to both readings, and bring in your own experiences with media portrayals as well, including how you or people you know have been affected.

2. Amy L. Beck's "Struggling for Perfection" on page 829 and Tiffany Shale's "Lasting Lessons in *The Bluest Eye*" on page 340

   • Discuss how both Pecola Breedlove and women today are affected by standards of beauty. What do they hope to gain? Refer specifically to both selections in your response. How have you been affected by society's standards of physical perfection?

3. Amy L. Beck's "Struggling for Perfection" on page 829 and Dave Barry's "The Ugly Truth about Beauty" on page 817

   • Discuss the authors' different approaches to a similar topic. Analyze the differences, and discuss which piece is more effective to you and why.

4. Amy L. Beck's "Struggling for Perfection" on page 829 and Brent Staples's "Just Walk on By: Black Men and Public Space" on page 834

   • How have the two different groups the authors portray been negatively affected by portrayals in the media? Bring in references from each reading along with your experiences of how the media can cause people to have incorrect, and sometimes dangerous, perceptions of themselves and others.

Follow the steps in the Writing Guide below to help you prewrite, draft, revise, and edit your cause and effect essay. Check off each step as you complete it.

WRITING GUIDE: CAUSE AND EFFECT

STEPS IN CAUSE AND EFFECT	HOW TO DO THE STEPS
Focus.	☐ Think about an event or situation that matters to you and whether you want to describe its causes, its effects, or both. Review the four basics of good cause and effect on page 272.
Prewrite to explore your topic. See Chapter 4 for more on prewriting.	☐ State what your purpose for writing is—to explain the causes, effects, or both. ☐ Use the ring diagram or clustering to get ideas about the causes or effects of your topic.
Write a thesis statement. The thesis statement in a cause and effect essay often includes the topic and an indicator of whether you will be discussing causes, effects, or both. Topic + indication of cause/ effect = ⎡Thesis⎤ ⎡A blog ruined my marriage.⎤ See Chapter 5 for more on writing a thesis statement.	☐ Write a thesis statement that includes your topic and an indicator of cause, effect, or both.

STEPS IN CAUSE AND EFFECT	HOW TO DO THE STEPS
Support your thesis statement. The major support for a cause and effect essay consists of the explanations of the causes or effects. See Chapter 6 for more on supporting a thesis statement.	☐ List the most important causes and effects of the event or situation mentioned in your thesis. ☐ For each cause or effect, give an example and details about how it caused or resulted from the event or situation. ☐ Add other causes or effects that you think of, and delete any that are weak or won't make sense to your readers.
Make a plan. See Chapter 7 for more on planning.	☐ Make a plan or an outline that presents your causes or effects according to order of importance or some other logical order. (See the diagram on p. 276.)
Write a draft. See Chapter 8 for more on drafting.	☐ Write an introduction that includes your thesis statement. See if you can use one of the introductory techniques in Chapter 8. ☐ Write topic sentences for each paragraph, and give detailed examples or explanations of the cause or effect that you are presenting in that paragraph. ☐ Write a concluding paragraph that makes an observation about the topic and its causes or effects, based on the points you have made in your essay. ☐ Title your essay.
Revise your draft. See Chapter 9 for more on revising a draft.	☐ Ask another person to read and comment on your draft. ☐ See if your thesis statement and introduction could be clearer or more interesting to your readers. ☐ Reread the body of your essay to make sure the causes or effects really have caused the topic or resulted from it. ☐ Reread your conclusion to make sure it reinforces your main point. ☐ Add transitions to connect your ideas. ☐ Make at least five changes to your draft to improve unity, support, or coherence (see pp. 127–40). ☐ Check to make sure the draft follows the four basics of good cause and effect.
Edit your draft. See Parts Four through Seven for more on editing.	☐ Use the spell checker and grammar checker on your computer, but also reread your essay carefully to catch any errors. ☐ Look for errors in grammar, spelling, and punctuation. Focus first on fragments, run-ons, subject-verb agreement, verb problems, and other areas where you often make mistakes. ☐ Ask yourself: Is this the best I can do?

You Know This

Whenever you try to convince someone to do or avoid doing something, you use argument.

- You persuade a friend to lend you some money.
- You understand the argument being made in a public-service ad.

In the United States 5,000 children die each year from unintentional gun injuries, 300 of them are younger than 10.

18

Argument

Writing That Persuades

Understand What Argument Is

Argument is writing that takes a position on an issue and offers reasons and supporting evidence to convince someone else to accept, or at least consider, that position. Argument is also used to persuade someone to take an action (or not to take an action).

■■ **FOUR BASICS OF GOOD ARGUMENT**

1. It takes a strong and definite position on an issue or advises a particular action.
2. It gives good reasons and supporting evidence to defend the position or recommended action.
3. It considers opposing views.
4. It has enthusiasm and energy from start to finish.

In the following paragraph, each number corresponds to one of the four basics of good argument.

1 The drinking age should be lowered from twenty-one to eighteen. **2** The government gives eighteen-year-olds the right to vote. If they are adult enough to vote for the people and policies that run this country, they should be mature enough to have a drink. **2** The U.S. penal system also regards eighteen-year-olds as adults. If an eighteen-year-old commits a crime and goes to trial, he or she is tried and sentenced as an adult, not as a minor. That means that if the crime is murder, an eighteen-year-old could receive the death penalty. Eighteen-year-olds are not given special treatment. Most important is the fact that at eighteen, individuals can enlist in the armed forces and go to war. The government considers them old enough to die for their country but not old enough to have a drink? This makes no sense. **3** Opponents to lowering the drinking age justify their position by saying that if the age is lowered, teenagers will start drinking even earlier. However, there is no evidence to show that legal age is a major influence on teenage drinking. Other factors involved, such as peer pressure and the availability of fake IDs, have more impact on whether teenagers drink. While the government does need to address the issue of teenage drinking, forbidding eighteen-year-olds to drink while granting them other, more important rights and responsibilities at the same age is neither consistent nor reasonable.

4 Writing is enthusiastic and energetic

Putting together a good argument is one of the most useful skills you can learn. Knowing how to argue well will equip you to defend effectively what you believe and to convince others to agree with you. We present an argument to persuade someone to give us a job, to buy something we're selling, or to give us more time to finish a task. And we argue when something important is at stake, like keeping a job or protecting our rights. To argue effectively, we need to do more than just say what we want or believe; we need to give solid reasons and evidence.

Argument is the method you use to persuade people to see things your way or at least to understand your position. Argument helps you to take action in problem situations rather than to stand by, silent and frustrated. Although knowing how to argue won't eliminate all such situations, it will help you to defend your position.

Many situations require good argument skills.

COLLEGE An exit essay from a writing course contains the following instruction: "Develop a well-balanced argument on the subject of free speech on the Internet."

WORK You present reasons why you should get a raise.

EVERYDAY LIFE You convince a large company that it has made a mistake on your bill.

Main Point in Argument

Your **main point** in an argument is the position you take on the issue you are writing about. When you are free to choose an issue, choose something you care about strongly. But even when you are assigned an issue, find something about it that you feel strongly about and take a definite position. You should approach your argument feeling committed to and enthusiastic about your position. To help you get there, consider the tips below:

Tips for Building Energy and Enthusiasm

- Imagine yourself arguing your position with someone who holds the opposite position.
- Imagine that your whole grade rests on persuading your teacher that your position is correct.
- Imagine how this issue could affect you or your family personally.
- Imagine that you are representing a large group of people who very much care about the issue and whose lives will be forever changed by it. It's up to you to win their case.

Take a few minutes to think about the issue, talk it over with a partner, or jot down ideas related to it. Once you have decided on your position and have built up some energy for it, write a thesis statement that includes the issue and your position on it.

Issue + Position = | Thesis statement |

| The drinking age should be lowered from twenty-one to eighteen. |

Issue + Position = | Thesis statement |

| The current minimum wage is not enough to live on. |

Issue + Position = | Thesis statement |

| The most important thing about a marriage is that two people love and respect each other, not what sex they are. |

Sometimes the thesis combines the issue and the position, as in the following statements:

Issue/position = | Thesis statement |

| Soldiers should not be forced to stay in war zones beyond their terms. |

Issue/position = | Thesis statement |

| All eighteen-year-olds should be drafted into the military. |

Try to make the thesis statement for any argument as specific as possible to help guide your writing and your readers.

VAGUE   Our health-care system is disgraceful.

MORE SPECIFIC Two key reforms would make health care more
                   affordable for all.

[The paper would detail the two reforms.]

Many thesis statements for arguments use words such as the following because they clearly express a position:

could (not)   ought (not)

must (not)   requires

must have   should (not)

needs   would

■ **PRACTICE 1   WRITING A STATEMENT OF YOUR POSITION** . . . .

Write your position on the following issues:

A ban on junk food and sugary drinks at elementary and high schools

_____

Mandatory drug testing as a requirement for employment

_____

Free college courses for prisoners

_____

Now, take one of the position statements that you just wrote, and put more energy into it.

_____

_____

Support in Argument

However strongly you may feel about an issue, if you don't provide solid **support** for your position, you will not convince anyone to see it your way. As you develop support for your position, think carefully about your readers and the kind of information that will be most convincing to them.

Reasons and Evidence

■ For online exercises on main point and support, visit *Exercise Central* at **bedfordstmartins .com/realessays**.

The major support for your position consists of the **reasons** that you give for that position. These reasons must be backed up with **evidence**, such as facts, examples, and expert opinions. The success of your argument depends on the quality of the reasons and evidence that you present to support your position.

Facts are statements or observations that can be proved true. **Statistics**—numerical facts based on research—can be persuasive evidence to back up your position. **Examples** are specific experiences or pieces of information that support your position. **Expert opinion** is the opinion of someone who is considered an expert in the area you are writing about. *Note:* The fact that a person's opinion appears on a Web site does not necessarily mean that he or she has any expertise. When in doubt about a source's authority, consult your instructor or a research librarian.

■ For more on finding sources, using quotations, and citing sources, see Chapter 21.

POSITION	It pays to stay in college.
REASON	College graduates earn more than high school graduates.
EVIDENCE/ FACT	College graduates earn 68 percent more than high school graduates and 320 percent more than high school dropouts.
REASON	Students learn up-to-date skills that they will need to find a job.
EVIDENCE/ EXAMPLE	Understanding how to use technology in your field may make the difference between getting a job and coming in second.

REASON	An increasing number of jobs require college degrees.
EVIDENCE/ **EXPERT** **OPINION**	John Sterling, president of one of the largest recruiting agencies, said recently, "Ten years ago, a college degree was perceived as an advantage. Today, the college degree is the basic ticket of entry for the majority of jobs." [*Note:* When you use expert opinion, you need to identify the source of the quote.]

As you choose reasons and evidence to support your position, consider your readers. Are they likely to agree with you, to be uncommitted, or to be hostile? Choose the support that is most likely to convince them, drawing on outside sources (such as the library or Internet) as needed.

Opposing Positions

Part of your support for your position involves the opposing position: Acknowledge it, and present some evidence against it. If, for example, you are arguing in favor of lowering the drinking age to eighteen, you should not ignore the position that it should be kept at age twenty-one. If you don't say anything about the other position, you are leaving your argument unprotected. To defend your own position, show some weakness in the opposing position.

The writer of the paragraph on page 290 might consider the opposing position as follows:

POSITION	The drinking age should be lowered from twenty-one to eighteen.
OPPOSING **POSITION**	The drinking age should not be lowered because people begin drinking before the legal age. If the age were lowered to eighteen, more sixteen-year-olds would drink.

ACKNOWLEDGING THE OPPOSING POSITION: First, laws should not be based on the extent to which they are likely to be abused or broken. They should be based on what's right. Even so, there is no evidence to show that legal age is a major influence on teenage drinking. Other factors involved, such as peer pressure and the availability of fake IDs, have more impact on whether teenagers drink.

Tips for Supporting Your Position by Addressing the Opposing Position

- Visualize someone who holds the opposing position and what that person would say to defend it.
- In part of the body of your essay, acknowledge the opposing position. Do so politely; if you try to ridicule the opposing view, you will alienate people and immediately weaken your argument.
- Poke some holes in the opposing position by addressing it directly and showing what's wrong, or misguided, about the position. Again, do this politely; don't make your opposition look foolish.
- Return to the reasons and the evidence that support your position.

PRACTICE 2 ACKNOWLEDGING AND ADDRESSING THE OPPOSING VIEW . . . .

For each of the following positions, in the spaces indicated, state the opposing position and at least one point someone holding the opposing view might make against your position.

ISSUE: The "Three Strikes and You're Out" rule in some high schools that requires students to be expelled after three serious offenses

POSITION: Against it

OPPOSING POSITION: _____

POINT THAT SOMEONE HOLDING THE OPPOSING POSITION WOULD MAKE:

_____

ISSUE: Mandatory retirement at age sixty-seven

POSITION: In favor of it

OPPOSING POSITION: _____

POINT THAT SOMEONE HOLDING THE OPPOSING POSITION WOULD MAKE:

_____

ISSUE: Stricter gun control laws

POSITION: Against it

OPPOSING POSITION: _____

POINT THAT SOMEONE HOLDING THE OPPOSING POSITION WOULD MAKE:

_____

· ·

In a short essay, you may not be able to address all the points of the opposing view, but you should know what they are and address at least the most important ones. As you gather support for your position, keep the opposing position in mind, and follow the tips given in the box on page 296.

Faulty Reasoning

As you write and review the support for your position, be sure that your evidence is good and your reasoning is logical. Unfortunately, we are exposed to **faulty reasoning** all the time, especially in advertising. Certain kinds of errors in logic are so common that there is a name for them—**logical fallacies**. You don't need to remember the name, but you should be aware of what the common ones are as you form and evaluate your argument.

Either/Or Extremes: Assuming that there are only two extreme choices with nothing in between.

EXAMPLE: My country, love it or leave it.

[**Faulty reasoning:** Should people really either applaud everything a government does or move to a different country?]

Bad Analogy: Comparing items or circumstances that are not alike enough to make a meaningful comparison.

EXAMPLE: A human fetus should have the same rights as a human adult.

[**Faulty reasoning:** While some specific rights may be shared by a fetus and an adult, saying they should have all the same rights doesn't make sense because they are different in many ways. Should a fetus be able to vote, for example?]

Circular Reasoning: Supporting a position by restating part of it.

EXAMPLE: I deserve a raise because I need to make more money.

[**Faulty reasoning:** While this may be true, it won't help persuade your boss to give you a raise. You would need to offer reasons why you are worth more than you are being paid.]

"Everyone Knows":   Appealing to people's general desire to be like the majority by supporting a statement with a claim that all or most other people believe something. A common occurrence of this is when a child says to a parent, "Everybody else's parents are letting them do X." (For a good example of this kind of influence, see "In Praise of Peer Pressure" on p. 282.) This kind of faulty reasoning is also called "the bandwagon effect."

EXAMPLE: Everyone knows that all politicians are liars.

[**Faulty reasoning:** While some research studies might measure people's perceptions about how truthful politicians are, it is not likely that any study would reveal that 100 percent of all people believe that 100 percent of all politicians lie 100 percent of the time.]

Mistaken Causes or Effects: Assuming that one thing caused another simply because it occurred beforehand.

EXAMPLE: The opening of the new liquor superwarehouse caused old Mr. Jones to close up his shop.

[**Faulty reasoning:** Mr. Jones might have closed for a variety of reasons. Your assumption is not evidence of his real reason for closing.]

Overgeneralization: Making a broad statement that is not supported by enough evidence.

EXAMPLE: Having grown up with three brothers, I know firsthand that boys are more violent than girls.

[**Faulty reasoning:** A sample of one family is not enough to assume that all boys act in a particular way.]

Oversimplification: Making something seem very simple when it isn't.

EXAMPLE: If more parking spaces were available on campus, most students would come to class.

[**Faulty reasoning:** Students miss class for many reasons, so saying parking is the problem is too simple.]

Slippery Slope: Saying that something will create a chain reaction, even though there is no evidence that this will happen.

EXAMPLE: Using marijuana will lead to heroin addiction.

[**Faulty reasoning:** There is no overall evidence that one leads all the way to another. To make such a claim, proof of each step of the chain reaction must be given.]

"This, so That":   Pairing ideas or events that aren't logically connected.

> EXAMPLE: I trust my doctor, so I ask him advice about my finances.
>
> [**Faulty reasoning:** The fact that a medical adviser is trustworthy has no bearing on the doctor's financial reliability. This kind of faulty reasoning is also called a *non sequitur* (literally, "it doesn't follow").]

There are other kinds of faulty reasoning, but the ones above are some of the most common.

PRACTICE 3   IDENTIFYING FAULTY REASONING

Read the sentences below, and identify which kind of faulty reasoning each represents. In the space provided, explain why it is an example of faulty reasoning.

1. If medical costs continue to rise, no one will be able to afford health care.

   _____

   _____

2. Colleges should either lower their tuitions or give all students scholarships.

   _____

   _____

3. We can blame McDonald's for the increase in obesity in this country.

   _____

   _____

4. Most college students are binge drinkers.

   _____

   _____

5. If college were free, students would graduate within four years.

   _____

   _____

   _____

Organization in Argument

**ARGUMENT
AT A GLANCE**

| Thesis statement |
| Includes the issue (topic) and your position on it |

↓

| Reason 1 |
| Supporting examples, facts, and expert opinions |

↓

| Reason 2 |
| Supporting examples, facts, and expert opinions |

↓

| Reason 3 |
| Supporting examples, facts, and expert opinions |

↓

| Conclusion |
| Reminds readers of your position and makes a strong last attempt to convince them of that position |

Argument most often uses **order of importance** to organize reasons for the writer's position on the issue. Consider what you think your readers will find your most convincing reason. Arrange your reasons and evidence so that they build the strongest case for your position, and save the most convincing reason for last. Do not forget to acknowledge and address the opposing position somewhere in your argument. The plan for an argument often looks like the chart to the left.

As you write your argument, use transitions to move your readers from one reason or point to the next. In the box below are some transitions often used for argument.

Common Transitions in Argument

TRANSITIONS FROM ONE POINT TO ANOTHER	TRANSITIONS TO ADD EMPHASIS
also	above all
another fact to consider	best of all
another reason	especially
another thing	in fact
consider that	in particular
for example	more important
in addition	most important
in the first place	remember
	the last point to consider
	worst of all

Read and Analyze Argument

Before writing your own argument essay, read the following three examples—from college, the workplace, and everyday life—and answer the questions that accompany them. As you read, notice that argument uses many of the other kinds of writing you have studied to support a position. It may tell a story, give examples, describe something, explain how something works, break a large point into categories, define a term, compare two or more things, or show cause and effect.

In many ways, learning how to construct a good argument requires you to use everything you have learned about the various kinds of good writing. Being able to make a good case for or against something you believe may be the most important skill you learn in college. It is certainly one that you can apply to all other parts of your life.

Argument in College

The following essay was written in response to this assignment: *Take a position on some aspect of college life, and write a short essay defending that position.*

VOCABULARY
The following words are *italicized* in Donnie's essay: *mandatory, ratio, jeopardize, correspond,* and *penalized.* If you do not know their meanings, look them up in a dictionary.

ATTENDANCE IN COLLEGE CLASSES
Donnie Ney

1   Attendance in college classes should be optional, not *mandatory*. Students pay a lot of money for their courses, so they should be able to decide whether and how to take advantage of them. Also, although class participation can help many students, not all students learn through class participation. If they learn better on their own or if they already know the content of a course that's required for graduation, they should be able to decide for themselves whether to sit in class hearing about things they already have learned. Finally, optional attendance would benefit the students who want to go to class because the student-to-instructor *ratio* would be lower, and students would get more personal attention.

PAUSE: What reasons has Donnie included in this paragraph?

_____

_____

PAUSE: Note that Donnie briefly uses narration here.

PAUSE: Do you agree that paying for the course should give students the right to attend or not without a penalty?

_____

_____

2   First, students pay tuition, fees, and the cost of books and materials to enroll in a class. Because they have paid for the class, they should have the choice about whether to attend. Isn't it a basic right of a consumer to decide how to use the things they've bought and paid for? Also, students' lives are complicated, and there are many good reasons that they may have to miss classes, even if they want to attend. For example, this semester I have missed several classes because of my child's ongoing battle with severe asthma. I cannot *jeopardize* her health in order to get to a class. On the other hand, I do not want to fail because I have missed more than the allowed number of classes. Such a policy does not seem fair.

3   Also, it seems unfair to require students who already know the course content or who learn it on their own to waste their time hearing about it again. Although most students attend classes because they want to learn, there are some required courses that students have to take whether they want to or not. For example, I have had to attend basic computer classes to teach me procedures such as how to turn on a computer, what e-mail is, and how to access the Internet. I have known these things for years. Why should I sit through classes that repeat what I know when I could be spending my time doing the many things I really need to do? Why should I fail if I miss too many of these classes? Such policies do not benefit me or anyone else. In addition, although colleges do not like to admit this, attendance does not always *correspond* to grades. For example, some students can read and understand the materials assigned without any help from the teacher. If the goal of a college course is to learn, and a student can learn without attending class, why should that student need to attend lectures?

PAUSE: Have you ever experienced this situation?

_____

_____

4   The best reason for making attendance optional is that students who do choose to attend could benefit from smaller classes and more personal attention. Classes could include more one-on-one instruction, which might improve students' grades and their ability to understand and retain course content. Many students struggle with course content and really need more of the instructor's time. However, with large

PAUSE: Note that this benefit is an effect of Donnie's position.

classes, instructors don't have much chance to spend lots of time with individual students.

5   For all of these reasons, I believe that attendance should be optional in college courses. Students do not all learn in the same way. Some students learn best by studying a lot rather than sitting in class. With more study time and less class time, some students will achieve better results on tests. Attendance should be the students' choice. If they need to go to class to pass, they will attend; if they don't need to go to class to learn, they should not be *penalized*.

PAUSE: What, to you, is the most persuasive reason Donnie gives?

_____

_____

1. Double-underline the **thesis statement**.
2. Underline the **reasons** that Donnie uses to support his position.
3. What kind of **organization** does Donnie use? _____

_____

4. Does the essay include the **four basics of good argument**? Be ready to explain your answer.
5. Do you agree with Donnie's position? Are there other good reasons he could have given?

■ For a list of the four basics of good argument, see page 290.

Argument at Work

The following profile shows how the director of a nonprofit organization uses argument in his work

Shawn Brown
Founder, Diamond Educators

BACKGROUND: I had what is, unfortunately, a typical kind of life for many poor, urban youth who are caught up in gangs, drugs, and violence. My brother was murdered in a crossfire, and I lived with my mother with no father around. I was an athlete and got away with not doing much in school. I had my first kid at age fifteen and in that same year almost shot a rival who had disrespected me. I didn't, mainly because I remembered my coach, who'd warned me not to leave my son fatherless. This coach, Ed Powell, had a saying I still repeat often: "He who fails to plan, plans to fail." I was lucky to have Powell and a few other adults reach out to me, help me turn around, and get me on the track of education and a better life.

A few years ago, I got together a group of my friends, all college-educated African American men with families and steady jobs. We talked about how many young black men have no positive role models and decided that we wanted to help them the way we had been helped. From that meeting came Diamond Educators, a nonprofit organization that starts working with kids in third grade by teaching them how to behave, speak, and "play the game" in a way that will lead to success in life. Teens who are in the program give back by mentoring elementary school boys. The program is growing and has a great success record.

COLLEGE/DEGREE: B.A., Merrimack College

EMPLOYERS: Diamond Educators, Boston Private Industry Council (PIC)

WRITING AT WORK: In both positions, I write a lot. For Diamond Educators, I've written a mission statement, research projects, proposals for funding and support, and many other kinds of writing. For the PIC, I write reports, e-mail, letters, and assessments.

HOW SHAWN USES ARGUMENT: I use argument in both speech and writing to persuade the boys, members of the community, legal bodies, and potential donors. I have to think about who the person is, what he or she thinks, and how I can best make my case.

Shawn's Argument

Shawn wrote this letter to support the parole request of a young man he had worked with.

VOCABULARY
The following words are *italicized* in the letter: *parole, mentor, multicultural, adverse, cope, invaluable, dedication, mentees, transform, jeopardize, essential,* and *incarcerated.* If you don't know their meanings, look them up in a dictionary.

PAUSE: What do you think the next paragraph will be about?

To Whom It May Concern:

1   It is with enthusiasm that I am writing to support *parole* for Rodney Strong. In his work for Diamond Educators as a *mentor* to young men, he has made a positive contribution to the at-risk youth in the city of Boston.

2   Diamond Educators is a nonprofit mentoring program that serves at-risk young males who attend Boston public schools or who live in the inner-city neighborhoods of Boston. The mentors of the Diamond

Educators program are *multicultural* male educators and professionals who grew up in the city of Boston and who dealt with *adverse* conditions that the majority of our young minority males face every day, conditions that often result in bad life choices. The adverse conditions I refer to are living in an environment where young men *cope* with peer pressure to join a gang and involve themselves with drugs, crime, and violence; single-parent homes; and a lack of positive male role models. Our mentors help young men chart a course through their difficult situations. These mentors are an *invaluable* resource for our young, urban, minority males.

PAUSE: What conditions does Brown list as causes of bad life choices?

3   As a mentor, Rodney demonstrated commitment and *dedication* to our program and to our students. Rodney worked long hours, but he found time to meet and counsel his *mentees*. He showed his mentees the importance of meeting commitments, taking responsibility, and having a positive purpose in life. He was a good example of how positive peer relationships can *transform* lives.

PAUSE: Why does Shawn write about Diamond Educators here rather than talking about Rodney?

4   Rodney gave these young boys hope. He showed his mentees that by applying themselves and taking advantage of the resources available to them, they could achieve success in life. Many of the boys otherwise live without hope of any kind and choose paths that *jeopardize* their own well-being and that of others in the community. That hope is *essential* to becoming a productive member of the human community. Rodney is a leader with a strong will to achieve his own success and to help others find theirs.

5   The path to success for urban minority males is extremely difficult, and, as with many difficult courses, progress is not always direct and uninterrupted. Rodney stepped off course and made a poor decision when he committed a crime. However, he has demonstrated that he has learned from his mistake and is ready to return to his community as a positive force. He is ready to contribute to society, and to keep him *incarcerated* deprives us of a good man, a good leader, and a good role model for young men. His release will show his mentees that there is hope of a good, lawful life after jail.

PAUSE: Why is the last sentence here important to Shawn's argument?

PAUSE: Note that Shawn uses narration to suggest Rodney's future story.

6   Rodney is dedicated to being a good father and a good community influence. Unlike many who return to the community after incarceration, Rodney will not persist in a life of crime; he will return to his path of success and contribution. Keeping him from that serves no purpose.

7   I support Rodney Strong and will continue to support him after his return to the community. I urge you to consider his good work and to allow him to continue it.

Sincerely,

Shawn Brown, Cofounder

Diamond Educators

1. What is Shawn's **main point**? _____

_____

2. What reasons does Shawn use to **support** his position? _____

_____

_____

3. If you were a member of the parole board, would you be persuaded by Shawn's letter? What else could he have said?

4. How might more use of **narration** have made the argument

stronger? _____

_____

5. Does Shawn's letter include the **four basics of good argument**? Be ready to explain your answer.

Argument in Everyday Life

■ NOTE: Partly as a result of this letter and his internship, John received a full scholarship to Dartmouth College.

After a class discussion and assignment on the unfairness of federal financial aid regulations, student John Around Him wrote the following letter to Senator John Kerry. Senator Kerry not only responded to the letter, promising to work to change the federal financial aid system, but he also visited John's college class. Because of this contact, John is now working as a policy intern in Kerry's Massachusetts office.

VOCABULARY
The following words are *italicized* in the letter: *chaos, eligibility,* and *criteria.* If you don't know their meanings, look them up in a dictionary.

Dear Senator Kerry:

1   My name is John Around Him, and I am a student at Bunker Hill Community College in Boston, Massachusetts. I am Native American and a veteran of the war in Iraq. I know that you, as a veteran of the Vietnam War, can relate to putting your life on the line in an environment of gunfire, explosions, *chaos,* and confusion, wondering if the next second might be your last. For most young people, being in the middle of a dangerous war—being shot at and surrounded by death and violence—is not an appealing way to earn money for college. However, for students like me who do not qualify for federal financial aid, it may be the only way to go to college, and this is why I am writing to you. The federal financial aid system needs to be changed because it is not effective in helping students, especially low-income and minority students, pay for college.

PAUSE: How does John appeal to his audience here?

_____

_____

2   I grew up on the Pine Ridge Reservation in South Dakota and graduated from Little Wound High School in 2001. I was an average student, with a grade-point average of just under 3.0. I always wanted to go to college, but I asked myself, "How would I pay for it?" I lived with a single-parent father and with two other families, and my father would often help others who needed it. My father was a language teacher, not highly paid, so for me family financial support for college was out of the question. I had to find another answer.

PAUSE: Note that John uses narration in this paragraph.

3   When I turned to the federal financial aid system, I found that there is money to help some students pay for college, but none for a student like me. According to the College Board's report, "Trends in College Pricing, 2006," the average tuition, room, and board costs for public universities is $12,796 (though many are much more, as is the case here in Massachusetts)—way out of line for my family's finances. Yet according to the financial aid formula, my father made too much money.

4   The formulas used to determine a student's financial need are not realistic: They don't represent the average student's situation. For example, according to the formula, to be considered independent (which largely determines *eligibility*) a student must meet one of the following

criteria: He or she must be either twenty-four years of age or older, married, a veteran, or an orphan or ward of the court. Many students today, however, are financially independent as soon as they graduate from high school. In 2005, according to the National Center for Education Statistics, 64 percent of students at community colleges and 37 percent at public colleges and universities were financially independent. Fifty-eight percent of those students worked at least thirty-five hours per week, and 67 percent delayed entering college to earn money to help pay for it. Still, those under age twenty-four are not considered to be independent, and their family income is taken into consideration, even when the student receives no family support. As a result, many students have to try to meet one of the other eligibility requirements. For too many, the answer is joining the military, going to war.

PAUSE: Summarize what John says about the criteria for eligibility. What kind of evidence does John use in this paragraph?

_____

_____

5   I am not saying that students should not enlist in the military. Would I have signed on if I had received financial aid? I don't know. I support our troops and enjoyed my time in the service. The military's values and discipline and my experiences there have contributed to who I am today, and I am thankful for that. However, I don't believe that students should have to risk their lives to qualify for financial aid.

6   I am writing to you not only on my own behalf but for the well-being of my family and my country. The federal financial aid system ignores a majority of students in need of aid. Despite rising tuition costs, our financial aid options are slim, and more and more students aren't able to achieve a college education, our path to success. This problem is like a cancer; unless treated, it will spread and will hurt our nation's future.

PAUSE: Why is this conclusion effective?

_____

_____

Sincerely yours,

John Around Him

1. Double-underline the **thesis statement**.
2. According to John, what factors make the federal financial aid system ineffective?
3. What is your reaction to his letter? Is his argument persuasive?

4. Senator John Kerry is both a veteran and a senator from the state where John Around Him attends college. What other facts, if any, make this student's appeal to the senator likely to be effective? If you don't know anything about John Kerry, look up his biography before you answer.

_____

_____

5. What was one immediate effect of John's letter to Senator Kerry?

_____

_____

Critical Reading and Writing: Key College Skills

1. **Summary.** Briefly summarize each of the three selections, including the issue, the writer's position, and the reasons that he or she gives for taking that position.

2. **Analysis.** Review each piece's introduction and conclusion, which are both essential parts of a good argument. Which introduction do you think is the strongest and why? Which conclusion and why?

3. **Synthesis.** Review Donnie Ney's essay on "Attendance in College Classes" and John Around Him's letter to Senator John Kerry, both of which concern student rights. Take a position on whether students are fairly treated by institutions such as a college and the government, drawing on information in the two example arguments. Use your own experience, too.

4. **Evaluation.** Using the **four basics of good argument** as a measure, choose the selection that you think is the best example of a good argument, and explain why.

Write an Argument Essay

In this section you will write your own argument essay based on _one_ of the following assignments. Before you begin to write, review the four basics of good argument on page 290. Also, read the Tips for Tackling Argument in the box on the next page.

TIPS FOR TACKLING ARGUMENT

1. Read the assignment carefully, highlighting key words. An assignment that uses argument might say, *Do you agree or disagree with the following statement?*, *Defend or refute X*, or *Do you believe X? Why or why not?*

2. Carefully decide on your position and the evidence that you can use to support it.

3. Use any of the writing strategies you have learned to make your reasons forceful. Tell the background story, provide sensory details, give detailed examples, explain how something works, break things into categories with examples, define a term as you are using it, compare two or more things, or explain how one thing causes another. Respond in advance to objections that your reader might have.

4. Write a powerful conclusion, showing why your position is important.

 ASSIGNMENT 1 WRITING ABOUT COLLEGE, WORK, AND EVERYDAY LIFE . . . .

■ Use the diagram on page 300 to help you organize.

Write an argument essay on *one* of the following topics or on a topic of your own choice. Select an issue that you care about so that you can argue powerfully.

COLLEGE

- Persuade one of your teachers to raise the grade on your last assignment (in a course you are currently taking).
- Defend the following statement: "A college degree means something."
- Present your instructor with reasons why you should be able to make up a test that you missed.
- Write a letter to the Student Affairs office proposing a student service that does not currently exist.

WORK

- Argue against a company policy that you believe is unfair.
- Argue that you should get a promotion.
- Argue that an employer should or should not have the right to forbid office romances.
- Argue that employers should or should not monitor employee e-mail use.

EVERYDAY LIFE

- Argue against a rent increase.
- Argue for or against McDonald's being sued by obese people who have eaten there regularly.
- Take a stand on a local issue or policy that you believe is unfair.
- Write a letter to your congressional representative asking him or her to work to change a law or policy that you believe is unfair.

■ ASSIGNMENT 2 **WRITING ABOUT AN IMAGE** . . . .

The people in the photograph are protesting proposed reductions in federal rent subsidies for low-income tenants. In cities with high rental costs, the reductions will force many people out of their homes.

Choose a proposed change that threatens your personal security, and present an argument against it.

■ ASSIGNMENT 3 **WRITING TO SOLVE A PROBLEM** . . . .

THE PROBLEM: An alumnus has given your college a large donation that is intended to improve the quality of student life. The president has set up a committee to determine several possible uses for the money, and you are one of the students on that committee.

THE ASSIGNMENT: Working either on your own or with a small group, first decide on three possible uses of the money that would improve the quality of student life. Then, choose one of them, and write a letter to the president arguing for this use of the donation. Be sure to include solid reasons for your choice.

RESOURCES: To help you decide which of the three possible uses you will argue for, you might type into a search engine key words related to areas in need of improvement at your college (for example, *[your college] computer center*). List any Web sites that you use.

 ASSIGNMENT 4   WRITING ABOUT READINGS . . . .

The examples of argument in this chapter cover the issues of lowering the drinking age, eliminating mandatory class attendance in college, and revising unfair federal financial aid provisions. At the heart of each of these issues is a basic conflict between individual rights and institutional rules or laws. Keeping this in mind, choose *one* of the following assignments.

• Choose one of the issues covered in this chapter, and write your own pro or con argument on the issue, using the evidence that the reading presents but adding to it with your own. Find at least one other source (either in print or online) on the subject, and refer to that source to support your position. Be sure to document your sources.

• Choose a different issue that pits individual rights against institutional policies. Here are some examples of such topics:

    – Should physician-assisted suicide be legal? (See the readings in Chapter 51.)

    – Should a college have the right to censor the college newspaper?

    – Should military recruiters be allowed to visit high schools?

    – Should same-sex marriage be banned?

    – Should marijuana be legalized?

    – Should the government be able to continue wiretapping U.S. residents without a court order?

    – Should students have to pass standardized tests to graduate from high school?

    – Should junk food be banned from public elementary and high schools?

Write an essay responding to the question, and use at least one online or print source to support your position. Be sure to document the source.

- Choose another issue that is important to you. (If you can't think of one, try looking through a news magazine or newspaper, or go to **slate.com**, **salon.com**, **grist.org**, or another news source.) Write an argument defending your position on the issue, using at least one source. Document any source that you use.

■ ASSIGNMENT 5   ARGUMENT WRITING TESTS . . . .

Many states and colleges require students to take a timed writing test. Often the test calls for an argument essay on an assigned issue, and students must argue for or against the issue, as directed. Many people believe that a good writer should be able to argue either side of an issue regardless of his or her personal feelings. Choose one of the following questions, come up with evidence to support both sides of the issue, and write an essay defending one side or another. *Note:* Part of the requirement of the essay is to be able to support each side, so you will need to turn in the support you develop for each side of the position.

- Should car manufacturers be forced to improve fuel economy, even if they pass the costs onto consumers?
- Agree or disagree with the following statement: Rap musicians should be stopped from using lyrics that encourage violence and demean women.
- Should U.S. citizens be required to vote?

Follow the steps in the Writing Guide below to help you prewrite, draft, revise, and edit your argument. Check off each step as you complete it.

WRITING GUIDE: ARGUMENT	
STEPS IN ARGUMENT	**HOW TO DO THE STEPS**
Focus.	☐ Before and as you write, think about your position on an issue and the ways that you can persuade readers to see things your way. Review the four basics of good argument on page 290.
Prewrite to explore your topic. See Chapter 4 for more on prewriting (including freewriting).	☐ Use a prewriting technique to explore an issue that you care about and your position on it. Freewriting is a good technique for many people. ☐ Consider why the issue is important to you and how it affects you. ☐ Think about what reasons you have for your position. ☐ Take a few minutes to build some energy about the issue.

continued

STEPS IN ARGUMENT	HOW TO DO THE STEPS
Write a thesis statement. The thesis statement of an argument essay usually includes the issue and the writer's position on that issue. Issue + Position = Thesis The minimum wage should be raised. See Chapter 5 for more on writing a thesis statement.	☐ Consider your readers and their possible opinions. ☐ Write a thesis that includes the issue and your position.
Support your thesis statement. The major support for an argument consists of the reasons for the writer's position. These reasons must be backed by evidence, such as facts, examples, and expert opinions. See Chapter 6 for more on supporting a thesis statement.	☐ Think about your readers and the reasons that will convince them of your position. ☐ Use a prewriting technique to come up with good reasons for your position. ☐ Choose the most persuasive reasons, selecting at least three. (Drop reasons or evidence that are weak or not directly related to your position on the issue.) ☐ Back your reasons with facts, good examples, or expert opinions. (Consider whether you will need to use outside sources.) ☐ Consider and address opposing positions.
Make a plan. See Chapter 7 for more on planning.	☐ Write a plan or outline, arranging your reasons according to order of importance and saving the most important reason for last. (See the diagram on p. 300.)
Write a draft. See Chapter 8 for more on drafting.	☐ Write an introduction that gets your readers' interest and presents your thesis. See if you can use one of the introductory techniques in Chapter 8. ☐ Using your outline, write a topic sentence for each of your reasons. ☐ Write body paragraphs with supporting evidence for each of your reasons. ☐ Write a concluding paragraph that makes a final case for your position based on the reasons you have presented. ☐ Title your essay.
Revise your draft. See Chapter 9 for more on revising a draft.	☐ Ask another person to read and comment on your draft. ☐ Cut any reasons that don't directly support your point or that seem weak.

STEPS IN ARGUMENT	HOW TO DO THE STEPS
Revise your draft (cont.).	☐ Add reasons and evidence that might help convince readers of your position.
	☐ Add transitions to move readers smoothly from one reason to another.
	☐ Rewrite your thesis statement to make it more concrete and forceful.
	☐ Reread your introduction to make sure that it states your position with confidence and hooks your readers.
	☐ Reread your conclusion to make sure it reminds readers of your position and makes a final pitch for it.
	☐ Make sure that the essay as a whole is energetic and drives home your point.
	☐ Make at least five changes to your draft to improve its unity, support, or coherence (see pp. 127–40).
	☐ Check to make sure the draft follows the four basics of good argument.
Edit your draft. See Parts Four through Seven for more on editing.	☐ Use the spell checker and grammar checker on your computer, but also reread your essay carefully to catch any errors.
	☐ Look for errors in grammar, spelling, or punctuation. Focus first on sentence fragments, run-ons, errors in subject-verb agreement, verb errors, and other areas where you often make mistakes.
	☐ Ask yourself: Is this the best I can do?

Part Three
Special College Writing Projects

19

Writing under Pressure

Tests and Essay Exams

You Know This

You've taken tests under pressure.

- You study for the test for your driver's license.
- You practice and try out for a team.

You will need good reading and writing skills to do well on the many tests you will take in college. To become a good test-taker, you also need to develop good test-taking strategies.

Studying for Tests

Some students spend hours studying for a test that they then fail. Often, they have not studied efficiently. This chapter will give you tips on studying for tests and for taking essay exams and other timed writing assignments.

Here are five reliable tips to help you study for any exam:

TIPS FOR STUDYING

1. Ask about the test.
2. Study with a partner or a group.
3. Predict what will be on the exam.
4. Use study aids.
5. Review actively.

Ask about the Test

Ask your instructor about an upcoming test. Just make sure you ask reasonable questions.

ASK	NOT
• What part of the course or text will it cover?	• What's on the test?
• Will the format be multiple choice, short answer, or essay?	• You're not going to give us an essay question, are you?
• Will we be allowed to use notes or books?	• We can just look up the answers, right?
• What percentage of my course grade will this count for?	• Is this test important?
• Can you recommend what to review?	• Do I need to read the book? Is the stuff you said in class important?
• Will we have the whole period to complete the test?	• How long is it?
• I know I have to miss class that day (give your reason). Can I arrange to take the test at another time?	• Is there a makeup test?

Write down your instructor's answers to your questions. Don't rely on your memory. You will be busy enough remembering the material for the exam without having to remember what your instructor said.

Study with a Partner or a Group

Forming a study group is well worth the time and effort it takes. Setting a time to study with others guarantees that you'll study, and pooling ideas improves everyone's ability to predict what will be on the test. Do some preparation before group meetings so that you make the most of the study time. The tips on the following page can help study group members prepare for a meeting:

- Each person can take responsibility for a particular section of the material, preparing a list of five to ten questions that might be on the test. Questions and possible responses can then be discussed in the group.
- Each person can photocopy his or her notes on a particular chapter, section, or topic and distribute them to the members of the group.
- Each person can come up with a list of the five most important things he or she learned about the material to be covered on the test.
- Each person can make a list of things he or she doesn't understand.

Predict What Will Be on the Exam

Whether you are studying with other people or by yourself, make a list of what you think will be on the exam. Look over your notes, assignments, and any previous tests or quizzes. Try writing questions for that material, and then try answering your own questions.

If you are confused about any material, ask about it either in class, after class, or during your instructor's office hours. Your instructor will probably welcome questions by e-mail as well. Do not go into an exam knowing that you don't understand a major concept.

PRACTICE 1   PREDICTING THE CONTENT OF A TEST . . . .

Imagine that you are having a quiz in this class next week. With a partner or in a small group, identify three topics that might be on that quiz, and write one question for each.

TOPIC: Fragments

QUESTION: What are four kinds of sentence fragments?

TOPIC: _____

QUESTION: _____

TOPIC: _____

QUESTION: _____

TOPIC: _____

QUESTION: _____

Use Study Aids

Use one or more of the following study aids—or any other that is available to you—to ensure your success:

- Reread your notes, looking especially for anything you've underlined or marked in some other way.
- If you are being tested on material from your textbook, reread chapter reviews, summaries, and boxes containing key concepts.
- Review handouts from your instructor.
- Consider other ways to review material—audiotapes, videos, computer exercises, study guides, the course or textbook Web site, and so on.

Review Actively

■ For more on active, critical reading, see Chapter 2, pages 22–34.

The following are some suggestions for reviewing material actively:

- To review material from a book, take notes. Improve your retention by writing information in your own words.
- To review handouts, use a colored pen or highlighter to mark the most important ideas, most useful facts, and other key information.
- Say important material aloud. Many people learn well by hearing something in addition to seeing it.
- To review notes, rewrite them in other words or in another format. For example, if you've written an outline, transform it into a chart or diagram that shows the relationships among ideas (see, for example, the clustering diagram on p. 65).

Test-Taking Strategies

Good test-takers know how to manage the test-taking process. They start with studying, and after they have studied, they move on to the next steps.

STRATEGIES FOR TAKING EXAMS

1. Be prepared.
2. Manage your nerves.
3. Understand the directions.
4. Survey the whole exam before starting.
5. Develop a plan.

Be Prepared

If you have followed the advice in the first part of this chapter, you've already done the most important preparation. But don't arrive at the exam and discover that you've left something essential at home. Take some time the night before to think about what you need. Make a list of what to bring (pen? books? calculator? notebook? textbook? computer disk? watch?), and assemble everything so that it's ready to go.

Manage Your Nerves

Get as much rest as possible the night before the exam, and allow extra time to get to class. Arrive early enough to settle in. Sit up straight, take a deep breath, and remind yourself that you know the material: You're prepared; you're ready; you will pass. When your instructor starts to talk, look up and listen.

Understand the Directions

Misunderstanding or ignoring directions is a major reason students do poorly on exams, so please pay attention to the advice here. First, listen to the **spoken directions** your instructor gives. It's tempting to start flipping through the exam as soon as you get it rather than listening to what your instructor is saying. Resist the temptation. Your instructor may be giving you key advice or information that's not written elsewhere, and you may miss it if you're not paying attention.

Second, when you begin the test, carefully read the **written directions** for each part. Sometimes, students answer all of the questions in a section only to find out afterward that the directions said to answer only one or two. If you don't understand any part of the directions, be sure to ask your instructor for clarification.

Survey the Whole Exam before Starting

Look over the whole exam before doing anything. See how many parts the exam has, and make sure to look on both sides of all pages. Note the kinds of questions and the number of points each question or part is worth. The toughest questions (and the ones worth the most points) are often at the end, so you will want to leave enough time to answer those.

> **Language Note:** Read the whole test through for any vocabulary you don't understand or cultural issues you are not familiar with. If you have questions, go to the teacher, and ask for clarification.

Develop a Plan

First, **budget your time.** After surveying the whole test, write down how much time you will allow for each part. You might even find it helpful to calculate what time you want to start each section: Part 1 at 9:40, Part 2 at 9:55, and so on. Make sure you leave enough time for the parts with the highest point values, such as essay questions: They can take longer than you think they will. As you plan your time, keep in mind how much time you *really* have for the exam: A "two-hour" exam may be only one hour and fifty minutes once your instructor has finished giving directions. Remember also to leave a few minutes to check your work.

Second, **decide on an order**—where you should start, what you should do second, third, and so on. Start with the questions you can answer quickly and easily, but stay within your time budget on them.

Finally, **monitor your time** during the exam. If you find you're really stuck on a question and you're going way over your time budget, move on. If you have time at the end of the exam period, you can always go back to it.

Answering an Essay Question

An **essay question** requires writing several well-supported paragraphs in response to a question or prompt within a set amount of time.

Essay questions on an exam are usually worth more points than short-answer or multiple-choice questions, so they deserve special attention. Apply the following strategies to essay questions.

STRATEGIES FOR ANSWERING AN ESSAY QUESTION

1. Read and analyze the question.
2. Write a thesis statement.
3. Make an outline.
4. Write your answer.
5. Reread and revise your answer.

Read and Analyze the Question

Read an essay question carefully so that you know exactly what it calls for you to do. Look for three kinds of key words:

- Words that tell you *what subject* to write on.
- Words that tell you *how to write about it.*
- Words that tell you *how many parts* your answer should have.

Tells how many parts the answer should have

Discuss two major causes of personal bankruptcy in this country.

Tells how to write the response   Tells what subject to write about

Define and give examples of the phenomenon of global warming.

Tells how to write the response   Tells what subject to write about

The following chart translates some common types of essay questions into an action plan.

Analyzing Essay Questions

KEY WORDS	WHAT'S REQUIRED	SAMPLE ANSWER
"**Analyze** the theory of relativity."	Break into parts and discuss.	"The theory of relativity is made up of four components . . ."
"**Define** *carpetbaggers*."	State the meaning, and give examples.	"*Carpetbaggers* were people who. . . ."
"**Describe the steps** in taking a blood pressure reading."	List and explain the steps.	"To take a person's blood pressure, first. . . . Next, ... Finally, ..."
"**Discuss the causes of** poor air quality."	List and explain the causes.	"Poor air quality is caused by several different factors. . . ."

continued

KEY WORDS	WHAT'S REQUIRED	SAMPLE ANSWER
"Discuss the effects of ozone levels."	List and explain the effects.	"Ozone levels affect air quality in several different ways. . . ."
"Discuss the meaning of obesity."	Define and give examples.	"Obesity, which the NIH defines as having a body mass index of 30 or higher, is reaching epidemic proportions in some parts of the industrialized world. . . ."
"Compare obsession and compulsion."	List and give examples of how the two items are similar. (Note: Sometimes the word *compare* can mean to write about *both* similarities and differences. When in doubt, ask.)	"Obsession and compulsion are both. . . ." "Obsession and compulsion share some traits such as . . . , but they differ in. . . ."
"Discuss the similarities and differences between obsession and compulsion."	List and give examples of how the two items are similar *and* how they're different.	"Obsession and compulsion share some traits such as . . . , but they differ in. . . ."
"Contrast obsession and compulsion." *or* **"Discuss the differences between** obsession and compulsion."	List and give examples of how the two items are different.	"Obsession and compulsion are related disorders, but they are not the same. . . ."
"Evaluate John Smith's argument."	Make a judgment about the subject, and support that judgment with reasons, opinions, and evidence.	"John Smith's argument in favor of *X* has several weaknesses. . . ."

KEY WORDS	WHAT'S REQUIRED	SAMPLE ANSWER
"Explain the term *hyperactivity.*"	Define and give examples.	"*Hyperactivity* is a condition characterized by. . . ."
"Trace the development of the Industrial Revolution."	Explain the sequence of steps or stages of the subject.	"The Industrial Revolution in the United States began. . . ."
"Identify and discuss the major causes of *X.* "	List and give examples.	"The major causes of *X* are. . . ."
"Should sex education be taught?"	Argue for or against with reasons, opinions, and evidence.	"Sex education is essential to . . . because. . . ."
"Summarize the concept of equal rights."	Give a brief overview.	"In the United States, the concept of equal rights is the guarantee that. . . ."

PRACTICE 2   **IDENTIFYING KEY WORDS** . . . .

Read the following essay questions, and then circle the key words that tell what subject to write about, how to write about it, and how many parts to write. In the space below each item, explain what the question is asking the writer to do.

EXAMPLE: (Define) and (illustrate) (dependency.)
Give the meaning of the term dependency and give examples of it.

1. Identify three causes of the second war in Iraq.

_____

2. Trace the stages of grieving.

_____

3. Discuss the problem of the current energy crisis.

_____

4. Should drivers be banned from using handheld cell phones while driving? Why or why not?

_____

. . . .

Write a Thesis Statement

■ For more on writing a thesis statement, see Chapter 5.

Your response should include a thesis statement that is simple and clear. In the thesis statement, you may want to preview what you plan to cover in your answer because sometimes an instructor will give partial credit for information contained in the thesis even if you run out of time to explain fully.

The best way to stay on track in an essay exam is to write a thesis statement that contains the key words from the essay question and restates the question as a main idea. It also helps to reread your thesis statement several times as you write your exam response.

The following are possible thesis statements for the four essay questions from Practice 2. Because the answers would depend on material covered in a course or on particular student opinions, we have used blanks instead of specific answers.

Three major causes underlie the second Iraq war: _____,
_____, *and* _____.

People normally move through _____ *stages of grieving:*
_____, _____, _____,
(and however many there are).

The current energy crisis is a problem because it _____,
_____, *and* _____.

Drivers should be banned from using handheld cell phones while driving because of _____ *and* _____ (or however many reasons).

■ **PRACTICE 3   WRITING THESIS STATEMENTS** . . . .

Write possible thesis statements in response to the following sample essay exam questions. Even if you do not know the answer to the question, write a thesis statement that responds to the question and lets the reader know what you will cover (as in the possible answers above).

ESSAY EXAM QUESTION: Discuss the concept of First Amendment (free speech) protection as it relates to pornography on the Internet.

POSSIBLE THESIS STATEMENT: The protection of First Amendment rights is often cited as a reason not to ban pornography on the Internet.

1. Discuss the causes of the decline of the traditional "nuclear family" (two married parents and their children living under the same roof, without others).

   _____

2. Explain the effects of binge drinking.

   _____

3. Trace the development of the Industrial Revolution in Lowell, Massachusetts.

   _____

4. Describe the atmospheric conditions that precede a thunderstorm.

   _____

5. Discuss three advantages or three disadvantages of reliance on e-mail.

   _____

Make an Outline

Make a short, informal outline to map out your answer to an essay question or writing prompt. Include any important names, dates, or facts that occur to you. This outline will help you stick to your main points and remember essential details as you write.

■ For more on outlining, see Chapter 7.

The following short outline is for a possible essay on the causes for the decline of the traditional "nuclear family" (item 1 in Practice 3 above).

> *THESIS: Many forces have combined to cause a decline in the traditional "nuclear family," and they are not all negative.*
>
>   *CAUSE 1: High rate of divorce*
>
>   *% of marriages that end in divorce*
>
>   *CAUSE 2: Not as much social pressure to marry*
>
>   *Many famous couples have children without being married.*

CAUSE 3: *Families are defined in broader ways.*

Blended families

Single parents

Gay parents

CONCLUSION: *Many reasons: Restate causes; make an observation (concept of "family" has evolved)*

Write Your Answer

■ For more on the parts of an essay, see pages 49–51 and Chapters 7 and 8.

Your answer to an essay question should always be in essay form, with an introductory paragraph, several support points, and a concluding paragraph. It is a good idea to list all of your key points before providing details. Some teachers give partial credit for points that reflect your understanding of the topic, even if the points haven't been developed. At the very least, get down the thesis statement and then the first sentence of each support paragraph.

Here is an essay written by Brenda White of Quinsigamond Community College in response to the essay prompt "Discuss your role model."

Introduction states thesis and previews support points.

My role model is my best friend, Tanya, a single mother. Although young, unmarried parents are often looked down on in our society, Tanya has overcome many obstacles and is doing an excellent job raising her son. I admire her patience, independence, and willingness to work hard. With these qualities, she defies the stereotype of the teen parent.

Support point 1

Tanya could have made the choice to terminate her pregnancy, but she decided not to because she knew that she had the patience to raise a child, even under difficult circumstances. She has incredible patience with her son, Quentin. For example, when he's crying—even for a long time—she'll just rock him until he sleeps. Tanya also has patience with her friends. She understands that they have other things to do and can't always be counted on to watch Quentin. Tanya never gets mad if we can't help her out. She is also patient with her mother, who is very critical. Tanya's steady patience has gotten her through many difficult situations.

Independence is another trait that makes Tanya a good role model. She is raising her son without the help of her parents and mostly without Quentin's father. Tanya does not rely on others to care for her son or make decisions about his care; she does what needs to be done. She is also financially independent. She spends the money she earns wisely, only on things that are necessary. She pays her own tuition, rent, and, of course, the expenses of bringing up Quentin. Tanya has earned her independence and is wise about the actions she takes.

— Support point 2

Tanya is a very hard worker, pushing herself to the maximum. She works two jobs so she can provide for her growing son. Tanya also maintains an A average in her college courses. She has always gone beyond the normal, everyday achievements. For example, she graduated from high school on the honor roll while living on her own and supporting her son. She works hard and sticks to her belief that education is valuable. Tanya has gone beyond the traditional definition of hardworking.

— Support point 3

In some people's eyes, Tanya is just a single, teenage mother, a burden on society. But to me, Tanya is a wonderful role model. She has accomplished a lot in her young life. She has also gained control of her life and her surroundings by being patient, independent, and hardworking. Tanya is a single, teenage parent, but she is also a worthy role model.

Conclusion sums up and strengthens response to essay prompt.

Reread and Revise Your Answer

After you have finished writing your answer to an essay question, reread it carefully. Then, revise your response to make it clearer, more precise, and more detailed.

Teachers sometimes use a *scoring rubric*, which consists of the criteria—or standards—they use to judge the quality of an essay. Although scoring rubrics vary from one teacher to the next, most rubrics used to evaluate writing include some basic elements:

- Fulfills the assignment. (Has the writer followed the assignment and answered the question? Does the essay stay focused on the topic?)

- Contains a thesis statement. (Does the essay clearly state the topic and the writer's main point about it?)

- Contains accurate information. (Does the essay include correct answers or reliable information?)

- Provides adequate support for the thesis. (Is the thesis backed by major support points, which are in turn supported by examples and details?)

- Uses correct language and expression. (Is the essay free of major errors in grammar, mechanics, and usage?)

Scoring rubrics often have points or percentages attached to each element. A typical scoring rubric might look like this:

ELEMENT	TOTAL POINTS POSSIBLE	STUDENT SCORE
Adherence to assignment	20	18
Thesis statement	15	15
Accurate information	30	25
Development of ideas	25	20
Language and expression	10	10
TOTAL POINTS	**100**	**88**

■ For more on revising, see Chapter 9.

If your teacher provides you with a rubric, use it to set priorities as you review and revise your essay. Otherwise, consider the elements in the sample rubric as you revise your essay exam.

When you are writing by hand (rather than using a computer), revise your essay by neatly crossing out mistakes and adding extra words or sentences between the lines or in the margin, like this:

> *Groups of people living together have expectations about how*
>
> *the group should function and how to keep order within the group.*
>
> ~~*Societies need to have rules and laws.*~~ *This semester, we learned*
>
> *about social deviance, which is any behavior that does not conform to*
>
> *expectations of the group and which violates the group's sense of*
>
> *, those who break society's rules,*
> *order. For example, criminals* ^ *are social deviants. Rather than thinking*
>
> *that we can or should eliminate deviant behavior altogether, I agree*
>
> *with sociologist Emile Durkheim that deviance is* ~~*necessary.*~~ *a necessary*
> *element of any healthy social group.*

■ **WRITING ASSIGNMENTS** . . . .

Choose one of the following topics, and write an essay on it using the strategies for answering an essay question beginning on page 324. To practice with timed writing, give yourself a 50-minute time limit.

1. Write an essay agreeing or disagreeing with one of the following statements:

   > Schoolchildren have too many vacations.
   >
   > Most students cheat.
   >
   > People should be required to retire at age sixty-seven.
   >
   > People should live together before they get married.
   >
   > There are no valuable lessons to be learned from studying history.

2. Define *responsibility*.
3. Propose a solution to a major problem in your town or city.
4. Discuss a person who has had great influence on you.
5. Discuss an event that changed your life.

You Know This

You summarize and report on all kinds of things.

- You tell a classmate what happened during a class he or she missed.
- You tell a friend about an episode of a television program he or she missed.

20

Writing Summaries and Reports

Important College Writing Tasks

Writing a Summary

A **summary** is a condensed version of a piece of writing, a conversation, or an event. It presents main ideas and key support points in a brief form and in your own words.

> ### ▪▪ FOUR BASICS OF A GOOD SUMMARY
>
> **1.** It clearly identifies what is being summarized and presents its main idea.
> **2.** It concisely identifies the key support for the main idea.
> **3.** It includes any final observations or recommendations made in the original.
> **4.** It is written in your own words and is objective in tone, presenting information without opinions.

■ For more on citing and documenting sources, see Chapter 21. For more on summarizing, see Chapters 2 and 21.

If you are summarizing a piece of writing, read it carefully to make sure you understand the main idea and key points. Then, try to write the first draft of the summary without looking at the original. When you're done, check the summary for accuracy against the original. *Note:* You must always cite and document the source, even if you do not use quotations from it.

The following paragraph summarizes the reading on page 32. Read the original piece and then the summary. The numbers in the paragraph correspond to the four basics of a good summary.

1 In their book *Discovering Psychology,* Don H. Hockenbury and Sandra Hockenbury explain that the way we see color is determined by properties of light waves—hue, saturation, and brightness (94). **2** Hue is actually color, and the way we see color is determined by the wavelength of the light. Different wavelengths result in our seeing different colors. Saturation is how pure the light wave is. The more saturation, the deeper the color: Red is more saturated than pink, for example. Brightness is how intense the color looks and is caused by the strength of the light wave. **3** Although most of us think that the color of an item is built into that item—like our jeans are blue—the color is actually determined by the "wavelength of light that the object reflects" (94). The jeans reflect the wavelength of the blue on the spectrum of color, and dark blue jeans have a higher saturation and brightness than light blue jeans.

Source and relevant page number are cited.

4 Summary is in the writer's own words

Exact words from original are in quotation marks.

There are many uses for summarizing:

COLLEGE   You answer exam questions that ask you to summarize information.

WORK   You write a memo that summarizes the issues discussed and decisions made at a meeting.

EVERYDAY LIFE   You summarize for a partner your conversation with a plumber who was at your home to fix a pipe.

Follow the steps in the Writing Guide on the next page to help you with the summary assignments that follow it. Also, review the four basics of a good summary on page 334. Check off each step in the guide as you complete it.

Although this guide is geared to summaries of texts, you can also use it when summarizing films, events, and other nontext sources. First, note the key stages or details of the film, event, or whatever you are summarizing. Next, work through this guide, beginning with the "Review" step.

WRITING GUIDE: SUMMARY	
STEPS IN SUMMARIZING	**HOW TO DO THE STEPS**
Focus.	☐ As you read, think about how you will summarize the piece.
Read the selection you want to summarize.	☐ Highlight key points or put a check mark (✔) next to them.
	☐ Note the title and headings, words in **boldface** or *italics*, and boxed information or diagrams.
Review your highlighting and make notes. See Chapter 2 for advice on taking notes while reading.	☐ Note the author's main idea and the major events or support.
	☐ Jot down the details about the major events or support that will explain them to your readers.
	☐ Decide whether to quote specific parts of the original, and note any page references.
Make an outline. See Chapter 7 for more on outlining.	☐ Arrange the major events and details in a logical order.
Draft the summary. See Chapter 8 for more on drafting.	☐ As you write, refer to the original, but use your own words.
	☐ Include a thesis statement that expresses the author's main idea, and present a condensed version of the support for the thesis.
Revise the draft. See Chapter 9 for more on revising.	☐ Read your draft.
	☐ Make sure it includes the author's main idea and key points.
	☐ Add transitions to help your reader move smoothly from one key point to another.
	☐ Make sure you have given enough examples so that readers who haven't read the piece can understand the main idea.
	☐ Make sure you have cited the source of the piece, and if you have quoted from it, be sure to include the page reference (if it's a print work) and quotation marks. For more on using quotations, see page 363.
	☐ Make sure the summary (apart from direct quotations) is in your own words.
	☐ Check to make sure it follows the four basics of a good summary.
Edit your work. See Parts Four through Seven for editing advice.	☐ Check for errors in grammar, spelling, and punctuation.
	☐ Ask yourself: Is this the best I can do?

■ SUMMARY ASSIGNMENT ·

Read the article that follows, and use the Writing Guide on page 336 to write
a summary of it.

Survey Finds Many Firms Monitor Staff

Your employer could be watching you. Such are the findings of a
new study released last week by the American Management Association
(AMA) in New York. The survey of 1,626 large and midsize companies found that nearly 80 percent of major U.S. firms routinely check
their employees' e-mail, Internet, or telephone connections, and some
regularly videotape them at work.

"It's not just a matter of corporate curiosity," said Eric R. Greenberg, director of management studies at the American Management
Association. "Personal e-mail can clog a company's telecommunications
system, and sexually explicit or other inappropriate material downloaded
from the Internet can lead to claims of a hostile work environment."

Researchers have found that companies are more likely to conduct
random checks versus 24-hour surveillance of messages, phone conversations, or Internet usage. Even so, the AMA advises that employees use
discretion at work.

According to the survey, 63 percent of U.S. companies check
employees' Internet connections, up 54 percent since last year.
Forty-seven percent read workers' e-mail, up from 38 percent in
the year 2000. Forty percent have installed firewalls to prevent
employees from using the Internet inappropriately, up from
29 percent last year.

When asked whether they had fired workers because of
inappropriate use of electronic equipment, 27 percent of the
employers said they had dismissed staff for misuse of office
e-mail or Internet connections. Sixty-five percent of the companies had disciplined offenders. Ellen Bayer, the AMA's practice
leader on human rights issues, said the findings indicate that
privacy in the modern-day workplace is "largely illusory."

"In this era of open space cubicles, shared desk space,
networked computers, and teleworkers, it is hard to realistically
hold onto the belief in private space," said Bayer. She added that
some employees do not understand that their employers have a
legal right to monitor equipment that workers use on the job.

Employers also reported other forms of surveillance, such
as monitoring telephone numbers called (43 percent), logged
computer time (19 percent), and video surveillance for security
purposes (38 percent).

■ This article uses direct quotations from personal interviews conducted by the writer.

■ For an example of a summary of an essay-length piece, see page 37.

"In this era of open space cubicles, shared desk space, networked com-puters, and teleworkers, it is hard to realistically hold onto the belief in private space," said Bayer.

"In previous years, the growth in monitoring went hand in hand with increases in the share of employees gaining access to e-mail and the Internet," added AMA's Greenberg. "This year, the average share of employees with office connections barely grew at all, while monitoring of those activities rose by nearly 10 percent. It is important to note, however, that 90 percent of the companies engaging in any of these practices inform their employees that they are doing so."

But companies don't have to inform employees of any monitoring practice. In fact, most U.S. courts have ruled in favor of employers who routinely monitor telephones, computers, or other electronic equipment used on the job. It is best not to misuse company media: Your employer may be watching you.

> —Staff reporter, "Survey Finds Many Firms Monitor Staff," *Boston Sunday Globe*, April 29, 2001

■ MORE SUMMARY ASSIGNMENTS

■ For online exercises on summarizing, visit *Exercise Central* at **bedfordstmartins .com/realessays**.

1. Summarize the cover story of a recent issue of a magazine (print or online).

2. Summarize the plot of a movie you have seen recently.

3. Summarize an article from today's newspaper.

4. Summarize an essay or article, either from this book (see Part Eight) or from another book you use in a course.

5. Summarize Donnie Ney's argument essay from Chapter 18 (p. 301).

Writing a Report

A **report** usually begins with a summary that condenses a piece of writing, a conversation, or an event, and then it moves to some type of analysis. Recall that a summary is objective: You present a brief version without stating your opinions. In contrast, a report summarizes key points and also includes reactions to, opinions about, or recommendations based on the original piece.

▪▪ FOUR BASICS OF A GOOD REPORT

1. It identifies the title and author of the original piece in the first sentence or paragraph.

2. It summarizes the original piece, including the main idea and key support points or events.

3. It moves to the writer's reactions to the piece. This part of the report may relate the piece to the writer's own experiences, giving specific examples to support the responses.

4. It has a conclusion that evaluates the original piece on a variety of possible aspects — originality, realism, accuracy, intensity, interest, and so on. The conclusion usually gives a thumbs-up or thumbs-down for readers.

NOTE: Reports often use quotations for support in both the summary and the response sections.

In college classes, you may be assigned to write a book report. A student, Tiffany Shale, wrote the report that follows on Toni Morrison's best-selling novel *The Bluest Eye*. The numbers in it correspond to the four basics of a good report.

Before reading Tiffany's report, read her comments about her process for completing the assignment.

I knew I had to write a report on this book, so I read it in a different way than I would have otherwise. I kept a highlighter beside me when I read and turned down the pages where I highlighted things that might be important. The passages I highlighted really did help me write the report. If you note what's important as you read, it's easy to go back at the end and find quotes and key ideas.

Here's what I did to write the report:

1. I typed some notes about the highlights and their page numbers.

2. I wrote a short outline about what happened in the book.

3. I used the outline to write a summary of the plot. Then I put some of the highlighted stuff into the summary.

4. I wrote down some of my reactions to the book, including ones I'd jotted down while reading. I picked the ones I wanted to write about and wrote the section that gave details about my reactions.

continued

> *Then, I looked at my notes about the highlights and used any I could to support my reactions.*
>
> *5. I reread my draft and made changes.*
>
> *When I started the book, I thought it was stupid and didn't like it at all. But I knew I had to read it, and by the end I thought it was good. I don't think boys would like it, though. I felt bad for Pecola and what the world had done to her. Writing the report was hard, but when I finished, I really felt like I had understood the book, and I felt like I was doing real college work.*

■ Note that the present tense (Claudia's narrative *opens;* Pecola *is staying*) is used to describe the actions in a literary work.

Lasting Lessons in *The Bluest Eye*

1 In her first novel, *The Bluest Eye,* Toni Morrison writes about a time when racial and social prejudices were very strong. White people were more highly valued by society, and many African Americans learned to hate the characteristics that made them black. In *The Bluest Eye,* a young girl is destroyed by a society she longs to be part of.

Thesis statement

2 The tragic story of Pecola Breedlove is a flashback to 1941 told by two narrators. One is Claudia, a young girl whose family took in Pecola after her father burned down the family's house. Claudia's narrative opens each of the four parts of the book, which are arranged by seasons, starting with "Autumn" and ending with "Summer." In "Autumn," Pecola is staying with Claudia's family. In one scene, Frieda, Claudia's sister, and Pecola are admiring the image of Shirley Temple on a mug. Claudia doesn't like Shirley and talks about dolls she receives every Christmas. She says, "I destroyed white baby dolls. But the dismembering of dolls was not the true horror. The truly horrifying thing was the transference of the same impulses to little white girls" (22). Eventually, she learns to stop hating the white baby dolls and loves Shirley Temple. At the end of Claudia's autumn narrative, Pecola has started to menstruate. Frieda tells her that now she can have a baby, when someone loves her. Pecola asks, "How do you do that? I mean, get somebody to love you?" (31).

Topic sentence

Specific example

Direct quotation with page reference (see throughout)

Specific example

The omniscient narrator takes over, telling how Pecola's parents have a history of fighting violently. During the fights, Pecola wants to

Topic sentence

disappear and wonders why everyone either ignores or hates her. Every night, she prays for blue eyes because she believes that if she had blue eyes, like Shirley Temple or like white girls, people would love her. — Specific example

As the story continues, the reader learns more about the dismal history of Pecola's parents, who have learned to hate themselves and each other. — Topic sentence They neglect Pecola, reinforcing her view that no one loves her and intensifying her wish for blue eyes, the feature that she believes would transform her life. In one very ugly scene, Pecola's father rapes her, and her mother beats her when learning what happened. Pecola becomes pregnant, and Claudia and Frieda pray that her baby will be born healthy. But the baby dies. — Specific example

Abandoned and miserable, Pecola visits a sham mystic, begging him to give her blue eyes. — Topic sentence To get rid of a dog he hates, the mystic gives Pecola a poisoned piece of meat to feed the dog and tells her that if there is a sign, she will have blue eyes. The dog dies, and Pecola takes it as a sign. — Specific example But she is sickened by the dog's death.

In the final chapters of the book, Pecola is having a conversation with an imagined friend. She has gone mad. — Topic sentence But she believes that she has blue eyes and that people stare at her in envy. She fears, however, that perhaps someone else has bluer eyes, but her friend assures her she has "the bluest eyes." Morrison writes, "A little black girl yearns for the blue eyes of a little white girl, and the horror at the heart of her yearning is exceeded only by the evil of fulfillment" (204). Pecola gets her wish only by being destroyed. — Specific example

3 When I first started reading *The Bluest Eye,* I didn't like it, but now I realize that it is a fine book written by a talented author. — Topic sentence One part of Morrison's writing that impressed me was her use of symbols, like flower seeds and blue eyes. Claudia's first narrative begins, "Quiet as it's kept, there were no marigolds in the fall of 1941" (6). Claudia and Frieda plant marigold seeds and believe that if they grow, Pecola's baby will live. But they die, and so does the baby. In the last paragraph of the book, Claudia says, "I even think now that the land of the entire country was hostile to marigolds that year" (206). The marigold seeds are like Pecola, and just as the soil was hostile to them, society was hostile to Pecola, and they both — Specific example/ support

Specific support — die. The author often refers to blue eyes. They symbolize black women's wish to look white at a time when society's racism considered white features to be the ideal of beauty.

Topic sentence — I learned about history from the book. I knew people were prejudiced before, but I didn't know that many African Americans tried to be like whites. I didn't know that their attempts showed a self-hatred caused by racism, or that they hated those who were poorer and "blacker" than they were. In "Winter," Claudia writes about Maureen Peal, a new girl in school whom everyone loves. She is very light-skinned and dresses like white girls. In one scene, Maureen, Claudia, and Frieda come upon a group of boys who have surrounded Pecola and are making fun of her.

Specific support — Maureen breaks it up with just a look, after Claudia and Frieda have tried without luck. The boys hate Pecola because she is beneath them. As Morrison states, "It was their contempt for their own blackness that gave the first insult its teeth. . . . their exquisitely earned self-hatred was . . . sucked up into a fiery cone of scorn that had burned for all ages . . . and consumed whatever was in its path" (65). This book taught me about an important time that I didn't know about.

Topic sentence — What I most liked about *The Bluest Eye* is that I related to the story about people wanting to fit in, even if it means not being true to themselves. At first, Claudia doesn't love Shirley Temple, but she learns to love her and to dislike herself. Pecola just wants to be loved and thinks that if only she had blue eyes, she would be, but trying to be someone she isn't destroys her. I think many young people do things just to fit in because of pressure from their friends or other people's ideas of what is good. Morrison's book focuses on African Americans, but her lesson about not trying to be someone else applies to everyone.

Specific support —

Conclusion — **4** I think *The Bluest Eye* is an important book that is very well written. I would recommend that everyone read it because it has some important lessons not only about history but also about our lives today. I would like to read other books that Morrison has written.

Works Cited entry with publication information —

Works Cited

Morrison, Toni. *The Bluest Eye*. New York: Penguin, 1970.

Although many reports, like this one, begin with a summary and move on to an analysis, some writers weave the summary and analysis together. Look at newspaper or magazine reviews of books, films, and other works to see different ways that reports are constructed.

Many occasions call for your being able to report on things:

> ■ In reports, writers typically analyze and evaluate. For more on these and other typical college writing skills, see pages 38–40.

COLLEGE	An instructor in a business class assigns you to write a report based on a campus event, such as a presentation on marketing trends by a local professional.
WORK	Your manager asks you to review software from different suppliers who want your company's business. Your review must recommend which supplier to use.
EVERYDAY LIFE	You informally review a new restaurant or health club for your friends.

Follow the steps in the Writing Guide on the next page to help you with the report assignments below. Also, review the four basics of a good report (p. 339). Check off each step in the guide as you complete it.

Although this guide is geared to reports about texts, you can also use it when writing about films, events, and other nontext sources. First, note the key parts of the film, event, or whatever you are reporting on, and then jot down your reactions. Next, work through this guide, beginning with the "Review" step.

■ REPORT ASSIGNMENTS

1. Read an essay that your instructor assigns from Part Eight of this book, and write a report on it.

2. Write a review of a book that you have read for either this class or another one.

3. Write a review of a movie or live performance that you either very much liked or very much disliked.

4. Write a report that includes a summary of and reaction to a recent or proposed change in your town or on your campus.

5. Write a report of a class that you have taken recently.

WRITING GUIDE: REPORT	
STEPS IN WRITING REPORTS	**HOW TO DO THE STEPS**
Focus.	☐ Read with the idea in mind that you will be writing a report on the piece.
Read the piece you are to report on. See Chapter 2 for advice on reading.	☐ As you read, highlight key points or put a check mark (✔) next to them. ☐ Note the title and any headings, words in **boldface** or *italics,* and boxed information or diagrams.
Review your highlighting and make notes. See Chapter 2 for advice on taking notes while reading.	☐ Jot down the author's main idea and key points for the summary part of the report. ☐ Think about your reactions to the piece: What do *you* want to say about it? What did you learn? How does it relate to your experience? Would you recommend it to others? Why or why not? ☐ Write down your reactions and support for them. ☐ Note any sentences in the text that you may use in the report, including page numbers (if you are reporting on a print work).
Make an outline. See Chapter 7 for more on outlining.	☐ Organize your report, starting with the summary and explanation of major events and moving to your reactions to the piece. Or you can interweave the summary and analysis if that organization is more logical for your subject.
Draft the report. See Chapter 8 for more on drafting.	☐ Write the summary, referring to the original but using your own words. ☐ Write the reaction part of the report, evaluating the piece as well as relating it to your own experience. ☐ Use material from the original to explain or support your ideas. ☐ If you quote directly from the original, make sure to use quotation marks and page numbers (if you're reporting on a print source). For more on using quotations, see page 363. ☐ Write an introduction that includes a thesis statement with your stance on the piece. ☐ Write a concluding paragraph that restates your opinion of the piece and makes a recommendation. ☐ Title your report.

STEPS IN WRITING REPORTS	HOW TO DO THE STEPS
Revise the draft. See Chapter 9 for more on revising.	☐ Read your draft. ☐ Make sure it includes the author's main idea and key points. ☐ Consider your reactions and add details, either from your own experience or from the original piece. ☐ Add transitions to help your reader move smoothly from one key point to another. ☐ Make sure you have given enough examples so that readers who haven't read the piece can understand the main idea. ☐ Check to make sure it follows the four basics of a good report.
Edit your work. See Parts Four through Seven for editing advice.	☐ Check for errors in grammar, spelling, and punctuation. ☐ Ask yourself: Is this the best I can do?

You Know This

You have done your own research.

- You go online to learn more about an issue or product that interests you.
- You go online to research a health question or problem.

21
Writing the Research Essay
Using Outside Sources

■ Tammy S. Sugarman, a librarian at Georgia State University, provided many useful suggestions for this chapter.

This chapter will guide you through the process of writing a research essay. Throughout the chapter, we show how one student, Messelina Hernandez, worked through key steps in the process. Messelina's completed research essay on mandatory school uniforms appears on pages 376–79.

■ Visit **bedfordstmartins .com/researchroom** for complete resources to help you write and document a research paper.

STEPS TO WRITING A GOOD RESEARCH ESSAY

1. Make a schedule.
2. Choose a topic.
3. Find sources.
4. Evaluate sources.
5. Avoid plagiarism by taking careful notes.
6. Write a thesis statement.
7. Make an outline.
8. Write your essay.
9. Cite and document your sources.
10. Revise and edit your essay.

Make a Schedule

After you receive your assignment, make a schedule that divides your research assignment into small, manageable tasks. There is no way that you can do every step the day (or even a few days) before the assignment is due, so give yourself a reasonable amount of time.

You can use the following schedule as a model for making your own:

SAMPLE RESEARCH ESSAY SCHEDULE

Assignment: _____
          (Write out what your instructor has assigned.)

Length: _____

Draft due date: _____

Final due date: _____

My general topic: _____

My narrowed topic: _____

STEP	DO BY
Choose a topic.	_____
Find and evaluate sources.	_____
Take notes, keeping publication information for each source.	_____
Write a working thesis statement by answering a research question.	_____
Review all notes; choose the best support for your working thesis.	_____
Make an outline that includes your thesis and support.	_____
Write a draft, including a title.	_____
Review the draft; get feedback; add more support if needed.	_____
Revise the draft.	_____
Prepare a list of Works Cited using correct documentation form.	_____
Edit the revised draft.	_____
Submit the final copy.	_____

Choose a Topic

Your instructor may assign a topic, or you might be expected to think of your own. If you are free to choose your own topic, find a subject that you are personally interested in or curious about. If you need help, try asking yourself some of the following questions:

1. What is going on in my own life that I want to know more about?
2. What have I heard about lately that I'd like to know more about?
3. What am I interested in doing in the future, either personally or professionally, that I could investigate?
4. What famous person—living or deceased—most interests me?
5. What do I daydream about? What frightens me? What do I see as a threat to me or my family? What inspires or encourages me?
6. Is there something I do in my spare time (sports, music, computer games) that I'd like to know more about?

POSSIBLE TOPICS FOR A RESEARCH ESSAY

Assisted suicide	Marijuana for medical purposes
Causes of stress	Medical insurance
Childhood obesity	The minimum wage
Date rape	Music downloading
Dieting/eating disorders	Online dating services
Ethics: business/political/personal	Outsourcing jobs to foreign countries
Executive salaries	Patients' rights
The family in America	Pets and mental health
Gambling	Presidential campaigns
Gay/lesbian marriage/adoption	Reality television programs
Global warming	Rights of children of illegal immigrants
Gun control	Road rage
Identity theft	Sexual harassment
An illness	Standardized testing
Internet games	Violence in cities
Limiting cell phone use	Violence in the media
Mandatory drug testing	Women in military combat
Mandatory school uniforms	

When you have a general topic, jot down some answers to these questions:

1. Why is this topic interesting to me? How does it affect me? What do I hope to gain by exploring it?
2. What do I know about the topic? What do I want to find out?

Although a research essay may be longer than some of the other writing you have done, the topic still needs to be narrow enough to write about in the assigned length. It would be impossible, for example, to write a good five-page essay on the general topic "crime." A more specific topic—something like "neighborhood watch programs as crime deterrents"—is more manageable.

> ■ For more on narrowing a topic, see Chapter 4.

Before writing a working thesis statement, you need to learn more about your topic. It helps to come up with a **guiding research question** about your narrowed topic. This question—often a variation of "What do I want to find out?"—will help to guide and focus your research.

MESSELINA HERNANDEZ'S GUIDING RESEARCH QUESTION

Messelina chose school uniforms as her topic. She used the following research question to guide her research: *What are the effects of school uniforms?*

Find Sources

With both libraries and the Internet available to you, finding information is not a problem. Knowing how to find good, reliable sources of information, however, can be a challenge. The following strategies will help you.

Consult a Reference Librarian

Reference librarians are essential resources in helping to find appropriate information in both print and electronic forms. If your library allows it, schedule an appointment with the librarian. Before your appointment, jot down some questions to ask, such as those on the following list. Begin your conversation by telling the librarian your research topic.

QUESTIONS FOR THE LIBRARIAN

- How do I use the library's catalog? What information will it give me?
- Can I access the library catalog and article databases from home?
- What other reference tools would you recommend for research on my topic?
- Once I identify a source that might be useful, how do I find it?
- Can you recommend an Internet search engine that will help me find information on my topic? Can you recommend some useful key words to use?
- How can I tell whether a Web site is reliable?
- I've already found some articles related to my topic. Can you suggest some other places to look?

Use the Online Catalog or Card Catalog

■ For more on conducting keyword searches, see page 353.

Most libraries now list their holdings online rather than in a card **catalog,** but both systems give the same information—titles, authors, subjects, publication data, and call numbers. If you are working with a librarian, he or she may offer step-by-step instructions for using the online catalog. If you are working on your own, the Help menu is usually easy to find and easy to follow. Catalogs allow you to search by author, title, subject, or key word. If you are just beginning your research, you will probably use the keyword search because you may not know specific authors or titles.

Messelina Hernandez, whose research essay on mandatory school uniforms appears on pages 376–79, searched her library's online catalog using the key words *mandatory school uniforms.* Here is one book she found:

Author:	Hudson, David L., 1969-
Title:	Rights of Students
Published:	Philadelphia: Chelsea House Publishers, c2004
Location:	Briggs Nonfiction
Call #:	344.73/BRI
Status:	Available
Description:	120 p.; 23 cm./Part of "Point-Counterpoint" series
Contents:	Discusses constitutional rights in schools. Includes point/counterpoint discussion of mandatory school uniforms.
ISBN:	0-7910-7920-1
OCLC #:	ocm53376048

A **call number** is a book's library identification number. Knowing the call number will help you to locate a source in the library. Once you do locate the source, browse the shelves around it. Since a library's holdings are organized by subject, you may find other sources related to your topic nearby.

If the book is available only at another library, you can ask a librarian to have the book sent to your library.

Look at Your Library's Web Site

Many libraries have Web sites that can help researchers find useful information. The library's home page may have links to electronic research sources that it subscribes to and that are free to library users. It will also list the library's hours and resources, and it may offer research tips and other valuable information. It is a good idea to bookmark this site for future use.

Use Other Reference Materials

The reference section of the library has many resources that will help you find information on your topic. Here is a sampling of common reference sources. Most are available online or on CD-ROM.

Periodical Indexes and Databases

Magazines, journals, and newspapers are called **periodicals**. Periodical indexes help you locate information published in these sources. Online periodical indexes are called **periodical databases** and often include the full text of magazine, journal, or newspaper articles. If your topic is a current one, such as Messelina Hernandez's on mandatory school uniforms, you may find more information in periodicals than in books. Following are some of the most popular periodical indexes and databases:

- InfoTrac
- LexisNexis
- NewsBank
- *New York Times Index*
- ProQuest
- *Readers' Guide to Periodical Literature*

Specialized Indexes

Specialized indexes—in book form, online, or on CD-ROM—direct you to resources in various broad subject areas. A few of the many indexes are the following:

- *America: History and Life*
- *Biological Abstracts*
- Educational Resources Information Center (ERIC)
- *MLA International Bibliography* (language and literature)
- PsychLIT

Encyclopedias

While most instructors will want you to use more specialized sources, encyclopedias can be a good place to start your research because they give you an overview of a subject. You might also consult the bibliography that concludes most encyclopedia entries. Some encyclopedias, like the *Encyclopædia Britannica,* are available in print, online, and on CD-ROM.

In addition to general encyclopedias, your library may have specialized encyclopedias that give more detailed information on your topic. For instance, you might consult the *Encyclopedia of Psychology* for a research paper in a psychology course.

Statistical Sources

■ Visit **www.census .gov**, the official Web site of the U.S. Census Bureau, for current state and national statistical data related to population, economics, and geography.

Statistical data, or facts and figures, that are directly related to your thesis can provide sound support. As one example, the *Statistical Abstract of the United States* (published annually by the U.S. Census Bureau) can help you locate useful statistics related to social issues, population trends, economics, and other topics.

Use the Internet

The Internet, a vast global computer network, provides access to all kinds of information. The biggest part of the Internet is called the World Wide Web, which allows users to jump from site to site using hyperlinks. If you are new to using the Web, this section will offer some basics. You might also want to work with a librarian, a writing-center tutor, or a knowledgeable friend to help you navigate the Web. To get started, you can go to some sites that categorize information on the Web, such as the Internet Public Library (**www.ipl.org**) or the Librarians' Internet Index (**www.lii.org**).

NOTE: Some Internet sites charge fees for information (such as archived newspaper or magazine articles). Before using any of these, check to see if the sources are available free through your library.

Uniform Resource Locator (URL)

Every Web site has an address, called a **uniform resource locator** (URL). You may already be familiar with some frequently advertised URLs, such as **www.amazon.com** (the Internet address for bookseller Amazon.com) or the URL for your college's Web site. If you know the URL of a Web site that you think would be helpful to your research, enter it into the address field of your Web browser. (**Web browsers**, like Microsoft Internet Explorer and Netscape Navigator, are software programs that allow a computer to read Web pages.)

Search Engines and Searching with Key Words

If you do not know the URL of a particular site you want to visit or if you want to look at multiple Web sites related to your topic, you will need to use a search engine. Of the following commonly used search engines, Google is the most popular.

- Google (**www.google.com**)
- Yahoo (**www.yahoo.com**)
- America Online (**www.aol.com**)
- Ask.com (**www.ask.com**)
- MSN.com (**www.msn.com**)

To use a search engine, type in key words from your subject. Because the Web is large, adding specific key words or phrases and using an advanced-search option may reduce the number of entries (called *hits*) you have to sift through to find relevant information. Search engines typically have a Help feature that offers guidance in using the engine, selecting key words, and refining your search.

Google search using phrase in quotes

Refined Google search (phrase in quotes plus additional term— mandatory—and plus signs)

When Messelina Hernandez entered *school uniforms* as a search term in Google, her search netted about 9,710,000 hits. (She put quotation marks around *school uniforms* to tell Google she wanted items related to this phrase only, not to *school* and *uniforms* separately, which would have returned many more results not related to her research topic.) She immediately saw some irrelevant entries, such as those related to purchasing school uniforms.

Messelina then refined her search by adding the word *mandatory* to the phrase *school uniforms*. She added "+" signs before each term to indicate that both terms had to appear in every result. This strategy reduced the number of hits to about 58,000 and produced results more relevant to Messelina's research question.

Messelina's search helped her refine her research question:

> **MESSELINA HERNANDEZ'S REFINED RESEARCH QUESTION:** *What are the effects of mandatory school uniforms?*

Adding additional search terms can narrow a search even more.

When you discover a Web site that you might want to return to, save the URL so that you don't have to remember it each time you want to go to the site. Different browsers have different ways of saving URLs; choose "Bookmarks" in Netscape or Firefox, or choose "Favorites" in Internet Explorer.

Online Research Sites

Online research sites constitute another valuable source of information on how to do research. At **www.bedfordstmartins.com/researchroom** (see p. 356), the publisher of this book hosts the *Bedford Research Room*, which includes guided tutorials on research processes; advice on finding, evaluating, and documenting sources; tips on avoiding plagiarism; and more. Other useful sites include Purdue University's Online Writing Lab (OWL) at **http://owl.english.purdue.edu**. This site offers a variety of materials and resources for writers, including research information.

Interview People

Personal interviews can be excellent sources of information. Before interviewing anyone, however, plan carefully. First, consider what kind of person to interview. Do you want information from an expert on the subject or from someone directly affected by the issue? How would the experience or comments of each person help support your points? The person should be knowledgeable about the subject and have firsthand experience. When you have decided whom to interview, schedule an appointment.

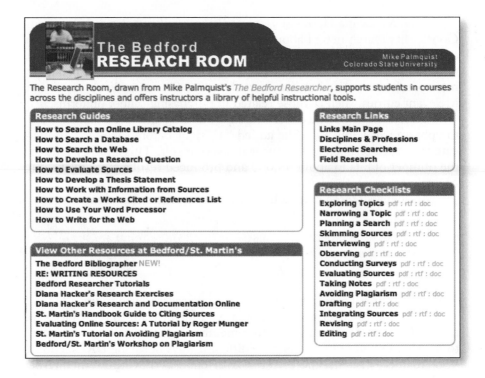

The Research Room, drawn from Mike Palmquist's *The Bedford Researcher*, supports students in courses across the disciplines and offers instructors a library of helpful instructional tools.

Research Guides

How to Search an Online Library Catalog
How to Search a Database
How to Search the Web
How to Develop a Research Question
How to Evaluate Sources
How to Develop a Thesis Statement
How to Work with Information from Sources
How to Create a Works Cited or References List
How to Use Your Word Processor
How to Write for the Web

View Other Resources at Bedford/St. Martin's

The Bedford Bibliographer NEW!
RE: WRITING RESOURCES
Bedford Researcher Tutorials
Diana Hacker's Research Exercises
Diana Hacker's Research and Documentation Online
St. Martin's Handbook Guide to Citing Sources
Evaluating Online Sources: A Tutorial by Roger Munger
St. Martin's Tutorial on Avoiding Plagiarism
Bedford/St. Martin's Workshop on Plagiarism

Research Links

Links Main Page
Disciplines & Professions
Electronic Searches
Field Research

Research Checklists

Exploring Topics pdf : rtf : doc
Narrowing a Topic pdf : rtf : doc
Planning a Search pdf : rtf : doc
Skimming Sources pdf : rtf : doc
Interviewing pdf : rtf : doc
Observing pdf : rtf : doc
Conducting Surveys pdf : rtf : doc
Evaluating Sources pdf : rtf : doc
Taking Notes pdf : rtf : doc
Avoiding Plagiarism pdf : rtf : doc
Drafting pdf : rtf : doc
Integrating Sources pdf : rtf : doc
Revising pdf : rtf : doc
Editing pdf : rtf : doc

Next, to get ready for the interview, prepare a list of five to ten questions. Ask open-ended questions (What is your position on regulating cell-phone use by drivers?) rather than questions that require only a simple yes-or-no response (Do you favor regulating cell-phone use by drivers?). Leave space for notes about the person's responses and for additional questions that may occur to you during the interview. Include in your notes the person's full name and qualifications and the date of the interview.

As you conduct the interview, listen carefully, and write down any important ideas. If you plan to use any of the interviewee's exact words, put them in quotation marks in your notes. (For more on using direct quotes, see page 363 of this chapter and Chapter 39).

NOTE: If you plan to record an interview, get your subject's permission first. Recording what a person says without being granted permission is unethical and, in some states, against the law.

Evaluate Sources

Evaluating sources means judging them to determine how reliable and appropriate for your topic they are. Reliable sources present accurate, up-to-date information written by authors with appropriate credentials for the subject matter. Reliable sources support claims with evidence and use objective, reasonable language. Research materials found in a college library (books, journals, and newspapers, for example) are generally considered reliable sources.

Don't assume that an Internet source is reliable just because it exists. Anyone can create a Web site and put whatever he or she wants on it. When you're viewing a Web site, try to determine its purpose. A Web site set up solely to provide information may be more reliable than an online product advertisement. If you are searching the Web for information about the psychological benefits of weight loss, for example, you will find sources ranging from articles published by the *Journal of the American Medical Association* (reliable) to advertisements for miraculous weight-loss products (questionable). Whether you are doing research for a college course, a work assignment, or personal use, make sure that the sources you draw on are reliable and appropriate for your purpose.

■ **PRACTICE   EVALUATING WEB SITES** . . . .

A keyword search for attention-deficit/hyperactivity disorder (ADHD) would point a researcher to thousands of sites; the ones shown below and on page 358 are just samples. Which do you think contains more reliable information? Why?

· ·

❶ Site is sponsored by the makers of the ADHD drug Concerta.

❷ Links offer ADHD-related information and "success stories" supportive of the drug's use.

❸ No specific publication date or date of last update is given.

❶ Site is sponsored by the Centers for Disease Control, a U.S. government agency dedicated to protecting the health of American citizens.

❷ Objective presentation of information

❸ Links to current information

❹ Clear contact information

❺ Date of last update, showing that information is current

❻ Links to related information, including "ADHD references," with full information on the sources cited

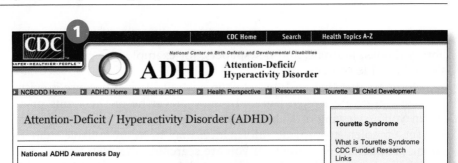

| CDC Home | Search | Health Topics A-Z |

National Center on Birth Defects and Developmental Disabilities

ADHD Attention-Deficit/Hyperactivity Disorder

▶ NCBDDD Home ▶ ADHD Home ▶ What is ADHD ▶ Health Perspective ▶ Resources ▶ Tourette ▶ Child Development

Attention-Deficit / Hyperactivity Disorder (ADHD)

National ADHD Awareness Day

Tuesday, **September 7, 2004** marks the inaugural National ADHD Awareness Day. In resolution S.370, the U.S. Senate recognized Attention-Deficit/Hyperactivity Disorder (ADHD) as a major public health concern and encouraged the federal government to raise public awareness about ADHD and to improve access to mental health services for children and adults with the illness. National ADHD Awareness Day highlights the significance of this disorder to many American children, families, and adults. For the actual Senate Resolution 370.

Attention-Deficit/Hyperactivity Disorder (ADHD) is one of the most common childhood behavioral disorders and can persist through adolescence and into adulthood. The causes are currently unknown.

Announcing
The National Resource Center on AD/HD

May 20, 2003 marked the official opening of the Children and Adults with Attention-Deficit/Hyperactivity Disorder's (CHADD) National Resource Center (NRC) on AD/HD, the country's first and only national clearinghouse dedicated to the evidence-based science and treatment of AD/HD. The clearinghouse is a collaboration between the CDC and CHADD, an advocacy organization serving individuals with AD/HD...

National Resource Center website, http://www.help4adhd.org has a toll-free number (800-233-4050). The Website answers many of your questions about AD/HD and directs you to other reliable sources online. New material is regularly being added. If you don't find the answers you are looking for, you can click on Ask a question about AD/HD, found on every page of this site. Your question will be directed to one of the knowledgeable Health Information Specialist for a response.

What is AD/HD?

According to the 2000 American Psychiatric Association's Diagnostic and Statistical Manual, Text Revision, of Mental Disorders-IV (DSM-IV-TR), ADHD is a Disruptive Behavior Disorder characterized by on-going inattention and/or hyperactivity-impulsivity occurring in several settings and more frequently and severely than is typical for individuals in the same stage of development. Symptoms begin before age 7 years and can cause serious difficulties in home, school or work life. ADHD can be managed through behavioral or medical interventions, or a combination of the two.

The National Center on Birth Defects and Developmental Disabilities has developed a research agenda in ADHD for CDC and/or other public agencies (click here for research agenda).

[ADHD References]

[Return to Top]

This page was last updated September 02, 2004

Tourette Syndrome

What is Tourette Syndrome
CDC Funded Research
Links

Report ❸

Report of the Surgeon General's Conference on Children's Mental Health: A National Action Agenda

Search Health Topics

Birth Defects
Developmental Disabilities
Human Development
Disability and Health
Hereditary Blood Disorders

Publications Search

Search by Author
Search by Keyword
Search by Title
Search by Year

Contact Us ❹

Thank you for visiting the CDC-NCBDDD Web site. In order to contact the National Center on Birth Defects and Developmental Disabilities, please click here

ADHD Home | What is ADHD? | Symptoms of ADHD | Peer Relationships | ADHD and Risk of Injuries | Public Health Perspective | Conference | Publications | ADHD References | Internet Links | CDC Funded Research | Contact Us

CDC Home | Search | Health Topics A-Z

Accessibility | Privacy Policy Notice

Centers for Disease Control and Prevention
National Center on Birth Defects and Developmental Disabilities

We promote the health of babies, children, and adults, and enhances the potential for full, productive living. Our work includes identifying the causes of birth defects and developmental disabilities, helping children to develop and reach their full potential, and promoting health and well-being among people of all ages with disabilities.

Here are some questions you can ask to evaluate a source. If you answer "no" to any of these questions, think twice about using the source.

QUESTIONS FOR EVALUATING A PRINT OR ELECTRONIC SOURCE

- Is the source up-to-date?
- Is the source reliable? Is it from a reputable publisher or Web site? (For Web sites, consider the URL extension; see the box below.)
- Is the information appropriate for your research topic?
- Is the author qualified to write reliably about the subject? If there is no information on the author, try an online search using the author's name.
- Who sponsored the publication or Web site? Be aware of the sponsor's motives (for example, to market a product) and the ways that they might affect the type of information presented.
- Does the information seem fair and objective? If there is a bias, does the author state his or her position up front?
- Does the author provide adequate support for key points, and does he or she cite the sources of this support?

■ For more information on evaluating online sources, visit **bedfordstmartins .com/researchroom**.

Guide to URL Extensions

EXTENSION	TYPE OF SITE	HOW RELIABLE?
.com	A commercial or business organization or a personal site	Varies. Consider whether you have heard of the organization, and be sure to read its home page or "About us" link carefully.
.edu	An educational institution	Varies. It may include student home pages and course materials of variable quality.
.gov	A government agency	Generally reliable
.net	A commercial or business organization or a personal site	Varies. This extension indicates just the provider, not anything about the source. Go to the source's home page to find out what you can about the author or the sponsor.
.org	A nonprofit organization	Generally reliable. Each volunteer or professional group promotes its own view or interests, however.

Avoid Plagiarism

Plagiarism is passing off someone else's ideas and information as your own. Turning in a paper written by someone else, whether it is from the Internet or written by a friend or family member who gives you permission, is deliberate plagiarism. Sometimes, however, students plagiarize by mistake because they have taken notes that do not distinguish a source's ideas from their own or that do not fully record source information, including publication data. As you find information for your research essay, do not rely on your memory to recall details about your sources; take good notes from the start. For more on how to avoid plagiarism, visit the Bedford Research Room at **bedfordstmartins.com/researchroom**.

NOTE: This section's advice on recording, citing, and documenting sources reflects Modern Language Association (MLA) style, the preferred style for the humanities.

Keep a Running Bibliography

A **bibliography** is a complete list, alphabetized by author, of the outside sources you consult. A **list of works cited** is a complete list, alphabetized by author, of the outside sources that you actually use in your essay. Most instructors require a list of works cited at the end of a research essay. Some may require a bibliography as well.

You can keep information for your bibliography and list of works cited on notecards or on your computer. Whatever method you use, be sure to record complete publication information for each source at the time you consult it; this will save you from having to look up this information again when you are preparing your list of works cited.

The following is a list of information to record for each source. For Messelina Hernandez's list of works cited, see page 379.

BOOKS	ARTICLES	WEB PAGES/OTHER ELECTRONIC SOURCES
Author name(s)	Author name(s)	Author name(s)
Title and subtitle	Title of article	Title of Web page/online material
—	Title of magazine, journal, or newspaper	Title of site/larger work (e.g., online periodical)
City of publication and publisher	—	Name of sponsoring organization OR database, provider, and subscribing institution (if any)

BOOKS	ARTICLES	WEB PAGES/OTHER ELECTRONIC SOURCES
Year of publication	Date of publication	Date of publication or latest update
—	Page number(s)	Page, section, or paragraph numbers (if provided)
—	—	Date on which you accessed the site
—	—	URL (online address)

You will probably integrate source material by summary, paraphrase, and direct quotation. As you take notes, record the method you are using so that you don't accidentally plagiarize.

Indirect Quotation: Summary

A summary puts the main point of a piece of writing in your own words. When you summarize, follow these guidelines:

■ For more on writing summaries, see Chapters 2 and 20.

- Make sure to identify the outside source clearly.

- Include in parentheses the page number(s), if available, of the entire section you have summarized. (You will need to provide full publication information later, in a list of works cited.)

SUMMARY OF AN ARTICLE

In "Effects of Student Uniforms on Attendance, Behavior Problems, Substance Abuse, and Academic Achievement," David L. Brunsma and Kerry A. Rockquemore report that mandatory school uniforms have no direct positive effects on substance abuse, behavior, or attendance. In fact, they claim that uniforms may have a negative effect on academic achievement (53–62). ———— Parenthetical reference

⎤ Identifying
⎦ information

Indirect Quotation: Paraphrase

Paraphrasing is restating another's ideas in your own words. Be careful when you paraphrase because it is easy to think you are using your own words when you are actually mixing your own and the source's. These guidelines can help:

- Don't look at the source while you are writing the paraphrase.

- Check your paraphrase against the original source to make sure you have not used the author's words or copied the author's sentence structure.

- Make sure to introduce the outside source—for example, "Marie Winn says that. . . ."
- Include in parentheses the page number(s), if available, of the section you have paraphrased. (You will need to provide full publication information later, in a list of works cited.)

Read the examples that follow to see acceptable and unacceptable paraphrases.

ORIGINAL SOURCE

Not unlike drugs or alcohol, the television experience allows the participant to blot out the real world and enter into a pleasurable and passive mental state. To be sure, other experiences, notably reading, also provide a temporary respite from reality. But it's much easier to stop reading and return to reality than to stop watching television. The entry into another world offered by reading includes an easily accessible return ticket. The entry via television does not. In this way television viewing, for those vulnerable to addiction, is more like drinking or taking drugs—once you start, it's hard to stop.

—from Marie Winn, *The Plug-In Drug*

UNACCEPTABLE PARAPHRASE (TOO CLOSE TO ORIGINAL)

Marie Winn says that like drugs or alcohol, television allows people to blot out reality and escape into the passive world of television. Reading also provides a break from the real world, but it's easier to put down a book than to turn off the television. Therefore, in people susceptible to addiction, television viewing is more like drinking or taking drugs than reading: It's much harder to stop once you've started.

This paraphrase is unacceptable for several reasons:

- The paraphrase too closely follows the wording of the original. (The writer has written the paraphrase while looking at the original source rather than expressing the ideas in his or her own words.)
- The writer hasn't included the page numbers of the source.

ACCEPTABLE PARAPHRASE

Identifying phrase ——————— Marie Winn says that although television and reading both offer a break from reality, television watching is harder to stop and can therefore be considered "addictive" in a way that reading

Parenthetical reference ——————— cannot (32).

The acceptable paraphrase presents Winn's basic ideas but in the writer's own words and structures. It also includes a parenthetical reference. The writer read Winn's paragraph but then wrote the paraphrase without looking at the original. Then, the writer checked the original again to make sure she hadn't missed any ideas or repeated words or sentence structures.

Direct Quotation

Use these guidelines when you write direct quotations:

- Record the exact words of the source.
- Include the name of the writer or speaker. If there is more than one writer or speaker, record all names.
- Enclose the writer's or speaker's words in quotation marks.
- For print sources, include the page number, if available, on which the quote appeared in the original source. The page number should go in parentheses after the end quotation mark but *before* the period. If the person quoted is not the author of the book or the article, give the author's name in parentheses along with the page number. If there are two or three authors, give all names.
- If a direct quotation is more than four typed lines or forty words, indent the whole quotation, and do not use quotation marks. Place the page number, in parentheses, *after* the final punctuation.

DIRECT QUOTATION   Identifying phrase   Quotation marks

According to Dr. Min Xiao, "The psychological benefits of a well-lit workspace are significant" (28).

Parenthetical reference

According to Dr. Min Xiao,

> The psychological benefits of a well-lit workspace are significant. Workers can see what they are doing better and don't have to squint or lean over their work to see it. Moreover, the light can provide a sense of well-being, simulating daylight. This is particularly important when workers are in cubicles in the middle of a floor with no natural light. (28)

■ For online exercises on summarizing, paraphrasing, and quoting, visit *Exercise Central* at **bedfordstmartins .com/realessays**.

On the next two pages, you can see one of Messelina Hernandez's original sources, a newspaper editorial she found online, with illustrations of how she summarized, paraphrased, quoted from it, and recorded publication information in her final paper.

http://www.dispatch.com/live/contentbe/dispatch/2006/01/16/20060116-A6-00.html

The Columbus Dispatch
dispatch.com

Keywords: [ ] SEARCH

HOME | NEWS | LOCAL | OPINION | OSU SPORTS | MORE SPORTS | BUSINESS | LIFE | ENTERTAINMENT | MULTIMEDIA | BLOGS | SERVICES

Sign up for newsletters | Search the archive

Dressed for success

Study shows high-school graduation rates rise when kids wear uniforms

Monday, January 16, 2006

If wearing uniforms increases highschool graduation rates, as a new study indicates, more school administrators should adopt this option. Even though the study was unable to link any improvements in test scores with students' attire, more diplomas will translate into increased job and training opportunities for the young people involved.

A high-school diploma is a key to success beyond the classroom.

Most significant, this particular study examined data in 64 high schools within eight of Ohio's largest urban public-school districts, where keeping kids in school is a real challenge. These districts — Akron, Canton, Cincinnati, Cleveland, Columbus, Dayton, Toledo and Youngstown — face a constant struggle to raise graduation rates.

But within these districts, the study of data from 1994 to 2002, comparing six high schools where students wore uniforms with similar schools without such standards, showed remarkable differences in students' attitudes.

While the mean graduation rates at the five schools where before- and after-uniform data could be analyzed rose 10.9 percentage points, rates at schools without uniforms fell 4.6 percentage points.

Suspensions dropped dramatically after students began wearing uniforms, and attendance generally improved, rising in four schools but dipping in two.

One school in Cleveland, three in Youngstown, one in Dayton and East High School in Columbus all began requiring uniforms in the 1997-98 school year and made up the group analyzed by Virginia Draa, assistant professor of human ecology at Youngstown State University.

Draa noted that East no longer requires uniforms but that it did throughout the study period and also showed some improvement in academics, as measured by proficiency test scores.

She conducted the research in connection with her dissertation for a doctorate in educational leadership.

She looked closely at schools with similar demographics and similar programs, making every effort to establish controls for other factors, such as tutoring, that could affect students' behavior and performance.

Her complete lack of any preconceived notion as to what the results would be add credibility to the study. In fact, as a former teacher in the Youngstown and Toledo public schools, she said she was "skeptical that they would have any impact," but now, she said, "I'm a convert to school uniforms."

She concluded that uniforms "do help in addressing problems with discipline and attendance," but added, "People should not expect miraculous improvements overnight in the school climate or even in one year."

As a professor of fashion and interiors merchandising, Draa has studied the social psychology of appearance and clothing, which shows that how people dress can influence how they behave and how they treat others.

Clearly, wearing uniforms at school can help create a more businesslike atmosphere that fosters learning. And, without the peer pressure to wear certain clothing, students apparently have less incentive to skip classes or drop out.

Columbus Public Schools established a dress code in the fall. That's a step in the right direction, but requiring uniforms might bring better results and be easier to administer.

WBNS (10TV) | Ohio News Network | Columbus Alive | 1460 The Fan | Mix 97.1 | BuckeyeXtra | ThisWeek Community Newspapers | TheBAG | Columbus Parent Magazine | Dispatch Español |

©2006, The Columbus Dispatch. Reproduction prohibited.
Home | Site map | Privacy policy | Advertise with Dispatch.com | Help!

Messelina's Thesis: Mandatory school uniforms offer extraordinary benefits to students and school systems, including improvements in students' self-esteem, attendance, academic performance, graduation rates, and safety.

Indirect Quotation: Summary

- **TYPICAL USE:** A summary briefly notes major evidence that supports your thesis.
- **EXAMPLE:** Messelina focuses on the major evidence in the editorial that supports her thesis—in this case, research that shows the benefits of school uniforms. Her introduction of this evidence and its source—the "glue" connecting the source information to the thesis—is underlined.

> <u>"Dressed for Success," a pro-uniform editorial in the Columbus Dispatch, highlights</u> Virginia Draa's 2006 study showing that graduation rates at sixty-four Ohio high schools improved after they implemented mandatory uniforms.

Indirect Quotation: Paraphrase

- **TYPICAL USE:** A paraphrase focuses on details that support your thesis, not on major evidence or overarching ideas.
- **EXAMPLE:** Messelina focuses on details that give specific examples and evidence. The words she uses to connect the paraphrase to her essay are underlined.

> <u>As noted in "Dressed for Success,"</u> Draa's study found that graduation rates at the schools rose by 10.9 percent between 1994 and 2002, while graduation rates at similar high schools dropped by 4.6 percent.

Direct Quotation

- **TYPICAL USE:** A direct quotation is used when the author's or speaker's words strongly support the thesis.
- **EXAMPLE:** Messelina uses quotations that support her thesis but avoids overquoting. Her connecting words are underlined.

> <u>The editorial concludes that</u> "more diplomas will translate into increased job and training opportunities for the young people. A high school diploma is a key to success beyond the classroom" ("Dressed for Success").

Works Cited Entry (MLA style)

"Dressed for Success." Editorial. Columbus Dispatch 16 Jan. 2006. 22 Jan. 2008 <http://www.dispatch.com/live/contentbe/dispatch/2006/01/16/20060116-A6-00.html>.

Write a Thesis Statement

■ For more on writing a thesis statement, see Chapter 5.

After you have taken notes on the sources you gathered, you should be ready to write a thesis statement, which states the main idea of your research essay. You can start by turning your guiding research question into a statement that answers the question, as Messelina does below. Note how she revises her thesis to make it more forceful and concrete.

> **MESSELINA HERNANDEZ'S GUIDING RESEARCH QUESTION:** *What are the effects of mandatory school uniforms?*
>
> **THESIS STATEMENT:** *Mandatory school uniforms have positive effects on students.*
>
> **REVISED THESIS STATEMENT:** *Mandatory school uniforms offer extraordinary benefits to students and school systems, including improvements in students' self-esteem, attendance, academic performance, graduation rates, and safety.*

As you write and revise your essay, your thesis statement may change, but having a good working one helps you focus your writing and see where you might need to do additional research.

Make an Outline

■ For more on outlining, see Chapter 7.

To organize your notes, you need to make an outline that supports your thesis. First, write down your thesis statement. Then, review your notes to decide what your three or four major support points will be. Write these under your thesis statement and number them. Under each major support point, write two or three supporting details, and number them.

Many students, like Messelina, use complete sentences in their outlines to help them remember what they want to say when they write a draft. As they write and revise their drafts, they can change the sentences and add further details.

MESSELINA HERNANDEZ'S OUTLINE

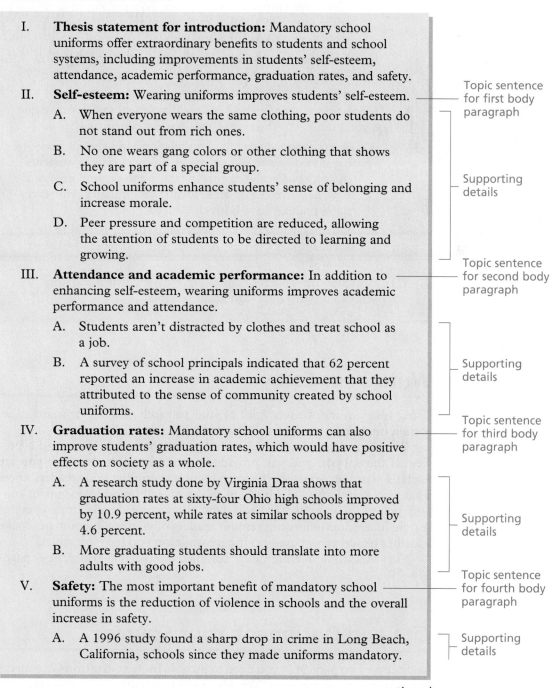

I.   **Thesis statement for introduction:** Mandatory school uniforms offer extraordinary benefits to students and school systems, including improvements in students' self-esteem, attendance, academic performance, graduation rates, and safety.

II. **Self-esteem:** Wearing uniforms improves students' self-esteem.

   A.   When everyone wears the same clothing, poor students do not stand out from rich ones.

   B.   No one wears gang colors or other clothing that shows they are part of a special group.

   C.   School uniforms enhance students' sense of belonging and increase morale.

   D.   Peer pressure and competition are reduced, allowing the attention of students to be directed to learning and growing.

III. **Attendance and academic performance:** In addition to enhancing self-esteem, wearing uniforms improves academic performance and attendance.

   A.   Students aren't distracted by clothes and treat school as a job.

   B.   A survey of school principals indicated that 62 percent reported an increase in academic achievement that they attributed to the sense of community created by school uniforms.

IV. **Graduation rates:** Mandatory school uniforms can also improve students' graduation rates, which would have positive effects on society as a whole.

   A.   A research study done by Virginia Draa shows that graduation rates at sixty-four Ohio high schools improved by 10.9 percent, while rates at similar schools dropped by 4.6 percent.

   B.   More graduating students should translate into more adults with good jobs.

V.   **Safety:** The most important benefit of mandatory school uniforms is the reduction of violence in schools and the overall increase in safety.

   A.   A 1996 study found a sharp drop in crime in Long Beach, California, schools since they made uniforms mandatory.

Topic sentence for first body paragraph

Supporting details

Topic sentence for second body paragraph

Supporting details

Topic sentence for third body paragraph

Supporting details

Topic sentence for fourth body paragraph

Supporting details

continued

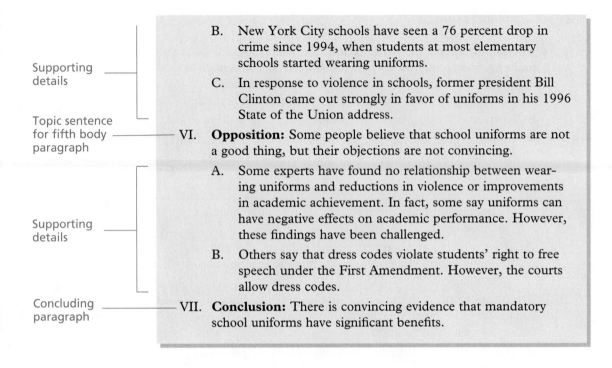

Supporting details

Topic sentence for fifth body paragraph

Supporting details

Concluding paragraph

B. New York City schools have seen a 76 percent drop in crime since 1994, when students at most elementary schools started wearing uniforms.

C. In response to violence in schools, former president Bill Clinton came out strongly in favor of uniforms in his 1996 State of the Union address.

VI. **Opposition:** Some people believe that school uniforms are not a good thing, but their objections are not convincing.

A. Some experts have found no relationship between wearing uniforms and reductions in violence or improvements in academic achievement. In fact, some say uniforms can have negative effects on academic performance. However, these findings have been challenged.

B. Others say that dress codes violate students' right to free speech under the First Amendment. However, the courts allow dress codes.

VII. **Conclusion:** There is convincing evidence that mandatory school uniforms have significant benefits.

Write Your Essay

Using your outline, write a draft of your research essay. (For more information on writing a draft, see Chapter 8.)

Your **introduction** should include your thesis statement and a preview of the support you will provide in the body of the essay. If you are taking a stand on an issue, the introduction should let your readers know what your position is. The **body** of the essay will present your major support points for your thesis backed by supporting details from your research. The **conclusion** will remind readers of your main point and make a further observation based on the information you have presented.

For Messelina Hernandez's completed research paper, see pages 376–79.

Cite and Document Your Sources

■ For more information on documenting sources, visit **bedfordstmartins .com/researchroom**.

As discussed on page 360, you need to include **in-text citations** of sources as you use them in the essay. You also need to document, or give credit to, your sources at the end of your research essay in a **list of works cited**.

Few people can remember the specifics of correct citation and documentation, so be sure to refer to this section or the reference text that your instructor prefers. Be sure to include all of the correct information, and pay attention to where punctuation marks such as commas, periods, and quotation marks should go.

There are several different systems of documentation. Most English professors prefer the Modern Language Association (MLA) system, which is used in this chapter. However, when you are writing a research paper in another course, you may be required to use another system. When in doubt, always ask your instructor.

Use In-Text Citations within Your Essay

In-text citations like the ones shown in this section are used for books and periodicals. For Web sites and other electronic sources, you typically will not be able to include page numbers, although you should note screen or paragraph numbers if these are used in the source.

When you refer to the author(s) in an introductory phrase, write just the relevant page number(s), if available, in parentheses at the end of the quotation.

DIRECT QUOTATION: In her book *Born to Buy,* Juliet B. Schor notes, "The world of children's marketing is filled with variants of the us-versus-them message" (53).

INDIRECT QUOTATION: In her book *Born to Buy,* Juliet B. Schor notes that marketing aimed at youth often sets children against adults (53).

When you do not refer to the author(s) in an introductory phrase, write the author's name followed by the page number(s), if available, at the end of the quotation. If an author is not named, use the title of the source.

DIRECT QUOTATION: "The world of children's marketing is filled with variants of the us-versus-them message" (Schor 53).

INDIRECT QUOTATION: Marketing aimed at youth often sets children against adults (Schor 53).

Use a List of Works Cited at the End of Your Essay

Books

BOOK BY ONE AUTHOR

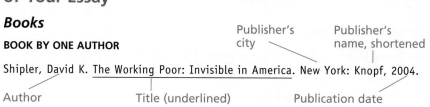

Publisher's city   Publisher's name, shortened

Shipler, David K. The Working Poor: Invisible in America. New York: Knopf, 2004.

Author   Title (underlined)   Publication date

WHAT TO LOOK FOR IN A BOOK

Title page (Publication city and date are sometimes on the copyright page.)

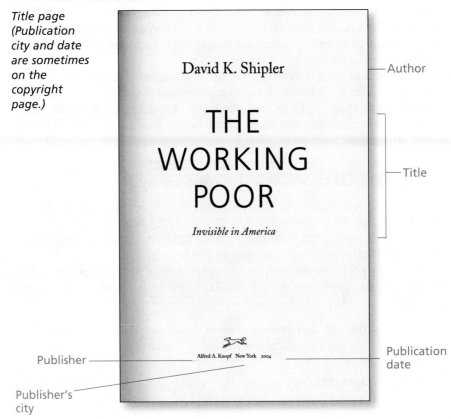

David K. Shipler — Author

THE WORKING POOR — Title

Invisible in America

Alfred A. Knopf New York 2004

Publisher

Publisher's city

Publication date

TWO OR MORE ENTRIES BY THE SAME AUTHOR

---. <u>Arab and Jew: Wounded Spirits in a Promised Land</u>. New York: Penguin, 2002.

Use three hyphens instead of repeating "Shipler, David K."

BOOK BY TWO OR THREE AUTHORS

Piccioto, Richard, and Daniel Paisner. <u>Last Man Down: A New York City Fire Chief and the Collapse of the World Trade Center</u>. New York: Berkley, 2002.

Quigley, Sharon, Gloria Florez, and Thomas McCann. <u>You Can Clean Almost Anything</u>. New York: Sutton, 1999.

BOOK WITH FOUR OR MORE AUTHORS

Roark, James L., et al. <u>The American Promise: A History of the United States</u>. 4th ed. Boston: Bedford/St. Martin's, 2009.

NOTE: *Et al.* means "and others."

BOOK WITH AN EDITOR

Tate, Parson, ed. Most Romantic Vacation Spots. Cheyenne: Chandler, 2000.

WORK IN AN ANTHOLOGY

Wright, Richard. "The Ethics of Living Jim Crow." The Bedford Introduction to Literature. Ed. Michael Meyer. 8th ed. Boston: Bedford/St. Martin's, 2008. 556-58.

ENCYCLOPEDIA ARTICLE

"Kosovo." Encyclopaedia Britannica. 16th ed. 1999.

Periodicals

MAGAZINE ARTICLE

Title of article   Title of periodical   Date

Netting, Jessa Forte. "Brazil's New Dinosaur." Discover Mar. 2005: 13.

Author

Page number (include page range for longer articles)

WHAT TO LOOK FOR IN A MAGAZINE ARTICLE

Title of article

Brazil's New Dinosaur

During his daily walk seven years ago, retired refrigerator repair-man Tolentino Marafiga spotted some unusual bones poking out of a road construction site in south-ern Brazil. It was a major find, pale-ontologists say: a new dinosaur species, one of the most primitive ever found.

The reptile walked on Earth 200 million to 225 million years ago, in the late Triassic, when dinosaurs were rare and new. Eight feet long and only 155 pounds, the lithe forest dweller was a delicate ancestor of the sauropods, the largest land animals that ever lived.

Like the most famous sauropod giant, *Brontosaurus,* the new dinosaur fed on plants, says Artemio Leal of Brazil's National Museum in Rio de Janeiro and lead author of the paper describing the find. A biped, it probably moved through conifer forests in a herd, shearing off bits of ferns and palmlike cycads with its ser-rated, spatulate teeth, suggests Leal.

The biggest surprise is that *Unaysaurus tolentinoi,* named for its discov-erer, was a close cousin of dinosaurs found in what is now Germany. This bol-sters the prevailing concept that all the world's continents were once jammed together as a single giant landmass called Pangaea.

Also intriguing is the dinosaur's well-preserved skull, with depressions and pro-trusions not seen before. The novel features helped paleontologists determine that the di-nosaur was a new species but raised other questions in the process, says Alexander Kell-ner, the paper's coauthor. "Sometimes pale-ontologists observe anatomic differences but cannot explain what their purposes were."

—*Jessa Forte Netting*

Author

Page number

DISCOVER MARCH 2005 **13**

Date

Title of periodical

NEWSPAPER ARTICLE

Fox, Maggie. "Scientists Report Experiment Creating Immune Cells."
<u>Boston Globe</u> 1 May 2002: A20.

EDITORIAL IN A MAGAZINE OR NEWSPAPER (author's name given)

Udall, Don. "When Someone Is Alive but Not Living." Editorial. <u>Newsweek</u>
14 June 1999: 12.

EDITORIAL IN A MAGAZINE OR NEWSPAPER (author's name not given)

"The Fall of a Telecom Gunslinger." Editorial. <u>New York Times</u> 1 May 2002: A22.

LETTER TO THE EDITOR IN A MAGAZINE OR NEWSPAPER (author's name given)

Vos, Peter. Letter. <u>Atlantic</u> Nov. 2004: 24.

Electronic Sources

Electronic sources include Web sites; databases or subscription services such as ERIC, InfoTrac, LexisNexis, and ProQuest; and electronic communications such as e-mail. Because electronic sources change often, always note the date you accessed or read the source as well as the date on which the source was posted or updated online, if this information is available.

PART OF A LARGER WEB SITE   Title of piece   Date of publication or last update

Author —— Rendall, Steve. "Meet the Stenographers: Press Shirks Duty to Scrutinize

Title of site —— Official Claims." <u>Fairness & Accuracy in Reporting</u>. Dec. 2004.

Access date —— 5 Jan. 2005 <http://www.fair.org/extra/0411/stenographers.html>. —— URL

NOTE: If the site sponsor is different from the site title, the sponsor's name should appear before the access date.

WHAT TO LOOK FOR IN A WEB SITE

URL ——————

Title of site ——————
(stands for Fairness & Accuracy in Reporting)

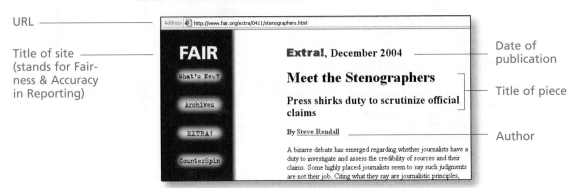

Date of publication

Title of piece

Author

ARTICLE FROM A DATABASE

Article title

Author

Rivero, Lisa. "Secrets of Successful Homeschooling." <u>Understanding Our Gifted</u> — Publication title

Volume and issue numbers — Database title

15.4 (2003): 8-11. <u>ERIC</u>. CSA Illumina. Boston Public Lib., Boston, MA. — Name and location of library

Date — Inclusive pages — Name of provider

3 Jan. 2005 <http://md2.csa.com>.

Access date   Main URL

WHAT TO LOOK FOR IN A DATABASE

Main URL   Name of provider

ARTICLE IN AN ONLINE PERIODICAL   Article title

Author——Weine, Stevan M. "Survivor Families and Their Strengths: Learning from Bosnians

Name of online periodical   Volume number

after Genocide." Other Voices: The (e)Journal of Cultural Criticism 2.1

Publication date ———— (2000). 1 May 2002 <http://www.othervoices.org/2.1/weine/bosnia.html>.

Access date   URL

E-MAIL OR ONLINE POSTING

■ For online exercises on documenting sources in MLA style, visit *Exercise Central* at **bedfordstmartins .com/realessays**.

Eisenhauer, Karen. "Learning Styles." E-mail to Susan Anker. 24 Apr. 2005.

Collins, Terence. "Effective Grammar Activities." Online posting. 14 Dec. 2001.
    CBW Listserv. 3 May 2002 <cbw-l@tc.umn.edu>.

Other Sources

PERSONAL INTERVIEW

Okayo, Margaret. Personal interview. 16 Apr. 2005.

SPEECH

Glenn, Cheryl. "Toward an Understanding of Silence and Silencing." Conf. on Coll.
    Composition and Communication Convention. Minneapolis Convention Center,
    Minneapolis. 13 Apr. 2000.

FILM, VIDEO, OR DVD

Million Dollar Baby. Dir. Clint Eastwood. Perf. Clint Eastwood, Hilary Swank, and
    Morgan Freeman. Warner Brothers, 2004.

TELEVISION OR RADIO PROGRAM

"Third-Day Story." West Wing. NBC. WCMH, Columbus. 3 Nov. 2004.

RECORDING

Keys, Alicia. "A Woman's Worth." Songs in A Minor. J-Records, 2001.

Revise and Edit Your Essay

After a break, reread your draft with fresh eyes and an open mind. Then, ask yourself these questions:

- Does my introduction state my thesis?
- Does each of the body paragraphs contain a topic sentence that directly supports my thesis? Do the supporting details in each paragraph relate to and explain the topic sentence?
- Do I provide a conclusion that reminds readers of my main point and makes a further observation?
- Have I included enough support for the thesis that readers are likely to see my topic the way I do? Is there anything else I could add to make my point?
- Do transitions help readers move from one idea to the next?
- Have I integrated source material smoothly into the essay? Do I need to smooth out anything that seems to be just dumped in?
- Have I reread the essay carefully, looking for errors in grammar, spelling, and punctuation?
- Have I cited and documented my sources?
- Are all of my citations and Works Cited entries in correct form (MLA or whatever style the instructor specifies)?
- Is this the best I can do?

For more on revising, see Chapter 9. When checking for grammar, spelling, and punctuation errors, consult Parts Four through Seven of this book. Look first at Chapter 22 beginning on page 385.

After reading the annotated student essay that follows, use the Writing Guide on page 380 to write your research essay.

Sample Student Research Essay

The student essay that follows is annotated to show both typical features of research essays (such as references to sources) and elements of good writing (such as the thesis statement and topic sentences). The paper also shows formatting (such as margins, spacing between lines, and placement of the title). Your instructor may specify different or additional formatting in class or in your syllabus.

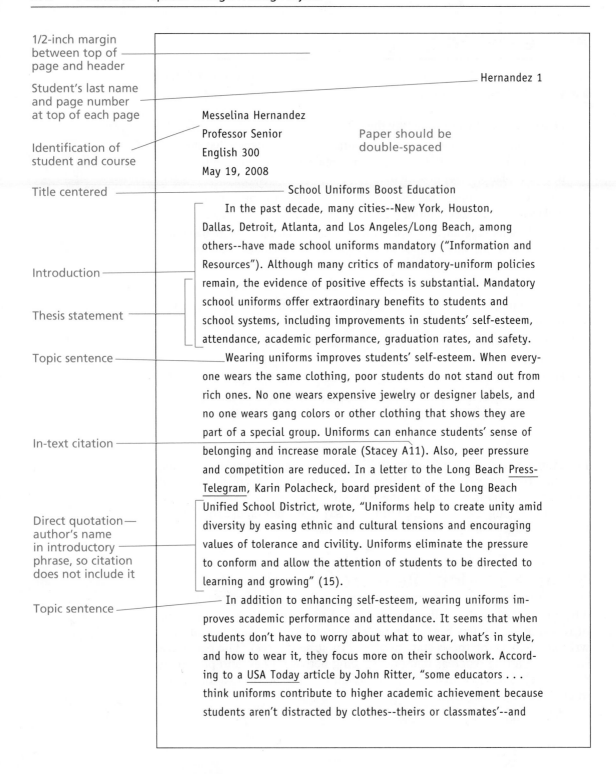

1/2-inch margin between top of page and header

Student's last name and page number at top of each page

Identification of student and course

Title centered

Introduction

Thesis statement

Topic sentence

In-text citation

Direct quotation— author's name in introductory phrase, so citation does not include it

Topic sentence

Hernandez 1

Messelina Hernandez
Professor Senior
English 300
May 19, 2008

Paper should be double-spaced

School Uniforms Boost Education

In the past decade, many cities--New York, Houston, Dallas, Detroit, Atlanta, and Los Angeles/Long Beach, among others--have made school uniforms mandatory ("Information and Resources"). Although many critics of mandatory-uniform policies remain, the evidence of positive effects is substantial. Mandatory school uniforms offer extraordinary benefits to students and school systems, including improvements in students' self-esteem, attendance, academic performance, graduation rates, and safety.

Wearing uniforms improves students' self-esteem. When everyone wears the same clothing, poor students do not stand out from rich ones. No one wears expensive jewelry or designer labels, and no one wears gang colors or other clothing that shows they are part of a special group. Uniforms can enhance students' sense of belonging and increase morale (Stacey A11). Also, peer pressure and competition are reduced. In a letter to the Long Beach Press-Telegram, Karin Polacheck, board president of the Long Beach Unified School District, wrote, "Uniforms help to create unity amid diversity by easing ethnic and cultural tensions and encouraging values of tolerance and civility. Uniforms eliminate the pressure to conform and allow the attention of students to be directed to learning and growing" (15).

In addition to enhancing self-esteem, wearing uniforms improves academic performance and attendance. It seems that when students don't have to worry about what to wear, what's in style, and how to wear it, they focus more on their schoolwork. According to a USA Today article by John Ritter, "some educators . . . think uniforms contribute to higher academic achievement because students aren't distracted by clothes--theirs or classmates'--and

Hernandez 2

they treat school as their job" (1A). Uniforms also improve students' test scores and attendance. A survey of school principals indicated that 62 percent reported an increase in academic achievement that they attributed to the sense of community created by school uniforms ("Information and Resources"). Apparently, when students feel more a part of the school community, they are more likely to attend school in the first place and are more likely to concentrate on learning when they are there.

    Mandatory school uniforms can also improve students' graduation rates, which would have positive effects on society as a whole. "Dressed for Success," a pro-uniform editorial in the Columbus Dispatch, highlights Virginia Draa's 2006 study showing that graduation rates at sixty-four Ohio high schools improved after they implemented mandatory uniforms. As noted in "Dressed for Success," Draa's study found that graduation rates at the schools rose by 10.9 percent between 1994 and 2002, while graduation rates at similar high schools dropped by 4.6 percent. The editorial concludes that "more diplomas will translate into increased job and training opportunities for the young people. A high school diploma is a key to success beyond the classroom" ("Dressed for Success").

    The most important benefit of mandatory school uniforms, however, is the reduction of violence in schools and the overall increase in safety. For example, in 1994, the Long Beach, California, school district became the first large urban system to adopt school uniforms. It drew extensive national attention and generated a good deal of controversy; however, the results were overwhelmingly positive. In a 1996 study of data from the Long Beach schools, the U.S. Department of Education found a 36 percent decline in overall crime in elementary and middle schools, a 50 percent decrease in weapons offenses, a 34 percent drop in assaults, and a 19 percent decline in vandalism ("School Uniformity" 40). Similarly, New York City schools have seen a

Indirect quotation, paraphrase

Summary

Paraphrase

Direct quote (For full text of article cited here, see p. 364.)

Topic sentence

Hernandez 3

76 percent drop in crime since 1994, when students in most elementary schools started wearing uniforms (Fanning). In a 1996 State of the Union Address, former president Bill Clinton drew more national attention to the issue when he said, "And if that means teenagers will stop killing each other over designer jackets, then public schools should be able to require school uniforms." Since then, many more schools have made school uniforms mandatory.

Acknowledgment of opposing view

Indirect quotation, summary

Some people believe that school uniforms are not a good thing, but their objections are not convincing. For instance, in a 1998 study, David L. Brunsma and Kerry A. Rockquemore found no relationship between wearing uniforms and reductions in violence or improvements in academic achievement; in fact, they reported that uniforms could be correlated with reduced academic performance (53-62). However, their analysis has since been

Summary

challenged (Bodine 69). Other experts say that dress codes violate students' right to free speech under the First Amendment and their liberty interest under the due process clause of the Fourteenth Amendment (Hudson 87; West 22). The courts have ruled, however, that schools may regulate what students wear. Others claim that most of the evidence of benefits of wearing school uniforms is not scientific. I would direct those opponents to the many studies that have found that there are direct benefits, starting with a bibliography that the National Association of Elementary School Principals provides on its Web site ("Information").

Conclusion reminding readers of main point

There is convincing evidence that mandatory school uniforms have significant benefits. If such a small change in policy can improve students' self-esteem, attendance, academic performance, graduation rates, and safety, why would anyone question it? The potential for positive change is well worth a try.

Hernandez 4

Works Cited

Bodine, Ann. "School Uniforms, Academic Achievement, and Uses of
　　Research." Journal of Educational Research 97.2 (2003): 67-72.

Brunsma, David L., and Kerry A. Rockquemore. "Effects of Student
　　Uniforms on Attendance, Behavior Problems, Substance
　　Abuse, and Academic Achievement." Journal of Educational
　　Research 92.1 (1998): 53-62.

Clinton, William Jefferson. State of the Union Address. Washington,
　　DC. 23 Jan. 1996.

"Dressed for Success." Editorial. Columbus Dispatch 16 Jan. 2006.
　　22 Jan. 2008 <http://www.dispatch.com/live/contentbe/
　　dispatch/2006/01/16/20060116-A6-00.html>.

Fanning, Karen. "To Wear or Not to Wear?" Scholastic News
　　11 May 1998. ProQuest Direct. Allan Hancock Coll. Lib., Santa
　　Maria. 27 Apr. 2004 <http://www.umi.com/proquest>.

Hudson, David L., Jr. Rights of Students. Philadelphia: Chelsea
　　House, 2004.

"Information and Resources: Public School Uniforms." National
　　Association of Elementary School Principals. 10 May 2004
　　<http://www.naesp.org>.

Polacheck, Karin. Letter. Press-Telegram Jan. 1996: 15.

Ritter, John. "Uniforms Changing Culture of the Nation's
　　Classrooms." USA Today 15 Oct. 1998: 1A.

"School Uniformity Yields High Marks." DSN Retailing Today
　　3 May 2004: 39-40.

Stacey, Julie. "Our View: Morale Is Up, Crime Is Down, and Kids
　　Can Concentrate on Learning Instead of Self-Protection." USA
　　Today 22 Aug. 1995: A11.

West, Charles K., et al. "Attitudes of Parents about School
　　Uniforms." Journal of Family and Consumer Sciences Mar.
　　1999. ProQuest Direct. Allan Hancock Coll. Lib., Santa Maria.
　　5 Apr. 2004 <http://www.umi.com/proquest/>.

■ Note that in Works
Cited entries, all lines
after the first one are
indented. Also, titles
of books, periodicals,
and Web sites are
underlined, and page
ranges are included
when available. URLs
are included for
Web-based sources.

Source without
author

After you have taken notes, found outside sources, and written a draft thesis statement, use the writing guide that follows to help you write your research essay.

WRITING GUIDE: RESEARCH ESSAY

STEPS IN WRITING THE RESEARCH ESSAY	HOW TO DO THE STEPS
Focus.	☐ Reread your guiding research question. ☐ Reread your working thesis, and revise it if it has changed based on your reading of outside sources.
Review your sources.	☐ Evaluate the support from outside sources: Are they strong sources? Do they support your thesis? ☐ Make sure that you have all the information to cite your sources accurately.
Review the range of your support. See Chapter 6 for more on supporting a thesis.	☐ Consider if you have enough facts, examples, and expert opinions. ☐ Find more kinds of support if you need it. ☐ Add your own thoughts to support your thesis based on what you have found out.
Make an outline. See Chapter 7 for more on making an outline.	☐ Write your thesis statement, and note what else you might say in your introductory paragraph. ☐ Write the main point you want to make in each of your support paragraphs. ☐ Decide what outside sources to use for each paragraph. ☐ Decide the order of paragraphs, saving what you believe is your strongest support for last.
Write a draft. See Chapter 8 for more on drafting.	☐ Write an introductory paragraph that describes your topic and includes your main point about that topic. If your essay is presenting your position on an issue, state your position clearly and with energy. (For more on argument, see Chapter 18.) ☐ Write topic sentences for each of your support paragraphs. ☐ Use your outside sources in your support paragraphs. ☐ Write a concluding paragraph that reviews the information you have provided, reviews your main point, and makes a final observation based on your findings. ☐ Title the essay.

STEPS IN WRITING THE RESEARCH ESSAY	HOW TO DO THE STEPS
Work your outside sources into the essay. • Indirect quotations (summary and paraphrase) **Ex:** In their article "Effects of Student Uniforms on Attendance . . . ," David L. Brunsma and Kerry A. Rockquemore state . . . (53–62). • Direct Quotation **Ex:** In a letter to the Long Beach *Press-Telegram,* Karin Polacheck wrote, "Uniforms help to create unity" (15).	☐ Use your own words. For more on summarizing, see Chapter 20. ☐ Introduce and identify the writer(s) or speaker(s) as in the example. ☐ Do *not* use quotation marks for indirect quotations. ☐ Give the page number(s) or the whole section you have summarized or paraphrased. The page numbers are in parentheses *before* the period. ☐ Use the *exact* words that are in the source. ☐ Introduce and identify the writer(s) or speaker(s). ☐ Use quotation marks before and after the speaker's or writer's exact words. For more on using quotation marks, see Chapter 39. ☐ Give the page number(s) where you found your quote. The page numbers are in parentheses after the last quotation mark but *before* the period. ☐ If the direct quotation is more than four typed lines or forty words, indent the whole quotation, and do *not* use quotation marks. Write the page number in parentheses *after* the period.
Revise your draft. See Chapter 9 for more on revising.	☐ Ask another person to read and comment on your draft. ☐ Review your support, and delete any points that don't relate directly to your thesis. ☐ If you feel your support is weak, find more, or expand on what you have. ☐ Add transitions to move your readers smoothly from one point to another. ☐ Rewrite your thesis statement to make it more concrete and forceful. ☐ Reread your introduction to be sure that it sets up your essay and makes readers want to continue. ☐ Reread your conclusion to be sure that it reminds your readers of your main point and support and makes a strong final observation.
Prepare a Works Cited list. See pages 368–74.	☐ List all of your outside sources, and be sure that they are formatted correctly.

continued

STEPS IN WRITING THE RESEARCH ESSAY	HOW TO DO THE STEPS
Edit your essay.	☐ Use the spell checker and grammar checker on your computer, but also reread your essay carefully to catch any errors. ☐ Reread your in-text citations and works cited list to be sure they are documented correctly. ☐ Find and correct errors in grammar, spelling, and punctuation. ☐ Ask yourself: Is this the best I can do?

Part Four

The Four Most Serious Errors

22

The Basic Sentence

An Overview

The Four Most Serious Errors

This book emphasizes the four grammar errors that people most often notice. These four errors may make your meaning harder to understand, and they give readers a bad impression of you. It's like going for a job interview in pajamas. People *will* notice.

■ **IDEA JOURNAL**
Write about any problems you have had with grammar in the past.

1. Fragments (see Chapter 23)
2. Run-ons (see Chapter 24)
3. Problems with subject-verb agreement (see Chapter 25)
4. Problems with verb form and tense (see Chapter 26)

If you can edit your writing to correct the four most serious errors, your sentences will be clearer, and your grades will improve. Learning how to correct these errors will make a big difference in your writing.

This chapter will review the basic elements of the sentence; the next four chapters cover the four most serious errors.

The Parts of Speech

There are seven basic parts of speech in English:

1. A **noun** names a person, place, or thing.

   Heroin is a drug.

■ In the examples in this chapter, subjects are underlined once and verbs are underlined twice.

385

2. A **pronoun** replaces a noun in a sentence. A pronoun can be the subject of a sentence (*I, you, he, she, it, we, they*), or it can be the object of a sentence (*me, you, him, her, us, them*). A pronoun can also show possession (*mine, yours, his, her, its, our, their*).

It causes addiction.

3. A **verb** tells what the subject does, or it links a subject to another word that describes it.

Heroin *causes* addiction. [The verb *causes* is what the subject *Heroin* does.]

It *is* dangerous. [The verb *is* links the subject *It* to a word that describes it: *dangerous*.]

4. An **adjective** describes a noun or pronoun.

[Heroin is *dangerous*. [The adjective *dangerous* describes the noun *Heroin*.]

It is *lethal*. [The adjective *lethal* describes the pronoun *It*.]

5. An **adverb** describes an adjective, a verb, or another adverb. Many adverbs end in -*ly*.

Heroin is *very* dangerous. [The adverb *very* describes the adjective *dangerous*.]

Addiction occurs *quickly*. [The adverb *quickly* describes the verb *occurs*.]

Addiction occurs *very* quickly. [The adverb *very* describes the adverb *quickly*.]

6. A **preposition** connects a noun, pronoun, or verb with some other information about it (*across, at, in, of, on, around, over,* and *to* are some prepositions).

Dealers often sell drugs *around* schools. [The preposition *around* connects the noun *drugs* with the noun *school*.]

7. A **conjunction** (for, and, nor, but, or, yet, so) connects words.

> **Language Note:** Any idea that ends with a period needs a subject and a verb to be a complete sentence. For a review of subjects and verbs, see pages 388–94.
>
> If you aren't sure about the order in which words in a sentence usually appear, see Chapter 33.

■ **PRACTICE 1   USING THE PARTS OF SPEECH** . . . .

In the following sentences, fill in each blank with a word that is the part of speech called for in parentheses after the blank. *Note:* Some verbs may be in the past tense, and some verbs may use a helping verb such as *is* or *was*.

■ For answers to odd-numbered practice items, see pages A-1–A-19 at the back of the book.

EXAMPLE: The ___*soccer*___ (adjective) ___*coach*___ (noun), a former drill sergeant, ___*demanded*___ (verb) that ___*she*___ (pronoun) arrive ___*promptly*___ (adverb) ___*for*___ (preposition) practice.

1. The young _____ (noun), who was new _____ (preposition) the school, _____ (verb) to join the debating _____ (conjunction) fencing clubs.

2. _____ (pronoun) dream _____ (verb) to play the _____ (noun) _____ (preposition) the _____ (adjective) band.

3. The _____ (noun) that _____ (adverb) went by _____ (verb) it difficult for the hotel's _____ (adjective) customers to sleep.

4. The _____ (adjective) _____ (noun), a recent addition _____ (preposition) the neighborhood, _____ (verb) the freshest fruit _____ (conjunction) vegetables that _____ (pronoun) had ever seen.

5. Shaking his head _____ (adverb), _____ (pronoun) looked up and _____ (verb) to get out _____ (preposition) the car.

The Basic Sentence

A **sentence** is the basic unit of written communication. A complete sentence written in standard English must have three elements:

- A **subject**
- A **verb**
- A **complete thought**

To edit your writing, you need a clear understanding of what a sentence *is* and what a sentence *is not*. You can find out if a group of words is a complete sentence by checking to see if it has a subject, a verb, and a complete thought.

Subjects

■ For a list of pronoun types, see page 496.

The **subject** of a sentence is the person, place, or thing that the sentence is about. The subject of the sentence can be a noun (a word that names the person, place, or thing) or a pronoun (a word that replaces the noun, such as *I, you, she,* or *they*).

> **Language Note:** English sentences always have a subject.
>
> **INCORRECT**   Is hot outside.
>
> **CORRECT**   It is hot outside.
>
> If you write sentences without any subject, see page 582.

To find the subject, ask yourself, "Who or what is the sentence about?"

PERSON AS SUBJECT   Vivian works for the police department.

[*Who* is the sentence about? *Vivian*]

THING AS SUBJECT   The tickets cost $65 apiece.

[*What* is the sentence about? The *tickets*]

> **Language Note:** The two sentences above use the word *the* before the noun (*the police department, the tickets*). *The, a,* and *an* are called *articles*. If you have trouble deciding which article to use with which nouns or if you often forget to use an article, see page 618.

A **compound subject** consists of two (or more) subjects joined by *and, or,* or *nor.*

TWO SUBJECTS	<u>Marty</u> and <u>Kim</u> <u><u>have</u></u> a new baby girl.
SEVERAL SUBJECTS	The <u>jacket</u>, <u>pants</u>, and <u>sweater</u> <u><u>match</u></u> perfectly.
SEVERAL SUBJECTS	<u>Kim</u>, <u>Juan</u>, or <u>Melba</u> <u><u>will bring</u></u> dessert.

A **prepositional phrase** is a word group that begins with a preposition and ends with a noun or pronoun. A **preposition** is a word that connects a noun, pronoun, or verb with some other information about it. The subject of a sentence is *never* in a prepositional phrase.

Language Note: If you have trouble deciding which prepositions to use, see page 622.

Preposition

The <u>check</u> <u><u>is</u></u> in the mail.

Prepositional phrase

The subject of the sentence is *check.* The subject can't be the word *mail,* which is in the prepositional phrase *in the mail.*

Preposition

<u>One</u> of my best friends <u><u>is</u></u> a circus clown.

Prepositional phrase

Although the word *friends* may seem to be the subject of the sentence, it isn't. *One* is the subject. The word *friends* can't be the subject because it is in the prepositional phrase *of my best friends.*

When you are looking for the subject of a sentence in your writing, it may help to cross out any prepositional phrases, as in the following sentences.

The <u>rules</u> ~~about smoking~~ <u><u>are posted</u></u> everywhere.

The <u>sound</u> ~~of lightning striking a tree~~ <u><u>is</u></u> like gunfire.

<u>Many</u> ~~of the students~~ <u><u>work</u></u> part-time.

Common Prepositions

about	beneath	like	to
above	beside	near	toward
across	between	next to	under
after	by	of	until
against	down	off	up
along	during	on	upon
among	except	out	with
around	for	outside	within
at	from	over	without
before	in	past	
behind	inside	since	
below	into	through	

PRACTICE 2   IDENTIFYING SUBJECTS AND PREPOSITIONAL PHRASES

In each of the following sentences, cross out any prepositional phrases, and underline the subject of the sentence.

EXAMPLE: ~~For several months~~, <u>Ronald</u> has been raising a guide dog ~~for the blind~~.

1. Many other people around the country are raising guide dog puppies.

2. However, Ronald's situation is unusual because he is in prison.

3. Ronald is participating in a program called Puppies Behind Bars.

4. The dog he is raising, a black Labrador puppy named Cooper, lives with Ronald twenty-four hours a day.

5. Whenever Ronald's cell is locked, Cooper stays in the cell with him.

6. In the cell, Ronald plays with the dog, rolling on the floor with him and talking to him in a high voice.

7. Ronald teaches Cooper manners and obedience before the start of Cooper's formal guide dog training.

8. In return, Ronald gains a sense of responsibility.

9. When he finishes his formal training, Cooper will be matched with a blind person.

10. Ronald believes that he and Cooper are contributing an important service to society.

■ For more practice, visit *Exercise Central* at **bedfordstmartins .com/realessays**.

Verbs

Every sentence has a **main verb,** the word or words that tell what the subject does or that link the subject to another word that describes it. Verbs do not always immediately follow the subject: Other words may come between the subject and the verb.

There are three kinds of verbs—action verbs, linking verbs, and helping verbs.

> **Language Note:** Be careful with *-ing* and *to* forms of verbs (*reading, to read*).
>
> **INCORRECT**   Terence loves to be reading.
>
> **CORRECT**   Terence loves reading. *or* Terence loves to read.
>
> If you make errors like this, see page 610.

Action Verbs

An **action verb** tells what action the subject performs.

To find the main action verb in a sentence, ask yourself, "What action does the subject perform?"

ACTION VERBS

The baby cried all night.

The building collapsed around midnight.

After work, we often go to Tallie's.

My aunt and uncle train service dogs.

Linking Verbs

A **linking verb** connects (links) the subject to a word or group of words that describe the subject. Linking verbs show no action. The most common linking verb is *be,* along with all its forms (*am, is, are,* and so on). Other linking verbs, such as *seem* and *become,* can usually be replaced by the corresponding form of *be,* and the sentence will still make sense.

To find linking verbs, ask yourself, "What word joins the subject and the words that describe the subject?"

LINKING VERBS

The dinner is delicious.

I felt great this morning.

This lasagna tastes just like my mother's.

The doctor looks extremely tired.

Some words can be either action verbs or linking verbs, depending on how they are used in a particular sentence.

ACTION VERB   The dog smelled Jake's shoes.

LINKING VERB   The dog smelled terrible.

Common Linking Verbs

FORMS OF *BE*	FORMS OF *BECOME* AND *SEEM*	FORMS OF SENSE VERBS
am	become, becomes	appear, appears
are	became	appeared
is	seem, seems	feel, feels, felt
was	seemed	look, looks
were		looked
		smell, smells
		smelled
		taste, tastes, tasted

Language Note: The verb *be* cannot be left out of sentences in English.

INCORRECT	Tonya well now.
CORRECT	Tonya **is** well now.

Helping Verbs

A **helping verb** joins with the main verb in the sentence to form the **complete verb**. The helping verb is often a form of the verb *be, have,* or *do*. A sentence may have more than one helping verb along with the main verb.

Helping verb	+	Main verb	=	Complete verb

HELPING VERBS + MAIN VERBS

Sunil was talking on his cell phone.

[The helping verb is *was*, and the main verb is *talking*. The complete verb is *was talking*.]

Charisse is taking three courses this semester.

Tomas has missed the last four meetings.

My brother might have passed the test.

Common Helping Verbs

FORMS OF *BE*	FORMS OF *HAVE*	FORMS OF *DO*	OTHER
am	have	do	can
are	has	does	could
been	had	did	may
being			might
is			must
was			should
were			will
			would

> **Language Note:** The verb *be* cannot be left out of sentences in English.
>
> **INCORRECT**   Greg studying tonight.
>
> **CORRECT**   Greg **is** studying tonight.

PRACTICE 3   IDENTIFYING THE VERB (ACTION, LINKING, OR HELPING + MAIN)

In the following sentences, underline each subject and double-underline each verb. Then, identify each verb as an action verb, a linking verb, or a helping verb + a main verb.

> **EXAMPLE:** At first, Miguel did not want to attend his high school
>
> reunion.   *helping verb + main verb*

1. Miguel's family moved to Ohio from Guatemala ten years ago.

2. He was the new kid at his high school that fall.

3. Miguel was learning English at that time.

4. The football players teased small, quiet boys like him.

5. After graduation, he was delighted to leave that part of his life behind.

6. Recently, the planning committee sent Miguel an invitation to his high school reunion.

7. His original plan had been to throw the invitation in the trash.

8. Instead, he is going to the reunion to satisfy his curiosity.

9. His family is proud of Miguel's college degree and his new career as a graphic artist.

10. Perhaps some of the other students at the reunion will finally get to know the real Miguel.

Complete Thoughts

A **complete thought** is an idea that is expressed in a sentence and that makes sense by itself, without other sentences. An incomplete thought leaves readers wondering what's going on.

INCOMPLETE THOUGHT	as I was leaving [*What's going on?*]
COMPLETE THOUGHT	The phone rang as I was leaving.
INCOMPLETE THOUGHT	the people selling the car [*What's going on?*]
COMPLETE THOUGHT	The people selling the car placed the ad.

To identify a complete thought, ask yourself, "Do I know what's going on, or do I have to ask a question to understand?"

INCOMPLETE THOUGHT in the apartment next door

[Do I know what's going on, or do I have to ask a question to understand? *You would have to ask a question, so this is not a complete thought.*]

COMPLETE THOUGHT Carlos lives in the apartment next door.

PRACTICE 4 IDENTIFYING COMPLETE THOUGHTS · · · · · · · · · · · ·

Some of the following items contain complete thoughts, and others do not. In the space to the left of each item, write either "C" for complete thought or "I" for incomplete thought. If you write "I," add words to make a sentence.

, he or she must return it in good condition.
EXAMPLE: ___*I*___ If someone wants to borrow the club's bike/
    ^

_____ 1. Although some prefer classic rock.

_____ 2. Eager to see the movie from its beginning.

_____ 3. Richard's late.

_____ 4. The arriving train.

_____ 5. There are apples.

_____ 6. Do not run.

___ 7. Playing loud music at a bus stop.

___ 8. They're right.

___ 9. Even with too many people signed up for the softball team.

___ 10. Instead of wearing a traditional tie.

Six Basic Sentence Patterns

In English, there are six basic sentence patterns, some of which you have already worked with in this chapter. Although there are other patterns, they build on these six.

1. Subject-Verb (S-V)

This is the most basic pattern, as you have already seen.

$$\text{S} \quad \text{V}$$
Airplanes pollute.

2. Subject-Linking Verb-Noun (S-LV-N)

$$\text{S} \quad \text{LV} \quad \text{N}$$
Fuel is a pollutant.

3. Subject-Linking Verb-Adjective (S-LV-ADJ)

$$\text{S} \quad \text{LV} \quad \text{ADJ}$$
Travel seems cheap.

4. Subject-Verb-Adverb (S-V-ADV)

$$\text{S} \quad \text{V} \quad \text{ADV}$$
Pollution costs dearly.

5. Subject-Verb-Direct Object (S-V-DO)

A *direct object* directly receives the action of the verb.

S   V   DO

It <u>degrades</u> ozone.

6. Subject-Verb-Indirect Object-Direct Object

An *indirect object* does not directly receive the action of the verb.

S   V   IO DO

<u>Biofuels</u> <u>offer</u> us hope.

PRACTICE 5   IDENTIFYING BASIC SENTENCE PATTERNS . . . .

In each of the following sentences, identify the basic sentence pattern by writing "S" above the subject, "V" above a verb, "LV" above a linking verb, "N" above a noun, "ADJ" above an adjective, "ADV" above an adverb, "DO" above a direct object, and "IO" above an indirect object.

S   V   IO   DO

EXAMPLE: **Dogs teach people manners.**

1. Dogs teach.

2. Dogs are natural coaches.

3. Dogs appear submissive.

4. They teach people lessons.

5. They instruct unintentionally.

6. They clearly teach.

7. Dogs give owners valuable lessons.

8. Dogs greet owners excitedly.

9. Dogs respond promptly.

10. Dogs are extremely polite.

Edit Paragraphs and Your Own Writing

■ EDITING REVIEW 1

Underline each subject, double-underline each verb, and correct the six incomplete thoughts.

(1) It can be easier to help others than many people think. (2) For example, donating hair. (3) Some people need donated hair in the form of wigs. (4) Who uses these wigs? (5) Mostly, children with cancer or other diseases that cause hair loss. (6) Donating is popular, especially with young girls. (7) More and more frequently, though, men and boys are contributing hair. (8) For example, one nonprofit organization. (9) It receives up to 2,000 locks of hair every week. (10) Unfortunately, most of the donated hair is unusable for this charity's wigs. (11) Because the charity's guidelines are quite strict. (12) Rejecting hair that is gray, wet, moldy, too short, or too processed. (13) It is able to sell some rejected hair to help meet the group's costs. (14) But continues to encourage donations. (15) Obviously, contributors feel they are getting more than they are giving.

■ **EDITING REVIEW 2** . . . .

Underline each subject, double-underline each verb, and correct the six incomplete thoughts.

(1) New parents commonly dress their baby boys in blue. (2) And their girls in pink. (3) Now, a recent study suggests that males actually do prefer blue and females prefer pink. (4) Or at least a redder shade of blue. (5) The study involved 208 men and women ages 20 to 26. (6) Who were asked to quickly select their preferred color. (7) Choosing from about 1,000 colored rectangles on a computer screen. (8) Women and men like blue. (9) According to the study. (10) However, women clearly express a greater preference for the pinker end of the blue color spectrum. (11) The researchers think that females may have developed a preference for more reddish colors. (12) Which resemble riper fruit and healthier faces.

■ **EDITING REVIEW 3** . . . .

In each blank, fill in a word that is the appropriate part of speech.

(1) Taking a peek __ a fellow passenger's computer screen is OK to do, right? (2) This is a serious question at a time when airplane flights __ tightly packed __ laptop use is common. (3) What if the _____ in the next seat is watching an offensive movie _____ headphones? (4) A recent survey _____ that 45 percent __ business travelers admit to peeking at someone else's laptop in a public place. (5) In many cases, it is _____ impossible to avoid getting a glimpse of a nearby screen. (6) So, what is the _____ etiquette for in-flight laptop use? (7) If you

are using ____ laptop, bring headphones. (8) Do not watch _____ that are in poor taste. (9) If a neighbor seems interested, invite _____ ___ to watch. (10) If you are sitting next to a laptop user, don't peek. (11) However, if the movie _____ is watching looks interesting, it is OK to ask _____ to watch. (12) If the sound is ___ high __ the content offensive, tell the laptop user. (13) If that does not work, ___ a flight attendant for assistance.

▪ EDITING REVIEW 4

In each sentence of the following paragraph, identify the basic sentence pattern by writing "S" above the subject, "V" above a verb, "LV" above a linking verb, "DO" above a direct object, and "IO" above an indirect object.

(1) It is afternoon. (2) At this hour, many people become drowsy. (3) Most fight this "post-lunch dip." (4) Some people nap. (5) Others give themselves a coffee transfusion. (6) Some try exercise. (7) The cleverest, however, use simple planning. (8) For these people, the "dip" is the time for simple, non-creative tasks. (9) They give their brains a well-deserved break. (10) Later in the afternoon, their energy returns. (11) At this point, they resume more complex tasks. (12) Sometimes, the path of least resistance is best.

23

Fragments

Incomplete Sentences

Understand What Fragments Are

A **sentence** is a group of words that has a subject and a verb and expresses a complete thought, independent of other sentences. A **fragment** is a group of words that is missing a subject or a verb or that does not express a complete thought.

SENTENCE   I am going to a concert on Friday at Memorial Arena.

FRAGMENT   I am going to a concert on Friday. *At Memorial Arena.*

[*At Memorial Arena* does not have a subject or a verb.]

> **Language Note:** Remember that any idea that ends with a period needs a subject and a verb to be complete. For a review of subjects and verbs, see pages 388–94.

In the Real World, Why Is It Important to Correct Fragments?

A fragment is one of the grammatical errors that people notice most, as the following example shows.

SITUATION: A student responds to an ad for a work-study position at the college.

■ **IDEA JOURNAL**
Without looking at this chapter, how would you define a fragment? How do you find a fragment in your writing?

■ In the examples in this chapter, subjects are underlined once and verbs are underlined twice.

Dear Professor Espinoza:

I am interested in the position for an assistant that I saw. On the work-study Web site. I have attached a résumé for you to review. That describes my experience. I would very much like to work for you next semester. Helping with your writing and research. I type very fast.

Thank you for your consideration.

Sincerely,

Carson Watson

Alex Espinoza
College Professor

(See Alex's Profile of Success on p. 191.)

RESPONSE: Alex Espinoza, the college professor who was profiled in Chapter 12, made the following response after reading Carson's letter.

If I had received this letter, I would not hire the writer. If Carson doesn't care about writing, why should I hire him? Bad writing is like walking out the door in your pajamas, unshaven, unshowered, and gross.

Find and Correct Fragments

To find fragments in your own writing, look for the five kinds of fragments in this chapter.

When you find a fragment, you can usually correct it in one of two ways.

WAYS TO CORRECT FRAGMENTS

- Add what is missing (a subject, a verb, or both).
- Attach the fragment to the sentence before or after it.

 PRACTICE 1   FINDING AND CORRECTING FRAGMENTS . . . .

Underline the three fragments in Carson Watson's letter above.

Fragments That Start with Prepositions

Whenever a preposition starts what you think is a sentence, check for a subject, a verb, and a complete thought. If any one of those is missing, you have a fragment.

■ For a list of common prepositions, see page 390.

FRAGMENT	The <u>plane</u> <u>crashed</u> into the house. *With a deafening roar.*

[*With a deafening roar* is a prepositional phrase that starts with the preposition *with* and ends with the noun *roar*. The phrase has neither a subject nor a verb. It is a fragment.]

FRAGMENT	<u>You</u> <u>should take</u> the second left and head west. *Toward the highway.*

[*Toward the highway* is a prepositional phrase that starts with the preposition *toward* and ends with the noun *highway*. The phrase has neither a subject nor a verb. It is a fragment.]

Remember, the subject of a sentence is *never* in a prepositional phrase (see p. 389).

Correct a fragment that starts with a preposition by connecting the fragment to the sentence either before or after it. If you connect a fragment to the sentence after it, put a comma after the fragment to join it to the sentence.

FRAGMENT	The <u>plane</u> <u>crashed</u> into the house. *From a height of eight hundred feet.*
CORRECTED	The <u>plane</u> <u>crashed</u> into the house. ^f^ From a height of eight hundred feet.
CORRECTED	From a height of eight hundred feet, the <u>plane</u> <u>crashed</u> into the house.

Fragments That Start with Dependent Words

A **dependent word** is the first word in a dependent clause, which does not express a complete thought even though it has a subject and a verb. Whenever a dependent word starts what you think is a sentence, look for a subject, a verb, and, especially, a complete thought.

Some dependent words are **subordinating conjunctions** (*after, because, before, since, until,* and so on).

FRAGMENT	<u>I</u> <u>completed</u> an application. *Because* the apartment was available.

■ For more practice
with correcting
fragments, visit
Exercise Central at
**bedfordstmartins
.com/realessays**.

[*Because* is a dependent word introducing the dependent clause *because the apartment was available*. The clause has a subject, *apartment*, and a verb, *was rented*, but it does not express a complete thought.]

CORRECTED   I completed an application because the apartment was available.

[The dependent clause is attached to the sentence before it.]

CORRECTED   Because the apartment was available, I completed an application.

[The dependent clause is in front of the sentence. Note that when the dependent clause comes at the beginning of the sentence, it needs a comma after it.]

Common Dependent Words

after	if	what(ever)
although	since	when(ever)
as	so that	where
because	that	whether
before	though	which(ever)
even though	unless	while
how	until	who/whose

Some dependent words are **relative pronouns** (*who, whose, which*). When a word group starts with *who, whose,* or *which,* it is not a complete sentence unless it is a question.

FRAGMENT   I visited my friend John. *Whose* brother is an astronaut.

[*Whose* is a relative pronoun starting a word group, so it is a fragment. If this phrase ended with a question mark ("Whose brother is an astronaut?"), it would be correct, but the writer is not asking a question.]

CORRECTED   I visited my friend John, whose brother is an astronaut.

Language Note: For help with forming questions, see Chapters 26 and 33.

■ **PRACTICE 2 CORRECTING FRAGMENTS THAT START
WITH PREPOSITIONS OR DEPENDENT WORDS** . . . .

In the following items, circle any prepositions or dependent words starting a
fragment. Then, correct the fragments by connecting them to the previous or
next sentence.

EXAMPLE: Most dogs are content to have a daily ~~walk.~~ *walk, while* (While) some
dogs need more.

1. Even after having a walk. These dogs become nervous and overly excited.

2. This, of course, greatly upsets the dogs' owners. Who have to deal with
   the messes that these agitated dogs leave around the home.

3. To address this growing need. A new type of service is springing up, especially in the larger cities of the country.

4. Because walking doesn't offer enough exercise for these high-spirited
   dogs. This new service provides someone to run with the dogs.

5. A runner will come to the owner's home and take the dog out for some
   vigorous exercise. At a price of around thirty to forty dollars.

6. Many of the runners are marathoners. With a large number also being
   actors, singers, writers, and students.

7. The runners have the chance to earn some much-needed cash. While they
   get some great exercise for both the dogs and themselves.

8. Some dogs, such as English bulldogs, are not good candidates for this
   service. Since they are not built for running.

9. But the larger dogs, especially young retrievers, Dalmatians, and Weimaraners, are perfect for this. If they're strong and healthy.

10. Many dog owners who use this service say it has solved a huge problem
    for them. With their exhausted dogs eagerly packing away their dinners
    and then lying down for the entire night.

■ For answers to
odd-numbered
practice exercises,
see pages A-1–A-19 at
the back of the book.

PRACTICE 3   CORRECTING FRAGMENTS THAT START WITH PREPOSITIONS OR DEPENDENT WORDS . . . .

Read the following paragraph, and circle the ten fragments that start with prepositions or dependent words. Then, correct the fragments.

For decades, scholars have argued. About when and how chickens reached the Americas. One theory is that Portuguese and Spanish settlers brought them. When they arrived after 1500. Another suggests that the chickens were brought over by Polynesian visitors before Columbus's voyages. Most scholars once believed that Portuguese and Spanish brought chickens to the Americas. Along with seeds, medicinal plants, and other necessities. Now, researchers think they finally know what happened. Thanks to some revealing evidence found on the coast of Chile, where chicken bones were discovered. Along with some pottery that was definitely dated between 1304 and 1424, or even earlier. Anthropologists performed a DNA analysis on the bones. Which revealed that the chickens from Chile had a close genetic relationship to chickens from several Polynesian sites. On the islands of Tonga and American Samoa. When these findings were published. Some anthropologists said the discovery supports the idea that Polynesians had by that time populated the Pacific and had even reached the Americas. Though the chicken bones matched Polynesian chickens. The pottery found with the bones was of the local Chilean style. However, it is still unclear whether it was the local Chileans or the visiting Polynesians. Who ate the chickens back then.

Fragments That Start with *-ing* Verb Forms

An *-ing* **verb form** (also called a **gerund**) is the form of a verb that ends in *-ing: walking, writing, swimming.* Unless it has a helping verb (*was walking, was writing, was swimming*), it can't be a complete verb in a sentence.

Sometimes an *-ing* verb form is used as a subject at the beginning of a complete sentence.

-*ING* FORM USED AS A SUBJECT

Swimming is a wonderful form of exercise.

[In this sentence, *swimming* is the subject and *is* is the verb.]

Running strains the knees.

[In this sentence, *running* is the subject, not the verb; *strains* is the verb.]

-*ING* FORM USED WITH A HELPING VERB AS A VERB

I *am working* every day this summer.

[In this sentence, *am* is the helping verb; *am working* is the complete verb.]

Tom *was running* when he saw the accident.

[In this sentence, *was* is the helping verb; *was running* is the complete verb.]

> **Language Note:** English uses both *-ing* verb forms (*Kara loves* ***singing***) and *infinitives* (*to* before the verb) (*Kara loves* ***to sing***). If these forms confuse you, pay special attention to this section and see also page 610.

Whenever a word group begins with a word in *-ing* form, look carefully to see if the word group contains a subject and a verb and if it expresses a complete thought.

FRAGMENT   Snoring so loudly I couldn't sleep.

[If *snoring* is the main verb, what is the subject? There isn't one. Is there a helping verb used with *snoring*? No. It is a fragment.]

FRAGMENT   *Hoping to make up for lost time.* I took a back road to school.

[If *hoping* is the main verb, what is the subject? There isn't one. Is there a helping verb used with *hoping*? No. It is a fragment.]

Correct a fragment that starts with an *-ing* verb form either by adding whatever sentence elements are missing (usually a subject and a helping verb) or by connecting the fragment to the sentence before or after it.

Usually, you will need to put a comma before or after the fragment to join it to the complete sentence.

***-ING* FRAGMENT**	The <u>audience</u> <u>applauded</u> for ten minutes. *Whistling and cheering wildly.*
CORRECTED	The <u>audience</u> <u>applauded</u> for ten minutes. _, ^wWhistling and cheering wildly. *They were whistling*
CORRECTED	The <u>audience</u> <u>applauded</u> for ten minutes. ~~Whistling~~ and cheering wildly.

***-ING* FRAGMENT**	*Working two jobs and going to school.* <u>I</u> <u>am</u> tired all the time.
CORRECTED	Working two jobs and going to school, <u>I</u> <u>am</u> tired all the time.
CORRECTED	*I am working* ~~Working~~ two jobs and going to school. <u>I</u> <u>am</u> tired all the time.

▨ PRACTICE 4   CORRECTING FRAGMENTS THAT START WITH *-ING* VERB FORMS ·

In the following items, circle any *-ing* verb that appears at the beginning of a word group. Then, correct any fragment either by adding the missing sentence elements or by connecting it to the sentence before or after it.

EXAMPLE: (Quilting) with a group of other women, ^{, m}My grandmother

found a social life and a creative outlet.

1. My grandmother spent her entire life. Living on a farm in eastern Wyoming.

2. Growing up during World War II. She learned from her mother how to sew her own clothes.

3. She was a natural seamstress. Creating shirts and dresses more beautiful than anything available in a store.

4. Joining a quilting circle at the age of twenty. My grandmother learned how to make quilts.

5. The quilting circle made quilts for special occasions. Using scraps of cloth left over from other sewing projects.

6. Laying the scraps out in an interesting pattern. The women then chose a traditional design for the stitching that joined the top and bottom parts of the quilt.

7. Celebrating the birth of her first child, my father. The quilting circle gave my grandmother a baby quilt that is now a treasured heirloom.

8. She told me that the quilt was made of memories. Incorporating fabric from her wedding dress, her maternity outfits, and all of the baby clothes she had stitched.

9. Looking at each bit of cloth in that quilt. My grandmother could still describe, years later, the garment she had made from it.

10. Trying to ensure that those memories would survive. I asked her to write down everything she recalled about my father's baby quilt.

. . . .

Fragments That Start with *to* and a Verb

An **infinitive** is the word *to* plus a verb—*to hire, to eat, to study*. These phrases are all called *infinitive forms*. Although they contain verbs, infinitive forms function as nouns, adjectives, or adverbs.

If a word group begins with *to* and a verb, it must have another verb or it is not a complete sentence.

FRAGMENT   I will go to the store later. *To buy a card.*

[The first word group is a sentence, with *I* as the subject and *will go* as the verb. There is no subject in the word group *to buy a card*, and there is no verb outside of the infinitive.]

FRAGMENT	Last week, a <u>couple</u> in New York <u>fulfilled</u> their wedding fantasy. *To get married on the top of the Empire State Building.*

[The first word group is a sentence, with *couple* as the subject, and *fulfilled* as the verb. In the second word group, there is no subject or verb outside of the infinitive.]

Correct a fragment that starts with *to* and a verb by connecting it to the sentence before or after it or by adding the missing sentence elements (a subject and a verb).

FRAGMENT	<u>Geri</u> <u>climbed</u> on the roof. *To watch the fireworks.*
CORRECTED	<u>Geri</u> <u>climbed</u> on the roof. *t*^To watch the fireworks.
CORRECTED	<u>Geri</u> <u>climbed</u> on the roof. ^*She wanted to* ~~To~~ watch the fireworks.
FRAGMENT	*To save on her monthly gas bills.* <u>Tammy</u> <u>sold</u> her SUV and got a Honda Civic Hybrid.
CORRECTED	To save on her monthly gas bills,/, <u>Tammy</u> <u>sold</u> her SUV and got a Honda Civic Hybrid.
CORRECTED	*Tammy wanted to* ^To save on her monthly gas bills. ~~Tammy~~ *She* <u>sold</u> her SUV and got a Honda Civic Hybrid.

> **Language Note:** Do not confuse the infinitive (*to* before the verb) with *that*.
>
> | | |
> |---|---|
> | **INCORRECT** | My <u>brother</u> <u>wants</u> *that* his girlfriend cook. |
> | **CORRECT** | My <u>brother</u> <u>wants</u> his girlfriend *to cook.* |

PRACTICE 5   FINDING AND CORRECTING FRAGMENTS THAT START WITH *TO* AND A VERB . . . .

In the following items, circle any examples of *to* and a verb that begin a word group. Then, correct each fragment either by adding the missing sentence elements or by connecting it to the previous or the next sentence.

EXAMPLE: In the 1940s, Joe Gold decided. *t*(To become) a member

of the Muscle Beach Weightlifting Club.

1. To lift weights. Bodybuilders then met at the Muscle Beach of Santa Monica in Los Angeles.

2. When Joe Gold thought of opening a gym in 1965, he knew exactly where. To locate it.

3. Muscle Beach had become known as Venice by then, but bodybuilders still went there. To lift railroad ties and buckets filled with concrete.

4. Gold invented several new workout machines. To give the bodybuilders more useful exercise.

5. To get the best possible workout. Arnold Schwarzenegger regularly went to Gold's Gym in Venice.

6. Schwarzenegger won the title of Mr. Universe and later successfully ran in an election. To become governor of California.

7. To have a realistic setting for the 1977 movie *Pumping Iron*. The filmmaker selected Gold's Gym.

8. *Pumping Iron*, featuring Schwarzenegger and other weight lifters, helped. To make Gold's Gym famous.

9. In the early 1970s, however, Joe Gold made a decision. To sell his original business along with the name *Gold's Gym* to another company.

10. Later, Gold went on. To create World Gym, which now has more than three hundred locations around the world.

Fragments That Start with Examples or Explanations

As you edit your writing, pay special attention to groups of words that are examples or explanations of information you presented in the previous sentences. These word groups may be fragments.

FRAGMENT   Shoppers <u>find</u> many ways to save money on food bills. *For example, using double coupons.*

[The second word group has no subject and no verb. The word *using* is an *-ing* verb form that needs either to be the subject of a sentence or to have a helping verb with it.]

FRAGMENT   <u>Parking</u> on this campus <u>is</u> a real nightmare. *Especially between 8:00 and 8:30 a.m.*

[The second word group has no subject and no verb.]

Finding fragments that start with examples or explanations can be difficult, because there is no single kind of word to look for. The following are a few starting words that may signal an example or explanation, but fragments that are examples or explanations do not always start with these words:

especially   for example   like   such as

When a group of words that you think is a sentence gives an example or explanation of information in the previous sentence, stop to see if it has a subject and a verb and if it expresses a complete thought. If it is missing any of these elements, it is a fragment.

FRAGMENT   The <u>Web</u> <u>has</u> many job search sites. *Such as Monster.com.*

[Does the second word group have a subject? No. A verb? No. It is a fragment.]

FRAGMENT   <u>I</u> <u>wish</u> I had something to eat from Chipotle's right now. *A giant burrito, for example.*

[Does the second word group have a subject? Yes, *burrito*. A verb? No. It is a fragment.]

FRAGMENT   <u>I</u> <u>pushed</u> seven different voice-mail buttons before I spoke to a real person. *Not a helpful one, though.*

[Does the second word group have a subject? Yes, *one*. A verb? No. It is a fragment.]

To correct a fragment that starts with an example or an explanation, connect it either to the previous sentence or to the next one. Sometimes, you can add the missing sentence elements (a subject, a verb, or both) instead. When you connect the fragment to a sentence, you may need to reword or to change some punctuation. For example, fragments that are examples and fragments that are negatives are often set off by commas.

FRAGMENT   The <u>Web</u> <u>has</u> many job search sites. *Such as Monster.com.*

CORRECTED   The <u>Web</u> <u>has</u> many job search sites, Such as Monster.com.

FRAGMENT   I <u>pushed</u> seven different voice-mail buttons before I spoke to a real person. *Not a helpful one, though.*

CORRECTED   I <u>pushed</u> seven different voice-mail buttons before I
                          , though not a helpful one.
              spoke to a real person. ~~Not a helpful one, though.~~

CORRECTED   I <u>pushed</u> seven different voice-mail buttons before I
                          He was not
              spoke to a real person. ~~Not~~ a helpful ~~one~~, though.

PRACTICE 6   CORRECTING FRAGMENTS THAT ARE EXAMPLES OR EXPLANATIONS · · · · · · · · · · · · · · · · ·

In the following items, circle any word groups that are examples or explanations. Then, correct each fragment either by connecting it to the previous sentence or by adding the missing sentence elements.

EXAMPLE: **Some studies estimate that the number of teenage girls suffering dating abuse is very high.** **Perhaps as many as one out of**
experiences some type of abuse from her boyfriend.
three girls,

1. Many parents believe that they would know if their daughters were being abused. Either physically or emotionally.

2. Most parents would certainly be concerned to see signs of violence on their children. Such as bruises or scratches.

3. A young man can be abusive without laying a finger on his girlfriend. A guy who monitors her actions and keeps her from spending time with other friends.

4. Abusive boyfriends often want to control their partners. Make sure that their girlfriends dress a certain way, for example.

5. Around her parents, a teenager's boyfriend may act like a perfect gentleman. Polite, attentive, and kind to the young woman.

6. When the couple is alone, however, he may be giving her verbal abuse. Like telling her that she is fat, stupid, and ugly.

7. A young woman with an abusive boyfriend may develop psychological problems that will be difficult to treat. Such as low self-esteem.

8. Parents should look for signs that their daughter needs help. Like slipping grades, loss of interest in her friends, and unwillingness to confide in parents.

9. Friends who think that a young woman is involved in an abusive relationship should try to be supportive of her. Not turn away even if she refuses to leave her boyfriend.

10. Young women need to know that help is available. From parents, guidance counselors, women's support services, and even the police, if necessary.

Edit Paragraphs and Your Own Writing

As you edit the following paragraphs and your own writing, use the Critical Thinking guide that follows. You may also want to refer to the chart on page 417.

CRITICAL THINKING: EDITING FOR FRAGMENTS

FOCUS
- Whenever you see one of the five trouble spots in your writing, stop to check for a possible fragment.

ASK
- Does the word group have a subject?
- Does it have a verb?
- Does it express a complete thought?

EDIT
- If your answer to any of these questions is "no," you have a fragment that you must correct.

Find and correct any fragments in the following paragraphs.

EDITING REVIEW 1 (5 fragments) . . . .

(1) Genetically modified foods are being marketed. (2) As the foods of the future. (3) For the past decade, gene technology has been advancing dramatically. (4) Inserting a gene from one species into the DNA of another species is easily possible. (5) A gene from a fish may be found. (6) To make tomatoes more resistant to disease. (7) Of course, genetic modification may have unintended effects. (8) As in the case of genetically modified corn. (9) Which may harm monarch butterfly caterpillars. (10) Arguing that the long-term effects of genetic modification may not be known for years to come. (11) Some scientists urge caution before marketing genetically modified foods.

EDITING REVIEW 2 (4 fragments) . . . .

(1) The term *organic* means different things. (2) To different people. (3) Organic foods are supposed to be grown without pesticides. (4) A method that reduces a farm's impact on the environment. (5) But is organic food a healthier choice for the person eating it? (6) Most people who buy organic food think so. (7) They pay premium prices for organic products because they think the food is good for their own well-being. (8) Not just that of the environment. (9) Surprisingly, however, some foods labeled organic today are highly processed. (10) The label merely means that the ingredients meet a certain government standard. (11) While guaranteeing nothing about the nutritional content or health benefits of the food.

EDITING REVIEW 3 (5 fragments) . . . .

(1) For several years. (2) The U.S. Department of Agriculture has permitted the irradiation of certain foods sold in American supermarkets. (3) Irradiating produce kills bacteria on the food. (4) Increasing its shelf life. (5) Without irradiation, a strawberry may last only a day or two after being purchased. (6) An irradiated strawberry, in contrast, can last a week or more. (7) Because the bacteria that would cause it to spoil are killed by radiation. (8) While some consumers worry about buying irradiated food. (9) Others dismiss these concerns as the effect of too many science-fiction movies. (10) In stores where irradiated fruits and vegetables are sold under banners announcing the radiation treatment. (11) The owners report a booming market.

EDITING REVIEW 4 (5 fragments and 4 formal English errors) . . . .

(1) Bacteria that resist antibiotics could be a real health threat in the next century. (2) Doctrz have begun 2 explain 2 their patients. (3) That antibiotics are useful only for certain kinds of infections and that patients must finish every course of antibiotics they start. (4) Antibiotic use in agriculture, however, has continued. (5) To increase. (6) The government does not even keep records. (7) Of antibiotic use in farm animals. (8) Mne cattle, pigs, and chickens get antibiotics for economic reasons. (9) Such as to keep them healthy and to make them grow faster. (10) Many scientists fear that antibiotic residue in the meat Americans eat may contribute to antibiotic resistance. (11) If so, agricultural antibiotics could eventually endanger human health.

■ **PRACTICE 7   EDITING YOUR OWN WRITING FOR FRAGMENTS** . . . . .

As a final practice, edit fragments in a piece of your own writing—a paper you are working on for this class, a paper you've already finished, a paper for another course, or a recent piece of writing from your work or everyday life. Use the Critical Thinking guide on page 414 and the chart below to help you.

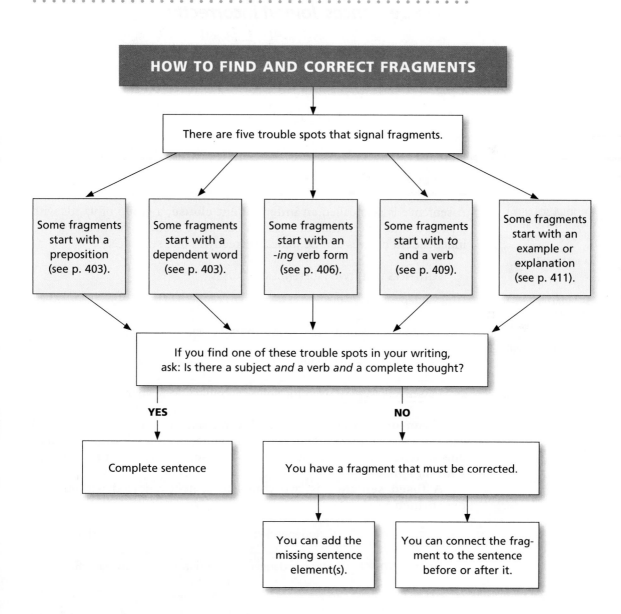

HOW TO FIND AND CORRECT FRAGMENTS

There are five trouble spots that signal fragments.

Some fragments start with a preposition (see p. 403).

Some fragments start with a dependent word (see p. 403).

Some fragments start with an -ing verb form (see p. 406).

Some fragments start with to and a verb (see p. 409).

Some fragments start with an example or explanation (see p. 411).

If you find one of these trouble spots in your writing, ask: Is there a subject *and* a verb *and* a complete thought?

YES

NO

Complete sentence

You have a fragment that must be corrected.

You can add the missing sentence element(s).

You can connect the fragment to the sentence before or after it.

24

Run-Ons

Two Sentences Joined Incorrectly

Understand What Run-Ons Are

■ IDEA JOURNAL
What is a run-on? Do you sometimes have to guess when to end a sentence?

A sentence is also called an **independent clause,** a group of words with a subject and a verb that expresses a complete thought. Sometimes, two independent clauses can be joined correctly in one sentence.

■ In the examples throughout this section, the subject is underlined once, and the verb is underlined twice.

SENTENCES WITH TWO INDEPENDENT CLAUSES

Independent clause   Independent clause

The fog was very thick, so the airport closed.

Independent clause   Independent clause

Passengers were delayed for hours, and many were angry.

A **run-on** is two sentences (each containing a subject and a verb and expressing a complete thought) that are joined incorrectly and written as one sentence. There are two kinds of run-ons—**fused sentences** and **comma splices.**

A **fused sentence** is two complete sentences joined without any punctuation.

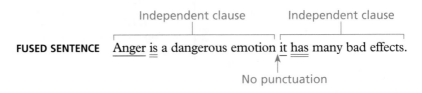

Independent clause   Independent clause

FUSED SENTENCE   Anger is a dangerous emotion it has many bad effects.

↑
No punctuation

418

A **comma splice** is two complete sentences joined by only a comma instead of a comma and one of the following words: *and, but, for, nor, or, so, yet.*

COMMA SPLICE   <u>Anger</u> <u>is</u> a dangerous emotion, <u>it</u> <u>has</u> many bad effects.

↑
Comma

In the Real World, Why Is It Important to Correct Run-Ons?

Run-ons are errors that many people, including instructors and employers, will notice, as the following example shows.

SITUATION: Marion is new to her position as a licensed practical nurse at a large hospital. Each day, she updates patients' records and writes brief summaries of their progress for other nurses. The following is a report that Marion wrote in her first week on the job.

> Trudari Kami is a premature infant she was born with a birth weight of 1.7 pounds her lungs were not fully developed, she was not able to breathe on her own. As of 2:15 a.m. on Thursday, April 6, she remains in stable condition her condition is still critical though she is being carefully monitored.

RESPONSE: Patty Maloney, the clinical nurse specialist profiled in Chapter 13, had the following response to Marion's report.

> I had to meet with Marion, who is obviously not sure how to communicate clearly in medical documents. I explained to her that what she had written was very difficult to understand, and I worked with her on editing the report so that the next person would understand what Marion was trying to say. I had to do this because the reports must be clear; otherwise, the next person might not be sure how to treat the baby.

Patty Maloney
Clinical Nurse
Specialist

(See Patty's Profile of Success on p. 208.)

Find and Correct Run-Ons

To find run-ons, focus on each sentence in your writing one at a time. Until you get used to finding run-ons, this step will take time, but after a while you will not make the error as often.

Read the paragraph on the next page. Does it include any run-ons?

_____ If so, how many? _____

The concert to benefit AIDS research included fabulous musicians and songs. One of the guitarists had six different guitars they were all acoustic. One had a shiny engraved silver shield on it, it flashed in the lights. The riffs the group played were fantastic. All of the songs were original, and many had to do with the loss of loved ones. At the end of some songs, the audience was hushed, too moved with emotion to begin the applause right away. When the concert was over, the listeners, many of them in tears, gave the performers a standing ovation.

■ **PRACTICE 1   FINDING RUN-ONS** . . . .

Find and underline the four run-ons in Marion's report on page 419.

. . . .

When you find a run-on in your writing, you can correct it in one of four ways.

WAYS TO CORRECT A RUN-ON

- Add a period.
- Add a semicolon.
- Add a comma and a coordinating conjunction.
- Add a dependent word.

Add a Period

You can correct a run-on by adding a period to make two separate sentences.

| S | + | V | . |

Independent clause

| S | + | V | . |

Independent clause

FUSED SENTENCES (corrected)

I <u>called</u> about my bill. I <u>got</u> four useless recorded messages.

I finally <u>hung up</u> my <u>question</u> <u>remained</u> unanswered.

COMMA SPLICES (corrected)

My sister found a guy she likes in a chat room, she plans to meet him.

I warned her that she should choose a public place, Applebee's at lunch would be good.

Add a Semicolon

A second way to correct a run-on is to join the two independent clauses into one sentence by adding a semicolon (;). Use a semicolon only when the two independent clauses express closely related ideas that make sense in a single combined sentence.

Independent clause   Independent clause

FUSED SENTENCES (corrected)

My father had a heart attack he is in the hospital.

My mother called 911 the ambulance was there in four minutes.

COMMA SPLICES (corrected)

The emergency room was different from the one on the show *ER*, the doctors and nurses were rude.

He was in the emergency room for over three hours, there was no bed for him.

A semicolon is sometimes used before a transition from one independent clause to another, and the transition word is followed by a comma.

TRANSITION BETWEEN SENTENCES

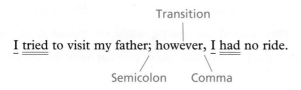

Transition

I tried to visit my father; however, I had no ride.

Semicolon   Comma

■ **PRACTICE 2 CORRECTING A RUN-ON BY ADDING A PERIOD OR A SEMICOLON** . . . .

For each of the following run-ons, indicate in the space to the left whether it is a fused sentence (FS) or a comma splice (CS). Then, correct the run-on by adding a period or a semicolon.

EXAMPLE: <u>*CS*</u> A cellular phone in the car can be a lifesaver in an

emergency; a cell phone may also contribute to an accident.

■ For answers to odd-numbered practice exercises, see pages A-1–A-19 at the back of the book.

_____ 1. The invention of cell phones made telephoning from a car possible, people could telephone for help if they were stranded on the highway.

_____ 2. Almost as soon as cell phones became common, people began to use them in traffic, some drivers were undoubtedly distracted by their telephones, creating a danger.

_____ 3. Some communities in the United States have banned drivers from talking on handheld cell phones, a driver must stop the car to place a call legally in those areas.

_____ 4. Cell-phone makers have come up with hands-free phones even in places with cell-phone restrictions, these phones can be used by the driver of a moving car.

_____ 5. No one debates that drivers can be distracted by cell phones some people wonder, however, whether the problem is really the fact that a driver is holding the phone.

_____ 6. If lawmakers simply want to make sure that drivers have their hands free, they should ban eating while driving as well, they could also stop people from shaving or putting on makeup behind the wheel.

_____ 7. Some people worry that drivers are distracted not by holding the telephone but by having a conversation a tense discussion with the boss or good news from a relative can take the driver's attention from traffic.

■ For more practice correcting run-ons, visit _Exercise Central_ at **bedfordstmartins .com/realessays**.

_____ 8. Cell-phone supporters argue that the same kinds of distractions can come from elsewhere in the car, music and talk radio, for example, can suddenly make a driver lose concentration.

_____ 9. There are differences, however, between talking on a cell phone and listening to music in the car, the telephone requires interaction from the driver, but the radio calls for passive listening.

_____ 10. Drivers who love making calls on the road will resist cell-phone restrictions many other people will feel safer in communities that do not allow driving while telephoning.

Add a Comma and a Coordinating Conjunction

A third way to correct a run-on is to add a comma and a **coordinating conjunction**: a link that joins independent clauses to form one sentence. Some people remember the seven coordinating conjunctions (_and, but, for, nor, or, so, yet_) by using the memory device of _fanboys_, for **f**or, **a**nd, **n**or, **b**ut, **o**r, **y**et, **s**o.

To correct a fused sentence, add both a comma and a coordinating conjunction. A comma splice already has a comma, so just add a coordinating conjunction that makes sense in the sentence.

■ **TIP:** Note that there is no comma _after_ a coordinating conjunction.

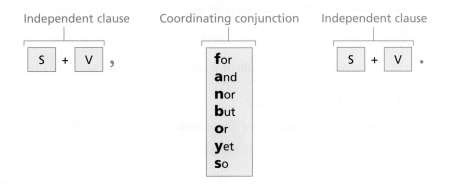

FUSED SENTENCES (corrected)

, but
We <u>warned</u> Tim to wear a seat belt ‸ he <u>refused</u>.

, and
<u>He</u> <u>hit</u> another car ‸ he <u>went</u> through the windshield.

COMMA SPLICES (corrected)

for
<u>He</u> <u>was</u> unbelievably lucky, ‸ <u>he</u> <u>got</u> just scrapes and bruises.

but
<u>He</u> <u>is</u> <u>driving</u> again, ‸ he always <u>buckles</u> his seat belt before starting the car.

Language Note: **Coordinating** conjunctions need to connect two independent clauses. They are not used to join a dependent and an independent clause.

Dependent clause

INCORRECT   Although we warned Tim to wear a seat belt, **but** <u>he</u> <u>refused</u>.

Independent clause

Independent clause   Independent clause

CORRECT   <u>We</u> <u>warned</u> Tim to wear a seat belt, **but** <u>he</u> <u>refused</u>.

PRACTICE 3   CORRECTING A RUN-ON BY ADDING A COMMA AND A COORDINATING CONJUNCTION . . . .

Correct each of the following run-ons. First, underline the subjects and double-underline the verbs to find the separate sentences. Then, add a comma (unless the run-on already includes one) and a coordinating conjunction.

EXAMPLE: <u>Tasmania</u>, an island off the coast of Australia, <u>is</u> the

but
home of many unusual kinds of wildlife, ‸ it also <u>has</u> <u>been</u> the site of

several oil spills.

1. Fairy penguins, a small breed of penguin, live in Tasmania these birds have often been the victims of oil spills.

2. The birds clean their feathers with their beaks they swallow the oil on their feathers.

3. Unfortunately, the penguins' attempts to clean off their feathers can be fatal crude oil is poisonous to penguins.

4. Wildlife conservationists in Tasmania expected future spills, they created a plan to save the penguins.

5. One of the conservationists created a pattern for a sweater for the penguins volunteers from around the world knitted these unusual sweaters.

6. The sweaters cover everything but the penguins' heads and feet, they can't lick the oil-poisoned feathers.

7. Most of the sweaters were made by elderly nursing-home residents in Tasmania, some were sent from as far away as Japan.

8. After future spills, a fairy penguin may wear a sweater it also might wear a tiny football jersey.

9. Some creative knitters made tuxedo-patterned sweaters a few of these penguin suits even have bow ties.

10. The penguins have a variety of protective outfits they don't like any of the garments.

Add a Dependent Word

The fourth way to correct a run-on is to make one of the complete sentences a dependent clause by adding a dependent word (a **subordinating conjunction** or a **relative pronoun**), such as *after, because, before, even though, if, though, unless,* or *when*. Choose the dependent word that best expresses the relationship between the two clauses.

Use a dependent word when the clause it begins is less important than or explains the other clause.

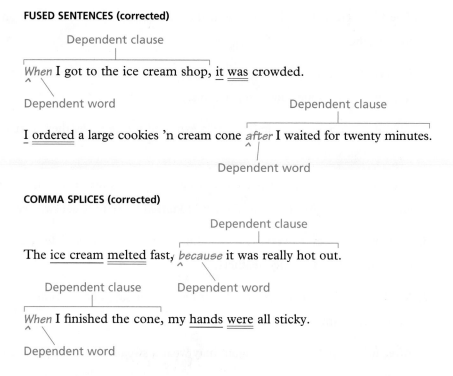

FUSED SENTENCES (corrected)

Dependent clause

When I got to the ice cream shop, it was crowded.

Dependent word

Dependent clause

I ordered a large cookies 'n cream cone *after* I waited for twenty minutes.

Dependent word

COMMA SPLICES (corrected)

Dependent clause

The ice cream melted fast, *because* it was really hot out.

Dependent clause   Dependent word

When I finished the cone, my hands were all sticky.

Dependent word

When the dependent clause starts off the sentence, you need to add a comma after it, as in the first and fourth sentences in the preceding examples. When the dependent clause is after the independent clause, there is no comma, as in the second and third examples.

Common Dependent Words

after	if	what(ever)
although	since	when(ever)
as	so that	where
because	that	whether
before	though	which(ever)
even though	unless	while
how	until	who/whose

■ PRACTICE 4 **CORRECTING A RUN-ON BY MAKING
A DEPENDENT CLAUSE** . . . .

Correct each of the following run-ons. First, underline the subjects and double-underline the verbs to find the separate sentences. Then, make one of the clauses dependent by adding a dependent word. Add a comma after the dependent clause if it comes first in the sentence.

EXAMPLE: Everyone knows where a compass points, it points
which is
toward the north.

1. This phenomenon is something we take for granted, it may be changing.

2. A change in magnetism is possible the earth's magnetic field is getting weaker.

3. Such a change happened before in the earth's history, magnetic materials pointed south instead of north for long periods.

4. A complete reversal could take thousands of years, some effects of the weaker magnetic field are already apparent.

5. The change in magnetism has affected some satellites, the satellites have been damaged.

6. Animals may also be affected some of them use the earth's magnetic field to sense where they are located.

7. Bees, pigeons, salmon, turtles, whales, newts, and even bacteria need the magnetic field to navigate, they will adjust to the magnetic change.

8. However, it could take five thousand to seven thousand years compasses would point south instead of north.

9. The processes affecting magnetism may unfold much more slowly, the magnetic change may not occur for millions of years.

10. The dinosaurs roamed the earth for about thirty-five million years, the earth's magnetic field did not change during all this time.

. . . .

A Word That Can Cause Run-Ons: *Then*

Many run-ons are caused by the word *then*. You can use *then* to join two sentences, but if you add it without the correct punctuation and/or joining word, the resulting sentence will be a run-on. Often, writers mistakenly use just a comma before *then*, but that makes a comma splice. To correct a run-on caused by the word *then*, you can use any of the four methods presented in this chapter.

COMMA SPLICE	I grabbed the remote, then I ate my pizza.
CORRECTED	I grabbed the remote. then I ate my pizza. [period added]
CORRECTED	I grabbed the remote; then I ate my pizza. [semicolon added]
CORRECTED	I grabbed the remote, then I ate my pizza. [coordinating conjunction *and* added]
CORRECTED	I grabbed the remote, then I ate my pizza. [dependent word *before* added to make a dependent clause]

Edit Paragraphs and Your Own Writing

As you edit the following paragraphs and your own writing, use the Critical Thinking guide that follows. You may also want to refer to the chart on page 433.

CRITICAL THINKING: EDITING FOR RUN-ONS

FOCUS
- Read each sentence aloud, and listen carefully as you read.

ASK
- Am I pausing in the middle of the sentence?
- If so, are there two subjects and two verbs?
- If so, are there two complete sentences in this sentence?
- If there are two sentences (independent clauses), are they separated by punctuation? If the answer is "no," the sentence is a **fused sentence**.
- If there is punctuation between the two independent clauses, is it a comma only, with no coordinating conjunction? If the answer is "yes," the sentence is a **comma splice**.

EDIT
- If the sentence is a run-on, correct it using one of the four methods for editing run-ons.

Find and correct any run-ons in the following paragraphs. Use which-ever of the four methods of correcting run-ons that seems best to you.

EDITING REVIEW 1 (6 run-ons) . . . .

(1) Your memory can play tricks on you. (2) It's often easy to forget things you want desperately to remember them. (3) You have probably had the experience of forgetting an acquaintance's name the name comes to your mind only when it's too late. (4) You have also probably been unable to find your keys once in a while, you put them down somewhere without thinking. (5) At other times, however, you may find it difficult to forget some things, you wish you could never think of them again. (6) If you have an annoying song in your mind, you may spend hours wishing desperately to forget it. (7) Sometimes, you may find yourself forced to relive your most embarrassing moment over and over again in your mind your memory won't let you leave that part of your past behind. (8) Some scholars believe that these annoying habits of memory evolved for a reason, it's hard to imagine, though, any good reason for developing the ability to forget where you left your keys.

EDITING REVIEW 2 (10 run-ons) . . . .

(1) There is one primary rule about cooking for astronauts, never make food that crumbles. (2) Looking for crumbs in a space station is no fun for the same reason, salt and pepper for astronauts are always in liquid form. (3) Space cuisine has come a long way since the first astronauts went up in 1961 those *Gemini* astronauts primarily had gelatin-coated food cubes and aluminum tubes of apple sauce. (4) They now get fresh fruit on occasion as well as such choices as shrimp cocktail, mashed potatoes with

bacon, green beans with garlic, and New Orleans jambalaya, they have to be especially careful with some food choices, though. (5) For example, the Russians often bring tomatoes when it is their turn to supply the space station it is not wise to bite right into a fresh tomato because it can squirt out juice which then has to be tracked down. (6) Every dish is eventually consumed, even if it is not liked, wasting food makes no sense when anything can happen in space. (7) NASA's current challenge is preparing and packaging food for the planned expeditions to Mars this food will have to have a five-year shelf life. (8) The food will be shot into space before the astronauts are, first the food will go up, which will take six months. (9) Getting the astronauts to Mars will take another six months, returning adds yet another six months, and delays have to be anticipated due to possible weather or mechanical problems. (10) A lot of thought is going into minimizing bacterial growth in the food bacteria is the last thing one wants on a space mission.

EDITING REVIEW 3 (12 run-ons) . . . .

(1) The number of bike riders is growing, especially in American cities increasing numbers of people are riding bikes to work and for exercise. (2) This makes it all the more important for drivers and bike riders to learn to share the road, every year, approximately 46,000 bike riders are injured in crashes with motor vehicles. (3) The good news is that most of these accidents are preventable, it takes special care on the part of both drivers and riders. (4) Car drivers need to recognize that bicycles have a legal right to use most roads bikes must ride on the shoulder when the speed limit is over fifty miles per hour. (5) When coming up on a cyclist,

slow down, when passing, give the bike at least three feet of clearance. (6) Be especially careful with young cyclists, even those on the sidewalks, they can suddenly dart out in traffic without looking. (7) When making a right turn, make sure there is no bicycle on the right, when waiting to turn left or at a stop sign, yield to a bicycle that has the right of way. (8) Check carefully for bicycles before opening a car door cyclists have been killed by headlong crashes into suddenly opened car doors. (9) Bike riders need to follow the same traffic rules that apply to drivers wait for a green light before crossing intersections and signal before all turns and stops. (10) Try to ride at least three feet from parked cars do not weave in and out between parked cars. (11) Don't ride wearing headphones or while talking on a cell phone, always wear a properly fitted bike helmet. (12) Increasing bike riding is a good sign for the environment and for Americans' expanding waistlines, for everyone's safety, both drivers and riders must vigilantly follow the rules of road-sharing.

EDITING REVIEW 4 (10 run-ons and 7 formal English errors) . . . .

(1) In times past, when a Ping-Pong player could not find someone to play against, that meant there was no Ping-Pong, those times are now over. (2) More and more, people are installing in their basements and garages the perfect Ping-Pong partner it is a robot that endlessly serves fast-moving Ping-Pong balls. (3) There R several dfrnt Ping-Pong robots on the market, they all do basically the same thing. (4) They pitch balls one by one to the person on the other side of the table the fancier ones have nets that can catch return balls and funnel them back to the automatic server. (5) The human player cn control the speed, placement, and spin of the

balls, the more elaborate models allow random serves or a programmed series of serves that can, for example, go 2 alternate sides of the table. (6) Some players feel that the robots cn b mo challenging to play against than a human opponent, it's hard to see where the ball is coming from. (7) Human players partially give away their intentions with their body position, the angle of the paddle, and the type of stroke none of these cues is visible with a robot server. (8) The ability of some robots to spin balls is also helpful, say some players the machine can be set to replay the exact same spinned serve repeatedly, allowing the person to better learn how to counter it. (9) The Ping-Pong robots with retrieving nets can save the human player time and effort some humans appreciate the break to pick up balls. (10) The relentless machine can provide an exhausting workout, of course, for many robot owners, this is the whole point.

PRACTICE 5 EDITING YOUR OWN WRITING FOR RUN-ONS . . . .

As a final practice, edit run-ons in a piece of your own writing—a paper you are working on for this class, a paper you've already finished, a paper for another course, or a recent piece of writing from your work or everyday life. Use the Critical Thinking guide on page 428 and the chart on page 433 to help you.

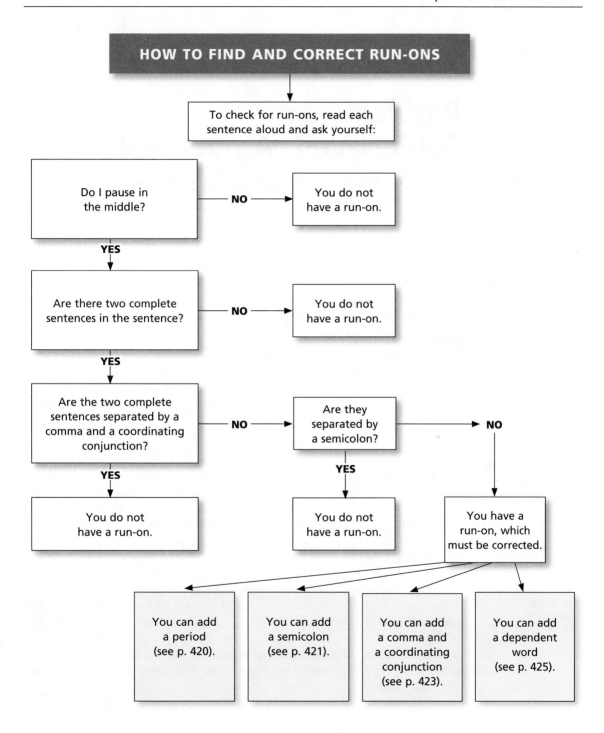

HOW TO FIND AND CORRECT RUN-ONS

To check for run-ons, read each sentence aloud and ask yourself:

Do I pause in the middle? —**NO**→ You do not have a run-on.

YES

Are there two complete sentences in the sentence? —**NO**→ You do not have a run-on.

YES

Are the two complete sentences separated by a comma and a coordinating conjunction? —**NO**→ Are they separated by a semicolon? →**NO**

YES

You do not have a run-on.

YES

You do not have a run-on.

You have a run-on, which must be corrected.

You can add a period (see p. 420).

You can add a semicolon (see p. 421).

You can add a comma and a coordinating conjunction (see p. 423).

You can add a dependent word (see p. 425).

25

Problems with Subject-Verb Agreement

When Subjects and Verbs Don't Match

Understand What Subject-Verb Agreement Is

■ **IDEA JOURNAL**
Write about a major disagreement you had with someone.

■ In the examples throughout this chapter, the subject is underlined once, and the verb is underlined twice.

■ For more on regular verbs and how they differ from irregular verbs, see Chapter 26.

In any sentence, **the subject and the verb must match—or agree—in number.** If the subject is singular (one person, place, or thing), then the verb must also be singular. If the subject is plural (more than one), the verb must also be plural.

SINGULAR   The <u>phone</u> <u>rings</u> constantly at work.

[The subject, *phone*, is singular—just one phone—so the verb must take the singular form: *rings*.]

PLURAL   The <u>phones</u> <u>ring</u> constantly at work.

[The subject, *phones*, is plural—more than one phone—so the verb must take the plural form: *ring*.]

Regular verbs, verbs that follow standard English patterns, have two forms in the present tense: one that does not add an ending and one that ends in *-s*. First-person (*I, we*) subjects, second-person (*you*) subjects, and plural subjects (more than one person, place, or thing) have verbs with no *-s* ending. Third-person singular subjects (*he, she, it,* and singular nouns) always have a verb that ends in *-s*. The chart that follows shows the differences.

Regular Verbs, Present Tense

	SINGULAR FORM	PLURAL FORM
First person	I walk.	We walk.
Second person	You walk.	You walk.
Third person	He/she/it walks.	They walk.
	Percy walks.	Percy and Don walk.
	The dog walks.	The dogs walk.

Language Note: Some nouns that don't end in -*s* are plural, so they need plural verbs. For example, *children* and *people* don't end in -*s*, but they mean more than one child or person, so they are plural.

INCORRECT	The people owns their apartments.
CORRECT	The people own their apartments.

In the Real World, Why Is It Important to Correct Subject-Verb Agreement Problems?

Like fragments and run-ons, subject-verb agreement errors are significant problems that can make a bad impression with instructors, employers, and others.

SITUATION: Part of Monique's work at the National Military Family Association involves helping people find and apply for various kinds of assistance. Below is a letter from a woman seeking help for her son who has returned from deployment in Iraq with symptoms of post-traumatic stress disorder.

Monique Rizer
Journalist, Development Associate

(See Monique's Profile of Success on p. 155.)

Dear X:

My son, Corporal Jonas Brown, were in Iraq. Now he is home, and he have many problems that is getting worse. He wake up every night screaming, and he cry and hold his head in his hands. Jonas, a young man who always work very hard, have not been able to hold a job. He is changed, and he need help before he hurt himself. His friends from the army talks to me and says as a veteran he are able to get free help. Please tell me what I should do.

RESPONSE: Many returning veterans suffer from post-traumatic stress disorder, and military psychiatric resources are stretched very thin. Unfortunately, the people who are most likely to get the help they need are the ones who can present their case well in writing. For example, when newspapers publish stories of veterans who suffer, those veterans often get help. But for someone like the mother who wrote this letter, the chances of getting a quick response aren't good. Her letter shows that she is not well educated and probably not able to work the system effectively.

Find and Correct Errors in Subject-Verb Agreement

To find problems with subject-verb agreement in your own writing, read carefully, and look for the five trouble spots covered in this chapter.

 PRACTICE 1   FINDING SUBJECT-VERB AGREEMENT PROBLEMS . . . .

Find and underline the twelve subject-verb agreement problems in the letter about Corporal Jonas Brown on page 435.

. . . .

The Verb Is a Form of *Be, Have,* or *Do*

The verbs *be, have,* and *do* do not follow the regular patterns for forming singular and plural forms; they are **irregular verbs**.

These verbs cause problems for people who use only one form of the verb in casual conversation: *You is the richest* (incorrect). *He is the richest* (correct). In college and at work, use the correct form of the verbs *be, have,* and *do* as shown in the charts on the next page.

                    are
You is the craziest person I've ever known.

                        has
Johnson have the best car in the lot.

                does
Valery do the bill paying on the first of every month.

Forms of the Verb **Be**

PRESENT TENSE	SINGULAR	PLURAL
First person	I am	we are
Second person	you are	you are
Third person	she/he/it is	they are
	the student/Joe is	the students are

PAST TENSE		
First person	I was	we were
Second person	you were	you were
Third person	she/he/it was	they were
	the student/Joe was	the students were

Forms of the Verb **Have**, *Present Tense*

	SINGULAR	PLURAL
First person	I have	we have
Second person	you have	you have
Third person	she/he/it has	they have
	the student/Joe has	the students have

Forms of the Verb **Do**, *Present Tense*

	SINGULAR	PLURAL
First person	I do	we do
Second person	you do	you do
Third person	she/he/it does	they do
	the student/Joe does	the students do

> ◼ **PRACTICE 2   CHOOSING THE CORRECT FORM OF *BE, HAVE,* OR *DO*** . . . .

In each sentence, underline the subject of the verb *be, have,* or *do,* and circle the correct form of the verb.

> **EXAMPLE:** The microwave <u>oven</u> (am /(is)/ are) a common fixture in most American <u>homes</u>.

◼ For answers to odd-numbered practice exercises, see pages A-1–A-19 at the back of the book.

1. Yet many people (has / have) concerns about the safety of this standard appliance.

2. They (am / is / are) worried that standing close to an operating microwave oven can expose them to harmful radiation.

3. Some microwave ovens (does / do) in fact leak radiation, but the levels that might be released are quite small.

4. The Center for Devices and Radiological Health, a unit of the U.S. Food and Drug Administration, (has / have) responsibility for regulating microwave oven safety.

5. According to the Center, the allowed amount of leakage from each microwave oven that reaches the market (am / is / are) far below the level of radiation that is harmful to humans.

◼ For more practice with subject-verb agreement, visit *Exercise Central* at **bedfordstmartins .com/realessays**.

6. Manufacturers of microwave ovens (does / do) even more to assure the safety of their products.

7. All microwave ovens (has / have) a type of door latch that prevents the production of microwaves whenever the latch is released.

8. Also, the doors of microwave ovens (am / is / are) lined with a metal mesh that stops microwaves from escaping.

9. Furthermore, the radiation level from a microwave oven (am / is / are) extremely low at a distance of even a foot from the oven.

10. Therefore, the radiation from an operating microwave oven (do / does) not pose a threat to anyone.

PRACTICE 3   USING THE CORRECT FORM OF *BE, HAVE,* OR *DO* . . . .

In each sentence, underline the subject and fill in the correct form of the verb (*be, have,* or *do*) indicated in parentheses.

EXAMPLE: Our <u>professor</u> _*has*_ (*have*) forty papers to grade this weekend.

1. Most students _____ (*be*) used to the idea that computers sometimes grade tests.

2. You _____ (*have*) probably taken standardized tests and filled in small ovals with a pencil.

3. A computer _____ (*do*) not have to be sophisticated to read the results of such tests.

4. Surprisingly, a new software program _____ (*be*) designed to grade student essays.

5. The program _____ (*have*) the ability to sort words in an essay and compare the essay to others in its database.

6. The software _____ (*do*) not check grammar or spelling.

7. Teachers _____ (*be*) still needed to supplement the computer grade, according to the software manufacturer.

8. If a computer grades your essay, you _____ (*have*) to write about one of five hundred specified topics.

9. A computer _____ (*do*) check the organization, clarity, and style of your writing.

10. Some teachers _____ (*be*) excited about their new computerized assistant, but I _____ (*do*) not like the idea of a computer grading my essays.

Words Come between the Subject and the Verb

When the subject and the verb aren't right next to each other, it can be difficult to make sure that they agree. Most often, what comes between the subject and the verb is either a prepositional phrase or a dependent clause.

Prepositional Phrase between the Subject and the Verb

■ For a list of common prepositions, see page 390.

A **prepositional phrase** starts with a preposition and ends with a noun or pronoun: The line *for the movie* went *around the corner.*

Remember, the subject of a sentence is never in a prepositional phrase. When you are looking for the subject, you can cross out any prepositional phrases. This strategy should help you find the real subject and decide whether it agrees with the verb.

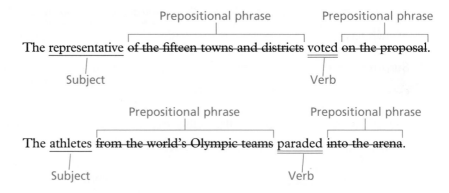

The representative of the fifteen towns and districts voted on the proposal.

The athletes from the world's Olympic teams paraded into the arena.

■ **PRACTICE 4   MAKING SUBJECTS AND VERBS AGREE WHEN THEY ARE SEPARATED BY A PREPOSITIONAL PHRASE** . . . . .

In each of the following sentences, first cross out the prepositional phrase between the subject and the verb, and then circle the correct form of the verb. Remember, the subject of a sentence is never in a prepositional phrase.

EXAMPLE: Twenty-eight million people in the United States (am / is / (are)) deaf or hard of hearing.

1. Most parents with hearing loss (has / have) children who can hear.

2. Many of these children (learns / learn) sign language as a first language.

3. Communication with words (comes / come) later.

4. Few people in the hearing world (understands / understand) the lives of deaf people completely.

5. Many deaf people in this country (feels / feel) closer to deaf people from other parts of the world than to hearing Americans.

6. The hearing children of deaf parents (comes / come) closer to understanding deaf culture than most hearing people.

7. A hearing child in a deaf household (resembles / resemble) a child of immigrant parents in many ways.

8. Adapting to two different cultures (makes / make) fitting in difficult for some young people.

9. Sometimes, ties to the hearing world and the deaf world (pulls / pull) in opposite directions.

10. Bridges between cultures (am / is / are) more easily built by people who understand both sides.

. . . .

Dependent Clause between the Subject and the Verb

A **dependent clause** has a subject and a verb, but it does not express a complete thought. When a dependent clause comes between the subject and the verb, it usually starts with the word *who, whose, whom, that,* or *which*.

The subject of a sentence is never in the dependent clause. When you are looking for the subject, you can cross out any dependent clauses.

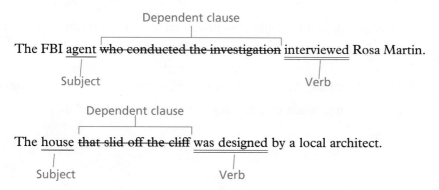

Dependent clause

The FBI agent ~~who conducted the investigation~~ interviewed Rosa Martin.

Subject   Verb

Dependent clause

The house ~~that slid off the cliff~~ was designed by a local architect.

Subject   Verb

PRACTICE 5 MAKING SUBJECTS AND VERBS AGREE WHEN THEY ARE SEPARATED BY A DEPENDENT CLAUSE . . . .

In each of the following sentences, cross out any dependent clauses. Then, correct any problems with subject-verb agreement. If a sentence has no problem, write "OK" next to it.

EXAMPLE: A person ~~who lies in job applications are~~ likely to get caught.
is

1. A résumé, which is a job applicant's first contact with many prospective employers, contain details about past work experience and education.

2. Many people who write résumés are tempted to exaggerate.

3. Perhaps an applicant who held a previous job for two months claim to have spent a year there.

4. A job title that sounds impressive look good on a résumé, whether or not it is accurate.

5. Often, a person who never received a college degree wants to add it to a résumé anyway.

6. A person who is considering untrue résumé additions need to think twice.

7. Employers who like a résumé checks the information provided by the applicant.

8. A résumé that contains false information goes in the reject pile.

9. In addition, many people who invent material on a résumé forgets the inventions when they face a prospective employer in an interview.

10. Even a company that does not check all of the information on résumés pays attention when interviewees seem to forget some of their qualifications.

The Sentence Has a Compound Subject

A **compound subject** consists of two (or more) subjects connected by *and, or,* or *nor* (as in *neither/nor* expressions). If two subjects are joined by *and,* they combine to become a plural subject, and the verb must take a plural form as well.

Subject   *and*   Subject   Plural form of verb

The director *and* the producer decide how the film will be made.

If two subjects are connected by *or* or *nor,* they are considered separate, and the verb should agree with the subject closest to it.

Subject   *or*   Singular subject   Singular form of verb

The director *or* the producer decides how the film will be made.

Subject   *nor*   Singular subject   Singular form of verb

Neither the director *nor* the producer wants to give up control.

Subject   *or*   Plural subject   Plural form of verb

The director *or* his assistants decide how the film will be made.

Subject   *nor*   Plural subject   Plural form of verb

Neither the director *nor* his assistants want to give up control.

PRACTICE 6 CHOOSING THE CORRECT VERB IN A SENTENCE WITH A COMPOUND SUBJECT . . . .

In each of the following sentences, underline the word (*and, or,* or *nor*) that joins the parts of the compound subject. Then, circle the correct form of the verb.

EXAMPLE: A child <u>and</u> an adult (has / (have)) different nutritional needs.

1. Fruits and vegetables (does / do) not make up enough of most Americans' diets.

2. The U.S. government and other organizations concerned with health and nutrition (recommends / recommend) that people eat at least five servings of fruits and vegetables a day.

3. Whole-grain cereal or bread (is / are) another important part of a healthy diet.

4. Neither vitamins nor fiber (is / are) found in many popular snack foods.

5. Potato chips and candy (contains / contain) few useful nutrients.

6. Neither fat nor sugar (helps / help) build a healthy body.

7. However, in small amounts, fat and sugar (contributes / contribute) beneficially by making food taste good.

8. Motivated dieters and certain health fanatics (eats / eat) nutritious food that tastes terrible.

9. Neither dieters nor health fanatics (is / are) likely to keep eating the unappetizing food for a lifetime.

10. Choosing nutritious food and preparing it well (allows / allow) a person to feel healthy and satisfied.

The Subject Is an Indefinite Pronoun

Indefinite pronouns, which refer to unspecified people or objects, are often singular, although there are exceptions.

When you find an indefinite pronoun in your writing, use the table on the next page to help you determine the correct verb form, singular or plural. If the pronoun may be singular or plural, you'll need to check whether the word it refers to is singular or plural to determine what verb form to use.

Everyone loves vacations.

[*Everyone* is always singular, so it takes the singular verb *loves*.]

Some of the wreckage was recovered after the crash.

[In this case, *some* is singular, referring to *wreckage,* so it takes the singular verb *was recovered*.]

Indefinite Pronouns

ALWAYS SINGULAR

anybody	everyone	nothing
anyone	everything	one (of)
anything	much	somebody
each (of)	neither (of)	someone
either (of)	nobody	something
everybody	no one	

MAY BE SINGULAR OR PLURAL

all	none
any	some

<u>Some</u> of the workers <u>were delayed</u> by the storm.

[In this case, *some* is plural, referring to *workers,* so it takes the plural verb *were delayed.*]

Often, an indefinite pronoun is followed by a prepositional phrase or a dependent clause; remember that the subject of a sentence is never found in either of these. To choose the correct verb, you can cross out the prepositional phrase or dependent clause to focus on the indefinite pronoun.

<u>All</u> ~~of my first day on the job~~ <u>was devoted</u> to filling out forms.

<u>Some</u> ~~who are longtime residents~~ <u>recommend</u> a rent strike.

■ **PRACTICE 7   CHOOSING THE CORRECT VERB WHEN THE SUBJECT IS AN INDEFINITE PRONOUN** . . . .

In each of the following sentences, underline the indefinite pronoun that is the subject, and cross out any prepositional phrases or dependent clauses that come between the subject and the verb. Then, circle the correct verb.

EXAMPLE: <u>One</u> ~~of the oldest types of exercise that people use to stay in shape~~ (**is**/ are) once again fashionable.

1. Many who choose this newly-trendy type of exercise, which is walking,

   (is / are) middle-aged or older.

2. Someone with aching joints, past injuries, or an aging body (want / wants) a relatively gentle form of exercise.

3. But everybody, even people who are young and in great shape, (need / needs) exercise that is safe, practical, and enjoyable.

4. Those who walk for aerobic exercise (sustain / sustains), on average, fewer fitness-related injuries than people who run.

5. Nobody with good sense or serious concern for his or her health (pursue / pursues) activities that might risk bodily damage.

6. Furthermore, anyone who sets aside the time and makes the effort to walk regularly (benefit / benefits) in several ways.

7. Some of today's active walkers (do / does) it to lose weight.

8. Anybody with a waistline problem, which is a category that includes too many people these days, (appreciate / appreciates) the opportunity to shed 300 calories by walking briskly for an hour.

9. Others who have the time for an energetic yet leisurely walk (enjoy / enjoys) looking at people, stores, and the outdoors as they exercise and observing the new and unusual around them.

10. Depending on their specific situations and preferences, many people want a steady, low-impact type of exercise, like walking, and many others choose something more strenuous and demanding, such as running; either type of exercise (help / helps) them to have a more active and healthy life.

The Verb Comes before the Subject

In most sentences, the subject comes before the verb. Two kinds of sentences reverse that order—questions and sentences that begin with *here* or *there*. In these two types of sentences, you need to check carefully for errors in subject-verb agreement.

Questions

In questions, the verb or part of the verb comes before the subject. To find the subject and verb, you can turn the question around as if you were going to answer it.

Where is the nearest gas station? The nearest gas station is . . .

Are the keys in the car? The keys are in the car.

> **Language Note:** Forming questions correctly is difficult for many people, especially those whose first language is not English. For charts that summarize how to correctly form questions, see Chapter 26.

Sentences That Begin with **Here** or **There**

When a sentence begins with *here* or *there,* the subject always follows the verb. Turn the sentence around to find the subject and verb.

Here are the hot dog rolls. The hot dog rolls are here.

There is a fly in my soup. A fly is in my soup.

> **Language Note:** *There is* and *there are* are common in English. If you have trouble using these expressions, see page 588.

■ **PRACTICE 8 CORRECTING A SENTENCE WHEN THE VERB COMES BEFORE THE SUBJECT** ·

Correct any problems with subject-verb agreement in the following sentences. If a sentence is already correct, write "OK" next to it.

EXAMPLE: There is several openings for bilingual applicants.

1. Where is the corporation's main offices located?

2. There is branch offices in Paris, Singapore, and Tokyo.

3. How well do the average employee abroad speak English?

4. What do the company manufacture?

5. How many languages are the manual written in?

6. Does the company employ college graduates as translators?

7. There is some machines that can do translation.

8. Does learning a second language give an applicant a special advantage?

9. There is never a disadvantage in knowing another language.

10. Here is the names of several qualified people.

Edit Paragraphs and Your Own Writing

As you edit the following paragraphs and your own writing, use the Critical Thinking guide that follows. You may also want to refer to the chart on page 451.

CRITICAL THINKING: EDITING FOR SUBJECT-VERB AGREEMENT
FOCUS • Whenever you see one of the five trouble spots in your writing, stop to check that the subject and the verb agree.
ASK • Where is the subject in this sentence? Where is the verb? • Do the subject and verb agree in number? (Are they both singular or both plural?)
EDIT • If you answer "no" to the agreement question, you need to correct the sentence.

Find and correct any problems with subject-verb agreement that you find in the following paragraphs.

■   EDITING REVIEW 1   (7 errors) . . . .

(1) School systems around the country is embracing educational standards. (2) The idea of standards sound reasonable. (3) Does anyone want to argue that students should not have to meet certain requirements to graduate? (4) A national standard for all American students have many supporters, too. (5) If the requirements for graduation in Oregon

and Tennessee is the same, everyone with a high school diploma gets a similar education. (6) There is a catch, of course. (7) Not everyone with a professional or personal interest in school quality is able to agree on these requirements. (8) Mathematics and writing is important, but so is music and physical education. (9) How is parents, teachers, and administrators ever going to find standards that everyone accepts?

EDITING REVIEW 2   (9 errors) . . . .

(1) Agreeing on school standards are only part of the battle over education. (2) How is students going to prove that they have met the standards before graduation? (3) The answer, in many cases, are testing. (4) School tests that are required by state law is becoming more and more common. (5) These tests are standardized, so all of the students taking an eighth-grade test in a particular state is given the same test. (6) Both the individual student and his or her school district is evaluated by the scores. (7) The parents of a student learns not only what their child's score is but also how the school compares with others around the state. (8) Then, children who need extra help is supposed to receive it, and schools with very low scores year after year becomes eligible for additional resources.

EDITING REVIEW 3   (6 errors) . . . .

(1) In reality, standardized tests for schools have many problems. (2) Most school districts that have a testing program uses tests that can be scored by a computer. (3) Computers cannot read, so the tests that they grade usually offers multiple-choice questions. (4) A multiple-choice test in science or mathematics do not allow students to demonstrate critical thinking. (5) How does students show their writing ability on such a test?

(6) There is tricks to answering multiple-choice questions that many students learn. (7) Frequently, a high score on such a test says more about the student's test-taking ability than about his or her knowledge of a subject. (8) Nevertheless, the quick results and low cost of a computer-graded multiple-choice test means that this imperfect testing system is used in many school systems.

EDITING REVIEW 4   (7 errors and 4 formal English errors)

(1) Another problem with standardized tests are that test material cn begin to change the curriculum. (2) Everyone who teaches want his or her students 2 get high scores on the tests. (3) For one thing, a teacher of underperforming students are likely to be criticized for not preparing them btr. (4) One result of teachers' fears are that they spend most of the class time preparing students for the test. (5) In some cases, the phenomenon of "teaching to the test" become school policy. (6) A creative teacher or one who has been teaching for years are no longer trusted to engage students with a subject. (7) Skul officials, who also want high scores for their districts, encourage teachers to focus on material that the test will cover. (8) Other material, which may be fascinating to students, are ignored because the test does not require it.

PRACTICE 9   EDITING YOUR OWN WRITING FOR SUBJECT-VERB AGREEMENT

As a final practice, edit for subject-verb agreement in a piece of your own writing—a paper you are working on for this class, a paper you've already finished, a paper for another course, or a recent piece of writing from your work or everyday life. Use the Critical Thinking guide on page 448 and the chart on page 451 to help you.

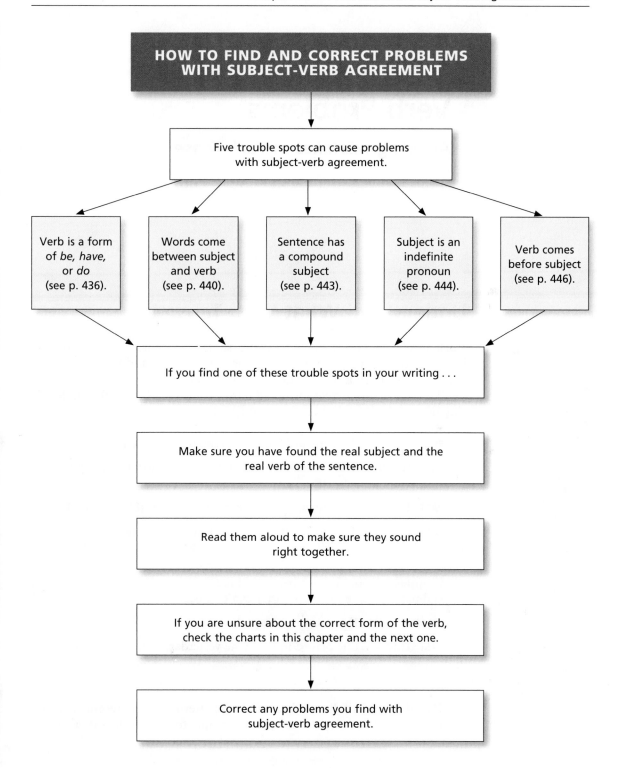

HOW TO FIND AND CORRECT PROBLEMS WITH SUBJECT-VERB AGREEMENT

Five trouble spots can cause problems with subject-verb agreement.

Verb is a form of *be, have,* or *do* (see p. 436).

Words come between subject and verb (see p. 440).

Sentence has a compound subject (see p. 443).

Subject is an indefinite pronoun (see p. 444).

Verb comes before subject (see p. 446).

If you find one of these trouble spots in your writing . . .

Make sure you have found the real subject and the real verb of the sentence.

Read them aloud to make sure they sound right together.

If you are unsure about the correct form of the verb, check the charts in this chapter and the next one.

Correct any problems you find with subject-verb agreement.

26

Verb Problems

Avoiding Mistakes in Verb Tense

Understand What Verb Tense Is

■ **IDEA JOURNAL**
Write about
something you did
yesterday. Then, write
about it again as
if you are going to
do it tomorrow.

Verb tense tells *when* the action of a sentence occurs—in the present, in the past, or in the future. Verbs change their form and use the helping verbs *have* or *be* to indicate different tenses.

To choose the correct form and tense, consider whether the subject is singular or plural *and* when the action occurs.

■ In the examples
throughout this
chapter, the subject is
underlined once, and
the verb is underlined
twice.

PRESENT TENSE	Teresa and I talk every day. [Plural subject]
PRESENT TENSE	She also talks to her mother every morning. [Singular subject]
PAST TENSE	Yesterday, they talked for two hours. [Plural subject]
FUTURE TENSE	Tomorrow, they will talk again. [Plural subject]

> **Language Note:** Remember to add the endings on present-tense and past-tense verbs, even if they can't be heard in speech.
>
> PRESENT TENSE Krystal play**s** varsity basketball.
>
> PAST TENSE She play**ed** in the game yesterday.

■ For more on
subject-verb agree-
ment and singular
versus plural verb
forms, see Chapter 25.

Regular verbs follow a few standard patterns in the present and past tenses, and their past-tense and past-participle forms end in *-ed* or *-d*.

Irregular verbs change spelling in the past-tense and past-participle forms. (For more on irregular verbs, see pp. 467–75.)

	REGULAR VERB: *WALK*	IRREGULAR VERB: *EAT*
Past tense	walked [I walk**ed**.]	ate [I ate.]
Past participle	walked [I have/had walk**ed**.]	eaten [I have/had eaten.]

In the Real World, Why Is It Important to Use Correct Verbs?

Errors in verb tense can create a negative impression of the writer, as the following example shows.

SITUATION: A student that Shawn has been working with shows him the script for an oral presentation he has to give in school the following week. Here is what the student wrote as an introduction:

Shawn Brown
Founder, Diamond Educators

(See Shawn's Profile of Success on p. 303.)

> Last week I done gone to the awards day for Diamond Educators and receive my first prize ever. I receive the prize because last semester I work with younger kids to help them do things right, like doing their homework and why it be important to go to school. Before I meet people at Diamond, I never understand why school matter. I believe that only fools cared about school, but now I know education can change my life. Trying to get a good education don't mean selling out: It mean making something of myself.

RESPONSE: The student has great ideas here, but there are lots of errors that will make people ignore his good ideas. He's writing more like he talks informally, and I tell people over and over that they need to know how and when to use "formal" English. It is important to achieving their own goals and to getting a better life.

Use Correct Verbs

Verbs have several tenses to express past, present, and future time. This section will explain what those tenses are and how to use them correctly when you write.

Regular Verbs

To avoid mistakes with regular verbs, understand the basic patterns for forming the present, past, and future tenses.

Present Tense

The **simple present tense** is used for actions that are happening at the same time that you are writing about them and about actions that are ongoing. There are two forms for the simple present tense of regular verbs—**-s ending** or **no added ending**. Use the *-s* ending when the subject is *she, he,* or *it,* or the name of one person or thing. Do not add any ending for other subjects.

Regular Verbs in the Simple Present Tense

	SINGULAR	PLURAL
First person	I laugh.	We laugh.
Second person	You laugh.	You laugh.
Third person	She/he/it laughs.	They laugh.
	The baby laughs.	The babies laugh.

PRACTICE 1   FINDING VERB ERRORS . . . .

Find and underline the eleven errors in the student's writing on page 453.

PRACTICE 2   USING THE SIMPLE PRESENT TENSE OF REGULAR VERBS . . . .

In each of the following sentences, first underline the subject, and then circle the correct verb form.

> **EXAMPLE:** Most elevator <u>riders</u> ((share)/ shares) a common complaint.

■ For answers to odd-numbered practice exercises, see pages A-1–A-19 at the back of the book.

1. Too often, elevator doors (open / opens) at practically every floor even when there are just a few people in the car.

2. Now, guests at one big hotel (enjoy / enjoys) faster, more direct elevator rides, thanks to a new "smart elevator" system.

3. The system (work / works) so well because it knows where people want to go before they get into their elevator car.

4. Whenever someone (want / wants) to take an elevator, he or she must first punch in the desired floor number at a keypad in the lobby.

5. A digital display then (indicate / indicates) the letter of the elevator car that will directly go to a floor close to the person's destination.

6. To ensure that guests don't get confused with the new system, employees of the hotel (help / helps) guests to use it correctly.

7. The hotel's managers (claim / claims) that the system reduces the average trip time by up to 30 percent.

8. However, some guests (express / expresses) irritation with the system.

9. They sometimes (wait / waits) a long time for an elevator, and then they cannot get into the first car that comes because it is not going near their floor.

10. Still, most people who use the system (consider / considers) it to be a welcome improvement in elevator technology.

■ For more practice with verbs, visit *Exercise Central* at **bedfordstmartins .com/realessays**.

Two other present-tense forms are the present progressive tense and the present perfect tense. The **present progressive tense** is used to describe actions that are in progress. It is formed as follows:

Present-tense form of *be* (helping verb)	+	Main verb with *-ing* ending

---

Present Progressive Tense

	SINGULAR	**PLURAL**
First person	I am laugh**ing**.	We are laugh**ing**.
Second person	You are laugh**ing**.	You are laugh**ing**.
Third person	She/he/it is laugh**ing**.	They are laugh**ing**.
	The baby is laugh**ing**.	The babies are laugh**ing**.

Language Note: Some languages, such as Russian, do not use the progressive tense. If your first language does not use the progressive tense, pay special attention to this section.

■ **PRACTICE 3   USING THE PRESENT PROGRESSIVE TENSE** . . . .

In each of the following sentences, underline the helping verb (a form of *be*), and fill in the correct form of the verb in parentheses.

> **EXAMPLE:** My grandmother is <u>*looking*</u> (*look*) into our family history.

1. She is _____ (*start*) with my grandfather's side of the family, the Mancinis.

2. To learn more about the Mancinis, she is _____ (*contact*) several of my grandfather's relatives to get birth documents and other information.

3. Also, she is _____ (*gather*) information about the Mancinis through genealogy sites on the Internet.

4. She is _____ (*learn*) a lot about my grandfather's ancestors; for instance, they were peasants who fled Italy around 1910 because of difficult living conditions.

5. My sister and I are _____ (*help*) our grandmother by looking at online records from Ellis Island.

6. Also, we are _____ (*think*) of taking a course in genealogical research at a local college.

7. Even our mother is _____ (*pitch*) in.

8. For example, she is _____ (*call*) older Mancinis to get family stories.

9. She is constantly _____ (*share*) the stories with my sister and me; for instance, she learned that our great-grandfather helped to organize a coal-miner strike soon after coming to America.

10. "These stories are _____ (*remind*) me of some modern Mancinis," she said. "We like to stir things up."

· ·

The **present perfect tense** is used for an action begun in the past that is ongoing into the present or that was completed at some unspecified time in the past. It is formed by using a **past participle,** a verb form that uses the helping verb *have*. The past participle of the verb *play*, for example, is *has played* or *have played*. The **present perfect** is formed as follows:

| Present-tense form of *have* (helping verb) | + | *Past participle* |

■ *Be* and *have* are irregular verbs. For more details on irregular verbs, see pages 467–75.

Present Perfect Tense

	SINGULAR	PLURAL
First person	I have laughed.	We have laughed.
Second person	You have laughed.	You have laughed.
Third person	She/he/it has laughed.	They have laughed.
	The baby has laughed.	The babies have laughed.

Language Note: Be careful not to leave out *have* when it is needed for the present perfect. Time-signal words like *since* or *for* may mean that the present perfect is needed.

| INCORRECT | Krystal *played* basketball since she was ten. |
| CORRECT | Krystal *has played* basketball since she was ten. |

■   **PRACTICE 4   USING THE PRESENT PERFECT TENSE** . . . .

In each of the following sentences, underline the helping verb (a form of *have*), and fill in the correct form of the verb in parentheses.

> **EXAMPLE:** My father <u>has</u> *served* (*serve*) in the army for twenty years.

1. My father's military career has _____ (*force*) our family to move many times.

2. We have _____ (*live*) in seven towns that I remember.

3. I have _____ (*attend*) three different high schools.

4. None of the towns has ever really _____ (*seem*) like home.

5. I have never _____ (*object*) to my family's traveling life.

6. None of us has ever _____ (*expect*) to stay in one place for long.

7. My closest friends have all _____ (*travel*) a lot, too.

8. One of them has _____ (*visit*) Egypt, Australia, Turkey, Pakistan, and seventeen other countries.

9. She has always _____ (*like*) the idea of becoming a travel agent.

10. But she has _____ (*decide*) to accept a position with a large international corporation that will allow her to travel.

. . . .

Past Tense

The **simple past tense** is used for actions that have already happened. An **-ed ending** is needed for all regular verbs in the past tense.

	SIMPLE PRESENT	SIMPLE PAST
First person	I <u>rush</u> to work.	I <u>rush**ed**</u> to work.
Second person	You <u>lock</u> the door.	You <u>lock**ed**</u> the door.
Third person	Rufus <u>seems</u> strange.	Rufus <u>seem**ed**</u> strange.

■ **PRACTICE 5   USING THE SIMPLE PAST TENSE** . . . .

In each of the following sentences, fill in the correct past-tense form of the verb in parentheses.

EXAMPLE: After the Revolutionary War _ended_ (*end*), American politicians _turned_ (*turn*) their anger against each other.

(1) In general, politicians after the war _____ (*decide*) to support either Alexander Hamilton, who favored a strong central government, or Thomas Jefferson, who advocated states' rights. (2) Rival politicians were _____ (*concern*) about the direction of the new democracy, so they _____ (*attack*) each other with great passion. (3) Few people _____ (*care*) about facts or honesty in their attacks. (4) Some politicians eagerly _____ (*challenge*) President George Washington and _____ (*call*) him a would-be king. (5) Hamilton _____ (*engage*) in personal attacks that were especially nasty. (6) In return, Hamilton's enemies _____ (*accuse*) him of planning to bring back the British monarchy.

(7) In six different instances, Hamilton _____ (*participate*) in fierce arguments that _____ (*stop*) just short of causing a duel. (8) He _____ (*fail*) to avoid a duel in his long dispute with Vice President Aaron Burr. (9) For years, Hamilton _____ (*charge*) Burr with being corrupt and dishonest. (10) When they _____ (*duel*) in 1804, each _____ (*fire*) a shot from a pistol. (11) Burr was not hit, but Hamilton was seriously wounded, and he _____ (*die*) the next day.

. . . .

SIMPLE PAST TENSE   My <u>car</u> <u>stalled</u>.

[The car stalled at some point in the past but does not stall now, in the present.]

PRESENT PERFECT TENSE   My <u>car</u> <u>has stalled</u> often.

[The car began to stall in the past but may continue to do so into the present.]

■ Be careful not to confuse the simple past tense with the present perfect tense (see p. 457).

PRACTICE 6   USING THE SIMPLE PAST TENSE AND PRESENT PERFECT TENSE . . . .

In each of the following sentences, circle the correct verb form.

EXAMPLE: Within the last twenty years, racial profiling (became / (has become)) a significant source of disagreement between law enforcement agencies and some communities of color.

1. Numerous charges of racial profiling (increased / have increased) the tension between local police and members of various ethnic groups.

2. Law enforcement agencies (used / have used) profiling for a long time.

3. With this practice, they (attempted / have attempted) to identify people who might be participating in criminal activity by their behavior and the conditions of a particular situation.

4. Once these "profiled" individuals (were singled out / have been singled out), the police questioned or searched them for drugs, guns, or other illegal material.

5. In 1998, an investigation of the New Jersey State Police (raised / has raised) the public's awareness of this issue.

6. The extensive publicity from this investigation (defined / has defined) racial profiling as the separating out of members of racial or ethnic groups for minor traffic or criminal offenses.

7. Investigators reviewing past law-enforcement activity concluded that the New Jersey State Police (violated / have violated) civil rights on numerous occasions.

8. Since this case was made public, other police departments (initiated / have initiated) investigations into their own possible profiling activities.

9. Similarly, communities (started / have started) to demand that the police be more accountable in their relationships with members of minority racial or ethnic groups.

10. The issue of profiling (endured / has endured) in the public mind and continues to be controversial.

· ·

Two other past-tense forms are the past progressive tense and the past perfect tense. The **past progressive tense** is used to describe actions that were ongoing in the past. It is formed as follows:

Past-tense form of *be* (helping verb)	+	Main verb with *-ing* ending

Past Progressive Tense

	SINGULAR	PLURAL
First person	I was laugh**ing**.	We were laugh**ing**.
Second person	You were laugh**ing**.	You were laugh**ing**.
Third person	She/he/it was laugh**ing**.	They were laugh**ing**.
	The baby was laugh**ing**.	The babies were laugh**ing**.

■ PRACTICE 7   USING THE PAST PROGRESSIVE TENSE · · · · · · · · · · ·

In each of the following sentences, first underline the helping verb (a form of *be*), and then fill in the correct form(s) of the verb in parentheses.

> **EXAMPLE:** Grandma and Grandpa still remember what they <u>were</u>
> <u>*doing*</u> (*do*) when Neil Armstrong became the first person
> to walk on the moon.

1. On that summer day in 1969, they were _____ (*climb*) up Mount Marcy, the highest mountain in New York State.

2. Neither of them was _____ (*intend*) to see that famous first moon walk.

3. They were both _____ (*focus*) on the difficult climb up the steep mountain.

4. Grandma, who exercised regularly, was _____ (*handle*) the hike pretty well.

5. But Grandpa was _____ (*have*) a lot of trouble with it.

6. By the time they got about halfway up the mountain, he was _____ (*ask*) to stop for a rest every few minutes.

7. Finally, he said he was _____ (*stop*) and going back down; Grandma went back down with him.

8. On the drive back to their house in New Jersey, they were _____ (*listen*) to the radio when they heard that Neil Armstrong would soon set foot on the moon.

9. They drove to the nearest diner, where people were _____ (*watch*) the moon landing on television.

10. About ten minutes after Grandma and Grandpa had each ordered hot chocolate, they were _____ (*experience*), along with most of the world, the first steps on the moon by a human.

· ·

The **past perfect tense** is used for an action that was begun in the past but was completed before some other past action took place. It is formed as follows:

■ *Be* and *have* are irregular verbs. For more details on irregular verbs, see pages 467–75.

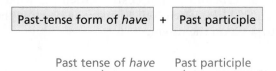

| Past-tense form of *have* | + | Past participle |

PAST PERFECT TENSE   My head had ached for a week before I called a doctor.

[Both of the actions (*head ached* and *I called*) happened in the past, but the ache happened before the calling.]

Be careful not to confuse the simple past tense with the past perfect tense.

SIMPLE PAST TENSE   My <u>car</u> <u>stalled</u>.

[One action (the car's stalling) occurred in the past.]

PAST PERFECT TENSE   By the time Jill arrived, my <u>car</u> <u>had stalled</u>.

[Two actions (Jill's arrival and the car's stalling) occurred in the past, but the car stalled before Jill's arrival.]

■ PRACTICE 8   USING THE PAST PERFECT TENSE . . . .

In each of the following sentences, circle the correct verb form. *Note:* Some of the verbs are irregular. For a chart showing forms of these verbs, see pages 469–72.

EXAMPLE: **By the time I reached home, rolling blackouts (darkened /** **(had darkened)) the city.**

1. The temperature was unseasonably hot when I (got / had gotten) out of bed that morning.

■ For more practice on the past and perfect tenses, see Chapter 33.

2. By noon, the air conditioners at the office (were running / had been running) at high power for three hours.

3. My boss told me that she (heard / had heard) that energy use that day was skyrocketing.

4. I (asked / had asked) how we could conserve energy.

5. I mentioned that I (just learned / had just learned) that some household and office machines use power even when they are turned off.

6. My boss (read / had read) the same information, so we unplugged computers in the office that were not in use.

7. We also (raised / had raised) the office temperature from sixty-eight degrees to seventy-two, and then we turned off some of the lights.

8. By late afternoon, we (did / had done) everything we could think of to save energy, but it was not enough.

9. We knew that the city (warned / had warned) residents that rolling blackouts were possible.

10. However, when the office (suddenly darkened / had suddenly darkened), everyone was stunned.

. . . .

Future Tense

The **simple future tense** is used for actions that will happen in the future. It is formed with the helping verb *will*.

Simple Future Tense		
	SINGULAR	**PLURAL**
First person	I will graduate in May.	We will graduate in May.
Second person	You will graduate in May.	You will graduate in May.
Third person	She/he/it will graduate in May.	They will graduate in May.
	My son will graduate in May.	My sons will graduate in May.

Two other future tense forms to be familiar with are the future progressive tense and the future perfect tense. The **future progressive tense** is used to describe actions in the future that are continuing. It is formed as follows:

Will + Be + Main verb with *-ing* ending

Future Progressive Tense

	SINGULAR	PLURAL
First person	I will be working Friday.	We will be working Friday.
Second person	You will be working Friday.	You will be working Friday.
Third person	She/he/it will be working Friday.	They will be working Friday.
	The boss will be working Friday.	The bosses will be working Friday.

The **future perfect tense** is used to describe actions that will be completed in the future before another action in the future. It is formed as follows:

$$\boxed{\textit{Will have}} \ + \ \boxed{\text{Past participle}}$$

Future Perfect Tense

	SINGULAR	PLURAL
First person	I will have finished by 10:00.	We will have finished by 10:00.
Second person	You will have finished by 10:00.	You will have finished by 10:00.
Third person	She/he/it will have finished by 10:00.	They will have finished by 10:00.
	The painter will have finished by 10:00.	The painters will have finished by 10:00.

PRACTICE 9　USING THE FUTURE TENSE . . . .

In each of the following sentences, circle the correct verb form. *Note:* Some of the verbs are irregular. For a chart showing forms of these verbs, see pages 469–72.

EXAMPLE: By Monday, Andrew (will pass / will be passing /(will have passed)) his driving test.

1. From then on, he (will use / will be using / will have used) his new car whenever he wants to get anywhere.

2. Andrew has already said he (will visit / will be visiting / will have visited) his friend Angela at her school one day next month.

3. Over the next few days, he also (will plan / will be planning / will have planned) visits to several other friends.

4. His car's manual says that his car (will need / will be needing / will have needed) servicing in six months.

5. By the time he leaves for his trip to Colorado next fall, he (will check / will be checking / will have checked) with his mechanic to make sure the car is in good condition.

6. Andrew has promised himself that, whenever something needs to be fixed on the car, he (will fix / will be fixing / will have fixed) it.

7. He learned this from seeing his older sister Carrie, who always (will wait / will be waiting / will have waited) until something in her car breaks before she concerns herself with it.

8. Andrew expects that next winter he (will receive / will be receiving / will have received) frequent emergency calls from his sister when her car breaks down.

9. By next spring, he expects that he (will rescue / will be rescuing / will have rescued) her several times.

10. But he also realizes that, even after having several breakdowns, Carrie still (will avoid / will be avoiding / will have avoided) dealing with any car problem until she absolutely must.

. . . .

Irregular Verbs

Unlike regular verbs, which have past-tense and past-participle forms that end in *-ed* or *-d,* **irregular verbs** change spelling in the past-tense and past-participle forms.

Present-Tense Irregular Verbs

Only a few verbs are irregular in the present tense. The ones most commonly used are the verbs *be* and *have.*

	BE		**HAVE**	
	SINGULAR	**PLURAL**	**SINGULAR**	**PLURAL**
First person	I am	we are	I have	we have
Second person	you are	you are	you have	you have
Third person	he/she/it is	they are	he/she/it has	they have
	the dog is	the dogs are	the dog has	the dogs have
	Chris is	Chris and Dan are	Chris has	Chris and Dan have

> **PRACTICE 10   USING *BE* AND *HAVE* IN THE PRESENT TENSE** . . . . . .

In each of the following sentences, fill in the correct form of the verb indicated in parentheses.

EXAMPLE: Disc golf ___*is*___ (*be*) played with Frisbees.

1. I _____ (*be*) a fanatical disc golfer.

2. The game _____ (*have*) eighteen holes, like regular golf, but uses a Frisbee instead of a ball.

3. A disc golf course _____ (*have*) fairways and holes.

4. A tee _____ (*be*) at the beginning of each fairway.

5. Players _____ (*be*) eager to get the Frisbee from the tee into a metal basket in the fewest possible throws.

6. Some disc golfers _____ (*have*) special Frisbees for teeing off and putting.

7. My brother, who also plays disc golf, _____ (*have*) thirty different Frisbees for the game.

8. His wife _____ (*be*) surprisingly patient with his enthusiasm for the sport.

9. "You _____ (*be*) in the middle of a second adolescence," she tells him.

10. However, she, too, _____ (*have*) formidable Frisbee technique.

. . . .

Past-Tense Irregular Verbs

As discussed earlier, the past-tense and past-participle forms of irregular verbs do not follow a standard pattern. For example, they do not use the -*ed* ending for past tense, although the past participle uses a helping verb, just as regular verbs do.

PRESENT TENSE	PAST TENSE	PAST PARTICIPLE
Tony makes hats.	Tony made hats.	Tony has/had made hats.
You write well.	You wrote well.	You have/had written well.
I ride a bike.	I rode a bike.	I have/had ridden a bike.

The verb *be* is tricky because it has two different forms for the past tense—*was* and *were*.

The Verb Be, *Past Tense*

	SINGULAR	PLURAL
First person	I was	we were
Second person	you were	you were
Third person	she/he/it was	they were
	the car was	the cars were
	Jolanda was	Jolanda and Ti were

■ **PRACTICE 11   USING PAST-TENSE FORMS OF THE VERB** *BE* . . . . . .

In the paragraph that follows, fill in each blank with the correct past-tense form of the verb *be*.

EXAMPLE: The many visitors to President Lincoln's White House
_____*were*_____ generally polite.

(1) Lincoln _____ respectful of his visitors as well, but they took up a great deal of his time. (2) Most of his visitors _____ politicians, army generals, journalists, job seekers, and relatives of Mrs. Lincoln. (3) Nearly every visitor _____ seeking something from the president, such as promotions, policy changes, or pardons. (4) Whenever a visitor came asking for nothing, Lincoln _____ clearly relieved. (5) Mrs. Lincoln's relatives _____ especially troublesome for the president. (6) Many of the Todds _____ Confederate sympathizers or even Confederate combatants. (7) Usually, though, a Todd visiting Lincoln _____ looking for a job. (8) Nearly everyone who had known Lincoln at some point in his life _____ welcomed by the president. (9) His manner _____ almost always so friendly and gracious that his visitors _____ quickly put at ease. (10) Contrary to the serious face in the Lincoln Memorial, whenever the president greeted a visitor, he _____ usually smiling.

As you write and edit, consult the following chart to make sure that you use the correct form of irregular verbs.

Irregular Verb Forms

PRESENT TENSE	PAST TENSE	PAST PARTICIPLE (with helping verb)
am/are/is	was/were	been
become	became	become

continued

PRESENT TENSE	PAST TENSE	PAST PARTICIPLE (with helping verb)
begin	began	begun
bite	bit	bitten
blow	blew	blown
break	broke	broken
bring	brought	brought
build	built	built
buy	bought	bought
catch	caught	caught
choose	chose	chosen
come	came	come
cost	cost	cost
do	did	done
draw	drew	drawn
drink	drank	drunk
drive	drove	driven
eat	ate	eaten
fall	fell	fallen
feed	fed	fed
feel	felt	felt
fight	fought	fought
find	found	found
forget	forgot	forgotten
freeze	froze	frozen
get	got	gotten
give	gave	given
go	went	gone
grow	grew	grown
have/has	had	had
hide	hid	hidden
hit	hit	hit
hold	held	held
hurt	hurt	hurt

PRESENT TENSE	PAST TENSE	PAST PARTICIPLE (with helping verb)
keep	kept	kept
know	knew	known
lay	laid	laid
leave	left	left
let	let	let
lie	lay	lain
light	lit	lit
lose	lost	lost
make	made	made
mean	meant	meant
meet	met	met
pay	paid	paid
put	put	put
quit	quit	quit
read	read	read
ride	rode	ridden
run	ran	run
say	said	said
see	saw	seen
sell	sold	sold
send	sent	sent
set (to place)	set	set
shake	shook	shaken
show	showed	shown
shut	shut	shut
sing	sang	sung
sink	sank	sunk
sit (to be seated)	sat	sat
sleep	slept	slept
speak	spoke	spoken
spend	spent	spent
stand	stood	stood

continued

PRESENT TENSE	PAST TENSE	PAST PARTICIPLE (with helping verb)
steal	stole	stolen
stick	stuck	stuck
sting	stung	stung
strike	struck	struck, stricken
swim	swam	swum
take	took	taken
teach	taught	taught
tear	tore	torn
tell	told	told
think	thought	thought
throw	threw	thrown
understand	understood	understood
wake	woke	woken
wear	wore	worn
win	won	won
write	wrote	written

PRACTICE 12   USING PAST-TENSE IRREGULAR VERBS · · · · · · · · · ·

In each of the following sentences, fill in the correct past-tense form of the irregular verb in parentheses. If you do not know the answer, find the word in the chart of irregular verb forms on pages 469–72.

> **EXAMPLE:** The *Titanic* ___*set*___ (*set*) out from England in 1912.

1. The White Star Line _____ (*build*) the *Titanic*, which was the biggest moving object in the world at that time.

2. The huge ship _____ (*hold*) over 2,200 passengers on its maiden voyage.

3. The newspapers _____ (*write*) that twenty lifeboats, which could hold 1,178 people altogether, hung from the upper deck of the *Titanic*.

4. The shipbuilders _____ (*feel*) that the giant liner was the safest ship in the world and that more lifeboats were simply unnecessary.

5. On April 14, 1912, during its first trip across the Atlantic, the *Titanic* _____ (*strike*) an iceberg.

6. The sharp ice _____ (*tear*) a gaping hole in the bottom of the ship.

7. Icy ocean water _____ (*begin*) to pour into the hold, dragging the *Titanic* down in the water.

8. Few passengers _____ (*understand*) the danger at first.

9. Half-empty lifeboats _____ (*leave*) the sinking ship while other passengers _____ (*stand*) on deck, refusing to depart.

10. Hundreds of people _____ (*freeze*) to death in the ocean before the nearest ship _____ (*come*) to rescue the *Titanic*'s 705 survivors.

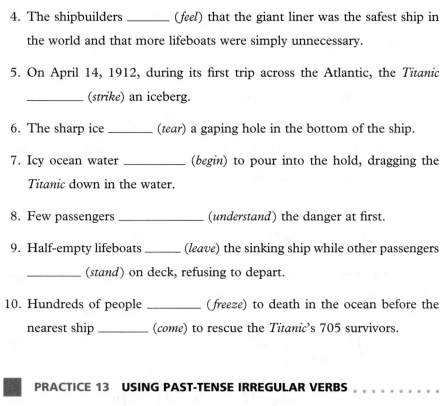

■ PRACTICE 13   **USING PAST-TENSE IRREGULAR VERBS** · · · · · · · · · · ·

In the following paragraph, replace any incorrect present-tense verb forms with the correct past-tense form of the verb. If you do not know the answer, look up the verbs in the chart of irregular verb forms on pages 469–72.

> EXAMPLE: Dewayne faced a judge and jury of his fellow high school
>   *hit*
> students after he ~~hits~~ a boy in the classroom.
>   ^

(1) Two years ago, my high school sets up a student court to give students a voice in disciplining rule breakers. (2) Before the court opened its doors, adults teach students about decision making and about courtroom procedures. (3) Some of us served as members of juries, and others become advocates or even judges. (4) I sit on a jury twice when I was a junior. (5) Then, last spring, my friend Dewayne appeared before the student court after he loses his temper and strikes a fellow student.

(6) I agreed to be his advocate because I think he truly regretted his behavior. (7) I tell the jury that he knew his violent reaction was a mistake. (8) The jury sends Dewayne for counseling to learn to manage his anger and made him write an apology to the other student. (9) After hearing the verdict, Dewayne shakes hands with all the jurors and thanked them for their fairness. (10) The experience makes me eager to learn more about America's system of justice.

PRACTICE 14 USING PAST-PARTICIPLE FORMS FOR IRREGULAR VERBS

In each of the following sentences, underline the helping verb (a form of *have*) and fill in the correct past-participle form of the verb in parentheses. If you do not know the correct form, find the word in the chart on pages 469–72.

> EXAMPLE: Hector <u>has</u> ___*found*___ (*find*) that a dot-com career has ups and downs.

1. By the time Hector graduated from college in 1998, he had _____ (*take*) dozens of hours of computer courses.

2. He had _____ (*choose*) a career in programming.

3. Before getting his diploma, Hector had _____ (*begin*) to work for an Internet service provider.

4. By the end of the summer, a rival online service had _____ (*steal*) Hector away from his employer.

5. His new bosses had _____ (*be*) in business for only a few months.

6. After a year, the company still never had _____ (*make*) a profit.

7. However, hundreds of investors had _____ (*buy*) shares of the company's stock.

8. By early 2000, the stock's price had _____ (*grow*) to more than fifty times its original worth.

■ For more practice on using past forms of irregular verbs, see Chapter 33.

9. Hector often wishes that he had _____ (*sell*) his shares then and retired a rich man.

10. Instead, the company went bankrupt, and Hector has _____ (*go*) to work for an old-fashioned but secure banking firm.

- -

Passive Voice

A sentence that is written in the **passive voice** has a subject that performs no action. Instead, the subject is acted upon. To create the passive voice, combine a form of the verb *be* with a past participle.

| *Be* (helping verb) | + | Past participle | = | Passive voice |

Be (helping verb)   Past participle

PASSIVE   The memo was written by an employee.

[The subject, *memo,* did not write itself. An employee wrote the memo, but the subject in the sentence, *memo,* performs no action.]

In sentences that use the **active voice**, the subject performs the action.

ACTIVE   An employee wrote the memo.

Use the passive voice when no one person performed the action, when you don't know who performed the action, or when you want to emphasize the receiver of the action. Use active voice whenever possible, and use passive voice sparingly.

PASSIVE   The dog was hit by a passing car.

[If the writer wants to focus on the dog as the receiver of the action, the passive voice is acceptable.]

ACTIVE   A passing car hit the dog.

Language Note: Don't confuse the passive voice with the present-perfect tense or past-perfect tense. The passive uses a form of the verb *be* (*is, was, were*), and the subject performs no action. The present-perfect tense and the past-perfect tense have subjects that perform an action, and they use a form of the verb *have*.

PASSIVE CORRECT   The <u>boat</u> <u>was crushed</u> by huge waves.

[The subject *boat* performs no action. The verb uses *was*, a form of *be*.]

PASSIVE INCORRECT   The <u>boat</u> <u>was been</u> crushed by huge waves.

[The verb in the passive voice should not use *two* forms of *be* (*was, been*). Use *was*.]

PRESENT PERFECT   Huge <u>waves</u> <u>have crushed</u> all the boats.

[The subject *waves* performs the action, *crushed,* using the present form of *have*.]

PAST PERFECT   Huge <u>waves</u> <u>had crushed</u> all the boats.

[The subject *waves* performed the action, *crushed,* using the past form of *have*.]

PRACTICE 15   CHANGING FROM PASSIVE VOICE TO ACTIVE VOICE

Rewrite the following sentences in the active voice.

EXAMPLE: *Officers control the*
The *Queen Mary 2,* the world's largest cruise ship, ~~can be controlled~~ with a joystick.

1. The *Queen Mary 2* is equipped with a grand lobby and an old-style three-story restaurant.

2. Its bridge, however, is filled with advanced consoles, screens, and joysticks.

3. The effects of the wind, waves, and ocean currents can be automatically corrected by the ship's computer systems.

4. During the ship's first docking in New York, the joystick was not touched by the captain.

5. He said the joystick would probably be used more by him in the future.

. . . .

Consistency of Verb Tense

Consistency of verb tense means that all the actions in a sentence that happen (or happened) at the same time are in the same tense. If all of the actions happen in the present, use the present tense for all verbs in the sentence. If all of the actions happened in the past, use the past tense for all verbs in the sentence.

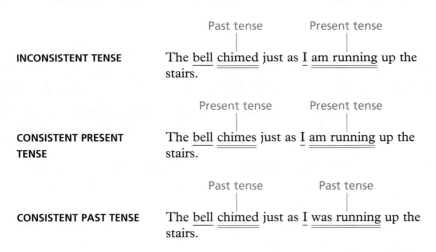

INCONSISTENT TENSE — The bell chimed just as I am running up the stairs.

CONSISTENT PRESENT TENSE — The bell chimes just as I am running up the stairs.

CONSISTENT PAST TENSE — The bell chimed just as I was running up the stairs.

PRACTICE 16   USING CONSISTENT TENSE . . . .

In each of the following items, double-underline the verbs in the sentence, and correct any unnecessary shifts in verb tense by writing the correct form of any incorrect verb in the blank space provided.

> **EXAMPLE:** ___use___ People either ride bicycles for leisurely journeys, or they used bikes for serious exercise.

1. _____ Those who want a good workout needed different kinds of equipment than those interested in an easy ride.

2. _____ For example, serious cyclists who had bikes with wide padded seats face the chance of injuries.

3. _____ A wide seat makes the rider shift from side to side, and it caused painful rubbing.

4. _____ In addition, the seat should have been high enough so that the rider cannot put his or her feet on the ground.

5. _____ Serious riders wore special shoes that snap onto the pedals to allow pushing up as well as pushing down.

6. _____ Serious money is also a factor because custom bicycles were expensive.

7. _____ Once an experienced cyclist chose the proper bicycle, he or she knows how to ride it properly.

8. _____ For instance, knowledgeable riders move around as they ride so that they exercised different muscle groups.

9. _____ The smart rider also kept his or her knees slightly bent, which eases the strain on the knees.

■ For more practices on verbs, see Chapter 33.

10. _____ Of course, those who just wished to have a fun ride through the park ignore all of this advice.

Verb Tense Reference Charts

English verbs, like verbs in most other languages, have different tenses to show when something happened: in the past, present, or future.

This section covers the most common tenses. The discussions of each tense start with a chart that tells you what time the tense is used for. The chart then shows how to use the tense in statements, negative sentences, and questions. You can use the verb charts both to learn tenses and to edit your own writing. Following the charts are lists of common errors to avoid.

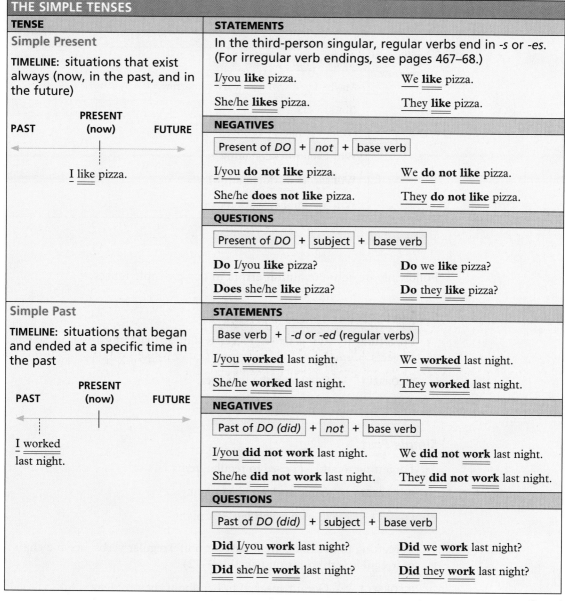

THE SIMPLE TENSES

TENSE	STATEMENTS
Simple Present **TIMELINE:** situations that exist always (now, in the past, and in the future) PRESENT PAST (now) FUTURE I like pizza.	In the third-person singular, regular verbs end in *-s* or *-es*. (For irregular verb endings, see pages 467–68.) I/you **like** pizza. We **like** pizza. She/he **likes** pizza. They **like** pizza.
	NEGATIVES
	Present of *DO* + *not* + base verb I/you **do not like** pizza. We **do not like** pizza. She/he **does not like** pizza. They **do not like** pizza.
	QUESTIONS
	Present of *DO* + subject + base verb **Do** I/you **like** pizza? **Do** we **like** pizza? **Does** she/he **like** pizza? **Do** they **like** pizza?
Simple Past **TIMELINE:** situations that began and ended at a specific time in the past PRESENT PAST (now) FUTURE I worked last night.	**STATEMENTS**
	Base verb + *-d* or *-ed* (regular verbs) I/you **worked** last night. We **worked** last night. She/he **worked** last night. They **worked** last night.
	NEGATIVES
	Past of *DO (did)* + *not* + base verb I/you **did not work** last night. We **did not work** last night. She/he **did not work** last night. They **did not work** last night.
	QUESTIONS
	Past of *DO (did)* + subject + base verb **Did** I/you **work** last night? **Did** we **work** last night? **Did** she/he **work** last night? **Did** they **work** last night?

continued

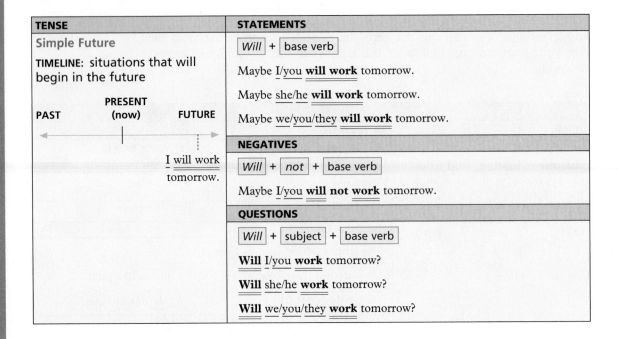

Following are some common errors in using simple tenses.

Simple Present

- Forgetting to add *-s* or *-es* to verbs that go with third-person singular subjects (*she/he/it*)

INCORRECT	She know the manager.
CORRECT	She knows the manager.

Simple Past

- Forgetting to add *-d* or *-ed* to regular verbs

INCORRECT	Gina work late last night.
CORRECT	Gina work**ed** late last night.

- Forgetting to use the correct past form of irregular verbs (see the chart of irregular verb forms on pages 469–72)

INCORRECT	Gerard speaked to her about the problem.
CORRECT	Gerard **spoke** to her about the problem.

- Forgetting to use the base verb without an ending for negative sentences

| INCORRECT | She does not [doesn't] wants money for helping. |
| CORRECT | She does not **want** money for helping. |

THE PROGRESSIVE TENSES

TENSE	STATEMENTS
Present Progressive **TIMELINE:** a situation that is in progress now but that started in the past PAST PRESENT (now) FUTURE I am typing.	Present of *BE* (*am*/*is*/*are*) + base verb ending in -*ing* I **am typing**. We **are typing**. You **are typing**. They **are typing**. She/he **is typing**.
	NEGATIVES
	Present of *BE* (*am*/*is*/*are*) + *not* + base verb ending in -*ing* I **am not typing**. We **are not typing**. You **are not typing**. They **are not typing**. She/he **is not typing**.
	QUESTIONS
	Present of *BE* (*am*/*is*/*are*) + subject + base verb ending in -*ing* **Am** I **typing**? **Are** we **typing**? **Are** you **typing**? **Are** they **typing**? **Is** she/he **typing**?
Past Progressive **TIMELINE:** a situation that started in the past and was in progress in the past PAST PRESENT (now) FUTURE raining arrival at restaurant	**STATEMENTS**
	Past of *BE* (*was*/*were*) + base verb ending in -*ing* It **was raining** when I got to the restaurant at 7:00. The students **were studying** all night.
	NEGATIVES
	Past of *BE* (*was*/*were*) + *not* + base verb ending in -*ing* It **was not raining** when I got to the restaurant at 7:00. The students **were not studying** all night.
	QUESTIONS
	Past of *BE* (*was*/*were*) + subject + base verb ending in -*ing* **Was** it **raining** when I got to the restaurant at 7:00? **Were** the students **studying** all night?

continued

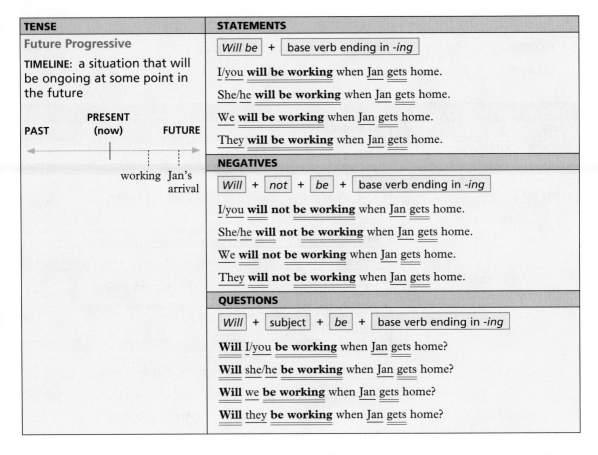

TENSE	STATEMENTS
Future Progressive **TIMELINE:** a situation that will be ongoing at some point in the future PRESENT (now) PAST ——————— FUTURE working Jan's arrival	*Will be* + base verb ending in *-ing* I/you **will be working** when Jan gets home. She/he **will be working** when Jan gets home. We **will be working** when Jan gets home. They **will be working** when Jan gets home.
	NEGATIVES
	Will + *not* + *be* + base verb ending in *-ing* I/you **will not be working** when Jan gets home. She/he **will not be working** when Jan gets home. We **will not be working** when Jan gets home. They **will not be working** when Jan gets home.
	QUESTIONS
	Will + subject + *be* + base verb ending in *-ing* **Will** I/you **be working** when Jan gets home? **Will** she/he **be working** when Jan gets home? **Will** we **be working** when Jan gets home? **Will** they **be working** when Jan gets home?

Following are some common errors in forming the present progressive.

- Forgetting to add *-ing* to the verb

  INCORRECT   I am type now.

  She/he is not work now.

  CORRECT   I am typ**ing** now.

  She/he is not work**ing** now.

■ For more practices on the progressive tenses, including forming negatives and questions, see pages 600–04.

- Forgetting to include a form of *be* (*am/is/are*)

  INCORRECT   He typing now.

  They typing now.

  CORRECT   He **is** typing now.

  They **are** typing now.

- Forgetting to use a form of *be* (*am/is/are*) to start questions

INCORRECT	They typing now?
CORRECT	**Are** they typing now?

THE PERFECT TENSES

TENSE	STATEMENTS
Present Perfect **TIMELINE:** a situation that began in the past and either is *still happening* or ended at an unknown time in the past PAST —— **PRESENT (now)** —— FUTURE I have attended every class.	Present of *HAVE* + past participle of base verb I/you **have attended** every class. She/he **has attended** every class. We **have attended** every class. They **have attended** every class.
	NEGATIVES
	Present of *HAVE* + *not* + past participle of base verb I/you **have not attended** every class. She/he **has not attended** every class. We **have not attended** every class. They **have not attended** every class.
	QUESTIONS
	Present of *HAVE* + subject + past participle of base verb **Have** I/you **attended** every class? **Has** she/he **attended** every class? **Have** we **attended** every class? **Have** they **attended** every class?
Past Perfect **TIMELINE:** a situation that began and ended before some other past situation occurred PAST —— **PRESENT (now)** —— FUTURE (somebody) Gil's left arrival	**STATEMENTS**
	Past of *HAVE* (*had*) + past participle of base verb I/you **had left** before Gil arrived. She/he **had left** before Gil arrived. We **had left** before Gil arrived. They **had left** before Gil arrived.

continued

TENSE	NEGATIVES
Past Perfect (cont.)	Past of *HAVE* (*had*) + *not* + past participle of base verb
	Usually used for "if" situations
	If you **had not left**, you would have seen him.
	If she/he **had not left**, she/he would have seen him.
	If we **had not left**, we would have seen him.
	If they **had not left**, they would have seen him.
	QUESTIONS
	Past of *HAVE* (*had*) + subject + past participle of base verb
	Had I/you **left** before Gil arrived?
	Had she/he **left** before Gil arrived?
	Had we **left** before Gil arrived?
	Had they **left** before Gil arrived?
Future Perfect **TIMELINE:** a situation that will be completed in the future before another future situation	**STATEMENTS**
	Will have + past participle of base verb
	I/you **will have graduated** before I/you move.
	She/he **will have graduated** before you move.
	We **will have graduated** before you move.
	They **will have graduated** before you move.
PAST PRESENT (now) FUTURE	**NEGATIVES**
graduation moving	*Will not have* + past participle of base verb
	I/you **will not have graduated** before I/you move.
	She/he **will not have graduated** before you move.
	We **will not have graduated** before you move.
	They **will not have graduated** before you move.
	QUESTIONS
	Will + subject + *have* + past participle of base verb
	Will I/you **have graduated** before I/you move?
	Will she/he **have graduated** before you move?
	Will we **have graduated** before you move?
	Will they **have graduated** before you move?

Following are some common errors in forming the perfect tense.

■ For more practices on the perfect tenses, including forming negatives and questions, see pages 605–09.

- Using *had* instead of *has* or *have* for the present perfect

INCORRECT	We **had** lived here since 2003.
CORRECT	We **have** lived here since 2003.

- Forgetting to use past participles (with *-d* or *-ed* endings for regular verbs)

INCORRECT	She has attend every class.
CORRECT	She has attend**ed** every class.

- Using *been* between *have* or *has* and the past participle of a base verb

INCORRECT	I have **been** attended every class.
CORRECT	I have attended every class.
INCORRECT	I will have **been** graduated before I move.
CORRECT	I will have graduated before I move.

MODAL AUXILIARIES/HELPING VERBS

HELPING VERB (MODAL AUXILIARY)	STATEMENTS
Modal auxiliaries join with a main (base) verb to make a complete verb.	Subject + helping verb + base verb PRESENT Dumbo can fly. PAST Forms vary — see below.
	NEGATIVES
	Subject + helping verb + *not* + base verb PRESENT Dumbo cannot fly. PAST Forms vary — see below.
	QUESTIONS
	Helping verb + subject + base verb PRESENT Can Dumbo fly? PAST Forms vary — see below.

continued

HELPING VERB (MODAL AUXILIARY)	STATEMENTS		
Can Means *ability*	PRESENT	Beth **can** work fast.	
	PAST	Beth **could** work fast.	
	NEGATIVES		
	PRESENT	Beth **can**not work fast.	
	PAST	Beth **could** not work fast.	
	QUESTIONS		
	PRESENT	**Can** Beth work fast?	
	PAST	**Could** Beth work fast?	
Could Means *possibility*. It can also be the past tense of *can*.	**STATEMENTS**		
	PRESENT	Beth **could** work fast if she had more time.	
	PAST	Beth **could** have worked fast if she had more time.	
	NEGATIVES		
	Can is used for present negatives. (See above.)		
	PAST	Beth **could** not have worked fast.	
	QUESTIONS		
	PRESENT	**Could** Beth work fast?	
	PAST	**Could** Beth have worked fast?	
May Means *permission* For past-tense forms, see *might*.	**STATEMENTS**		
	PRESENT	You **may** borrow my car.	
	NEGATIVES		
	PRESENT	You **may** not borrow my car.	
	QUESTIONS		
	PRESENT	**May** I borrow your car?	
Might Means *possibility*. It can also be the past tense of *may*.	**STATEMENTS**		
	PRESENT (with *be*): Lou **might** be asleep.		
	PAST (with *have* + past participle of *be*):		
	Lou **might** have been asleep.		
	FUTURE: Lou **might** sleep.		
	NEGATIVES		
	PRESENT (with *be*): Lou **might** not be asleep.		
	PAST (with *have* + past participle of *be*):		
	Lou **might** not have been asleep.		
	FUTURE: Lou **might** not sleep.		

HELPING VERB (MODAL AUXILIARY)	QUESTIONS
Might (cont.)	*Might* in questions is very formal and not often used.

	STATEMENTS
Must Means *necessary*	PRESENT: We **must** try.
	PAST (with *have* + past participle of base verb): We **must** have tried.
	NEGATIVES
	PRESENT: We **must** not try.
	PAST (with *have* + past participle of base verb): We **must** not have tried.
	QUESTIONS
	PRESENT: **Must** we try?
	Past-tense questions with *must* are unusual.

	STATEMENTS
Should Means *duty* or *expectation*	PRESENT: They **should** call.
	PAST (with *have* + past participle of base verb): They **should** have called.
	NEGATIVES
	PRESENT: They **should** not call.
	PAST (with *have* + past participle of base verb): They **should** not have called.
	QUESTIONS
	PRESENT: **Should** they call?
	PAST (with *have* + past participle of base verb): **Should** they have called?

	STATEMENTS
Will Means *intend to* (future) For past-tense forms, see *might.*	FUTURE: I **will** succeed.
	NEGATIVES
	FUTURE: I **will** not succeed.
	QUESTIONS
	FUTURE: **Will** I succeed?

	STATEMENTS
Would Means *prefer* or used to start a future request. It can also be the past tense of *will.*	PRESENT: I **would** like to travel.
	PAST (with *have* + past participle of base verb): I **would** have traveled if I had the money.

continued

HELPING VERB (MODAL AUXILIARY)	NEGATIVES
Would	PRESENT: I **would** not like to travel.
	PAST (with *have* + past participle of base verb):
	I **would** not have traveled if it hadn't been for you.
	QUESTIONS
	PRESENT: **Would** you like to travel?
	Or to start a request: **Would** you help me?
	PAST (with *have* + past participle of base verb):
	Would you have traveled with me if I had asked you?

■ For more practices on the modal auxiliaries (*can/could; may/might/must; should/will/would*), including forming negatives and questions, see pages 613–18.

Following are some common errors in using modal auxiliaries.

- Using more than one helping verb

  INCORRECT   They **will can** help.

  CORRECT   They **will** help. (future intention)

  They **can** help. (are able to)

- Using *to* between the helping verb and the main (base) verb

  INCORRECT   Emilio **might to** come with us.

  CORRECT   Emilio **might** come with us.

- Using *must* instead of *had to* in the past

  INCORRECT   She **must** work yesterday.

  CORRECT   She **had to** work yesterday.

- Forgetting to change *can* to *could* in the past negative

  INCORRECT   Last night, I **can**not sleep.

  CORRECT   Last night, I **could** not sleep.

- Forgetting to use *have* with *could/should/would* in the past tense

  INCORRECT   Tara **should** called last night.

  CORRECT   Tara **should have** called last night.

- Using *will* instead of *would* to express a preference in the present tense

INCORRECT   I **will** like to travel.

CORRECT   I **would** like to travel.

Edit Paragraphs and Your Own Writing

As you edit the following paragraphs and your own writing, use the Critical Thinking guide below and the Verb Tense Reference Charts that begin on page 478.

CRITICAL THINKING: EDITING FOR VERB PROBLEMS

FOCUS
- Read all of your sentences carefully, looking for verb problems.

ASK
- Is my sentence about the present? About the past? About something that happened before something else?
- Is each verb a regular verb or an irregular verb?
- Have I used the tense that tells the reader when the action happened?
- Have I used the correct form of the verb?
- If the verbs in the sentence are not all in the same tense, is it because the actions actually happened at different times?

EDIT
- Edit to correct any problems with verb form or verb tense.

Find and correct any problems with verb form or tense in the following paragraphs.

EDITING REVIEW 1 (7 errors) . . . .

(1) Since 1835, trapeze artists consider the triple somersault the most dangerous maneuver. (2) That year, a performer tried to do a triple somersault on a trapeze for the first time and dies in the attempt. (3) Only one person has managed to do the trick successfully in the next sixty-three

years. (4) That man, a trapeze artist named Armor, did a triple somersault in 1860 and is afraid to try it again. (5) According to circus legend, the second person to survive the triple, Ernie Clarke, once done a quadruple somersault in private. (6) Ernie Lane, the third person to complete a triple somersault, was later killed by the maneuver when his catcher missed. (7) Circus historians now believed that Alfredo Codona, a performer in the 1920s and 1930s, was the greatest master of the triple somersault. (8) He has went down in history as the King of Trapeze.

EDITING REVIEW 2 (8 errors) . . . .

(1) Many people go through life without even knowing that there is a record for peeling an apple or hopping on a pogo stick. (2) However, some people are very aware of such records, and ordinary folks around the world have did some peculiar things to qualify for the *Guinness Book of World Records*. (3) For example, a New Jersey disc jockey, Glen Jones, recently setted a new record for the longest continuous radio broadcast. (4) In the spring of 2001, he has stayed on the air for one hundred hours with only a few fifteen-minute breaks. (5) Another world record, for hopping up steps on a bicycle, is hold by Javier Zapata of Colombia. (6) He climbed 943 steps without letting his feet touch the ground, breaking a record that he has previously set. (7) Ashrita Furman of New York also be a record breaker. (8) She balanced a milk bottle on her head and then walks almost eighty-one miles around a track. (9) These strange endurance contests may not make Jones, Zapata, and Furman famous, but their names had entered the record book.

EDITING REVIEW 3 (9 errors) . . . .

(1) The Olympic Games first let women compete in swimming events in 1912, and with that, the swimsuit revolution begun. (2) In 1913, the first mass-produced women's swimsuit hit the market. (3) Before that year, women have only been able to wade at the beach in bathing costumes with long, baggy legs. (4) The 1913 suits, designed by Carl Jantzen, was ribbed one-piece outfits that allowed actual swimming. (5) An engineer, Louis Réard, comed up with the next major development in swimwear in 1946 while working in the lingerie business. (6) He has called it the "bikini," after a Pacific island used for testing the atomic bomb. (7) In the 1950s, few Americans had dared to wear bikinis, which was considered scandalous. (8) Two-piece swimsuits catch on in the 1960s and 1970s. (9) The bikini losted some popularity in the last decades of the twentieth century, but it has made a triumphant return in the new millennium.

EDITING REVIEW 4 (14 errors and 6 formal English errors) . . . .

(1) At most small colleges and universities, people got wherever they want to go by walking or riding their own bikes. (2) But students at one college who didn't have their own bikes or whose bikes were stole now had an alternative. (3) One of this college's new programs help students 2 get frm one place 2 another. (4) It is calling a shared bike program, and any member of the campus community can participate. (5) For a $10 fee, the participant received a key that will have unlocked any one of dozens of pink bikes that are park in various locations on campus. (6) The participant rides the pink bike to the desired destination, and

then locked the bike there. (7) The bike then is becoming available for the next participant who wants to use it. (8) The pink color of the bikes so far have not been a prob, even for the most masculine of campus men. (9) Actually, the bikes R pink cuz one of the school's colors was rose. (10) So now, for the participant who will have found one of the pink bikes, getting from one end of the campus to the other is simple.

 PRACTICE 17   EDITING YOUR OWN WRITING FOR CORRECT VERB TENSE AND FORM . . . .

As a final practice, edit for verb problems in a piece of your own writing—a paper you are working on for this class, a paper you've already finished, a paper for another course, or a recent piece of writing from your work or everyday life. Use the Verb Tense Reference Charts starting on page 478.

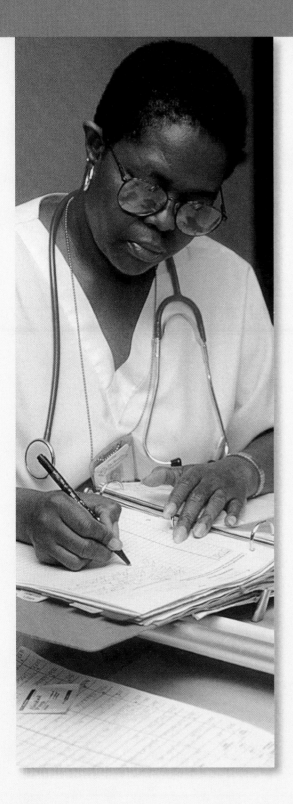

Part Five
Other Grammar Concerns

27

Pronouns

Using Substitutes for Nouns

Understand What Pronouns Are

Pronouns replace nouns (or other pronouns) in a sentence so that you do not have to repeat the nouns.

■ **IDEA JOURNAL**
Write about something you did with friends recently.

Tessa let me borrow *her* ~~Tessa's~~ jacket.

You have met Carl. *He* ~~Carl~~ is my cousin.

The noun (or pronoun) that a pronoun replaces is called the **antecedent.** The word *antecedent* means "something that comes before." In most cases, a pronoun refers to a specific antecedent nearby.

I filled out the (form.) It was complicated.

           Antecedent   Pronoun replacing antecedent

There are three basic types of pronouns—**subject** pronouns, **object** pronouns, and **possessive** pronouns. Note the pronouns in the following sentences.

        Object   Subject

The linebacker tackled him, and he went down hard.

Possessive

His shoulder was injured.

Pronoun Types

	SUBJECT	OBJECT	POSSESSIVE
First person (singular/plural)	I/we	me/us	my, mine/ our, ours
Second person (singular/plural)	you/you	you/you	your, yours/ your, yours
Third person (singular)	he, she, it	him, her, it	his, her, hers, its
Third person (plural)	they who/who	them whom/whom	their, theirs whose

Language Note: Notice that pronouns have gender (*he/she, him/ her, his/her/hers*). The pronoun must agree with the gender of the noun it refers to.

INCORRECT   Tonya lives with *his* cousin.

CORRECT   Tonya lives with *her* cousin.

Also, notice that English has different forms for subject and object pronouns, as shown in the preceding chart.

■ **PRACTICE 1   IDENTIFYING PRONOUNS** . . . .

In each of the following sentences, circle the pronoun, underline the antecedent (the noun to which the pronoun refers), and draw an arrow from the pronoun to the antecedent.

> **EXAMPLE:** My <u>uncle</u> is a hardworking entrepreneur who knew (he) could succeed with a business loan.

■ For more practice with pronouns, visit *Exercise Central* at **bedfordstmartins .com/realessays**.

1. Many poor people don't feel as if they can depend on big banks.

2. A bank in an underdeveloped area, however, needs to find customers wherever it can.

3. Microlending has become a popular banking trend. It has helped people in impoverished neighborhoods all over the world.

■ For more help with pronouns, see Chapter 33.

4. Microlending has succeeded because it involves lending very small amounts of money.

5. Many poor owners of small businesses use microlending to help them get their start.

6. For example, street vendors sell small quantities and earn small profits, so they may never save up enough to expand.

7. Yet a woman selling tacos from a cart may have enough experience to manage her own business successfully.

8. If the taco vendor gets a microloan, she may be able to open a storefront restaurant and earn larger profits.

9. After receiving a small loan, a young entrepreneur can make his or her business more successful.

■ Answers to odd-numbered practice items are at the back of the book.

10. According to my uncle, getting a microloan allowed him to pursue a childhood dream.

. . . .

Practice Using Pronouns Correctly

Check for Pronoun Agreement

A pronoun must agree with (match) the noun or pronoun it refers to in number: It must be singular (one) or plural (more than one). If it is singular, it must also match its noun or pronoun in gender (*he, she,* or *it*).

CONSISTENT   Sherry talked to *her* aunt.

[*Her* agrees with *Sherry* because both are singular and feminine.]

CONSISTENT   The Romanos sold *their* restaurant.

[*Their* agrees with *Romanos* because both are plural.]

Watch out for singular nouns that are not specific. If a noun is singular, the pronoun must be singular as well.

INCONSISTENT   Any athlete can tell you about *their* commitment to practice.

[*Athlete* is singular, but the pronoun *their* is plural.]

CONSISTENT   Any athlete can tell you about *his* or *her* commitment to practice.

[*Athlete* is singular, and so are the pronouns *his* and *her*.]

As an alternative to using the phrase *his or her,* make the subject plural if you can. (For more on this, see the note below.)

CONSISTENT   All athletes can tell you about *their* commitment to practice.

Two types of words often cause errors in pronoun agreement—indefinite pronouns and collective nouns.

Indefinite Pronouns

An **indefinite pronoun** does not refer to a specific person, place, or thing; it is general. Indefinite pronouns often take singular verbs. Whenever a pronoun refers to an indefinite person, place, or thing, check for agreement.

his
Someone forgot ~~their~~ coat.

his or her
Everybody practiced ~~their~~ lines.

NOTE: Although it is grammatically correct, using a masculine pronoun (*he, his,* or *him*) alone to refer to a singular indefinite pronoun such as *everyone* is now considered sexist. Here are two ways to avoid this problem:

1. Use *his or her.*

   Someone forgot his or her coat.

2. Change the sentence so that the pronoun refers to a plural noun or pronoun.

   The children forgot their coats.

Indefinite Pronouns

ALWAYS SINGULAR

anybody	everyone	nothing
anyone	everything	one (of)
anything	much	somebody
each (of)	neither (of)	someone
either (of)	nobody	something
everybody	no one	

MAY BE SINGULAR OR PLURAL

all	none
any	some

PRACTICE 2   USING INDEFINITE PRONOUNS . . . .

Circle the correct pronoun or group of words in parentheses.

(1) Everyone who has battled an addiction to alcohol has (his or her / their) own view of the best ways to stop drinking. (2) Millions of former problem drinkers have quit, and many have made (his or her / their) way through recovery programs. (3) Few begin the road to recovery without attending (his or her / their) first Alcoholics Anonymous (AA) meeting. (4) With its famous twelve-step program, AA has helped countless alcoholics, but someone who is not religious may find that (he or she / they) has difficulty with one of the twelve steps. (5) No one can complete the whole AA recovery program without turning (himself or herself / themselves) over to a "higher power." (6) In addition, everybody who joins AA is asked to admit that (he or she is / they are) powerless over alcohol. (7) Many object that (he or she needs / they need) to feel empowered rather than powerless in order to recover. (8) Anyone who does not feel

that (he or she / they) can believe in a higher power might participate instead in a group like Secular Organizations for Sobriety. (9) Some can take responsibility for (his or her / their) drinking and stop more easily with groups such as Smart Recovery. (10) Different approaches work for different people, but former problem drinkers offer this sober advice to others with alcohol problems: Anyone can quit drinking if (he or she wants / they want) to stop badly enough.

・・

Collective Nouns

A **collective noun** names a group that acts as a single unit.

Common Collective Nouns		
audience	company	group
class	crowd	jury
college	family	society
committee	government	team

Collective nouns are usually singular, so when you use a pronoun to refer to a collective noun, it too must usually be singular.

its
The class had ~~their~~ final exam at 8:00 a.m.

its
The group turned in ~~their~~ report.

If the people in a group are acting as individuals, however, the noun is plural and should be used with a plural pronoun.

The audience took *their* seats.

The drenched crowd huddled under *their* umbrellas.

PRACTICE 3   USING COLLECTIVE NOUNS AND PRONOUNS

Fill in the correct pronoun (*their* or *its*) in each of the following sentences.

EXAMPLE: The basketball team was playing all of __*its*__ games in a damp, dark gymnasium.

1. The downtown branch of the university needed to overhaul several buildings on _____ campus.

2. The theater department wanted to enlarge the auditorium used for _____ productions.

3. In the present theater, the audience had to wait in _____ seats until the performance was over and then exit through the stage door.

4. A sorority also needed more space to house _____ members.

5. In addition, the football team could not go to any out-of-town games because _____ bus had broken down.

6. The science teachers had to hold _____ office hours in the student cafeteria.

7. The university president appointed a commission to study renovations and agreed to abide by _____ findings.

8. The graduating class agreed to step up _____ fund-raising campaign.

9. One wealthy family donated _____ slightly used luxury car to a fund-raising auction.

10. A record homecoming crowd shouted _____ approval as the renovation plans were announced.

Make Pronoun Reference Clear

If the reader isn't sure what a pronoun refers to, the sentence may be confusing.

Avoid Ambiguous or Vague Pronoun References

In an **ambiguous pronoun reference**, the pronoun could refer to more than one noun.

AMBIGUOUS   Michelle told Carla that she should get a better hourly wage.

[Did Michelle tell Carla that Michelle herself should get a better hourly wage? Or did Michelle tell Carla that Carla should get a better hourly wage?]

EDITED   Michelle told Carla that she wanted a better hourly wage.

AMBIGUOUS   I threw my bag on the table and it broke.

[Was it the bag or the table that broke?]

EDITED   My bag broke when I threw it on the table.

In a **vague pronoun reference**, the pronoun does not refer clearly to any particular person or thing. To correct a vague pronoun reference, substitute a more specific noun for the pronoun.

VAGUE   After an accident at the intersection, they installed a traffic light.

[Who installed the traffic light?]

EDITED   After an accident at the intersection, the highway department installed a traffic light.

VAGUE   When I heard it, I laughed.

[Heard what?]

EDITED   When I heard the message, I laughed.

PRACTICE 4 AVOIDING AMBIGUOUS OR VAGUE PRONOUN REFERENCES

Edit each of the following sentences to eliminate any ambiguous or vague pronoun references. Some sentences may be revised correctly in more than one way.

scientists

EXAMPLE: In a recent study, ~~they~~ found that people do not always

see objects that are in unexpected places.

1. In a psychology study, volunteers watched a video of two basketball teams, and they had to count the number of passes.

2. As the volunteers focused on the players, some of them did not notice a person in a gorilla suit walking onto the basketball court.

3. Later, when the volunteers met with the researchers, many of them asked, "What gorilla?"

4. By the end of the study, the researchers had learned that if it was unexpected, many people simply could not see it.

5. The way the human brain processes visual information may keep people from using it wisely.

6. For example, if a car crosses into the lane facing oncoming traffic, it may not register in the mind of a driver who expects a routine trip.

7. A stop sign appearing at an intersection cannot prevent an accident if drivers do not see it.

8. Before the psychology study, they thought that drivers who missed signs of danger were simply not paying attention.

9. However, the study indicates that drivers make mistakes because they may not see them ahead.

10. Traffic safety regulations cannot make people's brains and eyes work differently, but they can make them wear seat belts.

Avoid Repetitious Pronoun References

In a **repetitious pronoun reference**, the pronoun repeats a reference to a noun rather than replacing the noun. Remove the repetitious pronoun.

The police officer ~~he~~ told me I had not stopped at the sign.

The sign, ~~it~~ was hidden by a tree.

> **Language Note:** In some languages, like Spanish, it is correct to repeat the noun with a pronoun. In formal English, however, a pronoun is used to replace a noun, not to repeat it.
>
> **INCORRECT**   My son he is a police officer.
>
> **CORRECT**   My son is a police officer.

■ **PRACTICE 5   AVOIDING REPETITIOUS PRONOUN REFERENCES** . . . .

Correct any repetitious pronoun references in the following sentences.

EXAMPLE: The science of robotics ~~it~~ already has practical applications.

1. Robots ~~they~~ have been part of many science-fiction classics, from *The Jetsons* to *Star Wars*.

2. Is there any child who ~~he~~ hasn't wished for a robot friend, a robot tutor, or a robot maid?

3. In some industries, robots ~~they~~ are already part of the workforce.

4. Robots ~~they~~ make sushi for some Japanese fast-food restaurant chains.

5. Additionally, a factory might use robots to handle substances that ~~they~~ are dangerous for humans to touch.

6. But business ~~it~~ is not the only area in which the robot population is increasing.

7. Some children who ~~they~~ wanted a robot friend have already gotten their wish.

8. Toy manufacturers have created a robot dog that it can respond to human commands.

9. The robot dog it was first on many holiday and birthday gift lists for children in the past few years.

10. Also, some house-cleaning robots they are on the market; for example, one vacuums floors.

Use the Right Type of Pronoun

As you can see on the chart on page 496, there are several types of pronouns—*subject* pronouns, *object* pronouns, and *possessive* pronouns, each of which has a different function.

Subject Pronouns

Subject pronouns serve as the subject of a verb.

■ For more on subjects, see Chapter 22.

She took my parking space.

I honked my horn.

> **Language Note:** Some languages omit subject pronouns, but English sentences always have a stated or written subject.
>
> **INCORRECT** Hates cleaning.
>
> **CORRECT** *He* hates cleaning.

Object Pronouns

Object pronouns either receive the action of a verb (the object of the verb) or are part of a prepositional phrase (the object of the preposition).

OBJECT OF THE VERB	Carolyn asked *me* to drive.
	Carolyn gave *me* the keys.
OBJECT OF THE PREPOSITION	Carolyn gave the keys to *me*.

Possessive Pronouns

Possessive pronouns show ownership. Note that you never need an apostrophe with a possessive pronoun.

> Giselle is *my* best friend.

> That jacket is *hers*.

Certain kinds of sentences can make choosing the right type of pronoun a little more difficult—ones that have compound subjects or objects; ones that make a comparison; and ones where you have to choose between *who* or *whom*.

Pronouns Used with Compound Subjects and Objects

A **compound subject** has more than one subject joined by a conjunction such as *and* or *or*. A **compound object** has more than one object joined by a conjunction.

COMPOUND SUBJECT	Tim and *I* work together.
COMPOUND OBJECT	Kayla baked the cookies for Jim and *me*.

To decide what type of pronoun to use in a compound construction, try leaving out the other part of the compound and the conjunction. Then, say the sentence aloud to yourself.

> ~~Jerome and~~ (me / (I)) like chili dogs.
>
> [Think: *I* like chili dogs.]

> The package was for ~~Karen and~~ (she / (her)).
>
> [Think: The package was for *her*.]

When you are writing about yourself and others, always put the others first, choosing the correct type of pronoun.

INCORRECT	*Me* and my friends went to the movies.
CORRECT	My friends and *I* went to the movies.

[Sentence puts others first and uses the subject pronoun, *I*]

INCORRECT	Gene bought the tickets for *I* and my friends.
CORRECT	Gene bought the tickets for my friends and *me*.

[Sentence puts others first and uses the object pronoun, *me*]

If a pronoun is part of a compound object in a prepositional phrase, use an object pronoun.

> Please keep that information just between you and *me*.
>
> [*Between you and me* is a prepositional phrase, so it uses the object pronoun, *me*.]

Many people make the mistake of writing *between you and I*. The correct pronoun is the object pronoun, *me*.

 PRACTICE 6   EDITING PRONOUNS IN COMPOUND CONSTRUCTIONS . . . .

Edit each sentence using the proper type of pronoun. If a sentence is already correct, write "C" next to it.

>   *she*   *I*
> **EXAMPLE:** Megan and I love soda, and ~~her~~ and ~~me~~ regularly have
>
>   two cans a day each.

1. However, a TV program on dental health started making she and I rethink our soda-drinking habit.

2. Her and me paid close attention as we watched a dentist, Dr. Jenine Summers, and her assistant, Ian, conduct an experiment.

3. Dr. Summers asked Ian to place a tooth in a bottle of soda, and her and him observed what happened to the tooth.

4. Megan and me watched as time-elapse photography showed how the tooth changed from day to day.

5. The result of the experiment surprised her and I.

6. At the end of the experiment, Dr. Summers and Ian looked in the bottle of soda for the tooth, and she and he showed that it had disappeared.

7. Them and us said "Wow" at the same time.

8. Dr. Summers explained how acids in the soda broke down the tooth; her comments about soda's sugar content were equally shocking to Megan and me.

9. Megan and me learned that each can of soda we drink contains about ten teaspoons of sugar, which creates even more tooth-dissolving acid and contributes to weight gain.

10. Therefore, us and some other friends have decided to ban soda from our refrigerators.

- -

Pronouns Used in Comparisons

Using the wrong type of pronoun in comparisons can give a sentence an unintended meaning. Editing sentences that contain comparisons can be tricky because comparisons often imply words that aren't actually included in the sentence.

To find comparisons, look for the words *than* or *as*. To decide whether to use a subject or object pronoun in a comparison, try adding the implied words and saying the sentence aloud.

Bill likes Chinese food more than *I*.

[This sentence means Bill likes Chinese food more than I like it. The implied word after *I* is *do*.]

Bill likes Chinese food more than *me*.

[This sentence means Bill likes Chinese food more than he likes me. The implied words after *than* are *he likes*.]

The professor knows more than (us /(we)).

[Think: The professor knows more than *we know*.]

Jen likes other professors more than (he /(him)).

[Think: Jen likes other professors more than *she likes him*.]

■ **PRACTICE 7   EDITING PRONOUNS IN COMPARISONS** . . . .

Edit each sentence using the correct pronoun type. If a sentence is correct, put a "C" next to it.

EXAMPLE: Clarissa was my friend before college, so few roommates
            she
            at school got along better than ~~her~~ and I.

1. We saw how some other roommates had conflicts right away, and we were happy that we got along better than them.

2. However, Clarissa, who is about a year younger than me, began to change during our freshman year.

3. She became romantically involved with Brad, and she eventually began to care more for he than me.

4. Apparently, this was clear to everyone except me.

5. I couldn't understand why she wanted to spend more time with him than with I.

6. For as long as I could remember, no two people were more inseparable than us.

7. Another friend of mine, Haley, solved the problem, and no one could have been as gentle with my feelings as her.

8. Haley had a few of the same classes as me, and we had begun to study together.

9. She pointed out that a similar conflict had developed between she and a lifelong friend, but understanding and open communication had saved their friendship.

10. Haley helped me to accept Clarissa and Brad's new relationship and to recognize that the change could mean growth for me as well as for them.

Choosing between **Who and Whom**

Who is always a subject; use it if the pronoun performs an action. *Whom* is always an object; use it if the pronoun does not perform any action.

WHO = SUBJECT   Janis is the friend *who* introduced me to Billy.

WHOM = OBJECT   Billy is the man *whom* I met last night.

In most cases, for sentences where the pronoun is followed by a verb, use *who*. When the pronoun is followed by a noun or pronoun, use *whom*.

The person (who / whom) spoke was boring.

[The pronoun is followed by the verb *spoke*. Use *who*.]

The person (who / whom) I met was boring.

[The pronoun is followed by another pronoun: *I*. Use *whom*.]

Whoever is a subject pronoun; *whomever* is an object pronoun.

▪ PRACTICE 8   CHOOSING BETWEEN *WHO* AND *WHOM* . . . .

In each sentence, circle the correct word, *who* or *whom*.

> **EXAMPLE:** Most people think it was Thomas Alva Edison (who /
> whom) invented the electric light bulb.

1. Edison is certainly the one (who / whom) became famous for his electric light bulb, but he did not invent it.

2. The inventor to (who / whom) this credit belongs is the English chemist Humphry Davy.

3. It was Davy for (who / whom), in 1809, a charged strip of charcoal took on a satisfying glow after he connected it to a battery with wires.

4. An English physicist named Joseph Wilson Swan, (who / whom) is also largely unknown, advanced this development in 1878 by creating an electric light bulb that glowed for 13.5 hours.

5. Three years earlier, Henry Woodward and Matthew Evans had patented a light bulb, and it was then Edison (who / whom) purchased their patent and in 1879 devised a carbon filament that burned for 40 hours.

Make Pronouns Consistent

Pronouns have to be consistent in **person**, which is the point of view a writer uses. Pronouns may be in first person (*I, we*); second person (*you*); or third person (*he, she, it,* or *they*). (See the chart on page 496.)

INCONSISTENT PERSON   *I* wanted to use the copy machine, but the attendant said *you* had to have an access code.

[The sentence starts in the first person (*I*) but shifts to the second person (*you*).]

CONSISTENT PERSON   *I* wanted to use the copy machine, but the attendant said *I* had to have an access code.

[The sentence stays with the first person, *I*.]

INCONSISTENT PERSON   After *a caller* presses 1, *you* get a recording.

[The sentence starts with the third person (*a caller*) but shifts to the second person (*you*).]

CONSISTENT PERSON   After *a caller* presses 1, *he or she* gets a recording.

CONSISTENT PERSON,   After *callers* press 1, *they* get a recording.
PLURAL

[In these last two examples, the sentence stays with the third person.]

PRACTICE 9   MAKING PRONOUNS CONSISTENT IN PERSON · · · · · ·

In the following items, correct the shifts in person. There may be more than one way to correct some sentences.

> **EXAMPLE:** I have a younger brother with an allergy to peanuts, so
> $\overset{I}{\underset{\wedge}{you}}$ have to be very careful with his food.

1. Experts agree that the percentage of people with allergies to foods is rising, but we don't know why.

2. Someone who has a mild allergic reaction the first time you eat a food may develop more severe allergies from future contacts with the food.

3. If a person has a severe allergy to a food and unknowingly eats even a small amount of that food, you could die.

4. However, if people with allergies are protected from any contact with the food for several years, his or her allergies may disappear or become milder.

5. When a child has severe allergies, their parents can be extremely cautious.

6. My little brother is severely allergic to peanuts, so you are not allowed to eat anything containing peanuts while he is nearby.

7. He carries an adrenaline pen that can save your life if you go into shock from a food allergy.

8. I love peanut butter, but you can't eat a peanut butter sandwich in my house.

9. My mother will not take my brother to any public place where you can even smell peanuts.

10. Some people think that her precautions are extreme, but she knows that you can't be too careful when your child's life is at stake.

Edit Paragraphs and Your Own Writing

Edit the following paragraphs for pronoun errors, referring to the chart on page 516 as you need to.

EDITING REVIEW 1 (14 errors)

(1) When a store makes a mistake with an order, the customer should complain to them. (2) But some people they are more effective than others at complaining. (3) A good example of this was when Gary, whom is in charge of facilities for his social club, ordered a barbecue grill. (4) When Gary called to place his order, he was pleased because you were connected to a sales person right away. (5) The ordering process between he and the sales person went smoothly, including the store's offer of free assembly of the barbecue, but things went downhill after that. (6) When Gary went to the store on the agreed-upon day to pick up the assembled barbecue, they

told him it was not assembled. (7) Gary lost his temper and screamed at the store manager, causing several nearby customers to abandon the products he or she was going to buy. (8) Gary kept yelling and the store manager kept calmly responding, but he soon angrily stormed out to the parking lot and drove away. (9) Therefore, the social club did not get their barbecue grill that day. (10) After Gary explained this to Natalie, the club's president, she said she didn't know who to blame more, Gary or the store manager. (11) She was better at diplomacy than him, so him and her agreed that Natalie would communicate with the store from then on. (12) When calling the store, Natalie she was polite, patient, and firm in discussing with the manager how to correct the situation. (13) The result was that they delivered the barbecue grill that same day, and the store manager gave the club a 10 percent discount on the purchase.

EDITING REVIEW 2 (11 errors) . . . .

(1) If someone arrives home carrying a heavy bag of groceries, they often have to struggle to find and get out the house keys to open the door. (2) Life just got a little easier for that person because of a new type of door lock that allows he or she to enter with just the swipe of a finger. (3) The lock is a scanner that stores the fingerprints of those whom are authorized to have access. (4) If the person's fingerprint matches a stored print, the lock it slides open. (5) The user does not need to do any wiring to install the lock, and it needs only four AA batteries to operate it. (6) Using radio waves, the lock detects distances between ridges and valleys of a finger just below the skin's surface, so it doesn't even matter if they have a minor cut or scratch. (7) While it may be possible for criminals to somehow get a photocopy of a homeowner's fingerprint, him or her is unlikely to get

this opportunity. (8) Furthermore, the person who the lock is intended for will never have this fingerprint information hacked because it is stored only by the lock itself and not in a central computer. (9) Homeowners with this device no longer need to remember their house keys because his or her fingerprints are always with him or her. (10) There is one thing homeowners do have to remember, though; you have to make sure there are always fresh batteries in the lock.

EDITING REVIEW 3 (11 errors)

(1) NASA recently had trouble finding enough volunteers for experiments designed to test how well you could counteract the effects of weightlessness. (2) The recruits were asked if he or she would lie down in bed for three weeks. (3) Each volunteer also had to have their feet about five inches higher than their heads. (4) The subjects they could not get up, ate while supported by one elbow, used bedpans, and showered lying down on a waterproof cart. (5) When people lie down for three weeks, your muscles and bones can weaken, just as in real weightlessness. (6) To see if this weakening can be counteracted, they had some subjects spin around on a centrifuge bed for thirty times a minute for one hour each day, which simulated gravity. (7) In order to test the comparative effects of the centrifuge on men and women, subjects were studied in male-female pairs, but only one such pair showed any difference. (8) (He was affected more than her.) (9) From the start, the project was hampered by their inability to recruit more than ten subjects. (10) Most of the researchers, whom had hoped for thirty participants, were puzzled by the small number of volunteers. (11) But one scientist, for who this was no surprise,

noted that the centrifuge experience, combined with three weeks of lying in bed, probably scared off a lot of people. (12) She also wondered if many people could take so much time off from his or her job.

EDITING REVIEW 4 (12 errors) . . . .

(1) For those whom have some clothes they no longer want, there is now a new way to put those clothes to use. (2) A trend called clothes swapping allows a person to donate their unwanted but still usable clothing in exchange for someone else's clothes. (3) People they are swapping clothes in many American cities and even in other countries. (4) It started in the 1990s when groups of women would get together and someone would bring along their unwanted clothes to see if anyone else wanted them. (5) But now there are advertised clothes swaps, and it draws men as well as women. (6) At some swap events, they require a donation of clothes in order to enter; at others, there might be an admission fee. (7) There is also the chance of finding a smelly or dirty tee shirt as you rummage through a stack of clothing. (8) But most swaps have a rule that participants clean and press his or her donated clothing. (9) The attraction it is a combination of the thrill of bartering and the anticipation of coming across some free clothes that fit one's size and personality. (10) Swaps don't have changing rooms, so they just put on an item over the clothes they are already wearing and ask others whom are nearby how it looks. (11) Getting clothes at no cost is, of course, the main advantage, but participants are also aware that, if they look awful when tried on at home, they can simply be donated at the next swap.

**PRACTICE 10   EDITING YOUR OWN WRITING
FOR PRONOUN USE** . . . .

As a final practice, edit for pronoun use in a piece of your own writing—a paper you are working on for this course, a paper you've already finished, a paper for another course, a recent piece of writing from your work or everyday life, or your idea journal entry. You may want to use the following chart as you edit.

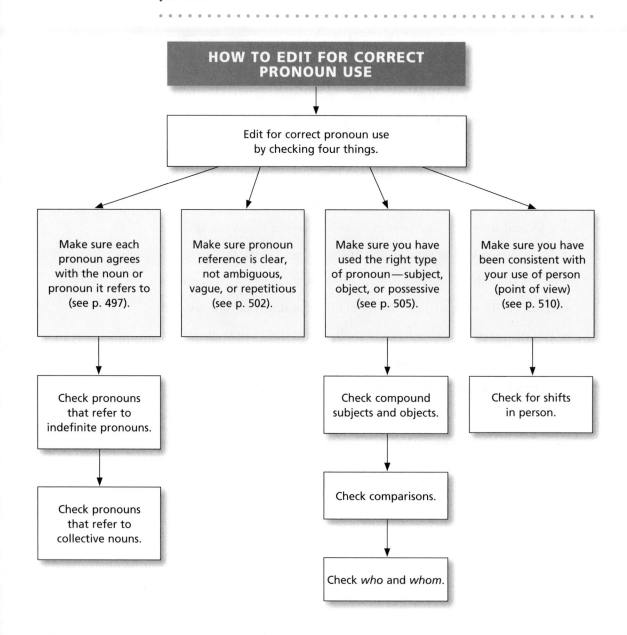

HOW TO EDIT FOR CORRECT PRONOUN USE

Edit for correct pronoun use by checking four things.

Make sure each pronoun agrees with the noun or pronoun it refers to (see p. 497).

Make sure pronoun reference is clear, not ambiguous, vague, or repetitious (see p. 502).

Make sure you have used the right type of pronoun—subject, object, or possessive (see p. 505).

Make sure you have been consistent with your use of person (point of view) (see p. 510).

Check pronouns that refer to indefinite pronouns.

Check compound subjects and objects.

Check for shifts in person.

Check pronouns that refer to collective nouns.

Check comparisons.

Check *who* and *whom*.

28

Adjectives and Adverbs

Describing **Which One?** *or* **How?**

Understand What Adjectives and Adverbs Are

Adjectives describe nouns (words that name people, places, or things) and pronouns (words that replace nouns). They add information about what kind, which one, or how many.

■ **IDEA JOURNAL**
Describe—in as much detail as possible—either a person or a room.

City traffic was *terrible* last night.

The highway was *congested* for *three* miles.

Two huge old tractor trailers had collided.

Language Note: In English, adjectives do not indicate whether the word they modify is singular or plural, unless the adjective is a number.

INCORRECT   My two new classes are *hards*.

[The adjective *two* is fine because it is a number, but the adjective *hard* should not end in *s*.]

CORRECT   My two new classes are *hard*.

517

Adverbs describe verbs (words that tell what happens in a sentence), adjectives, or other adverbs. They add information about how, how much, when, where, why, or to what extent. Adverbs often end with *-ly*.

MODIFYING VERB	Dave drives *aggressively*.
MODIFYING ADJECTIVE	The *extremely* old woman swims every day.
MODIFYING ANOTHER ADVERB	Dave drives *very* aggressively.

Adjectives usually come *before* the words they modify; adverbs come either before or after. You can also use more than one adjective or adverb to modify a word.

adj   adj   adj   noun   verb   adv   adv

The homeless, dirty, old man was talking loudly and crazily to himself.

> **Language Note:** Sometimes, students confuse the *-ed* and *-ing* forms of adjectives. Common examples are *bored/boring, confused/confusing, excited/exciting*, and *interested/interesting*. Often, the *-ed* form describes a person's reaction, while the *-ing* form describes the thing being reacted to.
>
> | | |
> |---|---|
> | **INCORRECT** | James is *interesting* in all sports. [James isn't interesting; sports are.] |
> | **CORRECT** | James *is interested* in all sports. [*Is interested* describes James's reaction to sports.] |
>
> Another common confusion is between when to use an adjective and when to use an adverb. Remember that adverbs modify verbs, adjectives, and other adverbs but not nouns. Adverbs often end in *-ly*.
>
> | | |
> |---|---|
> | **INCORRECT** | James is a *carefully* driver. |
>
> [The word *carefully* should not be used to describe a noun, *driver*. The noun *driver* should be modified by an adjective, *careful*. The adverb *carefully* can be used to modify a verb, *drives*.]
>
> | | |
> |---|---|
> | **CORRECT** | James is a *careful* driver. |
> | | James drives *carefully*. |

Practice Using Adjectives and Adverbs Correctly

Choosing between Adjective and Adverb Forms

Many adverbs are formed by adding *-ly* to the end of an adjective.

■ For coordinate adjectives, see Chapter 37.

ADJECTIVE	ADVERB
The *new* student introduced himself.	The couple is *newly* married.
That is an *honest* answer.	Please answer *honestly*.

To decide whether to use an adjective form or an adverb form, find the word you want to describe. If that word is a noun or a pronoun, use the adjective form. If it is a verb, an adjective, or another adverb, use the adverb form.

 PRACTICE 1 CHOOSING BETWEEN ADJECTIVE AND ADVERB FORMS . . . .

In each sentence, underline the word or phrase in the sentence that is being described, and then circle the correct word in parentheses.

■ Answers to odd-numbered practice items are at the back of the book.

> **EXAMPLE:** Teenagers who want a summer job (usual /(usually)) can
> find work.

■ For more practice with adjectives and adverbs, visit *Exercise Central* at **bedfordstmartins .com/realessays**.

1. Even in a slowing economy, many summer jobs for unskilled workers are (easy / easily) to find.

2. Of course, teenage workers without much experience should not have (extreme / extremely) rigid requirements for a summer job.

3. Fast-food restaurants (frequent / frequently) employ teenagers.

4. The wages at a fast-food restaurant will not be (high / highly) for a starting position, however.

5. In addition, the work may not be very (interesting / interestingly).

6. However, teenagers can learn (valuable / valuably) lessons from going to almost any job.

7. Arriving on time and behaving (responsible / responsibly) will impress any supervisor.

8. Working (close / closely) with other employees also may teach a teenage worker to get along with people who are not friends or family.

9. Earning money can make a high school student feel more (financial / financially) independent.

10. Saving for college tuition is one way in which a teenager can use money from a summer job (wise / wisely).

. . . .

Using Adjectives and Adverbs in Comparisons

To compare two persons, places, or things, use the **comparative** form of adjectives or adverbs.

Sheehan drives *faster* than I do.

Francis is *more gullible* than Destina is.

Comparative and Superlative Forms

ADJECTIVE OR ADVERB	COMPARATIVE	SUPERLATIVE
ADVERBS AND ADJECTIVES OF ONE SYLLABLE		
tall	taller	tallest
fast	faster	fastest
ADJECTIVES ENDING IN *Y*		
happy	happier	happiest
silly	sillier	silliest
ADVERBS AND ADJECTIVES OF MORE THAN ONE SYLLABLE		
graceful	more graceful	most graceful
gracefully	more gracefully	most gracefully
intelligent	more intelligent	most intelligent
intelligently	more intelligently	most intelligently

To compare three or more persons, places, or things, use the **super-lative** form of adjectives or adverbs.

Sheehan drives the *fastest* of all our friends.

Francis is the *most gullible* of the children.

Comparatives and superlatives can be formed either by adding an ending to an adjective or adverb or by adding a word. If an adjective or adverb is short (one syllable), add *-er* to form the comparative and *-est* to form the superlative. Also use this pattern for adjectives that end in *y* (but change the *y* to *i* before adding *-er* or *-est*). If an adjective or adverb has more than one syllable, add the word *more* to make the comparative and the word *most* to make the superlative.

Use either an ending (*-er* or *-est*) or an extra word (*more* or *most*) to form a comparative or superlative—not both at once.

One of the ~~most~~ easiest ways to beat stress is to exercise regularly.

It is ~~more~~ harder to study late at night than during the day.

> **Language Note:** Some languages, such as Spanish, always use words meaning *more* or *most* in comparisons, even when there is already the equivalent of an *-er* or *-est* ending on an adjective or adverb. That is not true of English. If there is an *-er* or *-est* ending on an adjective or adverb, do not use *more* or *most*.

■ **PRACTICE 2   USING COMPARATIVES AND SUPERLATIVES** . . . .

In the space provided in each sentence, write the correct form of the adjective or adverb in parentheses. You may need to add *more* or *most* to some adjectives and adverbs.

EXAMPLE: One of the ___*most loved*___ (*loved*) treats is chocolate.

1. Some people think that Americans are the _____ (*big*) consumers of chocolate in the world.

2. Actually, the people who eat the _____ (*great*) amount of chocolate are the British.

3. In fact, the British are nearly 40 percent _____ (*fond*) of chocolate than Americans are.

4. British chocolate makers are concerned because they expected British people's chocolate consumption to grow _____ (*robustly*) than it has in recent years.

5. However, a small company that makes chocolate with organically grown ingredients has experienced some of the _____ (*healthy*) sales of all chocolate manufacturers in recent years.

6. Even though this organic chocolate is _____ (*expensive*) than regular chocolate, people are willing to pay the price.

7. People have come to expect that organic foods will carry a _____ (*high*) price than conventional foods.

8. Another type of chocolate is also enjoying _____ (*strong*) sales in Britain than regular chocolate.

9. This chocolate does not contain the vegetable solids found in most British chocolate; therefore, it is considered by some chocolate lovers to be _____ (*pure*) than the standard product.

10. This "real" chocolate is expensive, but its sales are expected to continue to grow _____ (*fast*) than sales of other premium chocolates.

Using *Good, Well, Bad,* and *Badly*

Four common adjectives and adverbs have irregular forms—*good, well, bad,* and *badly.*

People often are confused about whether to use *good* or *well. Good* is an adjective, so use it to describe a noun or pronoun. *Well* is an adverb, so use it to describe a verb or an adjective.

Forms of Good, Well, Bad, *and* Badly

	COMPARATIVE	SUPERLATIVE
ADJECTIVE		
good	better	best
bad	worse	worst
ADVERB		
well	better	best
badly	worse	worst

ADJECTIVE	She is a *good* friend.
ADVERB	He works *well* with his colleagues.

Well can also be an adjective to describe someone's health:

I am not feeling *well* today.

▪ PRACTICE 3   USING *GOOD* AND *WELL* . . . .

Complete each sentence by circling the correct word in parentheses. Underline the word that *good* or *well* modifies.

EXAMPLE: A ((good) / well) storyteller can hold an audience's attention.

1. Mark Twain's ability to tell an amusing story is (good / well) known.

2. Twain's famous story "The Notorious Jumping Frog of Calaveras County" is a (good / well) example of traditional American tale-telling.

3. The story is narrated by an Easterner whose proper speech contrasts (good / well) with the country dialect of Simon Wheeler, a storyteller he meets.

4. Wheeler may not be (good / well) educated, but he is a master of the tall tale.

5. The narrator claims that Wheeler has told him a "monotonous" story, but the tale is apparently (good / well) enough for the narrator to repeat.

6. The frog in the story is famous for being a (good / well) jumper.

7. Wheeler explains that the frog's owner lives (good / well) by gambling on the frog's jumping ability.

8. The frog's owner, Jim Smiley, makes the mistake of leaving the frog with a man whom Smiley does not know (good / well).

9. The stranger makes the frog swallow heavy shot so that he can no longer jump (good / well).

10. In Twain's story, Simon Wheeler has such a (good / well) time telling stories that the narrator has to escape from him at the end.

PRACTICE 4   USING COMPARATIVE AND SUPERLATIVE FORMS OF *GOOD* AND *BAD* . . . .

Complete each sentence by circling the correct comparative or superlative form of *good* or *bad* in parentheses.

EXAMPLE: The (better /(best)) way my family found to learn about another culture was to allow an exchange student to live in our home.

1. Simone, a French high school student, spent last summer getting to know the United States (better / best) by living with my family.

2. She had studied English since the age of five, and her understanding of grammar was (better / best) than mine.

3. She told me that she had the (worse / worst) accent of any student in her English classes, but I liked the way she spoke.

4. Her accent was certainly no (worse / worst) than mine would be if I tried to speak French.

5. My (worse / worst) fear was that she would find our lives boring.

6. However, the exchange program's administrator explained that the (better / best) way for Simone to learn about our country was for us to do ordinary things.

7. For me, the (better / best) part of Simone's visit was the chance to see my world through fresh eyes.

8. I felt (better / best) about my summer job, trips to the supermarket, and afternoon swims at the pool because Simone found all of these things exotic and fascinating.

9. Simone even liked summer reruns on television; she claimed that French television was much (worse / worst).

10. The (worse / worst) part of the visit was having to say goodbye to Simone at the end of the summer.

Edit Paragraphs and Your Own Writing

Edit the following paragraphs for adjective and adverb errors, referring to the chart on page 530 as you need to.

EDITING REVIEW 1 (9 errors)

(1) For an average European in the Middle Ages, wearing stripes was not simple a fashion mistake. (2) According to Michel Pastoureau, a scholar of the medieval period, wearing stripes was one of the worse things a European Christian could do in the thirteenth and fourteenth centuries. (3) Stripes might be taken as a sign that the wearer was more sillier than

other people; jesters, for example, often wore them. (4) Prostitutes also wore striped clothes, so stripes might be seen as an indication that the person was sinfuller than others. (5) Wearing stripes was dangerousest for clergymen. (6) At least one clergyman in fourteenth-century France was executed because he had been foolishly enough to wear striped clothes. (7) Carmelite monks who wore striped cloaks were frequent attacked, and several popes insisted that the monks change to a more simple costume. (8) People in medieval Europe certainly took their clothing serious. (9) The only reason some people don't wear stripes today is that they are afraid of looking fat.

EDITING REVIEW 2 (14 errors) . . . .

(1) Many people no longer find it embarrassingly to admit that they have seen a psychotherapist. (2) Some patients argue that it is gooder to seek mental help than to suffer silently. (3) Others seem to feel that needing a therapist is a sign that their lives are interestinger than other people's. (4) At any rate, the stigma that some people once attached to psychotherapy is disappearing quick. (5) Therapists have lately become visibler in popular culture, and this visibility may result in even wider acceptance of psychotherapy. (6) For example, when a mobster on the cable television show *The Sopranos* asks a therapist to treat his panic attacks, viewers see that the most tough of men is still able to discuss his relationships and feelings with a mental health specialist. (7) If Tony Soprano can do it, what ordinary person is going to feel badly about seeking help for ordinary problems?

(8) However, people considering seeing a therapist are not the only ones who love to watch Tony Soprano trying to work through his

problems. (9) Indeed, *The Sopranos,* which was one of the bigger hits ever on cable television, included many psychologists in its audience. (10) One online magazine regular published a therapist's analysis of each episode. (11) Other therapists chatted online about whether or not the psychologist on the television show is practicing psychology. (12) The audiences of psychological professionals seem to agree that therapy is portrayed accurater on the show than in many popular films. (13) As they point out, at least the therapist is not in love with her patient, unlike several psychiatrists in recently movies. (14) Although Mr. Soprano, like many actual therapy patients, does things that are not good for his mental health, his therapist thinks that he is functioning best now than before. (15) If he ever honest discussed his criminal day job with her, even the therapists tuning in might have had trouble figuring out the bestest possible response.

■ EDITING REVIEW 3 (12 errors) . . . .

(1) For as long as most Americans could remember, everyone assumed that the food and other products people bought could be used safe. (2) But not long ago, newspaper articles began reporting how several brands of pet food sold regular in stores were making cats and dogs sick. (3) Some pets actual died from eating this food. (4) Investigators eventual traced this contaminated pet food to a real dangerous ingredient called melamine, which was supplied by several companies based in China. (5) There followed a major recall of this contaminated pet food, allowing consumers to feel more calm about the safety of store products. (6) However, soon after that, Americans learned that firms in China also were using hazardous ingredients in some toothpastes and drugs and

dangerous levels of lead in paint (which can be poisonous when ingested by children) on some good-selling toys. (7) However, foreign companies using worst ingredients to cut costs don't appear to be the only danger to American consumers. (8) Recently, contaminate spinach from California sickened more than one hundred people. (9) Have food and other products available in stores become unsafer than they used to be? (10) Are there good safeguards in place to assure consumers that contaminated products will not reach store shelves easy? (11) For now, the answer seems to be that the reporting of a free press is what is helping Americans stay informed good about the safety of the products they buy.

EDITING REVIEW 4 (14 errors)

(1) In large and small parks across the country, a common sight is a pair of chess players quiet and intent studying the pieces on the board between them. (2) But lately, chess in the park has been taken to a newest level. (3) "Street chess," as it is typical called, is no longer recreation; instead, it is most like a business. (4) Normal, it is the same people, mainly men, who are at their chess boards every day. (5) These players—some call them hustlers—take on anybody who is willing to try to beat them, usual for a wager of about $5. (6) Most of them are real skilled and able to defeat just about any opponent who challenges them. (7) Some play bad sometimes and lose a game deliberate so that their regular customers will keep coming back. (8) But most hustlers play to win all the time, even if they hold back sometimes to avoid embarrassing or discouraging their customers. (9) Players say that, general, the police do not bother them, but most hustlers still find it best to use street aliases than their real

names. (10) One player claims never to play for money, adding that he gives lessons for $45 an hour. (11) Some players treat the pastime casual, playing only when they're in the mood. (12) But for many hustlers, street chess is their life; they start during the day, every day, and continue good into the next morning.

PRACTICE 5 EDITING YOUR OWN WRITING FOR CORRECT ADJECTIVES AND ADVERBS

As a final practice, edit a piece of your own writing for correct use of adjectives and adverbs. It can be a paper you are working on for this course, a paper you've already finished, a paper for another course, a recent piece of writing from your work or everyday life, or your idea journal entry. You may want to use the chart on page 530 as you edit.

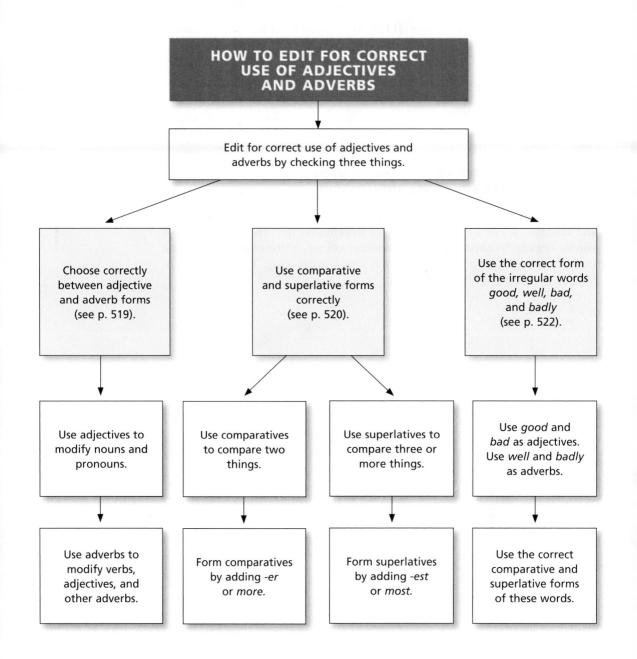

HOW TO EDIT FOR CORRECT USE OF ADJECTIVES AND ADVERBS

Edit for correct use of adjectives and adverbs by checking three things.

Choose correctly between adjective and adverb forms (see p. 519).

Use comparative and superlative forms correctly (see p. 520).

Use the correct form of the irregular words *good, well, bad,* and *badly* (see p. 522).

Use adjectives to modify nouns and pronouns.

Use comparatives to compare two things.

Use superlatives to compare three or more things.

Use *good* and *bad* as adjectives. Use *well* and *badly* as adverbs.

Use adverbs to modify verbs, adjectives, and other adverbs.

Form comparatives by adding *-er* or *more.*

Form superlatives by adding *-est* or *most.*

Use the correct comparative and superlative forms of these words.

29

Misplaced and Dangling Modifiers

Avoiding Confusing Descriptions

Understand What Misplaced and Dangling Modifiers Are

Modifiers are words or word groups that describe other words in a sentence. Unless the modifier is near the words it modifies, the sentence can be misleading or unintentionally funny.

■ IDEA JOURNAL
Write about how a person gets power or respect.

Misplaced Modifiers

A **misplaced modifier**, because it is not correctly placed in the sentence, describes the wrong word or words. To correct a misplaced modifier, move the modifier as close as possible to the word or words it modifies. The safest choice is often to put the modifier directly before the sentence element it modifies.

MISPLACED   Rudy saw my dog *driving his car on the highway*.

[Was my dog driving a car? No, Rudy was, so the modifier must come right before or right after his name.]

CORRECT   *Driving his car on the highway*, Rudy saw my dog.

MISPLACED   Claudia could not see the stop sign *without sunglasses*.

[Did the sign need sunglasses? No, Claudia did.]

CORRECT   *Without sunglasses*, Claudia could not see the stop sign.

Four constructions in particular often lead to misplaced modifiers:

1. **Modifiers such as *only, almost, hardly, nearly,* and *just***

    ordered only
    I ~~only ordered~~ half a pound.
    ^

                       almost
    Molly ~~almost~~ slept for ten hours.
                          ^

2. **Modifiers that start with *-ing* verbs**

    Using cash,
    Timothy bought the car. ~~using cash.~~
    ^   ^

    Wearing an oven mitt,
    Elena took out the hot pizza. ~~wearing an oven mitt.~~
    ^   ^

    [Note that when you move the phrase beginning with an *-ing* verb to the beginning of the sentence, you need to follow it with a comma.]

    Looking out the window of the plane, they
    ~~They~~ saw the Grand Canyon. ~~looking out the window of the plane.~~
    ^   ^

3. **Modifiers that are prepositional phrases**

              to the house for his sister.
    Jim was carrying the bags ~~for his sister to the house.~~
                             ^

              for ice cream in her glove compartment.
    Julie found money ~~in her glove compartment for ice cream.~~
                     ^

    With binoculars, we
    ~~We~~ saw the rare bird. ~~with binoculars.~~
    ^   ^

■ For more on how to use relative pronouns—*who, which,* and *that*—see page 592.

4. **Modifiers that are clauses starting with *who, whose, that,* or *which***

                    that was missing
    I finally found the sock stuck to a T-shirt. ~~that was missing.~~
                                    ^   ^

          who call people during dinner
    Telemarketers are sure to be annoying. ~~who call people during dinner.~~
                 ^   ^

    that I recently bought
    The computer died. ~~that I recently bought.~~
                  ^   ^

Dangling Modifiers

A **dangling modifier** "dangles" because the word or words it is supposed to modify are not in the sentence. Dangling modifiers usually appear at the beginning of a sentence and may seem to modify the noun or pronoun that immediately follow—but they don't.

Correct dangling modifiers either by adding the word being modified right after the opening modifier or by adding the word being modified to the opening modifier. Note that to correct a dangling modifier, you might have to reword the sentence.

DANGLING   *Talking on the telephone,* the dinner burned.

[Was the dinner talking on the telephone? No.]

CORRECT   *While Sharon was talking on the telephone,* the dinner burned.

The dinner burned *while Sharon was talking on the telephone.*

DANGLING   *While waiting in line,* the alarms went off.

[Were the alarms waiting in line? No.]

CORRECT   *While waiting in line,* I heard the alarms go off.

While I was waiting in line, the alarms went off.

Even if readers can guess what you are trying to say, misplaced and dangling modifiers are awkward. Be sure to look for and correct any misplaced and dangling modifiers in your writing.

Practice Correcting Misplaced and Dangling Modifiers

 PRACTICE 1   CORRECTING MISPLACED MODIFIERS . . . .

Find and correct any misplaced modifiers in the following sentences. If a sentence is correct, write a "C" next to it.

who work in U.S. hospitals

EXAMPLE: Many nurses are being trained to perform therapeutic

touch. ~~who work in U.S. hospitals.~~

1. Are there energy fields that can be touched by trained professionals in a human body?

2. People claim to be able to feel and move invisible energy fields who practice therapeutic touch.

■ For more practice with correcting mis-placed and dangling modifiers, visit *Exercise Central* at **bedfordstmartins .com/realessays**.

3. According to believers in therapeutic touch, an energy field can cause pain and illness that is out of alignment.

4. A practitioner treating a patient does not touch the sick person.

5. After a session of therapeutic touch, many patients just report that they felt better without knowing why.

6. Emily Rosa, the twelve-year-old daughter of a nurse, made news when her experiment appeared in an important medical journal to test practitioners of therapeutic touch.

7. In her experiment, practitioners were supposed to use the invisible energy field to determine when her hands were near theirs who could not see Emily.

8. Even though guessing should have allowed a 50 percent accuracy rating, the practitioners Emily tested were correct only 44 percent of the time.

9. Anyone who can demonstrate the ability to detect a human energy field can claim a million-dollar prize in a similar experiment.

10. The prize has not been awarded yet, which is offered by a foundation that investigates supernatural claims.

■ **PRACTICE 2 CORRECTING DANGLING MODIFIERS** . . . .

Find and correct any dangling modifiers in the following sentences. If a sentence is correct, write "C" next to it. It may be necessary to add new words or ideas to some sentences.

EXAMPLE: Selling a used car, a resale ~~will bring a better price~~ than a trade-in.
the owner will get a better price for

1. Trading in a used car, a buyer will offer a better price if the car is clean.

2. Hiring a professional detailer, a used car can be given a more polished appearance.

3. Looking like new, the owner can get the best price for a trade-in or a resale.

4. With essential repairs completed, a used car should be in good working order to be sold.

5. Approved as safe and drivable by a reputable mechanic, minor mechanical problems may not have to be fixed.

6. Winning points for honesty, prospective buyers should know about a used car's minor problems.

7. Deducted from the asking price, the owner can be fair with a buyer.

8. No matter how expensive, decorative lighting and other details usually do not add to the value of a car.

9. With higher than usual mileage, the owner may have to reduce the asking price.

10. Advertising in a local newspaper, a used car is likely to reach its target market.

Edit Paragraphs and Your Own Writing

Edit the following paragraphs for misplaced and dangling modifiers, referring to the chart on page 538 as you need to.

EDITING REVIEW 1

(1) When ordering items online, shipping and handling costs can make or break a business. (2) By charging too much, customers may abandon their order. (3) A customer may never return to the site who feels that shipping and handling charges are too high. (4) Most people

have shipped packages, so they know how much shipping costs at least occasionally. (5) Going too far in the other direction, some online customers get free shipping and handling. (6) The sites lose money that offer free shipping and may have to either close down for good or start charging shipping fees. (7) Most shipping companies charge by weight. (8) Buying from the sites that use these shippers, the online sites must either charge a flat fee, which may be too much or too little, or make the customer wait until the order is complete to find out the shipping fee. (9) Neither option is perfect, so a business must choose the least unattractive solution that wants to keep expanding its online customer base.

EDITING REVIEW 2 . . . .

MEMO

To: All staff

From: Sara Hollister

Re: Dress code

(1) After encouraging employees to wear casual clothing on Fridays, the casual dress code was soon in force all week long. (2) With some uncertainty about what was appropriate casual wear, a memo was circulated last year with guidelines for dress. (3) Wearing khakis and polo shirts, suits and ties became very rare in the halls of Wilson and Hollister. (4) Some younger staff members almost never wore anything but jeans. (5) Arriving in the office in a Hawaiian shirt, some employees hardly recognized Mr. Wilson without his trademark pinstriped suit. (6) Believing that informality improved productivity and morale, the casual dress code was well liked.

(7) The company must recommend for several reasons changes in the dress policy now. (8) The human resources department feels that the

relaxed attitude toward dress may have contributed to the recent increases in absenteeism and lateness at Wilson and Hollister. (9) Other problems have also surfaced. (10) Clients have sometimes expressed surprise who have dropped in unexpectedly. (11) Hoping to keep their respect and their business, the clients appear to feel more comfortable with employees in suits. (12) Finally, fearing an increase in sexual harassment, sleeveless shirts, shorts, miniskirts, and halter tops will no longer be permitted. (13) Human resources almost recommends a complete change in the casual-dress policy. (14) While continuing to wear casual clothing on Friday, business attire Monday through Thursday, is effective immediately. (15) As an employee who prefers casual clothing, this news is rather sad, but the decision is for the best. (16) Certain that you will understand the necessity for these changes, your cooperation is appreciated.

PRACTICE 3   EDITING YOUR OWN WRITING FOR MISPLACED AND DANGLING MODIFIERS

As a final practice, edit a piece of your own writing for misplaced and dangling modifiers. It can be a paper you are working on for this course, a paper you've already finished, a paper for another course, a recent piece of writing from your work or everyday life, or your idea journal entry. You may want to use the chart on page 538 as you edit.

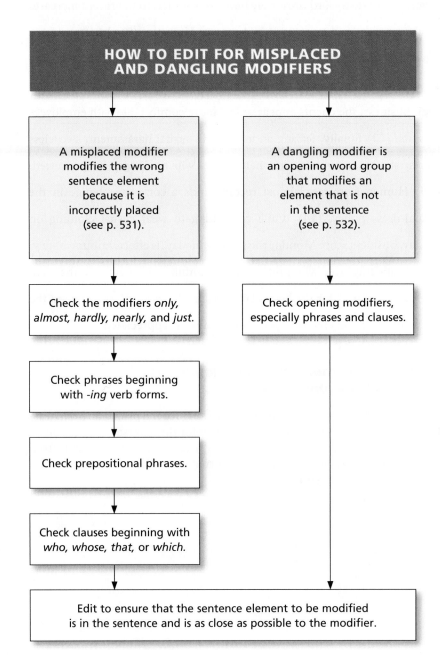

HOW TO EDIT FOR MISPLACED AND DANGLING MODIFIERS

A misplaced modifier modifies the wrong sentence element because it is incorrectly placed (see p. 531).

A dangling modifier is an opening word group that modifies an element that is not in the sentence (see p. 532).

Check the modifiers *only, almost, hardly, nearly,* and *just.*

Check opening modifiers, especially phrases and clauses.

Check phrases beginning with *-ing* verb forms.

Check prepositional phrases.

Check clauses beginning with *who, whose, that,* or *which.*

Edit to ensure that the sentence element to be modified is in the sentence and is as close as possible to the modifier.

30

Coordination and Subordination

Joining Ideas

Understand Coordination and Subordination

Coordination is used to join two sentences with related ideas, using *for, and, nor, but, or, so,* or *yet.* The two sentences you join will still be independent clauses—complete sentences—joined with a comma and a coordinating conjunction.

■ **IDEA JOURNAL**
Write about a family story—an incident that is told repeatedly.

TWO SENTENCES	The internship at the magazine is very prestigious. Many interns have gone on to get good jobs.

independent clause

JOINED THROUGH COORDINATION	The internship at the magazine is very prestigious, *and* many interns have gone on to get good jobs.

independent clause

Subordination is also used to join two sentences with related ideas, using a dependent word such as *although, because, if,* or *that.* The resulting sentence will have one independent clause (a complete sentence) and one dependent clause (not a complete sentence).

TWO SENTENCES	The internship was advertised last week. The magazine received many calls about it.

539

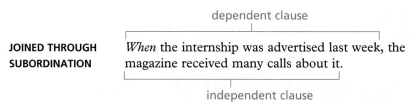

dependent clause

JOINED THROUGH
SUBORDINATION   *When* the internship was advertised last week, the magazine received many calls about it.

independent clause

[Adding the word *when* makes the first sentence dependent, or subordinate, to the second sentence.]

Both coordination and subordination are ways to join short, choppy sentences to get better rhythm and flow in your writing.

Practice Using Coordination and Subordination

Using Coordinating Conjunctions

Conjunctions join words, phrases, or clauses. **Coordinating conjunctions** (*and, but, for, nor, or, so,* and *yet*) join independent clauses. You can remember them by keeping the word *fanboys* in mind: **f**or, **a**nd, **n**or, **b**ut, **o**r, **y**et, **s**o. Choose the conjunction that makes the most sense, and make sure to put a comma before it when joining two independent clauses.

Independent clause	Coordinating conjunction , **f**or , **a**nd , **n**or , **b**ut , **o**r , **y**et , **s**o	Independent clause

My friend is coming   , and   I'm excited to see her.

[*And* simply joins two ideas.]

We were best friends   , but   I haven't seen her for years.

[*But* indicates a contrast.]

I'm a little nervous, for we may not have anything in common anymore. [*For* indicates a reason or cause.]

We haven't talked much, nor have we written. [*Nor* indicates a negative.]

Maybe we will pick up our friendship, or we may be like strangers. [*Or* indicates alternatives.]

We are meeting tonight, so we will know soon. [*So* indicates a result.]

It's hard to keep old friends, yet they are very important. [*Yet* indicates a reason.]

■ **PRACTICE 1 JOINING IDEAS WITH COORDINATING CONJUNCTIONS** ·

In each of the following sentences, fill in the blank with an appropriate coordinating conjunction. There may be more than one correct answer for some sentences.

■ Answers to odd-numbered practice items are at the back of the book.

> **EXAMPLE:** Millions of people get motion sickness while traveling, ___*and*___ it can turn an enjoyable experience into a nightmare.

1. Nearly 60 percent of children get carsick or airsick, _____ many also get sick on amusement park rides.

2. Some amusement park operators are aware of this, _____ a major theme park recently handed out "stomach distress" bags to customers.

3. Most people have experienced motion sickness at one time or another, _____ there are ways of easing or even avoiding its effects.

4. Motion sickness happens when a person's eyes and ears sense that she is moving one way, _____ her brain detects movement in another way.

5. When in a car, you want to see the car's movement while you are feeling it, _____ sit in the front seat and watch the road.

6. On a ship, you need to find a level point to focus on, _____ you should keep your eyes on the horizon.

■ For more practice with coordination and subordination, visit *Exercise Central* at **bedfordstmartins .com/realessays**.

7. When you are flying, choose a window seat, _____ look outside to watch and sense the plane's movement.

8. You can get a prescription for medication to prevent motion sickness, _____ you can also find some effective over-the-counter medications.

9. Taking ginger may be an even better way to prevent motion sickness, _____ you can simply buy ginger tea or raw ginger at a supermarket.

10. If you use a medication, be sure to take it one hour before you travel, _____ there may not be enough time for it to take effect.

PRACTICE 2 COMBINING SENTENCES WITH COORDINATING CONJUNCTIONS

Combine each pair of sentences into a single sentence by using a comma and a coordinating conjunction. In some cases, there may be more than one correct answer.

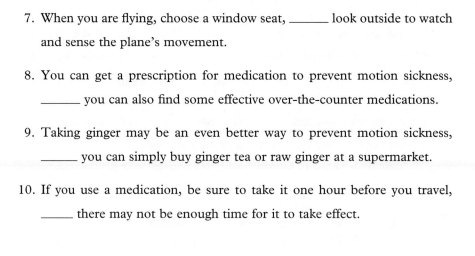

EXAMPLE: Americans have recently experienced unpleasant shocks at the gas station. People in the United States still pay
, but people
lower gas prices than much of the world.

1. Gasoline prices are lower in the United States than in many other industrialized countries. Most Americans do not find this news comforting.

2. People in the United States are used to low gas prices. Many drivers feel cheated when prices increase.

3. European drivers pay more than five dollars a gallon for gasoline. Gas prices in Asia have been triple those in the United States.

4. Canadians also pay higher gas prices than Americans pay. The taxes on gasoline are higher in Canada than they are in this country.

5. Few people would argue that gasoline prices in the United States are too low. The reason for these relatively cheap prices is that gasoline is not heavily taxed.

6. In many countries, taxes on gasoline support social services. The money may also pay for research on reducing air pollution.

7. Gasoline taxes can help to pay for roads. They can raise money for research into fuel efficiency.

8. However, taxes on gasoline are very unpopular with most drivers. Politicians are not eager to vote for gasoline taxes.

9. Many Americans do not want to pay gas taxes of even two or three cents per gallon. Most also do not want to spend tax money on mass transit systems.

10. Gasoline prices will probably never be as high in the United States as they are in Asia. A few Americans are not sure that this is a good thing.

Using Semicolons

A **semicolon** is a punctuation mark that can join two sentences through coordination. When you use a semicolon, make sure that the ideas in the two sentences are closely related.

EQUAL IDEA	;	EQUAL IDEA
My computer crashed	;	I lost all of my files.
I had just finished my paper	;	I will have to redo it.

A semicolon alone does not tell readers much about the relationship between the two ideas. Use a **conjunctive adverb** after the semicolon to give more information about the relationship. Put a comma after the conjunctive adverb.

The following are some of the most common conjunctive adverbs, along with a few examples of how they are used.

Independent clause	; afterward, ; also, ; as a result, ; besides, ; consequently, ; frequently, ; however, ; in addition, ; in fact, ; instead, ; still, ; then, ; therefore,	Independent clause

My computer crashed	; as a result,	I lost all my files.
I should have made backup files	; however,	I had not.
The information is lost	; therefore,	I will have to try to rebuild the files.

PRACTICE 3   JOINING IDEAS WITH SEMICOLONS . . . .

Join each pair of sentences by using a semicolon alone.

EXAMPLE: In the wake of recent scandals, many businesses are using
                                                                                            ; graphology
new techniques to identify questionable job candidates./ ~~Graphology~~
is one such technique.

1. Graphology involves identifying personality features on the basis of a person's handwriting. These features include honesty, responsibility, and loyalty.

2. Graphology is now used widely in Europe. Many American graphologists, too, say their business has grown significantly in recent years.

3. An owner of a jewelry store turned to a graphology consultant following an increase in employee theft. He says that handwriting analysis helped to identify the thieves.

4. Many scientists and doctors, however, believe that graphology is not reliable or scientific at all. They state that there is no evidence that graphology can uncover a person's true character.

5. Nevertheless, even some job seekers are beginning to use graphology to help them find work. One says he submitted his handwriting analysis report along with his résumé and got the job he wanted.

PRACTICE 4 COMBINING SENTENCES WITH SEMICOLONS AND CONNECTING WORDS (Conjunctive adverbs) . . . .

Combine each pair of sentences by using a semicolon and a connecting word followed by a comma. Choose a conjunctive adverb that makes sense for the relationship between the two ideas. In some cases, there may be more than one correct answer.

EXAMPLE: Most people do not own a gas mask. *; however, after* ~~After~~ 9/11, some may feel more comfortable having one available.

1. Two inventors believed that Americans would welcome the opportunity to have a gas mask. They invented one that is part of a baseball cap.

2. Professional gas masks are costly, heavy, and hard to use. Most consumers would not find them appealing.

3. The new baseball-cap gas mask is small and lightweight. It can fit in the corner of a drawer, in a coat pocket, or in a briefcase.

4. This mask can easily fit children as well as adults. It may sell for as little as twenty dollars.

5. The wearer slips a thin sheet of transparent plastic attached to the hat over his or her head. The plastic sheet can be tied shut at the back of the neck.

6. Air from the outside is pulled in by a tiny fan. The air is forced through a filter of activated carbon in the hat's brim.

7. The inventors say that the plastic sheet allows the wearer to see clearly. It does not make the wearer feel too closed in.

8. The mask is not intended for long-term use. It is meant to be worn for about fifteen to thirty minutes.

9. The goal is to allow the wearer to get out of the contaminated area quickly. The wearer can simply slip on the mask and then move into fresh air.

10. The inventors are now looking for a company to make the new gas mask. Consumers will be able to obtain the gas masks from the manufacturer.

. . . .

Using Subordinating Conjunctions

Conjunctions join words, phrases, or clauses. **Subordinating conjunctions** join two sentences, making the one after the dependent word a dependent clause.

Choose the conjunction that makes the most sense with the two sentences. Here are some of the most common subordinating conjunctions.

Independent clause	after	once	Dependent clause
	although	since	
	as	so that	
	as if	unless	
	because	until	
	before	when	
	even though	whenever	
	if	where	
	if only	while	
	now that		

I decided to go to work	although	I had a terrible cold.
I hate to miss a day	unless	I absolutely can't get there.

When the dependent clause ends a sentence (as in the preceding examples), it usually does not need to be preceded by a comma unless it is showing a contrast. When the dependent clause begins a sentence, use a comma to separate it from the rest of the sentence.

Subordinating conjunction	Subordinate idea	,	Main idea
Although	I had a terrible cold	,	I decided to go to work.
Unless	I absolutely can't get there	,	I hate to miss a day.

▮ **PRACTICE 5   JOINING IDEAS THROUGH SUBORDINATION** . . . .

In the following sentences, fill in the blank with an appropriate subordinating conjunction. In some cases, there may be more than one correct answer.

EXAMPLE: Smokey Bear spent most of his life in the National Zoo in Washington, D.C., __*where*__ he received so much mail that he had his own zip code.

1. Smokey Bear began reminding people that "Only you can prevent forest fires" in 1944 _____ government officials during World War II were concerned about preserving valuable resources like trees.

2. However, Smokey Bear existed only as a cartoon _____ a tragedy occurred six years later.

3. _____ a fire destroyed part of Lincoln National Forest in 1950, forest rangers found a badly burned bear cub clinging to a tree.

4. The "real" Smokey Bear became a celebrity _____ the public heard his story.

5. After his death, Smokey Bear's body was returned to New Mexico _____ he could be buried near his former home.

6. The character of Smokey Bear has been used continuously in U.S. fire safety campaigns _____ it first appeared more than fifty years ago.

7. Smokey has also appeared in public service announcements in Mexico, _____ he is known as Simon.

8. Recently, Smokey's famous line was changed to "Only you can prevent wildfires" _____ research indicated that most adults did not believe they could cause a wildfire.

9. However, humans can easily set fires _____ they discard cigarettes carelessly, burn trash on windy days, or even park a car with a catalytic converter in a dry field.

10. _____ the campaign heads into its seventh decade, Smokey is as recognizable to most Americans as Mickey Mouse and Santa Claus.

PRACTICE 6 COMBINING SENTENCES THROUGH SUBORDINATION . . . .

Combine each pair of sentences into a single sentence by using an appropriate subordinating conjunction either at the beginning or between the two sentences.

EXAMPLE: *Although* Michael had heard about lengthy delays for some air ^*travelers, he* travelers. He had never experienced one himself.
^

1. His turn came on a flight back to school in Austin from Minneapolis. He was staying with his family during winter break.

2. The flight took off on time and was going smoothly. He had heard some fellow passengers talking about a possible storm in the Austin area.

3. He paid no attention to the rumors. The pilot announced to the passengers that the flight was landing in Wichita, Kansas, due to severe weather in Austin.

4. According to the pilot, they would be taking off again soon. He expected the weather in Texas to clear.

5. Michael sat in his seat and tried to sleep. He heard some people ask the flight attendants to allow the passengers to wait in the air terminal.

6. Everyone had waited over two hours. The flight crew told the passengers to go out to the air terminal.

7. Five hours later, Michael and his fellow passengers still didn't know when they would be able to resume their flight. There were no announcements from anybody about what would happen next.

8. An announcement finally came. The passengers learned that the bad weather in Texas prevented the flight from continuing on to Austin.

9. Michael was already upset by the hours-long delay with no announcements. He was even angrier at the thought of sleeping overnight in the air terminal.

10. He was sitting uncomfortably in his terminal seat, feeling hopeless. A few other passengers asked him if he wanted to join them in renting a car to complete the trip to Austin, which he did.

Edit Paragraphs and Your Own Writing

Join the underlined sentences by using either coordination or subordination, referring to the chart on page 552 as you need to. Be sure to punctuate correctly.

EDITING REVIEW 1 (6 sets of sentences to be joined)

(1) A patient misunderstands a doctor's explanation and recommendations. (2) There can be serious consequences. (3) If medications are not properly used or preventive measures are not taken, health risks

increase. (4) <u>These problems are common with people of all ages, races, and educational levels.</u> (5) <u>They are especially prevalent among the elderly.</u> (6) The individual patient, of course, is affected in a personal and sometimes life-threatening way, but society in general also has to pay for the resulting increased medical costs. (7) <u>A patient follows these simple guidelines.</u> (8) <u>He or she can better understand what is wrong and what to do about it.</u> (9) First of all, make absolutely sure that the doctor's instructions are understandable. (10) <u>The doctor will probably ask if there are any questions.</u> (11) <u>Think over each step of the instructions, and ask for a clearer explanation of anything that's confusing.</u> (12) Repeat the instructions back to the doctor and ask, "Is that right?" (13) <u>Another tip is to take notes on what the doctor recommends.</u> (14) <u>Either write the notes yourself or bring along someone else to jot them down.</u> (15) It is easy to feel intimidated by being partially unclothed in the examination room. (16) <u>Ask to hear the necessary instructions in the doctor's office.</u> (17) <u>You are fully clothed.</u> (18) Finally, follow the doctor's instructions carefully, for recovery depends just as much on the patient as on the doctor.

EDITING REVIEW 2 (7 sets of sentences to be joined) . . . .

(1) Al-Qurain is a community in the small Middle Eastern country of Kuwait. (2) <u>Thirty years ago, Kuwait City officials began to use an abandoned quarry in al-Qurain as a garbage dump.</u> (3) <u>None of them thought the area would ever be populated.</u> (4) Fifteen years ago, the government began to build subsidized housing in al-Qurain. (5) <u>The dump was supposed to be closed.</u> (6) <u>Kuwaitis continued to use the al-Qurain landfill.</u> (7) People soon lived all around the foul-smelling garbage pit.

(8) Residents of the area were teased and insulted for living in the neighborhood. (9) Al-Qurain now houses sixty thousand people.

(10) For years, the dump sickened people around it. (11) Sometimes the garbage caught fire and sent fumes into the homes nearby. (12) Finally, the Kuwaiti Environmental Protection Agency decided to try to help. (13) The agency gets little government funding. (14) It needed to rely on donations for the cleanup effort. (15) Soon, a mountain of garbage had been removed. (16) The leveled site was covered with pebbles from the desert. (17) Engineers found a way to siphon methane gas from the seventy-five-foot-deep garbage pit. (18) Kuwait is famous for oil production. (19) A methane-powered generator may soon provide electricity for al-Qurain residents. (20) The air in the neighborhood now ranks among the country's cleanest. (21) For many environmentalists and residents of this neighborhood, the cleanup of al-Qurain is almost a miracle.

PRACTICE 7   EDITING YOUR OWN WRITING FOR COORDINATION AND SUBORDINATION

As a final practice, edit a piece of your own writing for coordination and subordination. It can be a paper you are working on for this course, a paper you've already finished, a paper for another course, a recent piece of writing from your work or everyday life, or your idea journal entry. You may want to use the chart on page 552 as you edit.

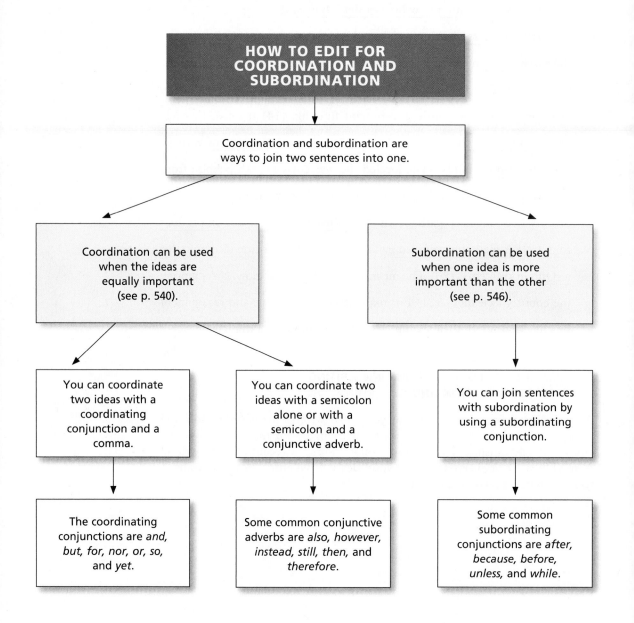

HOW TO EDIT FOR COORDINATION AND SUBORDINATION

Coordination and subordination are ways to join two sentences into one.

Coordination can be used when the ideas are equally important (see p. 540).

Subordination can be used when one idea is more important than the other (see p. 546).

You can coordinate two ideas with a coordinating conjunction and a comma.

You can coordinate two ideas with a semicolon alone or with a semicolon and a conjunctive adverb.

You can join sentences with subordination by using a subordinating conjunction.

The coordinating conjunctions are *and, but, for, nor, or, so,* and *yet*.

Some common conjunctive adverbs are *also, however, instead, still, then,* and *therefore*.

Some common subordinating conjunctions are *after, because, before, unless,* and *while*.

31

Parallelism

Balancing Ideas

Understand What Parallelism Is

Parallelism in writing means that similar parts in a sentence are balanced by having the same structure. Put nouns with nouns, verbs with verbs, and phrases with phrases.

NOT PARALLEL	I like <u>math</u> more than <u>studying English</u>.

[*Math* is a noun, but *studying English* is a phrase.]

PARALLEL	I like <u>math</u> more than <u>English</u>.

NOT PARALLEL	In class, we <u>read</u>, <u>worked</u> in groups, and <u>were writing</u> an essay.

[Verbs must be in the same tense to be parallel.]

PARALLEL	In class, we <u>read</u>, <u>worked</u> in groups, and <u>wrote</u> an essay.

NOT PARALLEL	Last night we went <u>to a movie</u> and <u>dancing at a club</u>.

[*To a movie* and *dancing at a club* are both phrases, but they have different forms. *To a movie* should be paired with another prepositional phrase: *to a dance club*.]

PARALLEL	Last night we went <u>to a movie</u> and <u>to a dance club</u>.

■ **IDEA JOURNAL**
Write about a movie you saw recently, and explain why you liked or disliked it.

Practice Writing Parallel Sentences

Parallelism in Pairs and Lists

When two or more items in a series are joined by the word *and* or *or,* use a similar form for each item.

NOT PARALLEL	The fund-raiser included <u>a bake sale</u> and <u>also holding an auction</u>.
PARALLEL	The fund-raiser included <u>a bake sale</u> and <u>an auction</u>.
NOT PARALLEL	Students got items for the auction <u>from local businesses</u>, <u>from their families</u>, and <u>ran an advertisement in the newspaper</u>.
PARALLEL	Students got items for the auction <u>from local businesses</u>, <u>from their families</u>, and <u>from people who responded to a newspaper advertisement</u>.

■ PRACTICE 1   MAKING PAIRS AND LISTS PARALLEL . . . .

In each sentence, underline the parts of the sentence that should be parallel. Then, edit the sentence to make it parallel.

EXAMPLE: Being a single parent can make the morning routine
                                      and stressful
difficult, ~~and it can be stressful~~ without the proper
                        ^
organization.

■ Answers to odd-numbered practice items are at the back of the book.

1. This is important because the beginning of the day affects you, and your children are affected as well.

2. Get a good start by planning ahead, setting a few rules, and also be sure to keep a cool head.

3. On the night before, make as many preparations for morning as possible, including preparing lunches, getting out clothes, and it's important to organize schoolbooks.

4. A quick cold breakfast can be easy, tasty, and it can provide good nutrition.

5. Cold cereal with milk and fruit, for example, is delicious and has the added advantage of giving you plenty of vitamins and minerals.

6. Allowing the kids to watch TV in the morning can cause all sorts of problems, or you can let the TV work to your advantage.

7. Set a rule that the kids must eat breakfast, wash up, be sure of brushing their teeth, get dressed, and put their shoes on before they turn on the TV.

8. Prevent frantic, last-minute searches by establishing specific places for the items each of you needs for the day, such as car keys, backpacks, all pairs of shoes that the kids will wear during the day, and coats.

9. Save for the evening time-consuming, stressful tasks such as teaching a child to tie shoes or becoming a referee who can objectively discuss both sides in a dispute between kids.

10. Set aside some "myself time," in which you stop rushing around, taking a deep breath, and calmly prepare for your day.

■ For more practice with parallelism, visit *Exercise Central* at **bedfordstmartins .com/realessays**.

Parallelism in Comparisons

In comparisons, the items being compared should have parallel structures. Comparisons often use the words *than* or *as*. When you edit for parallelism, make sure that the items on either side of the comparison word are parallel.

NOT PARALLEL   Driving downtown is as fast as the bus.

PARALLEL   Driving downtown is as fast as taking the bus.

NOT PARALLEL   Running is more tiring than walks.

PARALLEL   Running is more tiring than walking. *Or,*

A run is more tiring than a walk.

To make the parts of a sentence parallel, you may need to add or drop a word or two.

NOT PARALLEL	<u>A multiple-choice test</u> is easier than <u>answering an essay question</u>.
PARALLEL, WORD ADDED	<u>*Taking* a multiple-choice test</u> is easier than <u>answering an essay question</u>.
NOT PARALLEL	<u>The cost</u> of a train ticket is less than <u>to pay the cost</u> of a plane ticket.
PARALLEL, WORDS DROPPED	<u>The cost</u> of a train ticket is less than <u>the cost</u> of a plane ticket.

■ **PRACTICE 2   MAKING COMPARISONS PARALLEL** . . . .

In each sentence, underline the parts of the sentence that should be parallel. Then, edit the sentence to make it parallel.

EXAMPLE: <u>New appliances</u> are usually much more energy-efficient than <u>~~running~~ old ones</u>.

1. For many people, getting the household electric bill is more worrisome than to pay the rent each month.

2. The amount of the rent bill usually changes much less from month to month than what an energy company charges.

3. Saving money appeals to many consumers more than to use less electricity.

4. Compact fluorescent light bulbs use less energy than continuing to use regular incandescent bulbs.

5. In most households, running the refrigerator uses more energy than the use of all other appliances.

6. Many people worry that buying a new refrigerator is more expensive than if they simply keep the old one.

7. However, an energy-efficient new refrigerator uses much less electricity than running an inefficient older model.

8. Some new refrigerators use only as much energy as keeping a 75-watt light bulb burning.

9. Householders might spend less money to buy an efficient new refrigerator than it would take to run the old one for another five years.

10. Researching information about energy efficiency can save consumers as much money as when they remember to turn off lights and air conditioners.

. . . .

Parallelism with Certain Paired Words

When a sentence uses certain paired words called **correlative conjunctions**, the items joined by these paired words must be parallel. Correlative conjunctions, shown below, link two equal elements and show the relationship between them.

both . . . and	neither . . . nor	rather . . . than
either . . . or	not only . . . but also	

NOT PARALLEL	Brianna dislikes *both* <u>fruit</u> *and* <u>eating vegetables</u>.
PARALLEL	Brianna dislikes *both* <u>fruit</u> *and* <u>vegetables</u>.
NOT PARALLEL	She would *rather* <u>eat</u> popcorn every night *than* <u>to cook</u>.
PARALLEL	She would *rather* <u>eat</u> popcorn every night *than* <u>cook</u>.

PRACTICE 3 MAKING SENTENCES WITH PAIRED WORDS PARALLEL . . . .

In each sentence, circle the paired words and underline the parts of the sentence that should be parallel. Then, edit the sentence to make it parallel. You may need to change the second part of the correlative conjunction.

EXAMPLE: A recent survey of young women reported that a majority of them would ⟨rather⟩ lose twenty pounds permanently ⟨than⟩ to live to be ninety.

1. People in the United States are both pressed for time and have gotten used to convenient but fattening foods.

2. Many Americans are neither willing to exercise regularly nor do they have to do anything physical during a normal day.

3. Being overweight can be unhealthy, but many Americans would rather look thinner than to stay the same size and get in better shape.

4. In fact, some Americans are not only out of shape but are dangerously obsessed with being thin.

5. The idea that thinner is better affects both overweight people and it even influences people of normal weight.

6. In their quest to lose weight, many Americans have tried either fad diets or have taken prescription drugs.

7. Dozens of healthy, average-sized Americans in the past ten years have died from either surgical procedures to remove fat or they have died from dangerous diet drugs.

8. A thin person is neither guaranteed to be attractive nor is he or she necessarily healthy.

9. Some people who are larger than average are not only in good health but also can be physically fit.

10. Americans who would rather pay for risky drugs and surgery than eating moderately and exercising may have hazardous priorities.

▪ PRACTICE 4   **COMPLETING SENTENCES WITH
PAIRED WORDS** ·

The following items contain only the first part of a correlative conjunction. Complete the correlative conjunction, and add more information to form a whole sentence. Make sure that the structures on both sides of the correlative conjunction are parallel.

EXAMPLE: I am both enthusiastic about your company _and eager to_
work for you .

1. I could bring to this job not only youthful enthusiasm _____

   _____ .

2. I am willing to work either in your Chicago office _____

   _____ .

3. My current job neither encourages creativity _____ .

4. I would rather work in a difficult job _____ .

5. In college I learned a lot both from my classes _____ .

· ·

Edit Paragraphs and Your Own Writing

Edit the following paragraphs for parallelism, referring to the chart on page 562 as you need to.

▪ **EDITING REVIEW 1 (8 errors)** · · · · · · · · · · · · · · · · · ·

(1) Some employees who want to advance their careers would rather transfer within their company than looking for a new job elsewhere. (2) In-house job changes are possible, but employees should be sure that they both meet the criteria of the job and to avoid making their present boss angry. (3) Because businesses invest money in each person they

hire, many companies would rather hire from within and not bring an outsider into a position. (4) By hiring an employee from another department, a company neither needs to make an investment in a new employee but may also prevent the current employee from leaving. (5) Transfers usually go more smoothly now than in the past; however, an in-house job move can still require diplomacy and being honest. (6) Experts caution employees who are considering an in-house transfer to tell their current manager the truth and that they should discuss their wish to transfer with the potential new manager. (7) Employees should neither threaten to quit if they do not get the new job nor is it a good idea to spread the word around the department that they are anxious to leave their present job. (8) Employees' goals for in-house transfers should be career advancement and making sure that they create no bad feelings with the move.

EDITING REVIEW 2 (10 errors) . . . .

(1) Black motorists frequently arouse police suspicion either when driving in neighborhoods that are mainly white or when they are driving an expensive car. (2) A higher percentage of African Americans than among people who are white are pulled over by the police. (3) Many African Americans feel insulted, endangered, and react with anger when they are stopped randomly. (4) African Americans are liable to be singled out by police who suspect they are criminals not only while in a car but African Americans also report being wrongly stopped on foot. (5) Racial profiling is illegal yet a fairly common phenomenon. (6) According to a 2001 poll, among black women the figure is 25 percent, and 52 percent of black men have been stopped by police. (7) Victims of racial profiling have

done nothing wrong, yet they are made to feel that others are either afraid or do not trust them. (8) Law-abiding African Americans should neither expect such treatment nor should they put up with it from public officials who are supposed to protect citizens. (9) Police departments around the country must make their employees aware that automatically stopping, asking them questions, and searching African Americans will not be tolerated. (10) Treating all citizens fairly is a more important American value than that there is a high arrest rate for the police.

PRACTICE 5 EDITING YOUR OWN WRITING FOR PARALLELISM

As a final practice, edit a piece of your own writing for parallelism. It can be a paper you are working on for this course, a paper you've already finished, a paper for another course, a recent piece of writing from your work or everyday life, or your idea journal entry. You may want to use the chart on page 562 as you edit.

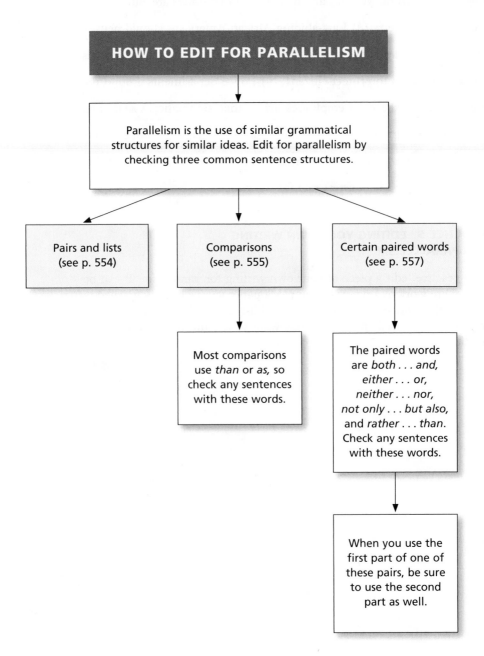

HOW TO EDIT FOR PARALLELISM

Parallelism is the use of similar grammatical structures for similar ideas. Edit for parallelism by checking three common sentence structures.

Pairs and lists (see p. 554)

Comparisons (see p. 555)

Certain paired words (see p. 557)

Most comparisons use *than* or *as*, so check any sentences with these words.

The paired words are *both . . . and, either . . . or, neither . . . nor, not only . . . but also,* and *rather . . . than.* Check any sentences with these words.

When you use the first part of one of these pairs, be sure to use the second part as well.

32

Sentence Variety

Putting Rhythm in Your Writing

Understand What Sentence Variety Is

Having **sentence variety** in your writing means using assorted sentence patterns, lengths, and rhythms. Sometimes writers use too many short, simple sentences, thinking that short is always easier to understand than long. In fact, that is not true, as the following examples show.

■ **IDEA JOURNAL**
Write about something that made you angry.

WITH SHORT, SIMPLE SENTENCES

Age discrimination can exist even in unpaid jobs. The newspaper today reported that a magazine has been accused of age discrimination. The magazine is the *Atlantic Monthly*. A woman was told she was too old to be an unpaid intern. The woman was forty-one. The position was for a senior in college. The woman was a senior. She had raised three children before going to college. She is suing the magazine. The next day, another woman, age fifty-one, reported that the same thing had happened to her a year earlier. She had filed a discrimination suit. The suit was brought to court by the Council on Age Discrimination. The magazine never showed up. The court never took any follow-up action against the magazine. Apparently, the matter was not of great importance to either the magazine or the justice system.

WITH SENTENCE VARIETY

Age discrimination can exist even in unpaid jobs. The newspaper today reported that a forty-one-year-old woman has accused a magazine, the *Atlantic Monthly,* of age discrimination. This woman, who raised three children before going to college and is now in her senior year, was told she was too old to be an unpaid intern, even though the position was for a college senior. She is suing the magazine. The next day, another woman, age fifty-one, reported that the same thing had happened to her a year earlier, and she, too, had filed an age discrimination suit. The suit was brought to court by the Council on Age Discrimination, but the magazine didn't appear for the court date, and the court never took any follow-up action. Apparently, the matter was not of great importance to either the magazine or the justice system.

Sentence variety is what gives your writing good rhythm and flow.

Practice Creating Sentence Variety

■ For two additional techniques used to achieve sentence variety, coordination and subordination, see Chapter 30.

To create sentence variety, write sentences of different types and lengths. Because many writers tend to write short sentences that start with the subject, this chapter will focus on techniques for starting with something other than the subject and for writing a variety of longer sentences.

Remember that the goal is to use variety to achieve a good rhythm. Do not simply change all your sentences from one pattern to another, or you still won't have variety.

Start Some Sentences with Adverbs

■ For more about adverbs, see Chapter 28.

Adverbs are words that describe verbs, adjectives, or other adverbs; they often end with -*ly*. As long as the meaning is clear, you can place an adverb at the beginning of a sentence or near the word it describes. An adverb at the beginning is usually followed by a comma.

■ Answers to odd-numbered practice items are at the back of the book.

ADVERB AT BEGINNING	*Frequently,* stories about haunted houses surface at Halloween.
ADVERB NEAR A VERB	Stories about haunted houses *frequently* surface at Halloween.
ADVERB AT BEGINNING	*Often,* these tales reveal the life stories of former inhabitants.
ADVERB NEAR A VERB	These tales *often* reveal the life stories of former inhabitants.

■ **PRACTICE 1   STARTING SENTENCES WITH AN ADVERB** . . . .

Edit each sentence so that it begins with an adverb.

        Frequently, hurricanes

     EXAMPLE: ~~Hurricanes frequently~~ strike barrier islands.
               ^

1. Harsh weather takes a toll annually on sandy beaches.

2. That island house formerly stood on solid ground.

3. The ocean eventually washed the ground out from under it.

4. The house was finally condemned as unsafe.

5. It is now going to be demolished.

> ■ For more practice with sentence variety, visit *Exercise Central* at **bedfordstmartins.com/realessays**.

■ **PRACTICE 2   STARTING SENTENCES WITH AN ADVERB** . . . .

This practice continues the story from the previous exercise. In each sentence, fill in the blank with an adverb that makes sense, adding a comma when necessary. There may be several good choices for each item.

     EXAMPLE: ___*Fortunately,*___ no one was living in the house at the time.

1. _____ a row of houses stood on the east side of the channel.

2. _____ a hurricane washed away most of the land nearby.

3. _____ most of the houses vanished.

4. _____ the house stood alone on a sandy peninsula.

5. _____ maps of the island were redrawn.

■ **PRACTICE 3   WRITING SENTENCES THAT START WITH AN ADVERB** . . . .

Write three more sentences that start with an adverb, using commas as necessary. Choose from the following adverbs: *amazingly, frequently, gently, lovingly, luckily, often, quietly, sadly, stupidly.*

     EXAMPLE: ___*Luckily, I remembered to save my file on a disk.*___

1. _____

2. _____

3. _____

Join Ideas Using an *-ing* Verb Form

One way to combine sentences is to turn one of them into a phrase using an *-ing* **verb form** (such as *walking* or *racing*). The *-ing* verb form indicates that the two parts of the sentence are happening at the same time. The more important idea (the one you want to emphasize) should be in the main clause, not in the phrase you make by adding the *-ing* verb form.

TWO SENTENCES	Jonah did well in the high jump. He came in second.
JOINED WITH *-ING* VERB FORM	Jonah did well in the high jump, coming in second.

To combine sentences this way, add *-ing* to the verb in one of the sentences and delete the subject. You now have a phrase that can be added to the beginning or the end of the other sentence, depending on what makes sense.

He also won the long jump. ̸He broke the record.
                          , breaking

If you add the phrase to the end of a sentence, you will usually need to put a comma before it unless the phrase is essential to the meaning of the sentence, as in the following example.

The thief broke into the apartment. ̸The thief used a crowbar.
                                  using

If you add a phrase starting with an *-ing* verb form to the beginning of a sentence, put a comma after it. Be sure that the word being modified follows immediately after the phrase. Otherwise, you will create a dangling modifier.

TWO SENTENCES	I dropped my bag. My groceries spilled.
DANGLING MODIFIER	Dropping my bag, my groceries spilled.
EDITED	Dropping my bag, I spilled my groceries.

■ **PRACTICE 4   JOINING IDEAS USING AN *-ING* VERB FORM** . . . .

Combine each pair of sentences into a single sentence by using an *-ing* verb
form. Add or delete words if necessary.

Imagining that

EXAMPLE: ~~Many fans of rap music~~ imagine it is a recent

    ^

              , many fans

development. ~~They~~ are not aware that the roots of this

            ^

music go back centuries.

1. Folk poets wandered from village to village in West Africa hundreds of
   years before the birth of the United States. They rhythmically recited stories and tales with the accompaniment of a drum and a few instruments.

2. Rap music uses rhymes and wordplay with a rhythmic delivery to build
   on this heritage. Its lyrics often deal with matters of race, socioeconomic
   class, and gender.

3. Many fans trace the beginning of modern-day rap to a Jamaican immigrant to the Bronx in New York. They still revere Kool Herc, a DJ in the
   1970s who originated the new sound in America.

4. Kool Herc recited lyrics to go along with the songs that he was playing as
   a DJ. He introduced this innovative music at private parties and then later
   at well-known dance halls.

5. In the 1980s, rappers' lyrics focused on sharp sociopolitical content. They
   captivated listeners with increasingly creative wordplay.

6. Rap songwriters developed a rougher, more sinister edge in the 1990s.
   They began narrating personal street experiences mixed with social commentary.

7. Today, rap music has branched out in several directions. Today, it has
   southern, northern, midwestern, and even international rap forms alongside the more established styles from the East and West coasts.

8. Perhaps consciously and perhaps not, rappers extensively use forms of wordplay that are also found in classical poetry. They call on such literary devices as double meanings, alliteration, similes, and metaphors.

9. Rap artists emphasize frequently the themes of wealth and class. Nearly all popular rappers in the United States are African American.

10. Rap has gained a solid foothold in American culture. It is now widely accepted as a form of mainstream American music.

PRACTICE 5 JOINING IDEAS USING AN *-ING* VERB FORM

Fill in the blank in each sentence with an appropriate *-ing* verb form. There are many possible ways to complete each sentence.

EXAMPLE: ___Owning___ **the rights to the character Spider-Man, Marvel Enterprises has been making big money lately.**

1. ____________ from losses of tens of millions of dollars a year, Marvel now turns a profit of more than $150 million a year, thanks to Spider-Man.

2. Marvel dominates the comic-book market, ____________ sixty comic books a month.

3. ____________ 83 percent of its profits from licensing its characters for films and related merchandise, Marvel makes only 15 percent of its profits from comic-book sales.

4. Marvel keeps tight control of the characters it licenses to filmmakers, ____________ no costume changes or added superpowers without Marvel's approval.

5. ____________ any film studio from having Spider-Man kill anyone, for example, Marvel maintains the character as it believes he should be.

■ **PRACTICE 6   JOINING IDEAS USING AN *-ING* VERB FORM** . . . .

Write two sets of sentences, and join each set using an *-ing* verb form.

EXAMPLE: a. *Teresa signed on to eBay.com.* _____

 b. *She used her password.* _____

COMBINED: *Using her password, Teresa signed on to eBay.com.* _____

 Teresa signed on to eBay.com using her password. _____

1. **a.** _____

 b. _____

 COMBINED: _____

 _____

2. **a.** _____

 b. _____

 COMBINED: _____

 _____

Join Ideas Using an *-ed* Verb Form

Another way to combine sentences is to turn one of them into a phrase using an **-ed verb form** (such as *waited* or *walked*). You can join sentences this way if one of them has a form of *be* as a helping verb along with the *-ed* verb form.

■ For more on helping verbs, see Chapters 22, 26, and 33.

TWO SENTENCES	Leonardo da Vinci was a man of many talents. He was noted most often for his painting.
JOINED WITH *-ED* VERB FORM	Noted most often for his painting, Leonardo da Vinci was a man of many talents.

To combine sentences this way, drop the subject and the helping verb from a sentence that has an *-ed* verb form. You now have a modifying phrase that can be added to the beginning or the end of the other sentence, depending on what makes the most sense.

Interested   *, Leonardo*
~~Leonardo was interested~~ in many areas, ~~He~~ investigated problems of

geology, botany, mechanics, and hydraulics.

■ For more on finding and correcting dangling modifiers, see Chapter 29.

If you add a phrase that begins with an *-ed* verb form to the beginning of a sentence, put a comma after it. Be sure the word that the phrase modifies follows immediately, or you will create a dangling modifier. Sometimes, you will need to change the word that the phrase modifies from a pronoun to a noun, as in the previous example.

■   **PRACTICE 7   JOINING IDEAS USING AN *-ED* VERB FORM** . . . .

Combine each pair of sentences into a single sentence by using an *-ed* verb form.

Hatched
EXAMPLE: ~~Alligators are hatched~~ from eggs when they are only a

, alligators
few inches long, ~~Alligators~~ can reach a length of ten feet or more as

adults.

1. An alligator was spotted in a pond in Central Park in New York City. Many New Yorkers refused to believe in the existence of the alligator.

2. Alligators were released by their owners for growing too large to be pets. These alligators were sometimes said to be living in New York City sewers.

3. Rumors were believed by some gullible people. The rumors about giant sewer alligators were untrue.

4. The story of the alligator in Central Park was denied by city officials. The story sounded like another wild rumor.

5. Central Park alligator sightings were reported by several New Yorkers. The sightings were confirmed when a television news crew filmed a reptile in the pond.

6. A professional alligator wrestler was hired to catch the reptile. He came to New York from Florida.

7. The pond in Central Park was surrounded by news cameras and curious onlookers. It was brightly lit just before 11:00 p.m. on the day the alligator wrestler arrived.

8. The creature was captured in just a few minutes by the alligator wrestler's wife. The so-called alligator turned out to be a spectacled caiman, a species native to Central and South America.

9. Some New Yorkers were surprised to find that the caiman was only two feet long. They may have felt a bit foolish for expecting to see a giant alligator in the park.

10. The caiman was removed from Central Park. It soon found a home in a warmer climate.

PRACTICE 8   JOINING IDEAS USING AN *-ED* VERB FORM · · · · · · · · · ·

Fill in the blank in each sentence with an appropriate *-ed* verb form. There are several possible ways to complete each sentence.

> **EXAMPLE:** ___*Enjoyed*___ **by many people around the world, online gambling is an increasingly popular recreational option.**

1. _____ regularly by Europeans, this venue for gambling is more difficult for Americans to access.

2. _____ by some U.S. states, online gambling is a major worry of the government.

3. _____ that Internet gambling can be used for hiding large exchanges of money, the U.S. Justice Department has asked major Internet search engines to remove advertising for online gambling operations.

4. Also _____ to legalizing online gambling in the United States, some antigambling activists think the speed of the Internet makes it more likely for problem gamblers to give in to their addiction.

5. _____ a harmless pastime by some, easy-access online gambling can arguably ruin even more lives than it already has.

■   **PRACTICE 9   JOINING IDEAS USING AN -*ED* VERB FORM** . . . .

Write two sets of sentences, and join them using an -*ed* verb form.

EXAMPLE: a.   *Lee is training for the Boston Marathon.*

b.   *It is believed to have the most difficult hill to run.*

COMBINED: *Lee is training for the Boston Marathon, believed to have the*

most difficult hill to run.

1. a. _____

b. _____

COMBINED: _____

_____

2. a. _____

b. _____

COMBINED: _____

_____

Join Ideas Using an Appositive

An **appositive** is a phrase that renames a noun. Appositives, which are nouns or noun phrases, can be used to combine two sentences into one.

TWO SENTENCES   Elvis Presley continues to be popular many years after his death. He is "the King."

| JOINED WITH AN APPOSITIVE | Elvis Presley, "the King," continues to be popular many years after his death. |

[The phrase *"the King"* renames the noun *Elvis Presley*.]

To combine two sentences this way, turn the sentence that renames the noun into a phrase by dropping its subject and verb. The appositive phrase can appear anywhere in the sentence, but it should be placed before or after the noun it renames. Use a comma or commas to set off the appositive.

Millions of people visit Elvis's home *, Graceland,* each year. ~~It is called Graceland.~~

▇ **PRACTICE 10   JOINING IDEAS USING AN APPOSITIVE** . . . .

Combine each pair of sentences into a single sentence by using an appositive. Be sure to use a comma or commas to set off the appositive.

EXAMPLE: William Shakespeare *, one of the greatest writers in the English language,* was famous and financially comfortable during his lifetime. ~~Shakespeare was one of the greatest writers in the English language.~~

1. Shakespeare grew up in Stratford, England. He was the son of a former town leader.

2. Shakespeare attended the local grammar school until his father could no longer afford it. His father was a poor manager of money.

3. In 1582, Shakespeare, just eighteen, married twenty-six-year-old Anne Hathaway. She was a farmer's daughter.

4. Three years later, he left for London. London was the center of England's theater world.

5. Young Shakespeare was once a simple country boy. He soon became involved in acting, writing, and managing for one of London's theater companies.

6. By 1592, he was famous enough to be criticized in writing by one of the leading playwrights of the time. This playwright was Robert Greene.

7. Greene's publisher soon printed a public apology for the criticism. This was proof that Shakespeare had won the respect of some influential figures.

8. Shakespeare is said to have performed for Queen Elizabeth I. She was a theater fan and supporter.

9. Eventually, Shakespeare returned to Stratford and purchased a large home where he lived until his death in 1616. The house was called New Place.

10. Shakespeare remains highly popular today, and more than 250 movies have been made of his plays or about his life. His life is a rich enough source of drama for any movie producer.

PRACTICE 11   JOINING IDEAS USING AN APPOSITIVE . . . .

Fill in the blank in each sentence with an appropriate appositive. There are many possible ways to complete each sentence.

> **EXAMPLE:** My sister Clara, <u> *a busy mother of three* </u>, loves to watch soap operas.

1. Clara's favorite show, _____, comes on at three o'clock in the afternoon.

2. Clara, _____, rarely has the time to sit down in front of the television for the broadcast.

3. Instead, she programs her VCR, _____, and tapes the show for later.

4. Clara's husband, _____, used to tease her for watching the soaps.

5. But while he was recovering from the flu recently, he found her stack of tapes, _____, and Clara insists that he watched every show of the previous season.

Join Ideas Using an Adjective Clause

An **adjective clause** is a group of words with a subject and a verb that describes a noun. Adjective clauses often begin with the word *who, which,* or *that* and can be used to combine two sentences into one.

TWO SENTENCES	Lorene owns an art and framing store. She is a good friend of mine.
JOINED WITH AN ADJECTIVE CLAUSE	Lorene, who is a good friend of mine, owns an art and framing store.

To join sentences this way, use *who, which,* or *that* to replace the subject of a sentence that describes a noun that is in the other sentence. Once you have made this change, you have an adjective clause that you can move so that it follows the noun it describes. The sentence with the idea you want to emphasize should become the main clause. The less important idea should be in the adjective clause.

■ Use *who* to refer to a person, *which* to refer to places or things (but not to people), and *that* for places or things.

TWO SENTENCES	Rosalind is director of human services for the town of Marlborough. Marlborough is her hometown.

[The more important idea here is that Rosalind is director of human services. The less important idea is that the town is her hometown.]

JOINED WITH AN ADJECTIVE CLAUSE	Rosalind is director of human services for the town of Marlborough, which is her hometown.

NOTE: If an adjective clause can be taken out of a sentence without completely changing the meaning of the sentence, put commas around the clause.

Lorene, who is a good friend of mine, owns an art and framing store.

[The phrase *who is a good friend of mine* adds information about Lorene, but it is not essential; the sentence *Lorene owns an art and framing store* means almost the same thing as the sentence in the example.]

If an adjective clause is essential to the meaning of a sentence, do not put commas around it.

The meat was recalled for possible salmonella poisoning. I ate it yesterday.

The meat that I ate yesterday was recalled for possible salmonella poisoning.

[The clause *that I ate yesterday* is an essential piece of information. The sentence *The meat was recalled for possible salmonella poisoning* changes significantly with the adjective clause *that I ate yesterday.*]

PRACTICE 12 JOINING IDEAS USING AN ADJECTIVE CLAUSE . . . .

Combine each pair of sentences into a single sentence by using an adjective clause beginning with *who, which,* or *that.*

Allergies that

EXAMPLE: ~~Some allergies~~ cause sneezing, itching, and watery eyes╱

~~They~~ can make people very uncomfortable.

1. Cats produce a protein. It keeps their skin soft.

2. This protein makes some people itch and sneeze. The protein is the reason for most allergic reactions to cats.

3. Some cat lovers are allergic to cats. They can control their allergies with medication.

4. Allergic cat lovers may get another option from a new company. The company wants to create a genetically engineered cat.

5. Scientists have successfully cloned mice. Some mice have been genetically engineered for scientific study.

6. Researchers may soon have the technology to clone cats. Cats could be genetically engineered to remove the allergen.

7. Many people have allergic reactions to cats. According to cat experts, more than 10 percent of those people are allergic to something other than the skin-softening protein.

8. A single gene produces a cat's skin-softening protein. Scientists are not sure whether the gene is necessary for the cat's good health.

9. However, owning a genetically engineered cat would allow an allergic person to avoid taking allergy medications. The medications can sometimes cause dangerous side effects.

10. Cloning and genetic engineering raise ethical questions. These are difficult to answer.

PRACTICE 13   JOINING IDEAS USING AN ADJECTIVE CLAUSE . . . .

Fill in the blank in each of the following sentences with an appropriate adjective clause. Add commas, if necessary. There are many possible ways to complete each sentence.

EXAMPLE: Interactive television ___*, which has started to become available*___ *to consumers,* is a potential threat to viewers' privacy.

1. Many Web sites _____ try to make a profit by selling information about visitors to the site.

2. Consumers _____ must provide information to retail Web sites before being allowed to complete a purchase.

3. Consumer privacy _____ is suffering further with interactive television.

4. A viewer _____ may not realize that the broadcaster is collecting information about him or her.

5. The sale of personal information _____ _____ can bring huge profits.

. . . .

Edit Paragraphs and Your Own Writing

Create sentence variety in the following paragraphs by joining at least two sentences in each of the paragraphs. Try to use several of the techniques discussed in this chapter. There are many possible ways to edit each paragraph. You may want to refer to the chart on page 581.

 EDITING REVIEW 1 . . . .

(1) Rats might be nicer creatures than people think. (2) It's certainly hard to love and appreciate rats. (3) They carry serious diseases like

typhus, salmonella poisoning, and bubonic plague. (4) Rats have such huge appetites that it has been estimated that they destroy as much as one-third of humans' food supplies every year. (5) It has been estimated that rats have been responsible for ten million deaths over the past century alone. (6) Rats in the laboratory should probably be given credit for saving as many lives as wild rats have taken.

(7) Rats are used widely in laboratory research. (8) Rats have many similarities to humans. (9) Young rats are ticklish. (10) When a rat pup is gently scratched at certain spots, such as the nape of the neck, it will squeal. (11) The squeal can be heard only with an ultrasound scan. (12) The squeal has a similar soundgram pattern to that of a human giggle. (13) Rats can get addicted to the same drugs that humans do. (14) Rats crave alcohol, nicotine, amphetamine, and cocaine. (15) Rats can also overindulge. (16) They can continue consuming food or drugs until they die.

(17) Studies also show that rats, similar to humans, have personalities. (18) They can be sad or cheerful depending on how they were raised and their circumstances. (19) Rats that have been raised in stable, caring conditions tend to be optimists. (20) Rats reared in uneven and unreliable conditions are likely to be pessimists. (21) Both types of rats can learn to connect a certain sound with getting food. (22) They also can associate another sound with no food. (23) However, when they hear a new sound, the two types of rats react differently. (24) The new sound is not associated with either food or no food. (25) The optimist will run to the food dispenser. (26) It is expecting to be fed. (27) The pessimist will go somewhere else. (28) It is expecting nothing.

(29) Rats can express kindness. (30) Researchers put pairs of female rats who were littermates in a cage but separated by wire mesh. (31) In each half of the cage, a rat could pull a lever that would deliver food to her sister but not to herself. (32) Each rat learned to be a giver of food and a recipient of a gift of food from her sister. (33) Then, one of the rats was replaced by an unfamiliar and unrelated rat that had never learned about the food gift process. (34) Those rats who had recently received food gifts were 21 percent more likely to pull the lever to give food to their new, unknown partners. (35) The researchers believe that these rats were generous only because another rat had just been kind to them. (36) Perhaps there is more to the rodents than previously thought.

EDITING REVIEW 2

(1) Employees once wanted nothing more than to stay at their jobs as long as possible. (2) They also viewed career advancement as a high priority. (3) The optimal situation was to be valued on the job. (4) This brought rewards of satisfaction and money as well as the attainment of higher rungs on the corporate ladder. (5) Today's young employees are going in a different direction. (6) Young workers these days have some expectations that few, if any, jobs could satisfy.

(7) A twenty-eight-year-old designer at an architecture firm had two weeks of vacation every year. (8) This is the standard vacation for most young employees. (9) Employees are commonly encouraged to take only one of these weeks off at a time. (10) Many have trouble finding time to take any vacation at all. (11) The designer arranged to take a job with another firm. (12) He then resigned from his current firm. (13) His new

firm agreed that he could begin work in four weeks. (14) He then left on a leisurely motorcycle trip beginning in the South, swinging over to the Rocky Mountains and returning across the Great Plains. (15) He chose an alternative to the entry-level two-week vacation. (16) He quit, went on an adventure, and then started a new job.

(17) A thirty-three-year-old bankruptcy lawyer was focused on a similar quest. (18) She quit her job, had an extended visit with her family, traveled for four months through New Zealand, Australia, Southeast Asia, and central Europe and then found a new job at a different law firm. (19) In another telling example, a software engineer, thirty-two, worked hard with little vacation during the ten years he was with his company. (20) He quit to live his dream of visiting all fifty-eight national parks. (21) His skills were in demand. (22) He did not worry about finding another job but was concerned about getting burned out again. (23) Growing up in a time of relative prosperity and economic stability, these workers can usually find new jobs. (24) This is perhaps a major difference between today's young employees and the generation before them.

(25) A twenty-seven-year-old minister and his wife left their posts in Colorado Springs for new positions at a church in Philadelphia. (26) They took six weeks off between jobs. (27) They say the six weeks of unemployment was healthy. (28) They maintain that they are not defined by what they do but by who they are. (29) They are emblematic of their generation of workers. (30) They took time off to renew relationships and pursue experiences that helped them reach a comfortable balance between work and life.

**PRACTICE 14   EDITING YOUR OWN WRITING
FOR SENTENCE VARIETY** . . . .

As a final practice, edit a piece of your own writing for sentence variety. It can be a paper you are working on for this course, a paper you've already finished, a paper for another course, a recent piece of writing from your work or everyday life, or your idea journal entry. You may want to use the following chart as you edit.

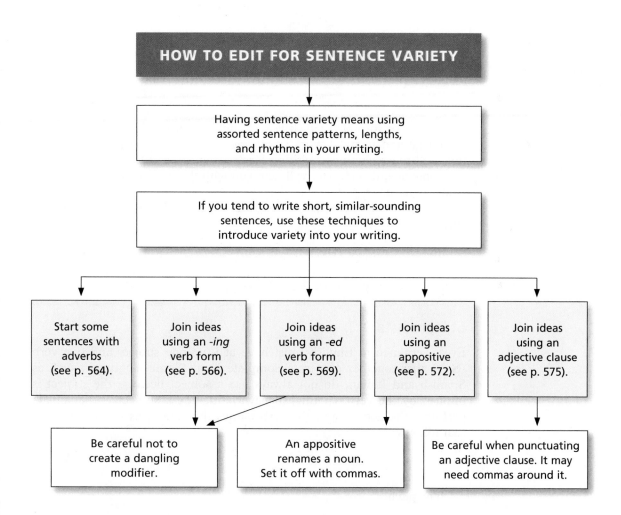

HOW TO EDIT FOR SENTENCE VARIETY

Having sentence variety means using assorted sentence patterns, lengths, and rhythms in your writing.

If you tend to write short, similar-sounding sentences, use these techniques to introduce variety into your writing.

Start some sentences with adverbs (see p. 564).

Join ideas using an *-ing* verb form (see p. 566).

Join ideas using an *-ed* verb form (see p. 569).

Join ideas using an appositive (see p. 572).

Join ideas using an adjective clause (see p. 575).

Be careful not to create a dangling modifier.

An appositive renames a noun. Set it off with commas.

Be careful when punctuating an adjective clause. It may need commas around it.

33

Formal English and ESL

Grammar Trouble Spots for Multilingual Students

■ **IDEA JOURNAL**
Write about a cultural or religious family tradition.

Academic, or formal, English is the English you will be expected to use in college and in most work situations, especially in writing. If you are not used to speaking and writing formal English or if English is not your first language, this chapter will help you with the most common problems students have.

NOTE: In this chapter, we use the word *English* to refer to formal English.

Basic Sentence Patterns

Statements

Every sentence in English must have at least one subject and one verb **(S-V)** that together express a complete idea. (Some languages, such as Spanish and Italian, do not always use a subject because the subject is implied by the verb. In English, always include a subject.) The subject performs the action, and the verb names the action, as in the sentence that follows.

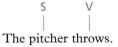

S   V

The pitcher throws.

Other English sentence patterns build on that structure. One of the most common patterns is subject-verb-object **(S-V-O)**.

The pitcher throws the ball.

There are two kinds of objects.

- A *direct object* receives the action of the verb.

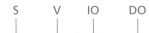

The pitcher throws the ball.

[The ball directly receives the action of the verb *throws*.]

- An *indirect object* does not receive the action of the verb. Instead, the action is performed *for* or *to* the person.

The pitcher throws me the ball.

or

The pitcher throws the ball to me.

[In both of these sentences, the word *me* doesn't receive the action of the verb, *throws*. The action is performed *to* the person.]

■ For other common English sentence patterns, see Chapter 22.

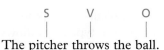 **PRACTICE 1   SENTENCE PATTERNS** . . . .

Label the subject (S), verb (V), direct object (DO), and indirect object (IO) in the following three sentences.

1. John sent the letter.

2. John sent Beth the letter.

3. John sent the letter to Beth.

. . . .

Note that the **S-V-O** pattern differs from the sentence patterns in some other languages. For example, in some languages (like Arabic) the pattern may be **S-O-V**; other languages don't have as strictly defined a word order (Spanish, Italian, and Russian, for example).

■ For more on
prepositions, see
pages 622–26. For
more on the parts
of sentences, see
Chapter 22.

Another common sentence pattern is subject-verb-prepositional phrase. In standard English, the prepositional phrase typically follows the subject and verb.

S   V   Prepositional phrase

Lilah went to the movies.

■ **PRACTICE 2 USING CORRECT WORD ORDER** . . . .

■ Answers to odd-
numbered practice
items are at the back
of the book.

Read each of the sentences that follow. If the sentence is correct, write "C" in the blank to the left of it. If it is incorrect, write "I" and rewrite the sentence using correct word order.

EXAMPLE: __I__ The ball to me Sara threw.

REVISION: _Sara threw the ball to me._

____ 1. Sports Sara likes a lot.

REVISION: _____

■ For more
practice with ESL
grammar issues, visit
Exercise Central at
**bedfordstmartins
.com/realessays**.

____ 2. To baseball camp she went this spring.

REVISION: _____

____ 3. At the camp, she met many other good players.

REVISION: _____

____ 4. At the end of camp, she gave to the other players her address.

REVISION: _____

_____

____ 5. With them she will try to stay in touch.

REVISION: _____

Negatives

To form a negative statement, use one of these words, often with a helping verb such as *can/could, does/did, has/have,* or *should/will/would.*

never	nobody	no one	nowhere
no	none	not	

Notice in the example sentences that the word *not* comes *after* the helping verb.

SENTENCE	The baby can talk.
NEGATIVE	The baby ~~no can~~ talk. *(cannot)*
SENTENCE	The store sells cigarettes.
NEGATIVE	The store ~~no~~ sells cigarettes. *(does not)*
SENTENCE	Jonah talks too much.
NEGATIVE	Jonah not talks too much. *(does)*
SENTENCE	Johnetta will call.
NEGATIVE	Johnetta ~~no~~ will call. *(not)*
SENTENCE	Caroline called.
NEGATIVE	Caroline ~~no~~ did call. *(not)*
SENTENCE	Paul will come.
NEGATIVE	Paul ~~no~~ will come. *(not)*

Common Helping Verbs

FORMS OF *BE*	FORMS OF *HAVE*	FORMS OF *DO*	OTHER VERBS
am	have	do	can
are	has	does	could
been	had	did	may
being			might
is			must
was			should
were			will

The helping verb cannot be omitted in expressions using *not*.

■ For more on help-ing verbs and their forms, see Chapter 22.

INCORRECT	The store *not sell* cigarettes.
CORRECT	The store *does not sell* cigarettes.

[*Does,* a form of the helping verb *do,* must come before *not.*]

CORRECT   The store *is not selling* cigarettes.

[*Is,* a form of *be,* must come before *not.*]

Double negatives are not standard in English.

INCORRECT   Johnetta *will not call no one.*

CORRECT   Johnetta *will not call anyone.*

CORRECT   Johnetta *will call no one.*

INCORRECT   Shane *does not have no* ride.

CORRECT   Shane *does not have a* ride

CORRECT   Shane *has no* ride.

When forming a negative in the simple past tense, use the past tense of the helping verb *do.*

did + *not* + base verb without an *-ed* = negative past tense

SENTENCE   I *talked* to Kayla last night.

[*Talked* is the past tense.]

NEGATIVE   I *did not* talk to Kayla last night.

[Note that *talk* in this sentence does not have an *-ed* ending because the helping verb *did* conveys that past.]

■ For forming nega-
tives in other tenses,
see pages 478–88 and
596–608.

SENTENCE   Kerry *passed* the test.

NEGATIVE   Kerry *did not* pass the test.

■ PRACTICE 3   **FORMING NEGATIVES** . . . .

Rewrite the sentences to make them negative.

                                                        not
EXAMPLE: **Jamal's computer is working too quickly.**
                                                        ^

1. It starts up as fast as it used to.

2. Jamal remembers how fast it once started.

3. He is definitely happy with its speed now.

4. He wants to spend the money for a new computer.

5. He earned enough money last year from his part-time job to pay for it.

6. His health allowed him to work for many hours.

7. He expects his computer to speed up all by itself.

8. Jamal's friends are very sympathetic about his problem.

9. Most of their computers are still as fast as his.

10. He tries to complain about it too much.

. . . .

Questions

To turn a statement into a question, move the helping verb so that it comes before the subject. Add a question mark (**?**) to the end of the question.

STATEMENT	Danh *can work* late.
QUESTION	*Can* Danh *work* late?

If the only verb in the statement is a form of *be*, it should be moved before the subject.

STATEMENT	Phuong *is* smart.	Jamie *is* at work.
QUESTION	*Is* Phuong smart?	*Is* Jamie at work?

If there is no helping verb or form of *be* in the statement, add a form of *do* and put it before the subject. Be sure to end the question with a question mark (**?**).

STATEMENT	Norah sings in the choir.
QUESTION	*Does* Norah sing in the choir?
STATEMENT	Amy visited the elderly woman.
QUESTION	*Did* Amy visit the elderly woman?
STATEMENT	The building burned.
QUESTION	*Did* the building burn?

Notice that the verb *visited* changed to *visit* and the verb *burned* to *burn* once the helping verb *did* was added.

■ For more on questions, see Chapters 25 and 26.

> **Language Note:** *Do* is used with *I, you, we,* and *they. Does* is used with *he, she,* and *it.*
>
> **EXAMPLES**   *Do* [I, you, we, they] practice every day?
>
> *Does* [he, she, it] sound terrible?

PRACTICE 4   USING QUESTIONS . . . .

Rewrite the sentences to make them into questions.

EXAMPLE: ~~All~~ *Are all* students ~~are~~ invited to work at our campus radio station./

1. You host a program on the station.

2. Any student can submit a proposal to host a program.

3. You submitted your proposal to host in your freshman year.

4. You were able to get on the air that same year.

5. You had many problems with your program in that first year.

6. People actually listen to your program on the station.

7. Preparing your program is both fun and hard work.

8. I should prepare my program ideas right away.

9. I must be careful to prepare enough content to fill an entire time slot.

10. New radio hosts usually get time slots in the middle of the night.

There Is and There Are

English sentences often include *there is* or *there are* to indicate the existence of something.

There is a man at the door.   [You could also say, *A man is at the door.*]

There are many men in the class.   [You could also say, *Many men are in the class.*]

When a sentence includes the words *there is* or *there are,* the verb (*is, are*) comes before the noun it goes with. The verb must agree with the noun in number. For example, the first sentence above uses the singular verb *is* to agree with the singular noun *man,* and the second sentence uses the plural verb *are* to agree with the plural noun *men.*

Language Note: The *there is/there are* structure does not exist in some other languages, so speakers of those languages sometimes leave out these words when writing in English.

INCORRECT	My mother said much work to do.
	Much work to do.
CORRECT	My mother said *there is* much work to do.
	There is much work to do.

In questions, the word order in *there is* and *there are* is inverted.

STATEMENTS	*There is* plenty to eat.
	There are some things to do.
QUESTIONS	*Is there* plenty to eat?
	Are there some things to do?

PRACTICE 5   USING *THERE IS* AND *THERE ARE* . . . .

In each of the following sentences, fill in the blank with *there is* or *there are.* Remember that these words are inverted in questions.

EXAMPLE: **Although my parents are busy constantly, they say**
____*there is*____ **always more that can be done.**

1. Every morning, _____ flowers to water and weeds to pull.

2. Later in the day, _____ more chores, like mowing the lawn or cleaning out the garage.

3. I always ask, " _____ anything I can do?"

4. They are too polite to say that _____ work that they need help with.

5. If _____ more productive parents in the world, I'd be surprised.

· ·

Pronouns

■ For more on pronouns, see Chapter 27.

Pronouns replace nouns or other pronouns in a sentence so that you do not have to repeat them. There are three types of pronouns:

- **Subject pronouns** serve as the subject of the verb (and every English sentence must have a subject).

  Jonah is my cousin. ~~Jonah~~ lives next door to me.

He

- **Object pronouns** receive the action of the verb or are part of a prepositional phrase.

  Jonah asked *me* for a ride.

  [The object pronoun *me* receives the action of the verb, *asked*.]

  Jonah is my cousin. He lives next door *to me*.

  [*To me* is the prepositional phrase; *me* is the object pronoun.]

- **Possessive pronouns** show ownership.

  Jonah is *my* cousin.

Use the following chart to check which type of pronoun to use.

Pronoun Types

SUBJECT		OBJECT		POSSESSIVE	
SINGULAR	**PLURAL**	**SINGULAR**	**PLURAL**	**SINGULAR**	**PLURAL**
I	we	me	us	my/mine	our/ours
you	you	you	you	your/yours	your/yours
he/she/it	they	him/her/it	them	his/her/hers/its	theirs
RELATIVE PRONOUNS					
who, which, that					

The singular pronouns *he/she, him/her,* and *his/hers* show gender. *He, him,* and *his* are masculine pronouns; *she, her,* and *hers* are feminine.

Here are some examples of common pronoun errors, with corrections.

Confusing Subject and Object Pronouns

Use a subject pronoun for the word that *performs* the action of the verb, and use an object pronoun for the word that *receives* the action.

> *She*
> Dora is a good student. ~~Her~~ gets all A's.

[The pronoun performs the action *gets,* so it should be the subject pronoun, *she.*]

> *her*
> Tomas gave the keys to she.

[The pronoun receives the action of *gave,* so it should be the object pronoun, *her.*]

Confusing Gender

Use masculine pronouns to replace masculine nouns and feminine pronouns to replace feminine nouns.

> *He*
> Gordon passed the test. ~~She~~ got a B.

[*Gordon* is a masculine noun, so the pronoun must be masculine.]

> *him*
> The iPod belongs to Michael. Carla gave it to ~~her~~.

[*Michael* is masculine, so the pronoun must be masculine.]

Leaving Out a Pronoun

Some sentences use the pronoun *it* as the subject or object. Do not leave *it* out of the sentence.

> *It is*
> Is my birthday today.

> *It will*
> Annahita will travel by bus. ~~Will~~ arrive at 3:00.

> *it*
> I tried calamari last night and liked very much.

Using a Pronoun to Repeat a Subject

Pronouns *replace* a noun, so do not use both a subject noun and a pronoun.

The boss ~~he~~ is very mean.

[*Boss* is the subject noun, so the sentence does not also need a subject pronoun.]

The baseball ~~it~~ broke the window.

[*Baseball* is the subject, so no pronoun is needed.]

Using Relative Pronouns

The words *who, which,* and *that* are **relative pronouns**. Use relative pronouns in a phrase or clause that gives more information about the subject.

- Use *who* to refer to a person or people.

  The man *who* owns the building is strange.

- Use *which* to refer to nonliving things.

  The building, *which* was just painted, is for sale.

- Use *that* to refer to either people or nonliving things. (Note that *who* is the preferred pronoun to refer to a person or people.)

  The building *that* my uncle owns is for sale.

  The present *that* you gave me is great.

■ **PRACTICE 6 USING THE CORRECT PRONOUN TYPE** . . . .

Fill in the blanks in the sentences with the correct type of pronoun (subject, object, or possessive). Use the chart on page 590 to help you.

> **EXAMPLE:** Working in a foreign country after graduation can help
> ___*your*___ future career opportunities.

1. My friend Felicia said she taught English in Japan for a year after _____

   graduation.

2. Felicia was the one in _____ group _____ was always cautious about

   trying new things.

3. _____ was a little nervous at the beginning of her year abroad, but

   _____ soon became interesting and rewarding.

4. Not only did her students learn from _____, but she said she learned from _____ as well.

5. Living in a foreign country for a year is a great way to learn _____ language.

6. Another friend, Jared, said _____ Spanish became fluent after he traveled through Chile for a year.

7. Jared is someone _____ spirit of adventure _____ have always admired.

8. As he backpacked around the country, he met _____ people and spoke _____ language.

9. Jared told me that working abroad probably wouldn't make much money for _____, but _____ would give me something worth more than money.

10. He worked at picking grapes and cooking in a restaurant, and he said _____ gave _____ some priceless experience.

11. _____ was not experience _____ seems very professional, but he says it helped _____ to grow.

12. Upon _____ return, Jared wanted a job at a company at _____ he could continue to grow.

13. He met with several job interviewers, for _____ there was always one main topic of interest: his time in Chile.

14. Most of _____ told _____ his foreign travel demonstrated his resourcefulness, independence, and strength of character.

15. My Chinese studies have interested _____ in working in China, a country _____ I would love to get to know from the inside.

Verbs

Learning how to use the various verb tenses and verb forms is a challenge for everyone (I know from trying to learn Spanish for the past few years). This section will give you examples and practices that build on what you learned in Chapter 26. To complete the practices, you will need to refer to the verb charts in that chapter (see pages with green bands down the side).

The Simple Tenses

The Simple Present

Use the simple present to describe situations that exist now.

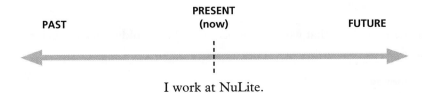

PAST

PRESENT
(now)

FUTURE

I work at NuLite.

Be and Have, Simple Present.   These two verbs can be confusing because they work differently in English in the simple present than they do in some other languages, such as Spanish.

BE		HAVE	
SINGULAR	**PLURAL**	**SINGULAR**	**PLURAL**
I *am*	We *are*	I *have*	We *have*
You *are*	You *are*	You *have*	You *have*
He/she/it *is*	They *are*	He/she/it *has*	They *have*

English uses *be* and *have* as follows:

- To express *age,* use *be.*

INCORRECT	I *have* twenty-two years.

CORRECT	I *am* twenty-two.

  I *am* twenty-two years old.

- To express *emotion,* use *be.*

  INCORRECT   She *has* sadness.

  CORRECT   She *is* sad. [Note that the word that expresses the emotion changes. You do not need an ending.]

- To express a *physical condition,* use *be.*

  INCORRECT   They *have* hunger.

  CORRECT   They *are* hungry. [The physical condition is first expressed by a noun (*hunger*) and then by an adjective (*hungry*).]

- To express family size, use *have.*

  INCORRECT   In my family, we *are* eight.

  CORRECT   In my family, we *have* eight people.
  My family *has* eight people.

The exception to this rule is when the description of family size begins with the words *there are* (a form of the verb *be*):

  CORRECT   In my family, *there are* eight people.

PRACTICE 7   USING *BE* AND *HAVE* IN THE SIMPLE PRESENT TENSE . . . .

Circle the correct verb in each of the following sentences.

    EXAMPLE: There ((are) / have) four of us in our dorm suite.

1. Each of us (is / has) favorite candidates in the upcoming election.

2. Every one of us (is / has) at least eighteen years old.

3. We finally (are / have) the chance to vote.

4. Nadia (is / has) especially proud to be casting her ballot.

5. I (am / have) also excited to have my opinion counted.

6. But some of our friends (are / have) not voting on Election Day.

7. They (are / have) no interest in who gets elected.

8. We (are / have) upset about their lack of interest.

9. In a democracy, every citizen (is / has) the right and, we believe, the obligation to vote.

10. Voting (is / has) an important way of strengthening our democracy.

Negatives. To form the simple present negative of any verb, add the present form of *do* (*does*), the negative *not,* and the verb without an ending.

subject + *do not/does not* + base form of verb

PRESENT	NEGATIVE
Jill *believes* everything she reads. [The verb *believe* has the present-tense ending *s.*]	Jill *does not believe* everything she reads. [In the negative, the present is expressed by the present tense of *do* (*does*). The verb *believe* does not have an ending.]
Carson and Manny *build* houses.	Carson and Manny *do not build* houses.

Questions. To form a question in the simple present tense, add the present-tense form of *do* (*does*), followed by the subject, followed by the verb without an ending.

do/does + subject + base form of verb

Does Jill *believe* everything she reads?

Do Carson and Manny *build* houses?

Negative Questions. *doesn't/don't* + subject + base form of verb

Doesn't Jill *believe* everything she reads?

Don't Carson and Manny *build* houses?

■   **PRACTICE 8   USING THE SIMPLE PRESENT TENSE** . . . .

On a separate piece of paper, rewrite each of the following sentences in two forms—in a negative form and as a question. Note that some sentences use regular verbs and some use irregular verbs. You may need to refer to the chart of irregular verbs on pages 469–72.

EXAMPLE: Kevin maintains two different blogs.

(negative)   _Kevin does not maintain two different blogs._

(question)   _Does Kevin maintain two different blogs?_

1. He writes his "public" blog for anyone who wants to see it.

2. He even tells his parents to read it.

3. He writes there about politics, his courses, and some music he likes.

4. He chooses topics that are rather general for this blog.

5. This blog gets comments from a wide range of people.

6. Kevin makes his other blog much more personal.

7. He gives only his close friends access to this blog.

8. He includes his thoughts about specific events and his views on life in general.

9. He uses incorrect grammar and loose organization for his entries here.

10. He finds that he learns and grows a lot from writing both of his blogs.

. . . .

The Simple Past

Use the simple past to describe situations that began and ended in the past.

I worked at NuLite Company.

Regular verbs in the simple past are formed by adding *-ed*; if the verb already ends in *e*, add only *d*.

PRESENT	PAST
Karina plays in the band.	Karina *played* in the band.
Toby practices every day.	Toby *practiced* every day.

Irregular past-tense verbs do not follow that rule: They are formed in other ways. For a chart of irregular past-tense verbs, see pages 469–72.

Negatives.   To form the simple past of any verb, add the past form of *do* (*did*), the negative *not*, and the verb without an ending.

$$\boxed{\text{subject}} \; + \; \boxed{\textit{did not}} \; + \; \boxed{\text{base verb}}$$

Selena *did not call*. [The verb *did*—the past tense of *do*—expresses the past. The verb *call* is the base verb with no *-ed* ending.]

Terry *did not run* in the race. [*Run* is the base form of the verb. The past is expressed by the verb *did*.]

Questions.   To form a question in the simple past, add the past form of *do* (*did*) and the verb without an ending.

$$\boxed{\textit{did}} \; + \; \boxed{\text{subject}} \; + \; \boxed{\text{base verb}}$$

Did Selena *call* her mother? [The verb *did*—the past tense of *do*—expresses the past. The verb *call* has no past ending; it is the base form.]

Did Terry and Jan *run* in the race?

Negative Questions. $\boxed{\textit{didn't}} \; + \; \boxed{\text{subject}} \; + \; \boxed{\text{base verb}}$

Didn't Selena call her mother?

Didn't Terry and Jan *run* in the race?

■   **PRACTICE 9   USING THE SIMPLE PAST TENSE** . . . .

On a separate piece of paper, rewrite each of the following sentences to express three forms—the past tense, a past negative, and a past question. Note that some sentences use regular verbs and some use irregular verbs. You may need to refer to the chart of irregular verbs on pages 469–72.

EXAMPLE: Terri likes to drive long distances.

(past)   *Terri liked to drive long distances.*

(past negative)   *Terri did not like to drive long distances.*

(past question)   *Did Terri like to drive long distances?*

1. She especially enjoys highway driving.

2. The rest of us love to sleep on the long drive to the city.

3. Luis annoys all of us by his snoring.

4. The sound of his snoring gets loud and irritating.

5. Genine calls out Luis's name.

6. This makes his snoring louder.

7. Genine pokes Luis's arm gently.

8. Luis wakes up angrily.

9. We choose to stay awake for the rest of the drive.

10. This keeps the peace between Luis and the rest of us.

· ·

Be, **Past Negative.**   The verb *be* can be confusing in the past tense, especially when it is used in a negative statement. The chart that follows shows how to form the negative past of the verb *be*.

BE, PAST TENSE, NEGATIVE	
SINGULAR	**PLURAL**
I *was* not	We *were* not
You *were* not	You *were* not
He/she/it *was* not	They *were* not

The Simple Future

The future tense is used to describe situations that will happen in the future. It is easier to form than the present and past tenses. Form the simple future using this formula:

| *will* | + | base form of verb |

I *will finish* soon.   We *will finish* soon.

You *will finish* soon.   You *will finish* soon.

He/she/it *will finish* soon. They *will finish* soon.

The Progressive Tenses

The Present Progressive

Use the present progressive to describe situations that are happening now but began in the past.

PAST   PRESENT
                        (now)   FUTURE

I am studying too much.

Statements. | subject | + | *am/are/is* | + | base verb with *-ing* ending |

SIMPLE PRESENT	PRESENT PROGRESSIVE
I *study* too much.	I *am studying* too much.
They *sing* in the choir.	They *are singing* in the choir.

Negatives. | subject | + | *am not/is not/are not* | + | base verb with *-ing* ending |

I *am not studying* too much.

They *are not singing* in the choir.

Questions. | *am/is/are* | + | subject | + | base verb with *-ing* ending |

Am I *studying* too much?

Are they *singing* in the choir?

Negative questions. | *isn't/aren't* | + | subject | + | base verb with *-ing* ending |

Isn't he *studying* too much?

Aren't they *singing* in the choir?

PRACTICE 10   USING THE PRESENT PROGRESSIVE TENSE . . . .

On a separate piece of paper, rewrite each of the sentences below in three forms—present progressive, present progressive negative, and present progressive question.

EXAMPLE:	We hike up a fairly high mountain.

(present progressive)   *We are hiking up a fairly high mountain.*

(present progressive   *We are not hiking up a fairly high mountain.*
negative)

(present progressive   *Are we hiking up a fairly high mountain?*
question)

1. I bring a lot of water for the hike.

2. Roger takes chocolate bars along in his backpack.

3. He gives away chocolate to anyone who wants it.

4. I try to do without a chocolate snack on this hike.

5. This winding trail gets steep.

6. I feel a need for a chocolate boost of energy.

7. I ask Roger for one of his energy bars.

8. He searches his backpack for any remaining chocolate.

9. Roger's chocolate helps me to keep on climbing.

10. Several of us thank Roger for his generosity and thoughtful preparation.

The Past Progressive

Use the past progressive to describe situations that were going on in the past.

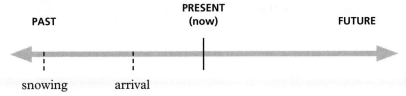

It was snowing when we arrived.

Statements.   subject + *was* + base verb with *-ing* ending

SIMPLE PAST	PAST PROGRESSIVE
The car *started* slowly.	The car *was starting* slowly last week.
We *parked* next to the restaurant.	We *were parking* when the car stalled.

Negatives.   subject + *was not/were not* + base verb with *-ing* ending

The car *was not starting* slowly last week.

We *were not parking* when the car stalled.

Questions.   *was/were* + subject + base verb with *-ing* ending

Was the car *starting* slowly last week?

Were we *parking* when the car stalled?

Negative questions.

wasn't/weren't + subject + base verb with *-ing* ending

Wasn't the car *starting* slowly last week?

Weren't we *parking* when the car stalled?

The Future Progressive

Use the future progressive to describe situations that began and ended before some other situation that happened.

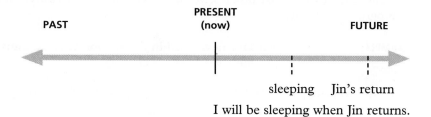

PAST ← → FUTURE
PRESENT (now)

sleeping   Jin's return

I will be sleeping when Jin returns.

The future progressive describes situations that will be ongoing in the future. It is easier to form than the present and past progressive tenses. Form the progressive future using this formula:

will be + base form of verb with *-ing* ending

I *will be finishing* soon.   We *will be finishing* soon.

You *will be finishing* soon.   You *will be finishing* soon.

He/she/it *will be finishing* soon. They *will be finishing* soon.

Negatives.   subject + *will not be* + base form of verb with *-ing* ending

I *will not be finishing* soon.   They *will not be finishing* soon.

Questions.   *will* + subject + *be* + base form of verb with *-ing* ending

Will you *be finishing* soon?   *Will* they *be finishing* soon?

Negative questions.

won't + subject + *be* + base form of verb with *-ing* ending

Won't you *be finishing* soon?   *Won't* they *be finishing* soon?

PRACTICE 11 USING THE PAST AND FUTURE PROGRESSIVE TENSES . . . .

On a separate sheet of paper, rewrite each of the following sentences in four forms—past progressive, past progressive negative, future progressive, and future progressive negative.

EXAMPLE: Samantha worked in the school cafeteria during the spring semester.

(past progressive)
Samantha was working in the school cafeteria during the spring semester.

(past progressive negative)
Samantha was not working in the school cafeteria during the spring semester.

(future progressive)
Samantha will be working in the school cafeteria during the spring semester.

(future progressive negative)
Samantha will not be working in the school cafeteria during the spring semester.

1. At first, she washed dishes, pots, and pans.

2. Soon, she staffed the cash register.

3. Then, Samantha assisted the chefs in the kitchen.

4. Later, Samantha served students at the sandwich and wrap counter.

5. In the end, she did the job she wanted most of all.

6. Samantha learned to cook for large numbers of people.

7. She followed the directions of the experienced chefs.

8. In the beginning, she memorized all of the cafeteria recipes.

9. After a while, she began to create her own recipes.

10. By the end of the semester, Samantha managed one of the cafeteria crews.

The Perfect Tenses

The Present Perfect

Use the present perfect to describe situations that started in the past and are still happening.

PAST   **PRESENT (now)**   **FUTURE**

We have known the Sanchez family for years.

Before you do this section, you might want to review past participles in Chapter 26. A past participle is the past form of the verb used with a helping verb.

Statements.   subject   +   *has/have*   +   past participle of base verb

SIMPLE PRESENT	PRESENT PERFECT
Dona *works* every night.	Dona *has worked* every night this week. [Dona started working earlier in the week and is still working.]
We *know* the Sanchez family.	We *have known* the Sanchez family for years.

Negatives.   subject   +   *has not/have not*   +   past participle of base verb

Dona *has not worked* every night this week.

We *have not known* the Sanchez family for very long.

Questions.   *has/have*   +   subject   +   past participle of base verb

Has Dona *worked* every night this week?

Have we *known* the Sanchez family for years?

Negative questions.

  hasn't/haven't   +   subject   +   past participle of base verb

Hasn't Dona *worked* every night this week?

Haven't we *known* the Sanchez family for years?

Sometimes people confuse the **simple past** with the **present perfect**. The simple past describes situations that began and ended in the past, while the present perfect describes situations that began in the past and are still happening.

SIMPLE PAST	PRESENT PERFECT
Dona *worked* every night last week. [Last week is over, so what Dona did happened and ended in the past.]	Dona *has worked* every night this week. [Dona began working at night earlier in the week and is still working at night.]

 PRACTICE 12 USING THE PRESENT-PERFECT TENSE . . . .

On a separate sheet of paper, rewrite each of the sentences below in three forms—present-perfect statement, present-perfect negative, and present-perfect question.

EXAMPLE: Jenna always likes to play challenging board games.

(present-perfect statement) *Jenna has always liked to play challenging board games.*

(present-perfect negative) *Jenna has not always liked to play challenging board games.*

(present-perfect question) *Has Jenna always liked to play challenging board games?*

1. Many of her friends also enjoy these games.

2. Sometimes, they play games far into the night.

3. Jenna decides to start a club for game players.

4. She goes through all the procedures for starting a school club.

5. She reserves a large room for every Sunday afternoon.

6. Jenna brings all of the games she owns to the gatherings.

7. She welcomes everyone to bring their own games as well.

8. The players make sure to emphasize the enjoyment of each other's company.

9. They keep it from getting overly competitive.

10. Their club develops a devoted following.

• •

The Past Perfect

Use the past perfect to describe situations that began and ended before some other situation happened.

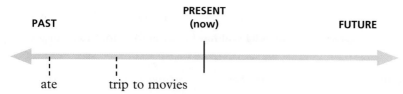

I had eaten before I went to the movies.

Statements. subject + had + past participle of base verb

PRESENT PERFECT	PAST PERFECT
Julia *has finished* the test.	Julia *had finished* the test before I started.
We *have voted*.	We *had voted* before the crowds arrived.

Negatives. subject + had not + past participle of base verb

Julia *had not finished* her test before I started.

We *had not voted* before the crowds arrived.

Questions. had + subject + past participle of base verb

Had Julia *finished* the test before I started?

Had they *voted* before the crowds arrived?

Negative questions.   *hadn't* + subject + past participle of base verb

Hadn't Julia *finished* the test before I started?

Hadn't they *voted* before the crowds arrived?

The Future Perfect

Use the future perfect to describe situations that begin and end before another situation begins.

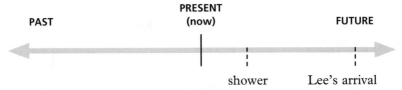

I will have showered before Lee comes.

Statements.   subject + *will have* + past participle of base verb

PRESENT PERFECT	FUTURE PERFECT
The teacher *has graded* the tests.	The teacher *will have graded* the tests before she returns them.
The runners *have finished* the race.	The runners *will have finished* the race before rush hour.

Negatives.   subject + *will not have* + past participle of base verb

The teacher *will not have graded* the tests before she returns them.

The runners *will not have finished* the race before rush hour.

Questions.   *will* + subject + *have* + past participle of base verb

Will the teacher *have graded* the test before she returns them?

Will the runners *have finished* the race before rush hour?

Negative questions.   *won't* + subject + *have* + past participle of base verb

Won't the teacher *have graded* the test before she returns them?

Won't the runners *have finished* the race before rush hour?

PRACTICE 13   USING THE PAST AND FUTURE PERFECT TENSES . . . .

On a separate piece of paper, rewrite each of the sentences below in four forms—past perfect, past-perfect negative, future perfect, and future-perfect negative. Use the phrase(s) provided in parentheses if necessary for meaning.

EXAMPLE:	The train has left the station. (before I got there/before I get there)

(past perfect) — *The train had left the station before I got there.*

(past-perfect negative) — *The train had not left the station before I got there.*

(future perfect) — *The train will have left the station before I get there.*

(future-perfect negative) — *The train will not have left the station before I get there.*

1. Jorge has finished his ice cream. (*by closing time*)

2. The bears have gone to sleep. (*after their morning feeding/before their morning feeding*)

3. Selena has called the doctor. (*after taking her temperature*)

4. The race has ended. (*almost before it started/almost before it starts*)

5. The battery has failed. (*before we got a new one/before we get a new one*)

6. Our team has played harder. (*after hearing that our rival lost their game/after hearing that our rival loses their game*)

7. You have completed your research. (*when I turned in my paper/when I turn in my paper*)

8. Victor has arranged a summer internship. (*by the end of the semester*)

9. He has eaten his main course. (*after his dessert*)

10. The new statistics have arrived. (*in time to include them in our report*)

Gerunds and Infinitives

A **gerund** is a verb form that ends in *-ing* and acts as a noun. An **infinitive** is a verb form that is preceded by the word *to*. Gerunds and infinitives cannot be the main verbs in sentences; each sentence must have another word that is the main verb.

GERUND   I like *running*.

[*Like* is the main verb, and *running* is a gerund.]

INFINITIVE   I like *to run*.

[*Like* is the main verb, and *to run* is an infinitive.]

How do you decide whether to use a gerund or an infinitive? The decision often depends on the main verb in a sentence. Some verbs can be followed by either a gerund or an infinitive.

■ To improve your ability to write and speak standard English, read magazines and your local newspaper, and listen to television and radio news programs. Read magazines and newspaper articles aloud; it will help your pronunciation.

Verbs That Are Followed by Either a Gerund or an Infinitive

begin	forget	like	remember	stop
continue	hate	love	start	try

Sometimes, using an infinitive or gerund after one of the verbs listed in the preceding box results in the same meaning.

GERUND   I love *listening* to Ray Charles.

INFINITIVE   I love *to listen* to Ray Charles.

Other times, however, the meaning changes depending on whether you use an infinitive or a gerund.

INFINITIVE   Mario stopped to smoke.

[This sentence means that Mario stopped what he was doing and smoked a cigarette.]

GERUND   Mario stopped smoking.

[This sentence means that Mario no longer smokes cigarettes.]

Verbs That Are Followed by an Infinitive

agree	decide	need	refuse
ask	expect	offer	want
beg	fail	plan	
choose	hope	pretend	
claim	manage	promise	

Tony *expects to get* a raise.

Lana *plans to adopt* a child.

Verbs That Are Followed by a Gerund

admit	discuss	keep	risk
avoid	enjoy	miss	suggest
consider	finish	practice	
deny	imagine	quit	

Football players *avoid injuring* themselves.

Imagine sitting on a beach in Hawaii.

Don't use the base form of the verb when you need a gerund or an infinitive.

INCORRECT, BASE VERB	CORRECT, GERUND	CORRECT, INFINITIVE
Cook is my favorite activity. [*Cook* is the base form of the verb, not a noun; it can't function as the subject of the sentence.]	*Cooking* is my favorite activity. [*Cooking* is a gerund that can serve as the subject of the sentence.]	
Play piano is fun.	*Playing* piano is fun.	
My goal is *graduate* from college.		My goal is *to graduate* from college. [*To graduate* is an infinitive that can serve as the subject of the sentence.]

continued

INCORRECT, BASE VERB	CORRECT, GERUND	CORRECT, INFINITIVE
I need take vacation. [There is already a verb, *need,* in the sentence, so there can't be another verb that shows the action of the subject, *I.*]		I need *to take* a vacation.

▇ **PRACTICE 14   USING GERUNDS AND INFINITIVES** . . . .

Fill in the blanks with the correct gerund or infinitive.

> EXAMPLE: ___Drinking___ (Drink) coffee is part of Alex's morning ritual.

1. He expects _____ (start) every day with a fresh cup.

2. _____ (Make) fresh coffee takes him a few minutes every morning.

3. He does not want _____ (wake up) any earlier than necessary.

4. But he enjoys _____ (feel) alert and lively in the morning.

5. So he has decided _____ (take) the extra time in the morning _____ (prepare) his coffee.

6. At one time, Alex tried to avoid _____ (have) coffee in the morning.

7. He soon came _____ (regret) this because he disliked _____ (feel) sleepy all morning.

8. In this way, he learned _____ (use) coffee as his morning stimulant.

9. In the evenings, though, he refuses _____ (drink) coffee because it sometimes keeps him from _____ (sleep) through the night.

10. Instead, he tends _____ (ask) for decaffeinated coffee at night.

■ **PRACTICE 15   USING GERUNDS AND INFINITIVES** . . . .

Correct the sentences that use a base verb when a gerund or an infinitive is needed. Three of the sentences are correct.

EXAMPLE: Gabriella enjoys ~~spend~~ *spending* time with her roommate Paige.

1. They both prefer listen to the same kind of music.

2. Neither of them wants go to bed early.

3. Like Paige, Gabriella delays do her homework as long as she can.

4. Each of them also dislikes practicing on her musical instrument.

5. But Gabriella admits notice one thing that bothers her about Paige.

6. Paige cannot bear arriving anywhere on time.

7. On the other hand, Gabriella refuses be late ever.

8. At first, Gabriella attempted to force Paige to be on time.

9. After a while, however, Gabriella has learned accept Paige's habitual lateness.

10. Gabriella now realizes that being in a relationship often includes tolerate unimportant differences.

Modal Auxiliaries

Modal verbs are helping verbs that express the writer's attitude about an action. There aren't many modal auxiliaries to learn—just the ones in the chart that follows.

MODAL AUXILIARIES	MEANING	EXAMPLE
can	ability	I can sing.
could	possibility	I could sing.
may	permission	You may sing.

continued

MODAL AUXILIARIES	MEANING	EXAMPLE
might	possibility	I might sing.
must	obligation	I must sing.
should	advice or expectation	I should sing.
will	intention	I will sing.
would (often with the verb *like*)	desire, intention	I would sing.

For this section, you will need to refer to the charts on pages 485–88, which give you statements, negatives, and questions for all of the modal auxiliaries.

Should/Must

As you see in the chart, *should* means that an action is expected or recommended. *Must* means that an action is required; it is an obligation.

> Tomorrow, I *should* go to class. [The writer has a choice about whether to go or not.]

> Tomorrow, I *must* go to class. [The writer has no choice about going to class: It is necessary.]

Read the two sentences that follow, and explain their meaning.

> My grandmother *should* eat more.

> My grandmother *must* eat more.

Two common student errors when using *should* or *must* are the following:

Using the Infinitive Instead of the Base Verb.   The infinitive is *to + the base verb*. The base verb does not have *to* before it. When using *should* and *must*, use the base verb.

INCORRECT	CORRECT
Children should *to obey* their parents.	Children should *obey* their parents.
They must *to work* late.	They must *work* late.

Using Two Modals.   Using two modal auxiliaries together in a sentence is incorrect in English. Use only one.

INCORRECT	CORRECT	CORRECT
I *must should* study harder.	I *must* study harder.	I *should* study harder.

Could/Would

Could means a possibility that an action will happen; *would* means an intention that an action happen. The meanings are similar, but the words are not interchangeable.

Gina *could* go to bed early. [Gina has the ability to go to bed early; it is possible that she will.]

Gina *would* like to go to bed early. [Gina has the wish and intention to go to bed early, but she might not be able to.]

Read the two sentences that follow, and explain their meaning.

Next semester, I *could* take two courses.

Next semester, I *would* like to take two courses.

Two common student errors when using *could* or *would* are the following:

Using a Gerund Instead of an Infinitive or the Base Verb.   A gerund is a verb form that ends in *-ing* and functions as a noun in a sentence. When using the modal auxiliary *could*, follow it with the base verb. When using *would*, follow it with the infinitive (*to* + base verb), not a gerund.

INCORRECT	CORRECT
Today, I could *winning* the lottery.	Today, I could *win* the lottery.
I would like *graduating* in 2010.	I would like *to graduate* in 2010.

Omitting the Modal.   Just as you don't want to use two modal auxiliaries together in a sentence, you also don't want to forget a modal when it is required to show intention.

INCORRECT	CORRECT	CORRECT
Next month, I *like* to take a vacation.	Next month, I *would like* to take a vacation.	
Tomorrow, I *help* you.	Tomorrow, I *could help* you.	Tomorrow, I *can help* you.

Modals and Present-Perfect Verbs

Present-perfect verbs use the helping verb *has* or *have* and the past participle of the base verb. When the sentence has a modal auxiliary before the verb, the helping verb is always *have*, not *had*.

PRESENT-PERFECT VERB	MODAL AND PRESENT-PERFECT VERB
I *have called* an ambulance.	I *could have called* an ambulance.
You *have lied* to me.	You *may have lied* to me.
Kyle *has gone* to the store.	Kyle *might have gone* to the store.
We *have visited* the hospital.	We *should have visited* the hospital.
They *have brought* a gift.	They *must have brought* a gift.

Three common problems students have when using modals and present-perfect verbs are the following:

Using *Had* Instead of *Have*. Always use *have*.

INCORRECT	CORRECT
Sharon *could had won*.	Sharon *could have* won.
I *might had got* that job.	I *might have gotten* that job.
You *should had seen* the show.	You *should have seen* the show.
We *would had missed* the bus.	We *would have missed* the bus.
They *must had seen* the accident.	They *must have seen* the accident.

Omitting *Have*.

INCORRECT	CORRECT
I *could worked* last night.	I *could have worked* last night.
He *might walked* home.	He *might have walked* home.
You *should answered* the phone.	You *should have answered* the phone.
We *would liked* to go.	We *would have liked* to go.
They *must planned* the surprise.	They *must have planned* the surprise.

Using the Past-Perfect Verb *Have*. The verb *have* can be a helping verb with the base verb in the past perfect, and it can also be the main verb. When it is the main verb, use the past-participle form of the verb: *had*. This is what you do with all modals and past-perfect verbs (modal + helping verb *have* + past participle of the verb). It can be confusing when the verb is *have* because its past participle is *had,* which can result in sentences that use *have had* together:

I *could have had* dessert.

You *should have had* a bigger lunch.

Jane *might have had* a cold.

We *should have had* dinner before class.

They *could have had* car touble.

PRACTICE 16   **USING MODAL AUXILIARIES** . . . .

Using the charts on pages 485–88 and 613–16, fill in the blanks in the following sentences. Note that the last three items ask you to fill in a modal and a past-perfect verb.

> **EXAMPLE:** Emelia __*should*__ know by now that computers __*can*__ be unreliable.

1. She did know that her new computer _____ do many things that her old computer was not capable of doing.

2. Emelia _____ have trusted the computer if its screen did not go blank several times a day.

3. It _____ also give her messages saying "Error" or even "Fatal error."

4. Her older sister said that whenever that happened, Emelia _____ restart the computer.

5. After restarting, she _____ often say to herself, "When I get rich, I _____ hire an assistant to worry about my computer."

6. On this Monday morning, however, restarting _____ not solve the problem.

7. Finally, she realized that she _____ call the computer's technical support service.

For the next three questions, fill in a modal and a past-perfect verb in parentheses.

8. The technician _____ (arrive) early the next morning, but he was late.

9. If he had had the necessary replacement parts, he _____ (fix) the computer right then.

10. Emelia now believes that if she had called for technical support earlier, she probably _____ (have) her computer in working order by now.

Articles

Articles announce a noun. English uses only three articles: *a, an,* and *the.* The same articles are used for both masculine and feminine nouns.

> **Language Note:** Articles (*a, an, the*) are not used in Russian or in many Asian languages. If you aren't sure when to use an article or which one to use, pay close attention to this section.

Using Definite and Indefinite Articles

The is a **definite article** and is used before a specific person, place, or thing. *A* and *an* are **indefinite articles** and are used with a person, place, or thing whose specific identity is not known.

DEFINITE ARTICLE   *The* man knocked on *the* door.

[A specific man knocked on a specific door.]

INDEFINITE ARTICLE   *A* man knocked on *a* door.

[Some man knocked on some door. We don't know what man or what door.]

DEFINITE ARTICLE	*The* hostess showed us to our seats.
INDEFINITE ARTICLE	*A* hostess showed us to our seats.

When the word following the article begins with a vowel (*a, e, i, o, u*), use *an* instead of *a*.

An energetic hostess showed us to our seats.

Using Articles with Count and Noncount Nouns

To use the correct article, you need to know what count and noncount nouns are. **Count nouns** name things that can be counted. **Noncount nouns** name things that cannot be counted.

COUNT NOUN	I sold ten of the *CDs* on eBay.
NONCOUNT NOUN	I sold lots of *music* on eBay.

[A *CD* can be counted; *music* cannot.]

Here are some examples of count and noncount nouns. This is just a brief list; all nouns in English are either count or noncount. To help determine if a noun is count or noncount, try adding *s*. Most count nouns form a plural by adding *s*; noncount nouns do not have plural forms.

COUNT	NONCOUNT		
apple/apples	advice	homework	rain
chair/chairs	beauty	honey	rice
dollar/dollars	equipment	information	salt
letter/letters	flour	jewelry	sand
smile/smiles	furniture	mail	spaghetti
tree/trees	grass	milk	sunlight
	grief	money	thunder
	happiness	postage	wealth
	health	poverty	

Articles with Count and Noncount Nouns

COUNT NOUNS	ARTICLE USED
SINGULAR *Specific* →	***the*** I want to read *the book* on taxes that you recommended. [The sentence refers to one particular book—the one that was recommended.] I can't stay in *the sun* very long. [There is only one sun.]
Not specific →	***a*** or ***an*** I want to read *a book* on taxes. [It could be any book on taxes.]
PLURAL *Specific* →	***the*** I enjoyed *the books* we read. [The sentence refers to a particular group of books—the ones we read.]
Not specific →	**no article** or ***some*** I usually enjoy *books*. [The sentence refers to books in general.] She found *some books*. [We don't know which books she found.]

NONCOUNT NOUNS	ARTICLE USED
SINGULAR *Specific* →	***the*** My son ate all *the food* we bought. [The sentence refers to particular food—the food we bought.]
Not specific →	**no article** or ***some*** There is *food* all over the kitchen. [The reader doesn't know what food the sentence refers to.] Give *some food* to the neighbors. [The sentence refers to an indefinite quantity of food.]

**PRACTICE 17   USING THE CORRECT ARTICLE
WITH COUNT AND NONCOUNT NOUNS** . . . .

Circle the correct article (or choose "no article") for each of the following sentences.

> **EXAMPLE:** Just about everyone has used (a / an / the /(no article)) spices at one time or another, but not many people are aware of the long and interesting history of these additives.

1. Scientists believe that as long ago as 50,000 B.C.E., people were using spices to improve (a / an / the / no article) taste of food.

2. This first use might have been (a / an / the / no article) accident, occurring when someone wrapped meat in leaves before roasting it to keep ash off of the flesh.

3. (A / An / The / no article) cook discovered that the leaves transferred a pleasant flavor to the meat.

4. In addition to flavoring foods, (a / an / the / no article) spices also became valued for their medicinal and deodorizing properties.

5. Eventually, spices became so prized—and expensive—that only (a / an / the / no article) richest people could afford them.

6. In fact, (a / an / the / no article) peppercorns were sometimes used as money in medieval times.

7. (A / An / The / no article) high cost of spices was partly the result of duties charged at major trading points in Asia and Europe.

8. Fortunately, we can now get just about any spice we want in the grocery store at (a / an / the / no article) reasonable price.

9. Although (a / an / the / no article) spices are now used largely for flavoring, consumers have shown renewed interest in their medicinal properties.

10. Researchers have started to look into whether (a / an / the / no article) health benefits claimed for certain spices have any basis in fact.

PRACTICE 18   EDITING NOUNS AND ARTICLES . . . .

Edit the following paragraph, adding and changing articles and nouns as necessary.

EXAMPLE: Restaurant work is not an easy way to earn the money.

(1) I am waitress at the restaurant four days a week. (2) My shift is at lunchtimes, and it is usually very busy then. (3) There is a university close by, so the many college students eat at my restaurant because it serves cheap foods. (4) I am college student too; however, some of my student customers do not treat me as a equal. (5) They seem to think that it is okay to be rude to person serving them. (6) Many of them do not tip me well even though I am very good waitress and take good cares of my customers. (7) I do not make high salaries, so I need the tips from my customers to make good living. (8) I understand that college students often have no moneys. (9) However, I think that peoples who cannot afford to leave tip should not eat in a restaurant.

Prepositions

■ For more on prepositions, see Chapter 22. For a list of prepositions, see page 390.

A **preposition** is a word (such as *of, above, between, about*) that connects a noun, pronoun, or verb with other information about it. The correct preposition to use is often determined by idiom or common practice rather than by the preposition's actual meaning.

An **idiom** is any combination of words that is always used the same way, even though there is no logical or grammatical explanation for it. The best way to learn English idioms is to listen and read as much as possible and then to practice writing and speaking the correct forms.

Prepositions after Adjectives

Certain prepositions often come after certain adjectives. Here are some common examples:

afraid of	full of	responsible for
ashamed of	happy about	scared of
aware of	interested in	sorry about/sorry for
confused by	nervous about	tired of
embarrassed about	proud of	worried about
excited about	reminded of	

Tanya is excited ~~of~~ *about* going to Mexico.

However, she is afraid ~~by~~ *of* taking time off.

Prepositions after Verbs

Many verbs in English consist of a verb plus a preposition (or an adverb). The meaning of these combinations is not usually the literal meaning the verb and the preposition would each have on its own. Often, the meaning of the verb changes completely depending on which preposition is used with it.

You must *take out* the trash. [*take out* = bring to a different location]

You must *take in* the exciting sights of New York City. [*take in* = observe]

Here are a few common examples:

call in (telephone)	You can *call in* your order.
call off (cancel)	They *called off* the pool party.
call on (choose)	The teacher always *calls on* me.
drop in (visit)	*Drop in* when you are in the area.
drop off (leave behind)	Cherry will *drop off* the car.
drop out (quit)	Too many students *drop out* of school.
fight against (combat)	He tried to *fight against* the proposal.
fight for (defend)	We need to *fight for* our rights.

fill in (refill)	Please *fill in* the holes in the ground.
fill out (complete)	Please *fill out* this application form.
fill up (make something full)	Don't *fill up* with junk food.
find out (discover)	Did you *find out* what happened?
give up (forfeit)	Don't *give up* your place in line.
go over (review)	He wants to *go over* our speeches.
grow up (mature)	All children *grow up*.
hand in (submit)	You may *hand in* your homework now.
lock up (secure)	Don't forget to *lock up* before you go to bed.
look up (check)	I *looked up* the word in the dictionary.
pick out (choose)	Sandy *picked out* a puppy.
pick up (take or collect)	When do you *pick up* the keys?
put off (postpone)	I often *put off* doing dishes.
sign in (register, leaving name)	I have to *sign in* to work.
sign out (borrow, leaving name)	I want to *sign out* a book.
sign up (register for)	Cressia *signed up* for three classes.
think about (consider)	Patsy sometimes *thinks about* moving.
turn in (submit)	Please *turn in* your homework now.

▪ PRACTICE 19   EDITING PREPOSITIONS . . . .

Edit the following sentences to make sure that the correct prepositions are used.

                                                   for

EXAMPLE: Several U.S. presidents have said that they were sorry of

the mistreatment of Japanese Americans during World War II.

1. During World War II, more than 120,000 Japanese Americans were locked down in internment camps.

2. Many young Japanese Americans still chose to sign away for the U.S. military.

3. These soldiers often had to fight for prejudice as well as the enemy.

4. About eight hundred Japanese American soldiers gave in their lives during the fighting.

5. After the war, many Japanese Americans who had been interned were ashamed for their experience.

6. More than fifty years after the war, some Americans of Japanese descent became interested on creating a memorial to the Japanese Americans of the war years.

7. They wanted to make other Americans aware on the sacrifices of Japanese Americans during World War II.

8. A city full with memorials to the country's past, Washington, D.C., was chosen to be the site of the National Japanese American Memorial, unveiled in 2000.

9. For the center of the memorial park, the designers picked on a sculpture by a Japanese American artist, Nina Akamu, featuring two cranes tangled in barbed wire.

10. Visitors to the park are now reminded on Japanese Americans' struggle for acceptance in the United States.

■ **PRACTICE 20   EDITING PREPOSITIONS** . . . .

Edit the following paragraph to make sure that the correct prepositions are used.

(1) Students who are anxious on mathematics take fewer math classes and perform worse in them than students who do not have math anxiety. (2) Scientists once believed that students were afraid about math because they were not good at it, but that belief was incorrect. (3) It turns up

that worry prevents students from understanding mathematics as well as they could. (4) Fear interferes in the working memory that is necessary for math, making students less able to think about math problems. (5) Starting on about the age of twelve, students with math anxiety become less able to compensate for the loss of working memory. (6) The good news is that effective treatment is available for math anxiety. (7) Students who once thought they would never be able to understand math may someday find up that they can conquer their anxiety and cope with numbers.

Edit Paragraphs and Your Own Writing

Edit the following paragraphs as indicated, referring to the charts on the pages with green bands down the side in Chapter 26 as you need them.

▪ EDITING REVIEW 1 (13 errors)

Edit the following paragraphs for errors in the use of nouns, pronouns, prepositions, and idioms.

(1) Everyone knows that people who are driving should not do anything else. (2) On spite of that, people often engage in risky behavior when driving, such as eating, arguing with someone else in the car, or looking at a map while driving fast on a highway. (3) One of the most common form of distraction while driving is holding a cell phone while talking or typing a text message. (4) Some drivers they keep trying to do more and more as they drive. (5) On the driver's side of his cars, they are installing G.P.S. navigation screens, portable DVD players, and even computer keyboards and screens. (6) The trouble is that the more of

these device a driver can see and reach, the greater the risk of that driver's attention getting distracted to driving.

(7) The risk can be high. (8) According to estimates by the National Highway Traffic Safety Administration, 80 percent of vehicle crash and 65 percent of close calls are partly due on driver distraction. (9) While automakers point to consumer demand as her reason for including more electronics for the driver, some car companies say they are making driving safer by increasing their offerings of hands-free phone systems and by making voice-activated technology easier to use. (10) One car manufacturer he recently introduced a feature in a concept minivan—one that is not in production—that attempts of address this problem. (11) It is a button that the driver she can push to instantly shut off all unnecessary electronic devices in the car. (12) Perhaps driving would get safer if more driver just say to their electronics, "Enough!"

▉ **EDITING REVIEW 2 (12 errors)** . . . .

Edit the following paragraphs for errors in the use of verbs.

(1) One of the most fascinating mysteries in nature be the annual fall migration of monarch butterflies. (2) Every autumn, many of these bright orange butterflies must travel all the way from Canada and the northern United States to Mexico. (3) In central Mexico, they will spend the winter; the next spring, they beginning their return journey. (4) But the monarch butterflies that leave Canada in the fall will not be the same butterflies that to return in the spring. (5) The butterflies that get back to Canada in spring will have been the great-grandchildren of those that had left in the fall.

(6) In the spring, the butterflies that flew from Canada to Mexico begin to mate and start back north. (7) But they only would have gotten to Texas, where they lay their eggs and soon die. (8) The daughters that are then born in Texas fly on to the northern United States, where they breed, lay their eggs, and die. (9) The next generation, the grandchildren, continue the northward migration to Canada, and then they breed and die. (10) Their offspring are the great-grandchildren of the butterflies that will have left Canada in the previous autumn.

(11) So the question remains: How do these subsequent generations of monarchs know where they must to go? (12) The answer, unfortunately, is that nobody knew for sure. (13) One theory assumes that the butterflies somehow use the sun's position to figure out the general direction in which they should go. (14) When the butterflies need to navigate in the mountains of central Mexico, the theory states that the insects follow the smell of the dead bodies of butterflies that flying this route before. (15) However, some scientists do not believe that the odors of the dead bodies last for a year. (16) For now, all anyone can do is enjoying the spectacular monarchs as they briefly visit our backyards, and wonder how they would manage their mysterious 4,000-mile-long journey.

■ **EDITING REVIEW 3 (12 errors)** . . . .

Edit the following paragraphs for errors in the use of verbs.

(1) E-mail is a young form of communication, and many of its conventions are still to evolve. (2) One of the most important conventions is the sign-off one should make to end an e-mail message. (3) Before electronic communications, every third grader is learning the proper sign-offs

to a personal or business letter. (4) Most people would usually close a letter with "Sincerely," "Yours truly," or "Love." (5) With e-mail, those old conventions changed into no conventions at all, and sign-offs now seem to do more than simply end messages.

(6) Some e-mailers look carefully at the sign-offs as indicators of how well the relationship will be to go. (7) One businesswoman described what happening to the e-mail sign-offs as her contract negotiations with a client will have begun to go badly. (8) In the beginning, she and her client used sign-offs like, "I look forward to hearing from you soon" and "Warmest regards." (9) But as difficulties are arising, the sign-off became "Regards." (10) The deal eventually will have been made, but the businesswoman still has lingering bad feelings about the sign-offs. (11) She said she usually choosing sign-offs according to how cordial she feels about the other person. (12) So, she often to select one of the following sign-offs: "Warmest regards," "All the best," or just "Sincerely." (13) One businessman, after to think carefully about what should be the friendliest and most appropriate sign-off, now has used "Warmly." (14) What do you use?

PRACTICE 21   EDITING YOUR OWN WRITING . . . .

As a final practice, edit a piece of your own writing—a paper you are working on for this course, a paper you've already finished, a paper for another course, a recent piece of your writing from your work or everyday life, or your idea journal entry. Refer to information in this chapter, along with the verb charts in Chapter 26.

Part Six
Word Use

34

Word Choice

Avoiding Language Pitfalls

Understand the Importance of Choosing Words Carefully

In conversation, much of your meaning is conveyed by your facial expression, your tone of voice, and your gestures. In writing, you have only the words on the page to make your point, so you must choose them carefully. If you use vague or inappropriate words, your readers may not understand you. Carefully chosen, precise words tell your readers exactly what you mean.

Two resources will help you find the best words for your meaning—a dictionary and a thesaurus.

■ **IDEA JOURNAL**
Describe your working habits.

Dictionary

You need a dictionary. For a very small investment, you can get a complete resource for all kinds of useful information about words—spelling, division of words into syllables, pronunciation, parts of speech, other forms of words, definitions, and examples of use.

The following is a part of a dictionary entry:

Spelling and end-of-line division	Pronunciation	Parts of speech

Other forms —

Definition —

Example —

con • crete (kon´ krēt, kong´- krēt, kon krēt´, kong- krēt´), *adj., n., v.* **-cret • ed, -cret • ing**, *adj.* **1.** constituting an actual thing or instance; real; perceptible; substantial: *concrete proof.* **2.** pertaining to or concerned with realities or actual instances rather than abstractions; particular as opposed to general: *concrete proposals.* **3.** referring to an actual substance or thing, as opposed to an abstract quality: The words *cat, water,* and *teacher* are concrete, whereas the words *truth, excellence,* and *adulthood* are abstract. . . .

—*Random House Webster's College Dictionary*

Thesaurus

■ To look up words in both the dictionary and the thesaurus on the Web, visit Merriam-Webster Online at **www.m-w.com**.

A thesaurus gives *synonyms* (words that have the same meaning) for the words you look up. Like dictionaries, thesauruses come in inexpensive and even electronic editions. Use a thesaurus when you can't find the right word for what you mean. Be careful, however, to choose a word that has the precise meaning you intend. If you are not sure how a word should be used, look it up in the dictionary.

Concrete, *adj.* 1. Particular, specific, single, certain, special, unique, sole, peculiar, individual, separate, isolated, distinct, exact, precise, direct, strict, minute; definite, plain, evident, obvious; pointed, emphasized; restrictive, limiting, limited, well-defined, clear-cut, fixed, finite; determining, conclusive, decided.

—J. I. Rodale, *The Synonym Finder*

Practice Avoiding Four Common Word-Choice Problems

Four common problems with word choice can make it difficult for readers to understand your point. You can avoid them by using specific words that fit your meaning and make your writing clearer.

Language Note: Make sure to use the right kinds of words—nouns to name a person, place, or thing; adjectives to describe nouns; adverbs to describe adjectives or other adverbs.

N

INCORRECT   Tyra seems *sadness*.

[*Sadness* is a noun. The kind of word needed to modify the noun, *Tyra*, is an adjective.]

ADJ

CORRECT   Tyra seems *sad*.

Vague and Abstract Words

Your words need to create a clear picture for your readers. **Vague and abstract words** are too general to make an impression. Here are some common vague and abstract words.

Vague and Abstract Words

a lot	dumb	OK (okay)	stuff
awesome	good	old	thing
awful	great	person	very
bad	happy	pretty	whatever
beautiful	house	sad	young
big	job	school	
car	nice	small	

When you see one of these words or another general word in your writing, try to replace it with a concrete or more specific word. A **concrete word** names something that can be seen, heard, felt, tasted, or smelled. A **specific word** names a particular individual or quality. Compare these two sentences:

VAGUE AND ABSTRACT   It was a beautiful day.

CONCRETE AND SPECIFIC   The sky was a bright, cloudless blue; the sun was shimmering; and the temperature was a perfect 78 degrees.

The first version is too general to be interesting. The second version creates a clear, strong image.

Some words are so vague that it is best to avoid them altogether.

VAGUE AND ABSTRACT   It's like *whatever*.

[This sentence is neither concrete nor specific.]

> **PRACTICE 1   AVOIDING VAGUE AND ABSTRACT WORDS** . . . .

■ For more practice with word choice, visit *Exercise Central* at **bedfordstmartins.com/realessays**.

In the following sentences, underline any words that are vague or abstract. Then, edit each sentence by replacing any vague or abstract words with concrete, specific ones. You may invent any details you like.

                                  drums in the pit band for our drama club's musicals.
EXAMPLE: Jessica <u>plays</u> <u>at club events.</u>
                          ^

1. Others play as well.

2. The club stages them often.

■ Answers to odd-numbered practice items are at the back of the book.

3. The last one was good.

4. At first, Jessica was troubled.

5. But after, she was happy.

6. Playing in a pit band is strange.

7. The music can also be hard.

8. However, she thinks it's great.

9. Next semester, they'll do a new one.

10. Jessica is preparing for it.

Slang

Slang is informal and casual language that is shared by a particular group. Slang should be used only in informal and casual situations. Avoid it when you write, especially for college classes or at work. Use language that is appropriate for your audience and purpose.

SLANG	EDITED
I'm going to *chill* at home.	I'm going to relax at home.
I *dumped* Destina.	I told Destina that I wanted to end our relationship.
I've been working *crazy* hard on my research project.	I've been working extremely hard on my research project.

If you are not sure if a word is slang, check an online source, such as **www.slangsite.com** or **www.manythings.org**.

 PRACTICE 2   AVOIDING SLANG . . . .

In the following sentences, underline any slang words. Then, edit the sentences by replacing the slang with language appropriate for a formal audience and purpose. Imagine, for example, that you are writing to a supervisor at work.

                                            aware of

EXAMPLE: As a cafeteria cashier, I am uniquely ~~clued in to~~ students'

         eating habits.

1. I realize that our food service managers think it is cool to serve exactly the foods that students want.

2. However, every day I see firsthand that most of our students are living on a wacko diet.

3. For instance, I know one dude who eats nothing but potato chips and bread.

4. He is certain it's no biggie that he never eats any fruit or veggies, and there are many students like him.

5. I am not proposing that we become nutritional cops and dictate to students what they should eat.

6. I have no desire to rat on students just because they choose to eat nothing but nutritionally devoid foods once in a while.

7. But in our effort to save a few bucks, it seems to me that we are depriving students of many important food choices that would enrich their diets.

8. For example, a significantly expanded fruit and salad station would allow our vegetarians an opportunity to do their thing.

9. Adding more healthy food choices might also help students to realize that awesome nutrition can be both sensible and fashionable.

10. I hope you don't feel that I am screwing up by making such a flap about this, but it is only because I want our students to be as healthy as possible.

. . . .

Wordy Language

Sometimes people think that using more words or using big words will make them sound smart and important. But using too many words in a piece of writing can obscure or weaken the point.

Wordy language includes phrases that contain too many words, unnecessarily modify a statement, or use slightly different words without adding any new ideas. It also includes overblown language — unnecessarily complicated words and phrases that are often used to make the writer or writing sound important.

WORDY	We have no openings *at this point in time.*
EDITED	We have no openings now.

[The phrase *at this point in time* uses five words to express what could be said in one word — *now.*]

WORDY	*In the opinion of this writer,* tuition is too high.
EDITED	Tuition is too high.

[The qualifying phrase *in the opinion of this writer* is not necessary and weakens the statement.]

WORDY	In our advertising, we will *utilize* the *superlative photographic images* of ArtSense.
EDITED	Our advertising will use ArtSense photographs.

[The words *utilize* and *superlative photographic images* are overblown.]

Common Wordy Expressions

WORDY	EDITED
A great number of	Many
A large number of	Many
As a result of	Because
At that time	Then
At the conclusion of	At the end
At this point in time	Now
Due to the fact that	Because
In order to	To
In spite of the fact that	Although
In the event that	If
In this day and age	Now
In this paper I will show that	(Just make the point; don't announce it.)
It is my opinion that	I think (or just make the point)
The fact of the matter is that	(Just state the point.)

PRACTICE 3 AVOIDING WORDY LANGUAGE . . . .

In the following sentences, underline the wordy language. Then, edit each sentence to make it more concise.

EXAMPLE: ~~The fact of the matter is that~~ <u>all</u> *All* drivers get angry some-

times, but nobody has ever heard of a car getting angry.

1. At this point in time, that may be changing, thanks to four Japanese inventors.

2. They are the people who have recently patented a car that can look angry and appear to cry, laugh, or wink.

3. The patent application describes a car with an antenna that wags, headlights that become dimmer and then grow brighter in an expressive fashion, and ornaments that look like eyebrows, eyelids, and tears.

4. The car would seem to be "sleeping" at the point in time in which its headlights, or eyes, are closed, and the antenna is limp.

5. In order to have the vehicle express anger, the car's hood would glow red as the eyebrows light up.

6. The operator of the motor vehicle would be able to make the car "wink" by dimming one headlight and vibrating the antenna.

7. In the event that the driver wants the car to "cry," he or she could make the hood dark blue, shade the headlights, and show a blinking "tear" light.

8. The inventors believe that orange is the best color to show happiness and that red is the best color for anger, in spite of the fact that others may disagree.

9. The inventors say that their ideas could be applied not just to cars but could also be taken advantage of for motorcycles, ships, or aircraft.

10. Critics of the expressive car have put forward the opinion that it might be too distracting to other drivers.

Clichés

Clichés are phrases used so often that people no longer pay attention to them. To get your point across and to get your readers' attention, replace clichés with fresh language that precisely expresses your meaning.

CLICHÉS	EDITED
Passing the state police exam is no *walk in the park*.	Passing the state police exam requires careful preparation.
I was *sweating bullets* until the grades were posted.	I was anxious until the grades were posted.

COMMON CLICHÉS

as big as a house	last but not least
as hard as a rock	more trouble than it's worth
as light as a feather	no way on earth
best/worst of times	110 percent
better late than never	playing with fire
break the ice	spoiled brat
climb the corporate ladder	spoiled rotten
crystal clear	starting from scratch
drop in the bucket	sweating blood/bullets
easier said than done	24/7
hell on earth	work like a dog

There are hundreds of clichés. To check if you have used a cliché, go to **www.clichesite.com**.

■ PRACTICE 4   **AVOIDING CLICHÉS** . . . .

In the following sentences, underline the clichés. Then, edit each sentence by replacing the clichés with fresh, precise language.

EXAMPLE: The camping trip started out ~~as smooth as silk.~~
                                                    perfectly.

1. Anthony, Matthew, and Stephen were as slow as molasses when they began hiking, but once they got used to their heavy backpacks, they were able to walk faster.

2. The cumbersome tent Matthew carried was heavy, but they had all agreed beforehand not to buy a lightweight backpacking tent because money doesn't grow on trees.

3. Feeling it was better to be safe than sorry, Stephen had packed nearly everything he had in double plastic bags.

4. He had gotten caught in the rain on a previous backpacking trip, and getting everything soaked was so unpleasant that he wouldn't wish it on his worst enemy.

5. Anthony confidently said the weather report did not mention rain, but Stephen, looking up at the increasingly cloudy sky, said they should not count their chickens before they hatch.

6. First, they felt an occasional drop of mist, then light sprinkles, and soon it was raining cats and dogs.

7. They continued hiking toward their campsite, and they noticed that the temperature had dropped abruptly, and it became bone-chillingly cold.

8. Stephen glanced over at Anthony and Matthew, and they each looked like something the cat had dragged in.

9. Finally, they turned back, and by the time they got to their car, they felt as though they had been run ragged.

10. As they sat in their dorm's kitchen sipping hot chocolate, Matthew gazed at the thunderstorm outside and thought to himself that there's no place like home.

. . . .

Edit Paragraphs and Your Own Writing

Edit the following paragraphs for vague and abstract language, slang, wordiness, or clichés, referring to the chart on page 646 as you need to.

■ **EDITING REVIEW 1 (23 possible edits)** . . . .

(1) Although people don't hear much about hobos in this day and age of tightly sealed boxcars, there was a time not long ago when hobos were a distinct segment of American culture. (2) Even then, however, few knew the handles of any hobos. (3) But to those who followed such social currents, there was one hobo who stood above the crowd—Steam Train Maury. (4) By the time he hung up his spurs from his hobo wanderings, he was crowned the king of the hobos five times, and eventually he achieved the status of Grand Patriarch of the Hobos.

(5) Hailing from Kansas in 1917 as Maurice W. Graham, Steam Train Maury was the product of a troubled family. (6) He spent much of his youth shifting from here to there. (7) In 1931, at the age of fourteen, he jumped on a train and at this point in time he began his first time as a hobo. (8) After riding the rails and bouncing about for several years, he became a cement mason, operated his own school for masons in Toledo, Ohio, and later served as a medical technician during World War II. (9) By 1971, he hooked up with a wife and had two children, but he also developed hip problems and was unable to work much, and he became dissatisfied with his life. (10) Now fifty-four, he hopped on a freight train with the vague intention and confused impression that he'd just relive his hobo life for a few weeks and then return home. (11) Those two weeks morphed into ten years during which Steam Train Maury became a hobo legend. (12) By 1981, Mr. Graham had cowritten a book about his sometimes exciting, sometimes boring, and sometimes frightening life as a hobo, helped to found the Hobo Foundation, and took part in establishing the Hobo Museum in Britt, Iowa. (13) At the National Hobo Convention held in Britt, which was celebrated every single year, he was

named the hobo king in 1973, 1975, 1976, 1978, and 1981. (14) In 2004, he was crowned as the Grand Patriarch of the Hobos, a title so prized that he was the only person ever to have won it.

(15) Hobos have been hopping trains for free rides ever since the Civil War, when wandering field workers and laborers took a significant and some say vital role in building the American West. (16) Later, some hobos, as a joke, named themselves "Tourist Union Local 63." (17) In 1900, the big shots from Britt, Iowa, offered their town for Local 63's hobo convention. (18) In the following decades, Britt became known as the "hobo town," and by 1933, it was widely publicizing its four-day hobo convention and drawing tens of thousands to the several widely varied events that were created just for the occasion. (19) This was during the Great Depression, when more than a million people were sneaking onto trains in a no-win search for work.

(20) Mr. Graham always emphasized a gussied-up view of the hobo existence, the perspective that moved author John Steinbeck to call hobos "the last free men." (21) One of the typical and often-repeated examples of Mr. Graham's stories was that of a character called the Pennsylvania Kid, who shaved with a piece of glass from a Coke bottle. (22) When asked if it was true that some hobos used deodorant, Mr. Graham cracked that it was a shame but he didn't know what to do about it. (23) Steam Train Maury croaked of a stroke in 2006 at the age of eighty-nine. (24) Making a fitting and appropriate use of the hobos' term for death, he had "taken the westbound."

EDITING REVIEW 2 (22 possible edits) . . . .

(1) Do humans have a thing or two to learn from honeybees? (2) A research study suggests that these hard-working insects may be hotshots

at decision making. (3) This becomes evident when a hive of honeybees keeps growing and growing so much that it eventually outgrows its home. (4) When that happens, the old queen shoves off, accompanied by a swarm of about 10,000 bees. (5) Their challenge at this critical and decisive moment is to find the best possible location for the new hive. (6) According to the study, the bees, in the vast majority of cases in which this happens, end up making good decisions.

(7) How do they swing that? (8) Do they in one way or another vote or have a method of coming to a consensus? (9) As a means of discerning the answer to this, the researchers conducted several experiments as they observed the honeybees making their decision. (10) While the swarm took a breather huddling together on a tree branch, scout bees searched for suitable locations. (11) As the scout bees wended their way back, each scout did a waggle dance to highlight what she had found. (12) Apparently, during this process, some scouts flip flopped and ended up dancing to support other scouts' finds. (13) The researchers concluded that the swarm doesn't wait for each and every one of the scouts to settle on one location. (14) Instead, the swarm senses when a sufficient and satisfactory number of scouts, perhaps fifteen or twenty, have agreed on one site. (15) At that point, the entire swarm gets ready to make their move. (16) For an approximate period of an hour, the bees warm up their flight muscles, and during this time, the remaining scouts usually decide to support the chosen site. (17) In this way, a solid consensus is achieved, and, in most cases, it is the coolest possible location for the new hive.

(18) As a result of these experiments, the researchers note that the bees' process works because it makes sense. (19) The inside story is brought to the group by independent individuals. (20) In the free marketplace

of waggle dancing, they openly chew the fat over it and eventually arrive at a mutual decision. (21) The fact of the matter is that it is almost always the right decision. (22) Are humans capable of pulling this off?

PRACTICE 5   EDITING YOUR OWN WRITING FOR WORD CHOICE . . .

As a final practice, edit a piece of your own writing for word choice. It can be a paper you are working on for this course, a paper you've already finished, a paper for another course, a recent piece of writing from your work or everyday life, or your idea journal entry. You may want to use the following chart as you edit.

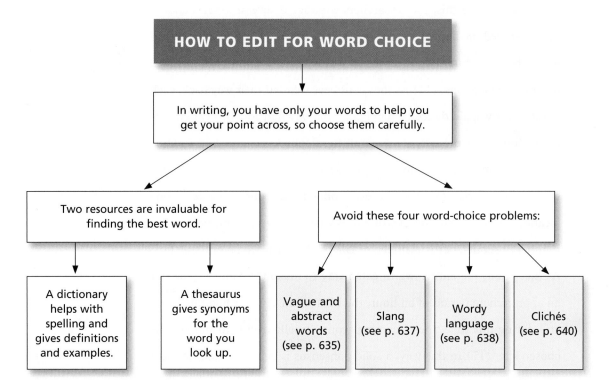

HOW TO EDIT FOR WORD CHOICE

In writing, you have only your words to help you get your point across, so choose them carefully.

Two resources are invaluable for finding the best word.

Avoid these four word-choice problems:

A dictionary helps with spelling and gives definitions and examples.

A thesaurus gives synonyms for the word you look up.

Vague and abstract words (see p. 635)

Slang (see p. 637)

Wordy language (see p. 638)

Clichés (see p. 640)

35

Commonly Confused Words

Avoiding Mistakes with Sound-Alikes

Understand Why Certain Words Are Commonly Confused

Certain words in English are confusing because they sound alike and may have similar meanings. In writing, words that sound alike may be spelled differently, and readers rely on the spelling to understand what you mean. Edit your writing carefully to make sure that you have used the correct words.

■ **IDEA JOURNAL**
Write about something you and a friend or family member disagree about. Explain your friend's opinion as well as your own.

STRATEGIES FOR EDITING SOUND-ALIKES

1. Proofread carefully, using the techniques on page 662.
2. Use a dictionary to find the meaning of words you are unsure of.
3. Focus on finding and correcting mistakes you make with the twenty-seven sets of commonly confused words covered in this chapter.
4. Develop a personal list of sound-alikes that confuse you. Before you turn in any piece of writing, consult your personal list to make sure you have used the correct words.

Practice Using Commonly Confused Words Correctly

Study the different meanings and spellings of these twenty-seven sets of commonly confused words. Complete the sentence after each set of words, filling in each blank with the correct word.

A/An/And

a: used before a word that begins with a consonant sound

A bat was living behind the shutter.

an: used before a word that begins with a vowel sound

An elderly lady sat beside me.

and: used to join two words

My sister *and* I went to the amusement park.

A friend *and* I got lost in *an* old maze.

Most classrooms have _____ worn-out chair _____ _____ old desk for the teacher.

Accept/Except

accept: to agree to receive or admit (verb)

I plan to *accept* the offer.

except: but, other than (conjunction)

The whole family was there *except* my brother.

I *accept* all your requests *except* the one to borrow my car.

Do not _____ anything from people at airports _____ from family members.

Advice/Advise

advice: opinion (noun)

I would like your *advice* on this decision.

advise: to give an opinion (verb)

My boyfriend *advises* me about car repairs.

Please *advise* me what to do; your *advice* is always helpful.

_____ me of your plans, particularly if you don't follow my _____.

Affect/Effect

affect: to have an impact on, to change something (verb)

> The whole region was *affected* by the drought.

effect: a result (noun)

> The lack of water will have a tremendous *effect* on many businesses.

The sunny weather has had a positive *effect* on people's moods, but it will negatively *affect* the economy.

Since this year's drought will _____ the cost of food, we'll be feeling

its _____ personally.

Are/Our

are: a form of the verb *be*

> The flowers *are* ready to bloom.

our: a pronoun showing ownership

> I am proud of *our* garden.

Gardens *are* rare in *our* neighborhood.

_____ bulbs _____ arriving this week.

By/Buy

by: next to or before

> I'll be standing *by* the door.

> We have to be at the restaurant *by* eight o'clock.

buy: to purchase (verb)

> I would like to *buy* a new car.

By the time I'm ready to leave the dollar store, I have found too much I want to *buy*.

I have decided to _____ the model _____ the showroom entrance.

Conscience/Conscious

conscience: a personal sense of right and wrong (noun)

> My *conscience* keeps me from doing bad things.

■ Remember that one of the words is *con-science;* the other is not.

■ Some commonly confused words—such as *conscience* and *conscious, loose* and *lose,* and *of* and *have*—sound similar but not exactly alike. To avoid confusing these words, practice pronouncing them correctly.

conscious: awake, aware (adjective)

> The patient is now *conscious.*

> Shelly was *conscious* of Sam's feelings.

Danny made a *conscious* decision to listen to his *conscience.*

The burglar was _____ that someone else was in the house and

for a moment felt a twinge of _____.

Fine/Find

fine: of high quality (adjective); feeling well (adverb); a penalty for breaking a law (noun)

> She works in the *fine* jewelry department.

> After taking some aspirin, Shana felt *fine.*

> The *fine* for exceeding the speed limit is $100.

find: to locate, discover (verb)

> Can you help me *find* the key?

You will *find* a *fine* leather jacket in the coat department.

A _____ partner is hard to _____.

Its/It's

■ If you are not sure whether to use *its* or *it's* in a sentence, try substituting *it is.* If the sentence doesn't make sense with *it is,* use *its.*

its: a pronoun showing ownership

> The bird went back to *its* nest.

it's: a contraction of the words *it is*

> *It's* important for you to be on time.

It's amazing to see a butterfly come out of *its* cocoon.

_____ good news for us that the bus changed _____ route.

Knew/New/Know/No

knew: understood; recognized (past tense of the verb *know*)

> I *knew* we took the wrong turn.

new: unused, recent (adjective)

> Jane has a *new* boyfriend.

know: to understand, to have knowledge of (verb)

I *know* him from work.

no: used to form a negative

There are *no* other classes at that time.

I *knew* that Jason would need *new* shoes.

The _____ employee already _____ some of the other employees.

There is *no* way to *know* what will happen.

Do you _____ what _____ means?

Loose/Lose

loose: baggy, not fixed in place (adjective)

That button is *loose.*

lose: to misplace, to forfeit possession of (verb)

I don't want to *lose* my job.

If the muffler is *loose,* you might *lose* it.

You will _____ that bracelet if it's too _____.

Mind/Mine

mind: to object to (verb); the thinking or feeling part of one's brain (noun)

I don't *mind* loud music.

Sometimes I think I am losing my *mind.*

mine: belonging to me (pronoun); a source of ore and minerals (noun)

That parking space is *mine.*

That store is a gold *mine.*

Keep in *mind* that the sweater is *mine.*

Your _____ is a lot sharper than _____.

Of/Have

of: coming from; caused by; part of a group; made from (preposition)

The president *of* the company pleaded guilty to embezzlement.

■ Do not use *of* after *would, should, could,* and *might.* Use *have* after those words.

have: to possess (verb; also used as a helping verb)

Do you *have* a schedule?

Jeannie should *have* been here by now.

I would *have* helped if you had told me you were out *of* change.

Joe might _____ been part _____ the band.

Passed/Past

passed: went by or went ahead (past tense of the verb *pass*)

Tim *passed* us a minute ago.

past: time that has gone by (noun); gone by, over, just beyond (preposition)

The school is just *past* the traffic light.

This *past* school year, I *passed* all of my exams.

If you go _____ the church, you have _____ the right turn.

Peace/Piece

peace: no disagreement; calm

The sleeping infant is at *peace.*

piece: a part of something larger

May I have a *piece* of paper?

We will have no *peace* until we give the dog a *piece* of that bread.

Selling his _____ of land will give Uncle Joe _____ of mind.

Principal/Principle

principal: main or chief (adjective); head of a school or a leader of an organization (noun)

Making sales calls is your *principal* responsibility.

Darla is a *principal* of the company.

Mr. Tucker is the *principal* of the Sawyer School.

principle: a standard of beliefs or behaviors (noun)

The issue is really a matter of *principle.*

The *principle* at stake is the *principal* issue of the court case.

The _____ problem with many criminals is that they do not

have good _____.

Quiet/Quite/Quit

quiet: soft in sound; not noisy (adjective)

The library was very *quiet.*

quite: completely, very (adverb)

I have had *quite* enough to eat after that half-pounder and fries.

quit: to stop (verb)

Will you please *quit* bothering me?

It is not *quite* time to *quit* yet.

The machine _____ running, and the office was _____.

Right/Write

right: correct; in a direction opposite from left (adjective)

Are you sure this is the *right* way?

Take a *right* after the bridge.

write: to put words on paper (verb)

I will *write* soon.

Please be sure to *write* the *right* address.

_____ your name in the _____ column.

Set/Sit

set: a collection of something (noun); to place an object somewhere (verb)

Junior has a great train *set.*

Please *set* the package on the table.

sit: to rest with one's rear end supported by a chair or other surface

You can *sit* right over there.

Set your coat down before you *sit.*

Let's _____ and look over my _____ of travel photos.

Suppose/Supposed

suppose: to imagine or assume to be true

Suppose you could go anywhere in the world.

I *suppose* you want some dinner.

supposed: past tense of *suppose;* intended

The clerk *supposed* the man was over twenty-one.

The meeting was *supposed* to be over by noon.

You are *supposed* to call when you are going to be late, but I *suppose* that's too much to expect.

I was _____ to take the ten o'clock train, but I _____ the eleven o'clock is okay.

Than/Then

than: a word used to compare two or more things or persons

Joanne makes more money *than* I do.

then: at a certain time

I will look forward to seeing you *then.*

I weigh a lot more *than* I used to back *then.*

If you want to lose weight, _____ you will have to eat less _____ you do now.

Their/There/They're

■ If you aren't sure whether to use *their* or *they're,* substitute *they are.* If the sentence doesn't make sense, use *their.*

their: a pronoun showing ownership

Their new apartment has two bedrooms.

there: a word indicating location or existence

Your desk is over *there.*

There is more work than I can handle.

they're: a contraction of the words *they are*

They're going to Hawaii.

Their windows are open, and *there* is a breeze, so *they're* not hot.

_____ going to be away, so my friend will be staying _____ and taking care of _____ cat.

Though/Through/Threw

though: however; nevertheless; in spite of (conjunction)

I'll be there, *though* I might be a little late.

through: finished with (adjective); from one side to the other (preposition)

Jenna is *through* with school in May.

Go *through* the first set of doors.

threw: hurled, tossed (past tense of the verb *throw*)

She *threw* away the garbage.

Jimmy *threw* the ball, and it went *through* the window, *though* he had not aimed it there.

_____ she loved him, she _____ him out because she couldn't

go _____ any more pain.

To/Too/Two

to: a word indicating a direction or movement (preposition); part of the infinitive form of a verb

I am going *to* the food store.

Do you want *to* see a movie?

too: also; more than enough; very (adverb)

Toni was sick *too*.

The car was going *too* fast.

two: the number between one and three

There are *two* tables.

They went *to* a restaurant and ordered *too* much food for *two* people.

The _____ friends started _____ dance, but it was _____ crowded

to move.

Use/Used

use: to employ or put into service (verb)

I *use* this grill all the time.

used: past tense of the verb *use*. *Used to* can indicate a past fact or state, or it can mean "familiar with."

I *used* the grill last night to cook chicken.

I *used* to do yoga.

I am *used* to juggling school and work.

Paolo *used* to be a farmer, so he knows how to *use* all the equipment.

When you last _____ the oven, what did you _____ it for?

Who's/Whose

■ If you aren't sure whether to use *whose* or *who's*, substitute *who is*. If the sentence doesn't make sense, use *whose*.

who's: a contraction of the words *who is* or *who has*

Who's hungry?

Who's been here the longest?

whose: a pronoun showing ownership

Whose bag is this?

The person *whose* name is first on the list is the one *who's* going next.

_____ the man _____ shoes are on the table?

Your/You're

■ If you aren't sure whether to use *your* or *you're*, substitute *you are*. If the sentence doesn't make sense, use *your*.

your: a pronoun showing ownership

I like *your* shirt.

you're: a contraction of the words *you are*

You're going to run out of gas.

You're about to get paint all over *your* hands.

_____ teacher says _____ always late to class.

PRACTICE 1   USING THE RIGHT WORD . . . .

In each of the following items, circle the correct word in parentheses.

EXAMPLE: (You're / (Your)) résumé is a critical computer file.

1. I tell all my friends to back up important data on (their / there) computers.

2. Unfortunately, I sometimes forget to take my own (advice / advise).

3. My computer had a serious crash, and now I cannot (find / fine) the most recent copy of my résumé.

4. I should (have / of) made a hard copy and a backup on a disk, but I didn't.

5. Today I have (a / an / and) interview for a job I really want, and I can't locate any résumés (accept / except) one from 2003.

6. (Loosing / Losing) a résumé is not the end of the world, but it will be (quiet / quite) a job reconstructing it.

7. It took me hours to (right / write) and proofread my most recent résumé.

8. This morning, I quickly (set / sit) down some information to give to the interviewer, but this version is sloppier (than / then) the résumé I (use / used) to have.

9. (Though / Through) I believe that I am well qualified for this job, I'm afraid that this résumé may have a bad (affect / effect) on my chances of being hired.

10. An interviewer (who's / whose) task is to hire the best person must pay attention (to / too / two) small details.

■ For more practice with commonly confused words, visit *Exercise Central* at **bedfordstmartins .com/realessays**.

Edit Paragraphs and Your Own Writing

Edit the following paragraphs for commonly confused words.

■ EDITING REVIEW 1 (18 errors)

(1) Most people no that Americans love to drive there cars. (2) However, many people may not be conscience of how much the government does to support our car culture. (3) For instance, the United States would never of had so many good highways without federal and state assistance for road construction and maintenance. (4) New highways are usually

paid for mainly buy tax money. (5) It is rare for a new road too be paid for with tolls, which would come exclusively from the people driving on it. (6) Americans also expect they're roads to be well maintained, and they may right to their representatives to complain about potholes and aging road surfaces. (7) The government is even responsible for keeping gas prices lower here then in most other industrialized nations.

(8) Few people mine that the government assists drivers in these ways. (9) Some would argue that its a government's job to help pay for transportation. (10) However, other forms of transportation in this country are often past over when Congress hands out funds. (11) Amtrak, the U.S. railroad, may soon loose virtually all government funds, even though many government officials are skeptical of it's ability to keep operating without government assistance. (12) Accept for a few places like New York and San Francisco, most U.S. cities do not have good mass transit systems. (13) Americans who's travels have taken them to certain parts of the world praise the national train systems and city transit systems they find there. (14) As traffic gets worse in our nation's urban and suburban areas, some people fine it odd that the United States does not invest more in transportation that would allow people to leave there cars at home.

▮ **EDITING REVIEW 2 (14 errors)** . . . .

(1) Hoping to keep are nation's blood supply safe, the U.S. government has placed restrictions on donating blood. (2) Anyone whose spent more than five years in Europe or more than three months in England since 1980 is not allowed to give blood. (3) Officials hope that asking about time in Europe will help them fine people who might of been

exposed to mad cow disease. (4) Men are also asked whether they have had sexual relations with other men in the passed ten years. (5) If they have, their asked not to give blood. (6) This is suppose to protect the blood supply from the AIDS virus. (7) Of course, they're are some problems with these restrictions. (8) First, know one knows how much exposure to infected meat can give a person mad cow disease, and know one is sure how long the disease can hide in a human body. (9) Second, many gay men our not infected with HIV, and many women, who are not asked about sexual activity, are infected. (10) Restricting certain groups of people from giving blood may not do anything to protect the blood supply, but it will certainly effect the amount of blood available. (11) Is it better to allow the blood supply to become dangerously low then to allow people who's blood might carry a disease to donate blood?

PRACTICE 2 EDITING YOUR OWN WRITING FOR COMMONLY CONFUSED WORDS

As a final practice, edit a piece of your own writing for commonly confused words. It can be a paper you are working on for this course, a paper you've already finished, a paper for another course, a recent piece of writing from your work or everyday life, or your idea journal entry. Add any misused words you find to your personal list of confusing words.

36

Spelling
Using the Right Letters

Understand the Importance of Spelling Correctly

■ **IDEA JOURNAL**
Describe a place in your town or city.

Unfortunately, spelling errors are easy for readers to spot, and they make a bad impression. Fortunately, practice greatly improves spelling.

Read the following paragraph, the body of a follow-up letter one student wrote to a prospective employer after an interview:

> Thank you for the oportunity to meet about the summer internship at Margate Associates. I hope you will find that my coursework in graphic design and my excellant communication skills make me a promiseing candidate for the position. I look forward to hearing from you soon. I am happy to provide you with referances if you need them.

 PRACTICE 1 FINDING SPELLING ERRORS . . . .

■ For more spelling practice, visit *Exercise Central* at **bedfordstmartins .com/realessays**.

Underline the four spelling errors in the preceding paragraph. In the space provided, write the correct spelling of each word.

_____

. . . .

If you are serious about improving your spelling, you need to have a dictionary and a spelling list (a list of words you often misspell)—and you need to use them.

A **dictionary** contains the correct spellings of words, along with information on how they are pronounced, what they mean, and where they came from. When proofreading your papers, use a current dictionary either in print or online. The following are two popular online dictionaries:

- Merriam-Webster Online at **www.m-w.com**. This dictionary has a wildcard search feature. If you are fairly sure how the beginning of a word is spelled, you can enter those letters and then an asterisk (*) and get a list of the words that begin with the letters. From the list, you can choose the word you want.

- Your Dictionary at **www.yourdictionary.com**. This site features specialty dictionaries for business, computers, law, medicine, and other fields.

If you have trouble finding words in a regular dictionary, get a spelling dictionary, which is designed to help you find a word even if you have no idea how to spell it. Checking a dictionary is the single most important thing you can do to improve your spelling.

■ For a sample dictionary entry, see page 634.

Keeping a **spelling list** will help you edit your papers and learn how to write the words correctly. From this list of words you often misspell, identify your personal spelling "demons"—the five to ten words that you misspell most frequently. Write these words, spelled correctly, on an index card, and keep the card somewhere handy so that you can consult it whenever you write.

Practice Spelling Correctly

Don't try to correct your grammar, improve your message, and check your spelling at the same time. Instead, do separate proofreading passes for each editing task.

Most word-processing programs have a **spell checker** that finds and highlights a word that may be misspelled and suggests other spellings. However, no spell checker can catch every mistake. A spell checker ignores anything it recognizes as a word, so it will not help you find words that are misused or misspellings that are also words. For example, a spell checker would not highlight any of the problems in the following phrases:

Just to it.	(Correct: Just do it.)
The strap is lose.	(Correct: The strap is loose.)
my writing coarse	(Correct: my writing course)

Use the following **proofreading techniques** to focus on the spelling of one word at a time. Different techniques work for different people, so try them all and then decide which ones work for you.

PROOFREADING TECHNIQUES

- Put a piece of paper or a ruler under the line you are reading.
- Cut a "window" in an index card that is about the size of a long word (such as *misunderstanding*), and place it over your writing to focus on one word or phrase at a time.
- Proofread your paper backward, one word at a time.
- If you are using a computer, print out a version of your paper that looks noticeably different: Make the words larger, make the margins larger, triple-space the lines, or do all of these. Read this version carefully.
- Read your paper aloud. This strategy will help you if you tend to leave words out.
- Exchange papers with a partner. Your only task as you proofread your partner's paper should be to identify possible misspellings.

After you proofread each word in your paper, look at your personal spelling list and your list of demon words one more time. If you used any of these words in your paper, go back and check their spelling again. (Most word-processing programs allow you to search for specific words using Find or Search commands from the Edit menu.) You may be surprised to find that you missed seeing the same old spelling mistakes.

PRACTICE 2   FINDING AND CORRECTING SPELLING MISTAKES . . . .

Take a paper you are working on, and find and correct any spelling errors using the tools discussed previously—a dictionary, your personal spelling list, proofreading techniques, and a spell checker. How many spelling mistakes did you find? Were you surprised? How was the experience different from what you normally do to edit for spelling?

Five Steps to Better Spelling

Learning to find and correct spelling mistakes that you have already made is only half the battle. You also need to become a better speller so that you do not make so many mistakes in the first place. Here are five ways to do so.

Step 1. Master Ten Troublemakers

The ten words on the following list were identified by writing teachers as the words most commonly misspelled. Because there are only ten, you should be able to memorize them.

INCORRECT	CORRECT
alot	a lot
argue ment	argument
defina te, defe nite	defin i te
develope	develop
lit e	ligh t
nece s ary, ne s esary	ne c e ss ary
reci e ve	rec ei ve
sep e rate	sep a rate
surpri z e, suprise	su r pri s e
until l	until

Step 2. Master Your Personal Spelling Demons

Once you know what your personal spelling demons are, you can master them. Try some of the following techniques.

- Create a memory aid—an explanation or saying that will remind you of the correct spelling. For example, "*surprise* is no *prize*" may remind you to spell *surprise* with an *s,* not a *z.*
- Break the word into parts, and try to master each part. You can break it into syllables (*Feb ru ar y*) or separate the prefixes and endings (*dis appoint ment*).
- Write the word correctly ten times.
- Write a paragraph in which you use the word at least three times.
- Say the letters of the word out loud. See if there's a rhythm or a rhyme you can memorize.
- Say the whole word out loud, emphasizing each letter and syllable even if that's not the way you normally say it. For example, say *prob a bly* instead of *prob ly.* Try to pronounce the word this way in your head each time you spell it.
- Ask a partner to give you a spelling test.

Step 3. Master Commonly Confused Words

Refer back to Chapter 35, which covers twenty-seven sets of words that are commonly confused because they sound alike, such as *write/right* and *its/it's*. If you can master these commonly confused words, you will avoid many spelling mistakes.

Step 4. Learn Six Spelling Rules

If you can remember the following six rules, you can avoid or correct many of the spelling errors in your writing.

Before the six rules, here is a quick review of vowels and consonants.

Vowels: *a e i o u* and sometimes *y*

Consonants: all the letters that are not vowels

The letter *y* can be either a vowel or a consonant. It is a vowel when it sounds like the *y* in *fly* or *hungry*. It is a consonant when it sounds like the *y* in *yellow*.

Rule 1. *I* before *e*/Except after *c*/Or when sounded like *a*/As in *neighbor* or *weigh*.

Many people repeat this rhyme to themselves as they decide whether a word is spelled with an *ie* or an *ei*.

piece (*i* before *e*)   receive (except after *c*)   eight (sounds like *a*)

EXCEPTIONS: either, neither, foreign, height, seize, society, their, weird

Rule 2. Drop the final *e* when adding an ending that begins with a vowel.

hope + ing = hoping   imagine + ation = imagination

Keep the final *e* when adding an ending that begins with a consonant.

achieve + ment = achievement   definite + ly = definitely

EXCEPTIONS: argument, awful, simply, truly (and others)

Rule 3.   When adding an ending to a word that ends in *y*, change the *y* to *i* when a consonant comes before the *y*.

lonely + est = loneliest   apology + ize = apologize

ha**pp**y + er = happ**i**er   likely + hood = likelihood

Do not change the *y* when a vowel comes before the *y*.

boy + ish = boyish   survey + or = surveyor

pay + ment = payment   buy + er = buyer

EXCEPTIONS   1. When adding *-ing* to a word ending in *y*, always keep the *y*, even if a consonant comes before it: study + ing = studying.

2. Other exceptions include *daily, dryer, said,* and *paid.*

Rule 4.   When adding an ending that starts with a vowel to a one-syllable word, double the final consonant only if the word ends with a consonant-vowel-consonant.

chop + ed = chopped   **sh**op + ing = shopping

hot + er = hotter   st**rap** + ed = strapped

Do not double the final consonant if the word ends with some other combination.

VOWEL-VOWEL-CONSONANT	VOWEL-CONSONANT-CONSONANT
cl**ean** + est = cleanest	sl**ick** + er = slicker
p**oor** + er = poorer	te**ach** + er = teacher
cl**ear** + ed = cleared	l**ast** + ed = lasted

Rule 5.   When adding an ending that starts with a vowel to a word of two or more syllables, double the final consonant only if the word ends with a consonant-vowel-consonant and the stress is on the last syllable.

ad**mit** + ing = admitting   cont**rol** + er = controller

ad**mit** + ed = admitted

Do not double the final consonant in other cases.

problem + atic = problematic   offer + ed = offered
understand + ing = understanding

Rule 6.   Add *s* to most words, including words that end in *o* preceded by a vowel.

MOST WORDS	WORDS THAT END IN VOWEL PLUS *O*
book + s = books	vid**eo** + s = videos
college + s = colleges	ster**eo** + s = stereos
jump + s = jumps	rad**io** + s = radios

Add *-es* to words that end in *s, -sh, -ch,* or *x* and *o* preceded by a consonant.

WORDS THAT END IN *S, -SH, -CH,* OR *X*	WORDS THAT END IN CONSONANT PLUS *O*
class + es = class**es**	pota**to** + es = potato**es**
push + es = push**es**	he**ro** + es = hero**es**
ben**ch** + es = bench**es**	**go** + es = go**es**
fa**x** + es = fax**es**	

EXCEPTIONS: pianos, solos (and others)

Step 5: Consult a Spelling List

The following is a list of the one hundred most commonly misspelled words. Consult this as you proofread your writing.

One Hundred Commonly Misspelled Words

absence	analyze	basically	career
achieve	answer	beautiful	category
across	appetite	beginning	chief
aisle	argument	believe	column
a lot	athlete	business	coming
already	awful	calendar	commitment

conscious	finally	marriage	schedule
convenient	foreign	meant	scissors
cruelty	friend	muscle	secretary
daughter	government	necessary	separate
definite	grief	ninety	sincerely
describe	guidance	noticeable	sophomore
dictionary	harass	occasion	succeed
different	height	occurrence	successful
disappoint	humorous	perform	surprise
dollar	illegal	physically	truly
eighth	immediately	prejudice	until
embarrass	independent	probably	usually
environment	interest	psychology	vacuum
especially	jewelry	receive	valuable
exaggerate	judgment	recognize	vegetable
excellent	knowledge	recommend	weight
exercise	license	restaurant	weird
fascinate	lightning	rhythm	writing
February	loneliness	roommate	written

Edit Paragraphs and Your Own Writing

Find and correct any spelling mistakes in the following paragraphs.

■ **EDITING REVIEW 1 (40 errors)** . . . .

(1) Americans have always been an inventive peeple and, in recent years, it seems as though there creative inspiration is stronger then it has ever been. (2) The U.S. Patent Office is now recieving the highest amount of patent applications in its histery, with the number of applications topping 400,000 anually. (3) To put this in purspective, in 1986, about 125,000 patent applications were fild, and the number of applications

has steadily increased since then. (4) It is not difacult to see why, with the prolifiration of available electronic gadgets, most of which involve numrous patent applications to protect their innovateive technology. (5) Many of the wondrus devices that are incorporatted into the latest cars, televisions, radioes, personal media plaiers, cell phones, and cameras are waiting for patent approval. (6) Therein lyes a big problem for the Patent Office, which now has a backlog of 700,000 applications and an avrage patent review time of 31 months.

(7) To get better control of the approval prosess, the Patent Office is gradualy tightening its ruleses, requireing inventors to provide more information and allowing the public greater acess to reveiw applications. (8) In addition, the office is approving a lowwer percentige of the applications it gets, from approveing 72 percent of applications in 2000 to only about 50 percent approved in 2007. (9) Inventers can improve they're chances of haveing a sucessful application by following a few sensable guidlines. (10) Be sure the invention is truley new and usefull, and describe it clearly and understandibly. (11) Then, move on to other venturs because the Patent Office's anser will not come speedely.

■ **EDITING REVIEW 2 (35 errors)** . . . .

(1) Most parents regularly tell their children to sit up strait, but is siting in a 90-degree posture really necesary? (2) More importent, is sitting up straight good for a purson's back? (3) Now, the long-held beleif that people will put a strain on their backs if they sit at anything other then a 90-degree angle has been prooven wrong. (4) Severel studys have shown that sitting up straight with the thighs parralel to the ground hieghtens the stress on the lumbar disks in the lower back. (5) Scientists first recognised

this by measureing the pressure on the backs of volunters as they sat in varius positions. (6) This reveeled that a reclining position placed the lest strain on the back and reduced the pressure asociated with back problems.

(7) Numberous seperate studies subsequently confirmed this, but their was no direct vizual evidence of how this worked until scientists were finaly able to use magnetic imaging resonance (MRI) machines. (8) In an MRI study, researchers had volunteers sit in three diffrent positions. (9) Two of the positions, sitting upright and sitting with the body bent forwerd, caused the most exaggerated spinal disk movment, during which the inturnal disk material was moved out of alignment. (10) For the therd position, the subjects sat back at a 135-degree angel with their feet on the flor. (11) This position produced the least back strain, indicateing that leening back while sitting is beter for the back than sitting up straight.

▮ PRACTICE 3 **EDITING YOUR OWN WRITING FOR SPELLING** . . . . . .

As a final practice, edit a piece of your own writing for spelling, using the techniques described in this chapter. It can be a paper you are working on for this course, a paper you've already finished, a paper for another course, a recent piece of writing from work or everyday life, or your idea journal entry.

Part Seven

Punctuation and Capitalization

37

Commas

,

Understand What Commas Do

Commas (,) are punctuation marks that help readers understand a sentence. Read aloud the following three sentences. How does the use of commas change the meaning?

■ **IDEA JOURNAL**
Write about some things you enjoy doing.

NO COMMA   After you call Jim I'll leave for the restaurant.

ONE COMMA   After you call Jim, I'll leave for the restaurant.

TWO COMMAS   After you call, Jim, I'll leave for the restaurant.

Commas signal particular meanings to your readers, so it is important that you understand when and how to use them.

Practice Using Commas Correctly

Commas between Items in a Series

Use commas to separate three or more items in a series. This includes the last item in the series, which usually has *and* before it.

item , item , item , and item

When you go to the store, please pick up *milk, bread, orange juice,* and *bananas.*

Last semester I took *math, reading,* and *composition.*

Students may take the course as a *regular classroom course,* as an *online course,* or as a *distance learning course.*

A comma is not always used before the final item in a series. In college writing, however, it is always best to include it.

Commas between Coordinate Adjectives

Coordinate adjectives are two or more adjectives that independently modify the same noun and are separated by commas. Coordinate adjectives can be separated by the word *and.*

We had an entire month of *cold, damp, grey* weather.

The car is *old, battered,* and *rusty.*

Do *not* use a comma between the final adjective and the noun it modifies.

INCORRECT	It was a *long, hard, complicated,* test.
CORRECT	It was a *long, hard, complicated* test.

Cumulative adjectives modify the same noun but form a unit and are not separated by commas. Cumulative adjectives cannot be joined by the word *and.*

Our team wants to win the *big regional sales* trophy.

All of the words in italics are adjectives, but they build on each other. Moving left from *trophy,* each adjective becomes part of a larger unit.

1. *Sales* describes the trophy.
2. The next word to the left, *regional,* describes not just the trophy but the *sales* trophy.
3. The next word to the left, *big,* describes the *regional sales* trophy.

The team didn't want to win just a *big* trophy or just a *regional* trophy or just a *sales* trophy. The team wanted the *big regional sales* trophy.

To summarize the rule: Use a comma to separate two or more coordinate adjectives. Do not use commas to separate cumulative adjectives.

■ **PRACTICE 1   USING COMMAS IN A SERIES
AND WITH ADJECTIVES** . . . .

Add commas where they are needed in the following sentences. If the sentence is correct, write "C" next to it.

> **EXAMPLE:** The short, slim conductor stepped up to the elaborate,
>
> colorful podium.

1. We had prepared a wholesome flavorful meal for the children their parents and their friends.

■ Answers to odd-numbered practice items are at the back of the book.

2. Lucas has painted three large pictures for the unfurnished boring living room.

3. The huge confusing and annoying airport desperately needed renovating.

4. These young plants might not survive the gusting unpredictable wind.

5. I have several urgent e-mail messages from Mr. Toland Ms. Fry and my father.

6. Please bake us some of your tasty rich chocolate chip cookies.

■ For more practice using commas, visit *Exercise Central* at **bedfordstmartins .com/realessays**.

7. Our scholarly English professor was once a professional baseball player.

8. She loves to take long slow walks in the rain.

9. Thomas has no phone no food no television and hardly anything else in his tiny uncomfortable one-room apartment.

10. The early morning edition of the newspaper arrives before I leave for my exciting new part-time job.

11. Driving on this endless dull unsafe highway can be unpleasant.

12. Jeffrey is a lazy gorgeous and cuddly cat.

13. Plentiful exercise combined with a healthy nutritious diet will have you fit fairly quickly.

14. The funny animated movie was based on a well-written graphic novel.

15. We always buy rich high-calorie candy bars when we go to the movies.

Commas in Compound Sentences

■ The words *and, but, for, nor, or, so,* and *yet* are called coordinating conjunctions. See Chapter 30 for more details.

A **compound sentence** contains two independent clauses (sentences) joined by one of these words—*and, but, for, nor, or, so, yet*. Use a comma before the joining word to separate the two clauses.

| Sentence , | *and / but / for / nor / or / so / yet* | sentence. |

Tom missed class yesterday**,** *and* he called to ask me what he missed.

I would have been happy to help him**,** *but* I was absent too.

I told him I wasn't there**,** *so* he said he would e-mail the professor.

A comma is not needed if the word *and, but, for, nor, or, so,* or *yet* joins two sentence elements that are not independent clauses.

> **Language Note:** A comma by itself cannot separate two sentences: Doing so creates a run-on (see Chapter 24).

PRACTICE 2 USING COMMAS IN COMPOUND SENTENCES

Edit the following compound sentences by adding commas where they are needed. If a sentence is already correct, put a "C" next to it.

EXAMPLE: The population of the United States is getting older, but

the number of people trained to care for the elderly is declining.

1. Working in a nursing home is a difficult job for elderly patients can seldom do much for themselves.

2. The labor is physically difficult and it can also be mentally draining.

3. Few trained nurses and nurse's aides want nursing-home jobs for the pay is also usually lower than that offered by hospitals.

4. Nursing-home workers have high turnover rates and the facilities are constantly in need of new personnel.

5. More workers will be needed as the baby boomers become elderly yet there is already a shortage of people willing to do the work.

6. A director sometimes must hire undertrained workers or the nursing home will face a severe staff shortage.

7. Workers without education and training may have difficulty understanding a doctor's orders, so the patients' care may suffer.

8. Home health aides and hospice workers are also in short supply and the need for such workers is growing every day.

9. Solving these problems will be difficult for long-term care for the elderly is already very expensive.

10. People caring for elderly patients must get better pay or no one will be available to do the work in a few years.

. . . .

Commas after Introductory Word Groups

Use a comma after an introductory word or word group. An introductory word group can be a word, a phrase, or a clause. The comma lets your readers know when the main part of the sentence is starting.

| Introductory word or word group |**,**| main part of sentence. |

INTRODUCTORY WORD   *Finally,* I finished the job.

INTRODUCTORY PHRASE   *According to the paper,* the crime rate went down.

INTRODUCTORY CLAUSE   *As you know,* the store is going out of business.

PRACTICE 3 USING COMMAS AFTER INTRODUCTORY WORD GROUPS

In each item, underline any introductory word or word group. Then, add commas after introductory word groups where they are needed.

EXAMPLE: <u>Every year</u>, more than two hundred motorists die in collisions with animals.

1. Along roadsides all across the country drivers see the bodies of animals hit by cars.

2. Usually the victims are common species, such as deer and raccoons.

3. Of course hitting a deer is not only disturbing but also potentially harmful or fatal to the occupants of a car.

4. However the deer population has not suffered much of a decline from traffic accidents.

5. On the other hand drivers in wilderness areas may accidentally kill endangered species.

6. For instance experts believe that 65 percent of the population of Florida panthers has been killed on highways in the past twenty years.

7. Maintaining the world's largest network of roads the U.S. Forest Service tries to balance the needs of humans and wildlife.

8. To get access to wilderness areas humans, many of whom strongly favor protecting the environment, need roads.

9. Unfortunately wilderness roads may isolate populations of animals that will not cross them and kill animals that make the attempt.

10. Although expensive underpasses and overpasses have been successful in some areas at reducing human collisions with animals.

Commas around Appositives and Interrupters

An **appositive,** a phrase that renames a noun, comes directly before or after the noun.

■ For more on appositives, see pages 572–74.

> Dick, *my neighbor,* has a new job.
>
> Apartment prices are high at Riverview, *the new complex.*

An **interrupter** is an aside or transition that interrupts the flow of a sentence and does not affect its meaning.

> Campus parking fees, *you should know,* are going up by 30 percent.
>
> A six-month sticker will now be $45, *if you can believe it.*

An interrupter that appears at the beginning of a sentence can be treated the same as an introductory word group.

> *As a matter of fact,* the fees are the highest of any of the campuses in the city.

Putting commas around appositives and interrupters tells readers that these elements give extra information but are not essential to the meaning of a sentence. If an appositive or interrupter is in the middle of a sentence, set it off with a pair of commas, one before and one after. If an appositive or interrupter comes at the beginning or end of a sentence, separate it from the rest of the sentence with one comma.

> *Incidentally,* your raise has been approved.
>
> Your raise, *incidentally,* has been approved.
>
> Your raise has been approved, *incidentally.*

Sometimes, an appositive is essential to the meaning of a sentence. When a sentence would not have the same meaning without the appositive, the appositive should not be set off with commas.

> The actor *John Travolta* has never won an Academy Award.
>
> [The sentence *The actor has never won an Academy Award* does not have the same meaning.]
>
> The lawyer *Clarence Darrow* was one of history's greatest speakers.
>
> [The sentence *The lawyer was one of history's greatest speakers* does not have the same meaning.]

PRACTICE 4   USING COMMAS TO SET OFF APPOSITIVES AND INTERRUPTERS . . . .

Underline any appositives or interrupters in the following sentences. Then use commas to set them off.

> EXAMPLE: The reason for the delay, <u>a mechanical problem with the airplane,</u> was not mentioned.

1. Road rage as most people know occurs when angry drivers overreact.

2. Another phenomenon air rage involves out-of-control and often intoxicated passengers on an airplane.

3. One famous air rage incident a confrontation between a drunken businessman and a flight attendant ended with the passenger tied to his seat for the rest of the flight.

4. Ground rage like air rage is a term used for incidents between airline passengers and airline employees.

5. Ground rage as the name suggests occurs in the terminal, not in the air.

6. Gate agents the people who check tickets and allow passengers to board the plane are frequent victims of ground rage.

7. Oversold seats a common occurrence in air travel can mean that some passengers are forced to miss a flight.

8. Passengers many of whom are on a tight schedule or have a connecting flight to catch find delayed flights infuriating as well.

9. Some delayed or bumped passengers take out their anger on the gate agent a convenient target.

10. Although some airline employees may not be helpful or friendly, their attitudes do not excuse passengers who commit assault a serious crime.

Commas around Adjective Clauses

An **adjective clause** is a group of words that often begins with *who, which,* or *that;* has a subject and verb; and describes the noun that comes before it in a sentence. An adjective clause may or may not be set off from the rest of the sentence by commas depending on its meaning in the sentence.

If an adjective clause can be taken out of a sentence without completely changing the meaning, put commas around the clause.

The mayor**,** *who was recently elected***,** has no political experience.

SuperShop**,** *which is the largest supermarket in town***,** was recently bought by Big Boy Markets.

I have an appointment with Dr. Kling**,** *who is the specialist.*

If an adjective clause is essential to the meaning of a sentence, do not put commas around it. You can tell whether a clause is essential by taking it out and seeing if the meaning of the sentence changes significantly, as it would if you took the clauses out of the following examples:

The hair salon *that I liked* recently closed.

Salesclerks *who sell liquor to minors* are breaking the law.

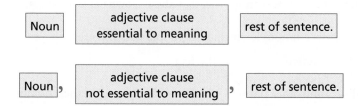

Use *who* to refer to a person; *which* to refer to places or things (but not to people); and *that* for people, places, or things. When referring to a person, *who* is preferable to *that.*

■ For more on adjective clauses, see pages 575–77.

PRACTICE 5   USING COMMAS TO SET OFF ADJECTIVE CLAUSES . . . .

Edit the following sentences by putting any needed commas around adjective clauses. Remember that if an adjective clause is essential to the meaning of the sentence, you should not use commas. If a sentence is already correct, put a "C" next to it.

EXAMPLE: Stephen King, who understands how to frighten his readers, has depicted evil clowns in his work.

1. The only thing that terrifies Maria is a person dressed as a clown.

2. The fear of clowns which is called *coulrophobia* is fairly common.

3. Some young children who develop this fear are not prepared adequately before seeing a clown for the first time.

4. Clowns who usually wear heavy makeup and brightly colored wigs do not look like ordinary people.

5. Clowns also make sudden movements that can frighten children.

6. Most children who fear clowns will get over their phobia as they grow up.

7. Such people who may never love clowns will still be able to tolerate having them around.

8. Many adults have seen movies that show clowns as evil killers.

9. Few adults admit to having coulrophobia which is most effectively treated when the sufferer confronts the fear.

10. Unlike some other phobias which can trap people in their homes or make them unable to work coulrophobia has little effect on most sufferers, who are not likely to meet clowns frequently in everyday life.

Other Uses for Commas

Commas with Quotation Marks

■ For more on quotation marks, see Chapter 39.

Quotation marks are used to show that you are using a direct quotation, repeating exactly what someone said or wrote. Generally, use commas to set off the words inside quotation marks from the rest of the sentence.

"Excuse me," said the old woman in back of me.

"Did you know," she asked, "that you just cut in front of me?"

I exclaimed, "Oh, no. I'm so sorry!"

Notice that a comma never comes directly *after* a quotation mark.

Commas in Addresses

Use commas to separate the elements of an address included in a sentence. However, do not use a comma before a zip code.

My address is 4498 Main Street, Bolton, Massachusetts 01740.

If a sentence continues after the address, put a comma after the address. Also, use a comma after individual elements used to name a geographical location such as a city and state.

The house was moved from Cripple Creek, Colorado, to the lot on Forest Street.

Commas in Dates

Separate the day from the year with a comma. If you give only the month and year, do not separate them with a comma.

She wrote the letter on April 1, 2005.

The next session is in January 2010.

If a sentence continues after a date that includes the day, put a comma after the date.

He waited until April 15, 2005, to file his 2004 tax return.

Commas with Names

Put commas around the name of someone you are addressing by name.

Don, I want you to come look at this.

Unfortunately, Marie, you need to finish the report by next week.

Commas with Yes *or* No

Put a comma after the word *yes* or *no* in response to a question.

No, that isn't what I meant.

PRACTICE 6 USING COMMAS

Edit the following sentences by adding commas where they are needed. If a sentence is already correct, put a "C" next to it.

EXAMPLE: The new regulations of telemarketing went into effect on

April 1, 2001.

1. My sister asked "James do you get a lot of telemarketing calls?"

2. "Yes I do" I replied "and they always come at dinnertime."

3. She told me that new laws that could help me protect my privacy had taken effect in April 2001.

4. I wrote to the governor's office in Albany New York for information about the telemarketing registry.

5. My address which is 21 Highland Road Binghamton New York has now been added to the state registry.

6. For a while I still got occasional calls that began with an unfamiliar voice saying "James I have an exciting offer for you."

7. I simply replied "No I have news for you."

8. I pointed out that on August 11 2009 I had added my name and address to a list of people who do not want to receive calls about exciting offers.

9. "As you probably know" I told my unwanted callers "it is illegal for you to contact me in this way."

10. The marketing calls had stopped completely by November 1.

Edit Paragraphs and Your Own Writing

Edit the following paragraphs by adding commas where they are needed.

■ EDITING REVIEW 1 (17 commas) . . . .

(1) Everyone who uses cleaning products at home has probably seen warning labels on those products for most household cleaners contain harsh chemicals. (2) The warnings which are required by law are so common that many users probably ignore them. (3) However all cleaning products should be used with care and some of them can seriously injure children or anyone else who misuses them. (4) Drain cleaners toilet bowl cleaners and chlorine bleach can all cause serious damage to skin eyes and other sensitive tissue. (5) Glass cleaners can react with bleach to produce toxic fumes. (6) Alternative cleansers nontoxic products that can be made from items in an average kitchen are cheaper than brand-name cleaning products and usually work just as well. (7) For most cleaning jobs a solution of vinegar and water or baking soda and water is effective. (8) A plunger can often fix a clogged drain as well as a drain cleaner can and club soda cleans windows nicely. (9) As for air fresheners one expert advises "Open your windows." (10) Economy efficiency and safety are three excellent reasons for choosing homemade cleansers.

■ EDITING REVIEW 2 (39 commas) . . . .

(1) A few days ago I received an e-mail that told a terrifying story. (2) At a large discount store in Austin Texas a four-year-old girl had disappeared and her mother had asked for the store employees' help in finding the child. (3) Thinking quickly the employees locked all of the

doors posted an employee at every exit and systematically searched the store. (4) The child who was found in a bathroom was safe but half of her head had been shaved. (5) In addition someone had changed her clothes so it seemed obvious that an abductor had been trying to slip her out of the store unnoticed. (6) The e-mail message which came from a distant acquaintance ended by advising me "Don't let your children out of your sight!"

(7) Later that day I was talking to my neighbor and I happened to mention the message. (8) She too had seen it and the story had shocked her. (9) Something about the story made me suspicious however so I decided to do some Internet research. (10) I found a site that discussed urban legends Internet hoaxes and chain letters. (11) On the site I discovered an exact copy of the e-mail I had received. (12) I also learned that my neighbor and I were not the first people to fall for this hoax for Ann Landers had even printed a version of it several years earlier. (13) When she learned that she had been fooled she printed a retraction a column explaining that the story was fictional. (14) A reader wrote to her and said "Reminding people to be cautious is one thing. Scaring them is another."

(15) After doing the research I felt better about the scary e-mail story but I felt sad that we are so distrustful of one another. (16) Such stories can make us fear that potential abductors are everywhere. (17) Thirty years ago most parents were not usually afraid to let children walk to school alone or play outside but today's parents rarely let children out of their sight until the kids are in their teens. (18) The difference is not in the number of abductions of children a very small number that has

remained nearly constant over the decades. (19) No the difference is that people now hear about these unusual and terrifying instances over and over. (20) Eventually they reach the conclusion that these stories must be true and they are convinced that such dreadful things must happen frequently. (21) The e-mail I had received was contributing I decided to this climate of irrational fear. (22) "Ann Landers's reader was right" I said to myself. (23) "We should teach our children caution but we can harm them and ourselves by making them believe that evil strangers are lurking around every corner."

PRACTICE 7 EDITING YOUR OWN WRITING FOR COMMAS · · · · · ·

As a final practice, edit a piece of your own writing for commas. It can be a paper you are working on for this course, a paper you've already finished, a paper for another course, a recent piece of writing from your work or everyday life, or your idea journal entry.

38

Apostrophes

,

Understand What Apostrophes Do

■ **IDEA JOURNAL**
Write about some possessions that you and others in your family value.

An **apostrophe** (') is a punctuation mark that either shows ownership (*Susan's*) or indicates that a letter has been intentionally left out to form a contraction (*I'm, that's, they're*). Although an apostrophe looks like a comma (,), it is not used for the same purpose, and it is written higher on the line than commas are.

apostrophe'   comma,

Practice Using Apostrophes Correctly

Apostrophes to Show Ownership

■ To understand this chapter, you need to know what nouns and pronouns are. For a review, see Chapters 22, 27, and 33.

- **Add 's to a singular noun to show ownership even if the noun already ends in s.**

  Darcy's car is being repaired.

  Joan got all the information she needed from the hotel's Web site.

  Chris's house is only a mile away.

- **If a noun is plural and ends in *s*, just add an apostrophe to show ownership. If it is plural but does not end in *s*, add *'s*.**

  The actors' outfits were dazzling. [More than one actor]

  Seven boys' coats were left at the school.

  The children's toys were all broken.

- **The placement of an apostrophe makes a difference in meaning.**

  My neighbor's twelve cats are howling. [One neighbor who has twelve cats]

  My neighbors' twelve cats are howling. [Two or more neighbors who together have twelve cats]

- **Do not use an apostrophe to form the plural of a noun.**

  Use the stair's or the elevator.

  All of the plant's in the garden are blooming.

- **Do not use an apostrophe with a possessive pronoun. These pronouns already show ownership (possession).**

  Do you want to take my car or your's?

  That basket is our's.

Possessive Pronouns

my	his	its	their
mine	her	our	theirs
your	hers	ours	whose
yours			

Its *or* It's

The single most common error with apostrophes and pronouns is confusing *its* (a possessive pronoun) with *it's* (a contraction meaning "it is"). Whenever you write *it's*, test to see if it's correct by reading it aloud as *it is*.

■ Answers to odd-
numbered practice
items are at the back
of the book.

■ PRACTICE 1   USING APOSTROPHES TO SHOW OWNERSHIP ·······

Edit the following sentences by adding *'s* or an apostrophe alone to show ownership and by crossing out any incorrect use of an apostrophe or *'s*.

> *Fevers*   *body's*
> **EXAMPLE:** **Fever's** are an important part of the human ~~bodys~~ system
>   ^   ^
> of defense against infection.

1. A thermometers indicator mark at 98.6 degrees is supposed to show a persons normal body temperature.

2. However, normal body temperature can range from 97 degrees to 100.4 degrees, so most doctors view of a temperature lower than 100.5 is that its not a fever at all.

3. Fever's help the body combat virus's and stimulate the immune system.

4. Unless a persons temperature is raised by an outside source, the bodys regulatory system will not usually let a fever go higher than 106 degrees.

■ For more practice
with apostrophe
usage, visit
Exercise Central at
bedfordstmartins
.com/realessays.

5. A fevers appearance is not necessarily a reason to take fever-reducing medication's, which can lower a bodys temperature without doing anything to fight the infection.

6. Taking fever-reducing drug's can actually make an illness take longer to run it's course.

7. Many doctors' do not recommend using any drugs to treat a fever if its lower than 102 degrees.

8. Parents should know that childrens fevers can go higher than their's.

9. Some parents fears of fever are so intense that they suffer from "fever phobia" and overreact to their childrens' symptoms.

10. Fever phobia can cause parent's to give their child extra medicine, but overdoses of ibuprofen and other fever reducers can impair the livers' ability to work properly and can therefore complicate the childs sickness.

Apostrophes in Contractions

A **contraction** is formed by joining two words and leaving out one or more of the letters. When writing a contraction, put an apostrophe where the letter or letters have been left out, not between the two words.

NOTE: In academic writing, contractions are rarely used.

Carol's studying to be a nurse. = *Carol is* studying to be a nurse.

I'll go when you come back. = *I will* go when you come back.

Be sure to put the apostrophe in the right place.

Don does'n't work here anymore.

Common Contractions

aren't = are not	she'll = she will
can't = cannot	she's = she is, she has
couldn't = could not	there's = there is, there has
didn't = did not	they'd = they would, they had
doesn't = does not	they'll = they will
don't = do not	they're = they are
he'd = he would, he had	they've = they have
he'll = he will	who'd = who would, who had
he's = he is, he has	who'll = who will
I'd = I would, I had	who's = who is, who has
I'll = I will	won't = will not
I'm = I am	wouldn't = would not
I've = I have	you'd = you would, you had
isn't = is not	you'll = you will
it's = it is, it has	you're = you are
let's = let us	you've = you have
she'd = she would, she had	

■ Do not use contractions in formal papers or reports for college or work.

> **Language Note:** Contractions that include a *be* verb cannot be followed by the base verb or the helping verbs *can, does,* or *has.*
>
> **INCORRECT**   She's *work* late. Dan's *has* sick.
>
> **CORRECT**   She's *working* late. Dan's sick.

PRACTICE 2   USING APOSTROPHES IN CONTRACTIONS . . . .

Read each sentence carefully, looking for any words that have missing letters. Edit these words by adding apostrophes where needed. Or, if apostrophes are misplaced, cross out and correct the error.

It's
EXAMPLE: ~~Its~~ sadly true that some athletes will use performance-
enhancing drugs if they can get away with it.

1. Those who do often say theyre using these drugs because their competitors are probably using them too.

2. Performance-enhancing drugs help some athletes win competitions, but for other athletes, these drugs arent enough to ensure victory.

3. Most athletes taking steroids and other substances say they would'nt use these drugs if they could be certain that their opponents are'nt using them.

4. Wholl be the one to put a stop to this drug use?

5. If sports organizations do'nt eliminate drug use, we all know whos the loser.

6. Youre the loser, Im the loser, and all athletes are the losers.

7. When even one athlete gets away with using drugs, we ca'nt trust that any athletic competition has been won fairly.

8. Youve got to take a stand, Ive got to take a stand, and anyone who believes in fairness has got to take a stand.

9. Lets eliminate performance-enhancing drugs now.

10. If we all are'nt ready to unite against drug use in sports, we might as well change the word *athlete* to *actor*.

. . . .

Apostrophes with Letters, Numbers, and Time

- **Use *'s* to make letters and numbers plural. The apostrophe prevents confusion or misreading.**

  Mississippi has four i*'*s.

  In women's shoes, size 8*'*s are more common than size 10*'*s.

- **Use an apostrophe or *'s* in certain expressions in which time nouns are treated as if they possess something.**

  I get two weeks*'* vacation next year.

  Last year*'*s prices were very good.

▨ **PRACTICE 3   USING APOSTROPHES WITH LETTERS, NUMBERS, AND TIME** . . . .

Edit the following sentences by adding apostrophes where needed and fixing incorrectly used apostrophes.

> **EXAMPLE:** I just updated my blog by entering the last three ~~week's~~ *weeks'*
>
> worth of entries.

1. Next months schedule is less busy, so I think I'll be able to keep my blog current then.

2. Arthur's blog offers an entire winters worth of detail on his social life.

3. His blog is a little hard to read because he always leaves out certain letters, such as as, es, and os.

4. Katie's blog also gets confusing when she puts all of her 4s and 8s in Roman numerals.

5. When Manny's computer was stolen, he lost notes for his blog and two year's work on his novel.

Edit Paragraphs and Your Own Writing

Edit the following paragraphs by adding apostrophes where needed and crossing out incorrectly used apostrophes. If a sentence is already correct, put a "C" after it.

■ EDITING REVIEW 1 (15 errors)

(1) Some of the first discussion's of global warming focused attention on one of the gases that contributes to the greenhouse effect: methane. (2) Like other greenhouse gases, methane helps to keep the earths' heat trapped in our atmosphere, and the temperature of the earth goes up as a result. (3) Humans are'nt the only producers of methane; its also a by-product of cow's digestion of their food. (4) For a while, many Americans knowledge of global warming didnt go much further than cow jokes. (5) As scientists' have become more convinced that global warming is real and a potential threat to human's, our knowledge of the causes of the greenhouse effect has expanded. (6) Cows arent completely off the hook, but theyre far less guilty of contributing to global warming than humans and cars are. (7) The amount of methane produced by cows' adds up to about 3 percent of the total amount of greenhouse gases produced by people. (8) Getting a cow to change it's diet wo'nt solve the worlds warming problem.

■ **EDITING REVIEW 2 (11 errors)** . . . .

(1) In March of 2001, the keyless entry systems of cars in Bremerton, Washington, suddenly stopped working, and no one knows why. (2) The cars locks were supposed to respond when their owner's pushed a button, and all at once they wouldnt. (3) After a few days wait, the entry systems began functioning again. (4) Many resident's of Bremerton, the home of a Navy shipyard, were convinced that the militarys technological activity had affected the cars, but Navy official's denied it. (5) Other people wondered if radio transmissions might have jammed the frequency and prevented the keyless systems' from functioning. (6) Fortunately, people whose cars have keyless entry systems were'nt locked out for those days. (7) These owners simply had to resort to a backup system to open and lock their car's — its called a "key."

■ **PRACTICE 4   EDITING YOUR OWN WRITING FOR APOSTROPHES** . . .

As a final practice, edit a piece of your own writing for apostrophes. It can be a paper you are working on for this course, a paper you've already finished, a paper for another course, a recent piece of writing from your work or everyday life, or your idea journal entry.

39

Quotation Marks

" "

Understand What Quotation Marks Do

■ **IDEA JOURNAL**
Write about a conversation you had today.

Quotation marks (" ") are punctuation marks with two common uses in college writing: They are used with some quotations, and they are used to set off titles. They always appear in pairs.

A **quotation** is the report of another person's words. There are two types of quotations: **direct quotations** (the exact repetition, word for word, of what someone said or wrote) and **indirect quotations** (a restatement of what someone said or wrote, not word for word). Quotation marks are used only for direct quotations.

■ To understand this chapter, you need to know what a sentence is. For a review, see Chapter 22.

DIRECT QUOTATION	George said, "I'm getting a haircut."
INDIRECT QUOTATION	George said that he was getting a haircut.

Practice Using Quotation Marks Correctly

Quotation Marks for Direct Quotations

When you write a direct quotation, you need to use quotation marks around the quoted words. These marks tell readers that the words used are exactly what was said or written.

Quoted words are usually combined with words that identify who is speaking. The identifying words can come after the quoted words, before them, or in the middle. Here are some guidelines for capitalization and punctuation:

- Capitalize the first letter in a complete sentence that's being quoted, even if it comes after some identifying words.

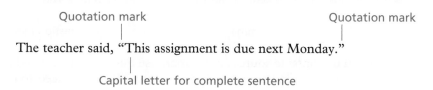

- Do not capitalize the first letter in a quotation if it's not the first word in the complete sentence.

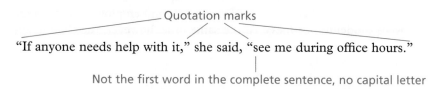

- If it is a complete sentence and its source is clear, you can let a quotation stand on its own, without any identifying words.

  Speaker (teacher) known

  "My office hours are on the first page of your syllabus."

- Attach identifying words to a quotation with a comma; these identifying words cannot be a sentence on their own.

  Identifying words attached with comma
  |
  A student asked, "May we e-mail questions?"

- Always put quotation marks *after* commas and periods. Put quotation marks after question marks and exclamation points if they are part of the quoted sentence.

  ■ For more on commas with quotation marks, see page 682.

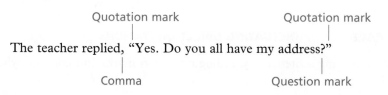

- If a question mark or exclamation point is part of your own sentence, put it after the quotation mark.

Quotation mark   Quotation mark

What famous athlete joked, "I didn't really say everything I said"?

Comma   Question mark

■ For information about how to use quotations in research papers, see Chapter 21.

When you use outside sources in a paper, use quotation marks to indicate the exact words that you quote from a source. You also need to cite, or give credit to, the source.

■ For more on citing and documenting sources, see pages 368–75.

The government needs to ensure that when a company fails, employees' pensions are protected. A recent article in the *Boston Globe* reported, "When Polaroid collapsed, pension funds and employee stock programs were suddenly worthless. At the same time, however, the chief financial officer walked away with a package worth more than $2 million" (Richardson B3).

Setting Off a Quotation within Another Quotation

Sometimes you may directly quote someone who quotes what someone else said or wrote. Put **single quotation marks** (' ') around the quotation within a quotation so that readers understand who said what.

The student handbook said, "Students must be given the opportunity to make up work missed for excused absences."

Terry's entire quotation

Terry told his instructor, "I'm sorry I missed the exam, but I would like to take a makeup exam. Our student handbook says, 'Students must be given the opportunity to make up work missed for excused absences,' and I have a good reason."

Here, Terry is including a quotation from the student handbook.

■ Answers to odd-numbered practice items are at the back of the book.

 PRACTICE 1   PUNCTUATING DIRECT QUOTATIONS · · · · · · · · · · · ·

Edit the following sentences by adding quotation marks and commas where needed.

EXAMPLE: At a meeting of a self-help group, the leader, Brooke, stood up and said, "We are all here because each of us is suffering from an eating disorder."

1. Looking around the room, Allison said I thought only teenage girls had eating disorders. There are people here of all ages, including several men.

2. Yes, there are men here said Brooke. Only some of us are teenage girls.

3. I'm forty years old, not a teenager, and not a girl Patrick said. However, I have an eating disorder.

4. Allison said You don't look like you have an eating disorder. You are not super skinny.

5. I eat too much said Patrick. I'm a compulsive eater.

6. When you say I'm a compulsive eater I don't know what you mean said Allison.

7. The dictionary defines *compulsive* as related to a psychological obsession, said Brooke.

8. Evan suddenly shouted We're all doing this because we're trying to hurt our families and friends!

9. That is one myth we're going to talk about said Brooke. In fact, people with eating disorders are hurting themselves. They are usually upset that their families and friends are worried about them.

10. Why did it suddenly get quiet when Brooke said Does this sound right to any of you?

■ For more practice with quotation marks, visit *Exercise Central* at **bedfordstmartins .com/realessays**.

No Quotation Marks for Indirect Quotations

When you report what someone said or wrote but do not use the person's exact words, you are writing an indirect quotation. Do not use quotation marks for indirect quotations. Indirect quotations often begin with the word *that*.

INDIRECT QUOTATION	Sophie said that the exam was postponed.
DIRECT QUOTATION	Sophie said, "The exam was postponed."
INDIRECT QUOTATION	The boy asked me what time it was.
DIRECT QUOTATION	"What time is it?" asked the boy.
INDIRECT QUOTATION	Carolyn told me that she had an accident.
DIRECT QUOTATION	Carolyn told me, "I had an accident."

■ **PRACTICE 2   PUNCTUATING DIRECT AND INDIRECT QUOTATIONS** . . . .

Edit the following sentences by adding quotation marks where needed and crossing out quotation marks that are incorrectly used. If a sentence is already correct, put a "C" next to it.

EXAMPLE: Sarita told me that ̷"she met her new boyfriend through an online dating service."̷

1. I never thought I would use the Internet for dating, but it really worked, she said.

2. Sarita remembered "how easy it was to look up profiles of men with her interests and to pick the best candidates."

3. She said, I could tell right away if I wasn't going to have anything in common with a person.

4. "I could also tell a lot about a guy's personality by the way he expressed himself," she added.

5. Sarita said the hardest part of the experience was going on trial dates to see if her original impressions of candidates were correct.

6. She knew that there was no future with one man when he arrived a half hour late and told her, I had something else to do first.

7. "He apparently thought that I was happy to wait around for him forever," she said exasperatedly.

8. Sarita told me that "I should think about online dating."

9. I found a great person, she said, and you could too.

10. I told her that I appreciated the advice but that I'm happy being single right now.

. . . .

Quotation Marks for Certain Titles

When referring to a short work such as a magazine or newspaper article, a chapter in a book, a short story, an essay, a song, or a poem, put quotation marks around the title of the work.

NEWSPAPER ARTICLE	"Mayor Warns of Budget Cuts"
SHORT STORY	"Everyday Use"
ESSAY	"Mother Tongue"

Usually, titles of longer works—such as novels, books, magazines, newspapers, movies, television programs, and CDs—are underlined or italicized. The titles of sacred books such as the Bible or the Koran are neither underlined, italicized, nor surrounded by quotation marks.

BOOK	The Chocolate War or *The Chocolate War*
NEWSPAPER	the Washington Post or the *Washington Post*
	[Do not underline, italicize, or capitalize the word *the* before the name of a newspaper or magazine, even if it is part of the title. But do capitalize *The* when it is the first word in titles of books, movies, and other sources.]

If you are writing a paper with many outside sources, your instructor will probably refer you to a particular system of citing sources. Follow that system's guidelines when you use titles in your paper.

NOTE: Do not put quotation marks around the title of a paper you write.

PRACTICE 3 **USING QUOTATION MARKS FOR TITLES** . . . .

Edit the following sentences by adding quotation marks around titles as needed. Underline any book, magazine, or newspaper titles.

EXAMPLE: Tyler walked down the aisle of the bus, humming "When the Saints Go Marching In" and wondering how he'd keep from getting bored on the long bus ride home.

1. He sat down and noticed that the woman sitting next to him was holding the Dallas Morning News.

2. Glancing at his neighbor's newspaper, he saw that she was reading an article called Best Bets for Winter Gardening.

3. He noticed that the passenger sitting directly in front of him was carefully going through Imitation of Spenser, John Keats's first poem.

4. The boy sitting in front of his neighbor was working on exercises from a book titled Rapid Math Tips and Tricks, and he suddenly cried out I won!

5. Tiring of his little game, Tyler took out his sociology textbook and began reading his next assigned chapter, The Economy and Politics.

Edit Paragraphs and Your Own Writing

Edit the following paragraphs by adding quotation marks where needed and crossing out any incorrectly used quotation marks. Underline any book, magazine, or newspaper titles. Correct any errors in punctuation.

 EDITING REVIEW 1 (17 errors) . . . .

(1) Here is one I've loved for years, said Evi, as she held up a CD called "Kind of Blue" by the "jazz trumpeter" Miles Davis. (2) Charlie, who was also flipping through the jazz CDs, said that "he had gone through

a Miles Davis phase but wasn't so interested in Miles's music now." (3) Shortly after they moved into the main section of the store, Charlie pulled out a book and opened it to an essay titled <u>Shooting an Elephant</u>. (4) "Reading this had a big effect on me", he said, adding that "he eventually read most of what George Orwell had written." (5) They were browsing through the rows of books when Evi stopped and said, this is what led me to read all of Dylan Thomas's poetry. (6) Taking a book from the shelf, she opened it to a poem titled Do Not Go Gentle into That Good Night, noting that "It was written for Thomas's dying father." (7) Pointing to a line in the poem, she said, when Thomas writes Rage, rage against the dying of the light, he is talking to his father, to himself, and to me, bringing all of us into that special moment. (8) They continued on silently until Charlie exclaimed look at this—a book about the making of the Beatles's Sgt. Pepper's Lonely Hearts Club Band! (9) Evi reached for another copy of the book, saying that "her father had introduced her to the Beatles's music when she was ten and that it had been one of her favorite albums ever since." (10) Charlie picked up a copy of "Rolling Stone magazine" as they walked to the checkout counter, and he said a trip to the bookstore turned out to be a lot more fun than I thought it would be.

EDITING REVIEW 2 (18 errors) . . . .

(1) "Did you know that people our age could experience a life crisis"? my twenty-five-year-old friend Beth asked as we browsed at the newsstand. (2) She showed me an article called The Trouble with Being 25 in a magazine she was looking at.

(3) I told her that "she was crazy." (4) You wait until midlife for your crisis, silly, I said. (5) I was imagining a middle-aged businessman

suddenly buying an expensive sports car and driving around listening to Prince singing Little Red Corvette.

(6) Beth pointed out that she had plenty of anxiety about being twenty-five. (7) It's as if people look at me and think I'm still basically a teenager, yet I have a grown-up job and grown-up responsibilities to go with it, she said.

(8) I asked her "what kinds of responsibilities she was talking about." (9) I have rent and bills to pay, she said, and I'm trying to decide if I should take a couple of classes at night to get a better job. (10) She thought for a moment and then added, "And sooner or later I'll need to figure out whether I want to get married and have children". (11) She picked up a newspaper and idly turned the pages until she found a head-line that said Confusion Reigns among Young Singles.

(12) "Wow! You're right"! I blurted out. (13) It's a good thing you read those stupid magazines, I said to Beth. (14) I was only partly kidding when I added that "she and I would never have realized that we were sup-posed to be having a crisis if we hadn't read about it."

(15) Let's do something to celebrate, said Beth. (16) That's why we spent the rest of the afternoon sitting around my kitchen table drinking coffee, listening to Beck singing Loser, and reading out loud to each other from How to Tell If You're Ready to Settle Down in the new issue of Cosmopolitan.

PRACTICE 4   EDITING YOUR OWN WRITING FOR QUOTATION MARKS

As a final practice, edit a piece of your own writing for quotation marks. It can be a paper you are working on for this course, a paper you've already finished, a paper for another course, a recent piece of writing from your work or everyday life, or your idea journal entry.

40

Other Punctuation

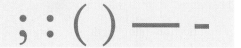

Understand What Punctuation Does

Punctuation helps readers understand your writing. If you use punctuation incorrectly, you send readers a confusing message—or, even worse, a wrong one. This chapter covers five marks of punctuation that people sometimes use incorrectly. Knowing what these marks do in a sentence can help you avoid such mistakes.

■ **IDEA JOURNAL**
Write to someone about to enter your college, giving him or her five good pieces of advice.

■ To understand this chapter, you need to know what sentences and independent clauses are. For a review, see Chapters 22 and 24.

SEMICOLON ;	Joins two independent clauses into one sentence
	Separates complete items in a list that already has commas within individual items
COLON :	Introduces a list
	Announces an explanation or example
PARENTHESES ( )	Set off extra information that is not essential to the sentence
DASH —	Sets off words for emphasis
	Indicates a pause
HYPHEN -	Joins two or more words that together form a single description
	Shows a word break at the end of a line

Practice Using Punctuation Correctly

Semicolon ;

Semicolons to Join Independent Clauses (Sentences)

Use a semicolon to join very closely related sentences and make them into one sentence.

> In an interview, hold your head up and don't slouch; it is important to look alert.

> Make good eye contact; looking down is not appropriate in an interview.

> **Language Note:** Do not use a comma instead of a semicolon to join two independent clauses: That would create a run-on (see Chapter 24).

Semicolons When Items in a Series Contain Commas

■ For more on using semicolons to join sentences, see Chapter 30.

Use a semicolon to separate list items that themselves contain commas. Otherwise, it is difficult for readers to tell where one item ends and another begins.

> I have a cousin who lives in Devon, England; another cousin who lives in Derry, New Hampshire; and a third cousin who lives in Freeport, Maine.

Colon :

Colons before Lists

Use a colon to introduce a list after an independent clause.

> In the United States, three ice cream flavors are the most popular: vanilla, chocolate, and strawberry.

> I have three stops to make on the way home: the grocery store, the post office, and the police station.

Colons before Explanations or Examples

Use a colon after an independent clause to let readers know that you are about to provide an explanation or example of what you just wrote. If the explanation or example is also an independent clause, capitalize the first letter after the colon.

Sometimes, the choice of cereals is overwhelming: My supermarket carries at least five different types of raisin bran.

I use one criterion to choose a cereal: price.

NOTE: A colon in a sentence must follow an independent clause. A common misuse is to place a colon after a phrase instead of an independent clause. Watch out especially for colons following the phrases *such as* or *for example*.

An independent clause contains a subject and a verb, and it expresses a complete thought. It can stand on its own as a sentence.

INCORRECT	The resort offers many activities, such as: snorkeling, golf, and windsurfing.
CORRECT	The resort offers many activities: snorkeling, golf, and windsurfing.
CORRECT	The resort offers many activities, such as snorkeling, golf, and windsurfing.
INCORRECT	Suzy has many talents. For example: writing, drawing, and painting.
CORRECT	Suzy has many talents: writing, drawing, and painting.

Colons in Business Correspondence

Use a colon after a greeting (called a *salutation*) in a business letter and after the standard heading lines at the beginning of a memorandum.

Dear Mr. Latimer:

To: Craig Kleinman

From: Susan Anker

Parentheses ( )

Use two parentheses to set off information that is not essential to the meaning of a sentence. Parentheses are always used in pairs and should be used sparingly.

My grandfather's most successful invention (his first) was the electric blanket.

My worst habit (and also the hardest to break) is interrupting.

When people speak too slowly, I often finish their sentences (at least in my mind).

Dash —

Use dashes as you use parentheses: to set off additional information, particularly information that you want to emphasize.

> The essay question —— worth 50 percent of the whole exam —— will be open book.

> Your answers should be well developed, and points —— 2 per error —— will be deducted for major grammar mistakes.

A dash can also indicate a pause, much as a comma does.

> My son wants to buy a car —— more power to him.

Make a dash by typing two hyphens together. Do not leave any extra spaces around a dash.

Hyphen -

Hyphens to Join Words That Form a Single Description

Use a hyphen to join words that together form a single description of a person, place, or thing.

■ If you are unsure about whether or how to hyphenate a word or phrase, consult a dictionary or your instructor.

> The eighty-year-old smoker was considered a high-risk patient.

> I followed the company's decision-making procedure.

> I can't wait to see my end-of-the-year grade.

Hyphens to Divide a Word at the End of a Line

Use a hyphen to divide a word when part of the word must continue on the next line. Most word-processing programs do this automatically, but if you are writing by hand, you need to insert hyphens yourself.

> If you give me the receipt for your purchase, I will imme-
> diately issue a refund.

If you are not sure where to break a word, look it up in a dictionary. The word's main entry will show you where you can break the word: dic • tio • nary. If you still aren't confident that you are putting the hyphen in the right place, don't break the word; write it all on the next line.

Edit Paragraphs and Your Own Writing

Edit the following paragraphs by adding semicolons, colons, parentheses, dashes, and hyphens where needed. Keep in mind that more than one type of punctuation may be acceptable in some places.

■ **EDITING REVIEW 1 (15 errors)** . . . .

(1) To avoid predators, many butterflies and moths randomly change directions as they fly about, but this is not their only strategy they also display striking colors like radiant and shiny reds, oranges, and blues and camouflage themselves in effective disguises. (2) For example, some butterflies have streaks composed of many dazzling colors across their wings to emphasize the speed of their flight sending a message that they're hard to catch. (3) Other butterflies use bold, attention getting color patterns to signal that they are poisonous to eat Some are truly poisonous and some are faking. (4) There are also species that attempt to look distasteful by imitating something that is not nutritious a bit of bird dropping, a dead leaf, or rotting vegetation. (5) One moth, *Oxytenis modestia,* is especially enterprising in its disguises In its first four caterpillar stages it looks like a bird dropping, even including fake seeds in it the fifth stage imitates a green snake with a fake large head and two fake eyes and the adult *Oxytenis* moth looks like a leaf, and because it breeds twice a year, mimics the appropriate leaf for the season. (6) *Oxytenis* moths that hatch in the dry season look like dry dead leaves those hatching in the rainy season look dark and moldy. (7) Several butterflies combine camouflage with eye catching display for example, *Pieria helvetia* has front wings that are bland and dull, but its hind wings are bright red. (8) When it is resting, its wings are closed, and it can hardly be seen, but when a predator threatens, it

■ For more practice with the punctuation covered in this chapter, visit **bedfordstmartins .com/realessays**.

bursts into rapid, dramatic flight its red patches make it conspicuously visible. (9) However, then it suddenly sets down again, folds its wings in, and seemingly disappears a clever magic act. (10) Birds and monkeys do their best to see past these disguises because, according to one researcher one who will do anything for his research, moths taste something like raw shrimp.

EDITING REVIEW 2 (19 errors) . . . .

(1) Caitlin had just gotten home from the video game store where she had a part time job during summer vacation when she received an unusual e-mail message titled "Request for Your Services." (2) The sender was Henry Otabe a man she didn't know and he said he wanted to engage Caitlin's services for a diplomatically sensitive task. (3) He said he would be visiting Washington, D.C., from Cameroon for three weeks on business and he wanted to be sure the U.S. State Department didn't waste his time as it had on past visits with needless bureaucratic paperwork. (4) He would require her help for four hours a day for the three week trip he asked how much she would charge. (5) Caitlin was suspicious about the message, but she also realized it could make sense for several reasons She was a graduate student in international relations she had interned twice at the U.S. State Department, with whose organizational structure she was familiar and she knew people on the diplomatic staffs of several African countries, including Cameroon. (6) Two days later, she e-mailed back agreeing to the task and mentioning a hefty fee what did she have to lose, she figured and she also asked for specific dates and times. (7) Three days later, Mr. Otabe sent her a message saying that he would arrive in about one month he added that, if she would confirm by

e-mail her agreement to their arrangement, he would send her an advance payment of $8,000 to reserve her time and services. (8) Two weeks passed and the check had not yet arrived which was no surprise to Caitlin, but she did receive an e-mail explaining that he was delayed due to unforeseen business and family concerns however, he had made the following arrangements Caitlin would immediately be sent a cashier's check for $10,000 instead of $8,000, and as soon as she received it, she should send $3,200 to his agent for prearrival necessities he included an address in Madrid. (9) Caitlin quickly received the $10,000 cashier's check which looked quite authentic and she took it to her bank she wanted to know if it was legitimate before she tried to cash it. (10) Three days later, Caitlin received a call from her bank's security department the check was fraudulent. (11) She e-mailed to Mr. Otabe telling him the check was fraudulent she got no reply.

■ For more practice with the punctuation covered in this chapter, visit **bedfordstmartins .com/realessays**.

■ PRACTICE 1 EDITING YOUR OWN WRITING FOR OTHER PUNCTUATION MARKS · · · · · · · · · · · · · · · ·

As a final practice, edit a piece of your own writing for semicolons, colons, parentheses, dashes, and hyphens. It can be a paper you are working on for this course, a paper you've already finished, a paper for another course, a piece of writing from your work or everyday life, or your idea journal entry. You may want to try more than one way to use these marks of punctuation in your writing.

41

Capitalization

Using Capital Letters

Understand Capitalization

■ **IDEA JOURNAL**
Write a guide to your family: their names, where they live, where they grew up, and where they work.

There are three basic rules of capitalization: Capitalize the first letter of

- every new sentence.
- names of specific people, places, dates, and things.
- important words in titles.

If you can remember these three rules, you will avoid the most common errors in capitalization.

Practice Capitalization

Capitalization of Sentences

■ Answers to odd-numbered practice items are at the back of the book.

Capitalize the first letter in each new sentence, including the first word in a direct quotation.

Mary was surprised when she saw all the people.

She asked, "What's going on here?"

■ PRACTICE 1   **CAPITALIZING THE FIRST WORD IN A SENTENCE** . . . . .

Edit the following paragraph, changing lowercase letters to capital letters as needed. If a sentence is already correct, put a "C" next to it.

■ For more practice with capitalization, visit *Exercise Central* at **bedfordstmartins .com/realessays**.

(1) Many fans of classic films point to 1939 as the greatest year in cinema history. (2) Moviegoers that year were mesmerized by Rhett Butler telling Scarlett O'Hara, "frankly, my dear, I don't give a damn." (3) the same year, audiences thrilled to the story of little Dorothy, who clicked her heels together and chanted, "there's no place like home." (4) the films of 1939 still make movie buffs shake their heads and mutter, "they don't make movies like that anymore!"

Capitalization of Names of Specific People, Places, Dates, and Things

Capitalize the first letter in names of specific people, places, dates, and things. Do not capitalize general words such as *college* as opposed to the specific name: *Lincoln College*. Look at the examples for each group.

People

Capitalize the first letter in names of specific people and in titles used with names of specific people.

■ The word *president* is not capitalized unless it comes directly before a name as part of that person's title: President George W. Bush.

SPECIFIC	NOT SPECIFIC
Carol Schopfer	my friend
Dr. D'Ambrosio	the physician
Professor Shute	your professor
Aunt Jane, Mother	my aunt, my mother

The name of a family member is capitalized when the family member is being addressed directly or when the family title is standing in for a first name.

Good to see you, Dad.

I see Mother is now taking classes.

In other instances, do not capitalize.

It is my father's birthday.

My mother is taking classes.

Places

Capitalize the first letter in names of specific buildings, streets, cities, states, regions, and countries.

SPECIFIC	NOT SPECIFIC
Bolton Police Department	the police department
Washington Street	our street
Boston, Massachusetts	my hometown
Texas	this state
the West	the western part of the country
Italy	that country

Do not capitalize directions in a sentence: *Drive south for five blocks.*

Dates

Capitalize the first letter in the names of days, months, and holidays. Do not capitalize the names of the seasons (winter, spring, summer, fall).

SPECIFIC	NOT SPECIFIC
Monday	today
January 4	winter
Presidents' Day	my birthday

Language Note: The first letter of all days, months, and proper names is capitalized.

Today is Tuesday, March 10.

Organizations, Companies, and Groups

SPECIFIC	NOT SPECIFIC
Santa Monica College	my college
Toys"R"Us	the toy store
Merrimack Players	the theater group

Languages, Nationalities, and Religions

SPECIFIC	NOT SPECIFIC
English, Greek, Spanish	my first language
Christianity, Buddhism	your religion

■ The names of languages should be capitalized even if you aren't referring to a specific course: *I am taking nutrition and Spanish.*

Language Note: The first letter of all languages and nationalities is capitalized.

Gina speaks Italian, but she is Chinese.

Courses

SPECIFIC	NOT SPECIFIC
English 100	a writing course
Nutrition 100	the basic nutrition course

Commercial Products

SPECIFIC	NOT SPECIFIC
Diet Coke	a diet cola
Hershey bar	a chocolate bar

PRACTICE 2   **CAPITALIZING NOUNS** . . . .

Edit the following sentences by adding capitalization as needed or removing capitalization where it is inappropriate.

EXAMPLE: My ~~H~~igh ~~S~~chool had a painting by Birger Sandzen on
display in an ~~A~~rt classroom.

1. Lindsborg is a small town in McPherson county, Kansas, that calls itself "little sweden, U.S.A."

2. Lindsborg's Restaurant, the Swedish crown, serves Swedish Meatballs at its sunday smorgasbord.

3. The Town's most famous resident was probably a swedish immigrant Artist named Birger Sandzen.

4. He read a book by the founder of Bethany college in lindsborg and came to kansas to teach at the College in 1894.

5. Sandzen intended to stay in kansas for two or three years, but he loved the great plains and ended up remaining in lindsborg for the rest of his life.

6. Sandzen taught Art, but he also taught Languages, and he sang as a Tenor with the Bethany oratorio society.

7. Although Sandzen worked mainly in the midwest, the Rocky mountains, and other less populous parts of The United States, he exhibited widely.

8. His show at the Babcock galleries in new york received an enthusiastic Critical response.

9. Sandzen's use of color showed the beauty of the landscapes of the west.

10. Sandzen's name may not be familiar to every Art Lover, but his works— which are found in private collections, at Schools in Kansas, and at the Sandzen memorial gallery in Lindsborg—are quite valuable today.

Capitalization of Titles

Capitalize the first word and all other important words in titles of books, movies, television programs, magazines, newspapers, articles, stories, songs, papers, poems, legislation, and so on. Words that do not need to be capitalized (unless they are the first word) include articles (*the, a, an*); coordinating conjunctions (*and, but, for, nor, or, so, yet*); and prepositions.

■ For more on punctuating titles, see page 701. For a list of common prepositions, see page 390.

American Idol is a very popular television program.

Newsweek and *Time* often have similar cover stories.

"Once More to the Lake" is one of Chuck's favorite essays.

■ PRACTICE 3   **CAPITALIZING TITLES** . . . .

Edit the following sentences by capitalizing titles as needed.

                           I   N E   B   G   T

       EXAMPLE: Kermit the Frog sang "it's not easy being green" in *the*

           M   M

           muppet movie.

1. The television show *sesame street*, which began in 1969, brought innovative programming to children.

2. My favorite among the show's friendly puppets, known as the Muppets, was Ernie, who liked to sing "rubber ducky."

3. The popular Muppets Kermit the Frog and Miss Piggy starred in several films, including one based on Charles Dickens's classic *a christmas carol* and one based on Robert Louis Stevenson's *treasure island*.

4. The show contained no advertising, but magazines such as *sesame street parents* and toys based on the characters sold widely.

5. "Elmo's world," a segment added to the show in the 1990s, introduced the small red monster who would become one of the most popular toys in history.

Edit Paragraphs and Your Own Writing

Edit the following paragraphs by capitalizing as needed and removing any unnecessary capitalization.

■   **EDITING REVIEW 1 (88 errors)** . . . .

(1) in Robert louis Stevenson's 1886 novella "the strange case of dr. jekyll and mr. hyde," a doctor uses Himself as the subject of an experiment and the results are Disastrous. (2) The novella was a Great Success, but stevenson didn't originate the idea of Doctors experimenting on themselves.

(3) one of the earliest known examples of self-experimentation goes back to the sixteenth Century, when santorio santorio, of padua, italy, weighed himself every Day for thirty Years. (4) By weighing everything he ate and drank as well as his Bodily Discharges, Santorio discovered that the Human body continually and imperceptibly loses large amounts of Fluid. (5) today, that Loss, called *insensible perspiration,* is routinely measured in Hospital patients.

(6) A Key Breakthrough to the modern age of Cardiology was made in 1929 by a german, dr. werner forssmann, who as a Surgical Resident at a medical facility called the august victoria home, near berlin, conducted a daring self-experiment by inserting a thin tube into one of his Veins and slid the tube into his own Heart. (7) This idea was later developed by other Researchers into the Technique of cardiac catheterization. (8) Dr. forssmann, who used catheters on himself nine times, shared a nobel prize in 1956 for his Pioneering Experiments.

(9) An important innovation in Anesthesia occurred when a Dentist in connecticut, Horace wells, watched a demonstration in which a

Volunteer inhaled Nitrous Oxide, cut his own leg, and felt no pain until the effects of the Gas wore off. (10) dr. wells then had one of his own teeth extracted after he had inhaled the Chemical, which people later commonly called "Laughing Gas." (11) he was amazed to have no Pain during his extraction, declaring, "it is the greatest discovery ever made." (12) Others' self-experimentation later aided the Development of ether, chloroform, and additional Anesthetics.

(13) In Medical circles, many people believe that major walter reed experimented on himself in the early 1900s as the Leader of the group in cuba that discovered that Mosquitoes transmit yellow fever. (14) in fact, Dr. reed said he would allow mosquitoes to infect him to test the Theory, but he returned to the united states before this was done. (15) Instead, other Members of his Team conducted the mosquito experiment on themselves, with one dying and another barely surviving. (16) after these self-experimenters proved the crucial Connection between mosquitoes and yellow fever, dr. reed returned to Cuba, but he never did perform the experiment on himself.

■ EDITING REVIEW 2 (99 errors) . . . .

(1) It is a remote spot in North Central Pennsylvania, and it has changed little over the past few Centuries. (2) But on certain nights, especially when there is a New Moon and the Sky is clear, hundreds of people gather there to see a Show that has been running for Eons. (3) it is cherry springs state park, and it is becoming one of the Prime locations for stargazing in the Eastern Half of the country.

(4) On Summer nights at the Park, it is not unusual to hear from somewhere in the darkness a statement like, "take a look at this; the milky

way is so bright that i can see my shadow!" (5) some visitors can easily pick out well-known sights, such as the big dipper, orion, and casseopeia, from the 10,000 Stars overhead, but for those who cannot, there are usually several Amateur Astronomers present who are happy to provide a quick course in astronomy 101. (6) Many of these Enthusiasts regularly set up their Telescopes on clear nights and invite Anyone who wishes to have a look.

(7) Cherry springs is growing in popularity for Eastern stargazers, but those from other regions of the country, particularly the american west, also have their pick from some excellent spots, including mauna kea in hawaii, utah's natural bridges national Monument and bryce canyon national Park, and chaco culture national historical Park in new mexico. (8) What the Best Stargazing Locations have in common is an effort to preserve their area from encroaching Light Pollution. (9) The international dark-sky association, an organization that works to reduce light pollution, has noted that the Administrators of Cherry Springs are especially appreciative of the importance of blocking out light.

(10) The site for the dark-sky area was made accessible to the public after the Park Manager, chip harrison, learned from astronomy enthusiasts frequenting the park that satellite photos of the World's surface at night showed that Cherry Springs was in a very black area containing few light sources. (11) The Primary Area used for stargazing is basically a fifty-acre lawn with short Pine Trees along its edges; it offers practically a horizon-to-horizon view. (12) in addition, along the Road that runs through the park, there are Earthen ledges and trees to block out light from nearby traffic.

(13) Visitors to Cherry Springs are expected to follow certain Rules of Star Party Etiquette. (14) All flashlights must have Red Filters, and they must always be pointed downward. (15) People should shield or turn off the Trunk, Door, and Dome Lights in their cars, and all Headlights should be off until cars are well away from the dark-sky field. (16) all Children must be carefully controlled because the Equipment that stargazers use is Privately Owned and sensitive. (17) Finally, when planning to visit cherry springs or any other Stargazing Site, start out early because the Best Time to Arrive is before dark to allow everyone's eyes to adjust.

PRACTICE 4   EDITING YOUR OWN WRITING FOR CAPITALIZATION

As a final practice, edit a piece of your own writing for capitalization. It can be a paper you are working on for this course, a paper you've already finished, a paper for another course, a recent piece of writing from your work or everyday life, or your idea journal entry.

Editing Review Test 1
The Four Most Serious Errors (Chapters 22–26)

If you need help, turn back to the chapters indicated.

DIRECTIONS: Each of the underlined word groups contains one or more errors. As you identify each error, write in the space the number of the word group containing the error. Then, edit the underlined word groups to correct the errors.

Two fragments _____   Two verb problems _____

Two run-ons _____   Four subject-verb
agreement errors _____

1 One opponent faces the other, during their personal battle, nobody else in the universe exist. **2** An attack prompts an immediate defense, often followed by a counterattack. **3** Starting the cycle again. **4** In an age of precision-guided, pilotless missiles and laser weapons, there would seem to be no place for fencing. **5** Yet in recent years, fencing had been experiencing a surge in popularity among women and men of all ages. **6** That is partly because, with training and dedicated practice, even someone who is elderly or not adept at other sports can often learn to hold his or her own quite well in a fencing encounter.

7 Most beginning fencers are equipped with a training sword and protective equipment that include a glove, face mask, knee socks, knickers, and a special gray jacket. **8** The jacket is woven with wire mesh for use with an electronic scoreboard. **9** At the tip of the sword will be a button instead of a sharp point. **10** This is for safety, it is also useful for keeping track of valid hits. **11** When the button contacts a valid target on the jacket of an opponent, an electric signal courses through the sword to a wire in the attacker's hand guard. **12** From the hand guard the wire runs to the back of the fencer's jacket up to an apparatus mounted on the ceiling where the hit is registered. **13** Causing a red light to go on. **14** In a typical match, the first fencer to score five valid hits on an opponent win. **15** All in all, fencing provide strenuous exercise, competition, excitement, and a never-ending challenge.

Editing Review Test 2

The Four Most Serious Errors (Chapters 22–26)

If you need help, turn back to the chapters indicated.

DIRECTIONS: Find the errors in the selection below. Some word groups may contain more than one error. As you identify each error, write in the space the number of the word group containing the error. Then, edit the selection to correct the errors.

Two fragments _____   Two verb problems _____

Two run-ons _____   Four subject-verb
agreement errors _____

1 Finding a poisonous snake is not something most people go out of their way to do that is exactly the goal of some scientists. **2** They are looking for precisely what everyone else wants to avoid: the snakes' venom. **3** This is not a hunt for excitement or a dangerous thrill, it is a search for a medical breakthrough. **4** For over thirty years, scientists have been using snake venom to create new drugs. **5** One type of venom, for example, has provide a key ingredient for treating congestive heart failure.

6 A snake creates venom in special glands in its upper jaw. **7** In latching onto prey, the snake squeezes these glands and release the venom. **8** Molecules from the venom then attacks the prey from the inside. **9** Some venom molecules cause muscle cells to relax. **10** Which cuts off the victim's oxygen supply. **11** Other molecules will have induced the victim's immune system to attack its own organs. **12** Most venoms contain a combination of such molecules.

13 In recent years, researchers have discovered how certain genes in venom relaxes the muscles in the prey's aorta, which pumps blood to the body's organs. **14** Relaxing these muscles prevent the aorta from contracting, which lowers the blood pressure and allows time for deadly toxins to attack the victim's bloodstream. **15** Scientists are now trying to use these muscle-relaxing toxins to humans' advantage. **16** Controlled relaxation of the blood vessels around the heart helps blood flow more easily. **17** Reducing the effects of congestive heart failure.

· ·

Editing Review Test 3

The Four Most Serious Errors (Chapters 22–26); Other Grammar Concerns (Chapters 27–33)

If you need help, turn back to the chapters indicated.

DIRECTIONS: Each of the underlined word groups contains one or more errors. As you identify each error, write in the space the number of the word group containing the error. Then, edit the underlined word groups to correct the errors.

Two fragments _____   One verb problem _____

One run-on _____   One pronoun error _____

One adjective error _____   One parallelism error _____

Three subject-verb agreement
errors _____

1 Anyone who has ever gotten lost in a maze knows what a frightening experience it can be. 2 But it is also challenging, exciting, and there is no problem with safety because few people ever got lost in them for long. 3 Mazes have become more popular than ever in recent years in the United States and in many countries around the world.

4 Mazes can be made of many different types of materials perhaps the larger number of them are made of corn stalks. 5 Corn mazes have become big business in some farming communities. 6 Building mazes are one way for farmers to market his farms as popular entertainment. 7 The point of this for some farmers are to adapt the small farm so that it can remain competitive in today's economy. 8 Some farms are expanding on the maze idea by turning a section of land into small theme parks. 9 Complete with hay rides, petting zoos, and pig races. 10 Mazes are usually the major attraction, however, and many are quite elaborate. 11 There are mazes shaped like butterflies, crowns, and sheriff's badges. 12 Some mazes even includes such features as double-decker bridges.

13 Other mazes are designed to teach people about various farm crops and how they are grown. 14 Whether entertaining, educational, or both. 15 Mazes have become a significant way of raising people's awareness of and interest in farming.

Editing Review Test 4

The Four Most Serious Errors (Chapters 22–26); Other Grammar Concerns (Chapters 27–33)

If you need help, turn back to the chapters indicated.

DIRECTIONS: Find the errors in the selection below. Some word groups may contain more than one error. As you identify each error, write in the space the number of the word group containing the error. Then, edit the selection to correct the errors.

Two fragments _____   One run-on _____

One subject-verb agreement error _____   Two pronoun errors _____

One misplaced/dangling modifier _____   Two coordination/subordination _____

Two uses of inappropriately informal
or casual language _____

1 Some say there are two kinds of video game players. 2 Those who use strategy guides and those who don't. 3 Many gamers consider the use of a strategy guide to be laziness or outright cheating; the publishing of these guides is a solid and growing business.

4 The creation of a strategy guide begins when early copies of the game arrives at the home or office of the guide's author. 5 Mixed with the excitement of trying out a new game is the realization that the finished guide is due to the publisher in four months and that the clock is ticking. 6 The author usually begins by spending many hours playing the game. 7 Trying out as many tactics as they can devise. 8 The game's designers usually provide plenty of help while the guide is being developed. 9 But guide authors must be able to get by on their own because there are times when they are just too busy to respond.

10 Published strategy guides face tough competition from a variety of free online sources. 11 A key advantage guide publishers have over free online content providers, however, is the assistance they receive from the game companies. 12 Many gamers, especially noobs, use a combination of free online help and published strategy guides.

13 Strategy guides have been popular with gamers for several years; the guide authors often do not share in this popularity. **14** One author explains that his publisher sometimes asks him to sign the strategy guides he wrote at trade shows. **15** The problem is that some people who buy the guide there specifically ask him *not* to sign it. **16** He says he's cool with that, working on the guides is its own reward.

· ·

Editing Review Test 5

The Four Most Serious Errors (Chapters 22–26);
Other Grammar Concerns (Chapters 27–33);
Word Use (Chapters 34–36)

If you need help, turn back to the chapters indicated.

DIRECTIONS: Each of the underlined word groups contains one or more errors. As you identify each error, write in the space the number of the word group containing the error. Then, edit the underlined word groups to correct the errors.

One run-on _____   One verb problem _____

One word choice error _____   Two pronoun errors _____

One adjective error _____   One spelling error _____

One subject-verb agreement error _____   One misplaced/dangling modifier _____

Two commonly confused word errors _____

    1 Nobody want to go through life frightened that criminals might be lurking around every corner. 2 But criminals do exist, and it makes sense to take precautions to avoid being victimized. 3 There are prudent measures that you can work into you're everyday routines that can help prevent you from becoming a victim to some common scams.

    4 First of all, don't give out financial information, such as your bank account or Social Security number, to anyone who you didn't know and trust. 5 It is surprisingly easy to create a fake Social Security card and then a fake birth certificate to go with it. 6 Using these fake documents, the local motor vehicle department will issue a new driver's license with your name and the criminal's photo.

    7 You've probably heard of some of the standard e-mail scams, one of which involves a so-called deposed Nigerian leader who offers to pay you a substantial sum if you help him transfer his fortune out of his country. 8 Many of these scams use the same trick to get people to beleive the sender is honest, the criminal will send a postdated check for a share in the fortune in return for a check from the victim that is allegedly necessary to unfreeze the funds. 9 Needless to say, the criminal's checks always bounce. 10 If you receive e-mail solicitations of any kind, don't play with fire.

11 Do thorough background checks on the sender before sending any money or information.

12 In addition, when its time to discard your old computer, remove the hard drive first to prevent thieves from recovering any vital data.

    13 On the positive side, you can relax a bit about your household trash. **14** Most identity theft cases they do not start with scammers rummaging through trash. **15** Instead, scammers use computer spyware or steal outgoing mail because they find these methods more easy.

Editing Review Test 6

The Four Most Serious Errors (Chapters 22–26); Other Grammar Concerns (Chapters 27–33); Word Use (Chapters 34–36)

If you need help, turn back to the chapters indicated.

DIRECTIONS: Find the errors in the selection below. Some word groups may contain more than one error. As you identify each error, write in the space the number of the word group containing the error. Then, edit the selection to correct the errors.

Two run-ons _____

One subject-verb agreement error _____

One parallelism error _____

Two commonly confused words errors _____

One use of inappropriately informal or casual language _____

One verb problem _____

One pronoun error _____

Two spelling errors _____

1 Eastern Egg Rock, a remote, treeless island off the coast of southern Maine, was for much of the twentieth century inhabited by a huge population of gulls. **2** By the mid-1980s, the gulls have been the dominant bird species they're for about a hundred years. **3** But before that, the island was primarily the home of arctic terns and puffins. **4** By the late nineteenth century, hunting had reduced the tern and puffin populations to nonviable levels, the gulls had taken over. **5** In 1973, the National Audubon Society decided to launch an experiment to try to bring puffins and terns back to Eastern Egg Rock. **6** Since then, Project Puffin has proven so sucessful that biologists from all over the world now come to check it out.

7 The Audubon's team focused on restoring the nesting enviroment and to control predators. **8** The team moved puffin chicks from successful colonies in Newfoundland too carefully built burrows and fed them by hand. **9** Decoys and recorded calls helped to attract puffins and terns to the nests. **10** Team members stayed on the island during every breeding season. **11** The large gulls don't like to nest around people this helped prevent them from returning. **12** There are now seventy pairs of breeding puffins on Eastern Egg Rock. **13** In addition, there are sizable populations of terns, storm petrels, and black guillemots.

14 Birdlife conservation efforts like Project Puffin seems to be having a significant effect worldwide. **15** A recent study found that, in the last century, thirty-one species of birds were saved from extinction due to conservation programs.

. . . .

Editing Review Test 7

The Four Most Serious Errors (Chapters 22–26); Other Grammar Concerns (Chapters 27–33); Word Use (Chapters 34–36); Punctuation and Capitalization (Chapters 37–41)

If you need help, turn back to the chapters indicated.

DIRECTIONS: Each of the underlined word groups contains one or more errors. As you identify each error, write in the space the number of the word group containing the error. Then, edit the underlined word groups to correct the errors.

One run-on _____   One verb problem _____

Two apostrophe errors _____   One pronoun error _____

One adverb error _____   One quotation marks error _____

One subject-verb agreement error _____   One capitalization error _____

One commonly confused word error _____   One comma error _____

One semicolon error _____

1 Todays young people, like young people of all Generations, spend its time differently

from the way their parents spent it. 2 One example of this is a phenomenon called 'multitasking.'

3 When having a conversation, some teenagers and young adults commonly had given assurances

that they are truly paying attention despite the music they are hearing through their headphones.

4 For many, doing homework is now combined with instant messaging, talking over a cell phone,

browsing through an online social network, returning e-mails, watching television, and, of course,

listening to music.

5 Doing more than one thing simultaneous is nothing new for human beings parents have

always been able to prepare meals while keeping an eye on their babies. 6 Ever since radio became

commonplace in the 1930s, people have worked or played while listening. 7 But as our capacity

for interpersonal connectivity has expanded, with the invention of each knew electronic device, the

speed and complexity of multitasking has risen dramatically. 8 In the 1980s, many young people

would have said that their most important possession was a so-called boom box—a portable stereo system. 9 Today, the most favored device by far is the computer. 10 <u>This is because the</u> <u>computer provides not only a radio and CD/DVD player but also instant messaging, Internet</u> <u>searches; movies, e-mail, games, and social networking.</u>

11 Is all this a good thing? 12 <u>Studies have indicated that the quality of what people</u> <u>produce and the depth of their thinking diminishes as they focus on increasing numbers</u> <u>of tasks.</u> 13 Other research shows that people who try to do two or more tasks simultaneously take longer to accomplish their tasks than if they had done them one at a time. 14 <u>Nevertheless,</u> <u>young peoples' multitasking seems to be here to stay, and it may be only in its infancy.</u>

- -

Editing Review Test 8

The Four Most Serious Errors (Chapters 22–26); Other Grammar Concerns (Chapters 27–33); Word Use (Chapters 34–36); Punctuation and Capitalization (Chapters 37–41)

If you need help, turn back to the chapters indicated.

DIRECTIONS: Find the errors in the selection below. Some word groups may contain more than one error. As you identify each error, write in the space the number of the word group containing the error. Then, edit the selection to correct the errors.

One run-on _____

One pronoun error _____

Two comma errors _____

One apostrophe error _____

One use of inappropriately informal or casual language _____

One capitalization error _____

One commonly confused word _____

One semicolon error _____

One verb problem _____

One adverb error _____

One spelling error _____

One misplaced/dangling modifier _____

Two hyphen errors _____

1 Some parents buy turtles for their children to keep as pets, but, apart from that, most adults probably don't think about them at all. 2 Yet, these slow clumsy creatures possess two remarkable qualities that many people love to have. 3 Turtles are indestructible, and they can nearly live for Centuries.

4 Most people attribute turtles' sturdiness to their tough shells, but turtles are tough in other important ways as well. 5 A turtle can go without food or liquid for months at a time. 6 It's heart doesn't need to beat constantly, so a turtle can virtually turn it on (or off) whenever it wants, turtles are built to survive through floods, heat waves, famines, ice ages, and predators' attacks.

7 In March, 2006, a 250 year old turtle died in a zoo in Calcutta. 8 Scientists have recently discovered that, unlike nearly every other animal studied, a turtles organs resist breaking down or

becoming less efficient over time. **9** A turtle that is over 100-years-old can have a liver, lungs, and kidneys that are nearly identical to those of a turtle in its teens.

10 Although turtles resist disease and predators extremely good, many turtle populations are now facing dire threats they have never had to deal with before; threats from humans. **11** Every year, zillions of turtles are killed by automobiles on new roads built across turtles' migrational pathways. **12** People are also steadily iliminating habitats on which turtles depend and, in some areas, hunting them nearly to extinction in order to sell their valuable shells and meat. **13** The resilient turtle might finally have met its match in humans.

. . . .

Editing Review Test 9

The Four Most Serious Errors (Chapters 22–26); Other Grammar Concerns (Chapters 27–33); Word Use (Chapters 34–36); Punctuation and Capitalization (Chapters 37–41)

If you need help, turn back to the chapters indicated.

DIRECTIONS: Find the errors in the selection below. Some word groups may contain more than one error. As you identify each error, write in the space the number of the word group containing the error. Then, edit the selection to correct the errors.

One fragment _____

One run-on _____

One pronoun error _____

One parallelism error _____

One apostrophe error _____

One spelling error _____

One dash error _____

One semicolon error _____

One parentheses error _____

One use of inappropriately informal or casual language _____

1 One of the most common afflictions people have is an allergy to pets. **2** Some whom are allergic simply refuse to have pets that can trigger a reaction, these pets include cats, dogs, birds, rabbits, gerbils, hamsters, and horses. **3** Instead, allergic people may keep pets that do not ordinarily cause an allergic reaction, such as fish, turtles, frogs, and lizards. **4** However, most pet-allergic people who are ga-ga about pets just go ahead and bring them into their homes anyway. **5** For these pet-allergic pet lovers, there are some good ways to reduce the allergens in a home to tolerable levels.

6 Allergens are spread from a pets saliva, urine, skin secretions, and dander the dead skin particles that animals continually shed. **7** These allergens disperse directly into the air. **8** The best way to minimize pet allergies is to limit where the pet goes in the home. **9** Here is the single most important rule; no pets in the bedroom. **10** Also, keep pets off of the furniture; instead—get a dog or cat its own floor cushion, and choose a cushion with a washable cover. **11** Rabbits, birds, gerbils, and hamsters need to be in their cages. **12** Another key is to thoroughly and frequently clean the pet, the areas where it spends most of its time, and it's extremely important to clean the bedrooms.

13 Install an air purifier in your bedroom and, if necesary, in other rooms where the pet is allowed.

14 Regularly clean the top blades of ceiling fans. **15** Which are one of the main spreaders of allergens. **16** In many cases, with sufficient care and effort, pets and pet-allergic humans can coexist.

Editing Review Test 10

The Four Most Serious Errors (Chapters 22–26);
Other Grammar Concerns (Chapters 27–33);
Word Use (Chapters 34–36); Punctuation and
Capitalization (Chapters 37–41)

If you need help, turn
back to the chapters
indicated.

DIRECTIONS: Find the errors in the selection below. Some word groups may contain more than one error. As you identify each error, write in the space the number of the word group containing the error. Then, edit the selection to correct the errors.

One fragment _____   Two spelling errors _____

One pronoun error _____   One comma error _____

One coordination/subordination error _____   One semicolon error _____

One subject-verb agreement error _____   One colon error _____

One commonly confused words error _____   One apostrophe error _____

1 People are arriving at airports earlier then they used to and spending more time there, and that has created an unexpected problem for travelers and airport managers. 2 People wait for their flights; increasing numbers of them is using their cell phones and laptop computers. 3 This is not a problem in terms of cell phone and wireless Internet access because most airports can easily make these networks available. 4 The problem occurs when cell phone and laptop users run out of battery power and need to plug into an electrical outlet. 5 In many airports including some of the most heavily used ones, there are not alot of outlets to go around.

6 Despite travelers' annoyance, many don't complain to airport personnel about not having enough outlets. 7 Most travelers mistakingly think that he or she are not allowed to use the outlets. 8 Assuming the outlets are only for airport management and cleaning staff. 9 Airport managers are definitely aware of the problem and are trying various ways of resolving it, including adding outlets in public seating areas and even in snack bars.

10 In the meantime, it's not unusual to see airport travelers carefully searching all the walls around them for a free outlet. 11 One experienced airport user offers other travelers this

advice, Think like airport cleaning staff. **12** Look for the best place to plug in a vacuum cleaner. **13** Often, he says, theres an outlet in a pillar; or behind some seats on a wall. **14** An especially kind traveler brings along an extension cord with three extra outlets and invites others to share in the connection. **15** Until the airports catch up on outlet availability, these makeshift solutions will have to do.

Part Eight

Readings for Writers

42

Introduction to the Readings

In this part of the book, you will find twenty-one essays (in Chapters 43–51) that demonstrate the types of writing you have studied—narration, illustration, description, process analysis, classification, definition, comparison and contrast, cause and effect, and argument. Chapter 51 presents a mini-casebook of readings on the theme of assisted suicide.

These readings are more than just good models of writing. They also tell great stories, argue passionately about controversial issues, and present a wide range of perspectives and information. These essays can also provide you with ideas for your own writing, both in and out of school. Most important, they offer you a chance to become a better reader and writer by examining how others write.

How Can These Readings Help You?

Reading the essays in this part of the book will help you develop several different abilities.

Your Ability to Write

The essays in this section are good examples of the types of the writing you are doing in your writing course. Looking at how someone else states main ideas, provides supporting details, organizes ideas, and introduces and concludes an essay will help you write better essays. The essays can also help you choose writing topics: As you react to an author's ideas, you may discover ideas of your own to explore. It's a good idea to keep a reading journal to record these ideas.

Your Ability to Read Critically

Critical reading means that you ask yourself why the author has made these points in this way and whether you agree. To help you read critically, the essays in this section contain many notes and questions. Soon you will find that questioning, checking, and probing come naturally to you. For more advice on critical reading, see Chapter 2.

Your Ability to Understand Other Experiences and Points of View

The authors of these selections represent various ages, genders, races, cultures, and experiences, and their writing reflects their many differences. Increasingly, employers value social skills, communication skills, and the ability to work as part of a team. Being able to understand new and different viewpoints can help you work well in a group. Another benefit may be more personal: As you read more and learn to see things through other people's eyes, you may discover new perspectives on your own life.

Your Ability to Help Yourself

Much practical information about living in the modern world is contained in written form, either print or electronic. As a good reader, you will be able to find whatever kinds of information you need. The list of topics is endless—making money, investing, starting your own business, finding a job, raising a family, treating an illness, protecting yourself from unfairness, buying a car at the best price, and so on. When you read well, you can find help to get what you need.

43

Narration

Each essay in this chapter uses narration to make its main point. As you read these essays, consider how they achieve the four basics of good narration that are listed below and discussed in Chapter 10 of this book.

■ **IDEA JOURNAL**
Write about something you did because of peer or family pressure.

■■ FOUR BASICS OF GOOD NARRATION

1. It reveals something of importance to you (your **main point**).
2. It includes all of the major events of the story (**primary support**).
3. It uses details to bring the story to life for your audience (**supporting details**).
4. It presents the events in a clear order, usually according to when they happened.

Langston Hughes

Salvation

Langston Hughes was born in 1902 in Joplin, Missouri, and spent his high school years in Cleveland, Ohio. Later, he studied engineering at Columbia University, but he eventually dropped out, soon becoming a central figure in the Harlem Renaissance, a period of creative innovation by writers, artists, and musicians in the African American section of New York. Hughes died in 1967. While he is primarily known as a poet, he was also a prolific writer of stories, plays, and essays.

In this excerpt from his autobiography, *The Big Sea,* Hughes recounts a childhood struggle to fulfill others' expectations while remaining true to his own ideas about being "saved."

GUIDING QUESTION
Was Hughes saved, or not?

PAUSE: Based on the first paragraph, predict what this essay will be about.

1   I was saved from sin when I was going on thirteen. But not really saved. It happened like this. There was a big revival at my Auntie Reed's church. Every night for weeks there had been much preaching, singing, praying, and shouting, and some very hardened sinners had been brought to Christ, and the membership of the church had grown by leaps and bounds. Then just before the revival ended, they held a special meeting for children, "to bring the young lambs to the fold." My aunt spoke of it for days ahead. That night I was escorted to the front row and placed on the mourners' bench with all the other young sinners, who had not yet been brought to Jesus.

2   My aunt told me that when you were saved you saw a light, and something happened to you inside! And Jesus came into your life! And God was with you from then on! She said you could see and hear and feel Jesus in your soul. I believed her. I had heard a great many old people say the same thing and it seemed to me they ought to know. So I sat there calmly in the hot, crowded church, waiting for Jesus to come to me.

3   The preacher preached a wonderful rhythmical sermon, all moans and shouts and lonely cries and dire pictures of hell, and then he sang a song about the ninety and nine safe in the fold, but one little lamb was left out in the cold. Then he said: "Won't you come? Won't you come to Jesus? Young lambs, won't you come?" And he held out his arms to all us young sinners there on the mourners' bench. And the little girls cried. And some of them jumped up and went to Jesus right away. But most of us just sat there.

4   A great many old people came and knelt around us and prayed, old women with jet-black faces and braided hair, old men with work-gnarled hands. And the church sang a song about the lower lights are burning, some poor sinners to be saved. And the whole building rocked with prayer and song.

5   Still I kept waiting to *see* Jesus.

6   Finally all the young people had gone to the altar and were saved, but one boy and me. He was a rounder's[1] son named Westley. Westley

[1] **rounder:** a man with a bad character

and I were surrounded by sisters and deacons praying. It was very hot in the church, and getting late now. Finally Westley said to me in a whisper: "God damn! I'm tired o' sitting here. Let's get up and be saved." So he got up and was saved.

7   Then I was left all alone on the mourners' bench. My aunt came and knelt at my knees and cried, while prayers and songs swirled all around me in the little church. The whole congregation prayed for me alone, in a mighty wail of moans and voices. And I kept waiting serenely for Jesus, waiting, waiting—but he didn't come. I wanted to see him, but nothing happened to me. Nothing! I wanted something to happen to me, but nothing happened.

8   I heard the songs and the minister saying: "Why don't you come? My dear child, why don't you come to Jesus? Jesus is waiting for you. He wants you. Why don't you come? Sister Reed, what is this child's name?"

PAUSE: What do you think Hughes might do next?

_____

_____

9   "Langston," my aunt sobbed.

10   "Langston, why don't you come? Why don't you come and be saved? Oh, Lamb of God! Why don't you come?"

11   Now it was really getting late. I began to be ashamed of myself, holding everything up so long. I began to wonder what God thought about Westley, who certainly hadn't seen Jesus either, but who was now sitting proudly on the platform, swinging his knickerbockered[2] legs and grinning down at me, surrounded by deacons and old women on their knees praying. God had not struck Westley dead for taking his name in vain or for lying in the temple. So I decided that maybe to save further trouble, I'd better lie, too, and say that Jesus had come, and get up and be saved.

PAUSE: Why did Hughes get up to be saved?

_____

_____

12   So I got up.

13   Suddenly the whole room broke into a sea of shouting, as they saw me rise. Waves of rejoicing swept the place. Women leaped in the air. My aunt threw her arms around me. The minister took me by the hand and led me to the platform.

14   When things quieted down, in a hushed silence, punctuated by a few ecstatic "Amens," all the new young lambs were blessed in the name of God. Then joyous singing filled the room.

15   That night, for the last time in my life but one—for I was a big boy twelve years old—I cried. I cried, in bed alone, and couldn't stop. I buried my head under the quilts, but my aunt heard me. She woke up and told my uncle I was crying because the Holy Ghost had come into my life, and because I had seen Jesus. But I was really crying because I

PAUSE: Summarize Hughes's feelings.

_____

_____

[2] **knickerbockered:** wearing a pair of knee-length pants popular for boys in the early twentieth century

couldn't bear to tell her that I had lied, that I had deceived everybody in the church, and I hadn't seen Jesus, and that now I didn't believe there was a Jesus any more, since he didn't come to help me.

■ SUMMARIZE AND RESPOND ·

In your reading journal or elsewhere, summarize the main point of "Salvation." Then, go back and check off support for this main idea. Next, write a brief summary (three to five sentences) of the essay. Finally, jot down your initial response to the essay. What do you think Hughes wanted to communicate to readers by relating this story from his youth? What did you learn about Hughes as a young person?

■ CHECK YOUR COMPREHENSION ·

1. Which of the following would be the best alternative title for this essay?
   a. "Auntie Reed's Church"
   b. "The Power of Prayer"
   c. "Waiting for Jesus"
   d. "Westley and Me"

2. The main idea of this essay is that
   a. most religious people are hypocrites.
   b. a good preacher can stir a congregation to be saved.
   c. Hughes had a very religious upbringing that affected him throughout his lifetime.
   d. Hughes lost his faith because he didn't see Jesus when he pretended to be saved.

3. According to Hughes, his aunt
   a. deeply wanted him to be saved.
   b. raised him for most of his childhood.
   c. was herself saved when she was twelve years old.
   d. knew why Hughes was really crying after the revival meeting.

4. If you are unfamiliar with the following words, use a dictionary to check their meanings: escorted (para. 1); dire (3); gnarled (4); congregation, serenely (7); deacons (11); deceived (15).

■ **READ CRITICALLY** . . . .

1. How can you tell that Hughes truly wanted to be "brought to Christ" (para. 1)?

2. Why did Hughes finally join the other children who had been "saved"?

3. What does the fact that Hughes cried after the revival service tell you about him?

4. What is the purpose of the exclamation points after the first three sentences of paragraph 2?

5. Note where Hughes uses direct quotation in the essay. What is the effect of these quotations?

■ **WRITE AN ESSAY** . . . .

Write an essay about a time in your youth when you desperately wanted to experience or achieve something but failed to do so. In addition to narrating the events that occurred, share the thoughts and feelings you had at the time.

. . . .

Uzodinma Iweala

A Close Encounter

Born in Washington, D.C., in 1982 to Nigerian parents serving in the diplomatic corps, Uzodinma Iweala spent most of his childhood in the United States and attended Harvard College, where he received a number of honors, including the Hoopes Prize for outstanding undergraduate thesis. Shortly after graduating, Iweala published the novel *Beast of No Nation* (2005), for which *Granta* magazine named him one of America's twenty best young novelists. In an interview with Barnes & Noble about his writing process, Iweala said, "Well, first I write everything by hand. . . . I then type up all I've written, print it out, and completely rewrite between the lines. When I'm finally ready to revise to a final draft, it becomes an affair involving colored pens, highlighters, stickies, and sometimes even scissors. I also like to read what

I've written aloud to people" (**www.barnesandnoble.com/writers/writerdetails.asp?cid=1458920**). Iweala is currently a student at Columbia University.

"A Close Encounter" first appeared as a "Lives" column in the *New York Times Magazine* in November 2005.

GUIDING QUESTION

Why does Iweala feel out of place in Nigeria?

1   I return to Nigeria after graduating from college. I have been to Abuja, the capital, a couple of times, but that was before my mother was appointed minister of finance.

2   Two weeks into my stay, on a rare occasion when my mother has time to chat, I tell her that I'm bored. Her response: "Here are the car keys. Go and buy some fruit." Overjoyed, I jump into the car, salute the heavily armed security at the gate and speed off in search of—fruit.

PAUSE: Underline details in this paragraph that suggest the economic differences between Iweala and the boy selling bananas and nuts.

3   The young boy sees me, or rather he sees the car first—a silver BMW—and quickly springs up from his spot under a small tree, eager to sell his bunches of bananas and bottles of roasted peanuts. His dingy shirt hangs low over too-short shorts. His sucked-in cheeks and puckered lips suggest that although he appears to be about twelve, he already knows the sourness of life. By the time I stop the car, he is at the passenger door, grunting: "Banana 300 naira (roughly $2). Groundnut 200 naira. Sah!" I look skeptically at his black-striped bananas and bargain him down to 200 total for the fruit and nuts. When he agrees, I reach for my wallet and hand him a crisp 500 naira note. He doesn't have change, so I tell him not to worry. He is grateful and smiles a row of perfect teeth.

4   When, two weeks later, I see this same boy, I am more aware of my position in Nigerian society. Security people at the house have told me: "You are the son of a minister! Kai! You should enjoy this country!" But it's hard to find enjoyment in a place where it's not that rare to see a little boy who should be in school standing on the corner selling fruit in the intense heat. My parents have raised me and my three siblings to be aware of the privilege we have been afforded and the responsibility it brings. "To whom much is given . . ." my grandfather always says.[1] And I have been given much, from education at the best schools in the United States to this car and its twelve speakers, which have changed the way I listen to music. But I worry about what is expected of me.

PAUSE: Why might Iweala be concerned about what is expected of him?

---

[1] **"To whom much is given . . .":** a passage from Luke 12:8 in the Christian Bible. The quotation continues with "of him much shall be required."

5   I pull over and wind down my window. He wears the same shirt and shorts and has a bunch of bananas and a bottle of peanuts ready. I wave them away. "What's up?" I ask him. He answers in broken English: "I dey oh. But I no get money to buy book for school." I reach into my wallet and pull out two fresh 500 naira notes. "Will this help?" I ask. He looks around nervously before sticking his hand into the car to take the bills. One thousand naira is a lot of money to someone whose family probably makes about 50,000 naira ($380) or less each year. "Thank you, sah," he says. "Thank you very much, oh!"

6   Later, I say to my mother: "That's the way it works? He doesn't have any money, so I dash him some. Trickle-down economics, right?"[2] My mother winces when anyone speaks of the slow progress of the economic reforms. "No, I'm trying to better his situation first," she says. The next morning, the Secret Service officers caution me, "Sometimes in this place, when you give a little, people think you're a fountain of opportunity."[3]

7   It's true that people will take advantage of you in Nigeria, but this happens everywhere in the world. I wonder if my little friend actually used the money for schoolbooks. What if he's a fraud? And then I wonder about my own motives. Did I give to alleviate my own guilt? Am I using him? Later, I realize that I don't know his name or the least bit about him nor did I think to ask.

PAUSE: How would you summarize the feelings that Iweala expresses in this paragraph?

_____

_____

8   Over the next six months, I am busy working in a refugee camp in northern Nigeria, biking across France and Spain and writing. Sometime after I return, I go for a drive, and I see the boy standing on the road next to a man who sells exotic birds. He jumps up and down to get my attention and has a big smile ready when I roll down the window.

9   "Oga sah!" he says. "Long time."

10   "Are you in school now?" I ask.

11   He nods.

12   "That's good," I say. A silence falls as we look at each other, and then I realize what he wants. "Here," I hold out a 500 naira note. "Take this."

13   He shakes his head vigorously and steps back as if offended. "What's wrong?" I ask. "It's a gift."

PAUSE: Why might the boy refuse Iweala's money?

_____

_____

14   He shakes his head again and brings his hand from behind his back. His face glistens with sweat. He drops a bunch of bananas and a bottle of peanuts in the front seat before he says, "I've been waiting to give these to you."

[2] **trickle-down economics:** an economic theory that was favored in the 1980s by the administration of President Ronald Reagan. The theory claimed that tax cuts for the wealthy would encourage them to spend more money, which then would "trickle down" to small businesses and average wage earners.

[3] **fountain of opportunity:** someone or something that can supply endless new opportunities (in this context, more money)

■ **SUMMARIZE AND RESPOND** . . . .

In your reading journal or elsewhere, summarize the main point of "A Close Encounter." Then, go back and check off support for this main idea. Next, write a brief summary (three to five sentences) of the essay. Finally, jot down your initial response to the reading. What impression of Iweala do you come away with? Of the boy selling bananas and nuts? What does their "close encounter" make you think about?

■ **CHECK YOUR COMPREHENSION** . . . .

1. Which of the following would be the best alternative title for this essay?

   a. "The Value of Money"

   b. "A Nigerian Politician's Son"

   c. "Connecting across the Nigerian Economic Divide"

   d. "Nigeria: A Land in Transition"

2. What is the main idea of this essay?

   a. The author wants to give readers a sense of the complicated nature of his relation to others in Nigeria.

   b. The author wants readers to share his feeling that economic inequality in Nigeria is the fault of politicians.

   c. The author hopes to show readers that he and his family deserve their privileged status because they are better educated than most Nigerians.

   d. The author wishes to convince readers that those who are privileged should share with others less fortunate.

3. Iweala's personal conflict stems partly from the fact that

   a. his mother's position rarely allows her time to chat with him.

   b. he was cheated by the boy selling bananas and nuts.

   c. people in Nigeria take advantage of others more often than Americans do.

   d. his family's high income gives him a privileged position in his country.

4. If you are unfamiliar with the following words, use a dictionary to check their meanings: dingy (para. 3); skeptically (3); afforded (4); winces (6); alleviate (7).

■ **READ CRITICALLY** . . . .

1. What is Iweala's attitude toward the boy he writes about? Point to specific passages in the article that support your interpretation.

2. What impression of the writer do you take away from this reading? What words would you use to describe him? Point to specific parts of the essay that create this impression for you.

3. Mark the transitions that Iweala uses in the essay to show the passage of time. How effective do you find his use of transitions?

4. Note Iweala's use of direct quotations. What do these contribute to his story?

5. In paragraph 4, Iweala writes that he worries about "what is expected of me." What does he mean? How do you think he should act, given the responsibility that he feels his privilege brings?

■ **WRITE AN ESSAY** . . . .

Write an essay about a time when you experienced a "close encounter" with another person across lines of class, race, culture, or other basic differences. How did you respond to those differences? Were you able to resolve them? Like Iweala, you should allow readers to see into your own thoughts regarding the encounter.

Narration: Linked Readings

■ **THE PRESSURE TO CONFORM** . . . .

Each of the following readings focuses on various aspects of the pressures people feel to conform:

> Langston Hughes, "Salvation" (this chapter, p. 745)
>
> Kathleen Vail, "Words That Wound" (Chapter 44, p. 759)
>
> Malcolm X, "My First Conk" (Chapter 46, p. 776)

Read the selections, and draw from at least one in addition to "Salvation" to write an essay titled "The Pressure to Conform in Our Society." You can refer to your own experience, but make sure to use material from the essays as well.

FEELING FOREIGN . . . .

Each of the following readings focuses on various aspects of feeling foreign or, in Mukherjee's essay, how people from other countries adapt to a new one.

Uzodinma Iweala, "A Close Encounter" (this chapter, p. 749)

Alex Espinoza, "An American in Mexico" (Chapter 45, p. 766)

Bharati Mukherjee, "Two Ways to Belong in America" (Chapter 49, p. 822)

Read the selections, and draw from at least one in addition to "A Close Encounter" to write an essay titled "Feeling Foreign." You can use the term *foreign* in the sense of being either from another country or in a new situation (such as starting at a new job or a new school).

44

Illustration

Each essay in this chapter uses illustration to get its main point across. As you read these essays, consider how they achieve the four basics of good illustration that are listed below and discussed in Chapter 11 of this book.

■ **IDEA JOURNAL**
Write about a time that you were bullied or hurt by what someone said about you.

> ## ▰ FOUR BASICS OF GOOD ILLUSTRATION
> 1. It has a point to illustrate.
> 2. It gives specific examples to show, explain, or prove the point.
> 3. It gives details to support these examples.
> 4. It uses enough examples to get the writer's point across.

Ellen Goodman
Nightmare of Feature Creep

A native of Newton, Massachusetts, Ellen Goodman (b. 1941) earned her bachelor's degree from Radcliffe College in 1963. She began her career in journalism as a researcher at *Newsweek* magazine at a time when few women became news writers and later was a reporter for the *Detroit Free Press*. She began writing a column for the *Boston Globe* in 1967 that went into syndication in 1976 and now appears on the op-ed page in over four hundred newspapers nationwide. Goodman has published six collections of her columns and two other works of nonfiction—*Turning Points* (1979), about changing women's roles, and *I Know Just What You Mean: The Power of Friendship in Women's Lives* (2000). Among many awards, Goodman received the Pulitzer Prize for Commentary in 1980.

Goodman is often praised for her directness, clarity, and sincerity. The following column from 2006 also reveals Goodman's witty side.

GUIDING QUESTION

What does the toothbrush that Goodman describes symbolize to her?

PAUSE: Based on this opening, predict what you think Goodman's attitude toward the high-tech toothbrush will be. Why?

_____

_____

PAUSE: Summarize Goodman's main point in paragraphs 5 and 6.

_____

_____

1   The origin of this species of rant was a toothbrush. A new toothbrush. A new toothbrush that came with an instructional DVD. The user of this advanced piece of dental equipment had been brushing his teeth lo these many years without any educational aids at all. But now he was the proud owner of an "IntelliClean System" equipped with packets of paste to be downloaded into the toothbrush's hard drive.

2   The good news is that his toothbrush—excuse me, his cleaning system—does not connect his fillings to the Internet or allow instant messaging with other people's bicuspids. But a toothbrush with a DVD and a "quad pacer" was the last straw, the final reminder of the ongoing "complexification" of everyday life—a word that can now be found in Wikipedia.

3   How did every simple piece of earthly equipment become stratospherically[1] high-tech? How did progress become associated with the number of features whose main feature is frustration?

4   Have you seen my new cell phone that can take pictures, handle e-mail, tell time, wake me up, get me the news, beat me in video games, and generally make me feel incompetent? It reminds me of a *New Yorker* cartoon of a man going into a store asking, "Do you have any phones that make phone calls?"

5   Once upon a time there were coffee makers that made, well, coffee. They now let you program, bump, and grind more kinds of espresso, americano, latte, and cappuccino at more times of day than a barista at Starbucks. You cannot drink that coffee while you are driving because you need that hand and a direct help line to Bangalore[2] just to use your car radio, which is now located on a dashboard that resembles the cockpit of a 747.

6   Shall we tell the children about the old days when you could walk into any stranger's house and actually turn on the TV? The on/off button in my home has been replaced by three remote controls that must be operated in perfect synchrony just to watch *Blue's Clues*.

7   I could get a universal remote for the cable, VCR, and DVD player that would make me unable to use them with one device instead of

[1] **stratospherically:** related to the part of the atmosphere that extends from 7 to 31 miles above the earth's surface; thus, very high

[2] **Bangalore:** a city in India

three. Or I could buy a new refrigerator which, for no apparent reason, has a television set where the kids' artwork used to be displayed.

8   The culprit of complexification is feature creep, a technological kudzu[3] that has taken over the gadget near you. Feature creep has led to what Roland Rust of the University of Maryland calls feature fatigue, a phrase inspired by the gift of a mouse pad that had been loaded with everything from a calculator to a radio. The only thing it couldn't do was brush his teeth. Maybe.

9   Rust tossed the better mouse pad in the bin and wrote a report on feature fatigue for the *Harvard Business Review*. A complexification guru, he blames engineers who love to load this stuff. And he blames consumers whose eyes are bigger than their abilities. In the store, he says, capability is a big deal. At home, usability is.

PAUSE: Underline what Rust suggests are the causes of feature creep.

10   It turns out that getting any new equipment is rather like getting a new baby. It all looks so easy when you're in the hospital. But when you get home, you don't have a clue what to do with it. One survey showed that 56 percent of consumers who bought a high-tech device were overwhelmed by it.

11   Let's be frank. Our daily lives have become more complicated. Americans moonlight[4] in the self-service economy—pumping our own overpriced gas, checking out our own groceries, printing our own pictures. Not to mention picking our Medicare prescription plans and 401(k)s.[5]

12   But faced with gadgets test-marketed on 14-year-olds, we now blame ourselves for being tech-unsavvy rather than blaming tech for being user-unfriendly. The way I figure it, I could have learned Mandarin[6] in the amount of time I spent updating software and hardware over the past decade. The difference is that I could still speak Mandarin, but the technological languages of the past three decades are now as extinct as the Xerox Telecopier.

13   Rust says that his model of simplicity is his automatic garage door opener. It goes up. It goes down. I don't have a garage. My model, I blush to confess, was always the toothbrush. It goes up and down. Of course, that was before it had a DVD.

PAUSE: What is Goodman's point in noting these "models of simplicity"?

_____

_____

14   Now I am sure that somewhere there is an engineer creating a toothbrush with an LCD, an MP3 player, and the capacity to instant message from my mouth to yours. Beware, the feature creep is coming to a molar near you.

---

[3] **kudzu:** a vine that is known for taking over the areas it infests

[4] **moonlight:** in this context, to work at a second job in addition to one's primary job

[5] **401(k)s:** retirement-related investment plans

[6] **Mandarin:** the official spoken language of China

SUMMARIZE AND RESPOND . . . .

In your reading journal or elsewhere, summarize the main point of "Nightmare of Feature Creep." Then, go back and check off support for this main idea. Next, write a brief summary (three to five sentences) of the essay. Finally, jot down your initial response to the reading. Do you find Goodman's presentation amusing, or not? To what extent do you agree with her?

 CHECK YOUR COMPREHENSION . . . .

1. Which of the following would be the best alternative title for the essay?

    a. "Modern Technology: Enhancing Daily Life"

    b. "A Rant about a High-Tech Toothbrush"

    c. "The Complexification of Everyday Life"

    d. "Why Do We Buy User-Unfriendly Gadgets?"

2. The main idea of this essay is that

    a. consumer electronics are increasingly loaded with extra features that make them more difficult to use but do not contribute to their usefulness.

    b. the daily lives of most Americans have become more and more complicated as we increasingly must perform tasks that others used to be paid to do.

    c. it is likely that in the future people will be able to send instant messages while brushing their teeth.

    d. feature creep, despite its problems, is the inevitable result of modern engineering.

3. One reason that Goodman is critical of feature creep is that it

    a. causes people to pay more for the products they buy.

    b. makes products user-unfriendly.

    c. has the potential to intrude on people's privacy.

    d. is a model of simplicity.

4. If you are unfamiliar with the following words, use a dictionary to check their meanings: rant (para. 1); bicuspids (2); culprit (8); guru (9); molar (14).

■ **READ CRITICALLY** . . . .

1. How do you think Goodman expected readers would respond to her essay? What does she seem to assume about her audience?

2. Does Goodman provide enough pertinent examples to convince you of her point? Why, or why not?

3. In paragraph 12, Goodman writes about the time she has spent "updating software and hardware over the past decade." What does this paragraph contribute to her main point?

4. Note places in the essay where Goodman uses exaggeration. What is the effect of this exaggeration?

5. In paragraphs 8, 9, and 13, Goodman refers to the work of Roland Rust of the University of Maryland. Why does she do so?

■ **WRITE AN ESSAY** . . . .

Write an essay on the topic of feature creep, focusing on examples drawn from your experience. First, think about what electronic products you rely on, how often you regularly use all the features they offer, and how much they frustrate you. In your essay, you may support Goodman's opinion, challenge it, or come down somewhere in the middle.

. . . .

Kathleen Vail
Words That Wound

Kathleen Vail was born in Pittsburgh, Pennsylvania, and received a bachelor's degree in journalism from California University of Pennsylvania. She has worked as an education reporter at daily newspapers in Pennsylvania, North Carolina, and Virginia, and in 1994 she became an assistant editor at the *American School Board Journal: The Source for School Leaders.* She has been managing editor there since 2006. Vail lives in Springfield, Virginia, with her husband and two sons.

Originally published in the *American School Board Journal,* "Words That Wound" focuses on school bullying and its sometimes devastating consequences.

GUIDING QUESTION
What examples of bullying does Vail give?

PAUSE: Based on these two opening paragraphs, what do you predict that this essay will be about?

1   Brian Head saw only one way out. On the final day of his life, during economics class, the fifteen-year-old stood up and pointed a semiautomatic handgun at himself. Before he pulled the trigger, he said his last words, "I can't take this anymore."

2   Brian's father, William Head, has no doubt why his child chose to take his life in front of a classroom full of students five years ago. Brian wanted everyone to know the source of his pain, the suffering he could no longer endure. The Woodstock, GA, teen, overweight with thick glasses, had been systematically abused by school bullies since elementary school. Death was the only relief he could imagine. "Children can't vote or organize, leave or run away," says Head. "They are trapped."

3   For many students, school is a torture chamber from which there is no escape. Every day, 160,000 children stay home from school because they are afraid of being bullied, according to the National Association of School Psychologists. In a study of junior high school students from small Midwestern towns, nearly 77 percent of the students reported they'd been victims of bullies at school—14 percent saying they'd experienced severe reactions to the abuse. "Bullying is a crime of violence," says June Arnette, associate director of the National School Safety Center. "It's an imbalance of power, sustained over a period of time."

4   Yet even in the face of this suffering, even after Brian Head's suicide five years ago, even after it was revealed this past spring that a culture of bullying might have played a part in the Columbine High School shootings,[1] bullying remains for the most part unacknowledged, underreported, and minimized by schools. Adults are unaware of the extent and nature of the problem, says Nancy Mullin-Rindler, associate director of the Project on Teasing and Bullying in the Elementary Grades at Wellesley College Center for Research for Women. "They underestimate the import. They feel it's a normal part of growing up, that it's character-building."

5   After his son's death, William Head became a crusader against bullying, founding an effort called Kids Hope to prevent others from suffering as Brian had. Unfortunately, bullying claimed another victim in the small town of Woodstock: thirteen-year-old Josh Belluardo. Last November, on the bus ride home from school, Josh's neighbor, fifteen-year-old Jonathan Miller, taunted him and threw wads of paper at him. He followed Josh off the school bus, hit the younger boy in the back of the head, and kicked him in the stomach. Josh spent the last two days of his life in a coma before dying of his injuries. Miller, it turns out, had been suspended nearly twenty times for offenses such as pushing and

[1] **Columbine High School shootings:** the April 1999 shootings at Columbine High School in Littleton, Colorado, in which two male students killed twelve students and a teacher, injured twenty-three others, and killed themselves

taunting other students and cursing at a teacher. He's now serving a life sentence for felony murder while his case is on appeal.

6   Bullying doesn't have to result in death to be harmful. Bullying and harassment are major distractions from learning, according to the National School Safety Center. Victims' grades suffer, and fear can lead to chronic absenteeism, truancy, or dropping out. Bullies also affect children who aren't victimized: Bystanders feel guilty and helpless for not standing up to the bully. They feel unsafe, unable to take action. They also can be drawn into bullying behavior by peer pressure. "Any time there is a climate of fear, the learning process will be compromised," says Arnette.

PAUSE: Underline the ways that bullying can be harmful, according to Vail.

7   A full 70 percent of children believe teachers handle episodes of bullying "poorly," according to a study by John Hoover at the University of North Dakota at Grand Forks. It's no wonder kids are reluctant to tell adults about bullying incidents. "Children feel no one will take them seriously," says Robin Kowalski, professor of psychology at Western Carolina University, Cullowhee, NC, who's done research on teasing behavior.

8   Martha Rizzo, who lives in a suburb of Cincinnati, calls bullying the "dirty little secret" of her school district. Both her son and daughter were teased in school. Two boys in her son's sixth-grade class began taunting him because he wore sweatpants instead of jeans. They began to intimidate him during class. Once they knocked the pencil out of his hand during a spelling test when the teacher's back was turned. He failed the test. Rizzo made an appointment with the school counselor. The counselor told her he could do nothing about the behavior of the bullies and suggested she get counseling for her son instead. "Schools say they do something, but they don't, and it continues," says Rizzo. "We go in with the same problem over and over again."

9   Anna Billoit of Louisiana went to her son's middle school teachers when her son, who had asthma and was overweight, was being bullied by his classmates. Some of the teachers made the situation worse, she says. One male teacher suggested to her that the teasing would help her son mature. "His attitude was, 'Suck it up, take it like a man,'" says Billoit.

10   Much bullying goes on in so-called transition areas where there is little or no adult supervision: hallways, locker rooms, restrooms, cafeterias, playgrounds, buses, and bus stops. When abuse happens away from adult eyes, it's hard to prove that the abuse occurred. Often, though, bullies harass their victims in the open, in full view of teachers and other adults. Some teachers will ignore the behavior, silently condoning.[2] But even when adults try to deal with the problem, they sometimes make

---

[2] **condoning:** approving

PAUSE: Why can confronting bullies in front of their peers be counter-productive, according to Vail?

things worse for the victim by not handling the situation properly. Confronting bullies in front of their peers only enhances the bullies' prestige and power. And bullies often step up the abuse after being disciplined. "People know it happens, but there's no structured way to deal with it," says Mullin-Rindler. "There's lots of confusion about what to do and what is the best approach."

11   Societal expectations play a part in adult reactions to childhood bullying. Many teachers and administrators buy into a widespread belief that bullying is a normal part of childhood and that children are better off working out such problems on their own. But this belief sends a dangerous message to children, says Head. Telling victims they must protect themselves from bullies shows children that adults can't and won't protect them. And, he points out, it's an attitude adults would never tolerate themselves. "If you go to work and get slapped on the back of the head, you wouldn't expect your supervisor to say, 'It's your problem—you need to learn to deal with it yourself,'" says Head. "It's a human rights issue."

PAUSE: What do you think of the point made here about teachers' "secret admiration for the strong kids"?

12   Ignoring bullying is only part of the problem. Some teachers go further by blaming the victims for their abuse by letting their own dislike for the victimized child show. "There's a lot of secret admiration for the strong kids," says Eileen Faucette of Augusta, GA. Her daughter was teased so badly in the classroom that she was afraid to go to the blackboard or raise her hand to answer a question. The abuse happened in front of the teacher, who did nothing to stop it.

13   Head also encountered a blame-the-victim attitude toward his son. Brian would get into trouble for fighting at school, but when Head and his wife investigated what happened, they usually found that Brian had been attacked by other students. The school, Head said, wanted to punish Brian along with his attackers. "The school calls it fighting," Head says. "But it's actually assault and battery."

PAUSE: Think about a time when you witnessed bullying behavior. How did you feel?

14   And changes are coming. This past April, five months after Josh Belluardo's death, the Georgia State Legislature passed an anti-bullying law. The law defines bullying as "any willful attempt or threat to inflict injury on another person when accompanied by an apparent present ability to do so" or "any intentional display of force such as would give the victim reason to fear or expect immediate bodily harm." Schools are required to send students to an alternative school if they commit a third act of bullying in a school year. The law also requires school systems to adopt anti-bullying policies and to post the policies in middle and high schools.

15   Head was consulted by the state representatives who sponsored the bill, but he believes the measure won't go far enough. He urges schools to treat bullying behavior as a violation of the state criminal law against assault, stalking, and threatening and to call police when the law is broken.

16   He knows it's too late for Brian, too late for Josh, too late for the teens who died in Littleton. But he continues to work, to educate and lobby on the devastating effects of bullying so that his son's death will not have been in vain.

17   "We should come clean and say what we've done in the past is wrong," says Head. "Now we will guarantee we'll protect the rights of students."

▮ SUMMARIZE AND RESPOND ·

In your reading journal or elsewhere, summarize the main point of "Words That Wound." Then go back and check off support for this main idea. Next, write a brief summary (three to five sentences) of the reading. Finally, jot down your initial response to the selection. How do your own experiences with teasing and bullying in school affect your response?

▮ CHECK YOUR COMPREHENSION ·

1. Which of the following would be the best alternative title for this essay?

   a. "Bullying in Elementary School"

   b. "The Tragic Story of a Bullied Teen"

   c. "The Causes of Adolescent Suicide"

   d. "Bullying: A Serious Problem"

2. The main idea of this essay is that

   a. educators and policymakers need to realize that bullying has serious negative consequences and take steps to reduce its occurrence.

   b. bullying should be made a criminal offense like assault, battery, stalking, and threatening.

   c. adults who tolerate bullying among schoolchildren would never tolerate the same kind of behavior if it were inflicted in the workplace.

   d. bullying is common in school settings because teachers, counselors, and administrators can do little about it.

3. According to Vail, teachers who ignore bullying

   a. are afraid to intervene.

   b. send the signal that they see nothing wrong with it.

   c. believe that parents have the responsibility for getting help for their children.

   d. were probably bullies themselves.

4. If you are unfamiliar with the following words, use a dictionary to check their meanings: endure (para. 2); import (4); crusader, taunted, coma (5); distractions, chronic, truancy, compromised (6); intimidate (8); prestige (10); devastating (16).

 READ CRITICALLY . . . .

1. Evaluate Vail's opening. How effective do you find it as a way of introducing her main point?

2. Identify each of the examples that Vail presents. Do these examples convince you that the problem of bullying is serious and widespread? Why or why not?

3. Consider the statistics that Vail offers in paragraphs 3 and 7. What do they contribute to the essay? Which other kinds of statistics would you like to see?

4. In paragraph 12, Vail writes about "blaming the victims." What does she mean, and how does this idea contribute to the main point she is making?

5. In what ways does Vail tie her conclusion back to the opening part of her essay? What is the effect of this conclusion?

 WRITE AN ESSAY . . . .

Write an essay developing your own ideas about what schools can do to reduce bullying among students. What policies might they adopt, and how could they enforce those policies? What could be done to stop the bullying that takes place in so-called transitional areas where students have no adult supervision? Use examples, either real or hypothetical, to help readers see that your plan would work.

Illustration: Linked Readings

 THE PRESSURE TO CONFORM . . . .

Each of the following readings focuses on various aspects of the pressures people feel to conform:

Read the selections, and draw from at least one in addition to "Words That Wound" to write an essay titled "The Pressure to Conform in Our Society." You can refer to your own experience, but make sure to use material from the essays as well.

• •

45

Description

■ **IDEA JOURNAL**
Describe a place from your past (or a family member's past) that you have visited.

Each essay in this chapter uses description to get its main point across. As you read these essays, consider how they achieve the four basics of good description that are listed below and discussed in Chapter 12 of this book.

▪▪ FOUR BASICS OF GOOD DESCRIPTION

1. It creates a main impression—an overall effect, feeling, or image—about the topic.
2. It uses specific examples to support the main impression.
3. It supports those examples with details that appeal to the senses—sight, hearing, smell, taste, and touch.
4. It brings a person, place, or physical object to life for the reader.

Alex Espinoza

An American in Mexico

Alex Espinoza was born in Tijuana, Mexico, in 1971 and spent his childhood in La Puenté, a community near Los Angeles. He attended San Bernardino Community College and transferred to the University of California at Riverside, where he earned a bachelor of arts degree in creative writing. He went on to receive his master of fine arts degree from the University of California at Irvine, where he was editor of the university's literary magazine, *Faultline.* Currently a member of the English faculty at California State University at Fresno, Espinoza published his first novel, *Still Water Saints,* in 2007. Espinoza is one of the Profiles of Success included in this book (see p. 191).

"An American in Mexico" originally appeared on February 25, 2007, in the *New York Times Magazine.* In it, Espinoza recounts a visit to Mexico that he made with his mother to connect to his roots in Mexico.

■ **NOTE:** Alex Espinoza is a Profile of Success in Chapter 12.

GUIDING QUESTION
What expectations does Espinoza have for his visit to the house his mother built in Mexico? Are these expectations fulfilled or disappointed?

1   When my father came to the United States to work as a day laborer many years ago, he intended to move back to the village in Michoacán where my mother and seven of my siblings lived. He wired my mother money, some of which she used to build a house there in El Ojo de Agua on a parcel of land that has been in her family since before the Mexican revolution.[1] But at some point, my mother had enough of waiting for my father's return. She packed up what little she had and, with her children, traveled to Tijuana to be closer to him and to make visits easier. She stayed in Tijuana for several years—I was born there, the youngest of eleven children. Eventually, we moved to the three-bedroom house outside Los Angeles where I grew up.

2   My childhood was different from the childhood of most of my siblings. I rode my BMX bike through vacant lots, watched cable, and collected "Star Wars" action figures. They climbed mesquite trees, made handmade dolls from old rags, and stole chicken eggs from a neighbor's henhouse to sell for candy. They also shared hardships and misfortunes—hunger, long hours of working in the fields at young ages, the loss of two infant sisters.

3   Their connection to Mexico was close, deep, and also painful, something I simply could not grasp. Growing up, I felt no ties to El Ojo de Agua. I traveled into Mexico with my family as a child a few times, but I felt disconnected and uninterested during those trips—and was always eager to return to my American life. But as I grew older, I began to want to see the place most of my family called home, the place my siblings had talked about with such complicated feelings. Two years ago, at 33, I finally decided to go. I took my mother along; it had been more than 25 years since she had returned.

PAUSE: Summarize the main differences between Espinoza's childhood and his older siblings' childhoods.

PAUSE: Why do you suppose that Espinoza finally decided to visit his family's former home?

[1] **Mexican revolution:** a period of civil war lasting from 1910 to 1917

4   We flew into Mexico City, where we stayed for one day—strolling through parks and museums and visiting the Basilica of Our Lady of Guadalupe; there we watched the steady flow of devotees making their pilgrimages to the altar on their knees, their hands clasped in prayer. The next day, we traveled by bus to the city of La Piedad, where my uncle picked us up at the depot.

5   After many years in the U.S., my uncle had recently returned home to sell agricultural equipment to local farmers. He employed a maid named Chavela, who lived in one of the nearby villages. Chavela told me that her boyfriend had left for the United States about a month before but that weeks had gone by without news of his whereabouts. She said she hoped to save enough money to be able to go and find him. It made me think of the trip my mother took more than three decades earlier, traveling by train to Tijuana with her children to be near my father.

PAUSE: What do you predict that Espinoza and his mother might find when they reach the house?

6   It was threatening to rain the afternoon my uncle drove us out over unpaved roads to the old house. Many of the houses along the main road of the village were empty and dark, with overgrown weeds and broken fences. Now and again, I'd spot one with dim lights illuminating the small windows. Tricycles and toys might be scattered around the front yard, and a column of white smoke threaded out through a hole in the corrugated-metal roof.

7   Gradually, the houses vanished, giving way to tall cornstalks, and we reached the wooden fence marking the entrance to my grandfather's property. We drove up a short distance before stopping and getting out. I spotted a reservoir behind some trees, and the water glistened when the clouds broke enough to allow a few beams of sunlight to touch the surface.

8   The house my mother built was nothing more than four walls made of orange bricks surrounded by thickets of wild shrubs and grass. The windows had no glass, and the front door had been ripped from its hinges. My uncle said that the house was sometimes used as a stable for the livestock that grazed in the hills not far away. There were broken bottles on the dirt floor, and it smelled of urine and manure.

9   "I lived here," my mother said to me, as if she couldn't believe it herself. "Right here."

PAUSE: Why might the house have become "mythic" to Espinoza?

10   This was a place that had, over the years, become mythic[2] in my mind. But it was real. I touched the brick walls, and I saw the trees my siblings had climbed, the fields where they had worked. The soft mud gave way underneath my shoes. A clean set of my footprints remained.

11   I took pictures, and after the film was developed, I sat on the floor of my apartment back in California and took the photos out. I looked at each one and tried piecing them together, assembling a memory.

[2] **mythic:** unreal but often with wondrous associations

I really wanted to connect to that land the way my brothers and sisters had—to get a better sense of our shared past. I thought I could understand things like sacrifice, the small traces of ourselves we are forced to leave behind. But all that the pictures showed were indistinguishable[3] sections of walls, windows, and dark doorways.

[3] **indistinguishable:** impossible to tell apart

 SUMMARIZE AND RESPOND . . . .

In your reading journal or elsewhere, summarize the main point of "An American in Mexico." Then, go back and check off support for this main idea. Next, write a brief summary (three to five sentences) of the reading. Finally, jot down your initial response to the selection. How does Espinoza make you feel about his visit to the house that his mother built in Mexico many years earlier?

CHECK YOUR COMPREHENSION . . . .

1. Which of the following would be the best alternative title for this essay?

    a. "Growing Up the Youngest of a Large Family"

    b. "A Journey to My Mexican Past"

    c. "Photographs and Memory"

    d. "A Connection to the Past"

2. The main idea of this essay is that

    a. immigrants have an obligation to visit the places where their families originally lived.

    b. the younger children in immigrant families generally have a more privileged life than do their elder siblings.

    c. the author's attempt to make a connection to his family's former life in Mexico was not successful.

    d. photographs can never do justice to one's memories of a place.

3. The author's mother's response to visiting the house she built in Mexico is one of

    a. disgust that the place is so filthy.

    b. amazement that she once lived there.

    c. sadness that no one lives there any longer.

    d. anger toward her brother for allowing it to become shabby.

4. If you are unfamiliar with the following words, use a dictionary to check their meanings: disconnected (3); devotees, pilgrimages (4); illuminating, corrugated (6).

■ READ CRITICALLY

1. Espinoza begins his essay with a brief history of his immediate family. What purpose does this opening serve?

2. In paragraph 3, Espinoza refers to his siblings' feelings about their home in Mexico as "complicated." Why does he think that they might feel the way they do?

3. Note Espinoza's use of descriptive detail in paragraphs 6 to 8. To what senses does he appeal? What overall impression does he create?

4. Espinoza makes use of direct quotation only once in the essay, and he does so in a one-sentence paragraph (para. 9). Why do you suppose that he chose to do so? How would the effect be different if he had put what his mother said into his own words rather than quoting her directly?

5. Evaluate Espinoza's concluding paragraph. What impression does he seem to wish to create? What makes you think as you do?

■ WRITE AN ESSAY

Write an essay about a place that has special meaning for you. Your associations with the place may be either positive or negative or some combination of the two. Be sure to include the kinds of descriptive detail that will bring your subject to life for your readers and let them understand its significance.

Debra Marquart

Chores

Growing up on a rural North Dakota farm near the tiny hamlet of Napoleon in the 1960s and 1970s, Debra Marquart was a rebel from an early age. She escaped to college only to drop out and tour with rock and heavy-metal bands. Eventually returning to school, she completed a master's degree in English at Iowa State University and a master's degree in liberal arts at Moorhead State University in Minnesota. She published her first book of poetry, *Everything's a Verb,* in 1995, followed by a jazz-accompanied spoken-word CD, *A Regular Dervish,* in 1996. Now a member of the faculty at Iowa State's creative writing and environment program, she has written *The Hunger Bone: Rock & Roll Stories* (2000), a collection of short stories based on her experiences as a road musician, along with poetry and prose for a variety of journals. Her memoir, *The Horizontal World: Growing Up Wild in the Middle of Nowhere* (2006), received the Elle Lettres award from *Elle* magazine and the 2007 PEN USA Creative Nonfiction Award.

"Chores," adapted from *The Horizontal World,* originally appeared in *Orion* magazine. In it, Marquart describes in stark detail the experience of slaughtering chickens on her family's farm.

GUIDING QUESTION

Which descriptive details presented in this essay do you find most memorable?

1   Chores—even the word registers a feeling for the task at hand: "I've gotta go home and do chores." Never singular, always plural, a job that interrupts some fun you're having, then grows and grows like polyps[1] in an intestine. One syllable quickly spat out or yelled up creaky stair, the word *chores* describes a job so unsavory that to spend the energy using two syllables means you'd probably never get around to doing it.

PAUSE: What comes to your mind when you think of the word *chores*?

2   It's best to turn away from chores, pretend you didn't hear the call, hope someone else will do them, better to turn back to the softness and warmth of your own bed, back to the brush of cotton and the sweet downy smell of sheets, than to skitter across a cold wood floor in the dark, pull on the old clothes and worn smelly shoes, and go out into the drafty, shit-smeared places where chores are done.

3   I have been pulled from my bed in my white nightgown after I've disregarded my mother's first and second calls, my father's third call for chores. I have been taken down to the big backyard near the chicken coop to help with butchering the hens.

PAUSE: Based on this paragraph, what do you predict the author will describe in the essay?

4   My mother has already started. She is cutting necks. My grandmother kneels beside her, also cutting. Between them is a growing pile of chicken heads, wall-eyed, astonished open beaks, the stunned crop of white feathers against the pink wavy flesh of fading combs.

5   My oldest sister, Kate, is galloping around the yard like the cloaked angel of death, snaring chickens with a long wire leg-catcher. When she

[1] **polyps:** a type of tumor

traps them by the ankle, they squawk wildly, trying to catch the ground with the other leg and run away until she lifts them in the air and hands them, wings flapping, feathers flying loose, over to the neck cutters. In this way, my sister is god today.

6　　My second-oldest sister, Elizabeth, is retrieving the chickens from the headless places they have flown to. Around and around she runs, looking for the vivid sprays that will signal a chicken is nearby—blood rising in fountains on the white stucco walls of the chicken coop, blood bucking up against the trunks of cottonwoods, blood in soaked patches on the grass, the red-iron smell of oxidization strewn across the dewy green lawn.

7　　As the youngest girl, I stand on the edge of this slaughter, guarding the three loads of laundry my mother has risen early to wash, the whites now flapping on the line. My mother is quick with the knife; her blade is sharp. She places the chicken on the ground, pulls its wings back and severs the neck with one quick motion. Without turning to look up, she throws the bird into the air as if to separate herself from the act, then she grabs another live chicken.

PAUSE: Why do you suppose this memory is so vivid for Marquart?

_____

_____

8　　My grandmother kneels beside her, moving more slowly. She cuts off the head, then holds her hand around the chicken's neck, tilting it like a wine bottle she means to pour down to nothing. Under her knee, the chicken bumps and claws until all the electrical impulses that drive its muscles are finished. Beside her is a large red pool running down the hill. And so, it seems, there are at least two ways to butcher a chicken.

PAUSE: Underline the specific descriptive details Marquart uses in this paragraph.

9　　The water is already boiling in tubs up the hill in the barn where we go to pluck the feathers. Sitting in a circle, we grasp the upturned claws and dip the chickens in steaming water. The feathers come off in clumps and drop into another tub between us. The smell is complex—water meets wool meets vinegar meets dirt—like wet fur, like bad feet.

10　　We pluck the strong wing feathers with their deep roots and peel away the body's blanket of feathers. Then we rub the skin for the downy layer and pick away the tiny pinfeathers nestling inside the deep pockets of skin.

11　　Across the yard, Mother is in the milk house with the burning candle. She is the fire woman singeing the plucked bodies as she passes them over the flame. The room smells of sulfur, the deep-caked odor of burnt hair and flesh. Grandmother sits beside her, on a stool in front of the sink. She is the last one to receive the bodies.

12　　She places the chicken on its back before her and opens the bird's legs, looking for the soft spot unprotected by bone. "The pooper," she says, "the last part to go over the fence." She repeats these words all day again and again to keep us from fainting.

13   She draws a sharp blade across the film of skin between the legs. A world of steaming darkness spills out into which she must thrust her hand, extracting the long weave of intestines, the soft gray lungs, the heart, the liver, the tiny green row of developing egg yolks, the brown gizzard, all swimming in a gelatinous ooze. Carefully, she finds the small sac of bile, the green-black poison that, if ruptured, will ruin the meat of the bird, and she cuts it away.

14   Only she knows how to distinguish the edible from the throwaway parts. She crops the feet from the body with a hard crunch of her knife and trims away the claws, the dirt still packed tight under the nails from the chicken's constant scratching for food. We recoil when she places the trimmed yellow feet on the edible pile. She'll then take them home in a bag to Grandpa at the end of the day, and we have no idea what they do with them.

15   And when she holds the gizzard in her palm like a warm bun and draws a blade along the edge, turning the sac inside out to show us the chicken's last supper, I expect to see bottle caps, shiny pennies, diamond rings inside, but I find only an undigested clump of oats, a few tiny bits of gravel.

16   At the end of the day, we tuck in the wings and legs, slipping the naked birds into the dozens of water-filled milk cartons my mother has been saving all year for freezing the meat. She sets aside four of the biggest birds for frying that night.

17   "Mmm, girls," she says, "just think—fresh chicken."

18   "Ughh," I say to Grandmother as we walk the red wheelbarrow to the dump ground to bury the parts, the metallic tinge of blood still in my mouth.

19   "Do I really have to eat it?" I ask.

20   I could use a few days for amnesia[2] to set in. But Grandmother tells me I must. I must learn to know the taste of what my hands have done on my tongue.

PAUSE: Summarize the impression of her grandmother that Marquart creates.

_____

_____

[2] **amnesia:** a state of forgetfulness

SUMMARIZE AND RESPOND . . . .

In your reading journal or elsewhere, summarize the main point of "Chores." Then, go back and check off support for this main idea. Next, write a brief summary (three to five sentences) of the selection. Finally, jot down your initial response to the reading. To what extent do you share the feelings that the author expresses in her final paragraphs about not wanting to eat the chickens?

■ **CHECK YOUR COMPREHENSION** . . . .

1. Which of the following would be the best alternative title for this essay?
   a. "Jobs We'd Rather Avoid"
   b. "Butchering Day"
   c. "Bad Taste"
   d. "A Yard Full of Chickens"

2. The main idea of this essay is that
   a. it is only right to know where one's food actually comes from.
   b. chores are those tasks that nobody really wants to do.
   c. the author feels that her mother and grandmother do not understand her.
   d. butchering chickens on a family farm is a brutal and difficult job.

3. According to the author, when killing chickens her mother and grandmother
   a. apply different techniques.
   b. take pleasure in the task.
   c. want to get the job over with as quickly as possible.
   d. always do laundry first.

4. If you are unfamiliar with the following words, check a dictionary for their meanings: unsavory (para. 1); skitter (2); wall-eyed (4); gelatinous, ruptured (13); edible, recoil (14).

■ **READ CRITICALLY** . . . .

1. What purpose do the first two paragraphs serve? How do they relate to the rest of the essay?

2. Note Marquart's use of repetition in paragraph 6. What is the effect of this repetition?

3. In describing how her mother and grandmother cut the chickens' necks (paras. 7–8), what does Marquart's language suggest about their different attitudes toward the job?

4. Note Marquart's appeal to different senses in the essay. How would you evaluate her use of such appeals?

5. Where in the essay does Marquart give you a sense of what she was like as a child? What impression of her do you come away with?

 WRITE AN ESSAY . . . .

Write an essay describing an experience from your childhood that you remember vividly. You might choose something particularly pleasurable, something unpleasant or frightening, or something that happened once or many times—anything, as long as you can recall the experience in detail. Like Marquart's, your essay may use elements of narration, but your goal should be to appeal to your readers' senses of sight, sound, smell, taste, and touch.

Description: Linked Readings

FEELING FOREIGN . . . .

Each of the following readings focuses on various aspects of feeling foreign or, in Mukherjee's essay, the ways that people from other countries adapt to a new one.

Alex Espinoza, "An American in Mexico" (this chapter, p. 766)

Uzodinma Iweala, "A Close Encounter" (Chapter 43, p. 749)

Bharati Mukherjee, "Two Ways to Belong in America" (Chapter 49, p. 822)

Read the selections, and draw from at least one in addition to "An American in Mexico" to write an essay titled "Feeling Foreign." You can use the term *foreign* in the sense of being from another country or in the sense of being in a new situation, such as starting at a new job or a new school.

46

Process Analysis

■ **IDEA JOURNAL**
Write about a time
you felt pressured to
do something that
wasn't true to your-
self.

Each essay in this chapter uses process analysis to get its main point across. As you read these essays, consider how they achieve the four basics of good process analysis that are listed below and discussed in Chapter 13 of this book.

■■ FOUR BASICS OF GOOD PROCESS ANALYSIS

1. It helps readers either perform the steps themselves or understand how something works.
2. It presents the essential steps in the process.
3. It explains the steps in detail.
4. It arranges the steps in a logical order (usually in chronological order).

Malcolm X

My First Conk[1]

Malcolm X was born Malcolm Little in Omaha, Nebraska, in 1925. When a teacher told Malcolm that he would never fulfill his dream of becoming a lawyer because he was black, Malcolm lost interest in school, dropped out, and spent several years committing drug-related crimes. Malcolm turned his life around, though, when he was sentenced

[1] **conk:** a method of straightening curly hair

to prison on burglary charges, using the time to further his education and to study the teachings of the Nation of Islam, the Black Muslim movement in America. He also changed his surname from Little to X, suggesting that he could never know his true name—the African name of his ancestors who were made slaves. Malcolm X became an important leader of the Nation of Islam soon after his release from prison, but he later left the group to form his own, less radical religious and civil rights group. In 1964, Malcolm X was assassinated while giving a speech.

"My First Conk" is an excerpt from *The Autobiography of Malcolm X,* which Malcolm cowrote with his friend Alex Haley. Using vivid details to bring the painful process to life, Malcolm takes readers step by step through his first "conk"—a process that straightens curly hair.

GUIDING QUESTION
What main point does Malcolm X make about the process he analyzes?

1   Shorty soon decided that my hair was finally long enough to be conked.[2] He had promised to school me in how to beat the barbershop's three- and four-dollar price by making up congolene,[3] and then conking ourselves.

2   I took the little list of ingredients he had printed out for me, and went to a grocery store, where I got a can of Red Devil lye,[4] two eggs, and two medium-sized white potatoes. Then at a drugstore near the poolroom, I asked for a large jar of vaseline, a large bar of soap, a large-toothed comb and a fine-toothed comb, one of those rubber hoses with a metal spray-head, a rubber apron and a pair of gloves.

3   "Going to lay on that first conk?" the drugstore man asked me. I proudly told him, grinning, "Right!"

4   Shorty paid six dollars a week for a room in his cousin's shabby apartment. His cousin wasn't at home. "It's like the pad's mine, he spends so much time with his woman," Shorty said. "Now, you watch me—"

5   He peeled the potatoes and thin-sliced them into a quart-sized Mason fruit jar, then started stirring them with a wooden spoon as he gradually poured in a little over half the can of lye. "Never use a metal spoon; the lye will turn it black," he told me.

---

[2] **conked:** straightened

[3] **congolene:** a product used to straighten hair

[4] **lye:** a strong alkaline substance used in soaps and cleaners

6   A jelly-like, starchy-looking glop resulted from the lye and potatoes, and Shorty broke in the two eggs, stirring real fast—his own conk and dark face bent down close. The congolene turned pale-yellowish. "Feel the jar," Shorty said. I cupped my hand against the outside, and snatched it away. "Damn right, it's hot, that's the lye," he said. "So you know it's going to burn when I comb it in—it burns *bad*. But the longer you can stand it, the straighter the hair."

7   He made me sit down, and he tied the string of the new rubber apron tightly around my neck, and combed up my bush of hair. Then, from the big vaseline jar, he took a handful and massaged it hard all through my hair and into the scalp. He also thickly vaselined my neck, ears, and forehead. "When I get to washing out your head, be sure to tell me anywhere you feel any little stinging," Shorty warned me, washing his hands, then pulling on the rubber gloves, and tying on his own rubber apron. "You always got to remember that any congolene left in burns a sore into your head."

8   The congolene just felt warm when Shorty started combing it in. But then my head caught fire.

PAUSE: What is the main point of paragraphs 8–15?

9   I gritted my teeth and tried to pull the sides of the kitchen table together. The comb felt as if it was raking my skin off.

10   My eyes watered, my nose was running. I couldn't stand it any longer; I bolted to the washbasin. I was cursing Shorty with every name I could think of when he got the spray going and started soap-lathering my head.

11   He lathered and spray-rinsed, lathered and spray-rinsed, maybe ten or twelve times, each time gradually closing the hot-water faucet, until the rinse was cold, and that helped some.

12   "You feel any stinging spots?"

13   "No," I managed to say. My knees were trembling.

14   "Sit back down, then. I think we got it all out okay."

15   The flame came back as Shorty, with a thick towel, started drying my head, rubbing hard. *"Easy, man, easy,"* I kept shouting.

16   "The first time's always worst. You get used to it better before long. You took it real good, homeboy. You got a good conk."

17   When Shorty let me stand up and see in the mirror, my hair hung down in limp, damp strings. My scalp still flamed, but not as badly; I could bear it. He draped the towel around my shoulders, over my rubber apron, and began again vaselining my hair.

18   I could feel him combing, straight back, first the big comb, then the fine-tooth one.

19   Then, he was using a razor, very delicately, on the back of my neck. Then, finally, shaping the sideburns.

20   My first view in the mirror blotted out the hurting. I'd seen some pretty conks, but when it's the first time, on your *own* head, the transformation, after the lifetime of kinks, is staggering.

21   The mirror reflected Shorty behind me. We both were grinning and sweating. And on top of my head was this thick, smooth sheen of shining red hair—real red—as straight as any white man's.

22   How ridiculous I was! Stupid enough to stand there simply lost in admiration of my hair now looking "white," reflected in the mirror in Shorty's room. I vowed that I'd never again be without a conk, and I never was for many years.

23   This was my first really big step toward self-degradation:[5] When I endured all of that pain, literally burning my flesh to have it look like a white man's hair. I had joined that multitude of Negro men and women in America who are brainwashed into believing that the black people are "inferior"—and white people "superior"—that they will even violate and mutilate their God-created bodies to try to look "pretty" by white standards.

[5] **self-degradation:** loss of moral character or honor

> **PAUSE:** Why does Malcolm X refer to himself as "ridiculous" and "stupid" (para. 22) for being happy with his straightened hair?
>
> _____
>
> _____
>
> **PAUSE:** Do you think Malcolm X's ideas in this essay are still relevant today?
>
> _____
>
> _____

■ SUMMARIZE AND RESPOND ·

In your reading journal or elsewhere, summarize the main point of "My First Conk." Then go back and check off support for this main idea. Next, write a brief summary (three to five sentences) of the essay. Finally, jot down your initial response to the essay. Did it surprise you that a well-known black activist leader once wanted to look more like a white man? What is something you have done to conform to a particular group?

■ CHECK YOUR COMPREHENSION · · · · · · · · · · · · · · · · · ·

1. Which of the following would be the best alternative title for this essay?

   a. "The Pain of Conformity"

   b. "Why I Hated My First Conk"

   c. "Hairstyles of the Past"

   d. "Does Anyone Remember Congolene?"

2. The main idea of this essay is that

   a. most people regret something they have done to change their appearance.

   b. making a homemade conking solution is a dangerous process.

   c. when Malcolm X was younger, he wanted to straighten his hair.

   d. conking is a painful and degrading process that Malcolm X later regretted having gone through.

3. According to the author,

   a. he was very pleased when he first saw his straightened hair.

   b. Shorty helped him conk his hair the first time because he didn't have his family's approval.

   c. conking was such a painful experience that he never did it again.

   d. the conk didn't change the way he saw himself.

4. If you are unfamiliar with the following words, use a dictionary to check their meanings: shabby (para. 4); bolted (10); blotted, staggering (20); sheen (21); endured, brainwashed, inferior, mutilate (23).

READ CRITICALLY

1. What do you think is Malcolm X's purpose in analyzing the process of conking?

2. Reread paragraphs 6 through 11, underlining the details that Malcolm X uses to appeal to readers' senses. How do these details support his main point?

3. Without going into too much detail, list the major steps in the conking process.

4. Describe the author's attitude toward conking when he was a teenager. How and why do you think this attitude changed as he grew older?

5. Are the essay's final two paragraphs a good example of an effective conclusion? Why or why not?

WRITE AN ESSAY

Write an essay about a process you have gone through to change your appearance (dieting, tattooing, body piercing, or bodybuilding, for example). In your essay, explain why you made the decision to change your appearance, and then explain the process. In your conclusion, examine how your perception of the experience has changed over time.

Daniel Goleman

For Man and Beast, Language of Love Shares Many Traits

Born in 1946 in Stockton, California, Daniel Goleman received his B.A. degree from Amherst College and his Ph.D. in clinical psychology and human behavior from Harvard University. As a long-time science reporter for the *New York Times*, Goleman wrote often about the brain and studies in the behavioral sciences. In 1995, he published the best-selling and highly influential *Emotional Intelligence: Why It Can Matter More than IQ*, in which he argues that people who have empathy and the ability to love are most likely to be successful in life. His later books include *Working with Emotional Intelligence* (1998) and *Social Intelligence: The New Science of Human Relationships* (2006). Goleman lectures frequently to professional and business groups and on college campuses.

In the following essay, published on February 14, 1995, in the *New York Times,* Goleman explores mating rituals among humans and other animals.

GUIDING QUESTION
According to the essay, why do women and men who are interested in one another behave as they do?

1   With the same ethological[1] methods they have long used in studies of animals, scientists are turning their attention to the nuances of human courtship rituals — otherwise known as flirting.

2   By turning the ethologists' lens on human courtship, scientists are finding striking similarities with other species, suggesting that the non-verbal template[2] used by *Homo sapiens*[3] for attracting and approaching a prospective mate is to some extent part of a larger, shared animal heritage.

3   A woman parades past a crowded bar to the women's room, hips swaying, eyes resting momentarily on a likely man and then coyly looking away just as she notices his look. This scenario exemplifies a standard opening move in courtship, getting attention, said Dr. David Givens, an

PAUSE: Based on these two opening paragraphs, what process do you predict the essay will describe?

[1] **ethological:** relating to the study of animals

[2] **template:** a pattern

[3] ***Homo sapiens:*** the species of human beings

anthropologist in Washington who is writing a book about evolution and behavior. "In the first phase of courting, humans broadcast widely a nonverbal message that amounts to 'notice me,'" said Dr. Givens. "They do it through movement, through their dress, through gesture."

PAUSE: Do you think this is true? Why or why not?

4 From hundreds of hours of observations in bars and at parties, Dr. Givens discovered that women, more than men, tend to promenade, making numerous trips to the women's room, for instance, both to scout and to be seen.

5 A second nonverbal message in this earliest stage is, "I am harmless," Dr. Givens has found. The gestures and postures humans use to send this message are shared with other mammals, particularly primates.[4] Charles Darwin, who noted the same gestures in his 1859 book, *The Expressions of the Emotions in Man and Animals*, called them "submissive displays."

6 Perhaps the first serious study of flirting was done in the 1960s by Dr. Irenaus Eibl-Eibesfeldt, an eminent ethologist at the Max Planck Institute in Germany. Dr. Eibl-Eibesfeldt traveled to cultures around the world with a camera that took pictures from the side so he could stand near couples and take their pictures without their realizing they were being observed. In research in Samoa, Brazil, Paris, Sydney, and New York, Dr. Eibl-Eibesfeldt discovered an apparently universal non-verbal human vocabulary for flirting and courtship.

PAUSE: What signals do potential partners give each other early on, and why do they do so?

7 In humans, one such gesture is a palm-up placement of the hand, whether on a table or a knee, a reassuring sign of harmlessness. Another submissive display is the shoulder shrug, which, ethologists suggest, derives from an ancient vertebrate[5] reflex, a posture signifying helplessness. A posture combining the partly shrugged shoulder and a tilted head—which displays the vulnerability of the neck—is commonly seen when two people who are sexually drawn to each other are having their first conversation, Dr. Givens said.

8 Being playful and childish is another way potential lovers often communicate harmlessness. "You see the same thing in the gray wolf," said Dr. Givens.

9 When wolves encounter each other, they usually give a show of dominance, keeping their distance. But in a sexual encounter, they become playful and frisky, "like puppies," said Dr. Givens, "so they can accept closeness." The next step is a mutual show of submission, all of which paves the way for physical intimacy.

10 "We still go through the ritual of courtship much like our mammalian ancestors," said Dr. Givens. "These gestures are subcortical,

---

[4] **primates:** mammals that include humans, apes, and monkeys

[5] **vertebrate:** an animal with a backbone or spinal column

regulated by the more primitive part of our brain. They have nothing to do with the intellect, with our great neocortex."[6]

11   The nonverbal repertoire for flirting is "part of a natural sequence for courtship worldwide," said Dr. Helen Fisher, an anthropologist at Rutgers University in New Brunswick, N.J., and author of *The Anatomy of Love* (Fawcett, 1993). "Mothers don't teach this to their daughters."

12   "In evolutionary terms, the payoff for each sex in parental investment differs: To produce a child, a woman has an obligatory nine-month commitment, while for a man it's just one act of copulation," said Dr. David Buss, a psychologist at the University of Michigan in Ann Arbor and author of *The Evolution of Desire* (Basic Books, 1994). "For men in evolutionary terms, what pays is sexual access to a wide variety of women, while for women, it's having a man who will commit time and resources for helping raise children."

PAUSE: How do you respond to the point made in this paragraph?

_____

_____

13   From this view, the coyness of courtship is a way to "test a prospective partner for commitment," said Dr. Jane Lancaster, an anthropologist at the University of New Mexico in Albuquerque. "Women, in particular, need to be sure they're not going to be deserted."

14   Coyness is not seen in species where the female does not need the sustained help or resources of a male to raise her young, said Dr. Lancaster. In species where a single act of sex is the only contact a female requires with the father of her young, "there's a direct assertion of sexual interest by the female," said Dr. Lancaster.

15   But in species where two parents appreciably enhance the survival of offspring, "females don't want to mate with a male who will abandon them," said Dr. Lancaster. In such species, "the courtship dances are coy, a test to see if the male is willing to persist and pursue or simply wants a momentary dalliance," he said. "Instead of the female simply getting in a posture for mating, she repeats a promise-withdraw sequence, getting in the mating posture and then moving away."

16   In humans, flirtatious looks imitate this sequence. The coy look a woman gives a man is the beginning of a continuing series of approach-withdraw strategies that will unfold over the course of their courtship. These feminine stratagems signal the man, "I'm so hard to win that if you do win me, you won't have to worry about me getting pregnant by another male," said Dr. Lancaster.

PAUSE: What comparison is being made in this and the previous paragraph?

_____

_____

17   A taxonomy[7] of 52 "nonverbal solicitation behaviors" observed in flirting women has been created by Dr. Monica Moore, a psychologist at Webster University in St. Louis. In her research, conducted in singles bars, shopping malls, and other places young people go to meet those

[6] **neocortex:** the part of the brain that serves as the center of higher human functions

[7] **taxonomy:** a classification system

of the opposite sex, Dr. Moore has found that the women who send flirtatious signals most frequently are most likely to be approached by men—even more so than are women who are rated more attractive.

18   "It's not who's most physically appealing," said Dr. Moore, "but the woman who's signaling availability that men approach."

19   Flirting is the opening gambit in a continuing series of negotiations at every step of the way in courtship. Indeed, the first major negotiation point is signaled by the flirtatious look itself.

20   "When a man is looking at a woman and she senses it, her first decision is, 'Do I have further interest in him?'" said Dr. Beverly Palmer, a psychologist at California State University in Dominguez Hills who has studied flirting. "If so, by flirting she sends the next signal: 'I'm interested in you, and yes, you can approach me.'"

21   Once the first conversation begins, there is "a major escalation point," she said. "A large number of prospective pickups end here."

22   Though men may say they are well aware of the tentativeness of flirting, Dr. Buss's findings suggest a male tendency—at least among college-age men—toward wishful thinking in interpreting flirtatious looks. In settings where men and women go to meet someone of the opposite sex, Dr. Buss said, "we find that when you ask men what it means for a woman to smile at them, they interpret it as a sexual invitation."

23   "But when you ask women what it means," he continued, "they'll say it just indicates she wants to get to know him better."

24   In interviews with 208 college-age men and women published in the *Journal of Sex Research*, Dr. Buss and colleagues found that when it comes to seduction, "the sexual signals that work for a woman backfire for men."

25   "There's a huge sex difference in how effective different tactics are," he added.

26   Perhaps not surprisingly, the research showed that for women, direct sexual approaches—dressing seductively, dancing close, staring into a man's eyes—worked well in leading to sexual contact. But for men, similar direct strategies were failures.

27   Instead, for men, the less overtly seductive romantic stratagems fared best. "For men, the most effective approaches are displays of love and commitment," said Dr. Buss. "Telling her he really loves her, that he cares, and is committed."

PAUSE: How well do the flirtatious behaviors and responses described correspond to your own experience?

■   **SUMMARIZE AND RESPOND** . . . .

In your reading journal or elsewhere, summarize the main point of "For Man and Beast, Language of Love Shares Many Traits." Then, go back and check off support for this main idea. Next, write a brief summary (three to five sentences) of the reading. Finally, jot down your initial response to the selection. What information presented by Goleman did you find most thought provoking? Has your own behavior ever matched the kinds of behaviors he describes here?

■ **CHECK YOUR COMPREHENSION** . . . .

1. Which of the following would be the best alternative title for this essay?

   a. "The Biological Basis of Human Courtship Rituals"

   b. "Flirting: A Guide to Better Understanding the Signals"

   c. "Using Science to Help Find a Mate"

   d. "Flirting: Good Strategy or Bad?"

2. The main idea of this essay is that

   a. women have different ways of indicating interest in a potential part-ner than men do.

   b. one can become more successful at flirting by understanding the unconscious signals that are involved in courtship.

   c. many of the behaviors associated with flirting by humans have paral-lels in other species.

   d. men are likely to misread a woman's smile as an indication of her sexual availability.

3. One central point Goleman makes is that women

   a. learn flirting from their mothers.

   b. play the game of courtship as a way of making sure that a man is will-ing to commit to helping raise children.

   c. should realize that men sometimes use direct sexual approaches because they think that they work.

   d. who are more attractive are less likely to be approached by a man than those who are flirtatious.

4. If you are unfamiliar with the following words, use a dictionary to check their meanings: nuances (para. 1); heritage (2); coyly, scenario, exem-plifies (3); promenade (4); submissive (5); eminent (6); derives, vulner-ability (7); subcortical (10); repertoire (11); obligatory, copulation (12); appreciably, dalliance (15); stratagems (16); gambit (19); escalation (21); tentativeness (22); tactics (25); overtly (27).

READ CRITICALLY . . . .

1. How does Goleman give readers a broad perspective on the stages of human courtship? What techniques does he use to shift from describing the process to commenting on it?

2. What specific evidence is offered in the essay to suggest that human courtship rituals are the product of evolution? How convincing do you find this evidence?

3. How extensively does Goleman rely on the testimony of experts in this essay? How does he present the work of these experts? Does this strategy seem appropriate to you? Why or why not?

4. Why do you think that anthropologists and psychologists might be interested in studying human courtship rituals? What larger lessons might they hope to learn? Can you see any practical applications of such research?

5. To what extent does this essay support stereotypes regarding male and female behavior? What is your response to this aspect of the reading?

 WRITE AN ESSAY . . . .

Write an essay about a process involving human interaction. You might use Goleman's essay as a starting point and write in more detail about the stages that two people go through over the course of meeting, getting to know one another, and becoming partners. Or you could focus on the stages involved in the evolution of a friendship, the relationship between a parent and child, or another close relationship. You can base your essay on your own experience, but in presenting the process, explain it in terms of how it applies to people generally.

Process Analysis: Linked Readings

 THE PRESSURE TO CONFORM . . . .

Each of the following readings focuses on various aspects of the pressures people feel to conform:

Malcolm X, "My First Conk" (this chapter, p. 776)

Langston Hughes, "Salvation" (Chapter 43, p. 745)

Kathleen Vail, "Words That Wound" (Chapter 44, p. 759)

Read the selections, and draw from at least one in addition to "My First Conk" to write an essay titled "The Pressure to Conform in Our Society." You can refer to your own experience, but make sure to use material from the essays as well.

 CONCEPTIONS OF GENDER . . . .

Each of the following readings focuses on various aspects of the effects of gender on people's behaviors and lives.

Daniel Goleman, "For Man and Beast, Language of Love Shares Many Traits" (this chapter, p. 781)

Scott Russell Sanders, "The Men We Carry in Our Minds" (Chapter 47, p. 788)

Dave Barry, "The Ugly Truth about Beauty" (Chapter 49, p. 817)

Amy L. Beck, "Struggling for Perfection" (Chapter 50, p. 829)

Drawing from at least one selection in addition to "For Man and Beast, Language of Love Shares Many Traits," write an essay titled "How Gender Affects Behavior." You can refer to your own experience, but make sure to use material from the essays as well.

47

Classification

■ **IDEA JOURNAL**
Write about the different "languages" that you use in your life—with friends, with family, in college, and at work.

Each essay in this chapter uses classification to get its main point across. As you read these essays, consider how they achieve the four basics of good classification that are listed below and discussed in Chapter 14 of this book.

■ FOUR BASICS OF GOOD CLASSIFICATION

1. It makes sense of a group of people or items by organizing them into meaningful categories.
2. It has a purpose for sorting the people or items.
3. It uses a single organizing principle.
4. It gives detailed examples or explanations of the people or items that fit into each category.

Scott Russell Sanders
The Men We Carry in Our Minds

Since 1971, Scott Russell Sanders (b. 1945) has been an English professor at Indiana University. His observations of the midwestern landscape have informed several of his works, including his essay collection, *The Force of Spirit* (2000). In addition to nonfiction, Sanders writes novels, short stories, and children's books, and he has been awarded, among many other honors, a Lannan Literary Award and a Guggenheim Fellowship.

In "The Men We Carry in Our Minds," which first appeared in the *Milkweed Chronicle* in 1984, Sanders looks back at the men he knew during his boyhood in Tennessee. He considers how the hard lives they led challenge some common assumptions of feminism.

GUIDING QUESTION
Into what three categories does Sanders classify the sorts of men he grew up with?

1   "This must be a hard time for women," I say to my friend Anneke. "They have so many paths to choose from, and so many voices calling them."

2   "I think it's a lot harder for men," she replies.

3   "How do you figure that?"

4   "The women I know feel excited, innocent, like crusaders in a just cause. The men I know are eaten up with guilt."

5   We are sitting at the kitchen table drinking sassafras tea, our hands wrapped around the mugs because this April morning is cool and drizzly. "Like a Dutch morning," Anneke told me earlier. She is Dutch herself, a writer and midwife and peacemaker, with the round face and sad eyes of a woman in a Vermeer[1] painting who might be waiting for the rain to stop, for a door to open. She leans over to sniff a sprig of lilac, pale lavender, that rises from a vase of cobalt blue.

6   "Women feel such pressure to be everything, do everything," I say. "Career, kids, art, politics. Have their babies and get back to the office a week later. It's as if they're trying to overcome a million years' worth of evolution in one lifetime."

7   "But we help one another. We don't try to lumber on alone, like so many wounded grizzly bears, the way men do." Anneke sips her tea. I gave her the mug with owls on it, for wisdom. "And we have this deep-down sense that we're in the right—we've been held back, passed over, used—while men feel they're in the wrong. Men are the ones who've been discredited, who have to search their souls."

8   I search my soul. I discover guilty feelings aplenty—toward the poor, the Vietnamese, Native Americans, the whales, an endless list of debts—a guilt in each case that is as bright and unambiguous as a neon sign. But toward women I feel something more confused, a snarl of shame, envy, wary tenderness, and amazement. This muddle troubles me. To hide my unease I say, "You're right, it's tough being a man these days."

---

[1] **Vermeer:** a seventeenth-century Dutch painter known for depictions of people in moments of contemplation

9   "Don't laugh." Anneke frowns at me, mournful-eyed, through the sassafras steam. "I wouldn't be a man for anything. It's much easier being the victim. All the victim has to do is break free. The persecutor has to live with his past."

10   How deep is this past? I find myself wondering after Anneke has left. How much of an inheritance do I have to throw off? Is it just the beliefs I breathed in as a child? Do I have to scour memory back through father and grandfather? Through St. Paul?[2] Beyond Stonehenge[3] and into the twilit caves? I'm convinced the past we must contend with is deeper even than speech. When I think back on my childhood, on how I learned to see men and women, I have a sense of ancient, dizzying depths. The back roads of Tennessee and Ohio where I grew up were probably closer, in their sexual patterns, to the campsites of Stone Age hunters than to the genderless cities of the future into which we are rushing.

11   The first men, besides my father, I remember seeing were black convicts and white guards, in the cottonfield across the road from our farm on the outskirts of Memphis. I must have been three or four. The prisoners wore dingy gray-and-black zebra suits, heavy as canvas, sodden with sweat. Hatless, stooped, they chopped weeds in the fierce heat, row after row, breathing the acrid dust of boll-weevil[4] poison. The overseers wore dazzling white shirts and broad shadowy hats. The oiled barrels of their shotguns flashed in the sunlight. Their faces in memory are utterly blank. Of course those men, white and black, have become for me an emblem of racial hatred. But they have also come to stand for the twin poles of my early vision of manhood—the brute toiling animal and the boss.

12   When I was a boy, the men I knew labored with their bodies. They were marginal farmers, just scraping by, or welders, steelworkers, carpenters; they swept floors, dug ditches, mined coal, or drove trucks, their forearms ropy with muscle; they trained horses, stoked furnaces, built tires, stood on assembly lines wrestling parts onto cars and refrigerators. They got up before light, worked all day long whatever the weather, and when they came home at night they looked as though somebody had been whipping them. In the evenings and on weekends they worked on their own places, tilling gardens that were lumpy with clay, fixing broken-down cars, hammering on houses that were always too drafty, too leaky, too small.

PAUSE: What do you predict Sanders will do in the next few paragraphs of the essay?

PAUSE: How would you summarize the life of the working men that Sanders remembers from childhood?

---

[2] **St. Paul:** New Testament author who established strictures on the roles of husbands and wives

[3] **Stonehenge:** massive prehistoric monument in southern England

[4] **boll weevil:** parasite that destroys cotton plants

13   The bodies of the men I knew were twisted and maimed in ways visible and invisible. The nails of their hands were black and split, the hands tattooed with scars. Some had lost fingers. Heavy lifting had given many of them finicky backs and guts weak from hernias. Racing against conveyor belts had given them ulcers. Their ankles and knees ached from years of standing on concrete. Anyone who had worked for long around machines was hard of hearing. They squinted, and the skin of their faces was creased like the leather of old work gloves. There were times, studying them, when I dreaded growing up. Most of them coughed, from dust or cigarettes, and most of them drank cheap wine or whiskey, so their eyes looked bloodshot or bruised. The fathers of my friends always seemed older than the mothers. Men wore out sooner. Only women lived into old age.

14   As a boy I also knew another sort of men, who did not sweat and break down like mules. They were soldiers, and so far as I could tell they scarcely worked at all. During my early school years we lived on a military base, an arsenal in Ohio, and every day I saw GIs in the guard-shacks, on the stoops of barracks, at the wheels of olive drab Chevrolets. The chief fact of their lives was boredom. Long after I left the arsenal I came to recognize the sour smell the soldiers gave off as that of souls in limbo.[5] They were all waiting—for wars, for transfers, for leaves, for promotions, for the end of their hitch—like so many braves waiting for the hunt to begin. Unlike the warriors of older tribes, however, they would have no say about when the battle would start or how it would be waged. Their waiting was broken only when they practiced for war. They fired guns at targets, drove tanks across the churned-up fields of the military reservation, set off bombs in the wrecks of old fighter planes. I knew this was all play. But I also felt certain that when the hour for killing arrived, they would kill. When the real shooting started, many of them would die. This was what soldiers were *for*, just as a hammer was for driving nails.

PAUSE: Do you believe that soldiers have an easier life than do physical laborers?

15   Warriors and toilers: Those seemed, in my boyhood vision, to be the chief destinies for men. They weren't the only destinies, as I learned from having a few male teachers, from reading books, and from watching television. But the men on television—the politicians, the astronauts, the generals, the savvy lawyers, the philosophical doctors, the bosses who gave orders to both soldiers and laborers—seemed as remote and unreal to me as the figures in tapestries. I could no more imagine growing up to become one of these cool, potent creatures than I could imagine becoming a prince.

---

[5] **limbo:** in Roman Catholic teaching, a region eternally occupied by souls assigned to neither heaven nor hell

16   A nearer and more hopeful example was that of my father, who had escaped from a red-dirt farm to a tire factory, and from the assembly line to the front office. Eventually he dressed in a white shirt and tie. He carried himself as if he had been born to work with his mind. But his body, remembering the early years of slogging work, began to give out on him in his fifties, and it quit on him entirely before he turned sixty-five. Even such a partial escape from man's fate as he had accomplished did not seem possible for most of the boys I knew. They joined the army, stood in line for jobs in the smoky plants, helped build highways. They were bound to work as their fathers had worked, killing themselves or preparing to kill others.

17   A scholarship enabled me not only to attend college, a rare enough feat in my circle, but even to study in a university meant for children of the rich. Here I met for the first time young men who had assumed from birth that they would lead lives of comfort and power. And for the first time I met women who told me that men were guilty of having kept all the joys and privileges of the earth for themselves. I was baffled. What privileges? What joys? I thought about the maimed dismal lives of most of the men back home. What had they stolen from their wives and daughters? The right to go five days a week, twelve months a year, for thirty or forty years to a steel mill or a coal mine? The right to drop bombs and die in war? The right to feel every leak in the roof, every gap in the fence, every cough in the engine, as a wound they must mend? The right to feel, when the lay-off comes or the plant shuts down, not only afraid but ashamed?

PAUSE: Why was Sanders "slow to understand the deep grievances of women"?

18   I was slow to understand the deep grievances of women. This was because, as a boy, I had envied them. Before college, the only people I had ever known who were interested in art or music or literature, the only ones who read books, the only ones who ever seemed to enjoy a sense of ease and grace were the mothers and daughters. Like the menfolk, they fretted about money, they scrimped and made-do. But, when the pay stopped coming in, they were not the ones who had failed. Nor did they have to go to war, and that seemed to me a blessed fact. By comparison with the narrow, ironclad days of fathers, there was an expansiveness, I thought, in the days of mothers. They went to see neighbors, to shop in town, to run errands at school, at the library, at church. No doubt, had I looked harder at their lives, I would have envied them less. It was not my fate to become a woman, so it was easier for me to see the graces. Few of them held jobs outside the home, and those who did filled thankless roles as clerks and waitresses. I didn't see, then, what a prison a house could be, since houses seemed to me brighter, handsomer places than any factory. I did not realize—because such things

were never spoken of—how often women suffered from men's bullying. I did learn about the wretchedness of abandoned wives, single mothers, widows; but I also learned about the wretchedness of lone men. Even then I could see how exhausting it was for a mother to cater all day to the needs of young children. But if I had been asked, as a boy, to choose between tending a baby and tending a machine, I think I would have chosen the baby. (Having now tended both, I know I would choose the baby.)

19   So I was baffled when the women at college accused me and my sex of having cornered the world's pleasure. I think something like my bafflement has been felt by other boys (and by girls as well) who grew up in dirt-poor farm country, in mining country, in black ghettos, in Hispanic barrios,[6] in the shadows of factories, in third world nations—any place where the fate of men is as grim and bleak as the fate of women. Toilers and warriors. I realize now how ancient these identities are, how deep the tug they exert on men, the undertow of a thousand generations. The miseries I saw, as a boy, in the lives of nearly all men I continue to see in the lives of many—the body-breaking toil, the tedium, the call to be tough, the humiliating powerlessness, the battle for a living and for territory.

20   When the women I met at college thought about the joys and privileges of men, they did not carry in their minds the sort of men I had known in my childhood. They thought of their fathers, who were bankers, physicians, architects, stockbrokers, the big wheels of the big cities. These fathers rode the train to work or drove cars that cost more than any of my childhood houses. They were attended from morning to night by female helpers, wives and nurses and secretaries. They were never laid off, never short of cash at month's end, never lined up for welfare. These fathers made decisions that mattered. They ran the world.

21   The daughters of such men wanted to share in this power, this glory. So did I. They yearned for a say over their future, for jobs worthy of their abilities, for the right to live at peace, unmolested, whole. Yes, I thought, yes yes. The difference between me and these daughters was that they saw me, because of my sex, as destined from birth to become like their fathers, and therefore an enemy to their desires. But I knew better. I wasn't an enemy, in fact or in feeling. I was an ally. If I had known, then, how to tell them so, would they have believed me? Would they now?

PAUSE: Why might Sanders have concluded his essay with these questions?

---

[6] **barrios:** Spanish-speaking communities

■ **SUMMARIZE AND RESPOND** . . . .

In your reading journal or elsewhere, summarize the main point of "The Men We Carry in Our Minds." Then, go back and check off support for this main idea. Next, write a brief summary (three to five sentences) of the essay. Finally, jot down your initial response to the reading. To what extent do you believe that Sanders's categories of types of men still hold true today? To what extent do you feel that the positions held by men and women in society have changed (or remained the same) since this essay was written? How much sympathy do you have for the feelings Sanders expresses?

■ **CHECK YOUR COMPREHENSION** . . . .

1. Which of the following would be the best alternative title for this essay?

   a. "A Conversation with Anneke about Men and Women"

   b. "My Childhood on a Tennessee Farm"

   c. "A Scholarship Student's Reflections on the Differences between Men and Women"

   d. "The 'Privileges' of Being a Man"

2. The main idea of this essay is that

   a. men control most of the power in society and, therefore, lead more comfortable lives than women.

   b. it is difficult for a young man who grew up poor to see men as having more power than women.

   c. the balance of power between men and women has shifted significantly over the years so that men and women are now more nearly equal.

   d. access to education can create a more level playing field for those who grow up poor and those who grow up rich.

3. According to Sanders,

   a. his childhood observations led him to believe that women led easier lives than men did.

   b. when he went away to college, he felt a great deal of sympathy for the grievances of the women he met there.

   c. the "warriors and toilers" he observed in childhood provided role models for him later in life.

d. his father struggled throughout his life to provide a comfortable home environment for his family.

4. If you are unfamiliar with the following words, use a dictionary to check their meanings: midwife (para. 5); lumber (7); unambiguous, wary, muddle (8); persecutor (9); genderless (10); acrid (11); marginal (12); maimed, hernias (13); arsenal (14); tapestries (15); dismal (17); expansiveness, wretchedness (18); baffled, undertow, tedium (19).

READ CRITICALLY . . . .

1. In paragraphs 1–9, what point does Sanders's friend Anneke make about men and women in the United States at the time the essay was written in the early 1980s?

2. Why, in paragraph 8, does Sanders suggest that he chose to agree with Anneke about the place of men in relationship to women ("You're right, it's tough being a man these days") when this was not his true feeling?

3. What sorts of images of men did Sanders grow up with? How did these images affect his attitudes toward the position of women in society?

4. In what ways did the women he met in college challenge Sanders's views of the positions of men and women in society? Why does he think his viewpoint and that of the college women he met were so different? Why did he consider himself their "ally" rather than their "enemy" (para. 21)?

5. How does Sanders communicate a point about social class that goes beyond simply his own experiences?

WRITE AN ESSAY . . . .

Write an essay titled "The _____ I Carry in My Mind," filling in the blank with a specific label referring to people—for example, *teachers, students, parents, bosses, coworkers, friends* (or *boyfriends, girlfriends*). Be sure that you have enough examples of the subject you choose so that you can classify them into at least three categories, each of which you can name concretely (as Sanders names "warriors" and "toilers"). In your essay, focus primarily on defining these categories, using specific examples (at least one per category) as illustrations.

. . . .

Amy Tan
Mother Tongue

Amy Tan was born in Oakland, California, in 1952, several years after her mother and father emigrated from China. She studied at San Jose City College and later San Jose State University, receiving a B.A. with a double major in English and linguistics. In 1973, she earned an M.A. in linguistics from San Jose State. In 1989, Tan published her first novel, *The Joy Luck Club,* which was nominated for the National Book Award and the National Book Critics Circle Award. Tan's other books include *The Kitchen God's Wife* (1991) and *The Hundred Secret Senses* (1995). Her short stories and essays have been published in the *Atlantic, Grand Street, Harper's,* the *New Yorker,* and other publications.

In the following essay, which was selected for *The Best American Essays 1991,* Tan discusses the different kinds of English she uses, from academic discourse to the simple language she speaks with her mother.

GUIDING QUESTION

In what ways did Tan's mother's "limited" ability to speak English affect Tan as she was growing up?

1   I am not a scholar of English or literature. I cannot give you much more than personal opinions on the English language and its variations in this country or others.

2   I am a writer. And by that definition, I am someone who has always loved language. I am fascinated by language in daily life. I spend a great deal of my time thinking about the power of language—the way it can evoke an emotion, a visual image, a complex idea, or a simple truth. Language is the tool of my trade. And I use them all—all the Englishes I grew up with.

3   Recently, I was made keenly aware of the different Englishes I do use. I was giving a talk to a large group of people, the same talk I had already given to half a dozen other groups. The nature of the talk was about my writing, my life, and my book, *The Joy Luck Club.* The talk was going along well enough, until I remembered one major difference that made the whole talk sound wrong. My mother was in the room. And it was perhaps the first time she had heard me give a lengthy speech, using the kind of English I have never used with her. I was saying things like "The intersection of memory upon imagination" and "There is an aspect of my fiction that relates to thus-and-thus"—a speech filled with carefully wrought grammatical phrases, burdened, it suddenly seemed to

me, with nominalized forms, past perfect tenses, conditional phrases, all the forms of standard English that I had learned in school and through books, the forms of English I did not use at home with my mother.

4   Just last week, I was walking down the street with my mother, and I again found myself conscious of the English I was using, the English I do use with her. We were talking about the price of new and used furniture and I heard myself saying this: "Not waste money that way." My husband was with us as well, and he didn't notice any switch in my English. And then I realized why. It's because over the twenty years we've been together I've often used that same kind of English with him, and sometimes he even uses it with me. It has become our language of intimacy, a different sort of English that relates to family talk, the language I grew up with.

PAUSE: Summarize Tan's main point in paragraph 4.

_____
_____

5   So you'll have some idea of what this family talk I heard sounds like, I'll quote what my mother said during a recent conversation which I videotaped and then transcribed. During this conversation, my mother was talking about a political gangster in Shanghai[1] who had the same last name as her family's, Du, and how the gangster in his early years wanted to be adopted by her family, which was rich by comparison. Later, the gangster became more powerful, far richer than my mother's family, and one day showed up at my mother's wedding to pay his respects. Here's what she said in part:

6   "Du Yusong having business like fruit stand. Like off the street kind. He is Du like Du Zong—but not Tsung-ming Island people. The local people call putong, the river east side, he belong to that side local people. That man want to ask Du Zong father take him in like become own family. Du Zong father wasn't look down on him, but didn't take seriously, until that man big like become a mafia. Now important person, very hard to inviting him. Chinese way, came only to show respect, don't stay for dinner. Respect for making big celebration, he shows up. Mean gives lots of respect. Chinese custom. Chinese social life that way. If too important won't have to stay too long. He come to my wedding. I didn't see, I heard it. I gone to boy's side, they have YMCA dinner. Chinese age I was nineteen."

7   You should know that my mother's expressive command of English belies how much she actually understands. She reads the *Forbes* report,[2] listens to *Wall Street Week*, converses daily with her stockbroker, reads all of Shirley MacLaine's[3] books with ease—all kinds of things I can't

---

[1] **Shanghai:** a major city in eastern China

[2] ***Forbes* report:** a financial publication geared toward investors

[3] **Shirley MacLaine:** actress whose works of autobiography have often referred to her past lives

begin to understand. Yet some of my friends tell me they understand 50 percent of what my mother says. Some say they understand 80 to 90 percent. Some say they understand none of it, as if she were speaking pure Chinese. But to me, my mother's English is perfectly clear, perfectly natural. It's my mother tongue. Her language, as I hear it, is vivid, direct, full of observation and imagery. That was the language that helped shape the way I saw things, expressed things, made sense of the world.

8   Lately, I've been giving more thought to the kind of English my mother speaks. Like others, I have described it to people as "broken" or "fractured" English. But I wince when I say that. It has always bothered me that I can think of no other way to describe it other than "broken," as if it were damaged and needed to be fixed, as if it lacked a certain wholeness and soundness. I've heard other terms used, "limited English," for example. But they seem just as bad, as if everything is limited, including people's perceptions of the limited English speaker.

9   I know this for a fact, because when I was growing up, my mother's "limited" English limited *my* perception of her. I was ashamed of her English. I believed that her English reflected the quality of what she had to say. That is, because she expressed them imperfectly her thoughts were imperfect. And I had plenty of empirical[4] evidence to support me: the fact that people in department stores, at banks, and at restaurants did not take her seriously, did not give her good service, pretended not to understand her, or even acted as if they did not hear her.

10   My mother has long realized the limitations of her English as well. When I was fifteen, she used to have me call people on the phone to pretend I was she. In this guise, I was forced to ask for information or even to complain and yell at people who had been rude to her. One time it was a call to her stockbroker in New York. She had cashed out her small portfolio and it just so happened we were going to go to New York the next week, our very first trip outside California. I had to get on the phone and say in an adolescent voice that was not very convincing, "This is Mrs. Tan."

11   And my mother was standing in the back whispering loudly, "Why he don't send me check, already two weeks late. So mad he lie to me, losing me money."

12   And then I said in perfect English, "Yes, I'm getting rather concerned. You had agreed to send the check two weeks ago, but it hasn't arrived."

13   Then she began to talk more loudly. "What he want, I come to New York tell him front of his boss, you cheating me?" And I was trying to

PAUSE: In paragraphs 9–14, what evidence does Tan use to support her claim that others believed that her mother's English showed a lack of intelligence?

---

[4] **empirical:** based on direct experience or observation

calm her down, make her be quiet, while telling the stockbroker, "I can't tolerate any more excuses. If I don't receive the check immediately, I am going to have to speak to your manager when I'm in New York next week." And sure enough, the following week there we were in front of this astonished stockbroker, and I was sitting there red-faced and quiet, and my mother, the real Mrs. Tan, was shouting at his boss in her impeccable broken English.

14   We used a similar routine just five days ago, for a situation that was far less humorous. My mother had gone to the hospital for an appointment, to find out about a benign brain tumor a CAT scan[5] had revealed a month ago. She said she had spoken very good English, her best English, no mistakes. Still, she said, the hospital did not apologize when they said they had lost the CAT scan and she had come for nothing. She said they did not seem to have any sympathy when she told them she was anxious to know the exact diagnosis, since her husband and son had both died of brain tumors. She said they would not give her any more information until the next time and she would have to make another appointment for that. So she said she would not leave until the doctor called her daughter. She wouldn't budge. And when the doctor finally called her daughter, me, who spoke in perfect English—lo and behold—we had assurances the CAT scan would be found, promises that a conference call on Monday would be held, and apologies for any suffering my mother had gone through for a most regrettable mistake.

PAUSE: Have you or anyone you know not been taken seriously because of language, age, race, or some other trait?

15   I think my mother's English almost had an effect on limiting my possibilities in life as well. Sociologists and linguists probably will tell you that a person's developing language skills are more influenced by peers. But I do think that the language spoken in the family, especially in immigrant families which are more insular, plays a large role in shaping the language of the child. And I believe that it affected my results on achievement tests, IQ tests, and the SAT. While my English skills were never judged as poor, compared to math, English could not be considered my strong suit. In grade school I did moderately well, getting perhaps B's, sometimes B-pluses, in English and scoring perhaps in the sixtieth or seventieth percentile on achievement tests. But those scores were not good enough to override the opinion that my true abilities lay in math and science, because in those areas I achieved A's and scored in the ninetieth percentile or higher.

16   This was understandable. Math is precise; there is only one correct answer. Whereas, for me at least, the answers on English tests were always a judgment call, a matter of opinion and personal experience. Those tests were constructed around items like fill-in-the-blank sentence completion, such as "Even though Tom was _____, Mary

---

[5] **CAT scan:** a form of X-ray used to produce internal images of the body

PAUSE: What has been your experience with the kinds of English tests that Tan writes about in paragraphs 16–17?

_____

_____

thought he was _____." And the correct answer always seemed to be the most bland combinations of thoughts, for example, "Even though Tom was shy, Mary thought he was charming," with the grammatical structure "even though" limiting the correct answer to some sort of semantic[6] opposites, so you wouldn't get answers like, "Even though Tom was foolish, Mary thought he was ridiculous." Well, according to my mother, there were very few limitations as to what Tom could have been and what Mary might have thought of him. So I never did well on tests like that.

17   The same was true with word analogies, pairs of words in which you were supposed to find some sort of logical, semantic relationship—for example, "_Sunset_ is to _nightfall_ as _____ is to _____." And here you would be presented with a list of four possible pairs, one of which showed the same kind of relationship: _red_ is to _stoplight, bus_ is to _arrival, chills_ is to _fever, yawn_ is to _boring._ Well, I could never think that way. I knew what the tests were asking, but I could not block out of my mind the images already created by the first pair, "_sunset_ is to _nightfall_"—and I would see a burst of colors against a darkening sky, the moon rising, the lowering of a curtain of stars. And all the other pairs of words—red, bus, stoplight, boring—just threw up a mass of confusing images, making it impossible for me to sort out something as logical as saying: "A sunset precedes nightfall" is the same as "a chill precedes a fever." The only way I would have gotten that answer right would have been to imagine an associative situation, for example, my being disobedient and staying out past sunset, catching a chill at night, which turns into feverish pneumonia as punishment, which indeed did happen to me.

PAUSE: How do you think Tan might answer the questions she poses in paragraph 18?

_____

_____

18   I have been thinking about all this lately, about my mother's English, about achievement tests. Because lately I've been asked, as a writer, why there are not more Asian Americans represented in American literature. Why are there few Asian Americans enrolled in creative writing programs? Why do so many Chinese students go into engineering? Well, these are broad sociological questions I can't begin to answer. But I have noticed in surveys—in fact, just last week—that Asian students, as a whole, always do significantly better on math achievement tests than in English. And this makes me think that there are other Asian American students whose English spoken in the home might also be described as "broken" or "limited." And perhaps they also have teachers who are steering them away from writing and into math and science, which is what happened to me.

---

[6] **semantic:** related to the meaning of words

19   Fortunately, I happen to be rebellious in nature and enjoy the challenge of disproving assumptions made about me. I became an English major my first year in college, after being enrolled as pre-med. I started writing nonfiction as a freelancer the week after I was told by my former boss that writing was my worst skill and I should hone my talents toward account management.

PAUSE: How do you respond when people make assumptions about you?

20   But it wasn't until 1985 that I finally began to write fiction. And at first I wrote using what I thought to be wittily crafted sentences, sentences that would finally prove I had mastery over the English language. Here's an example from the first draft of a story that later made its way into *The Joy Luck Club,* but without this line: "That was my mental quandary[7] in its nascent[8] state." A terrible line, which I can barely pronounce.

21   Fortunately, for reasons I won't get into today, I later decided I should envision a reader for the stories I would write. And the reader I decided upon was my mother, because these were stories about mothers. So with this reader in mind—and in fact she did read my early drafts—I began to write stories using all the Englishes I grew up with: the English I spoke to my mother, which for lack of a better term might be described as "simple"; the English she used with me, which for lack of a better term might be described as "broken"; my translation of her Chinese, which could certainly be described as "watered down"; and what I imagined to be her translation of her Chinese if she could speak in perfect English, her internal language, and for that I sought to preserve the essence, but neither an English nor a Chinese structure. I wanted to capture what language ability tests can never reveal: her intent, her passion, her imagery, the rhythms of her speech, and the nature of her thoughts.

22   Apart from what any critic had to say about my writing, I knew I had succeeded where it counted when my mother finished reading my book and gave me her verdict: "So easy to read."

[7] **quandary:** a state of uncertainty

[8] **nascent:** developing; beginning to come into existence

SUMMARIZE AND RESPOND

In your reading journal or elsewhere, summarize the main point of "Mother Tongue." Then, go back and check off support for this main idea. Next, write a brief summary (three to five sentences) of the essay. Finally, jot down your initial response to the reading. What do you think of Tan's relationship with her mother? Do you think that Tan's mother's "limited" English has affected their relationship for the better, for the worse, or in some more complex way? What impression do you have of Tan herself?

■   **CHECK YOUR COMPREHENSION** . . . .

1. Which of the following would be the best alternative title for this essay?

    a. "The Englishes I Grew Up With"

    b. "My Mother's Difficulties Communicating in English"

    c. "How to Communicate with an Immigrant Parent"

    d. "A Writer's Fascination with the English Language"

2. The main idea of this essay is that

    a. children of immigrant parents have difficulties communicating in English because of their parents' "limited" command of the language.

    b. there is no single, proper way to speak English because different people communicate in different ways.

    c. teachers believe that Asian American students necessarily do better in math and science than they do in English and writing.

    d. the kind of English one uses may change in different contexts.

3. Tan concludes that

    a. to become a successful writer, she had to work harder than would someone who grew up in a home where English was the native language.

    b. her mother found her book easy to read because her mother grew up speaking Chinese.

    c. in finding her voice as a writer, she called on the memory of her mother and their communication with each other.

    d. to prove her mastery of the English language, she had to write in a way that her mother would find impossible to understand.

4. If you are unfamiliar with the following words, use a dictionary to check their meanings: evoke (para. 2); keenly, wrought, burdened (3); intimacy (4); belies (7); fractured (8); guise (10); impeccable (13); benign (14); linguists, insular (15); associative (17); freelancer, hone (19); wittily (20).

■   **READ CRITICALLY** . . . .

1. Why, when speaking with her husband, does Tan sometimes switch to the kind of English her mother speaks? What does this tell you of her feelings about her mother's way of speaking?

2. Why does Tan dislike using labels such as "broken" or "limited" in referring to the English her mother speaks?

3. In what ways does Tan say that the language spoken within immigrant families can limit the possibilities of the children in such families? Do you agree with her?

4. What, exactly, does Tan classify in this essay? What are the specific classifications she writes about?

5. Tan divides her essay into three sections, indicated by the spaces between paragraphs 7 and 8 and paragraphs 17 and 18. What is the focus of each of these sections? Why do you suppose she chose to organize her essay in this way?

■ WRITE AN ESSAY . . . .

Write an essay classifying your use of language in different situations—at home with family members, with friends outside of home, at school, in your workplace, and elsewhere that your language may change because of the circumstances in which you find yourself. For each situation, give examples of the kind of language you use that differ from the language you use in other situations.

Classification: Linked Readings

■ STEREOTYPES . . . .

Each of the following readings focuses on stereotypes.

Scott Russell Sanders, "The Men We Carry in Our Minds" (this chapter, p. 788)

Amy Tan, "Mother Tongue" (this chapter, p. 796)

Nancy Mairs, "On Being a Cripple" (Chapter 48, p. 805)

Brent Staples, "Just Walk on By: Black Men and Public Space" (Chapter 50, p. 834)

Read the selections, and draw from at least one in addition to "Mother Tongue" to write an essay titled "Stereotypes and Their Effects."

■   **CONCEPTIONS OF GENDER** . . . .

Each of the following readings focuses on various aspects of the effects of gender on people's behaviors and lives.

> Scott Russell Sanders, "The Men We Carry in Our Minds" (this chapter, p. 788)
>
> Daniel Goleman, "For Man and Beast, Language of Love Shares Many Traits" (Chapter 46, p. 781)
>
> Dave Barry, "The Ugly Truth about Beauty" (Chapter 49, p. 817)
>
> Amy L. Beck, "Struggling for Perfection" (Chapter 50, p. 829)

Read the selections, and draw from at least one in addition to "The Men We Carry in Our Minds" to write an essay titled "How Gender Affects Behavior." You can refer to your own experience, but make sure to use material from the essays as well.

. . . .

48

Definition

Each essay in this chapter uses definition to get its main point across. As you read these essays, consider how they achieve the four basics of good definition that are listed below and discussed in Chapter 15 of this book.

■ **IDEA JOURNAL**
What labels do people use to try to define you?

> ## ■■ FOUR BASICS OF GOOD DEFINITION
> **1.** It tells readers what term is being defined.
> **2.** It gives a clear basic definition.
> **3.** It uses examples to show what the writer means.
> **4.** It gives details about the examples that readers will understand.

Nancy Mairs
On Being a Cripple

In her essays, memoirs, and poetry, Nancy Mairs (b. 1943) often writes about multiple sclerosis and her experience, since 1993, of life in a wheelchair. Mairs attended Wheaton College and earned an M.F.A. and Ph.D. from the University of Arizona. Her essay collections include *Waist High in the World: A Life among the Nondisabled* (1996) and *A Troubled Guest* (2002).

This essay, from the collection *Plaintext* (1986), addresses the words we use to talk about people with disabilities. Mairs makes a case for honesty in language and explains what she means when she calls herself a cripple.

GUIDING QUESTION
How would you describe Mairs's attitude toward her disability?

To escape is nothing. Not to escape is nothing. —LOUISE BOGAN

PAUSE: Why might this incident in the women's room have prompted Mairs to write her essay?

1   The other day I was thinking of writing an essay on being a cripple. I was thinking hard in one of the stalls of the women's room in my office building, as I was shoving my shirt into my jeans and tugging up my zipper. Preoccupied, I flushed, picked up my book bag, took my cane down from the hook, and unlatched the door. So many movements unbalanced me, and as I pulled the door open I fell over backward, landing fully clothed on the toilet seat with my legs splayed in front of me: the old beetle-on-its-back routine. Saturday afternoon, the building deserted, I was free to laugh aloud as I wriggled back to my feet, my voice bouncing off the yellowish tiles from all directions. Had anyone been there with me, I'd have been still and faint and hot with chagrin. I decided that it was high time to write the essay.

2   First, the matter of semantics.[1] I am a cripple. I choose this word to name me. I choose from among several possibilities, the most common of which are "handicapped" and "disabled." I made the choice a number of years ago, without thinking, unaware of my motives for doing so. Even now, I'm not sure what those motives are, but I recognize that they are complex and not entirely flattering. People—crippled or not—wince at the word "cripple," as they do not at "handicapped" or "disabled." Perhaps I want them to wince. I want them to see me as a tough customer, one to whom the fates/gods/viruses have not been kind, but who can face the brutal truth of her existence squarely. As a cripple, I swagger.

3   But, to be fair to myself, a certain amount of honesty underlies my choice. "Cripple" seems to me a clean word, straightforward and precise. It has an honorable history, having made its first appearance in the Lindisfarne Gospel in the tenth century. As a lover of words, I like the accuracy with which it describes my condition: I have lost the full use of my limbs. "Disabled," by contrast, suggests any incapacity, physical or mental. And I certainly don't like "handicapped," which implies that I have deliberately been put at a disadvantage, by whom I can't imagine (my God is not a Handicapper General), in order to equalize chances in the great race of life. These words seem to me to be moving away from my condition, to be widening the gap between word and reality. Most remote is the recently coined euphemism[2] "differently abled," which partakes of the same semantic hopefulness that transformed countries from

---

[1] **semantics:** in general, the study of words; here, the choice of particular words

[2] **euphemism:** a word that puts a pleasant cover over an unpleasant condition

"undeveloped" to "underdeveloped," then to "less developed," and finally to "developing" nations. People have continued to starve in those countries during the shift. Some realities do not obey the dictates of language.

4   Mine is one of them. Whatever you call me, I remain crippled. But I don't care what you call me, so long as it isn't "differently abled," which strikes me as pure verbal garbage designed, by its ability to describe anyone, to describe no one. I subscribe to George Orwell's thesis that "the slovenliness[3] of our language makes it easier for us to have foolish thoughts." And I refuse to participate in the degeneration of the language to the extent that I deny that I have lost anything in the course of this calamitous disease; I refuse to pretend that the only differences between you and me are the various ordinary ones that distinguish any one person from another. But call me "disabled" or "handicapped" if you like. I have long since grown accustomed to them; and if they are vague, at least they hint at the truth. Moreover, I use them myself. Society is no readier to accept crippledness than to accept death, war, sex, sweat, or wrinkles. I would never refer to another person as a cripple. It is the word I use to name only myself.

5   I haven't always been crippled, a fact for which I am soundly grateful. To be whole of limb is, I know from experience, infinitely more pleasant and useful than to be crippled; and if that knowledge leaves one open to bitterness at my loss, the physical soundness I once enjoyed (though I did not enjoy it half enough) is well worth the occasional stab of regret. Though never any good at sports, I was a normally active child and young adult. I climbed trees, played hopscotch, jumped rope, skated, swam, rode my bicycle, sailed. I despised team sports, spending some of the wretchedest afternoons of my life, sweaty and humiliated, behind a field-hockey stick and under a basketball hoop. I tramped alone for miles along the bridle paths that webbed the woods behind the house I grew up in. I swayed through countless dim hours in the arms of one man or another under the scattered shot of light from mirrored balls, and gyrated through countless more as Tab Hunter and Johnny Mathis gave way to the Rolling Stones, Creedence Clearwater Revival, Cream. I walked down the aisle. I pushed baby carriages, changed tires in the rain, marched for peace.

6   When I was twenty-eight I started to trip and drop things. What at first seemed my natural clumsiness soon became too pronounced to shrug off. I consulted a neurologist, who told me that I had a brain tumor. A battery of tests, increasingly disagreeable, revealed no tumor. About a year and a half later I developed a blurred spot in one eye. I had, at last, the episodes "disseminated[4] in space and time" requisite

PAUSE: Why does Mairs dislike the terms *disabled, handicapped,* and *differently abled*?

---

[3] **slovenliness:** sloppiness

[4] **disseminated:** spread over

for a diagnosis: multiple sclerosis. I have never been sorry for the doctor's initial misdiagnosis, however. For almost a week, until the negative results of the tests were in, I thought that I was going to die right away. Every day for the past nearly ten years, then, has been a kind of gift. I accept all gifts.

7   Multiple sclerosis is a chronic[5] degenerative[6] disease of the central nervous system, in which the myelin that sheaths the nerves is somehow eaten away and scar tissue forms in its place, interrupting the nerves' signals. During its course, which is unpredictable and uncontrollable, one may lose vision, hearing, speech, the ability to walk, control of bladder and/or bowels, strength in any or all extremities,[7] sensitivity to touch, vibration, and/or pain, potency, coordination of movements—the list of possibilities is lengthy and, yes, horrifying. One may also lose one's sense of humor. That's the easiest to lose and the hardest to survive without. . . .

8   Like many women I know, I have always had an uneasy relationship with my body. I was not a popular child, largely, I think now, because I was peculiar: intelligent, intense, moody, shy, given to unexpected actions and inexplicable notions and emotions. But as I entered adolescence, I believed myself unpopular because I was homely: my breasts too flat, my mouth too wide, my hips too narrow, my clothing never quite right in fit or style. I was not, in fact, particularly ugly, old photographs inform me, though I was well off the ideal; but I carried this sense of self-alienation with me into adulthood, where it regenerated in response to the depredations of MS. Even with my brace I walk with a limp so pronounced that, seeing myself on the videotape of a television program on the disabled, I couldn't believe that anything but an inchworm could make progress humping along like that. My shoulders droop and my pelvis thrusts forward as I try to balance myself upright, throwing my frame into a bony S. As a result of contractures, one shoulder is higher than the other and I carry one arm bent in front of me, the fingers curled into a claw. My left arm and leg have wasted into pipestems, and I try always to keep them covered. When I think about how my body must look to others, especially to men, to whom I have been trained to display myself, I feel ludicrous, even loathsome.

9   At my age, however, I don't spend much time thinking about my appearance. The burning egocentricity of adolescence, which assures one that all the world is looking all the time, has passed, thank God, and I'm generally too caught up in what I'm doing to step back, as I

---

[5] **chronic:** marked by a long duration; always present

[6] **degenerative:** having a worsening effect; causing deterioration

[7] **extremities:** limbs of the body

used to, and watch myself as though upon a stage. I'm also too old to believe in the accuracy of self-image. I know that I'm not a hideous crone, that in fact, when I'm rested, well dressed, and well made up, I look fine. The self-loathing I feel is neither physically nor intellectually substantial. What I hate is not me but a disease.

10   I am not a disease.

11   And a disease is not—at least not singlehandedly—going to determine who I am, though at first it seemed to be going to. Adjusting to a chronic incurable illness, I have moved through a process similar to that outlined by Elisabeth Kübler-Ross in *On Death and Dying.* The major difference—and it is far more significant than most people recognize—is that I can't be sure of the outcome, as the terminally ill cancer patient can. Research studies indicate that, with proper medical care, I may achieve a "normal" life span. And in our society, with its vision of death as the ultimate evil, worse even than decrepitude, the response to such news is, "Oh well, at least you're not going to *die.*" Are there worse things than dying? I think that there may be.

12   I think of two women I know, both with MS, both enough older than I to have served me as models. One took to her bed several years ago and has been there ever since. Although she can sit in a high-backed wheelchair, because she is incontinent she refuses to go out at all, even though incontinence pants, which are readily available at any pharmacy, could protect her from embarrassment. Instead, she stays at home and insists that her husband, a small quiet man, a retired civil servant, stay there with her except for a quick weekly foray[8] to the supermarket. The other woman, whose illness was diagnosed when she was eighteen, a nursing student engaged to a young doctor, finished her training, married her doctor, accompanied him to Germany when he was in the service, bore three sons and a daughter, now grown and gone. When she can, she travels with her husband; she plays bridge, embroiders, swims regularly; she works, like me, as a symptomatic-patient instructor of medical students in neurology. Guess which woman I hope to be.

[8] **foray:** a trip, an outing

PAUSE: Why might Mairs have chosen to write this one-sentence paragraph (para. 10)?

▪ **SUMMARIZE AND RESPOND** . . . .

In your reading journal or elsewhere, summarize the main point of "On Being a Cripple." Then, go back and check off support for this main idea. Next, write a brief summary (three to five sentences) of the reading. Finally, jot down your initial response to the selection. What impression of Mairs do you come away with? What did you learn from her description of her disease? If you could write a note to Mairs, what would you say to her?

■ **CHECK YOUR COMPREHENSION** . . . .

1. Which of the following would be the best alternative title for this essay?

    a. "The Painfulness of a Disease"

    b. "Surviving with Multiple Sclerosis"

    c. "Learning to Laugh at My Disability"

    d. "Coping with Others' Attitudes toward Disability"

2. The main idea of this essay is that

    a. multiple sclerosis is an incurable disease of the central nervous system that can affect movement, vision, hearing, and speech.

    b. many labels are used to describe disabled people, but most such people prefer the term *crippled*.

    c. one needs a strong sense of humor and a circle of supportive friends to live with a disability.

    d. being disabled presents many difficulties and obstacles, but one can learn to cope with these challenges.

3. Mairs makes the point that

    a. she is grateful to have the memory of being able-bodied as a young woman.

    b. the greatest drawback to her disability is that it makes her feel unattractive.

    c. she feels doctors are not doing enough to discover a cure for multiple sclerosis.

    d. she believes everyone should use the word *crippled* rather than *disabled* or *handicapped*.

4. If you are unfamiliar with the following words, use a dictionary to check their meanings: splayed, chagrin (para. 1); wince, swagger (2); incapacity, partakes, dictates (3); degeneration, calamitous (4); gyrated (5); neurologist (6); inexplicable, regenerated, depredations, contractures, ludicrous, loathsome (8); crone (9); decrepitude (11); incontinent (12).

■ **READ CRITICALLY** . . . .

1. How effective do you find Mairs's opening paragraph as an introduction to the essay as a whole?

2. Why do you think Mairs devotes paragraphs 2–4 to discussing her use of the word *cripple* to describe herself? How do you respond to this section

of the essay? Mairs also objects to terms like *differently abled*, which do not tell the full truth about a condition. Can you think of other such words? Why do you think such words come into the language?

3. How would you evaluate "On Being a Cripple" as a definition essay? What have you learned from the essay that you did not know before?

4. Mairs writes at the end of paragraph 11, "Are there worse things than dying? I think that there may be." What does she mean? How do this question and answer lead into the subject of paragraph 12?

5. What do you think of Mairs's closing sentence? What image of Mairs does it leave you with?

WRITE AN ESSAY . . . .

Write an essay defining an important aspect of yourself. This definition might relate to a challenge you face in life, or it might focus on another facet of your identity—your family heritage, your membership in a particular group, a personality or physical trait that you believe sets you apart from many others you know. Think about titling your essay "On Being _____" and, as Mairs does, relating experiences that help communicate your definition to readers.

. . . .

Juliet B. Schor

Age Compression

Juliet B. Schor (b. 1955) is a professor of sociology at Boston College. Her research and writings focus on work and leisure activities and their relation to family life. Her books include the best-selling *The Overworked American: The Unexpected Decline of Leisure* (1993) and *The Overspent American: Why We Want What We Don't Need* (1999).

In this essay, Schor describes a marketing trend in which products designed for adults or teenagers are pitched to younger kids. It is an excerpt from her most recent book, *Born to Buy* (2004), a study of the commercial pressures placed on today's children.

GUIDING QUESTION
What is Schor's attitude toward age compression as a marketing strategy?

1   One of the hottest trends in youth marketing is age compression — the practice of taking products and marketing messages originally designed for older kids and targeting them to younger ones. Age compression includes offering teen products and genres, pitching gratuitous violence to the twelve-and-under crowd, cultivating brand preferences for items that were previously unbranded among younger kids, and developing creative alcohol and tobacco advertising that is not officially targeted to them but is widely seen and greatly loved by children. "By eight or nine they want 'N Sync," explained one tweening expert to me, in the days before that band was eclipsed by Justin Timberlake, Pink, and others.

PAUSE: Underline each example of age compression in paragraph 2.

2   Age compression is a sprawling trend. It can be seen in the import of television programming specifically designed for one-year-olds, which occurred, ironically, with Public Broadcasting's *Teletubbies*. It includes the marketing of designer clothes to kindergartners and first graders. It's the deliberate targeting of R-rated movies to kids as young as age nine, a practice the major movie studios were called on the carpet for by the Clinton administration in 2000. It's being driven by the recognition that many children nationwide are watching MTV and other teen and adult programming. One of my favorite MTV anecdotes comes from a third-grade teacher in Weston, Massachusetts, who reported that she started her social studies unit on Mexico by asking the class what they knew about the country. Six or seven raised their hands and answered, "That's the place where MTV's Spring Break takes place!" For those who haven't seen it, the program glorifies heavy partying, what it calls "bootylicious girls," erotic dancing, wet T-shirt contests, and binge drinking.

PAUSE: Do you agree that the social trends described in paragraph 3 are leading to age compression? Can you think of other trends that are a factor?

3   A common argument within the marketing world is that age compression is being caused by social trends that make contemporary children far more sophisticated than their predecessors. These include the increased responsibilities of kids in single-parent or divorced families, higher levels of exposure to adult media, children's facility[1] with new technology, early puberty, and the fact that kids know more earlier. In the 1980s, Hasbro sold its GI Joe action figure to boys aged eleven to fourteen. Now, Joe is rejected by eight-year-olds as too babyish. Twenty years ago, *Seventeen* magazine targeted sixteen-year-olds; now it aims at eleven and twelves. In a telling gesture, the toy industry has officially lowered its upper age target from fourteen to ten.

4   Marketers have even coined an acronym to describe these developments. It's KAGOY, which stands for Kids Are Getting Older Younger. The social trends become part of the license for treating kids as if they were adults. Indeed, some advertisers are even arguing that current approaches are too protective of children. In a presentation at the 2001

---

[1] **facility:** ability to use easily

annual Marketing to Kids Conference, executive Abigail Hirschhorn of DDB New York argued that it's time to stop talking down to kids and start "talking up" to them and that too much advertising denies kids what they really crave — the adult world. She argued for more "glamour, fashion, style, irony, and popular music."

5   Nowhere is age compression more evident than among the eight- to twelve-year-old target. Originally a strategy for selling to ten- to thirteen-year-olds, children as young as six are being targeted for tweening. And what is that exactly? Tweens are "in-between" teens and children, and tweening consists mainly of bringing teen products and entertainment to ever-younger audiences. If you're wondering why your daughter came home from kindergarten one day singing the words to a Britney Spears or Jennifer Lopez song, the answer is that she got tweened. Tween marketing has become a major focus of the industry, with its own conferences, research tools, databases, books, and specialty firms. Part of why tweening is so lucrative is that it involves bringing new, more expensive products to this younger group. It's working because tweens have growing purchasing power and influence with parents. The more the tween consumer world comes to resemble the teen world, with its comprehensive branding strategies and intense levels of consumer immersion, the more money there is to be made.

PAUSE: What is tweening, and how has it changed?

6   In some cases, it's the advertisers pushing the trend with their clients. But clients are also initiating the process. Mark Lapham (pseudonym),[2] president of a company that has focused almost exclusively on the teen market, says, "We're being asked all the time about it" by makers of school supplies, apparel manufacturers, cosmetics companies. Lapham explains how his clients are thinking: "Hey, we can actually sell a cosmetic, not just bubble gum lip gloss . . . we can sell foundation possibly . . . nail polish."

7   Abigail Hirschhorn's plea for industry change is well behind the times. Children are being exposed to plenty of glamour, fashion, style, irony, and popular music, that is, sex. Even the family-friendly Disney Channel is full of sexually suggestive outfits and dancing. One Radio Disney employee explained to me that the company keeps a careful watch on lyrics but is hands-off with the other stuff. A stroll down the 6X–12 aisles of girls' clothing will produce plenty of skimpy and revealing styles. People in advertising are well aware of these developments. Emma Gilding of Ogilvy & Mather recounted an experience she had during an in-home videotaping. The little girl was doing a Britney Spears imitation, with flirting and sexual grinding. Asked by Gilding what she wanted to be when she grew up, the three-year-old answered: "A sexy shirt girl." As researcher Mary Prescott (pseudonym) explained to me in the summer of 2001, "We're coming out of a trend now. Girl power turned into sex

PAUSE: Based on the second sentence, what do you predict paragraph 7 will be about?

[2] **pseudonym:** an assumed name, here to protect the identity of the speaker

power. A very sexy, dirty, dark thing. Parents were starting to panic." While Prescott felt that a reversal toward "puritanism" had already begun, other observers aren't so sure. Not long after Prescott's prediction, Abercrombie & Fitch came under fire for selling thong underwear with sexually suggestive phrases to seven- to fourteen-year-olds. And child development expert Diane Levin alerted parents to the introduction of World Wrestling Entertainment action figures recommended for age four and above, which include a male character with lipstick on his crotch, another male figure holding the severed head of a woman, and a female character with enormous breasts and a minimal simulated black leather outfit and whip. Four-year-olds are also targeted with toys tied to movies that carry PG-13 ratings.

PAUSE: Do you believe that these members of the industry really feel guilty? Why or why not?

8   Some industry insiders have begun to caution that tweening has gone too far. At the 2002 KidPower conference, Paul Kurnit spoke out publicly about companies "selling 'tude' to pre-teens and ushering in adolescence a bit sooner than otherwise." Privately, even more critical views were expressed to me. Mark Lapham revealed that he finds this "kind of an amazing thing . . . this is where personally my guilt comes out, like gosh, it's not really appropriate sometimes." But, he continues, "that's where society's going, what do you do?" Prescott, who is more deeply immersed in the world of tweening, confessed that "I am doing the most horrible thing in the world. We are targeting kids too young with too many inappropriate things. . . . It's not worth the almighty buck."

▮ SUMMARIZE AND RESPOND . . . .

In your reading journal or elsewhere, summarize the main point of "Age Compression." Then, go back and check off support for this main idea. Next, write a brief summary (three to five sentences) of the reading. Finally, jot down your initial response to the selection. Before reading this essay, had you already noticed instances of age compression in advertising and the entertainment media? Do you share Schor's concerns over such practices? Do you agree or disagree that age compression is simply a reflection of the times we live in? Why or why not?

▮ CHECK YOUR COMPREHENSION . . . .

1. Which of the following would be the best alternative title for this essay?

   a. "Growing Up with the Media"

   b. "Sex and Violence for Kids"

   c. "Capturing the Tween Consumer"

   d. "Are Kids Getting Older Younger?"

2. The main idea of this essay is that

   a. today more and more children are being treated as if they were adults.

   b. many marketers today focus on attracting young children to increasingly mature products.

   c. age compression is the result of contemporary children having more responsibilities than did children in the past.

   d. some marketers are beginning to feel guilty about targeting inappropriate products to young children.

3. Schor suggests that one reason for age compression is

   a. children today have increased exposure to teenage and adult media.

   b. marketers now have more respect for children than they did in the past.

   c. parents take too little responsibility for monitoring the shopping habits of their children.

   d. contemporary children believe that most toys are just too babyish to play with.

4. If you are unfamiliar with the following words, use a dictionary to check their meanings: genres, gratuitous (para. 1); predecessors (3); irony (4); puritanism (7).

READ CRITICALLY . . . .

1. What would you describe as Schor's purpose in this essay? Who might her intended audience be?

2. On the basis of this essay, what would you say drives marketers to target younger children as they do?

3. Why do you suppose two of Schor's sources, Mark Lapham and Mary Prescott, agreed to be quoted only if their real names weren't used?

4. Evaluate Schor's use of examples in the essay. What do they tell us about age compression in marketing?

5. One researcher quoted in the essay suggests that "a reversal toward 'puritanism'" has begun (para. 7). In looking at marketing toward children today, do you see any evidence of such a reversal?

WRITE AN ESSAY . . . .

Write an essay in which you focus on the kinds of products and entertainment media that are targeted toward consumers ages thirteen to seventeen. You may wish to refer to television commercials, print ads in magazines, in-school advertising, advertising on Internet sites, film trailers, and the like, as well as to particular products. Do you find any evidence of age compression in marketing to this older group of consumers?

Definition: Linked Readings

 STEREOTYPES . . . .

Each of the following readings focuses on stereotypes.

> Nancy Mairs, "On Being a Cripple" (this chapter, p. 805)
>
> Scott Russell Sanders, "The Men We Carry in Our Minds" (Chapter 47, p. 788)
>
> Amy Tan, "Mother Tongue" (Chapter 47, p. 796)
>
> Brent Staples, "Just Walk on By: Black Men and Public Space" (Chapter 50, p. 834)

Read the selections, and draw from at least one in addition to "On Being a Cripple" to write an essay titled "Stereotypes: Are They Wrong?" You can refer to your own experience, but make sure to use material from the essays as well.

49

Comparison and Contrast

Each essay in this chapter uses comparison and contrast to get its main point across. As you read these essays, consider how they achieve the four basics of good comparison and contrast that are listed below and discussed in Chapter 16 of this book.

■ **IDEA JOURNAL**
Compare your attitudes to those of an older person in your family.

> ## ▪▪ FOUR BASICS OF GOOD COMPARISON
> ##   AND CONTRAST
>
> **1.** It uses subjects that have enough in common to be usefully compared and contrasted.
>
> **2.** It serves a purpose—either to help readers make a decision or to understand the subjects.
>
> **3.** It presents several important, parallel points of comparison and contrast.
>
> **4.** It is organized either point by point or whole to whole (see pp. 255–56).

Dave Barry
The Ugly Truth about Beauty

According to the *New York Times*, humorist Dave Barry is "the funniest man in America." Born in 1947 in Armonk, New York, Barry earned a B.A. from Haverford College. He then worked for several years as a newspaper reporter and a lecturer on business writing before discovering his talent as a humor columnist. The columns he now writes for the

Miami Herald appear in newspapers nationwide, and his work has been collected in numerous books. Barry's hilarious observations on American life won him the Pulitzer Prize for Commentary in 1988.

In "The Ugly Truth about Beauty," first published in the *Philadelphia Inquirer Magazine* in 1998, Barry compares and contrasts men's and women's beauty routines. The essay humorously highlights differences in the ways that men and women view themselves.

GUIDING QUESTION

Why do men and women think of their looks differently?

1   If you're a man, at some point a woman will ask you how she looks.

2   "How do I look?" she'll ask.

3   You must be careful how you answer this question. The best technique is to form an honest yet sensitive opinion, then collapse on the floor with some kind of fatal seizure. Trust me, this is the easiest way out. Because you will never come up with the right answer.

PAUSE: Based on the first sentence of paragraph 4, how do you think Barry will go on to develop this essay?

4   The problem is that women generally do not think of their looks in the same way that men do. Most men form an opinion of how they look in seventh grade, and they stick to it for the rest of their lives. Some men form the opinion that they are irresistible stud muffins, and they do not change this opinion even when their faces sag and their noses bloat to the size of eggplants and their eyebrows grow together to form what appears to be a giant forehead-dwelling tropical caterpillar.

5   Most men, I believe, think of themselves as average-looking. Men will think this even if their faces cause heart failure in cattle at a range of three hundred yards. Being average does not bother them; average is fine, for men. This is why men never ask anybody how they look. Their primary form of beauty care is to shave themselves, which is essentially the same form of beauty care that they give to their lawns. If, at the end of his four-minute daily beauty regimen,[1] a man has managed to wipe most of the shaving cream out of his hair and is not bleeding too badly, he feels that he has done all he can, so he stops thinking about his appearance and devotes his mind to more critical issues, such as the Super Bowl.

6   Women do not look at themselves this way. If I had to express, in three words, what I believe most women think about their appearance, those words would be: "not good enough." No matter how attractive a woman may appear to be to others, when she looks at herself in the mirror, she thinks: woof. She thinks that at any moment a municipal

[1] **regimen:** routine

animal-control officer is going to throw a net over her and haul her off to the shelter.

7   Why do women have such low self-esteem? There are many complex psychological and societal reasons, by which I mean Barbie. Girls grow up playing with a doll proportioned such that, if it were a human, it would be seven feet tall and weigh eighty-one pounds, of which fifty-three pounds would be bosoms. This is a difficult appearance standard to live up to, especially when you contrast it with the standard set for little boys by their dolls . . . excuse me, by their action figures. Most of the action figures that my son played with when he was little were hideous-looking. For example, he was very fond of an action figure (part of the He-Man series) called "Buzz-Off," who was part human, part flying insect. Buzz-Off was not a looker. But he was extremely self-confident. You could not imagine Buzz-Off saying to the other action figures: "Do you think these wings make my hips look big?"

PAUSE: What two subjects does Barry contrast in paragraph 7?

_____

_____

8   But women grow up thinking they need to look like Barbie, which for most women is impossible, although there is a multibillion-dollar beauty industry devoted to convincing women that they must try. I once saw an *Oprah* show wherein supermodel Cindy Crawford dispensed makeup tips to the studio audience. Cindy had all these middle-aged women applying beauty products to their faces; she stressed how important it was to apply them in a certain way, using the tips of their fingers. All the women dutifully did this, even though it was obvious to any sane observer that, no matter how carefully they applied these products, they would never look remotely like Cindy Crawford, who is some kind of genetic mutation.

PAUSE: What is Barry's main point in paragraph 8?

_____

_____

9   I'm not saying that men are superior. I'm just saying that you're not going to get a group of middle-aged men to sit in a room and apply cosmetics to themselves under the instruction of Brad Pitt, in hopes of looking more like him. Men would realize that this task was pointless and demeaning.[2] They would find some way to bolster their self-esteem that did not require looking like Brad Pitt. They would say to Brad: "Oh YEAH? Well what do you know about LAWN CARE, pretty boy?"

10   Of course many women will argue that the reason they become obsessed with trying to look like Cindy Crawford is that men, being as shallow as a drop of spit, WANT women to look that way. To which I have two responses:

11   1. Hey, just because WE'RE idiots, that does not mean YOU have to be; and

12   2. Men don't even notice 97 percent of the beauty efforts you make anyway. Take fingernails. The average woman spends 5,000 hours per year worrying about her fingernails; I have never once, in more than

[2] **demeaning:** degrading, lowering one's character

forty years of listening to men talk about women, heard a man say, "She has a nice set of fingernails!" Many men would not notice if a woman had upward of four hands.

13   Anyway, to get back to my original point: If you're a man, and a woman asks you how she looks, you're in big trouble. Obviously, you can't say she looks bad. But you also can't say that she looks great, because she'll think you're lying, because she has spent countless hours, with the help of the multibillion-dollar beauty industry, obsessing about the differences between herself and Cindy Crawford. Also, she suspects that you're not qualified to judge anybody's appearance. This is because you have shaving cream in your hair.

 SUMMARIZE AND RESPOND . . . .

In your reading journal or elsewhere, summarize the main point of "The Ugly Truth about Beauty." Then, go back and check off support for this main idea. Next, write a brief summary (three to five sentences) of the essay. Finally, jot down your initial response to the essay. Do you agree with Barry's assessment of why there are differences in the ways men and women view themselves? What examples from your experience do or do not support his points?

 CHECK YOUR COMPREHENSION . . . .

1. Which of the following would be the best alternative title for this essay?

   a. "Barbie versus He-Man"

   b. "Men and Women: What They See in the Mirror"

   c. "It's Kinder to Lie"

   d. "The Beauty Industry's Dark Secret"

2. The main idea of this essay is that

   a. men don't know how to respond when women ask about their appearance.

   b. men don't care how much effort women put into their looks.

   c. because of society and the media, men and women view their physical appearances differently.

   d. childhood toys influence the way men and women think about their looks.

3. According to Barry,

   a. most men are concerned with how women view their appearance.

   b. women want men to be honest about their looks.

   c. most women are dissatisfied with their appearance.

   d. a woman's perception of her appearance is influenced by her moods and her female friends.

4. If you are unfamiliar with the following words, use a dictionary to check their meanings: societal, proportioned (para. 7); mutation (8); bolster (9).

READ CRITICALLY

1. Who is Barry's intended audience, and what do you think is his purpose in writing this essay?

2. In paragraphs 7 and 8, Barry discusses children's toys. Why did he choose these particular toys, and how do they help him explain his points of contrast?

3. What is Barry's attitude toward Cindy Crawford and Brad Pitt? Explain how he uses these examples to support his main point.

4. Explain the significance of the title. What do you think Barry would say is the ugly truth about beauty?

5. Why do you think the beauty industry is so successful? Support your answer with examples from this essay.

WRITE AN ESSAY

Look through your family photographs, or use the Internet or magazines to view men's and women's fashions over the last fifty years. Think about how fashions have changed, and write an essay that compares and contrasts fashion trends from two different decades. Use concrete examples to show differences and similarities in the two time periods' styles.

Bharati Mukherjee

Two Ways to Belong in America

Novelist Bharati Mukherjee (b. 1940) grew up in Calcutta, India, and in London. She learned to read by the time she was three years old and had written several short stories by the age of ten. A graduate of the University of Calcutta and the University of Borada in India, Mukherjee came to the United States in 1961 to attend the University of Iowa, where she earned an M.F.A. and later a Ph.D. in English and comparative literature. Married to the Canadian writer Clark Blaise, Mukherjee has taught at McGill University in Montreal and is now on the faculty of the University of California at Berkeley. Her novels include *Tiger's Daughter* (1971), *Jasmine* (1989), and *The Tree Bride* (2004), and she has also published the short-story collections *Darkness* (1975) and the award-winning *The Middleman and Other Stories* (1988). Much of her fiction focuses on the tensions that are inherent in the immigrant experience.

In the following essay, originally published in the *New York Times* in 1996, Mukherjee contrasts herself, a self-described "American of Bengali-Indian origin," with her sister, whose ties to India remain much stronger.

GUIDING QUESTION

How does the author's identity differ from her sister's?

PAUSE: Based on this opening paragraph, what do you predict will be the subject of Mukherjee's comparison and contrast?

1   This is a tale of two sisters from Calcutta,[1] Mira and Bharati, who have lived in the United States for some thirty-five years, but who find themselves on different sides in the current debate over the status of immigrants.[2] I am an American citizen, and she is not. I am moved that thousands of long-term residents are finally taking the oath of citizenship. She is not.

2   Mira arrived in Detroit in 1960 to study child psychology and preschool education. I followed her a year later to study creative writing at the University of Iowa. When we left India, we were almost identical in appearance and attitude. We dressed alike, in saris;[3] we expressed

[1] **Calcutta:** a city in India

[2] **the current debate over the status of immigrants:** the 1996 debate in Congress about legislation (ultimately defeated) to deny a number of benefits (such as Social Security payments) to legal immigrants who were not citizens, even though they had worked and paid taxes like any citizen

[3] **saris:** traditional dress for Indian women

identical views on politics, social issues, love, and marriage in the same Calcutta convent-school accent. We would endure our two years in America, secure our degrees, then return to India to marry the grooms of our father's choosing.

3   Instead, Mira married an Indian student in 1962 who was getting his business administration degree at Wayne State University. They soon acquired the labor certifications necessary for the green card[4] of hassle-free residence and employment.

4   Mira still lives in Detroit, works in the Southfield, Michigan, school system, and has become nationally recognized for her contributions in the fields of pre-school education and parent-teacher relationships. After thirty-six years as a legal immigrant in this country, she clings passionately to her Indian citizenship and hopes to go home to India when she retires.

5   In Iowa City in 1963, I married a fellow student, an American of Canadian parentage. Because of the accident of his North Dakota birth, I bypassed labor-certification requirements and the race-related "quota" system[5] that favored the applicant's country of origin over his or her merit. I was prepared for (and even welcomed) the emotional strain that came with marrying outside my ethnic community. In thirty-three years of marriage, we have lived in every part of North America. By choosing a husband who was not my father's selection, I was opting for fluidity, self-invention, blue jeans and T-shirts, and renouncing three thousand years (at least) of caste-observant,[6] "pure culture" marriage in the Mukherjee family. My books have often been read as unapologetic (and in some quarters as overenthusiastic) texts for cultural and psychological "mongrelization."[7] It's a word I celebrate.

6   Mira and I have stayed sisterly close by phone. In our regular Sunday morning conversations, we are unguardedly affectionate. I am her only blood relative on this continent. We expect to see each other through the looming crises of aging and ill health without being asked.

PAUSE: Summarize the primary differences between Mukherjee and her sister.

---

[4] **green card:** the informal term for a U.S. government-issued document granting lawful permanent residence (which is not the same as citizenship)

[5] **race-related "quota" system:** a system that grants legal status and citizenship to immigrants in part based on preset numbers. Only a certain number of legal immigrants from any given country are allowed entry per year. Immigrants who marry U.S. citizens are given preference over other immigrants, regardless of their countries of origin.

[6] **caste-observant:** dividing into social classes. For thousands of years, traditional Indian society has divided itself into castes, or social classes, with strict rules regarding relationships across these castes. Mukherjee and her sister were born into one of the upper castes.

[7] **"mongrelization":** the mixing of breeds. The term is derived from a mongrel dog, which is a mix of many breeds. The term often is used negatively.

Long before Vice President Gore's "Citizenship U.S.A."[8] drive, we'd had our polite arguments over the ethics of retaining an overseas citizenship while expecting the permanent protection and economic benefits that come with living and working in America.

7   Like well-raised sisters, we never said what was really on our minds, but we probably pitied one another. She, for the lack of structure in my life, the erasure of Indianness, the absence of an unvarying daily core. I, for the narrowness of her perspective, her uninvolvement with the mythic depths or the superficial pop culture of this society. But, now, with the scapegoatings[9] of "aliens" (documented or illegal) on the increase, and the targeting of long-term legal immigrants like Mira for new scrutiny and new self-consciousness, she and I find ourselves unable to maintain the same polite discretion. We were always unacknowledged adversaries, and we are now, more than ever, sisters.

PAUSE: How would you respond to Mukherjee's sister? Do you think her attitude is justified?

8   "I feel used," Mira raged on the phone the other night. "I feel manipulated and discarded. This is such an unfair way to treat a person who was invited to stay and work here because of her talent. My employer went to the I.N.S.[10] and petitioned for the labor certification. For over thirty years, I've invested my creativity and professional skills into the improvement of *this* country's pre-school system. I've obeyed all the rules, I've paid my taxes, I love my work, I love my students, I love the friends I've made. How dare America now change its rules in midstream? If America wants to make new rules curtailing benefits of legal immigrants, they should apply only to immigrants who arrive after those rules are already in place."

9   To my ears, it sounded like the description of a long-enduring, comfortable yet loveless marriage, without risk or recklessness. Have we the right to demand, and to expect, that we be loved? (That, to me, is the subtext of the arguments by immigration advocates.) My sister is an expatriate,[11] professionally generous and creative, socially courteous and gracious, and that's as far as her Americanization can go. She is here to maintain an identity, not to transform it.

10   I asked her if she would follow the example of others who have decided to become citizens because of the anti-immigration bills in Congress. And here, she surprised me. "If America wants to play the manipulative game, I'll play it, too," she snapped. "I'll become a U.S.

---

[8] **"Citizenship U.S.A." drive:** a campaign encouraging eligible immigrants to apply for citizenship, in part because it confers the right to vote

[9] **scapegoating:** making an object of blame

[10] **I.N.S.:** Immigration and Naturalization Service

[11] **expatriate:** a person residing in but not a citizen of a country that is different from the country of his or her birth and heritage

citizen for now, then change back to India when I'm ready to go home. I feel some kind of irrational attachment to India that I don't to America. Until all this hysteria against legal immigrants, I was totally happy. Having my green card meant I could visit any place in the world I wanted to and then come back to a job that's satisfying and that I do very well."

11   In one family, from two sisters alike as peas in a pod, there could not be a wider divergence of immigrant experience. America spoke to me—I married it—I embraced the demotion from expatriate aristocrat to immigrant nobody, surrendering those thousands of years of "pure culture," the saris, the delightfully accented English. She retained them all. Which of us is the freak?

12   Mira's voice, I realize, is the voice not just of the immigrant South Asian community but of an immigrant community of the millions who have stayed rooted in one job, one city, one house, one ancestral culture, one cuisine, for the entirety of their productive years. She speaks for greater numbers than I possibly can. Only the fluency of her English and the anger, rather than the fear, born of confidence from her education, differentiate her from the seamstresses, the domestics, the technicians, the shop owners, the millions of hard-working but effectively silenced documented immigrants as well as their less fortunate "illegal" brothers and sisters.

PAUSE: Summarize the point that Mukherjee makes in this paragraph.

_____

_____

13   Nearly twenty years ago, when I was living in my husband's ancestral homeland of Canada, I was always well-employed but never allowed to feel part of the local Quebec or larger Canadian society. Then, through a Green Paper[12] that invited a national referendum on the unwanted side effects of "nontraditional" immigration, the government officially turned against its immigrant communities, particularly those from South Asia.

14   I felt then the same sense of betrayal that Mira feels now. I will never forget the pain of that sudden turning, and the casual racist outbursts the Green Paper elicited. That sense of betrayal had its desired effect and drove me, and thousands like me, from the country.

15   Mira and I differ, however, in the ways in which we hope to interact with the country that we have chosen to live in. She is happier to live in America as an expatriate Indian than as an immigrant American. I need to feel like a part of the community I have adopted (as I tried to feel in Canada as well). I need to put roots down, to vote and make the difference that I can. The price that the immigrant willingly pays, and that the exile avoids, is the trauma of self-transformation.

PAUSE: Why might Mukherjee feel as she does about being "an immigrant American"?

_____

_____

[12] **Green Paper:** a document that is issued by the Canadian government to invite public discussion on an issue prior to establishing policy

SUMMARIZE AND RESPOND . . . .

In your reading journal or elsewhere, summarize the main point of "Two Ways to Belong in America." Then, go back and check off support for this main idea. Next, write a brief summary (three to five sentences) of the reading. Finally, jot down your initial response to the selection. Can you sympathize with Mira's continuing connection to her country of birth? What is your view of the place of immigrants in U.S. society?

 CHECK YOUR COMPREHENSION . . . .

1. Which of the following would be the best alternative title for this essay?

   a. "The Dilemma of Legal Residents in the United States"

   b. "Expatriate Indian or Immigrant American: A Choice"

   c. "Coming to America from India"

   d. "The Trauma of Self-Transformation"

2. The main idea of this essay is that

   a. Mukherjee and her sister view their position as immigrants in the United States very differently.

   b. Mukherjee and her sister are outraged by the fact that the U.S. government would take promised benefits away from legal immigrants.

   c. Mukherjee became an American citizen almost by accident because she married a man who happened to be born in the United States.

   d. Mukherjee faced a situation while living in Canada that was similar to the situation her sister later faced in the United States.

3. According to the essay, Mukherjee's sister hopes to

   a. become an American citizen.

   b. lobby for other immigrants whose situation is similar to hers.

   c. change people's minds about her immigrant status.

   d. return to India when she retires.

4. If you are unfamiliar with the following words, use a dictionary to check their meanings: certifications (para. 3); fluidity, unapologetic (5); unguardedly, looming (6); mythic, unacknowledged, adversaries (7); curtailing (8); subtext (9); hysteria (10); divergence, demotion (11); ancestral, referendum (13); betrayal (14).

■ **READ CRITICALLY** . . . .

1. In her five opening paragraphs, which organizational pattern for comparison and contrast does Mukherjee use? Why do you think she chose this pattern?

2. What impression of her sister does Mukherjee create for you? What leads you to this impression?

3. What impression do you take away of Mukherjee herself? What makes you think as you do?

4. In paragraph 12, Mukherjee puts the word *illegal* in quotation marks. Why do you think she does so? How does this tie into the larger point of this paragraph?

5. Evaluate Mukherjee's conclusion. How effectively does it summarize the essay's main ideas?

■ **WRITE AN ESSAY** . . . .

Write an essay comparing and contrasting yourself to a sibling, a relative you are close to, or a close friend. Like Mukherjee, make sure to establish a context for your relationship with the other person, and provide readers with details so that they can see the similarities and differences in your personalities, behaviors, and life choices.

Comparison and Contrast: Linked Readings

■ **CONCEPTIONS OF GENDER** . . . .

Each of the following readings focuses on various aspects of the effects of gender on people's behaviors and lives.

Dave Barry, "The Ugly Truth about Beauty" (this chapter, p. 817)

Daniel Goleman, "For Man and Beast, Language of Love Shares Many Traits" (Chapter 46, p. 781)

Scott Russell Sanders, "The Men We Carry in Our Minds" (Chapter 47, p. 788)

Amy L. Beck, "Struggling for Perfection" (Chapter 50, p. 829)

Read the selections, and draw from at least one in addition to "The Ugly Truth about Beauty" to write an essay titled "How Gender Affects Behavior." You can refer to your own experience, but make sure to use material from the essays as well.

 CHASING BEAUTY . . . .

Though they have very different tones, both of the following readings focus on women's quest for beauty or perfection.

Dave Barry, "The Ugly Truth about Beauty" (this chapter, p. 817)

Amy L. Beck, "Struggling for Perfection" (Chapter 50, p. 829)

Read the selections, and write an essay titled "The Dangers of Chasing Beauty and Perfection." You can refer to your own experience, but make sure to use material from the essays as well.

50

Cause and Effect

Each essay in this chapter uses cause and effect to get its main point across. As you read these essays, consider how they achieve the four basics of good cause and effect that are listed below and discussed in Chapter 17 of this book.

■ **IDEA JOURNAL**
What event or situation has influenced who you are?

> ▪▪ **FOUR BASICS OF GOOD CAUSE AND EFFECT**
> ▪▪
>
> 1. The main point reflects the writer's purpose—to explain causes, effects, or both.
> 2. If the purpose is to explain causes, it presents concrete causes.
> 3. If the purpose is to explain effects, it presents actual effects.
> 4. It gives readers clear and detailed examples or explanations of the causes and/or effects.

Amy L. Beck

Struggling for Perfection

Amy L. Beck was born in 1979 in Greenwich, Connecticut. After graduating from Harvard University in 2000, Beck joined Teach for America, a program that places recent college graduates in inner-city or rural schools, and she taught first graders in Long Beach, California, for two years. She has also worked in France as a researcher for the travel guide *Let's Go* and as an intern with the French Public Health Administration. Beck is currently a resident in pediatrics at the University of California, San Francisco.

In "Struggling for Perfection," which she wrote for the *Harvard Crimson* in 1998, Beck explores eating disorders and domestic abuse. How are these two problems linked? According to Beck, they are both partly caused by media images.

GUIDING QUESTION
What is the cause-and-effect relationship that Beck writes about?

1   Sex sells. This truth is a boon[1] for marketing gurus and the pornography industry but a rather unfortunate situation for women. Every issue of *Playboy*, every lewd poster, and even the Victoria's Secret catalog transform real women into ornaments, valued exclusively for their outward appearance. These publications are responsible for defining what is sexy and reinforce the belief that aesthetic[2] appeal is a woman's highest virtue.

PAUSE: After reading her second paragraph, what do you predict that Beck will do in her essay?

2   Some argue that the proliferation[3] of pornography and other sexually explicit images of women is both harmless for society and inevitable. Just this point was made in a recent *Crimson* column titled "In Defense of Hooters and the St. Pauli Girl." In the tone of an expert, the author boldly claims that the objectification[4] of women in the media does not affect the way men treat the real women in their lives, nor does it give those with pathological[5] tendencies "the decisive nudge into misogyny."[6] Furthermore, the author says, those women who feel pressure to conform to beauty standards set by the media are suffering from a classic psychosis in which they "confuse fiction with reality."

3   My first reaction was to ask how anyone could possibly believe that the pervasiveness[7] of pornography and sexually explicit depictions of women could fail to have any sort of effect on society. Having spent twelve weeks working in a psychiatric hospital last summer, I am writing from a starkly different perspective.

4   During my first eight weeks at the hospital, I worked on an eating disorder unit in constant contact with anorexics and bulimics. Many

[1] **boon:** a welcome benefit

[2] **aesthetic:** having to do with beauty

[3] **proliferation:** rapid growth

[4] **objectification:** the treatment of a person as an object

[5] **pathological:** abnormal, diseased

[6] **misogyny:** hatred of women

[7] **pervasiveness:** the extension or spread of one thing throughout something else

patients on the unit were so emaciated[8] that I could never accustom myself to their appearance; every time I saw them I experienced the same shock. Most had been in and out of countless other hospitals and treatment programs, improving slightly each time but always sliding back into eating-disordered behavior when released.

5   These people were truly at rock bottom, considered by many to be incurable. Their eating disorders had consumed them entirely, leaving no trace of the vibrant, intelligent people that once inhabited their now skeletal bodies. Certainly, these people also had family problems, alcoholic parents, histories of abuse and clinical depression, to name a few, all of which contribute to feelings of worthlessness and extremely low self-esteem—cited by experts as a major cause of eating disorders. What I find significant, however, is not the root of their problems but that these women (there were a few men, but never more than five percent of the patient population) turned to their bodies as a means of expression and self-healing. Profoundly influenced by the depiction of women by the fashion industry, they had been convinced that the only way to attain love, respect, and personal fulfillment was through a relentless pursuit of physical perfection. Most were perfectly aware that they would never look like a supermodel, but it was inconceivable not to try to do so. They found that they were good at dieting and that they were praised and rewarded for their success. And by the time things had gone too far, they had lost all sense of perspective.

PAUSE: Underline the sentence that best expresses the main point of paragraph 5.

6   Convinced by the media and popular culture to believe that, as women, they should look a certain way and that only if they looked that way would they be loved and respected, they turned to dieting as a means of personal fulfillment and self-definition. While cases as extreme as those I saw at the hospital are rare, many women experience milder but still debilitating[9] forms of eating disorders. They may never get sick enough to require hospitalization, but they nonetheless devote excessive mental and physical energy to diet and exercise, often jeopardizing their health in the process.

7   For my last four weeks at the hospital I transferred from eating disorders to a general psychology unit. The diagnoses varied, but the number of patients with histories of abuse was astounding. After listening to and reading countless case histories, I began to recognize the patterns. In many cases, domestic battering was chronic, occurring weekly or daily whenever the victim broke some sort of household rule, such as serving dinner late or dressing "too sexy." The majority of the sexual abuse victims had been raped by people close to them: relatives, ex-boyfriends,

PAUSE: Summarize the main point of paragraph 7.

_____

_____

[8] **emaciated:** extremely thin

[9] **debilitating:** weakening

or family friends. In one particularly striking case, a patient's boyfriend made her have sex with five of his friends on a frequent basis.

8   The men who committed these heinous crimes were rarely pathological rapists or batterers. Few would even be deemed mentally ill or classically misogynistic. Rather, they are men who view the real women in their lives in the same manner that they would view a *Playboy* model, a waitress at Hooters, or a prostitute—as objects that exist solely for their pleasure and convenience. These men are not genetically predisposed[10] to disrespect and abuse women. Their attitudes towards women were societally conditioned.

9   Some would argue that pornography did not contribute to these men's behavior towards women. I disagree. Rape and battery are not new problems, and objectification of women by the media reinforces historically entrenched beliefs that a woman's main reason for existence is procreation and the sexual pleasure of her mate. Pornographic magazines and lewd posters reduce women to a commodity[11] that can be purchased and owned, divorcing the physical manifestation[12] from the person within. The power of popular culture to affect how we eat, how we dress, and how we behave is enormous. Conceptions of gender are in no way immune to this phenomenon.

PAUSE: How are you and others you know affected by media images?

10   Certainly some of us are more affected by the media than others. Not all teenage girls develop anorexia, nor do all men who read *Playboy* abuse their wives. Nonetheless, the prevalence of both eating disorders and various forms of domestic and sexual abuse indicate major societal trends. The American Anorexia/Bulimia Association reports that 5 percent of women will develop a full-fledged eating disorder, while 15 percent have "substantially disordered eating." The Family Violence Prevention Program documents that 4 million American women were battered last year. And, yes, I am absolutely convinced that the objectification of women by the media is an integral part of both of these problems, presenting women with unrealistic role models while encouraging men to think of women solely in terms of their sexuality.

11   Women are up against a long history of devaluation and oppression, and, unfortunately, the feminist movements have been only partially successful in purging[13] those legacies. Sexually charged images of women in the media are not the only cause of this continuing problem, but they certainly play a central role.

[10] **predisposed:** inclined to something in advance

[11] **commodity:** a thing of use, value, or advantage

[12] **manifestation:** a visible presence, an outward show

[13] **purging:** removing something unwanted

SUMMARIZE AND RESPOND . . . .

In your reading journal or elsewhere, summarize the main point of "Struggling for Perfection." Then, go back and check off support for this main idea. Next, write a brief summary (three to five sentences) of the essay. Finally, jot down your initial response to the essay. Do you agree or disagree with Beck's points? What else do you think causes eating disorders and domestic abuse?

CHECK YOUR COMPREHENSION . . . .

1. Which of the following would be the best alternative title for this essay?

   a. "The Alarming Growth of Eating Disorders"

   b. "The Causes and Effects of Eating Disorders"

   c. "The Media's Influence on Eating Disorders and Domestic Abuse"

   d. "Pressure to Conform"

2. The main idea of this essay is that

   a. media images of women are not the only cause of eating disorders.

   b. publications such as *Playboy* and the Victoria's Secret catalog transform women into sexual objects.

   c. low self-esteem is a major cause of eating disorders.

   d. media images of women contribute to eating disorders and violence against females.

3. According to the author,

   a. women who try to look like supermodels are unable to tell the difference between fiction and reality.

   b. many of the women she met while working in the hospital had backgrounds that included abuse, family problems, and depression.

   c. patients with eating disorders are often incurable.

   d. feminist movements have been very successful in their attempts to lessen the prevalence of eating disorders and abuse against women.

4. If you are unfamiliar with the following words, use a dictionary to check their meanings: gurus, lewd (para. 1); inevitable, psychosis (2); anorexics, bulimics (4); depiction (5); chronic (7); heinous, genetically (8); entrenched, procreation (9); integral (10); devaluation, legacies (11).

■ **READ CRITICALLY** . . . .

1. Why do you think Beck begins her essay by discussing the column "In Defense of Hooters and the St. Pauli Girl" (para. 2)?

2. Media images of women lead to what two major problems, according to Beck? How are these problems linked?

3. Describe Beck's attitude toward men who commit domestic abuse. What examples from the essay support your response?

4. Does Beck provide clear links between media images of women and the effects of those images? Discuss some of the supporting details she uses to show these links.

5. Beck presents some statistics about eating disorders and domestic abuse. How does she use these statistics to make a further observation about her main point?

■ **WRITE AN ESSAY** . . . .

Beck acknowledges the fact that sexually charged media images of women are not the only cause of eating disorders and abuse. Write an essay about a different possible cause of one of these problems. You could also choose to write about a similar problem (what causes some men to take steroids, for example). If you addressed other causes of eating disorders and abuse for the Summarize and Respond section above, feel free to use those ideas.

. . . .

Brent Staples

Just Walk on By: Black Men and Public Space

Brent Staples was born in 1951 in Chester, Pennsylvania. After graduating from Widener University, he earned a Ph.D. in psychology from the University of Chicago. He is a member of the editorial board of the *New York Times,* writing commentary on politics and culture. In 1995, he published a memoir, *Parallel Time: Growing Up in Black and White* (1994).

In "Just Walk on By," Staples observes how people, particularly women, react to him when he goes out for a walk. This essay was first published in *Ms.* magazine.

GUIDING QUESTION
How does Staples affect people, and why?

1   My first victim was a woman—white, well dressed, probably in her early twenties. I came upon her late one evening on a deserted street in Hyde Park, a relatively affluent neighborhood in an otherwise mean, impoverished section of Chicago. As I swung onto the avenue behind her, there seemed to be a discreet, uninflammatory[1] distance between us. Not so. She cast back a worried glance. To her, the youngish black man—a broad six feet two inches with a beard and billowing hair, both hands shoved into the pockets of a bulky military jacket—seemed menacingly close. After a few more quick glimpses, she picked up her pace and was soon running in earnest. Within seconds she disappeared into a cross street.

PAUSE: After reading the title and the first paragraph, what do you predict Staples will write about in the rest of the essay?

2   That was more than a decade ago, I was twenty-two years old, a graduate student newly arrived at the University of Chicago. It was in the echo of that terrified woman's footfalls that I first began to know the unwieldy inheritance I'd come into—the ability to alter public space in ugly ways. It was clear that she thought herself the quarry[2] of a mugger, a rapist, or worse. Suffering a bout of insomnia, however, I was stalking sleep, not defenseless wayfarers. As a softy who is scarcely able to take a knife to a raw chicken—let alone hold one to a person's throat—I was surprised, embarrassed, and dismayed all at once. Her flight made me feel like an accomplice in tyranny.[3] It also made it clear that I was indistinguishable from the muggers who occasionally seeped into the area from the surrounding ghetto. That first encounter, and those that followed, signified that a vast, unnerving[4] gulf lay between nighttime pedestrians—particularly women—and me. And I soon gathered that being perceived as dangerous is a hazard in itself. I only needed to turn a corner into a dicey situation, or crowd some frightened, armed person in a foyer somewhere, or make an errant[5] move after being pulled over by a policeman. Where fear and weapons meet—and they often do in urban America—there is always the possibility of death.

3   In that first year, my first away from my hometown, I was to become thoroughly familiar with the language of fear. At dark, shadowy intersections, I could cross in front of a car stopped at a traffic light and elicit the *thunk, thunk, thunk, thunk* of the driver—black, white, male, or female—hammering down the door locks. On less traveled streets

[1] **uninflammatory:** unlikely to cause fear

[2] **quarry:** one that is chased, as in a hunt

[3] **tyranny:** the abuse of power

[4] **unnerving:** upsetting

[5] **errant:** stray, unintended

PAUSE: In paragraph 3, what does Staples mean by "standard unpleasantries"?

_____

_____

after dark, I grew accustomed to but never comfortable with people crossing to the other side of the street rather than pass me. Then there were the standard unpleasantries with policemen, doormen, bouncers, cabdrivers, and others whose business it is to screen out troublesome individuals _before_ there is any nastiness.

4   I moved to New York nearly two years ago and I have remained an avid night walker. In central Manhattan, the near-constant crowd cover minimizes tense one-on-one street encounters. Elsewhere—in SoHo, for example, where sidewalks are narrow and tightly spaced buildings shut out the sky—things can get very taut indeed.

5   After dark, on the warrenlike[6] streets of Brooklyn where I live, I often see women who fear the worst from me. They seem to have set their faces on neutral, and with their purse straps strung across their chests bandolier-style, they forge ahead as though bracing themselves against being tackled. I understand, of course, that the danger they perceive is not a hallucination. Women are particularly vulnerable to street violence, and young black males are drastically overrepresented among the perpetrators of that violence. Yet these truths are no solace against the kind of alienation that comes of being ever the suspect, a fearsome entity with whom pedestrians avoid making eye contact.

6   It is not altogether clear to me how I reached the ripe old age of twenty-two without being conscious of the lethality nighttime pedestrians attributed to me. Perhaps it was because in Chester, Pennsylvania, the small, angry industrial town where I came of age in the 1960s, I was scarcely noticeable against a backdrop of gang warfare, street knifings, and murders. I grew up one of the good boys, had perhaps a half-dozen fistfights. In retrospect, my shyness of combat has clear sources.

PAUSE: Summarize the point that Staples makes about himself in paragraphs 6 and 7.

_____

_____

7   As a boy, I saw countless tough guys locked away; I have since buried several, too. They were babies, really—a teenage cousin, a brother of twenty-two, a childhood friend in his mid-twenties—all gone down in episodes of bravado played out in the streets. I came to doubt the virtues of intimidation early on. I chose, perhaps unconsciously, to remain a shadow—timid, but a survivor.

8   The fearsomeness mistakenly attributed to me in public places often has a perilous flavor. The most frightening of these confusions occurred in the late 1970s and early 1980s, when I worked as a journalist in Chicago. One day, rushing into the office of a magazine I was writing for with a deadline story in hand, I was mistaken for a burglar. The office manager called security and, with an ad hoc[7] posse, pursued me through the labyrinthine halls, nearly to my editor's door. I had no way of proving who I was. I could only move briskly toward the company of someone who knew me.

[6] **warrenlike:** narrow and having many blind spots

[7] **ad hoc:** made up of whatever is available (Latin, _for this purpose_)

9   Another time I was on assignment for a local paper and killing time before an interview. I entered a jewelry store on the city's affluent Near North Side. The proprietor excused herself and returned with an enormous red Doberman pinscher straining at the end of a leash. She stood, the dog extended toward me, silent to my questions, her eyes bulging nearly out of her head. I took a cursory look around, nodded, and bade her good night.

10   Relatively speaking, however, I never fared as badly as another black male journalist. He went to nearby Waukegan, Illinois, a couple of summers ago to work on a story about a murderer who was born there. Mistaking the reporter for the killer, police officers hauled him from his car at gunpoint and but for his press credentials would probably have tried to book him. Such episodes are not uncommon. Black men trade tales like this all the time.

11   Over the years, I learned to smother the rage I felt at so often being taken for a criminal. Not to do so would surely have led to madness. I now take precautions to make myself less threatening. I move about with care, particularly late in the evening. I give a wide berth to nervous people on subway platforms during the wee hours, particularly when I have exchanged business clothes for jeans. If I happen to be entering a building behind some people who appear skittish,[8] I may walk by, letting them clear the lobby before I return, so as not to seem to be following them. I have been calm and extremely congenial[9] on those rare occasions when I've been pulled over by the police.

PAUSE: In paragraph 11, underline each of the precautions Staples says he takes to appear less threatening.

12   And on late-evening constitutionals[10] I employ what has proved to be an excellent tension-reducing measure: I whistle melodies from Beethoven and Vivaldi and the more popular classical composers. Even steely New Yorkers hunching toward nighttime destinations seem to relax, and occasionally they even join in the tune. Virtually everybody seems to sense that a mugger wouldn't be warbling bright, sunny selections from Vivaldi's *Four Seasons*. It is my equivalent of the cowbell that hikers wear when they know they are in bear country.

PAUSE: How do you respond to the image, in paragraph 12, of Staples whistling classical music as he walks at night?

_____

_____

[8] **skittish:** nervous, jumpy

[9] **congenial:** pleasant, agreeable

[10] **constitutionals:** walks taken for one's health

■   **SUMMARIZE AND RESPOND** . . . .

In your reading journal or elsewhere, summarize the main point of "Just Walk on By: Black Men and Public Space." Then, go back and check off support for this main idea. Next, write a brief summary (three to five sentences) of the reading. Finally, jot down your initial response to the selection. Did you find any of what Staples relates surprising, or do his observations match your own experience? Did reading about Staples's experiences change your attitudes in any way? What impression do you have of the writer himself?

■ CHECK YOUR COMPREHENSION . . . .

1. Which of the following would be the best alternative title for this essay?
   a. "Walking the Streets after Dark"
   b. "The Burdens of Racial Identity"
   c. "Being Mistaken for a Criminal Because of One's Skin"
   d. "How to Avoid Muggers and Other Street Criminals"

2. The main idea of this essay is that
   a. the author had to learn how to make himself appear less threatening to others.
   b. the author recognizes that strangers may be unjustifiably afraid of him because he is a black man.
   c. the author believes that people should try to see black men as individuals and not stereotype them as muggers.
   d. the author knew criminals as he was growing up but wants readers to understand that he himself is not one.

3. An important point that Staples makes in this essay is that
   a. the police and other authorities often stop black men for questioning for no good reason.
   b. he felt angry because of strangers' behavior toward him but found ways to suppress his anger.
   c. people in large cities like Chicago and New York are more likely than others to fear black men.
   d. he was once almost arrested because he was mistaken for a murderer he was writing a story about.

4. If you are unfamiliar with the following words, use a dictionary to check their meanings: menacingly (para. 1); unwieldy, insomnia, way-farers, dismayed, indistinguishable, dicey (2); hallucination, perpetra-tors, solace, alienation, entity (5); lethality, retrospect (6); bravado (7); perilous, posse, labyrinthine (8); affluent, cursory (9); credentials (10); warbling (12).

■ **READ CRITICALLY** . . . .

1. What, specifically, is the cause-and-effect relationship that Staples is describing in the essay? How well do you think he shows this relationship? What is the effect of the situation on Staples himself?

2. Why do you suppose Staples opens his essay by referring to "[m]y first victim"? What is the effect of this language?

3. Who would you say Staples imagined as his audience for this essay? What vision of himself does he seem to want his readers to come away with?

4. Why do you think Staples refers to the experience of another black man in paragraph 10, when all of his other examples are drawn from his own experience?

5. What is your response to Staples's final two paragraphs? To his final sentence? How would you evaluate this conclusion?

■ **WRITE AN ESSAY** . . . .

Write an essay, based on your own experiences, about the causes and effects of stereotypes and mistaken perceptions. You might focus on mistaken perceptions others have had of you or on mistaken perceptions you have had of others—or on both kinds of mistaken perceptions. You might also focus on instances of mistaken perceptions and stereotyping that you have witnessed. Be sure to establish clear cause-and-effect relationships.

Cause and Effect: Linked Readings

■ **CONCEPTIONS OF GENDER** . . . .

Each of the following readings focuses on various aspects of the effects of gender on people's behaviors and lives.

Amy L. Beck, "Struggling for Perfection" (this chapter, p. 829)

Daniel Goleman, "For Man and Beast, Language of Love Shares Many Traits" (Chapter 46, p. 781)

Scott Russell Sanders, "The Men We Carry in Our Minds" (Chapter 47, p. 788)

Dave Barry, "The Ugly Truth about Beauty" (Chapter 49, p. 817)

Read the selections, and draw from at least one in addition to "Struggling for Perfection" to write an essay titled "How Gender Affects Behavior." You can refer to your own experience, but make sure to use material from the essays as well.

■ **CHASING BEAUTY** . . . .

Though they have very different tones, both of the following readings focus on women's quest for beauty or perfection.

> Amy L. Beck, "Struggling for Perfection" (this chapter, p. 829)
>
> Dave Barry, "The Ugly Truth about Beauty" (Chapter 49, p. 817)

Read the selections, and write an essay titled "The Dangers of Chasing Beauty and Perfection." You can refer to your own experience, but make sure to use material from the essays as well.

■ **STEREOTYPES** . . . .

Each of the following readings focuses on stereotypes.

> Brent Staples, "Just Walk on By: Black Men and Public Space" (this chapter, p. 834)
>
> Scott Russell Sanders, "The Men We Carry in Our Minds" (Chapter 47, p. 788)
>
> Amy Tan, "Mother Tongue" (Chapter 47, p. 796)
>
> Nancy Mairs, "On Being a Cripple" (Chapter 48, p. 805)

Read the selections, and draw from at least one in addition to "Just Walk on By" to write an essay titled "Stereotypes: Are They Wrong?" You can refer to your own experience, but make sure to use material from the essays as well.

. . . .

51

Argument Casebook

Assisted Suicide

This chapter includes five essays on the issue of legalized assisted suicide. The first three, in favor of it, are written by a nurse, a doctor, and an individual with terminal cancer. Their essays argue that legal physician-assisted suicide is a humane choice and, in some cases, is the only way for people to maintain their dignity and humanity in the face of acute suffering. The last two essays, written by doctors, are against legalization of physician-assisted suicide. These essays reveal another side of what legal physician-assisted suicide could bring—not a humane end but rather the triumph of cost-effectiveness over compassionate end-of-life care.

As you will see when you read these five essays, physician-assisted suicide is not an easy issue. It is, however, an issue that has significance for all of us. Physical trauma can dramatically affect an individual's quality of life at any time. Any of us could be seriously injured in a traffic accident or suddenly afflicted with an untreatable disease.

Some of you may already have an opinion on physician-assisted suicide. As you read the essays, however, consider carefully the arguments that they present. Try to imagine that someone you love is the patient, and evaluate the arguments as though you were going to have to make a decision about the end of that person's life.

▪▪ FOUR BASICS OF GOOD ARGUMENT

1. It takes a strong and definite position on an issue or advises a particular action.
2. It gives good reasons and supporting evidence to defend the position or recommended action.
3. It considers opposing views.
4. It has enthusiasm and energy from start to finish.

Legalized Assisted Suicide: In Favor

Barbara Huttmann

A Crime of Compassion

Barbara Huttmann was middle-aged when she returned to school to study nursing, receiving her degree in 1976. She went on to earn a master's degree in nursing administration and later worked as an administrator for a health-care consulting firm. She is also the author of two books, *The Patient's Advocate* (1981) and *Code Blue: A Nurse's True Story* (1982), which recount her years in nursing school and her later years as a practicing nurse.

The following essay, adapted from *Code Blue* for *Newsweek* magazine in 1983, focuses on her decision to honor a patient's wishes to be allowed to die.

GUIDING QUESTION
What motivates Huttmann to act as she does?

1   "Murderer," a man shouted. "God help patients who get *you* for a nurse."

2   "What gives you the right to play God?" another one asked.

3   It was the *Phil Donahue Show*[1] where the guest is a fatted calf[2] and the audience a two-hundred-strong flock of vultures hungering to pick at the bones. I had told them about Mac, one of my favorite cancer patients. "We resuscitated[3] him fifty-two times in just one month. I refused to resuscitate him again. I simply sat there and held his hand while he died."

4   There wasn't time to explain that Mac was a young, witty, macho cop who walked into the hospital with thirty-two pounds of attack equipment, looking as if he could single-handedly protect the whole city, if not the entire state. "Can't get rid of this cough," he said. Otherwise, he felt great.

---

[1] ***Phil Donahue Show:*** one of the earliest audience-participation television talk shows. This show first aired in 1970 and ran through the mid-1990s.

[2] **fatted calf:** from the biblical parable of the prodigal son, in which a father kills a specially fed calf to celebrate the return of his son who had left home years earlier

[3] **resuscitated:** brought back to life

5   Before the day was over, tests confirmed that he had lung cancer. And before the year was over, I loved him, his wife, Maura, and their three kids as if they were my own. All the nurses loved him. And we all battled his disease for six months without ever giving death a thought. Six months isn't such a long time in the whole scheme of things, but it was long enough to see him lose his youth, his wit, his macho, his hair, his bowel and bladder control, his sense of taste and smell, and his ability to do the slightest thing for himself. It was also long enough to watch Maura's transformation from a young woman into a haggard, beaten old lady.

6   When Mac had wasted away to a sixty-pound skeleton kept alive by liquid food we poured down a tube, IV solutions we dripped into his veins, and oxygen we piped to a mask on his face, he begged us: "Mercy . . . for God's sake, please just let me go."

7   The first time he stopped breathing, the nurse pushed the button that calls a "code blue"[4] throughout the hospital and sends a team rushing to resuscitate the patient. Each time he stopped breathing, sometimes two or three times in one day, the code team came again. The doctors and technicians worked their miracles and walked away. The nurses stayed to wipe the saliva that drooled from his mouth, irrigate the big craters of bedsores that covered his hips, suction the lung fluids that threatened to drown him, clean the feces that burned his skin like lye, pour the liquid food down the tube attached to his stomach, put pillows between his knees to ease the bone-on-bone pain, turn him every hour to keep the bedsores from getting worse, and change his gown and linen every two hours to keep him from being soaked in perspiration.

> **PAUSE:** Underline the details that Huttmann provides in this paragraph to describe Mac's condition.

8   At night I went home and tried to scrub away the smell of decaying flesh that seemed woven into the fabric of my uniform. It was in my hair, the upholstery of my car—there was no washing it away. And every night I prayed that Mac would die, that his agonized eyes would never again plead with me to let him die.

9   Every morning I asked his doctor for a "no-code" order. Without that order, we had to resuscitate every patient who stopped breathing. His doctor was one of several who believe we must extend life as long as we have the means and knowledge to do it. To not do it is to be liable for negligence, at least in the eyes of many people, including some nurses. I thought about what it would be like to stand before a judge, accused of murder, if Mac stopped breathing and I didn't call a code.

> **PAUSE:** Summarize the main idea Huttmann is trying to communicate in this paragraph.
>
> _____
>
> _____

10   And after the fifty-second code, when Mac was still lucid enough to beg for death again, and Maura was crumbled in my arms again, and

---

[4] **code blue:** a signal that is used in hospitals to announce a patient's life-threatening emergency (usually cardiac arrest)

when no amount of pain medication stilled his moaning and agony, I wondered about a spiritual judge. Was all this misery and suffering supposed to be building character or infusing us all with the sense of humility that comes from impotence?

11   Had we, the whole medical community, become so arrogant that we believed in the illusion of salvation through science? Had we become so self-righteous that we thought meddling in God's work was our duty, our moral imperative, and our legal obligation? Did we really believe that we had the right to force "life" on a suffering man who had begged for the right to die?

PAUSE: What do you predict that Huttmann will do in the next few paragraphs?

12   Such questions haunted me more than ever early one morning when Maura went home to change her clothes and I was bathing Mac. He had been still for so long, I thought he at last had the blessed relief of coma. Then he opened his eyes and moaned, "Pain . . . no more . . . Barbara . . . do something . . . God, let me go."

13   The desperation in his eyes and voice riddled me with guilt. "I'll stop," I told him as I injected the pain medication.

14   I sat on the bed and held Mac's hand in mine. He pressed his bony fingers against my hand and muttered, "Thanks." Then there was one soft sigh, and I felt his hands go cold in mine. "Mac?" I whispered, as I waited for his chest to rise and fall again.

15   A clutch of panic banded my chest, drew my finger to the code button, urged me to do something, anything . . . but sit alone with death. I kept one finger on the button, without pressing it, as a waxen pallor slowly transformed his face from person to empty shell. Nothing I've ever done in my forty-seven years has taken so much effort as it took *not* to press that code button.

16   Eventually, when I was as sure as I could be that the code team would fail to bring him back, I entered the legal twilight zone and pushed the button. The team tried. And while they were trying, Maura walked into the room and shrieked, "No . . . don't let them do this to him . . . for God's sake . . . please, no more!"

17   Cradling her in my arms was like cradling myself, Mac, and all those patients and nurses who had been in this place before, who do the best they can in a death-defying society.

18   So a TV audience accused me of murder. Perhaps I am guilty. If a doctor had written a no-code order, which is the only *legal* alternative, would he have felt less guilty? Until there is legislation making it a criminal act to code a patient who has requested the right to die, we will all of us risk the same fate as Mac. For whatever reason, we developed the means to prolong life, and now we are forced to use it. We do not have the right to die.

PAUSE: What are your reactions to Huttmann's story?

SUMMARIZE AND RESPOND . . . .

In your reading journal or elsewhere, summarize the main point of "A Crime of Compassion." Then, go back and check off support for this main idea. Next, write a brief summary (three to five sentences) of the selection. Finally, jot down your initial response to the reading. Do you think that Huttmann's action makes her a "murderer"? Or do you sympathize with her decision? What makes you think as you do?

CHECK YOUR COMPREHENSION . . . .

1. Which of the following would be the best alternative title for this essay?

   a. "A Defense for Murder"

   b. "The Difficult Job of Being a Nurse"

   c. "The Right to Die"

   d. "Prolonging Life: The Responsibility of Medical Professionals"

2. The main idea of this essay is that

   a. the author believes that suffering patients who have no chance of recovery should not be kept alive artificially against their wishes.

   b. the author believes that television talk shows do not provide an adequate forum for discussing complex issues such as the right to die.

   c. the author believes that most readers do not understand all the tasks that are required of a nurse.

   d. the author believes that advances in medical science make it possible to prolong life and that doing so is the responsibility of medical professionals.

3. According to Huttmann, several medical professionals that she worked with when Mac was a patient felt that all patients must be resuscitated because

   a. it was the ethical thing to do.

   b. they had the medical expertise to do so.

   c. most patients wanted to be resuscitated.

   d. not to do so might have led to legal liability for negligence.

4. If you are unfamiliar with the following words, use a dictionary to check their meanings: vultures (para. 3); macho (4); haggard (5); feces (7); negligence (9); lucid, infusing, impotence (10); pallor (15).

■ READ CRITICALLY

1. Evaluate Huttmann's three opening paragraphs. What do they contribute to her essay? How and why does she refer back to them in her conclusion?

2. How well do you think Huttmann presents her patient Mac and his wife, Maura? How does she attempt to make their situation seem real to the reader?

3. What is the purpose of paragraph 9? Why do you think that Huttmann waits until this point in the essay to offer this information?

4. What is the effect of the questions that Huttmann poses in paragraphs 10 and 11? Why do you think she presents these thoughts as questions here?

5. What is your overall evaluation of Huttmann's argument? How effectively do you think she presents her case? How is her argument shaped by her role as a nurse? How do you explain your evaluation?

■ WRITE AN ESSAY

Write an essay about a belief that you have come to hold through personal experience but that many other people might disagree with or find controversial. Like Huttmann, show readers what happened to make you think as you do, and take a clear stand on the issue.

Marc Siegel

Treating the Pain by Ending a Life

Dr. Marc Siegel, a 1985 graduate of the School of Medicine and Biomedical Sciences at the State University of New York, Buffalo, is an associate professor at the New York University School of Medicine as well as a practicing internist. A prolific writer for general audiences, he writes a regular column, "The Unreal World," for the *Los Angeles Times* in which he explains the facts behind widely held but mistaken beliefs about medicine. His essays have appeared in the *Washington Post, USA Today,* and *Slate,* and he is a frequent guest on television news programs and National Public Radio. His books include *False Alarm: The Truth about the Epidemic of Fear* (2005), named one of the top twenty books of the year by *Discover* magazine, and *Bird Flu: Everything You Need to Know about the Next Pandemic* (2006).

"Treating the Pain by Ending a Life" first appeared in the *Boston Globe* in January 2006 shortly after the U.S. Supreme Court ruled in favor of the state of Oregon in a suit that the Bush administration brought over an Oregon state law permitting physician-assisted suicide.

GUIDING QUESTION

What does Siegel say are the two primary roles for a physician, and how do these two roles shape his argument?

1   The U.S. Supreme Court ruled this week that doctors in Oregon should not be charged with a crime for overdosing patients in the name of treating pain and hastening death. This decision should be applauded and must not be circumvented[1] by new laws.

2   Ten years ago, I assumed the care of a woman with advanced pancreatic cancer that had spread to her spine. She was a well-known writer, and we quickly became friends. I would travel to her apartment and visit her for hours there, something I'd rarely done before and haven't done since. She had a close group of friends who visited her constantly, and an Irish nursing agency that cared for her impeccably around the clock. At first, her cancer wasn't causing her pain, though it paralyzed her below the waist and bound her to her bed and wheelchair. Still, she enjoyed the visits, mine and everyone else's, until the fateful day when the cancer spread to her bones and began what was clearly an escalating pain. I dialed up the morphine[2] to compensate, until the day came when the amount of morphine necessary clearly hastened her death. I was able to predict roughly the time she would die, and her friends said their good-byes. I used morphine in the name of relieving suffering, not as a murder weapon. No one who knew her seemed upset by the trade-off, a tortured life for a peaceful death, and all thanked me for my care at the end.

PAUSE: How do you respond to the "trade-off" of "a tortured life for a peaceful death"?

_____

_____

3   Morphine and other narcotics suppress breathing and lower blood pressure. It is not unusual for physicians to use these drugs to relieve suffering and thereby accelerate death in terminal cases. What is unusual is

---

[1] **circumvented:** bypassed; gotten around

[2] **morphine:** a powerful pain-relieving medication

for doctors to be prosecuted for overdosing their patients deliberately in the name of this cause. Oregon has been the focus of the Bush administration's attempts to criminalize the activity, but this use of medications to knowingly end a tortured life is not confined to Oregon. It has been part of a physician's end-of-life role for many years, whether it is formalized in the law or not.

PAUSE: Summarize the central point of this paragraph.

4   Any effective physician has two fundamental roles. The first is to prolong life. The second is to ease suffering. In most situations, easing suffering is part of prolonging life, as when we guide a patient through an accident or a surgery and treat pain as part of ensuring survival. Sometimes, though, our two roles collide, and a decision must be made as to which to prioritize.[3] This decision is made, in part, by considering long-term outcome as well as the wishes of the patient. It is never a perfect situation, but we physicians have been making this determination for eons, and we cannot be penalized or prosecuted and still be expected to function.

5   In the Netherlands, active euthanasia[4] is legal, which means that a cancer patient who is still ambulatory and thinking clearly can ask a doctor for a lethal injection. I am not in favor of this policy, not because I believe that a person doesn't have a right to end his or her life when given a terminal diagnosis, but because I question the role of a physician in facilitating[5] this outcome. Such a role should not be assumed, because it is not strictly a part of relieving suffering.

PAUSE: Under what conditions, according to Siegel, should doctors be allowed to prescribe potentially lethal doses of narcotics to patients?

6   But this is not the same thing as the Oregon law, which allows a physician to participate when pain predominates, when the patient is in agony, when reducing morphine cannot bring back quality of life. When the only choice is pain or death, doctors routinely—with their patients' advance approval—help them choose death. The U.S. Supreme Court is wise to acknowledge one of our fundamental roles. We are not "Kevorkian-izing"[6] our doomed patients when we help ease their path from this world.

---

[3] **prioritize:** give greater importance to

[4] **active euthanasia:** the assistance in or hastening of death by using drugs or other means. In passive euthanasia, death is a side-effect of the treatment of pain or the withholding of other forms of treatment.

[5] **facilitating:** making easier

[6] **"Kevorkian-izing":** actively helping people commit suicide. Dr. Jack Kevorkian, a controversial figure in the debate over physician-assisted suicide, created several devices that allowed individuals to self-administer lethal dosages of drugs. Kevorkian, a trained physician whose medical license was revoked in 1991, claimed to have participated in the suicide of some 130 people and was convicted of second-degree murder in 1999.

SUMMARIZE AND RESPOND . . . .

In your reading journal or elsewhere, summarize the main point of "Treating the Pain by Ending a Life." Then, go back and check off support for this main idea. Next, write a brief summary (three to five sentences) of the essay. Finally, jot down your initial response to the reading. How sympathetic are you toward Siegel's beliefs about doctors' "end-of-life role"?

 CHECK YOUR COMPREHENSION . . . .

1. Which of the following would be the best alternative title for this essay?

   a. "A Doctor's Competing Roles: The Need to Prioritize"

   b. "The Right to Relieve a Patient's Suffering"

   c. "The Use of Morphine to Treat Pain"

   d. "Active Euthanasia"

2. The main idea of this essay is that

   a. doctors should not be barred from using narcotics to relieve the suffering of patients who are in incurable, unbearable pain—even if the narcotics prove to be lethal.

   b. a doctor's primary roles are to prolong life and to ease suffering.

   c. doctors should do everything in their power to save a patient's life.

   d. the patient's wishes are irrelevant when a doctor decides to administer a potentially lethal dosage of pain medication.

3. Siegel makes the point in the essay that he is opposed to

   a. the use of morphine and other narcotics.

   b. Oregon's law permitting doctors to administer narcotics to hasten a patient's death.

   c. active euthanasia.

   d. predicting when a patient will die.

4. If you are unfamiliar with the following words, use a dictionary to check their meanings: impeccably, compensate (para. 2); collide (4); predominates (6).

 READ CRITICALLY . . . .

1. What is the point of the example that Siegel writes about in paragraph 2? Why do you suppose that he decided to develop it in detail and include it early in the essay?

2. What is the purpose of paragraph 3? Does the information that Siegel offers here surprise you in any way?

3. What distinction does Siegel make between using drugs in potentially lethal doses to relieve pain and practicing active euthanasia, which is legal in the Netherlands? Why do you think that he feels the need to make this distinction?

4. Evaluate Siegel's final paragraph. How effectively do you think he makes his case here?

5. How would you define Siegel's intended audience? How does his perspective as a physician shape his argument?

▇ WRITE AN ESSAY ·

Write an essay in which you argue your views regarding another controversy in the practice of medicine—for example, the medical use of marijuana, animal testing and experimentation, condom distribution in schools to stem the spread of disease, human cloning, the publication of the names of people who are infected with HIV, the effectiveness of alternative medical practices, or the mandatory treatment of the dying children of parents whose religion forbids it. You may wish to do some research so that you have a good grasp of differing opinions on the issue.

· ·

Jerry Fensterman
I See Why Others Choose to Die

Jerry Fensterman with his son

Jerry Fensterman was a devoted father, husband, and golfer, among other things. He graduated from University of California, Santa Cruz, and received a graduate degree from University of California at Berkeley. His last and perhaps most satisfying job was as director of development at the Fenway Institute. After he was diagnosed with cancer, Fensterman found solace in writing. During his illness, his writing energized him, and he said that if his health improved, he would write seriously about topics that he thought were important. After Fensterman's death in 2007, his wife, Lisa Bevilaqua, sorted through his belongings and discovered journals that began in his years in college and continued beyond graduation. In these journals, Fensterman confronted a range of life issues and worked through problems of all sorts. He also left many letters for family and friends to read after his death. Fensterman discovered himself in the act of writing, and his writings during his terminal illness inspired others.

In the essay that follows, Fensterman offers a unique position on the issue of physician-assisted suicide, showing that complex questions rarely have simple black-and-white, one-size-fits-all answers.

GUIDING QUESTION

What kinds of changes, both physical and psychological, does Fensterman describe undergoing in the years following April 2004?

1   The U.S. Supreme Court's decision to let stand Oregon's law permitting physician-assisted suicide[1] is sure to fuel an ongoing national debate. Issues of life and death are deeply felt and inspire great passions. It would be wonderful, and unusual, if all those joining the fray would do so with the humility and gravity[2] the matter deserves.

2   I am approaching fifty, recently remarried, and the father of a terrific thirteen-year-old young man. By every measure, I enjoy a wonderful life. Or at least I did until April 2004, when I was diagnosed with kidney cancer. Surgery was my only hope to prevent its spread and save my life. The discovery of a new lump in December 2004 after two surgeries signaled that metastasis[3] was under way. My death sentence had been pronounced.

PAUSE: What do you predict will be Fensterman's position on physician-assisted suicide?

3   Life may be the most intense addiction on earth. From the moment I first heard the words "you have cancer," and again when I was told that it was spreading out of control, I recognized my addiction to life almost at the cellular level. I have tried since then, as I did before, to live life to the fullest. I also committed myself to doing everything within my power to extend my life.

4   Toward that end, I am participating in my third clinical trial in a year. I have gained some small benefit from it. I am, however, one of the

---

[1] **Oregon's law permitting physician-assisted suicide:** the Death with Dignity Act, the 1997 law that Oregon enacted to allow terminally ill Oregonians to end their lives through the voluntary self-administration of lethal medications that are expressly prescribed by a physician for that purpose. The U.S. Supreme Court struck down the Bush administration's legal challenge to the law in January 2006.

[2] **gravity:** seriousness

[3] **metastasis:** the process by which cancer spreads throughout the body

first people with my cancer to try this drug. Its median benefit seems to be only on the order of three months. So my expectations are modest. The side effects of these drugs are significant, as are the symptoms of the cancer's gallop through my body. All things considered, I believe I have earned my merit badge for "doing all one can in the face of death to stay alive."

PAUSE: Underline some of the changes that Fensterman describes he has gone through.

5   That the experience has changed me is obvious. I have a few scars, have lost 50 pounds, and my hair is thinner. I rely on oxygen nearly all the time, can no longer perform the job I loved, and have difficulty eating. More profoundly, my universe has contracted. Simply leaving home has become an enormous task, and travel is essentially out of the question. I can no longer run, swim, golf, ski, and play with my son. I haven't yet learned how to set goals or make plans for a future that probably consists of weeks or months, not years. I am also nearing a point where I will not be able to take care of my most basic needs.

PAUSE: Summarize Fensterman's main point in this paragraph.

_____

_____

6   Mine has been a long, difficult, and certain march to death. Thus, I have had ample time to reflect on my life, get my affairs in order, say everything I want to the people I love, and seek rapprochement with friends I have hurt or lost touch with. The bad news is that my pain and suffering have been drawn out, the rewarding aspects of life have inexorably shrunk, and I have watched my condition place an increasingly great physical and emotional burden on the people closest to me. While they have cared for me with great love and selflessness, I cannot abide how my illness has caused them hardship, in some cases dominating their lives and delaying their healing.

PAUSE: Underline Fensterman's thesis statement.

7   Perhaps the biggest and most profound change I have undergone is that my addiction to life has been "cured." I've kicked the habit! I now know how a feeling, loving, rational person could choose death over life, could choose to relieve his suffering as well as that of his loved ones a few months earlier than would happen naturally. I am not a religious person, but I consider myself and believe I have proved throughout my life to be a deeply moral person. Personally, I would not now choose physician-assisted suicide if it were available. I do not know if I ever would. Yet now, I understand in a manner that I never could have before why an enlightened society should, with thoughtful safeguards, allow the incurably ill to choose a merciful death.

PAUSE: How do you respond to Fensterman's argument?

_____

_____

8   The Supreme Court's ruling will inflame the debate over physician-assisted suicide. Besides adding my voice to this debate, I ask you to carefully search your soul before locking into any position. If you oppose physician-assisted suicide, first try to walk a mile in the shoes of those to whom you would deny this choice. For as surely as I'm now wearing them, they could one day just as easily be on your feet or those of someone you care deeply about.

■   **SUMMARIZE AND RESPOND** . . . .

In your reading journal or elsewhere, summarize the main point of "I See Why Others Choose to Die." Then, go back and check off support for this main idea. Next, write a brief summary (three to five sentences) of the essay. Finally, jot down your initial response to the essay. What impression of Fensterman does the essay create for you? How do you react to his basic argument?

■   **CHECK YOUR COMPREHENSION** . . . .

1. Which of the following would be the best alternative title for this essay?

   a. "Physician-Assisted Suicide: The Perspective of an Incurably Ill Patient"

   b. "Physician-Assisted Suicide: An Issue That Inspires Great Passions"

   c. "Life: The Most Intense Addiction on Earth"

   d. "How Illness Changed My Life"

2. The main idea of this essay is that

   a. the debate over physician-assisted suicide should be approached with great seriousness.

   b. people with incurable illnesses suffer physically, psychologically, and emotionally, but they are also able to escape their addiction to life.

   c. physician-assisted suicide should be legal, and people opposed to the practice should consider the wishes of those suffering incurable illnesses.

   d. the U.S. Supreme Court's ruling in favor of Oregon's law permitting physician-assisted suicide has fueled the debate over the practice.

3. Fensterman implies that some people who oppose physician-assisted suicide are

   a. humble.

   b. acting reasonably.

   c. overly passionate.

   d. no longer addicted to life.

4. If you are unfamiliar with the following words, use a dictionary to check their meanings: median (para. 4); rapprochement, inexorably (6); enlightened (7).

■ **READ CRITICALLY** . . . .

1. What do you think of Fensterman's suggestion in paragraph 3 that "[l]ife may be the most intense addiction on earth"? How do you react to the idea that he has "kicked the habit" (para. 7)? How well do you think this language serves his argument?

2. Fensterman waits until late in the essay to state his thesis. Why do you think that he might have chosen to position the thesis as he does? Do you find his choice appropriate given his purpose and audience?

3. In paragraphs 5 and 6, Fensterman describes the changes that suffering from an incurable illness have brought about in his life. What effect do these details have on his overall argument?

4. In paragraph 7, Fensterman writes that he is "not a religious person" but considers himself to be "a deeply moral person." Why do you think he reveals this about himself? How does this information affect your reading of his argument?

5. Evaluate Fensterman's concluding paragraph. Do you think that it will have its intended effect on those who oppose physician-assisted suicide? Why or why not?

■ **WRITE AN ESSAY** . . . .

Write an essay arguing for or against a controversial legal decision that you feel strongly about or that affects your life directly. Alternatively, you may choose to write about a particular law that you agree or disagree with and about which opinions differ. The issue can be one on the local, state, or federal level, but be sure to define it clearly for your readers. Feel free, as Fensterman does, to base your argument in part on personal experience. Keep in mind that, like Fensterman, you are writing to an audience that doesn't necessarily share your views.

Write an Essay in Favor of Legalized Physician-Assisted Suicide

Read the three essays that support physician-assisted suicide. Each of the authors has a different perspective on the subject. Drawing from at least two of the three essays, write your own argument supporting physician-assisted suicide. You may use your own experiences in your argument as well as outside sources. When you use material from the essays here or from another source, be sure to cite the source. (For information on citing sources, see Chapter 21.)

Your introduction should include a statement of your position on the issue. In the body of your essay, develop reasons for your opinion, using the essays and other sources. In your conclusion, summarize your reasons, and restate your opinion based on the evidence you have presented.

Legalized Assisted Suicide: Opposed

Marilyn Golden

Why Progressives Should Oppose the Legalization of Assisted Suicide

Marilyn Golden has been an advocate for the rights of the disabled since shortly after her graduation from Brandeis University, when she herself acquired a disability. She was closely involved with development of the Americans with Disabilities Act, which Congress passed in 1990. She also served for nine years as director of Access California, a clearinghouse for information on architectural accessibility for people with disabilities, and in 1996 was appointed by President Bill Clinton to the U.S. Architectural and Transportation Barriers and Compliance Board, a position she still holds. On the international front, she has served as codirector of the Disabled International Support Effort. The author of numerous articles and policy papers, Golden is currently a policy analyst with the Disability Rights Education and Defense Fund, the country's foremost advocacy group for disability civil rights, based in Berkeley, California.

The following essay originally appeared in *BeyondChron,* San Francisco's alternative online daily newspaper. In it, Golden takes a stand against the legalization of assisted suicide in California.

GUIDING QUESTION

What kinds of evidence and outside authorities does Golden cite to support her argument?

PAUSE: Do you think that legalizing assisted suicide is supported mostly by liberals?

1   There is a widespread public perception that those opposed to legalization of assisted suicide in California are religious conservatives, and that the logical position for a liberal is in support.

2   But Californians Against Assisted Suicide shows a diversity of political opinion that may be surprising to those who have not looked closely at the issue. In opposition are numerous disability rights organizations generally seen as liberal-leaning: the Southern California Cancer Pain Initiative, a group associated with the American Cancer Society; the American Medical Association and the California Medical Association; and the Coalition of Concerned Medical Professionals,[1] which does anti-poverty work in poor communities. Catholic organizations are in the mix, but no one could consider this a coalition of religious conservatives. They represent many groups coming together across the political spectrum. Why?

Managed Care and Assisted Suicide: A Deadly Mix

PAUSE: Underline the two sentences that best express Golden's argument in paragraph 3.

3   Perhaps the most significant reason is the deadly mix between assisted suicide and profit-driven managed health care. Again and again, health maintenance organizations (HMOs) and managed care bureaucracies[2] have overruled physicians' treatment decisions, sometimes hastening patients' deaths. The cost of the lethal medication generally used for assisted suicide is about $35 to $50, far cheaper than the cost of treatment for most long-term medical conditions. The incentive to save money by denying treatment already poses a significant danger. This danger would be far greater if assisted suicide were legal.

PAUSE: How might Lee's position have influenced her action?

4   Though the bill would prohibit insurance companies from coercing[3] patients, direct coercion is not necessary. If patients with limited finances are denied other treatment options, they are, in effect, being steered toward assisted death. It is no coincidence that the author of Oregon's assisted suicide law, Barbara Coombs Lee, was an HMO executive when she drafted it.

5   A 1998 study from Georgetown University's Center for Clinical Bioethics underscores the link between profit-driven managed health care and assisted suicide. The research found a strong link between cost-cutting pressure on physicians and their willingness to prescribe lethal drugs to patients, were it legal to do so. The study warns that there must be a "sobering degree of caution in legalizing [assisted suicide] in

[1] **Coalition of Concerned Medical Professionals:** a group that was formed in opposition to AB 654, a state bill that would have legalized assisted suicide in California. As of this writing, no such legislation has passed the California Assembly.

[2] **health maintenance organizations (HMOs) and managed care bureaucracies:** group health insurance plans that entitle members to the services of participating physicians, hospitals, and clinics for a flat fee, usually paid monthly. HMOs often are criticized for making treatment decisions based on considerations of profit.

[3] **coercing:** forcing

a medical care environment that is characterized by increasing pressure on physicians to control the cost of care."

Oregon Is a Deeply Flawed Model

6   The California bill is modeled after a nearly identical law that went into effect in Oregon in 1997. Assisted suicide advocates laud Oregon's example. But Oregon shines only if you don't look too closely. Californians concerned with good government have reason to be highly skeptical.

7   Each year, Oregon publishes a statistical report that leaves out more than it states. Several of these reports have included language such as "We cannot determine whether assisted suicide is being practiced outside the framework of the law." (In fact, the statute provides no resources or even authority to detect such violations.) All of the information in the report comes from doctors who prescribed the drugs, not from family members or friends who probably have additional information about the patients. The state doesn't even talk to doctors who refused to assist the very same patients, though these doctors may have viewed the patients as not meeting legal requirements. Autopsies are not required, so there's no way to know if the deceased was actually terminally ill, opening the door to another Dr. Kevorkian.[4] The state's research has never reported on several prominent cases inconsistent with the law—these cases came to light only via the media. Last month, an editorial in *The Oregonian* complained that the law's reporting system "seems rigged to avoid finding" the answers.

8   Also disturbing, end-of-life care in Oregon has been touted as improving because of this law, but when the full situation is taken into account, the claim lacks data, or the improvement has been explainable by other factors. For example, assisted-suicide advocates have lauded the increased use of hospice[5] care in Oregon—but hospice referrals increased dramatically across the U.S. during the same period. In July 2004, a study in the *Journal of Palliative Medicine* showed that dying patients in Oregon are nearly twice as likely to experience moderate or severe pain during the last week of life as similar Oregon patients around the time the Oregon law came into effect, suggesting a significant *decline* in care.

PAUSE: What, according to Golden, is troubling about Oregon's reporting system?

---

[4] **Dr. Kevorkian:** Dr. Jack Kevorkian, a controversial figure in the debate over physician-assisted suicide. He created several devices that allowed individuals to self-administer lethal dosages of drugs. Kevorkian, a trained physician whose license was revoked in 1991, claimed to have participated in the suicide of some 130 people and was convicted of second-degree murder in 1999.

[5] **hospice:** a program or facility that provides special care for people who are near the end of life

PAUSE: Why is Golden critical of the "good faith" standard?

9   Most troubling, the California bill and Oregon's law legalize negligence by means of the "good faith" standard, which says that no practitioners of assisted suicide will be subject of any legal liability if they act in good faith, something nearly impossible to disprove, making all other rules unenforceable. For everything else doctors do, they are liable if they are negligent. But on assisted suicide, even if negligent, health care practitioners cannot be found to be violating the law, as long as they practice in good faith.

10   There are many more reasons progressives[6] should oppose the legalization of assisted suicide. We must focus not on what we hope to have available for ourselves someday but, rather, on the significant dangers of legalizing assisted suicide in this society as it operates today. This column is sure to bring howls from those already ideologically supportive of legalization, but those who want to look deeper, beyond the simplistic mantras of choice and "right to die," are encouraged to read other articles and testimony that can be found in these locations:

- a longer article by this author at **http://dredf.org/assisted suicide.html**

- commentary by Dr. Herbert Hendin, Medical Director of the American Foundation for Suicide Prevention, at **http://www.psychiatrictimes.com/p040201b.html**

- testimony by Dr. Gregg Hamilton, Physicians for Compassionate Care, at **http://www.pccef.org/articles/art32HouseofLords .htm**

- analysis of the first six years of Oregon's assisted suicide law by the International Task Force on Euthanasia and Assisted Suicide at **http://internationaltaskforce.org/orrpt6.htm**

[6] **progressives:** people whose political philosophy leads them to advocate for social justice and the rights of workers and the lower classes

 SUMMARIZE AND RESPOND . . . .

In your reading journal or elsewhere, summarize the main point of "Why Progressives Should Oppose the Legalization of Assisted Suicide." Then, go back and check off support for this main idea. Next, write a brief summary (three to five sentences) of the selection. Finally, jot down your initial response to the reading. What do you think of the arguments that Golden makes here? Does anything in the essay tempt you to rethink your position on physician-assisted suicide? What might you say to Golden about her stand on this issue?

■ **CHECK YOUR COMPREHENSION** . . . .

1. Which of the following would be the best alternative title for this essay?

   a. "Conservative Opposition to Legalizing Physician-Assisted Suicide"

   b. "Physician-Assisted Suicide and Managed Care"

   c. "The Oregon Model of Physician-Assisted Suicide"

   d. "Liberals Should Rethink Their Position on the 'Right to Die'"

2. The main idea of this essay is that

   a. the California Assembly Judiciary Committee has begun conducting hearings on whether the state should legalize physician-assisted suicide.

   b. liberals in favor of assisted suicide should rethink their position based on its potential misuse under managed-care programs and problems that arise under governmental oversight.

   c. the Oregon model of physician-assisted suicide is deeply flawed because it does nothing to detect violations, it allows the only information about patients to come from the prescribing doctors, and it protects doctors from charges of negligence by a "good-faith" clause.

   d. although insurers could not force clients to seek assisted suicide, poor patients whose managed-care program denies them other treatment options are being pushed in that direction.

3. Golden makes the point that when physicians are pressured to cut costs,

   a. state governments should step in to make sure that patient treatment does not suffer.

   b. they are more likely to refer their patients to hospices.

   c. their practice may come under scrutiny for medical negligence.

   d. their willingness to participate in assisted suicide increases.

4. If you are unfamiliar with the following words, use a dictionary to check their meanings: coalition (para. 2); bureaucracies (3); skeptical (6); autopsies (7); lauded, palliative (8); negligence (9); ideologically, mantras (10).

■ **READ CRITICALLY** . . . .

1. In paragraph 2, why does Golden list the groups that have come together to oppose an assisted-suicide bill in California? What does this suggest to you about her intended audience?

2. Golden ends her second paragraph with a question. Why? What is the effect of this strategy?

3. In paragraph 4, Golden notes that the author of Oregon's assisted-suicide law is a former HMO executive. Why does she do so? What does this information make you think of the Oregon law? Is this a fair conclusion?

4. Why do you suppose that Golden focuses on the Oregon assisted-suicide law in paragraphs 6–9? How does she expect readers to respond?

5. Golden ends her argument with a list of "other articles and testimony" that oppose assisted suicide. What is her reason for doing so? Do you feel that you should seek out these other sources? Why or why not?

■ WRITE AN ESSAY ·

Write an essay in which you assume that your audience is made up of readers who share your general political views but disagree with you regarding the specific issue that you are writing about. For example, if your politics are conservative, you still might support amnesty for illegal immigrants, marriage for same-sex partners, or more money for prisoner rehabilitation. Try to convince an audience of conservatives to consider your position even if they don't embrace it. If your politics are liberal, you still might oppose the previously mentioned issues or another issue that liberals tend to support. Try to convince an audience of liberals that your differing views have merit. In either case, try to establish some common ground with your readers.

· ·

Herbert Hendin

The Case against Physician-Assisted Suicide: For the Right to End-of-Life Care

Born in New York City in 1926, psychiatrist Herbert Hendin received his bachelor's degree from Columbia University and his medical degree from New York University. A clinical professor of psychiatry at New York Medical College in Valhalla, New York, he was also a founding director of the American Foundation for Suicide Prevention in 1987, serving as its first president, its executive director, and its medical director. He currently acts as director of Suicide Prevention Projects for the foundation. Hendin's research has focused on suicide, post-traumatic stress disorder, substance abuse, and euthanasia, and his books include *Black Suicide* (1967), *Wounds of War: The Psychological Aftermath of Combat in Vietnam* (1984), *Living High: Daily Marijuana Use among Adults* (1987), *Suicide in America* (1996), and *Seduced by Death: Doctors, Patients, and the Dutch Cure* (1997).

In the following essay, originally published in *Psychiatric Times,* Hendin uses his access to studies of physician-assisted suicide in the Netherlands, where it has been practiced in some form since 1984, to make a case against its legalization elsewhere.

GUIDING QUESTION

Why does Hendin use information obtained from the Netherlands regarding physician-assisted suicide? What does this information contribute to his argument?

1   Euthanasia is a word coined from Greek in the seventeenth century to refer to an easy, painless, happy death. In modern times, however, it has come to mean a physician's causing a patient's death by injection of a lethal dose of medication. In physician-assisted suicide, the physician prescribes the lethal dose, knowing the patient intends to end his or her life.

PAUSE: Summarize the contrast that Hendin establishes in this opening paragraph.

_____

_____

2   Compassion for suffering patients and respect for patient autonomy[1] serve as the basis for the strongest arguments in favor of legalizing physician-assisted suicide. Compassion, however, is no guarantee against doing harm. A physician who does not know how to relieve a patient's suffering may compassionately, but inappropriately, agree to end the patient's life.

3   Patient autonomy is an illusion when physicians are not trained to assess and treat patient suffering. The choice for patients then becomes continued agony or a hastened death. Most physicians do not have such training. We have only recently recognized the need to train general physicians in palliative[2] care, training that teaches them how to relieve the suffering of patients with serious, life-threatening illnesses. Studies show that the less physicians know about palliative care, the more they favor assisted suicide or euthanasia; the more they know, the less they favor it.

PAUSE: Underline the sentence in this paragraph that best summarizes Hendin's main idea.

4   What happens to autonomy and compassion when assisted suicide and euthanasia are legally practiced? The Netherlands, the only country

[1] **autonomy:** freedom to act independently and to carry out one's own wishes

[2] **palliative:** concerned with easing pain

in which assisted suicide and euthanasia have had legal sanction for two decades, provides the best laboratory to help us evaluate what they mean in actuality. The Dutch experience served as a stimulus for an assisted-suicide law in Oregon—the one U.S. state to sanction it.

5   I was one of a few foreign researchers who had the opportunity to extensively study the situation in the Netherlands, discuss specific cases with leading Dutch practitioners, and interview Dutch government-sponsored euthanasia researchers about their work. We all independently concluded that guidelines established by the Dutch for the practice of assisted suicide and euthanasia were consistently violated and could not be enforced. In the guidelines, a competent patient who has unrelievable suffering makes a voluntary request to a physician. The physician, before going forward, must consult with another physician and must report the case to the authorities.

6   Concern over charges of abuse led the Dutch government to undertake studies of the practice in 1990, 1995, and in 2001 in which physicians' anonymity[3] was protected, and they were given immunity for anything they revealed. Violations of the guidelines then became evident. Half of Dutch doctors feel free to suggest euthanasia to their patients, which compromises the voluntariness of the process. Fifty percent of cases were not reported, which made regulation impossible. The most alarming concern has been the documentation of several thousand cases a year in which patients who have not given their consent have their lives ended by physicians. A quarter of physicians stated that they "terminated the lives of patients without an explicit request" from the patient. Another third of the physicians could conceive of doing so.

7   An illustration of a case presented to me as requiring euthanasia without consent involved a Dutch nun who was dying painfully of cancer. Her physician felt her religion prevented her from agreeing to euthanasia so he felt both justified and compassionate in ending her life without telling her he was doing so. Practicing assisted suicide and euthanasia appears to encourage physicians to think they know best who should live and who should die, an attitude that leads them to make such decisions without consulting patients—a practice that has no legal sanction in the Netherlands or anywhere else.

8   Compassion is not always involved. In one documented case, a patient with disseminated[4] breast cancer who had rejected the possibility of euthanasia had her life ended because, in the physician's words: "It could have taken another week before she died. I just needed this bed."

PAUSE: Based on this paragraph, what do you predict Hendin will discuss in the paragraphs that follow?

_____

_____

PAUSE: How do you respond to the behavior of the physician that Hendin describes in paragraph 7?

_____

_____

[3] **anonymity:** a state of not being identified by name

[4] **disseminated:** spread widely

9   The government-sanctioned studies suggest an erosion of medical standards in the care of terminally ill patients in the Netherlands when 50% of Dutch cases of assisted suicide and euthanasia are not reported, more than 50% of Dutch doctors feel free to suggest euthanasia to their patients, and 25% admit to ending patients' lives without their consent.

10   Euthanasia, intended originally for the exceptional case, became an accepted way of dealing with serious or terminal illness in the Netherlands. In the process, palliative care became one of the casualties, while hospice[5] care has lagged behind that of other countries. In testimony given before the British House of Lords, Zbigniew Zylicz, one of the few palliative care experts in the Netherlands, attributed Dutch deficiencies in palliative care to the easier alternative of euthanasia.

> **PAUSE:** Summarize Hendin's point about palliative care in this paragraph.

11   The World Health Organization has recommended that governments not consider assisted suicide and euthanasia until they have demonstrated the availability and practice of palliative care for their citizens. All states and all countries have a long way to go to achieve this goal.

12   People are only beginning to learn that, with well-trained doctors and nurses and good end-of-life care, it is possible to avoid the pain of the past experiences of many of their loved ones and to achieve a good death. The right to such care is the right that patients should demand and the challenge that every country needs to meet.

> **PAUSE:** What would you say a "good death" (para. 12) means to Hendin?

[5] **hospice:** a program or facility that provides special care for people who are near the end of life

---

■ **SUMMARIZE AND RESPOND** . . . .

In your reading journal or elsewhere, summarize the main point of "The Case against Physician-Assisted Suicide: For the Right to End-of-Life Care." Then, go back and check off support for this main idea. Next, write a brief summary (three to five sentences) of the essay. Finally, jot down your initial response to the selection. Were you surprised by the information given on assisted-suicide practices in the Netherlands? Do you agree with Hendin that these studies make a strong case against legalizing assisted suicide? Why or why not?

■ **CHECK YOUR COMPREHENSION** . . . .

1. Which of the following would be the best alternative title for this essay?

   a. "Physician-Assisted Suicide: A Lack of Compassion"

   b. "Guidelines to Be Followed in Cases of Physician-Assisted Suicide: An Overview"

    c.   "Physician-Assisted Suicide for Exceptional Cases Only"

    d.   "The Potential for Abuse in Physician-Assisted Suicide and the Need for Greater Palliative Care"

2. The main idea of this essay is that

    a.   physician-assisted suicide is acceptable only when a patient's suffering cannot be eased and the patient requests the prescription voluntarily.

    b.   rather than legalizing assisted suicide, the United States should work toward better end-of-life care for all patients.

    c.   most physicians lack compassion for their patients when it comes to assisted suicide.

    d.   the Dutch government's concern over potential abuses of that country's assisted-suicide laws led it to commission studies that allowed physicians to respond anonymously and without threat of punishment.

3. The Dutch government studied physician abuse of assisted-suicide laws and did *not* find that

    a.   many physicians performed assisted suicide only when they could remain anonymous.

    b.   physicians suggested assisted suicide to patients who had not brought the subject up themselves.

    c.   a large number of physicians did not report cases of assisted suicide to authorities.

    d.   some physicians felt that they could decide when patients should end their lives, whether out of compassion or because it was convenient.

4. If you are unfamiliar with the following words, use a dictionary to check their meanings: sanction (para. 4); immunity (6); erosion (9); casualties, deficiencies (10).

■ READ CRITICALLY . . . .

1. In his opening paragraph, why does Hendin contrast the original definition of *euthanasia* with how the word is currently used? How does this original definition tie into the larger point Hendin is making?

2. What is Hendin's strategy in paragraph 3? Do you find it is effective in terms of his overall argument?

3. How does Hendin establish his authority to make his particular case against physician-assisted suicide? Do you find his authority believable?

4. In paragraph 8, Hendin refers to a case in which a physician performed assisted suicide without a patient's consent and primarily for the doctor's convenience, not to relieve the patient's suffering. Do you find this example sufficient for the point Hendin is trying to make? Why or why not?

5. In his next-to-last paragraph, Hendin summarizes recommendations that were made by the World Health Organization. Why does he do so? Do you think that this passage serves its intended purpose?

WRITE AN ESSAY

Write an essay that argues for a position on one side of a debatable issue to which you can bring personal expertise and authority. Like Hendin, you should have knowledge of the topic that most of your audience will not have, either because you have learned things through research that others are not familiar with or because you have had life experiences that relatively few other people have shared. In your essay, be sure to establish your authority on the subject.

Write an Essay against Legalized Physician-Assisted Suicide

Read the essays by Golden and Hendin that argue against legalized physician-assisted suicide. Drawing from both essays, write your own argument against physician-assisted suicide. You may use your own experiences in your argument as well as outside sources. When you use material from the essays here or from another source, be sure to cite the source. (For information on citing sources, see Chapter 21.)

Your introduction should include a statement of your position on the issue. In the body of your essay, develop reasons for your opinion, using the essays and other sources. In your conclusion, summarize your reasons, and restate your opinion based on the evidence you have presented.

Write an Essay: What Do You Think?

Using material from at least four of the five essays in this chapter, write an essay either for or against legalized physician-assisted suicide.

In your introduction, state your position on the issue. In the body of your essay, acknowledge the opposite side of the issue—either pro (Huttmann, Siegel, and Fensterman) or con (Golden and Hendin). Use the appropriate selections to support your position, along with any relevant experiences you have had and outside sources you use. Cite all sources. (For information on citing sources, see Chapter 21.) In your conclusion, restate your position, review the reasons you have given, and make a last pitch for your side of the argument. As you write your argument, imagine that someone you love will be directly affected by the issue.

Appendix

Problem Solving in Writing

Some writing assignments, both in English and in other subjects, will require you to use problem-solving skills. Such assignments will ask you to read and analyze a problem in order to develop possible solutions, often by synthesizing information from various sources.

Problem-solving skills are necessary not only in college but also—and even more so—in the work world. Often, managers assign a team to work on and pose possible solutions to a problem that the organization faces. Also, problem-solving skills will help you in your everyday life when you run into a situation that you want to change.

Each of the chapters in Part Two includes problem-based writing assignments ("Writing to Solve a Problem"). These assignments offer you the opportunity to solve real-world problems by working alone or as part of a team. Use the following section to complete those assignments or to address any problem you may face in college, at work, or in your everyday life.

Problem Solving

Problem solving is the process of identifying a problem and figuring out a reasonable solution.

Problems range from minor inconveniences like finding a rip in the last clean shirt you have when you're running late to more serious problems such as being laid off from your job. While such problems disrupt our lives, they also give us opportunities to tackle difficult situations with confidence.

Too often, people are paralyzed by problems because they don't have strategies for attacking them. However, backing away from a problem rarely helps solve it. When you know how to approach a challenging situation, you are better able to take charge of your life.

Problem solving consists of five basic steps, which can be used effectively by both individuals and groups of people.

THE PROBLEM-SOLVING PROCESS

Understand the problem.

You should be able to say or write it in a brief statement or question.

EXAMPLE:

Your ten-year-old car needs a new transmission, which will cost at least $750. Do you keep the car or buy a new one?

Identify people or information that can help you solve the problem (resources).

EXAMPLES:

- Your mechanic
- Friends who have had similar car problems
- Car advice from print or Web sources

List the possible solutions.

EXAMPLES:

- Pay for the transmission repair.
- Buy a new car.

Evaluate the possible solutions.

1. Identify the steps each solution would require.
2. List possible obstacles for each solution (like money or time constraints).
3. List the advantages and disadvantages of the solutions.

EXAMPLES (considering only advantages and disadvantages):

- Pay for the transmission repair.

  Advantage: This would be cheaper than buying a new car.

  Disadvantage: The car may not last much longer, even with the new transmission.

- Buy a new car.

  Advantage: You'll have a reliable car.

  Disadvantage: This option is much more expensive.

↓

Choose the most reasonable solution, one that is realistic — the simpler the better. Be able to give reasons for your choice.

Solution: Pay for the transmission repair.

Reasons: You do not have money for a new car, and you don't want to assume more debt. Opinions from two mechanics indicate that your car should run for three to five more years with the new transmission. At that point, you'll be in a better position to buy a new car.

Answers to Odd-Numbered Editing Exercises

CHAPTER 22: THE BASIC SENTENCE
Practice 22-1, page 387
Possible answers:
1. student; at; wanted; and   3. cars; continually; made; angry   5. decisively; he; refused; of

Practice 22-2, page 390
Answers:
1. *Subject:* people; *prepositional phrase:* around the country   3. *Subject:* Ronald; *prepositional phrase:* in a program called Puppies Behind Bars   5. *Subject:* Cooper; *prepositional phrases:* in the cell; with him   7. *Subject:* Ronald; *prepositional phrases:* before the start; of Cooper's formal guide dog training   9. *Subject:* Cooper; *prepositional phrase:* with a blind person

Practice 22-3, page 394
Answers:
1. *Subject:* family; *action verb:* moved   3. *Subject:* Miguel; *helping verb + main verb:* was learning   5. *Subject:* he; *linking verb:* was   7. *Subject:* plan; *helping verb + main verb:* had been   9. *Subject:* family; *linking verb:* is

Practice 22-4, page 395
Answers and possible edits:
1. I (incomplete thought); Most young people like the very latest styles in music, although some prefer classic rock.   3. C (complete thought)   5. C (complete thought)   7. I (incomplete thought); Playing loud music at a bus stop ought to be illegal.   9. I (incomplete thought); Even with too many people signed up for the softball team, the coach gave everyone a chance to play.

Practice 22-5, page 397
Answers:
1. S-V   3. S-LV-ADJ   5. S-LV-ADV   7. S-V-IO-(ADJ)-DO   9. S-V-ADV

Editing Reviews, pages 398, 399
Possible edits:
1. (1) It can be easier to help others than many people think. (2) For example, a person can donate his or her hair. (3) Some people need donated hair in the form of wigs. (4) Who uses these wigs? (5) Mostly, children with cancer or other diseases that cause hair loss need wigs. (6) Donating is popular, especially with young girls. (7) More and more frequently, though, men and boys are contributing hair. (8/9) For example, one nonprofit organization receives up to 2,000 locks of hair every week. (10) Unfortunately, most of the donated hair is unusable for this charity's wigs. (11) The charity's guidelines are quite strict. (12) The organization must reject hair that is gray, wet, moldy, too short, or too processed. (13) It is able to sell some rejected hair to help meet the group's costs. (14) But the organization continues to encourage donations. (15) Obviously, contributors feel they are getting more than they are giving.

3. (1) Taking a peek at a fellow passenger's computer screen is OK to do, right? (2) This is a serious question at a time when airplane flights are tightly packed and laptop use is common. (3) What if the person in the next seat is watching an offensive movie without headphones? (4) A recent survey showed that 45 percent of business travelers admit to peeking at someone else's laptop in a public place. (5) In many cases, it is nearly impossible to avoid getting a glimpse of a nearby screen. (6) So, what is the proper etiquette for in-flight laptop use? (7) If you are using your laptop, bring headphones. (8) Do not watch movies that are in poor taste. (9) If a neighbor seems interested, invite him or her to watch. (10) If you are sitting next to a laptop user, don't peek. (11) However, if the movie he or she is watching looks interesting, it is OK to ask politely to watch. (12) If the sound is too high or the content offensive, tell the laptop user. (13) If that does not work, ask a flight attendant for assistance.

CHAPTER 23: FRAGMENTS
Practice 23-2, page 405
Answers:
1. *Dependent words:* Even after. Even after having a walk, these dogs become nervous and overly excited.   3. *Preposition:* To. To address this growing need, a new type of service is springing up, especially in the larger cities of the country.   5. *Preposition:* at. A runner will come to the owner's home and take the dog out for some vigorous exercise, at a price of around thirty to forty dollars.   7. *Dependent word:* while. The runners have the chance to earn some much-needed cash, while they get some great exercise for both the dogs and themselves.   9. *Dependent word:* if. But the larger dogs, especially young retrievers, Dalmatians, and Weimaraners, are perfect for this, if they're strong and healthy.

Practice 23-3, page 406
Possible edits:

For decades, scholars have argued about when and how chickens reached the Americas. One theory is that Portuguese and Spanish settlers brought them when they arrived after 1500. Another suggests that the chickens were brought over by Polynesian visitors before Columbus's voyages. Most scholars once believed that the Portuguese and Spanish brought chickens to the Americas, along with seeds, medicinal plants, and other necessities. Now, researchers think they finally know what happened, thanks to some revealing evidence found on the coast of Chile, where chicken bones were discovered, along with some pottery that was definitely dated between 1304 and 1424, or even earlier. Anthropologists performed a DNA analysis on the bones, which revealed that the chickens from Chile had a close genetic relationship to chickens from several Polynesian sites on the islands of Tonga and American Samoa. When these findings were published, some anthropologists said the discovery supports the idea that Polynesians had by that time populated the Pacific and had even reached the Americas. Though the chicken bones matched Polynesian chickens, the pottery found with the bones was of the local Chilean style. However, it is still unclear whether it was the local Chileans or the visiting Polynesians who ate the chickens back then.

Practice 23-4, page 408
Answers and possible edits:
1. -ing *verb:* living. My grandmother spent her entire life living on a farm in eastern Wyoming. **3.** -ing *verb:* creating. She was a natural seamstress. My grandmother created shirts and dresses more beautiful than anything available in a store. **5.** -ing *verb:* using. The quilting circle made quilts for special occasions using scraps of cloth left over from other sewing projects. **7.** -ing *verb:* Celebrating. Celebrating the birth of her first child, my father, the quilting circle gave my grandmother a baby quilt that is now a treasured heirloom. **9.** -ing *verb:* Looking. Looking at each bit of cloth in that quilt, my grandmother could still describe, years later, the garment she had made from it.

Practice 23-5, page 410
Answers and possible edits:
1. To + *verb:* To lift weights. To lift weights, bodybuilders then met at the Muscle Beach of Santa Monica in Los Angeles. **3.** To + *verb:* to lift. Muscle Beach had become known as Venice by then, but bodybuilders still went there to lift railroad ties and buckets filled with concrete. **5.** To + *verb:* To get. To get the best possible workout, Arnold Schwarzenegger regularly went to Gold's Gym in Venice. **7.** To + *verb:* To have. To have a realistic setting for the 1977 movie *Pumping Iron*, the filmmaker selected Gold's Gym. **9.** To + *verb:* to sell. In the early 1970s, however, Joe Gold made a decision to sell his original business along with the name *Gold's Gym* to another company.

Practice 23-6, page 413
Possible edits:
1. Many parents believe that they would know if their daughters were being abused, either physically or emotionally. **3.** A young man can be abusive without laying a finger on his girlfriend. He might monitor her actions and keep her from spending time with other friends. **5.** Around her parents, a teenager's boyfriend may act like a perfect gentleman. He may be polite, attentive, and kind to the young woman. **7.** A young woman with an abusive boyfriend may develop psychological problems that will be difficult to treat, such as low self-esteem. **9.** Friends who think that a young woman is involved in an abusive relationship should try to be supportive of her, not turn away even if she refuses to leave her boyfriend.

Editing Reviews, pages 415, 416
Possible edits:
1. (1/2) Genetically modified foods are being marketed as the foods of the future. (3) Correct (4) Correct (5/6) A gene from a fish may be found to make tomatoes more resistant to disease. (7/8/9) Of course, genetic modification may have unintended effects, as in the case of genetically modified corn, which may harm monarch butterfly caterpillars. (10/11) Arguing that the long-term effects of genetic modification may not be known for years to come, some scientists urge caution before marketing genetically modified foods.
3. (1/2) For several years, the U.S. Department of Agriculture has permitted the irradiation of certain foods sold in American supermarkets. (3/4) Irradiating produce kills bacteria on the food, increasing its shelf life. (5) Correct (6/7) An irradiated strawberry, in contrast, can last a week or more, because the bacteria that would cause it to spoil are killed by radiation. (8/9) While some consumers worry about buying irradiated food, others dismiss these concerns as the effect of too many science-fiction movies. (10/11) In stores where irradiated fruits and vegetables are sold under banners announcing the radiation treatment, the owners report a booming market.

CHAPTER 24: RUN-ONS
Practice 24-2, page 422
Answers and possible edits:
1. CS (comma splice). The invention of cell phones made telephoning from a car possible. People could telephone for help if they were stranded on the highway. **3.** CS (comma splice). Some communities in the United States have banned drivers from talking on handheld cell phones; a

driver must stop the car to place a call legally in those areas. **5.** FS (fused sentence). No one debates that drivers can be distracted by cell phones. Some people wonder, however, whether the problem is really the fact that a driver is holding the phone. **7.** FS (fused sentence). Some people worry that drivers are distracted not by holding the telephone, but by having a conversation. A tense discussion with the boss or good news from a relative can take the driver's attention from traffic. **9.** CS (comma splice). There are differences, however, between talking on a cell phone and listening to music in the car. The telephone requires interaction from the driver, but the radio calls for passive listening.

Practice 24-3, page 424

Answers and possible edits:
1. *Subjects:* penguins; birds. *Verbs:* live; have been. Fairy penguins, a small breed of penguin, live in Tasmania, and these birds have often been the victims of oil spills. **3.** *Subjects:* attempts; oil. *Verbs:* can be; is. Unfortunately, the penguins' attempts to clean off their feathers can be fatal, for crude oil is poisonous to penguins. **5.** *Subjects:* One; volunteers. *Verbs:* created; knitted. One of the conservationists created a pattern for a sweater for the penguins, and volunteers from around the world knitted these unusual sweaters. **7.** *Subjects:* Most; some. *Verbs:* were made; were sent. Most of the sweaters were made by elderly nursing-home residents in Tasmania, but some were sent from as far away as Japan. **9.** *Subjects:* knitters; few. *Verbs:* made; have. Some creative knitters made tuxedo-patterned sweaters, and a few of these penguin suits even have bow ties.

Practice 24-4, page 427

Answers and possible edits:
1. *Subjects:* phenomenon; it. *Verbs:* is; may be changing. Although this phenomenon is something we take for granted, it may be changing. **3.** *Subjects:* change; materials. *Verbs:* happened; pointed. Such a change happened before in the earth's history, when magnetic materials pointed south instead of north for long periods. **5.** *Subjects:* change; satellites. *Verbs:* has affected; have been. The change in magnetism has affected some satellites, which have been damaged. **7.** *Subjects:* bees, pigeons, salmon, turtles, whales, newts, bacteria; they. *Verbs:* need; will adjust. Because bees, pigeons, salmon, turtles, whales, newts, and even bacteria need the magnetic field to navigate, they will adjust to the magnetic change. **9.** *Subjects:* processes; change. *Verbs:* may unfold; may occur. The processes affecting magnetism may unfold much more slowly, so that the magnetic change may not occur for millions of years.

Editing Reviews, pages 429, 430

1. (1) Correct (2) It's often easy to forget things when you want desperately to remember them. (3) You have probably had the experience of forgetting an acquaintance's name, which comes to your mind only when it's too late. (4) You have also probably been unable to find your keys once in a while because you put them down somewhere without thinking. (5) At other times, however, you may find it difficult to forget some things even though you wish you could never think of them again. (6) Correct (7) Sometimes, you may find yourself forced to relive your most embarrassing moment over and over again in your mind; your memory won't let you leave that part of your past behind. (8) Some scholars believe that these annoying habits of memory evolved for a reason. It's hard to imagine, though, any good reason for developing the ability to forget where you left your keys.

3. (1) The number of bike riders is growing, especially in American cities because increasing numbers of people are riding bikes to work and for exercise. (2) This makes it all the more important for drivers and bike riders to learn to share the road. Every year, approximately 46,000 bike riders are injured in crashes with motor vehicles. (3) The good news is that most of these accidents are preventable, but it takes special care on the part of both drivers and riders. (4) Car drivers need to recognize that bicycles have a legal right to use most roads, although bikes must ride on the shoulder when the speed limit is over fifty miles per hour. (5) When coming up on a cyclist, slow down; when passing, give the bike at least three feet of clearance. (6) Be especially careful with young cyclists, even those on the sidewalks, because they can suddenly dart out in traffic without looking. (7) When making a right turn, make sure there is no bicycle on the right; when waiting to turn left or at a stop sign, yield to a bicycle that has the right of way. (8) Check carefully for bicycles before opening a car door. Cyclists have been killed by headlong crashes into suddenly opened car doors. (9) Bike riders need to follow the same traffic rules that apply to drivers. Wait for a green light before crossing intersections and signal before all turns and stops. (10) Try to ride at least three feet from parked cars; do not weave in and out between parked cars. (11) Don't ride wearing headphones or while talking on a cell phone, and always wear a properly fitted bike helmet. (12) Increasing bike riding is a good sign for the environment and for Americans' expanding waistlines, but for everyone's safety, both drivers and riders must vigilantly follow the rules of road-sharing.

CHAPTER 25: PROBLEMS WITH SUBJECT-VERB AGREEMENT

Practice 25-2, page 438

Answers:
1. *Subject:* people; *verb:* have **3.** *Subject:* ovens; *verb:* do **5.** *Subject:* amount; *verb:* is **7.** *Subject:* ovens; *verb:* have **9.** *Subject:* level; *verb:* does

Practice 25-3, page 439
Answers:
1. *Subject:* students; *verb:* are 3. *Subject:* computer; *verb:* does 5. *Subject:* program; *verb:* has 7. *Subject:* teachers; *verb:* are 9. *Subject:* computer; *verb:* does

Practice 25-4, page 440
Answers:
1. *Prepositional phrase:* with hearing loss; *verb:* have 3. *Prepositional phrase:* with words; *verb:* comes 5. *Prepositional phrase:* in this country; *verb:* feel 7. *Prepositional phrase:* in a deaf household; *verb:* resembles 9. *Prepositional phrase:* to the hearing world and the deaf world; *verb:* pull

Practice 25-5, page 442
Answers:
1. *Dependent clause:* which is a job applicant's first contact with many prospective employers; *verb:* contains 3. *Dependent clause:* who held a previous job for two months; *verb:* claims 5. *Dependent clause:* who never received a college degree; *verb* is OK 7. *Dependent clause:* who like a résumé; *verb:* check 9. *Dependent clause:* who invent material on a résumé; *verb:* forget

Practice 25-6, page 443
Answers:
1. *Subject joined by:* and; *verb:* do 3. *Subject joined by:* or; *verb:* is 5. *Subject joined by:* and; *verb:* contain 7. *Subject joined by:* and; *verb:* contribute 9. *Subject joined by:* nor; *verb:* are

Practice 25-7, page 445
Answers:
1. Many are middle-aged or older. 3. But everybody needs exercise that is safe, practical, and enjoyable. 5. Nobody pursues activities that might risk bodily damage. 7. Some do it to lose weight. 9. Others enjoy looking at people, stores, and the outdoors as they exercise and observing the new and unusual around them.

Practice 25-8, page 447
Answers:
1. Where are the corporation's main offices located? 3. How well does the average employee abroad speak English? 5. How many languages is the manual written in? 7. There are some machines that can do translation. 9. OK

Editing Reviews, pages 448, 449
Answers:
1. (1) School systems around the country are embracing educational standards. (2) The idea of standards sounds reasonable. (3) Correct (4) A national standard for all American students has many supporters, too. (5) If the requirements for graduation in Oregon and Tennessee are the same, everyone with a high school diploma gets a similar education. (6) Correct (7) Correct (8) Mathematics and writing are important, but so are music and physical education. (9) How are parents, teachers, and administrators ever going to find standards that everyone accepts?

3. (1) Correct (2) Most school districts that have a testing program use tests that can be scored by a computer. (3) Computers cannot read, so the tests that they grade usually offer multiple-choice questions. (4) A multiple-choice test in science or mathematics does not allow students to demonstrate critical thinking. (5) How do students show their writing ability on such a test? (6) There are tricks to answering multiple-choice questions that many students learn. (7) Correct (8) Nevertheless, the quick results and low cost of a computer-graded multiple-choice test mean that this imperfect testing system is used in many school systems.

CHAPTER 26: VERB PROBLEMS
Practice 26-2, page 454
Answers:
1. *Subject:* doors; *verb:* open 3. *Subject:* system; *verb:* works 5. *Subject:* display; *verb:* indicates 7. *Subject:* managers; *verb:* claim 9. *Subject:* They; *verb:* wait

Practice 26-3, page 456
Answers:
1. *Helping verb:* is; *main verb:* starting 3. *Helping verb:* is; *main verb:* gathering 5. *Helping verb:* are; *main verb:* helping 7. *Helping verb:* is; *main verb:* pitching 9. *Helping verb:* is; *main verb:* sharing

Practice 26-4, page 458
Answers:
1. *Helping verb:* has; *past participle:* forced 3. *Helping verb:* have; *past participle:* attended 5. *Helping verb:* have; *past participle:* objected 7. *Helping verb:* have; *past participle:* traveled 9. *Helping verb:* has; *past participle:* liked

Practice 26-5, page 459
Answers:
1. decided 3. cared 5. engaged 7. participated; stopped 9. charged 11. died

Practice 26-6, page 460
Answers:
1. have increased 3. have attempted 5. raised 7. violated 9. have started

Practice 26-7, page 461
Answers:
1. *Helping verb:* were; *main verb:* climbing 3. *Helping verb:* were; *main verb:* focusing 5. *Helping verb:* was; *main verb:* having 7. *Helping verb:* was; *main verb:* stopping 9. *Helping verb:* were; *main verb:* watching

Practice 26-8, page 463
Answers:
1. got 3. had heard 5. had just learned 7. raised 9. had warned

Practice 26-9, page 466
Answers:
1. will be using 3. will be planning 5. will have checked 7. will wait 9. will have rescued

Practice 26-10, page 467
Answers:
1. am 3. has 5. are 7. has 9. are

Practice 26-11, page 469
Answers:
1. was 3. was 5. were 7. was 9. was; were

Practice 26-12, page 472
Answers:
1. built 3. wrote 5. struck 7. began 9. left; stood

Practice 26-13, page 473
Answers:
1. Two years ago, my high school set up a student court to give students a voice in disciplining rule breakers. 3. Some of us served as members of juries, and others became advocates or even judges. 5. Then, last spring, my friend Dewayne appeared before the student court after he lost his temper and struck a fellow student. 7. I told the jury that he knew his violent reaction was a mistake. 9. After hearing the verdict, Dewayne shook hands with all the jurors and thanked them for their fairness.

Practice 26-14, page 474
Answers:
1. *Helping verb:* had; *past participle:* taken 3. *Helping verb:* had; *past participle:* begun 5. *Helping verb:* had; *past participle:* been 7. *Helping verb:* had; *past participle:* bought 9. *Helping verb:* had; *past participle:* sold

Practice 26-15, page 476
Possible edits:
1. The *Queen Mary 2* has a grand lobby and an old-style three-story restaurant. 3. The ship's computer systems can automatically correct the effects of the wind, waves, and ocean currents. 5. He said he would probably use the joystick more in the future.

Practice 26-16, page 477
Answers:
1. *Verbs:* want, needed; *corrected verb:* need 3. *Verbs:* makes, caused; *corrected verb:* causes 5. *Verbs:* wore, snap; *corrected verb:* wear 7. *Verbs:* chose, knows; *corrected verb:* chooses 9. *Verbs:* kept, eases; *corrected verb:* keeps

Editing Reviews, pages 489, 491
Answers:
1. (1) Since 1835, trapeze artists have considered the triple somersault the most dangerous maneuver. (2) That year, a performer tried to do a triple somersault on a trapeze for the first time and died in the attempt. (3) Only one person managed to do the trick successfully in the next sixty-three years. (4) That man, a trapeze artist named Armor, did a triple somersault in 1860 and was afraid to try it again. (5) According to circus legend, the second person to survive the triple, Ernie Clarke, once did a quadruple somersault in private. (6) Correct (7) Circus historians now believe that Alfredo Codona, a performer in the 1920s and 1930s, was the greatest master of the triple somersault. (8) He has gone down in history as the King of Trapeze.

3. (1) The Olympic Games first let women compete in swimming events in 1912, and with that, the swimsuit revolution began. (2) Correct (3) Before that year, women had only been able to wade at the beach in bathing costumes with long, baggy legs. (4) The 1913 suits, designed by Carl Jantzen, were ribbed one-piece outfits that allowed actual swimming. (5) An engineer, Louis Réard, came up with the next major development in swimwear in 1946 while working in the lingerie business. (6) He called it the "bikini," after a Pacific island used for testing the atomic bomb. (7) In the 1950s, few Americans dared to wear bikinis, which were considered scandalous. (8) Two-piece swimsuits caught on in the 1960s and 1970s. (9) The bikini lost some popularity in the last decades of the twentieth century, but it has made a triumphant return in the new millennium.

CHAPTER 27: PRONOUNS
Practice 27-1, page 496
Answers:
1. *Pronoun:* they; *noun:* people 3. *Pronoun:* it; *noun:* microlending 5. *Pronoun:* them; *noun:* owners 7. *Pronoun:* her; *noun:* woman 9. *Pronoun:* his or her; *noun:* entrepreneur

Practice 27-2, page 499
Answers:
1. his or her 3. their 5. himself or herself 7. they need 9. their

Practice 27-3, page 501
Answers:
1. its   **3.** their   **5.** its   **7.** its   **9.** its

Practice 27-4, page 502
Possible edits:
1. In a psychology study, volunteers who watched a video of two basketball teams had to count the number of passes. **3.** Later, when meeting with the researchers, many of the volunteers asked, "What gorilla?" **5.** The way the human brain processes visual information may keep people from using that information wisely. **7.** A stop sign appearing at an intersection cannot prevent an accident if drivers do not see the sign. **9.** However, the study indicates that drivers make mistakes because they may not see problems ahead.

Practice 27-5, page 504
Answers:
1. Robots have been part of many science-fiction classics, from *The Jetsons* to *Star Wars*. **3.** In some industries, robots are already part of the workforce. **5.** Additionally, a factory might use robots to handle substances that are dangerous for humans to touch. **7.** Some children who wanted a robot friend have already gotten their wish. **9.** The robot dog was first on many holiday and birthday gift lists for children in the past few years.

Practice 27-6, page 507
Answers:
1. However, a TV program on dental health started making her and me rethink our soda-drinking habit. **3.** Dr. Summers asked Ian to place a tooth in a bottle of soda, and she and he observed what happened to the tooth. **5.** The result of the experiment surprised her and me. **7.** They and we said "Wow" at the same time. **9.** Megan and I learned that each can of soda we drink contains about ten teaspoons of sugar, which creates even more tooth-dissolving acid and contributes to weight gain.

Practice 27-7, page 508
Answers:
1. We saw how some other roommates had conflicts right away, and we were happy that we got along better than they. **3.** She became romantically involved with Brad, and she eventually began to care more for him than me. **5.** I couldn't understand why she wanted to spend more time with him than with me. **7.** Another friend of mine, Haley, solved the problem, and no one could have been as gentle with my feelings as she. **9.** She pointed out that a similar conflict had developed between her and a lifelong friend, but understanding and open communication had saved their friendship.

Practice 27-8, page 510
Answers:
1. who   **3.** whom   **5.** who

Practice 27-9, page 511
Possible edits:
1. Experts agree that the percentage of people with allergies to foods is rising, but they don't know why. **3.** If a person has a severe allergy to a food and unknowingly eats even a small amount of that food, he or she could die. **5.** When children have severe allergies, their parents can be extremely cautious. **7.** He carries an adrenaline pen that can save his life if he goes into shock from a food allergy. **9.** My mother will not take my brother to any public place where she can even smell peanuts.

Editing Reviews, pages 512, 514
Possible edits:
1. (1) When a store makes a mistake with an order, the customer should complain to it. (2) But some people are more effective than others at complaining. (3) A good example of this was when Gary, who is in charge of facilities for his social club, ordered a barbecue grill. (4) When Gary called to place his order, he was pleased because he was connected to a sales person right away. (5) The ordering process between him and the sales person went smoothly, including the store's offer of free assembly of the barbecue, but things went downhill after that. (6) When Gary went to the store on the agreed-upon day to pick up the assembled barbecue, the store's manager told him it was not assembled. (7) Gary lost his temper and screamed at the store manager, causing several nearby customers to abandon the products they were going to buy. (8) Gary kept yelling and the store manager kept calmly responding, but Gary soon angrily stormed out to the parking lot and drove away. (9) Therefore, the social club did not get its barbecue grill that day. (10) After Gary explained this to Natalie, the club's president, she said she didn't know whom to blame more, Gary or the store manager. (11) She was better at diplomacy than he, so he and she agreed that Natalie would communicate with the store from then on. (12) When calling the store, Natalie was polite, patient, and firm in discussing with the manager how to correct the situation. (13) The result was that the store delivered the barbecue grill that same day, and the store manager gave the club a 10 percent discount on the purchase.

3. (1) NASA recently had trouble finding enough volunteers for experiments designed to test how well they could counteract the effects of weightlessness. (2) The recruits were asked if they would lie down in bed for three weeks. (3) The volunteers also had to have their feet about five inches higher than their heads. (4) The subjects could not get up, ate while supported by one elbow, used bedpans, and showered lying down on a waterproof cart. (5) When people lie down for three weeks, their muscles and bones can weaken, just as in real weightlessness. (6) To see if this weakening can be counteracted, the researchers had some subjects spin around on a centrifuge bed for thirty times a minute for one hour each day, which simulated gravity. (7) Correct (8) (He was affected more than she.) (9) From the start, the project was hampered by the researchers' inability to recruit more than ten subjects. (10) Most of the researchers, who had hoped for thirty participants, were puzzled by the small number of volunteers. (11) But one scientist, for whom this was no surprise, noted that the centrifuge experience, combined with three weeks of lying in bed, probably scared off a lot of people. (12) She also wondered if many people could take so much time off from their jobs.

CHAPTER 28: ADJECTIVES AND ADVERBS
Practice 28-1, page 519
Answers:

1. *Easy* modifies *jobs*. 3. *Frequently* modifies *employ*. 5. *Interesting* modifies *work*. 7. *Responsibly* modifies *behaving*. 9. *Financially* modifies *independent*.

Practice 28-2, page 521
Answers:

1. biggest 3. fonder 5. healthiest 7. higher 9. purer

Practice 28-3, page 523
Answers:

1. *Well* modifies *known*. 3. *Well* modifies *contrasts*. 5. *Good* modifies *tale*. 7. *Well* modifies *lives*. 9. *Well* modifies *jump*.

Practice 28-4, page 524
Answers:

1. better 3. worst 5. worst 7. best 9. worse

Editing Reviews, pages 525, 527
Answers:

1. (1) For an average European in the Middle Ages, wearing stripes was not simply a fashion mistake. (2) According to Michel Pastoureau, a scholar of the medieval period, wearing stripes was one of the worst things a European Christian could do in the thirteenth and fourteenth centuries. (3) Stripes might be taken as a sign that the wearer was sillier than other people; jesters, for example, often wore them. (4) Prostitutes also wore striped clothes, so stripes might be seen as an indication that the person was more sinful than others. (5) Wearing stripes was most dangerous for clergymen. (6) At least one clergyman in fourteenth-century France was executed because he had been foolish enough to wear striped clothes. (7) Carmelite monks who wore striped cloaks were frequently attacked, and several popes insisted that the monks change to a simpler costume. (8) People in medieval Europe certainly took their clothing seriously. (9) Correct

3. (1) For as long as most Americans could remember, everyone assumed that the food and other products people bought could be used safely. (2) But not long ago, newspaper articles began reporting how several brands of pet food sold regularly in stores were making cats and dogs sick. (3) Some pets actually died from eating this food. (4) Investigators eventually traced this contaminated pet food to a very dangerous ingredient called melamine, which was supplied by several companies based in China. (5) There followed a major recall of this contaminated pet food, allowing consumers to feel calmer about the safety of store products. (6) However, soon after that, Americans learned that firms in China also were using hazardous ingredients in some toothpastes and drugs and dangerous levels of lead in paint (which can be poisonous when ingested by children) on some best-selling toys (or "toys that sell well"). (7) However, foreign companies using bad ingredients to cut costs doesn't appear to be the only danger to American consumers. (8) Recently, contaminated spinach from California sickened more than one hundred people. (9) Have food and other products available in stores become less safe than they used to be? (10) Are there good safeguards in place to assure consumers that contaminated products will not reach store shelves easily? (11) For now, the answer seems to be that the reporting of a free press is what is helping Americans stay well informed about the safety of the products they buy.

CHAPTER 29: MISPLACED AND DANGLING MODIFIERS
Practice 29-1, page 533
Possible edits:

1. Are there energy fields in a human body that can be touched by trained professionals? 3. According to believers in therapeutic touch, an energy field that is out of alignment can cause pain and illness. 5. After a session of therapeutic touch, many patients report that they just felt better without knowing why. 7. In her experiment, practitioners who could not see Emily were supposed to use the invisible energy field to determine when her hands were near theirs. 9. Anyone who can demonstrate the ability to detect a human energy field in a similar experiment can claim a million-dollar prize.

Practice 29-2, page 534
Possible edits:

1. Trading in a used car, a seller will get a better price if the car is clean. 3. With the used car looking like new,

the owner can get the best price for a trade-in or a resale. **5.** Approved as safe and drivable by a reputable mechanic, a used car may still have minor mechanical problems that do not have to be fixed. **7.** By deducting the cost of repairing minor problems from the asking price, the owner can be fair with a buyer. **9.** With higher than usual mileage, a used car might need a reduced asking price.

Editing Review 1, page 535
Possible edits:

(1) Shipping and handling costs can make or break a business that sells online. (2) By charging too much, a site may force customers to abandon their order. (3) A customer who feels that shipping and handling charges are too high may never return to the site. (4) Most people have shipped packages at least occasionally, so they know how much shipping costs. (5) Going too far in the other direction, some online sites offer their customers free shipping and handling. (6) The sites that offer free shipping lose money and may have to either close down for good or start charging shipping fees. (7) Correct (8) Using these shippers, the online sites must either charge a flat fee, which may be too much or too little, or make the customer wait until the order is complete to find out the shipping fee. (9) Neither option is perfect, so a business that wants to keep expanding its online customer base must choose the least unattractive solution.

CHAPTER 30: COORDINATION AND SUBORDINATION
Practice 30-1, page 541
Possible edits:
1. and   **3.** yet   **5.** so   **7.** and   **9.** for

Practice 30-2, page 542
Possible edits:
1. Gasoline prices are lower in the United States than in many other industrialized countries, but most Americans do not find this news comforting. **3.** European drivers pay more than five dollars a gallon for gasoline, and gas prices in Asia have been triple those in the United States. **5.** Few people would argue that gasoline prices in the United States are too low, but the reason for these relatively cheap prices is that gasoline is not heavily taxed. **7.** Gasoline taxes can help to pay for roads, or they can raise money for research into fuel efficiency. **9.** Many Americans do not want to pay gas taxes of even two or three cents per gallon, nor do most want to spend tax money on mass transit systems.

Practice 30-3, page 544
Answers:
1. Graphology involves identifying personality features on the basis of a person's handwriting; these features include honesty, responsibility, and loyalty. **3.** An owner of a jewelry store turned to a graphology consultant following an increase in employee theft; he says that handwriting analysis helped to identify the thieves. **5.** Nevertheless, even some job seekers are beginning to use graphology to help them find work; one says he submitted his handwriting analysis report along with his résumé and got the job he wanted.

Practice 30-4, page 545
Possible edits:
1. Two inventors believed that Americans would welcome the opportunity to have a gas mask; as a result, they invented one that is part of a baseball cap. **3.** The new baseball-cap gas mask is small and lightweight; in fact, it can fit in the corner of a drawer, in a coat pocket, or in a briefcase. **5.** The wearer slips a thin sheet of transparent plastic attached to the hat over his or her head; then, the plastic sheet can be tied shut at the back of the neck. **7.** The inventors say that the plastic sheet allows the wearer to see clearly; also, it does not make the wearer feel too closed in. **9.** The goal is to allow the wearer to get out of the contaminated area quickly; consequently, the wearer can simply slip on the mask and then move into fresh air.

Practice 30-5, page 547
Possible edits:
1. because   **3.** after   **5.** so that   **7.** where   **9.** if

Practice 30-6, page 548
Possible edits:
1. His turn came on a flight back to school in Austin from Minneapolis, where he was staying with his family during winter break. **3.** He paid no attention to the rumors until the pilot announced to the passengers that the flight was landing in Wichita, Kansas, due to severe weather in Austin. **5.** As Michael sat in his seat and tried to sleep, he heard some people ask the flight attendants to allow the passengers to wait in the air terminal. **7.** Five hours later, Michael and his fellow passengers still didn't know when they would be able to resume their flight, since there were no announcements from anybody about what would happen next. **9.** If Michael was already upset by the hours-long delay with no announcements, he was even angrier at the thought of sleeping overnight in the air terminal.

Editing Review 1, page 549
Possible edits:

(1/2) Whenever a patient misunderstands a doctor's explanation and recommendations, there can be serious consequences. (3) Correct (4/5) These problems are common with people of all ages, races, and educational levels, but they are especially prevalent among the elderly. (6) Correct

(7/8) If a patient follows these simple guidelines, he or she can better understand what is wrong and what to do about it. (9) Correct (10/11) The doctor will probably ask if there are any questions, so think over each step of the instructions, and ask for a clearer explanation of anything that's confusing. (12) Correct (13/14) Another tip is to take notes on what the doctor recommends; either write the notes yourself or bring along someone else to jot them down. (15) Correct (16/17) Ask to hear the necessary instructions in the doctor's office when you are fully clothed. (18) Correct

CHAPTER 31: PARALLELISM
Practice 31-1, page 554
Answers and possible edits:
1. *Parts that should be parallel:* affects you/affected as well. This is important because the beginning of the day affects you and your children. **3.** *Parts that should be parallel:* preparing lunches/getting out clothes/it's important to organize schoolbooks. On the night before, make as many preparations for morning as possible, including preparing lunches, getting out clothes, and organizing schoolbooks. **5.** *Parts that should be parallel:* delicious/has the added advantage of giving you plenty of vitamins and minerals. Cold cereal with milk and fruit, for example, is delicious and vitamin- and mineral-rich. **7.** *Parts that should be parallel:* eat breakfast/wash up/be sure of brushing their teeth/get dressed/put their shoes on. Set a rule that the kids must eat breakfast, wash up, brush their teeth, get dressed, and put their shoes on before they turn on the TV. **9.** *Parts that should be parallel:* teaching a child to tie shoes/becoming a referee who can objectively discuss both sides in a dispute between kids. Save for the evening time-consuming, stressful tasks such as teaching a child to tie shoes or refereeing a dispute.

Practice 31-2, page 556
Answers and possible edits:
1. *Parts that should be parallel:* getting the household electric bill/to pay the rent. For many people, getting the household electric bill is more worrisome than paying the rent each month. **3.** *Parts that should be parallel:* saving money/to use less electricity. Saving money appeals to many consumers more than using less electricity. **5.** *Parts that should be parallel:* running the refrigerator/the use of all other appliances. In most households, running the refrigerator uses more energy than using all other appliances. **7.** *Parts that should be parallel:* an energy-efficient new refrigerator/running an inefficient older model. However, running an energy-efficient new refrigerator uses much less electricity than running an inefficient older model. **9.** *Parts that should be parallel:* to buy an efficient new refrigerator/it would take to run the old one for another five years. Householders

might spend less money to buy an efficient new refrigerator than to run the old one for another five years.

Practice 31-3, page 557
Answers and possible edits:
1. *Paired words:* both/and. *Parts that should be parallel:* pressed for time/have gotten used to convenient but fattening foods. People in the United States are both pressed for time and used to convenient but fattening foods. **3.** *Paired words:* rather/than. *Parts that should be parallel:* look thinner/to stay the same size and get in better shape. Being overweight can be unhealthy, but many Americans would rather look thinner than stay the same size and get in better shape. **5.** *Paired words:* both/and. *Parts that should be parallel:* overweight people/it even influences people of normal weight. The idea that thinner is better affects both overweight people and people of normal weight. **7.** *Paired words:* either/or. *Parts that should be parallel:* surgical procedures to remove fat/they have died from dangerous diet drugs. Dozens of healthy, average-sized Americans in the past ten years have died from either surgical procedures to remove fat or dangerous diet drugs. **9.** *Paired words:* not only/but also. *Parts that should be parallel:* in good health/can be physically fit. Some people who are larger than average are not only in good health but also physically fit.

Practice 31-4, page 559
Possible edits:
1. but also leadership experience   **3.** nor allows flexibility **5.** and from other students

Editing Review 1, page 559
Possible edits:
(1) Some employees who want to advance their careers would rather transfer within their company than look for a new job elsewhere. (2) In-house job changes are possible, but employees should be sure that they both meet the criteria of the job and avoid making their present boss angry. (3) Because businesses invest money in each person they hire, many companies would rather hire from within than bring an outsider into a position. (4) By hiring an employee from another department, a company neither needs to make an investment in a new employee nor loses a current employee. (5) Transfers usually go more smoothly now than in the past; however, an in-house job move can still require diplomacy and honesty. (6) Experts caution employees who are considering an in-house transfer to tell their current manager the truth and to discuss their wish to transfer with the potential new manager. (7) Employees should neither threaten to quit if they do not get the new job nor spread the word around the department that they are anxious to leave their present job. (8) Employees' goals for in-house

transfers should be advancing their careers and making sure that they create no bad feelings with the move.

CHAPTER 32: SENTENCE VARIETY

Practice 32-1, page 565
Answers:
1. Annually, harsh weather takes a toll on sandy beaches. 3. Eventually, the ocean washed the ground out from under it. 5. Now it is going to be demolished.

Practice 32-2, page 565
Possible edits:
1. Formerly, 3. Overnight, 5. Later,

Practice 32-4, page 567
Possible edits:
1. Wandering from village to village in West Africa hundreds of years before the birth of the United States, folk poets rhythmically recited stories and tales with the accompaniment of a drum and a few instruments. 3. Tracing the beginning of modern-day rap to a Jamaican immigrant to the Bronx in New York, many fans still revere Kool Herc, a DJ in the 1970s who originated the new sound in America. 5. In the 1980s, rappers' lyrics focused on sharp sociopolitical content, captivating listeners with increasingly creative wordplay. 7. Branching out in several directions, rap music today has southern, northern, midwestern, and even international rap forms alongside the more established styles from the East and West coasts. 9. Emphasizing frequently the themes of wealth and class, nearly all popular rappers in the United States are African American.

Practice 32-5, page 568
Possible answers:
1. Switching 3. Earning 5. Preventing

Practice 32-7, page 570
Possible edits:
1. Many New Yorkers refused to believe in the existence of an alligator spotted in a pond in Central Park in New York City. 3. Believed by some gullible people, the rumors about giant sewer alligators were untrue. 5. Reported by several New Yorkers, the Central Park alligator sightings were confirmed when a television news crew filmed a reptile in the pond. 7. Surrounded by news cameras and curious onlookers, the pond in Central Park was brightly lit just before 11:00 p.m. on the day the alligator wrestler arrived. 9. Surprised to find that the caiman was only two feet long, some New Yorkers may have felt a bit foolish for expecting to see a giant alligator in the park.

Practice 32-8, page 571
Possible edits:
1. Used 3. Concerned 5. Considered

Practice 32-10, page 573
Possible edits:
1. Shakespeare, the son of a former town leader, grew up in Stratford, England. 3. In 1582, Shakespeare, just eighteen, married twenty-six-year-old Anne Hathaway, a farmer's daughter. 5. Young Shakespeare, once a simple country boy, soon became involved in acting, writing, and managing for one of London's theater companies. 7. Greene's publisher soon printed a public apology for the criticism, proof that Shakespeare had won the respect of some influential figures. 9. Eventually, Shakespeare returned to Stratford and purchased a large home, New Place, where he lived until his death in 1616.

Practice 32-11, page 574
Possible edits:
1. *Love and Desire* 3. an aging but reliable machine 5. a pile over two feet high

Practice 32-12, page 576
Possible edits:
1. Cats produce a protein that keeps their skin soft. 3. Some cat lovers who are allergic to cats can control their allergies with medication. 5. Scientists have successfully cloned mice that have been genetically engineered for scientific study. 7. According to cat experts, more than 10 percent of those people who have allergic reactions to cats are allergic to something other than the skin-softening protein. 9. However, owning a genetically engineered cat would allow an allergic person to avoid taking allergy medications, which can sometimes cause dangerous side effects.

Practice 32-13, page 577
Possible edits:
1. that receive hundreds or thousands of hits each day 3. , which is becoming rarer every day, 5. , which companies use to target potential customers,

Editing Review 1, page 577
Possible edits:
(1/2) Rats, which might be nicer creatures than people think, are certainly hard to love and appreciate. (3/4) Not only do they carry serious diseases like typhus, salmonella poisoning, and bubonic plague, but rats have such huge appetites that it has been estimated that they destroy as much as one-third of humans' food supplies every year. (5/6) It has been estimated that rats have been responsible for ten

million deaths over the past century alone; however, rats in the laboratory should probably be given credit for saving as many lives as wild rats have taken.

(7/8) Used widely in laboratory research, rats have many similarities to humans. (9/10) Being ticklish, when a rat pup is gently scratched at certain spots, such as the nape of the neck, it will squeal. (11/12) The squeal, which can be heard only with an ultrasound scan, has a similar soundgram pattern to that of a human giggle. (13/14) Rats can get addicted to the same drugs that humans do, craving alcohol, nicotine, amphetamine, and cocaine. (15/16) Capable of overindulging, rats can continue consuming food or drugs until they die.

(17/18) Studies also show that rats, similar to humans, have personalities, being sad or cheerful depending on how they were raised and their circumstances. (19/20) Raised in stable, caring conditions, rats tend to be optimists, while rats reared in uneven and unreliable conditions are likely to be pessimists. (21/22) Both types of rats can learn to connect a certain sound with getting food, and they also can associate another sound with no food. (23/24) However, when they hear a new sound, not associated with either food or no food, the two types of rats react differently. (25/26) The optimist will run to the food dispenser, expecting to be fed. (27/28) The pessimist, expecting nothing, will go somewhere else.

(29/30) Demonstrating that rats can express kindness, researchers put pairs of female rats who were littermates in a cage but separated by wire mesh. (31/32) Trained so that in each half of the cage, a rat could pull a lever that would deliver food to her sister but not to herself, each rat learned to be a giver of food and a recipient of a gift of food from her sister. (33/34) Then, one of the rats was replaced by an unfamiliar and unrelated rat that had never learned about the food gift process, revealing that those rats who had recently received food gifts were 21 percent more likely to pull the lever to give food to their new, unknown partners. (35/36) The researchers, believing that these rats were generous only because another rat had just been kind to them, show us that perhaps there is more to the rodents than previously thought.

CHAPTER 33: FORMAL ENGLISH AND ESL

Practice 33-1, page 583
Answers:
1. *S:* John, *V:* sent, *DO:* letter **3.** *S:* John, *V:* sent, *DO:* letter, *IO:* Beth

Practice 33-2, page 584
Answers:
1. I (incorrect); Sara likes sports a lot. **3.** C (correct) **5.** I (incorrect); She will try to stay in touch with them.

Practice 33-3, page 586
Answers:
1. It does not start up as fast as it used to. **3.** He is definitely not happy with its speed now. **5.** He did not earn enough money last year from his part-time job to pay for it. **7.** He does not expect his computer to speed up all by itself. **9.** Most of their computers are still not as fast as his.

Practice 33-4, page 588
Answers:
1. Do you host a program on the station? **3.** Did you submit your proposal to host in your freshman year? **5.** Did you have many problems with your program in that first year? **7.** Is preparing your program both fun and hard work? **9.** Must I be careful to prepare enough content to fill an entire time slot?

Practice 33-5, page 589
Answers:
1. there are **3.** Is there **5.** there are

Practice 33-6, page 592
Answers:
1. her **3.** She; it **5.** its **7.** whose; I **9.** me; it **11.** It; that; him **13.** whom **15.** me; that

Practice 33-7, page 595
Answers:
1. has **3.** have **5.** am **7.** have **9.** has

Practice 33-8, page 597
Possible edits:
1. He does not write his "public" blog for anyone who wants to see it. Does he write his "public" blog for anyone who wants to see it? **3.** He does not write there about politics, his courses, and some music he likes. Does he write there about politics, his courses, and some music he likes? **5.** This blog does not get comments from a wide range of people. Does this blog get comments from a wide range of people? **7.** He does not give only his close friends access to this blog. Does he give only his close friends access to this blog? **9.** He does not use incorrect grammar and loose organization for his entries here. Does he use incorrect grammar and loose organization for his entries here?

Practice 33-9, page 598
Possible edits:
1. She especially enjoyed highway driving. She especially did not enjoy highway driving. Did she especially enjoy highway driving? **3.** Luis annoyed all of us by his snoring. Luis did not annoy all of us by his snoring. Did Luis annoy

all of us by his snoring? **5.** Genine called out Luis's name. Genine did not call out Luis's name. Did Genine call out Luis's name? **7.** Genine poked Luis's arm gently. Genine did not poke Luis's arm gently. Did Genine poke Luis's arm gently? **9.** We chose to stay awake for the rest of the drive. We did not choose to stay awake for the rest of the drive. Did we choose to stay awake for the rest of the drive?

Practice 33-10, page 601
Possible edits:
1. I am bringing a lot of water for the hike. I am not bringing a lot of water for the hike. Am I bringing a lot of water for the hike? **3.** He is giving away chocolate to anyone who wants it. He is not giving away chocolate to anyone who wants it. Is he giving away chocolate to anyone who wants it? **5.** This winding trail is getting steep. This winding trail is not getting steep. Is this winding trail getting steep? **7.** I am asking Roger for one of his energy bars. I am not asking Roger for one of his energy bars. Am I asking Roger for one of his energy bars? **9.** Roger's chocolate is helping me to keep on climbing. Roger's chocolate is not helping me to keep on climbing. Is Roger's chocolate helping me to keep on climbing?

Practice 33-11, page 604
Answers:
1. At first, she was washing dishes, pots, and pans. At first, she was not washing dishes, pots, and pans. At first, she will be washing dishes, pots, and pans. At first, she will not be washing dishes, pots, and pans. **3.** Then, Samantha was assisting the chefs in the kitchen. Then, Samantha was not assisting the chefs in the kitchen. Then, Samantha will be assisting the chefs in the kitchen. Then, Samantha will not be assisting the chefs in the kitchen. **5.** In the end, she was doing the job she wanted most of all. In the end, she was not doing the job she wanted most of all. In the end, she will be doing the job she wanted most of all. In the end, she will not be doing the job she wanted most of all. **7.** She was following the directions of the experienced chefs. She was not following the directions of the experienced chefs. She will be following the directions of the experienced chefs. She will not be following the directions of the experienced chefs. **9.** After a while, she was beginning to create her own recipes. After a while, she was not beginning to create her own recipes. After a while, she will be beginning to create her own recipes. After a while, she will not be beginning to create her own recipes.

Practice 33-12, page 606
Possible edits:
1. Many of her friends also have enjoyed these games. Many of her friends also have not enjoyed these games. Have

many of her friends also enjoyed these games? **3.** Jenna has decided to start a club for game players. Jenna has not decided to start a club for game players. Has Jenna decided to start a club for game players? **5.** She has reserved a large room for every Sunday afternoon. She has not reserved a large room for every Sunday afternoon. Has she reserved a large room for every Sunday afternoon? **7.** She has welcomed everyone to bring their own games as well. She has not welcomed everyone to bring their own games as well. Has she welcomed everyone to bring their own games as well? **9.** They have kept it from getting overly competitive. They have not kept it from getting overly competitive. Have they kept it from getting overly competitive?

Practice 33-13, page 609
Possible edits:
1. Jorge had finished his ice cream by closing time. Jorge had not finished his ice cream by closing time. Jorge will have finished his ice cream by closing time. Jorge will not have finished his ice cream by closing time. **3.** Selena had called the doctor after taking her temperature. Selena had not called the doctor after taking her temperature. Selena will have called the doctor after taking her temperature. Selena will not have called the doctor after taking her temperature. **5.** The battery had failed before we got a new one. The battery had not failed before we got a new one. The battery will have failed before we get a new one. The battery will not have failed before we get a new one. **7.** You had completed your research when I turned in my paper. You had not completed your research when I turned in my paper. You will have completed your research when I turn in my paper. You will not have completed your research when I turn in my paper. **9.** He had eaten his main course after his dessert. He had not eaten his main course after his dessert. He will have eaten his main course after his dessert. He will not have eaten his main course after his dessert.

Practice 33-14, page 612
Answers:
1. to start **3.** to wake up **5.** to take; to prepare **7.** to regret; feeling **9.** to drink; sleeping

Practice 33-15, page 613
Answers:
1. They both prefer to listen to the same kind of music. **3.** Like Paige, Gabriella delays doing her homework as long as she can. **5.** But Gabriella admits noticing one thing that bothers her about Paige. **7.** On the other hand, Gabriella refuses to be late ever. **9.** After a while, however, Gabriella has learned to accept Paige's habitual lateness.

Practice 33-16, page 617
Possible edits:
1. could 3. would 5. would; will 7. should 9. would have fixed

Practice 33-17, page 621
Answers:
1. the 3. The 5. the 7. The 9. no article

Practice 33-18, page 622
Answers:
1. I am a waitress at a restaurant four days a week. 3. There is a university close by, so many college students eat at my restaurant because it serves cheap food. 5. They seem to think that it is okay to be rude to the person serving them. 7. I do not make a high salary, so I need the tips from my customers to make a good living. 9. However, I think that people who cannot afford to leave a tip should not eat in a restaurant.

Practice 33-19, page 624
Answers:
1. During World War II, more than 120,000 Japanese Americans were locked up in internment camps. 3. These soldiers often had to fight against prejudice as well as the enemy. 5. After the war, many Japanese Americans who had been interned were ashamed of their experience. 7. They wanted to make other Americans aware of the sacrifices of Japanese Americans during World War II. 9. For the center of the memorial park, the designers picked out a sculpture by a Japanese American artist, Nina Akamu, featuring two cranes tangled in barbed wire.

Practice 33-20, page 625
Answers:
1. Students who are anxious about mathematics take fewer math classes and perform worse in them than students who do not have math anxiety. 3. It turns out that worry prevents students from understanding mathematics as well as they could. 5. Starting at about the age of twelve, students with math anxiety become less able to compensate for the loss of working memory. 7. Students who once thought they would never be able to understand math may someday find out that they can conquer their anxiety and cope with numbers.

Editing Reviews, pages 626, 628
Possible edits:
1. (1) Everyone knows that people who are driving should not do anything else. (2) In spite of that, people often engage in risky behavior when driving, such as eating, arguing with someone else in the car, or looking at a map while driving fast on a highway. (3) One of the most common forms of distraction while driving is holding a cell phone while talking or typing a text message. (4) Some drivers keep trying to do more and more as they drive. (5) On the driver's side of their cars, they are installing G.P.S. navigation screens, portable DVD players, and even computer keyboards and screens. (6) The trouble is that the more of these devices a driver can see and reach, the greater the risk of that driver's attention getting distracted from driving.

(7) Correct (8) According to estimates by the National Highway Traffic Safety Administration, 80 percent of vehicle crashes and 65 percent of close calls are partly due to driver distraction. (9) While automakers point to consumer demand as their reason for including more electronics for the driver, some car companies say they are making driving safer by increasing their offerings of hands-free phone systems and by making voice-activated technology easier to use. (10) One car manufacturer recently introduced a feature in a concept minivan — one that is not in production — that attempts to address this problem. (11) It is a button that the driver can push to instantly shut off all unnecessary electronic devices in the car. (12) Perhaps driving would get safer if more drivers just say to their electronics, "Enough!"

3. (1) E-mail is a young form of communication, and many of its conventions are still evolving. (2) One of the most important conventions is the sign-off one should make to end an e-mail message. (3) Before electronic communications, every third-grader learned the proper sign-offs to a personal or business letter. (4) Most people would usually close a letter with "Sincerely," "Yours truly," or "Love." (5) Correct

(6) Some e-mailers look carefully at the sign-offs as indicators of how well the relationship is going. (7) One businesswoman described what happened to the e-mail sign-offs as her contract negotiations with a client began to go badly. (8) In the beginning, she and her client used sign-offs like, "I look forward to hearing from you soon" and "Warmest regards." (9) But as difficulties arose, the sign-offs became "Regards." (10) The deal eventually was made, but the businesswoman still has lingering bad feelings about the sign-offs. (11) She said she usually chooses sign-offs according to how cordial she feels about the other person. (12) So, she often selects one of the following sign-offs: "Warmest regards," "All the best," or just "Sincerely." (13) One businessman, after thinking carefully about what would be the friendliest and most appropriate sign-off, now uses "Warmly." (14) Correct

CHAPTER 34: WORD CHOICE
Practice 34-1, page 636
Answers and possible edits:
1. *Vague or abstract words:* others, play. Erik plays clarinet, Lily plays violin, and several other talented musicians are

in the band as well.   **3.** *Vague or abstract words:* one, good. Last semester's play, <u>Thoroughly Modern Millie</u>, featured delightful singing and near-professional sound from the band.   **5.** *Vague or abstract word:* happy. But after she played at her first rehearsal, she was relieved that she could easily keep up with the others.   **7.** *Vague or abstract words:* music, hard. The musical score can also have tricky and unusual tempos that require precise counting.   **9.** *Vague or abstract words:* they'll do a new one. Next semester, the club will put on a production of <u>The Fantasticks</u>.

Practice 34-2, page 637
Answers and possible edits:
1. *Slang:* cool. I realize that our food service managers think it is smart to serve exactly the foods that students want.   **3.** *Slang:* dude. For instance, I know one man who eats nothing but potato chips and bread.   **5.** *Slang:* cops. I am not proposing that we become nutritional police and dictate to students what they should eat.   **7.** *Slang:* a few bucks. But in our effort to save money, it seems to me that we are depriving students of many important food choices that would enrich their diets.   **9.** *Slang:* awesome. Adding more healthy food choices might also help students to realize that good nutrition can be both sensible and fashionable.

Practice 34-3, page 639
Answers and possible edits:
1. *Wordy language:* At this point in time. That may be changing, thanks to four Japanese inventors.   **3.** *Wordy language:* become dimmer and then grow brighter in an expressive fashion. The patent application describes a car with an antenna that wags, headlights that dim and brighten expressively, and ornaments that look like eyebrows, eyelids, and tears.   **5.** *Wordy language:* In order to have the vehicle. To express anger, the car's hood would glow red as the eyebrows light up.   **7.** *Wordy language:* In the event that. If the driver wants the car to "cry," he or she could make the hood dark blue, shade the headlights, and show a blinking "tear" light.   **9.** *Wordy language:* could also be taken advantage of for. The inventors say that their ideas could be applied not just to cars but also to motorcycles, ships, or aircraft.

Practice 34-4, page 641
Answers and possible edits:
1. *Cliché:* as slow as molasses. Anthony, Matthew, and Stephen were quite slow when they began hiking, but once they got used to their heavy backpacks, they were able to walk faster.   **3.** *Cliché:* it was better to be safe than sorry. Just for extra safety, Stephen had packed nearly everything he had in double plastic bags.   **5.** *Cliché:* they should not count their chickens before they hatch. Anthony confidently said the weather report did not mention rain, but Stephen,

looking up at the increasingly cloudy sky, said that weather reports could be wrong.   **7.** *Cliché:* bone-chillingly cold. They continued hiking toward their campsite, and they noticed that the temperature had dropped abruptly, and it became extremely cold.   **9.** *Cliché:* run ragged. Finally, they turned back, and by the time they got to their car, they were exhausted.

Editing Review 1, page 643
Possible edits:

(1) Although people don't hear much about hobos in these days of tightly sealed boxcars, there was a time not long ago when hobos were a distinct segment of American culture. (2) Even then, however, few knew the names of any hobos. (3) But to those who followed such social currents, there was one hobo who stood out — Steam Train Maury. (4) By the time he retired from his hobo wanderings, he was crowned the king of the hobos five times, and eventually he achieved the status of Grand Patriarch of the Hobos.

(5) Born in Kansas in 1917 as Maurice W. Graham, Steam Train Maury was the product of a troubled family. (6) He spent much of his youth shifting among parents and various relatives. (7) In 1931, at the age of fourteen, he jumped on a train and began his first time as a hobo. (8) After hopping on trains and wandering for several years, he became a cement mason, operated his own school for masons in Toledo, Ohio, and later served as a medical technician during World War II. (9) By 1971, he had married and had two children, but he also developed hip problems and was unable to work much, and he became dissatisfied with his life. (10) Now fifty-four, he hopped on a freight train thinking he'd just relive his hobo life for a few weeks and then return home. (11) Those two weeks turned into ten years during which Steam Train Maury became a hobo legend. (12) By 1981, Mr. Graham had cowritten a book about his eventful life as a hobo, helped to found the Hobo Foundation, and took part in establishing the Hobo Museum in Britt, Iowa. (13) At the annual National Hobo Convention held in Britt, he was named the hobo king in 1973, 1975, 1976, 1978, and 1981. (14) In 2004, he was crowned Grand Patriarch of the Hobos, the only person ever to have won that title.

(15) Hobos have been hopping trains for free rides ever since the Civil War, when wandering field workers and laborers helped to build the American West. (16) Toward the end of the nineteenth century, some hobos, as a joke, named themselves "Tourist Union Local 63." (17) In 1900, officials from Britt, Iowa, offered their town for Local 63's hobo convention. (18) In the following decades, Britt became known as the "hobo town," and by 1933, it was widely publicizing its four-day hobo convention and drawing tens of thousands to the festivities. (19) This was during the

Great Depression, when more than a million people were sneaking onto trains in a desperate search for work.

(20) Mr. Graham always emphasized an idealized view of the hobo existence, the perspective that moved author John Steinbeck to call hobos "the last free men." (21) Typical of Mr. Graham's stories was that of a character called the Pennsylvania Kid, who shaved with a piece of glass from a Coke bottle. (22) When asked if it was true that some hobos used deodorant, Mr. Graham commented that it was a shame but he didn't know what to do about it. (23) Steam Train Maury died of a stroke in 2006 at the age of eighty-nine. (24) Using the hobos' term for death, he had "taken the westbound."

CHAPTER 35: COMMONLY CONFUSED WORDS
Practice 35-1, page 656
Answers:
1. their   3. find   5. an; except   7. write   9. though; effect

Editing Review 1, page 657
Answers:

(1) Most people know that Americans love to drive their cars. (2) However, many people may not be conscious of how much the government does to support our car culture. (3) For instance, the United States would never have had so many good highways without federal and state assistance for road construction and maintenance. (4) New highways are usually paid for mainly by tax money. (5) It is rare for a new road to be paid for with tolls, which would come exclusively from the people driving on it. (6) Americans also expect their roads to be well maintained, and they may write to their representatives to complain about potholes and aging road surfaces. (7) The government is even responsible for keeping gas prices lower here than in most other industrialized nations.

(8) Few people mind that the government assists drivers in these ways. (9) Some would argue that it's a government's job to help pay for transportation. (10) However, other forms of transportation in this country are often passed over when Congress hands out funds. (11) Amtrak, the U.S. railroad, may soon lose virtually all government funds, even though many government officials are skeptical of its ability to keep operating without government assistance. (12) Except for a few places like New York and San Francisco, most U.S. cities do not have good mass transit systems. (13) Americans whose travels have taken them to certain parts of the world praise the national train systems and city transit systems they find there. (14) As traffic gets worse in our nation's urban and suburban areas, some people find it odd that the United States does not invest more in transportation that would allow people to leave their cars at home.

CHAPTER 36: SPELLING
Practice 36-1, page 660
Spelling errors/corrections:
oportunity/opportunity, excellant/excellent, promiseing/promising, referances/references

Editing Review 1, page 667
Answers:

(1) Americans have always been an inventive people and, in recent years, it seems as though their creative inspiration is stronger than it has ever been. (2) The U.S. Patent Office is now receiving the highest amount of patent applications in its history, with the number of applications topping 400,000 annually. (3) To put this in perspective, in 1986, about 125,000 patent applications were filed, and the number of applications has steadily increased since then. (4) It is not difficult to see why, with the proliferation of available electronic gadgets, most of which involve numerous patent applications to protect their innovative technology. (5) Many of the wondrous devices that are incorporated into the latest cars, televisions, radios, personal media players, cell phones, and cameras are waiting for patent approval. (6) Therein lies a big problem for the Patent Office, which now has a backlog of 700,000 applications and an average patent review time of 31 months. (7) To get better control of the approval process, the Patent Office is gradually tightening its rules, requiring inventors to provide more information and allowing the public greater access to review applications. (8) In addition, the office is approving a lower percentage of the applications it gets, from approving 72 percent of applications in 2000 to only about 50 percent approved in 2007. (9) Inventors can improve their chances of having a successful application by following a few sensible guidelines. (10) Be sure the invention is truly new and useful, and describe it clearly and understandably. (11) Then, move on to other ventures because the Patent Office's answer will not come speedily.

CHAPTER 37: COMMAS
Practice 37-1, page 675
Answers:
1. We had prepared a wholesome, flavorful meal for the children, their parents, and their friends.   3. The huge, confusing, and annoying airport desperately needed renovating.   5. I have several urgent e-mail messages from Mr. Toland, Ms. Fry, and my father.   7. C   9. Thomas has no phone, no food, no television, and hardly anything else in his tiny, uncomfortable one-room apartment.   11. Driving on this endless, dull, unsafe highway can be unpleasant.   13. Plentiful exercise combined with a healthy, nutritious diet will have you fit fairly quickly.   15. We always buy rich, high-calorie candy bars when we go to the movies.

Practice 37-2, page 676
Answers:
1. Working in a nursing home is a difficult job, for elderly patients can seldom do much for themselves. 3. Few trained nurses and nurse's aides want nursing-home jobs, for the pay is also usually lower than that offered by hospitals. 5. More workers will be needed as the baby boomers become elderly, yet there is already a shortage of people willing to do the work. 7. C 9. Solving these problems will be difficult, for long-term care for the elderly is already very expensive.

Practice 37-3, page 678
Answers:
1. Along roadsides all across this country, drivers see the bodies of animals hit by cars. 3. Of course, hitting a deer is not only disturbing but also potentially harmful or fatal to the occupants of a car. 5. On the other hand, drivers in wilderness areas may accidentally kill endangered species. 7. Maintaining the world's largest network of roads, the U.S. Forest Service tries to balance the needs of humans and wildlife. 9. Unfortunately, wilderness roads may isolate populations of animals that will not cross them and kill animals that make the attempt.

Practice 37-4, page 680
Answers:
1. Road rage, as most people know, occurs when angry drivers overreact. 3. One famous air rage incident, a confrontation between a drunken businessman and a flight attendant, ended with the passenger tied to his seat for the rest of the flight. 5. Ground rage, as the name suggests, occurs in the terminal, not in the air. 7. Oversold seats, a common occurrence in air travel, can mean that some passengers are forced to miss a flight. 9. Some delayed or bumped passengers take out their anger on the gate agent, a convenient target.

Practice 37-5, page 681
Answers:
1. C 3. C 5. C 7. Such people, who may never love clowns, will still be able to tolerate having them around. 9. Few adults admit to having coulrophobia, which is most effectively treated when the sufferer confronts the fear.

Practice 37-6, page 684
Answers:
1. My sister asked, "James, do you get a lot of telemarketing calls?" 3. C 5. My address, which is 21 Highland Road, Binghamton, New York, has now been added to the state registry. 7. I simply replied, "No, I have news for you." 9. "As you probably know," I told my unwanted callers, "it is illegal for you to contact me in this way."

Editing Review 1, page 685
Answers:
(1) Everyone who uses cleaning products at home has probably seen warning labels on those products, for most household cleaners contain harsh chemicals. (2) The warnings, which are required by law, are so common that many users probably ignore them. (3) However, all cleaning products should be used with care, and some of them can seriously injure children or anyone else who misuses them. (4) Drain cleaners, toilet bowl cleaners, and chlorine bleach can all cause serious damage to skin, eyes, and other sensitive tissue. (5) Glass cleaners can react with bleach to produce toxic fumes. (6) Alternative cleansers, nontoxic products that can be made from items in an average kitchen, are cheaper than brand-name cleaning products and usually work just as well. (7) For most cleaning jobs, a solution of vinegar and water or baking soda and water is effective. (8) A plunger can often fix a clogged drain as well as a drain cleaner can, and club soda cleans windows nicely. (9) As for air fresheners, one expert advises, "Open your windows." (10) Economy, efficiency, and safety are three excellent reasons for choosing homemade cleansers.

CHAPTER 38: APOSTROPHES
Practice 38-1, page 690
Answers:
1. A thermometer's indicator mark at 98.6 degrees is supposed to show a person's normal body temperature. 3. Fevers help the body combat viruses and stimulate the immune system. 5. A fever's appearance is not necessarily a reason to take fever-reducing medications, which can lower a body's temperature without doing anything to fight the infection. 7. Many doctors do not recommend using any drugs to treat a fever if it's lower than 102 degrees. 9. Some parents' fears of fever are so intense that they suffer from "fever phobia" and overreact to their children's symptoms.

Practice 38-2, page 692
Answers:
1. Those who do often say they're using these drugs because their competitors are probably using them too. 3. Most athletes taking steroids and other substances say they wouldn't use these drugs if they could be certain that their opponents aren't using them. 5. If sports organizations don't eliminate drug use, we all know who's the loser. 7. When even one athlete gets away with using drugs, we can't trust that any athletic competition has been won fairly. 9. Let's eliminate performance-enhancing drugs now.

Practice 38-3, page 693
Answers:
1. Next month's schedule is less busy, so I think I'll be able to keep my blog current then. 3. His blog is a little hard

to read because he always leaves out certain letters, such as *a*'s, *e*'s, and *o*'s. **5.** When Manny's computer was stolen, he lost notes for his blog and two years' work on his novel.

Editing Review 1, page 694
Answers:

(1) Some of the first discussions of global warming focused attention on one of the gases that contributes to the greenhouse effect: methane. (2) Like other greenhouse gases, methane helps to keep the earth's heat trapped in our atmosphere, and the temperature of the earth goes up as a result. (3) Humans aren't the only producers of methane; it's also a by-product of cows' digestion of their food. (4) For a while, many Americans' knowledge of global warming didn't go much further than cow jokes. (5) As scientists have become more convinced that global warming is real and a potential threat to humans, our knowledge of the causes of the greenhouse effect has expanded. (6) Cows aren't completely off the hook, but they're far less guilty of contributing to global warming than humans and cars are. (7) The amount of methane produced by cows adds up to about 3 percent of the total amount of greenhouse gases produced by people. (8) Getting a cow to change its diet won't solve the world's warming problem.

CHAPTER 39: QUOTATION MARKS
Practice 39-1, page 698
Answers:
1. Looking around the room, Allison said, "I thought only teenage girls had eating disorders. There are people here of all ages, including several men." **3.** "I'm forty years old, not a teenager, and not a girl," Patrick said. "However, I have an eating disorder." **5.** "I eat too much," said Patrick. "I'm a compulsive eater." **7.** "The dictionary defines *compulsive* as 'related to a psychological obsession,'" said Brooke. **9.** "That is one myth we're going to talk about," said Brooke. "In fact, people with eating disorders are hurting themselves. They are usually upset that their families and friends are worried about them."

Practice 39-2, page 700
Answers:
1. "I never thought I would use the Internet for dating, but it really worked," she said. **3.** She said, "I could tell right away if I wasn't going to have anything in common with a person." **5.** C **7.** C **9.** "I found a great person," she said, "and you could too."

Practice 39-3, page 702
Answers:
1. He sat down and noticed that the woman sitting next to him was holding the <u>Dallas Morning News</u>. **3.** He noticed that the passenger sitting directly in front of him was carefully

going through "Imitation of Spenser," John Keats's first poem. **5.** Tiring of his little game, Tyler took out his sociology textbook and began reading his next assigned chapter, "The Economy and Politics."

Editing Review 1, page 702
Answers:

(1) "Here is one I've loved for years," said Evi, as she held up a CD called <u>Kind of Blue</u> by the jazz trumpeter Miles Davis. (2) Charlie, who was also flipping through the jazz CDs, said that he had gone through a Miles Davis phase but wasn't so interested in Miles's music now. (3) Shortly after they moved into the main section of the store, Charlie pulled out a book and opened it to an essay titled "Shooting an Elephant." (4) "Reading this had a big effect on me," he said, adding that he eventually read most of what George Orwell had written. (5) They were browsing through the rows of books when Evi stopped and said, "This is what led me to read all of Dylan Thomas's poetry." (6) Taking a book from the shelf, she opened it to a poem titled "Do Not Go Gentle into That Good Night," noting that it was written for Thomas's dying father. (7) Pointing to a line in the poem, she said, "When Thomas writes 'Rage, rage against the dying of the light,' he is talking to his father, to himself, and to me, bringing all of us into that special moment." (8) They continued on silently until Charlie exclaimed, "Look at this—a book about the making of the Beatles's <u>Sgt. Pepper's Lonely Hearts Club Band</u>!" (9) Evi reached for another copy of the book, saying that her father had introduced her to the Beatles's music when she was ten and that it had been one of her favorite albums ever since. (10) Charlie picked up a copy of <u>Rolling Stone</u> magazine as they walked to the checkout counter, and he said, "A trip to the bookstore turned out to be a lot more fun than I thought it would be."

CHAPTER 40: OTHER PUNCTUATION
Editing Review 1, page 709
Possible edits:

(1) To avoid predators, many butterflies and moths randomly change directions as they fly about, but this is not their only strategy; they also display striking colors (like radiant and shiny reds, oranges, and blues) and camouflage themselves in effective disguises. (2) For example, some butterflies have streaks composed of many dazzling colors across their wings to emphasize the speed of their flight—sending a message that they're hard to catch. (3) Other butterflies use bold, attention-getting color patterns to signal that they are poisonous to eat: Some are truly poisonous and some are faking. (4) There are also species that attempt to look distasteful by imitating something that is not nutritious: a bit of bird dropping, a dead leaf, or rotting vegetation. (5) One moth, *Oxytenis modestia*, is especially

enterprising in its disguises: In its first four caterpillar stages it looks like a bird dropping, even including fake seeds in it; the fifth stage imitates a green snake with a fake large head and two fake eyes; and the adult *Oxytenis* moth looks like a leaf, and because it breeds twice a year, mimics the appropriate leaf for the season. (6) *Oxytenis* moths that hatch in the dry season look like dry dead leaves; those hatching in the rainy season look dark and moldy. (7) Several butterflies combine camouflage with eye-catching display; for example, *Pieria helvetia* has front wings that are bland and dull, but its hind wings are bright red. (8) When it is resting, its wings are closed, and it can hardly be seen, but when a predator threatens, it bursts into rapid, dramatic flight—its red patches make it conspicuously visible. (9) However, then it suddenly sets down again, folds its wings in, and seemingly disappears—a clever magic act. (10) Birds and monkeys do their best to see past these disguises because, according to one researcher (one who will do anything for his research), moths taste something like raw shrimp.

CHAPTER 41: CAPITALIZATION
Practice 41-1, page 713
Answers:
(1) C (3) The same year, audiences thrilled to the story of little Dorothy, who clicked her heels together and chanted, "There's no place like home."

Practice 41-2, page 715
Answers:
1. Lindsborg is a small town in McPherson County, Kansas, that calls itself "Little Sweden, U.S.A." **3.** The town's most famous resident was probably a Swedish immigrant artist named Birger Sandzen. **5.** Sandzen intended to stay in Kansas for two or three years, but he loved the Great Plains and ended up remaining in Lindsborg for the rest of his life. **7.** Although Sandzen worked mainly in the Midwest, the Rocky Mountains, and other less populous parts of the United States, he exhibited widely. **9.** Sandzen's use of color showed the beauty of the landscapes of the West.

Practice 41-3, page 717
Answers:
1. The television show *Sesame Street*, which began in 1969, brought innovative programming to children. **3.** The popular Muppets Kermit the Frog and Miss Piggy starred in several films, including one based on Charles Dickens's classic *A Christmas Carol* and one based on Robert Louis Stevenson's *Treasure Island*. **5.** "Elmo's World," a segment added to the show in the 1990s, introduced the small red monster who would become one of the most popular toys in history.

Editing Review 1, page 718
Answers:
(1) In Robert Louis Stevenson's 1886 novella "The Strange Case of Dr. Jekyll and Mr. Hyde," a doctor uses himself as the subject of an experiment and the results are disastrous. (2) The novella was a great success, but Stevenson didn't originate the idea of doctors experimenting on themselves.

(3) One of the earliest known examples of self-experimentation goes back to the sixteenth century, when Santorio Santorio, of Padua, Italy, weighed himself every day for thirty years. (4) By weighing everything he ate and drank as well as his bodily discharges, Santorio discovered that the human body continually and imperceptibly loses large amounts of fluid. (5) Today, that loss, called insensible perspiration, is routinely measured in hospital patients.

(6) A key breakthrough to the modern age of cardiology was made in 1929 by a German, Dr. Werner Forssmann, who as a surgical resident at a medical facility called the August Victoria Home, near Berlin, conducted a daring self-experiment by inserting a thin tube into one of his veins and slid the tube into his own heart. (7) This idea was later developed by other researchers into the technique of cardiac catheterization. (8) Dr. Forssmann, who used catheters on himself nine times, shared a Nobel Prize in 1956 for his pioneering experiments.

(9) An important innovation in anesthesia occurred when a dentist in Connecticut, Horace Wells, watched a demonstration in which a volunteer inhaled nitrous oxide, cut his own leg, and felt no pain until the effects of the gas wore off. (10) Dr. Wells then had one of his own teeth extracted after he had inhaled the chemical, which people later commonly called "laughing gas." (11) He was amazed to have no pain during his extraction, declaring, "It is the greatest discovery ever made." (12) Others' self-experimentation later aided the development of ether, chloroform, and additional anesthetics.

(13) In medical circles, many people believe that Major Walter Reed experimented on himself in the early 1900s as the leader of the group in Cuba that discovered that mosquitoes transmit yellow fever. (14) In fact, Dr. Reed said he would allow mosquitoes to infect him to test the theory, but he returned to the United States before this was done. (15) Instead, other members of his team conducted the mosquito experiment on themselves, with one dying and another barely surviving. (16) After these self-experimenters proved the crucial connection between mosquitoes and yellow fever, Dr. Reed returned to Cuba, but he never did perform the experiment on himself.

EDITING REVIEW TESTS
Pages 723–37
Possible edits:

1. (1) One opponent faces the other, and during their personal battle, nobody else in the universe exists. (2/3) An attack prompts an immediate defense, often followed by a counterattack, starting the cycle again. (4) Correct (5) Yet in recent years, fencing has been experiencing a surge in popularity among women and men of all ages. (6) Correct (7) Most beginning fencers are equipped with a training sword and protective equipment that includes a glove, face mask, knee socks, knickers, and a special gray jacket. (8) Correct (9) At the tip of the sword is a button instead of a sharp point. (10) This is for safety, and it is also useful for keeping track of valid hits. (11) Correct (12/13) From the hand guard the wire runs to the back of the fencer's jacket up to an apparatus mounted on the ceiling where the hit is registered, causing a red light to go on. (14) In a typical match, the first fencer to score five valid hits on an opponent wins. (15) All in all, fencing provides strenuous exercise, competition, excitement, and a never-ending challenge.

3. (1) Correct (2) But it is also challenging, exciting, and safe because few people ever get lost in them for long. (3) Correct (4) Mazes can be made of many different types of materials, but perhaps the largest number of them are made of corn stalks. (5) Correct (6) Building mazes is one way for farmers to market their farms as popular entertainment. (7) The point of this for some farmers is to adapt the small farm so that it can remain competitive in today's economy. (8/9) Some farms are expanding on the maze idea by turning a section of their land into small theme parks, complete with hay rides, petting zoos, and pig races. (10) Correct (11) Correct (12) Some mazes even include such features as double-decker bridges. (13) Correct (14/15) Whether entertaining, educational, or both, mazes have become a significant way of raising people's awareness of and interest in farming.

5. (1) Nobody wants to go through life frightened that criminals might be lurking around every corner. (2) Correct (3) There are prudent measures that you can work into your everyday routines that can help prevent you from becoming a victim to some common scams. (4) First of all, don't give out financial information, such as your bank account or Social Security number, to anyone whom you don't know and trust. (5) Correct (6) Using these fake documents, a criminal can ask the local motor vehicle department to issue a new driver's license with your name and the criminal's photo. (7) Correct (8) Many of these scams use the same trick to get people to believe the sender is honest. The criminal will send a postdated check for a share in the fortune in return for a check from the victim that is allegedly necessary to unfreeze the funds. (9) Correct (10) If you receive e-mail solicitations of any kind, use extreme caution. (11) Correct (12) In addition, when it's time to discard your old computer, remove the hard drive first to prevent thieves from recovering any vital data. (13) Correct (14) Most identity theft cases do not start with scammers rummaging through trash. (15) Instead, scammers use computer spyware or steal outgoing mail because they find these methods easier.

7. (1) Today's young people, like young people of all generations, spend their time differently from the way their parents spent it. (2) One example of this is a phenomenon called "multitasking." (3) When having a conversation, some teenagers and young adults commonly give assurances that they are truly paying attention despite the music they are hearing through their headphones. (4) Correct (5) Doing more than one thing simultaneously is nothing new for human beings. Parents have always been able to prepare meals while keeping an eye on their babies. (6) Correct (7) But as our capacity for interpersonal connectivity has expanded with the invention of each new electronic device, the speed and complexity of multitasking has risen dramatically. (8) Correct (9) Correct (10) This is because the computer provides not only a radio and CD/DVD player but also instant messaging, Internet searches, movies, e-mail, games, and social networking. (11) Correct (12) Studies have indicated that the quality of what people produce and the depth of their thinking diminish as they focus on increasing numbers of tasks. (13) Correct (14) Nevertheless, young people's multitasking seems to be here to stay, and it may be only in its infancy.

9. (1) Correct (2) Some who are allergic simply refuse to have pets that can trigger a reaction. These pets include cats, dogs, birds, rabbits, gerbils, hamsters, and horses. (3) Correct (4) However, most pet-allergic people who love pets just go ahead and bring them into their homes anyway. (5) Correct (6) Allergens are spread from a pet's saliva, urine, skin secretions, and dander (the dead skin particles that animals continually shed). (7) Correct (8) Correct (9) Here is the single most important rule: no pets in the bedroom. (10) Also, keep pets off of the furniture; instead, get a dog or cat its own floor cushion, and choose a cushion with a washable cover. (11) Correct (12) Another key is to thoroughly and frequently clean the pet, the areas where it spends most of its time, and the bedrooms. (13) Install an air purifier in your bedroom and, if necessary, in other rooms where the pet is allowed. (14/15) Regularly clean the top blades of ceiling fans, which are one of the main spreaders of allergens. (16) Correct

Juliet B. Schor. "Age Compression." From *Born to Buy* by Juliet B. Schor. Copyright © 2004 by Juliet B. Schor. Reprinted with the permission of Scribner, an imprint of Simon & Schuster Adult Publishing Group. All rights reserved.

Christopher Shea. "In Praise of Peer Pressure [Cause and Effect in Everyday Life]." First published in the *Boston Globe*, April 29, 2007. Copyright © 2007 by Christopher Shea. Used by permission of the author.

Marc Siegel. "Treating the Pain by Ending a Life." First published in the *Boston Globe*, January 19, 2006. Copyright © 2006 by Marc Siegel. Used by permission of the author.

Rebecca Skloot. "Celebrity Teeth." First published in the *New York Times*, Sunday Magazine, December 11, 2005. Copyright © 2005 by Rebecca Skloot. Used by permission of the author.

Brent Staples. "Just Walk on By: Black Men and Public Space." Originally published in *Ms.* magazine. Used by permission of the author.

Amy Tan. "Mother Tongue." Copyright © 1990 by Amy Tan. First appeared in *The Threepenny Review*. Reprinted by permission of the author and the Sandra Dijkstra Literary Agency.

Lindsey Tanner. "Study says ads trick children's taste buds." First published by *Associated Press*, August 7, 2007. Copyright © 2007 by Associated Press. Used with permission of The Associated Press. All rights reserved.

Kathleen Vail. "Words That Wound." Reprinted with permission from *American School Board Journal*, September 1999. Copyright 1999 National School Boards Association. All rights reserved.

Photo Credits

Page 1: © Bob Daemmrich/The Image Works
Page 3: Martin Barraud/Taxi/Getty Images
Page 22: Reggie Casagrande/Digital Vision/Getty Images
Page 45: Tetra Images/Getty Images
Page 62: Photo by Robert Gauthier/Time & Life Pictures/Getty Images
Page 71: © Google, Inc. Used with permission.
Page 74: Amanda Marsalis/Taxi/Getty Images
Page 88: Marcus Clackson/Digital Vision/Getty Images
Page 100: Tom Grill/Photographers Choice/Getty Images
Page 110: Daniel Garcia/AFP/Getty Images
Page 125: Michael Blann/Stone/Getty Images
Page 145: Gary Conner/PhotoEdit
Page 147: Naum Kazhdan/The New York Times/Redux
Page 163: © Scott Roper/Corbis
Page 167: Richard Ambo/*The Honolulu Advertiser*
Page 181: Courtesy of AdCouncil. Reprinted with permission.

Page 185: Courtesy of Want Ad Publications, Inc. Reprinted with permission.
Page 198: Amy Eckert
Page 214: Courtesy of AdCouncil. Reprinted with permission.
Page 218: Image provided courtesy of Zappos.com, Inc. © 2008 Zappos.com, Inc.
Page 231: Courtesy of AdCouncil. Reprinted with permission.
Page 248: Andrew Scott/*Columbia College Chronicle*.
Page 252: © 2004 Consumers Union of U.S., Inc. Yonkers, NY 10703-1057, a nonprofit organization. Reprinted with permission from the October 2004 issue of *Consumer Reports Money Adviser* ™ for educational purposes only. No commercial use or reproduction permitted. www.ConsumerReports.org
Page 267: Photo courtesy of U.S. Army.
Page 268: © 2007 Consumers Union of U.S., Inc. Yonkers, NY 10703-1057, a nonprofit organization. Reprinted with permission from the November 2007 issue of *Consumer Reports*® for educational purposes only. No commercial use or reproduction permitted. www.ConsumerReports .org
Page 272: Emily Ortmans
Page 286: © Mark Richards/Corbis
Page 290: Martin O'Loughlin
Page 311: Boston Globe/Dina Rudick/Landov
Page 317: © Bob Daemmrich/The Image Works
Page 319: Rubberball/Getty Images
Page 334: PhotoAlto/Sigrid Olsson/Getty Images
Page 354: © Google, Inc.
Page 357: Courtesy of McNeil Consumer & Specialty Pharmaceuticals, a division of McNeil-PPC, Inc. www .concerta.net
Page 358: Courtesy of Centers for Disease Control and Prevention (CDC)
Page 364: Courtesy of *The Columbus Dispatch*
Page 370: Courtesy of Alfred A. Knopf
Page 371: Antonio Scorza/AFP/Getty Images
Page 372: Courtesy of FAIR/Extra!
Page 373: Courtesy of CSA
Page 383: Jason Reblando
Page 493: Richard Lord Enterprises, Inc./The Image Works
Page 631: Rachel Epstein/The Image Works
Page 671: Jeff Greenberg/PhotoEdit
Page 741: Jason Reblando
Page 745: Library of Congress
Page 749: Jamie Rose/The New York Times/Redux
Page 755: © Martha Stewart
Page 766: Courtesy of Alex Espinoza
Page 770: © Richard Koenig
Page 776: Library of Congress

Page 781: Courtesy of Daniel Goleman
Page 788: Courtesy of Christina Rahr
Page 796: A. E. Rodriguez/Getty Images
Page 805: © Jeff Smith
Page 811: Courtesy of Juliet Schor
Page 817: Raul Rubiera/Miami Herald
Page 822: © Jerry Bauer

Page 834: Courtesy of The New York Times. Reprinted with permission.
Page 846: Courtesy of Marc Siegel
Page 850: Courtesy of Lisa Bevilaqua
Page 855: Courtesy of Marilyn Golden
Page 860: Courtesy of Dr. Herbert M. Hendin

Index

Y

Correction Symbols

This chart lists typical symbols that instructors use to point out writing problems. The explanation of each symbol includes a step you can take to revise or edit your writing. Included also are suggested chapters to check for more help and information. If your instructor uses different symbols for some errors, write them in the left-hand column for future reference.

YOUR INSTRUCTOR'S SYMBOL	STANDARD SYMBOL	HOW TO REVISE OR EDIT (Numbers in boldface are chapters where you can find help)
	adj	Use correct adjective form **28**
	adv	Use correct adverb form **28**
	agr	Correct subject-verb agreement or pronoun agreement **25; 27**
	awk	Awkward expression: edit for clarity **9**
	cap	Use capital letter correctly **41**
	case	Use correct pronoun case **27**
	cliché	Replace overused phrase with fresh words **34**
	coh	Revise paragraph or essay for coherence **9**
	combine	Combine sentences **32**
	con t	Correct the inconsistent verb tense **26**
	coord	Use coordination correctly **30**
	cs	Comma splice: join the sentences correctly **24**
	d or dic	Diction: edit word choice **34**
	dev	Develop your paragraph or essay more completely **6; 9**
	dm	Revise to avoid a dangling modifier **29**
	frag	Attach the fragment to a sentence or make it a sentence **23**
	fs	Fused sentence: join the two sentences correctly **24**
	intro	Add or strengthen your introduction **8**
	ital	Use italics **39**
	lc	Use lowercase **41**
	mm	Revise to avoid a misplaced modifier **29**
	pl	Use the correct plural form of the verb **26**
	ref	Make pronoun reference clear **27**
	ro	Run-on sentence; join the two sentences correctly **24**
	sp	Correct the spelling error **35; 36**
	sub	Use subordination correctly **30**
	sup	Support your point with details, examples, or facts **6**
	tense	Correct the problem with verb tense **26**
	trans	Add a transition **9**
	ts	Add or strengthen your topic sentence or thesis statement **5**
	u	Revise paragraph or essay for unity **6; 9**
	w	Delete unnecessary words **34**
	?	Make your meaning clearer **9**
	,	Use comma correctly **37**
	; : ( ) - —	Use semicolon/colon/parentheses/hyphen/dash correctly **40**
	" "	Use quotation marks correctly **39**